Behavioral Counseling: Cases and Techniques

EDITED BY

JOHN D. KRUMBOLTZ AND CARL E. THORESEN
STANFORD UNIVERSITY

Holt, Rinehart and Winston, Inc.

NEW YORK · CHICAGO · SAN FRANCISCO · ATLANTA
DALLAS · MONTREAL · TORONTO · LONDON · SYDNEY

Library of Congress Catalog Card Number: 74-77811
ISBN 0-03-078205-8
Printed in the United States of America

01234   22   9876543

PREFACE

WE WANTED TO PREPARE a useful cookbook for counselors and psychologists. This book is as close as we could come considering the advanced state of our ignorance.

The primary purpose of the book is to provide counselors and psychologists with detailed descriptions of promising counseling techniques. We wanted counselors to have concrete examples of procedures that seem to have promise for helping clients. This is neither a theory nor a research book, though many of the ideas and procedures presented are based on research work related to various theoretical formulations.

The articles selected had to meet two criteria: (1) the technique seemed to have a great deal of promise for helping a client, and (2) the technique was described in sufficient detail that another counselor could duplicate the essential actions upon reading the report.

The authors were asked to be very specific. They were asked to include, when applicable, partial transcripts of interviews, specific assignments given to clients, exact words spoken in consultations with significant others in the client's life, detailed diagnostic information, actual copies of forms or instructions or sources where information could be obtained. Authors of case studies were asked to describe their actual observations as to how behavior had been changed.

Some authors were understandably reluctant to make an inference that their experimental technique or combination of techniques actually resulted in the behavior change observed. We assured them that these techniques would not be presented as final answers. The reader is cautioned that the degree to which any technique may or may not produce a desired behavior change cannot be determined by the evidence in this book. Considerable research work has been done on some of these techniques. For other techniques the research work is suggested or only just beginning. Clearly we are unable to make the inference with any known degree of certainty that the changed behavior in any case study was the result of whatever the counselor did.

The purpose of the book is not to provide proof that certain techniques work. It is only to describe techniques that at least one counselor thought were effective for changing certain behaviors of at least one client at one particular time. Our main hope is that counselors and psychologists who read this book will be encouraged to try, to modify, to evaluate, and to improve these ideas for themselves. Eventually, a definitive cookbook for counselors with tested recipes may be written. Right now, however, counselors and psychologists need to explore and develop some of the possible ingredients.

We expect that the book will be a useful text in training programs for counselors, school psychologists, clinical psychologists, counseling psychologists, and school social workers. Case materials from elementary, secondary, college, and adult levels are included.

The book is organized by types of techniques. But for the reader who wishes to work on a particular type of client problem we have included a Diagnostic Table of Contents. If a reader were particularly interested in techniques which might help, say, secondary school students with decision-making problems, he could consult the Diagnostic Table of Contents and find the pertinent articles.

Our procedure in constructing the book was first to identify potential authors from among counselors and psychologists doing exciting, innovative work. We asked them to write a detailed description of what they had done and what changes they had observed presumably as a result of their experimentation. Because of space limitations we could not include all the reports that were available. We also had to reduce the length of many reports. The book is not exhaustive. Many others are engaged in creative developments which are not described here, but which merit consideration.

In addition to the soliciting and editing of the manuscripts, we have prepared introductory sections which attempt to provide a perspective for these techniques and case studies. The book in its entirety represents a progress report of where behavioral counseling stands at this point in its development. Hopefully, new ideas and new developments in the years ahead will produce improved techniques. We constantly emphasize that the ideas presented here seem promising, deserve to be considered by counselors and psychologists, need to be evaluated systematically, and need to be improved.

Another editorial contribution is labeled "Editors' Notes." These notes are scattered throughout the book within each article and represent the opinions of the editors only. In these editors' notes we have attempted to call attention to important points, issue warnings or cautions about

potential dangers, suggest needed research studies, and express our en-
lightened prejudices.

The book will be successful to the extent that it stimulates counselors
and psychologists to try new and better ways of helping clients. We have
included examples of techniques which failed as well as of those which
seemed to succeed. The authors and editors are very much aware that
the techniques described are not perfect and that every response made
by the counselor was not necessarily helpful. The fact that errors can be
made without necessarily causing great damage may hopefully encourage
other counselors to try some new ideas.

Some day soon we may prepare a revised edition. We would welcome
communications from counselors and psychologists who have tried other
new ideas or extensions and modifications of the techniques in this book.

That a final manuscript could be sent off to the publisher is due in
large part to Mrs. Eleanor Worden, our good and faithful secretary. She
handled diligently the voluminous correspondence; retyped almost all
the manuscripts; gave authors and others the impression that the editors
were well organized; kept track of endless details; maintained files; and
through it all somehow kept a pleasant disposition. Without her help and
enthusiasm this book would never have appeared.

J.D.K.
C.E.T.

Stanford, California
June 1969

CONTENTS

PREFACE, iii
DIAGNOSTIC TABLE OF CONTENTS, xi

INTRODUCTION, 1

PART I. PROBLEM IDENTIFICATION IN BEHAVIORAL COUNSELING, 7

1. The "Inner Circle" Strategy: Identifying Crucial Problems, 19
   ARNOLD A. LAZARUS

PART II. REINFORCEMENT TECHNIQUES, 25

Arranging Reinforcement and Extinction Contingencies, 29

2. Modifying Hyperactive and Aggressive Behavior, 30
   BARBARA J. VANCE
3. Assuming Responsibility for Appropriate Classroom Behavior, 33
   WANDA K. CASTLE
4. Reducing Soiling Behavior in a Therapeutic Summer Camp, 36
   HENRY C. RICKARD AND JOHN L. GRIFFIN

Identifying Effective and Ineffective Reinforcers, 41

5. "The Reinforcement Menu": Finding Effective Reinforcers, 42
   MARVIN F. DALEY
6. Refusing Reinforcement, 45
   CLAIRE V. KORN

7. Reinforcement that Backfired, 49
BARBARA B. VARENHORST

Structuring and Reinforcement, 52

8. Commitment to Change: Structuring the Goals and Ground Rules for Counseling, 54
MARGARET H. HOOPES AND A. LYNN SCORESBY

9. Overcoming Procrastination, 58
MARGARET H. HOOPES

10. Improving Academic Performance, 64
A. LYNN SCORESBY

11. Formulating Educational and Vocational Goals, 70
T. ANTOINETTE RYAN

12. Structuring for Academic Success, 73
ADDIE FUHRIMAN

Role-Playing and Reinforcement, 79

13. Overcoming Fear of Speaking in a Group, 80
RAY E. HOSFORD

14. Helping a Client Speak Up in Class, 83
BARBARA B. VARENHORST

Using Behavior Contracts, 87

15. Systematic Exclusion: Eliminating Chronic Classroom Disruptions, 89
DAVID W. KEIRSEY

16. Applying Systematic Exclusion to a Case of Bizarre Behavior, 114
DAVID A. SHIER

17. Learning that Privileges Entail Responsibilities, 124
MICHAEL DINOFF AND HENRY C. RICKARD

Teaching Others to Use Reinforcement, 130

18. Establishing Reinforcement Techniques in the Classroom, 131
BARBARA SANBORN AND WILLIAM SCHUSTER

19. Teaching Teachers to Reinforce Student Participation, 152
RAY E. HOSFORD

20. Teaching Parents to be Behavior Modifiers in the Classroom, 155
G. R. PATTERSON

PART III. SOCIAL MODELING TECHNIQUES, 163

Live Models, 166

21. Eliminating Excessive Fears of the Environment through
    Contact Desensitization, 168
    BRUNHILDE RITTER

22. Developing Appropriate Social Behaviors of Juvenile
    Delinquents, 178
    IRWIN G. SARASON AND VICTOR J. GANZER

23. Using Behavioral Techniques with Autistic Children, 193
    WILLIAM E. STILWELL

Filmed Models, 200

24. Participating in Classroom Discussions, 202
    RAY E. HOSFORD AND DON L. SORENSON

25. Increasing Task-Oriented Behavior, 207
    STEWART B. NIXON

Audio Tape Recorded Models, 211

26. Exploring and Processing Information about Educational and
    Vocational Opportunities in Groups, 213
    NORMAN R. STEWART

27. Encouraging Constructive Use of Time, 234
    JAMES E. SMITH

28. Overcoming Underachievement, 241
    ALICE L. BEACH

Modeling Behavioral Methods with Teachers, 249

29. Helping Teachers Analyze and Remedy Problems, 250
    ROSEMARIE K. MOORE AND KENNETH SANNER

30. Consulting with the Classroom Teacher, 260
    DWIGHT L. GOODWIN

PART IV. COUNTERCONDITIONING, 265

31. Systematic Desensitization: Reducing Test Anxiety, 267
    JOHN R. EMERY

PART V. COGNITIVE TECHNIQUES, 289

Simulation, 291

32. Vocational Problem-Solving Experiences, 293
    JOHN D. KRUMBOLTZ AND LAWRENCE E. SHEPPARD

33. Learning the Consequences of Life's Decisions, 306
BARBARA B. VARENHORST

34. Self-Control through "Imaginal Aversive Contingency" and "One-Downsmanship": Enabling the Powerless to Accommodate Unreasonableness, 319
GERALD C. DAVISON

Planning, 328

35. Learning Decision-Making, 329
WILLIAM YABROFF

36. Developing Skills for Educational and Vocational Problems, 343
THOMAS M. MAGOON

Confrontation, 397

37. "Pounce": Learning Responsibility for One's Own Employment Problems, 399
ROBERT A. WALKER

38. Learning Job-Seeking Interview Skills, 414
JANICE A. PRAZAK

PART VI. MULTIPLE TECHNIQUES, 429

Interpersonal Problems, 431

39. Using Assertive Training, 433
DONALD R. NEUMAN

40. Reducing Heterosexual Anxiety, 442
THOMAS J. D'ZURILLA

41. Controlling Sexual and Interpersonal Anxieties, 454
DAVID L. GEISINGER

Academic Problems, 470

42. Reducing Test Anxiety, 471
FRANCINE T. WEINSTEIN

43. Improving Study Behaviors, 486
G. BRIAN JONES

REFERENCES, 499

INDEX, 509

DIAGNOSTIC
TABLE OF CONTENTS

DIRECTIONS: 1. Locate the type of client problem with which you are concerned in the lefthand column.
2. Locate the age level of the client in the top row.
3. The numbers in the intersecting squares refer to articles that describe relevant cases or techniques.
4. Additional ideas for help with the problem may be adapted from those listed in the same row under other age categories.

Problem	Age Level			
	Elementary	Secondary	College	Adult
Deficient Decision-Making Skills	17	17, 26, 32, 33, 35	8, 9, 10, 11, 36	29, 30
Ineffective Academic Skills	2, 5, 13, 15, 16, 19, 20, 24, 25, 30	3, 7, 18, 19, 27, 28	8, 9, 10, 11, 12, 31, 42, 43	15, 16, 29, 30
Inappropriate Social Skills	2, 4, 5, 13, 15, 16, 17, 23, 30	3, 7, 14, 17, 18, 22, 34	39, 40	15, 16, 29, 30, 37, 38, 41
Self-Defeating Fears and Anxieties	6, 13, 23, 24	1, 14, 34	31, 39, 40, 42	21, 38, 41

Introduction

WHAT IS BEHAVIORAL COUNSELING? Does it differ from any other kind of counseling? Would a counselor use behavioral counseling to help some clients and "brand X" counseling to help others?

Although behavioral counseling has much in common with other types of counseling, it offers certain features that distinguish it from other approaches (Krumboltz, 1966c). We think these distinctive features are desirable and should be characteristic of all approaches to counseling. In fact, we look forward to the time when we will no longer have to label one kind of counseling as "behavioral" but we will be able simply to refer to the profession of counseling. In the long run the demand will be for counseling services that have demonstrated their effectiveness, and counselors who are best able to help their clients will survive and prosper.

The characteristics of behavioral counseling are such that continued change and improvement are virtually inevitable. Behavioral counseling cannot remain static because its very nature requires constant growth.

ESSENTIAL FEATURES OF BEHAVIORAL COUNSELING

Four interrelated characteristics of the approach enable behavioral counselors to respond flexibly and adopt continuously improving procedures to help their clients.

Criteria for Formulating Counseling Goals

When a counseling goal is finally formulated in behavioral counseling, it must meet three criteria: (1) It must be a goal

1

desired by the client; (2) The counselor must be willing to help the client achieve this goal; (3) It must be possible to assess the extent to which the client achieves the goal (Krumboltz, 1966a, 1966b).

A client may wish to overcome some maladaptive behavior. For example, he may wish to be able to stand up for his own rights and not be treated as a "doormat" by his family, friends, and employer. He may wish to overcome a generalized anxiety, or some particular anxiety such as that associated with taking examinations or meeting new people. He may wish to learn how to make important personal decisions more effectively. Goals such as these do meet the three criteria. They are based on the client's wishes. In all probability at least some counselors would be willing to help the client accomplish these goals, and means are available to assess whether the desired behavior changes are accomplished.

Alternative approaches to counseling frequently state goals which do not meet these three criteria. For example, the goal of "self-actualization," desirable as it may be for all, is seldom requested by clients unless they have read certain documents in advance. A counselor agreeing to help a client "self-actualize" could not be sure to what he was agreeing, and it becomes exceedingly difficult to specify when, if ever, the client achieves self-actualization. As a general ideal, we subscribe fully to self-actualization. We want people to attain their full potential. But as a counseling goal, the abstract and ambiguous terminology makes it difficult for clients or counselors to know what they are trying to do and when they have succeeded. The general ideal, whether it is self-actualization or self-realization, needs to be analyzed into specific actions desired by each client so that the counselor and the client know where they are going and when they get there (Thoresen, 1968a).

Many counselors who would like to try behavioral counseling approaches have difficulty, however, precisely at this point. Their clients do not come to them with clearly stated behavior changes that they would like to accomplish. The first job of a counselor is to establish precisely what the goal is. Problems are not always self-evident. They must be constructed in such a way that they become solvable. A counselor must translate the complaint presented by the client into a solvable problem that meets the three criteria.

Tailoring Techniques to the Client

Behavioral counselors do not use the same technique with every client. They try to select a procedure or combination of procedures most likely to help a client accomplish his particular goals (Thoresen, 1966b).

A common stereotyped misconception of the behavioral counselor is that of a cold, impersonal machine dispensing either M & M's or the word "good" in a metallic voice (Thoresen, 1966a). Although the use of well-timed positive reinforcement is one frequently used tool, such reinforcement is not administered mechanically or impersonally primarily because impersonal attempts at reinforcement would not be helpful to clients. Basically, behavioral counselors are human beings who take genuine pleasure in seeing their clients make progress and cannot help but communicate their enthusiasm. Moreover, behavioral counselors do not confine themselves to the use of positive reinforcement. They also use modeling techniques, role-playing, cognitive structuring, simulation, confrontation, and counterconditioning, as well as variations and combinations of these and other techniques.

A behavioral counselor has no vested interest in any single technique. If one technique does not work, he tries something else. Alternative approaches to behavioral counseling, on the other hand, are generally characterized by a single method (Krumboltz, 1964). For example, if two years of psychoanalysis does not enable a client to achieve "real insight," then the only possible prescription is more years of psychoanalysis.

Experimenting with Procedures

There are no restrictions on the possible techniques behavioral counselors can try except, of course, ethical ones. Experimentation is an essential part of a counselor's job. The systematic testing of many procedures and variations on those procedures is necessary so that the profession can develop those techniques best suited for helping various kinds of clients. Thus, there is no "approved list" of techniques the use of which enables one to call himself a behavioral counselor. The door must be kept open to all procedures that might be helpful to the extent of encouraging those who may be trying some novel or "far-out" technique even if it does not fit the existing pattern of techniques. Variations of sensitivity training, sensory-aware-ness exercises, and marathon group therapy, for example, are not usually associated with behavioral counseling, but such procedures deserve the same careful evaluation as any others.

Sensitivity training might well become part of the repertoire of behavioral counselors if several conditions are met: (1) Has the client requested help in learning to perceive, describe accurately, and respond appropriately to the emotional states of others? (2) Is it possible to determine whether a client has in fact achieved this increased sensitivity? (3) Does sensitivity training produce the desired results for at least some clients more effectively than alternative procedures? If affirmative answers can be given to these three questions, then sensitivity training is clearly a part of behavioral counseling.

A technique is not a part of behavioral counseling if it is routinely given to every client without considering alternative methods of accomplishing the client's goals. Counseling is not behavioral if no means are available to assess the extent to which each client accomplishes his goal. It is not behavioral if the technique is advocated without scientific evidence as to its merits and without constant efforts to improve upon it.

The field of counseling and psychotherapy has suffered long enough from advocates of one-shot panaceas. Behavioral approaches must not establish another rigidified orthodoxy. The constant evaluating of possible improvements in both orthodox and unorthodox techniques will keep us from becoming one-pill physicians.

Improving Procedures on the Basis of Relevant Evidence

Behavioral counseling is a self-correcting system. Behavioral counselors may make mistakes. They may use the wrong procedure at the wrong time with the wrong client. They may fail to diagnose the difficulty accurately. But the results of their mistake will be immediately obvious to them. The client will not make progress; that is, relevant behaviors will not change. This feedback will enable the counselor to modify his procedures. As long as the client and the counselor are both agreed on what kinds of behavior changes the client is to accomplish, and as long as it is possible to assess in some manner the extent to which these changes are occurring, then it becomes possible for both client and counselor to evaluate the success of treatment.

Human behavior is exceedingly complex. It is not easy for a counselor to identify correctly all the factors that may elicit and maintain an inappropriate pattern of behavior. It is difficult for a counselor at times to intervene in a way that will enable the client to overcome factors in his environment that maintain an inappropriate type of behavior. Nevertheless, techniques that do not work can always be eliminated and new techniques can be tried. It is important to remember that the techniques that work for one client may not work for another.

At different points in counseling, both formal and informal evaluation are needed to test procedures. Informal evaluation often aids in generating hypotheses which can then be tested in more formal experiments. Over the years this constant testing, revision, and re-evaluation will create improved techniques.

Is this evaluation process any different from that associated with other approaches to counseling? Don't other counseling approaches evaluate their procedures scientifically? From the behavioral counselor's point of view, one-technique approaches to counseling seldom experiment in a way that leads to improvements in procedures. We may see studies, for example, in which subjects are randomly assigned to counseling or to a control group. Once in awhile (perhaps one time in twenty) the counseled group may have a higher criterion score on some instrument than the control group, but, because no alternative procedures are part of the design, there is considerable danger that a few affirmative results will result in rigidifying the one procedure still more (Thoresen, 1968b).

It is possible to design research to improve counseling procedures (Krumboltz, 1967); such research would consist of experimental tests of alternative counseling procedures, each of which seemed to have some likelihood of being successful. Furthermore, the experiments would need to test procedures for different kinds of clients and for different kinds of problems. Eventually we can discover the probability of success for using each technique to help each kind of client to accomplish each type of behavior change. At present, we are a long way from such precision in our knowledge, but we should not waste time performing research that does not advance us toward this precise and helpful knowledge.

PART I

Problem Identification
in Behavioral Counseling

BEHAVIORAL APPROACHES TO COUNSELING have often been accused of oversimplifying human problems (for example, Jourard, 1961; McCully, 1964; and Arbuckle, 1968). "Sure, you can get a client to speak more in class if you reinforce him for speaking, but how many clients come in to counselors specifically asking to speak more in class?" comment critics. "Sure, you can overcome snake phobias by desensitization, but how many clients come in complaining about their fear of snakes? How about the real life, pervasive problems of clients, problems of existence, of alienation, of despair?" Thus, some counselors view behavioral counseling as a limited collection of techniques confined to accomplishing rather trivial changes in behavior with a small number of clients who happen to request some particular change in behavior. Behavioral counselors themselves have probably unintentionally contributed to this misconception. Communication tends to be facilitated when rather simple examples are used; perhaps we have fallen into the trap of trying to facilitate communication and understanding through oversimplification. Let us try to correct the situation now.

Very seldom do clients begin by requesting help in accomplishing specific behavior changes. Very seldom does a client enter a counselor's office and state, "I want to learn to speak up in class," "I wish to reduce anxiety associated with viewing snakes," or "I wish to engage in information-seeking relevant to my career choice." When goals are so clearly and specifically expressed, it is relatively easy for a behavioral counselor to devise some kind of procedure that might help. But clients seldom behave this way. Most clients do not describe their difficulties in such simple, straightforward language. Most cannot specify what behavior they desire. They are usually confused and uncertain. Can a behavioral counselor help a client who does not know what he wants, who is confused and unhappy? Certainly. One of the most exciting characteristics of behavioral counseling is its capability for successfully resolving the highly complex problems of clients (Thoresen, 1968a).

The counselor begins by listening carefully to the client's concerns. The counselor tries to understand and assess the client's thoughts and feelings. He first tries to see things from the client's point of view. He communicates his understandings to the client and attempts to determine if he is accurately perceiving the client's thoughts and feelings.

But the behavioral counselor often does more initially than listen empathically and clarify perceptions of what the client is experiencing. He also seeks answers to questions. What precisely is going on in the client's everyday life? In what ways do others respond to the client's words, thoughts, and feelings? Much attention is directed to the client and the particulars of his living environment (Thoresen, 1968b).

For some clients the counselor's empathic understanding is enough. Listening without condemning may relieve guilt feelings. The sympathetic audience may enable the client to verbalize his plans and proceed without any further action by the counselor. All counselors must learn to be empathic listeners. But they must learn more. A good listener may suffice for some clients but not for most. Most clients need further assistance once the counselor understands their thoughts and feelings about their problems.

The counselor must help the client describe how he would like to act instead of the way in which he currently acts. The counselor must help the client translate his confusions and fears into a goal that the client would like to accomplish and which would begin to resolve the client's problems. This can be accomplished by focusing on specific behaviors in the client's present situation.

DIFFICULTIES IN FORMULATING GOALS

This process of translating amorphous feelings into specific goals is, of course, not easy. In the following sections we will examine seven stumbling blocks that counselors face in making the translation and see some ways they can step over them.

The Problem Is Someone Else's Behavior

Frequently the problem as presented by the client has nothing to do with his own behavior but is attributed entirely to deficiencies in someone else's behavior. School counselors are often confronted by teachers who say, "Johnny is always causing trouble in my class. He won't pay attention. He won't do what I tell him. You are a counselor. You talk to him and straighten him out." It is easy for a beginning counselor to make a serious mistake in accepting a referral from a teacher on this basis.

The first question a counselor must ask is, "Who is my client?" In almost all cases the answer should be, "My client is the person who brought me the problem." In this case, the client is actually the teacher, not Johnny. The teacher has far more resources for controlling the contingencies of reinforcement (the antecedents and consequences of behavior) in Johnny's life than does the counselor. If the counselor were to accept the referral on the teacher's terms (take Johnny out of class and talk with him in the counselor's office), it is unlikely that the counselor would accomplish very much in enabling Johnny and the teacher to develop harmonious working relations. A more fruitful approach would be for the counselor to reply to the teacher, "Yes, that does sound like a difficult problem. Maybe we can work on it together. Could you suggest a time when I might be able to visit your class to observe Johnny exhibiting this kind of behavior?" With this reply the counselor establishes himself as an ally of the teacher, his client, so that together they can work on the problem. The goal of the counseling then becomes one of discovering the types of action that the teacher (the client) can take in order to modify Johnny's inattentive and destructive behavior.

A similar situation exists for parents who bring their children to a counselor or child psychologist. The parent, like the teacher, hopes to shift responsibility on to someone else whom he or she can then blame if no progress is made. The parent, like the teacher, however, controls many more reinforcing contingencies than does any counselor or child psychologist. The client is the parent, not the child. The role of the counselor is then to work with the parent in creating an environment in which the child is able to learn and to experience reinforcing consequences for more appropriate types of behavior. The goal of the counseling is to help the parent change his behavior so that the child's behavior improves.

Not only do persons in authority (teachers, parents, and employers) complain about the behavior of those for whom they are responsible, but peers often complain about each other. Children complain about the behavior of their classmates, teachers about their colleagues, husbands and wives about their spouses. The picture presented to the counselor is one in which the presenter is virtuous—if only "they" would change *their* behavior, everything would be all right. The counselor is frequently asked for help in getting the "offending party" to come in for some counseling.

The counselor should continue to consider the person bringing the complaint as the client. Here is the person who is bothered sufficiently by the problem to bring it to the attention of a counselor. The counselor remains sympathetic toward the person bringing the complaint but, in effect, insists, "Let us see what *you* can do that might possibly help this person change his behavior."

Does this mean that the "offending party" in all of these cases is never to see the counselor? Not necessarily. There are many instances in which it is highly desirable for all individuals involved to talk with the counselor. It is usually best, however, for the counselor to avoid inviting the "offending party" to come in for counseling. The teacher may ask Johnny if he would be willing to discuss their problem with the counselor. Johnny may agree, wishing for a happier classroom atmosphere. The counselor then considers Johnny a client too. He can then help Johnny engage in behavior which will enable him to learn without antagonizing the teacher.

In all counseling situations the counselor must make a value judgment on whether he wishes to help a client achieve any given goal. The counselor's own interests, competencies, and ethical standards are involved (Krumboltz, 1965).

In summary, when a client presents as a problem someone else's behavior, the counselor must structure the situation so that the client himself accepts responsibility for engaging in some kind of behavior that might in turn remedy the difficulty. The client might elect to change the other person's behavior, tolerate it, or withdraw from it, but the decision and resulting action must be seen as the client's responsibility.

The Problem Is Expressed as a Feeling

Problems are usually presented to counselors as descriptions of feelings. The client may say, "I feel inadequate," "I feel unwanted and unloved," "I feel alienated and lonely." Just as a physician encourages his patient to "tell me where it hurts," so the counselor would encourage his client to describe in detail his emotional sensations. The counselor needs to listen to the client tell of his feelings in such a way that the counselor will be able to describe the problem and the feelings involved to the client with considerable accuracy.

This reflecting and clarifying of the client's problems and his feelings, this careful attending, serves two important purposes: (1) It guarantees that the counselor has accurately perceived the problem and the feelings of the client so that he can better assess what needs to be done; (2) It establishes the counselor as an important person in the client's life, one who is likely to be viewed as a social model and whose verbal responses may be effective reinforcers. A few clients even find that the clear and accurate reflection of their own problem is sufficient for them to resolve their own difficulties without further attention. Perhaps these few instances have reinforced many counselors on an intermittent schedule to believe that all clients can be treated by merely understanding their feelings. And sometimes clients fortuitously get better, independent of the counselor's efforts, thereby creating the belief—the superstition—that the counselor's listening caused the changes.

There are two basic ways of dealing with problems expressed as feelings:

TAKING ACTION INCOMPATIBLE WITH UNDESIRED FEELING

A person who feels unwanted and unloved may be perceiving the environment quite accurately. And if he talks about being unwanted and unloved in front of others, he probably drives them away. The general approach a counselor can take is to ask, "What could you do that would make at least some people want to have you around and be their friend?" Perhaps most people want to be loved and desired for themselves without the necessity of doing anything to deserve it. The truth of the matter, however, is that we want and love those people who do things we consider to be desirable. We do not usually love those who make us feel guilty, who punish us, who burden us, or who do nothing for us. There are countless ways to be useful and constructive in our society. Some ways pay money and some do not. Social service and political organizations are always looking for volunteer workers for worthy causes. The goal of counseling for such people is that they engage in different activities until they find some pattern of behavior that gives them the satisfactions they want. Merely talking about their loneliness with a counselor will not be sufficient. Some adults, for example, regularly try to "purchase friendship" this way but it seldom suffices.

Lonely people need to learn to take the initiative in meeting people. What does a lonely person *do* when he goes to a meeting of some organization or to a church service, for example? Does he merely stand there hoping that someone will come up and make him feel welcome? And would he know what to say if someone did greet him? He might learn to take the initiative and introduce himself to people near him, saying, "Hello, my name is _____. I'm new here."

People who feel inadequate need to develop skills. No one is inadequate in everything. One professor was once asked how he happened to have become the world's foremost authority on the ancient Greek poet Theocritus. He replied, "I'm the only one who has ever heard of him." There are an unlimited number of skills, hobbies, and interests at which one can become proficient. A counselor can help a person suffering from feelings of inadequacy to build some competency so that he can be outstanding in at least one small area.

ESTABLISHING MORE REALISTIC STANDARDS
FOR COMPARING FEELINGS

Feelings of inadequacy are often found, however, among extremely competent persons. Those who are loved may feel unloved, and those with many friends, lonely. Building behaviors incompatible with these feelings is one approach, but for some people it is not sufficient. These people frequently have levels of aspiration unrealistically high and consider their feelings to be quite unique and unshared by others. The truth of the matter is that we all have these feelings of inadequacy and loneliness but seldom do we express such feelings to one another. Our society does not generally reward the expression of such feelings. In subtle ways it actually punishes the expression of such feelings. Yet, each person knows how he alone feels. Since he hears none of his fellows describing feelings similar to his own, he assumes that his fellows do not share these feelings. Each of us thinks he is alone with his own particular set of unhappy feelings because he has no opportunity to learn that others share these feelings with him.

Perhaps one of the greatest values of counseling in groups is the opportunity it provides for the sharing of feelings (Krumboltz, 1968). The discovery that feelings of guilt, hostility, hatred, lust, fear, greed, and selfishness, mixed with desires for love, tenderness, and warmth are shared by his fellows is often a revealing experience for one who previously thought he was alone in these feelings. The goal of counseling is to enable the client and other clients to share their feelings openly with one another so that they can accurately perceive the extent to which these feelings are shared by others.

The problem of unrealistically high aspirations is a difficult one. High aspirations are undoubtedly instilled at an early age by perfectionistic mothers, fathers, and teachers, as well as mass media. To some extent the desire for perfection should not be discouraged, but some people who by objective standards appear to be successful actually lead unhappy lives because no amount of success can ever live up to the standards of perfection they have adopted. They are not as politically astute as the President of the United States, not as good a baseball player as Willie Mays, not as happily married as Sleeping Beauty and Prince Charming. The difficulty is that they compare their own successes with those of the most successful people in each field of endeavor. The counselor may sometimes help by bringing people like this into closer contact with the real world. Clients with such unrealistically high expectations can adopt as their goal behaviors which will enable them to learn about the true range of ability that exists in each of the areas of competency to which they aspire. Discovering the number of people who are less competent, less happy, and less privileged is one possible approach to this problem. ("I cried because I had no shoes until I met a man who had no feet.") The counselor must discover ways to help his client take constructive steps to accomplish his highest goals, develop alternative plans if necessary, and learn that frustrations and setbacks have always accompanied great accomplishments.

The Problem Is the Absence of a Goal

Many people do not know what they want. If they knew what they wanted they would be able to get it, but they are unable to make up their minds about a goal. A rich vocabulary has grown up around people in this category. They are said to be purposeless, alienated, other-directed. Among young people, occupational goals must be decided. Older people may have settled on occupational goals, achieved some measure of success in their occupations, but feel that their lives lack real purpose.

Sophisticated philosophers may dispute the "purpose of life" and "ultimate values." Our view is that purposes are made, not born. "Man's chief purpose," wrote Lewis Mumford, "is the creation and preservation of values . . . this is what gives significance, ultimately, to the individual human life." A life does not have a purpose built into it, a purpose that must somehow be discovered. Instead, people can adopt or construct purposes for their own lives. They can adopt purposes advocated by different political, religious, or social organizations. The purposes one may adopt or construct can include making a million dollars, teaching the blind, eradicating poverty, discovering beauty, stopping war, creating world unity, or finding truth. Most mature individuals have committed themselves to the attainment of some type of goal, in many instances a long-term goal that is in fact incapable of achievement during their own lifetimes. Their goals give purpose and meaning to their lives.

How do people come to adopt or construct goals for their own lives? What kind of experiences lead them to adopt one goal rather than another? People troubled by the absence of a goal might be encouraged to explore how other people have solved this particular problem. They might well be encouraged to experiment with different organizations and causes. They could attend meetings with people and test the goals and procedures of many organizations against their own desires. Reading biographies of key individuals to see how they formed goals for their own lives may often be instructive. The process of exploration must be an active one. The goal of the client is to engage in the type of exploration which will lead him to try on for size an alternative series of goals with the expectation that eventually he will adopt or construct some goal or combination of goals that will give meaning to his life.

The Problem Is that the Desired Behavior Is Undesirable

In certain rare instances a client may desire to achieve goals that the counselor is unwilling to help him achieve. For example, the client may be a brilliant high school student admitted to some of the best colleges in the country. He is about to decide that he will attend the local junior college because his current girl friend is going to be enrolled there. While the counselor recognizes the boy's right to make his own decisions and lead his own life, he feels that the boy is throwing away the chance for a brilliant career for reasons that he will very shortly regret. Should the counselor let the boy know of his opinion?

In general, we consider it unwise for counselors to try to sell one choice or another to clients facing a given decision. The counselor's job is to help the client consider the alternatives and to make sure the client is aware of all the consequences for each alternative. The final decision must be made by the client based on his own goals and values.

But what if the client asks for the opinion of the counselor? Suppose he says, "What would you do if you were in my shoes?" Should the counselor give a frank recommendation? In our opinion, yes. The request for an opinion is to be interpreted as a request for information. The client asking for a recommendation is in essence asking for one more bit of information, namely, what would the counselor do in his place. Our point of view is represented in the following testimony: "In the counseling I have received, I have always welcomed the opinion of my counselor, not that I have always followed his recommendation, but his opinion has always been an important factor that I have wanted to take into account in reaching my own decision."

No one can be forced to make a decision contrary to his own best judgment. The counselor's job is to help the client investigate and evaluate those factors that will influence his happiness and success in the years ahead. A thorough exploratory process means the evaluation not only of impartial information, but also a thorough exploration of the opinions of important people in the young person's life.

Who is to say what really will make the client happiest in the long run? The client must take responsibility for the success of his own decisions. The counselor's responsibility ends when

he has done all in his power to help his client learn to anticipate the probable consequences and weigh the values to be
gained and sacrificed by each of the alternatives being considered.

The Problem Is that the Client Does Not Know His Behavior Is Inappropriate

One of the dangers in counseling is that the counselor has
but one side of the story—his client's version of what is happening. People tend to distort events to place themselves in a
more favorable light and to justify their own actions. A counselor may be totally unable to determine from the client's
account exactly what the client should do in order to overcome
the particular difficulty being faced.

Consider the case of an attractive young lady who wants to
get married but finds that, although she attracts many dates,
no man continues to date her more than three times. She
blames the fickle nature of males, wants to know what to do
about it, but is totally unable to diagnose the difficulty. The
first goal of counseling in this situation would be for the client
to engage in behavior which would enable her to find out
exactly what she was doing that was causing men to avoid her.
The counselor might be unable to diagnose the difficulty himself because of his own personal commitments. Yet he must
help the client structure a course of action that will enable her
to find out what is wrong. Confrontation techniques might be
useful. One value of marathon group counseling is that in a
relatively short period of time, through enforced contact, members of a group are encouraged to tell one another exactly
what they think of each other and share ideas about ways to
improve.

Another technique available to school counselors consists of
the use of sociometric devices. For example, in the "guess who"
technique pupils are asked to nominate classmates who fit
various descriptions. Most people in our society are reluctant
to criticize another individual to his face. We seldom communicate our negative opinions directly to the person concerned. We may reject him in various subtle or not so subtle
ways, but almost never do we tell him why we are rejecting
him. It is believed (probably quite accurately) that frank,
critical evaluations will result in counteraggression against the
one voicing such criticisms. The result of this understandable

reluctance is that most people who engage in inappropriate behavior are not aware of exactly what it is they do that causes people to shun them. Diagnosing problems of this type is extremely difficult, but clearly, if the client is to make any improvement, he must know what the difficulty is.

Our three-dates-only client, if she had sufficient "ego strength," could ask one of her girlfriends to interview boyfriends who had deserted her in an endeavor to discover their reasons for doing so. The client could ask that these interview reports be transmitted either to the counselor or, depending on circumstances, to the client herself. But the identification of the difficulty is only the first step. Insight into the problem is seldom sufficient to overcome it. The diagnosis might be that the client is overly possessive, expresses jealousy, becomes bossy, attempts to demonstrate intellectual superiority, or any one of a number of possible behaviors which young men tend to avoid. Once the problem is identified, however, alternative ways of behaving can be learned.

The Problem Is a Choice Conflict

Another problem that is sometimes difficult to translate into behavioral objectives occurs when the client has a choice conflict—two desirable alternatives, both of which cannot be attained. It is the old problem of wanting to possess the eaten cake. A young man may wish to be promoted in his company and yet not wish to put in the extra effort and time required to do a top-notch job because of pressure from his fellow employees. He sees a conflict between his desire for promotion and his desire to be accepted by his fellow workers. Or a wife may no longer love her husband but may wish to maintain the financial security she enjoys as his wife. She may be torn between wanting to leave her husband and wanting to stay with him.

If requested by the client, the counselor's task is to help the client engage in a type of behavior that will enable him or her to resolve the conflict. Usually the client needs help in learning how to decide. The counselor might well begin by asking whether all possible alternatives had been considered. In almost every choice conflict there are more than two alternatives available. The ambitious but affiliative young man might well be able to devise ways to accomplish his work well without necessarily antagonizing his peers. The unhappy wife might well be able to devise ways of living somewhat more harmoniously with her husband or may be able to become more financially independent. All possible alternatives must be uncovered and considered. "Brainstorming" by both counselor and client may turn up possibilities neither would have thought of alone.

Once the possible alternatives are in the open the client can be encouraged to engage in activities which would test the feasibility of each possible alternative. The ambitious employee may experiment with taking some of his work home. The unhappy wife may try out some activities that she and her husband might enjoy together. The testing of alternative courses of action may eventually lead to a solution that these clients would find desirable.

The Problem Is a Vested Interest in Not Identifying Any Problem

Some clients may not even have a problem, but may merely want someone to listen to them talk. People who will listen indefinitely are few and far between, and the discovery that counselors are trained to do just this may seem a godsend to some verbose persons. A counselor must decide whether he wishes to have himself used in this manner. Some counselors might acquiesce, thinking this a worthwhile use of their time. Others might dismiss the client after a few sessions. A more constructive approach would be to help the client establish friendships of his own, friends who would listen to him—provided, of course, that he in turn learned to listen to them!

The client may be attempting to enhance his social status, his "image," by seeing a counselor. At present such prestige accrues more to those who undergo some kind of "therapy" such as psychoanalysis or psychiatric care, the cost of which identifies the client as a person of means. The client may have a personal interest in the counselor, perhaps a desire for a romantic attachment, but the client is not willing to express such desires explicitly. Sometimes the client finds a continuing relationship vicariously reinforcing. Other clients may wish to keep vital information from the counselor on the grounds that such information would prove embarrassing or detrimental to the client. Lazarus in Article 1 which follows has described an intriguing method for getting clients to describe what their real motives and concerns are. He calls it the "inner circle" strategy.

1

THE "INNER CIRCLE" STRATEGY: IDENTIFYING CRUCIAL PROBLEMS

Arnold A. Lazarus
TEMPLE UNIVERSITY MEDICAL SCHOOL

It is essential that the client bring meaningful material to the counselor's attention if successful counseling is to occur. Experienced counselors are aware that this truism may call for considerable skill and ingenuity when faced with particular individuals. Clients deliberately or sometimes inadvertently tend to digress; they may dwell on matters tangentially relevant or entirely beside the point. Others are inclined to conceal or distort crucial material. The present account describes a simple yet effective strategy for overcoming certain "resistances" so that clients may assume a greater willingness and ability to dwell on relevant personal issues.

Successful case reports frequently allude to the fact that the therapist was able to "ferret out relevant areas of deviant behavior" and thereafter to modify them successfully. The bulk of such reports focuses attention on the modification processes, but seldom describes the manner in which the significant dimensions of aberrant behavior were discovered. When confronted by a seemingly amorphous clinical history from which expert counselors extract specific areas of therapeutic relevance, trainees often ask: "How did you deduce that the client required desensitization to criticism and disapproval?", or "How did you realize that the problem was mainly sexual?" One answer, of course, is that the experienced counselor learns to be sensitive to certain cues and subtle responses of his client. This enables him to distinguish false and spurious leads from areas of genuine concern. The "easy" client who readily confides, confesses, and accepts counseling is obviously seldom a diagnostic or therapeutic problem. How to handle the skeptical or embarrassed and self-conscious individual is a matter that calls for more than sympathy, empathy, or a ready ear. These people need to be *taught* to confide, to be led into personal territory. Many clients need to learn what types of information can be shared and divulged both in a counseling situation and in other interpersonal settings.

The "inner circle" strategy seems very promising in developing the right therapeutic climate. It is a procedure which seems to induce confidence in the counselor and often undermines the client's neurotic guilts. The "inner circle" strategy also appears to enhance the process of problem identification by fostering the development of more intimate rapport. For illustrative purposes, the procedure will be described by referring in detail to an actual case.

CASE OF SALLY ANN

Sally Ann, age 15 years, the attractive only child of a wealthy economist and his wife, was described by her teacher as "moody, irritable . . . doing poor work . . . and aggressive." Previously she had been an excellent student, socially well-integrated and judgmentally sound. For over three months, however, she had been noticeably withdrawn; her grades had fallen sharply; she was involved in various personal clashes with other teachers and fellow students; and she threatened to commit suicide (according to her mother's report). The reason for Sally's abrupt change in behavior was first thought to be medical, but the examinations of both a prominent physician and an endocrinologist revealed no pathology. Sally Ann was accordingly referred for "counseling" and, not surprisingly, displayed hostility and suspicion toward the entire situation. Her attitude was openly belligerent. "I'm not nuts!" she protested. The usual reassurances that most processes of counseling and therapy are in fact not intended for psychotics elicited a petulant shrug. The "inner circle" strategy was immediately prompted by a subsequent rejoinder that she disliked the idea of someone "prying into my private affairs." The dialogue then continued more or less as follows:

Counselor: You know, I always feel uneasy about people who value their privacy so highly. I mean, what have most people really got to hide?

Sally Ann: Wouldn't you like to know!

Counselor: Seriously, most people make a big deal about their own hang-ups, but when you get down to it, there's nothing really terrible about them.

Sally Ann: What do you mean?

Counselor: Well, if someone was hiding the fact that he was a murderer or a blackmailer or something, I could understand his concern about not being found out, but most of us don't really have anything important to hide.

Sally Ann: I might just want to hide the fact that I had two helpings of ice cream for dinner. If I want to keep that to myself, I have a right to.

Counselor: Sure you do. There should be no compulsion to tell, but there should also be no compulsion *not* to tell. Perhaps I can explain my position more easily by means of a diagram.

(The following diagram is drawn on a blank card or a piece of scrap paper:)

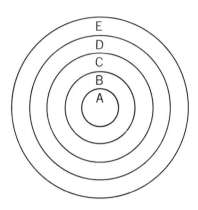

Counselor: Now this depicts the way many people function. Do you see the small inner circle marked A? Well, that represents the person's private territory, his own inner world, the part he shares with nobody. Okay? Now look at circle B. That's the part of his life, feelings, thoughts, and experiences that he shares only with his closest friends or confidants. In other words, his very closest friends are allowed free access to all or any information in E, D, C, or B, but nobody is allowed into A. Do you understand what I'm saying?

Sally Ann: Yes.

Counselor: Okay. Now look at circle C. The person will allow several good close friends to enter circle C. These good friends can go anywhere in E, D, and C, but they will not be allowed into B, which is reserved only for the person's very closest friends, and of course, nobody is allowed to enter circle A. The territory around D is for acquaintances (who are not allowed into C or B), and E represents the person's superficial contact with the world at large. The sort of information that may be gathered by minimal social contact. Do you follow me?

Sally Ann: Are you saying that this is normal?

Counselor: I'm not placing a value judgment on it. I'm merely saying that many people operate this way.

Sally Ann: What if nobody is allowed into A or B?

Counselor: Ah! Then A instead of being a small circle will be as large as "A + B." Such a person would presumably be so much on the

defensive that he wouldn't allow anyone to get really close to him. I don't think he'd be particularly happy.

Sally Ann: Why not?

Counselor: Well, because I feel that the truly happy and self-fulfilling people are those who don't make barriers around the inner circle A.

Sally Ann: You mean they just blab to everybody about everything?

Counselor: No. They are selective and discreet, but unlike most people, they don't reserve circle A only for themselves, but share this highly personal zone with certain loved and trusted persons.

Sally Ann: Mmm!

Counselor: Let's pause to consider the usual ingredients or the contents of circle A. What do you think it consists of? What are most people so busily keeping to themselves or so actively hiding from others? The information in circle A is usually made up of one or more of the following categories: sex, anger, dishonesty, financial matters, and issues of personal competence.

Sally Ann: Say that again.

Counselor: Well, let me elaborate. To some people, just about everything is private and secret. Their personalities can be depicted as a giant A circle and a narrow outer E circle. To use an earlier example you quoted, these people might just get sufficiently "personal" to tell you that they had ice cream or perhaps beefstew for lunch. If you asked them a question like, "What did you pay for your dog's collar?," they would avoid giving you a straight answer and might tell you to mind your own business or not to get so personal.

Sally Ann: Well, other people might be self-conscious about their age, or their religion, or their parents, or something else which might bother them more than sex or dishonesty—I forget the other things you mentioned.

Counselor: Agreed. What I'm saying is merely that most people in our culture regard as highly private and personal all matters relating to their own sexual deeds or feelings; their own aggressive or hostile impulses; any acts of dishonesty such as lying, cheating, or stealing; money matters such as their earnings, assets, or debts; and whether or not they consider themselves frauds or phonies, or if they really regard themselves as competent as they pretend to be.

Sally Ann: So I still don't see the point you're making.

Counselor: I am implying that since the contents of circle A are more or less the same for everybody, people shouldn't feel so negatively different from other members of the human race and use up so much energy keeping the world out of circle A. I mean everyone has lied or been dishonest in some way or another. . . .

Sally Ann: Okay, so what if circle A doesn't concern your own misdeeds but those of somebody else?

Counselor: I guess the key word here is *misdeeds*. Short of something like assault or murder, who's to say that it's definitely a misdeed? Most things are relative and purely a matter of opinion.

Sally Ann: All right! What would you say if I told you that I think my father is carrying on with another woman?

Counselor: First, I would say that he has his reasons, if the allegation is true. Secondly, I would want more evidence. Thirdly, I would want to know exactly why this bothers you so much and why you think you have a right to judge him.

For present purposes, there is no point in extending the counseling dialogue beyond this point. A crucial issue had finally been reached, and the first objective of problem identification had been fulfilled. A young girl was referred for counseling and arrived feeling angry and defensive. If the counselor had responded in a passive, less structured manner, would he have elicited such highly-charged information so rapidly, if at all?

For purposes of closure, it should be mentioned that Sally Ann's suspicions were unfounded. At the counselor's instigation, she confronted her father about her misgivings, and he satisfactorily accounted for those actions which had aroused his daughter's suspicions.

It became more obvious that Sally Ann was hypersensitive to many areas of dissension between her parents who in fact enjoyed a somewhat abrasive but basically sound relationship. A program of systematic desensitization to their somewhat frequent verbal altercations rendered her much less vulnerable in this regard. At the end of the next semester, her grade average was in the top ten percent, and her teacher commented on Sally Ann's "obvious adaptability."

It should be noted that the counselor assisted Sally Ann in preparing to confront her father. For example, Sally Ann was afraid that her father might become extremely irate and accuse her of being insolent and presumptuous, or at the opposite extreme, she feared that he might become excessively contrite and repentant. Role-playing procedures with the counselor playing the father prepared Sally Ann for a variety of likely and unlikely responses from her father.

ADVANTAGES OF THE "INNER CIRCLE" STRATEGY

To present the case of Sally Ann as a bright, 15-year-old whose grade average declined and whose interpersonal clashes appeared to be a function of her home situation is brief but accurate. To omit the "inner circle" strategy, which allows the counselor so much scope to get at the client's personal values and so many opportunities for subtle and meaningful communications, is to circumvent an area of "behavior modification" in some ways perhaps more crucial than specific counseling procedures.

Several counselors who have made use of this procedure have reported that they find that it immediately tends to focus their clients' attention on personal and relevant material. It appears to provide a double economy in that meaningful material is uncovered more rapidly and clients also seem to emerge with a "cognitive map" which helps them model future interpersonal relationships.

PART II

Reinforcement Techniques

PROBABLY THE MOST DISTINCTIVE FEATURE of behavioral counseling is its use of reinforcement techniques. The value of reinforcement, however, has long been recognized. Mark Twain once said, "I can live for two months on a good compliment." Shakespeare said, "Our praises are our wages."

Reinforcement appears to be a simple technique, but its apparent simplicity is deceptive. In simple animal studies psychologists can easily identify that food and water constitute effective reinforcers when administered to animals deprived of them for an interval of time. That is, a "hungry" animal given food after turning right in a maze will tend to turn right more frequently in the future. Food is said to be a reinforcer in these circumstances because the presentation of it following a response increases the frequency of that type of response in the future.

Animals will also learn to respond to conditioned reinforcers. When a click consistently precedes the presentation of food, animals will learn to modify their behavior if it is followed by a click. The click constitutes an effective conditioned reinforcer only if it is frequently associated with a more primary reinforcer.

Counselors are seldom in a position to use primary reinforcers though occasionally candy M & M's are used to reinforce a certain kind of behavior (for example, Articles 18 and 25). Counselors more often use conditioned reinforcers, usually certain types of words, because for most human beings in our society these words have been associated with more primary reinforcers in the past. The conditioning history of most individuals in families and schools has involved the association of primary reinforcers with such words as "good," "nice job," "fine work," "beautiful." These words would be like clicks to the animal who had associated them with more primary reinforcers. A person who had grown up in a culture where these words were not associated with primary reinforcers would not be able to respond appropriately to them until he had learned to make necessary translations.

Words of praise or approval cannot be used with the assurance that they will always be effective reinforcers. In the first place, not everyone in our society has grown up having these same words paired with more primary reinforcers. For some individuals kind words may have been used by people who were weak and powerless, while the powerful figures dealt out punishment and abuse during mealtime. Thus, words which are reinforcing for the majority of the population might be repudiated by a few who would respond to a harsher language.

A second reason for the sometimes unpredictable effectiveness of alleged reinforcers is that conditioned reinforcers gradually lose their effectiveness if used too frequently without pairing them with more primary reinforcement. A counselor who uses words of praise and approval too generously will find that the words have little impact. It is necessary to be discriminating in the use of reinforcers, using them only when one is sincerely pleased with specifically identified progress.

It is also necessary to arrange that these words of praise are accompanied by more substantial types of reinforcement. A counselor cannot rely upon words alone to reinforce approved behavior. The verbally approved behavior must also have positive consequences. That is, the individual being reinforced by the counselor with words must also experience more substantial rewards.

Suppose that a high school boy who wants to plan his future says, "I think I would like to find out more about accounting as a career," and the counselor replies, "Good." The counselor utters the word "good" in the hope that it will be a reinforcing stimulus which will encourage the boy to engage in some exploratory activity concerning a possible career choice. But is the word actually reinforcing? We have evidence from many studies that the word "good" when uttered soon after a response tends to increase the frequency of that response. But there are also many instances in which the word "good" did not have the desired effect. Some people seem to have better luck with it than others. It works with some people some of the time and not with other people at other times. All we can say with any assurance is that on the average, given certain conditions, the word "good" does seem to function as a reinforcer.

If the boy who talked about exploring accounting as a career did not explore further and did not even talk about further exploratory activity, we would have to conclude that the word "good" did not serve as a reinforcer in that instance. Strictly speaking we do not know whether any given stimulus actually serves as a reinforcer until we later observe whether it resulted in an increase in the response which it followed. From a practical point of view, however, we do know that certain classes of stimuli tend to serve a reinforcing function in a number of situations. The use of certain stimuli as possible reinforcers in counseling cannot be guaranteed to have any given result, but on the basis of past experience these stimuli seem highly likely to serve as reinforcers. In any given practical situation the counselor can only try and see.

Since the counselor is often not in a position to administer rewards himself, it is frequently advisable for him to arrange reinforcing circumstances in the client's natural environment. Thus, counselors are encouraged to work with teachers in structuring classroom environments where students will receive rewards and to work with parents who are in a still better position to help their children. The counselor's words may provide the initial impetus to start a new course of action, but they will not be sufficient to maintain a new pattern of behavior unless more substantial rewards are forthcoming to the individual.

Verbal rewards are seldom sufficient if the client does not wish to change in the same direction as the counselor. Agreement between counselor and client on the goals to be accomplished is usually a prerequisite for effective behavior change. Verbal reinforcement and support from a counselor can be extremely helpful to a client when used to support that client in making difficult behavior changes desired by that client. The same verbal symbols, however, can be totally ineffective and possibly even resented by a client when they are used in an effort to influence the client in ways that the client himself does not desire.

Another complexity is in defining the response to be reinforced. A response is clearly more than the simple contraction of a single muscle. Extremely complex patterns of behavior seem amenable to the influence of positive reinforcement. For example, when students are reinforced for talking about possible exploratory activities, they do in fact emit a wide variety of different responses. One of these patterns might consist of walking to the school library, asking the librarian for a book about a particular career, checking the book out of the library, reading the book, returning to the counselor and discussing the information. Some high school students can emit such a complicated pattern of behavior because they have learned over the years that all of these steps are part of what must be involved in obtaining further information about a career. However, for others who have not yet learned all the parts of this complicated response, a counselor's reinforcing talk about exploratory activity might not result in this complex pattern at all. It might be necessary to reinforce each substep in order to help some clients learn how to explore a career choice.

The complexity of patterns that may respond to reinforcement has no known limit. Whether a given pattern will respond to reinforcement for any particular student cannot be guaranteed in advance. It depends upon whether the student has learned the subresponses involved in the major response being reinforced. If reinforcing a complex pattern of behavior does not seem to yield the desired results, one possible difficulty may be that the pattern needs to be analyzed into its constituent elements and the student reinforced for performing each subpart.

Part II is designed to illustrate the wide variety of complex response patterns that counselors, psychologists, and teachers can influence through the use of a variety of reinforcers. Although the basic notion of reinforcement is a simple one, we will see that in actual practice its application is more difficult. Professional personnel who are dedicated to the welfare of each client will need to be more skillful and sensitive than ever.

Arranging Reinforcement
and Extinction Contingencies

THE KEY TO THE SUCCESSFUL use of reinforcement is proper timing. The reinforcer must be presented immediately following the desired behavior, and it must not be presented immediately following undesired behavior. The basic idea is extremely simple, but many teachers and counselors find it difficult to apply in practice.

Very frequently teachers ignore the productive task-oriented behavior that they are hoping to encourage and, instead, pay attention to a child only when he is causing difficulty. Attention from a powerful adult figure may frequently serve as a reinforcer to a child even when that attention may seem somewhat aversive to the adult. Article 2 by Vance provides a good example of how teachers with the best of intentions may ignore a child when he is doing well but attend to him when he is causing trouble. The counselor's role in this case was to reverse the process, helping the teachers to attend to the child when he was making improvements in his behavior and to ignore him when he was causing difficulty.

Article 3 by Castle describes a similar situation in junior high school. The problem again is one of proper timing. However, the counselor had to do more than merely time her own reinforcers properly. She had to arrange for both the teachers and the child's mother to cooperate in the proper timing of their reinforcers. If the teachers or parents are reinforcing the undesirable behavior, then the counselor alone is virtually powerless to help the child. It's like bailing a ruptured boat with a thimble. Castle shows how the cooperative efforts of counselor, teacher, and parent, all focused on the same problem behavior, can produce some significant changes.

In a rather unusual case which still illustrates the basic principles, Rickard and Griffin, in Article 4, report how soiling behavior has been modified through the use of well-timed reinforcing contingencies. Rickard and Griffin show how the cooperative efforts of several camp counselors and even the cooperation of other campers themselves are combined to contribute to a difficult case in toilet training. When the contingencies of reinforcement used in the camp are not followed by similar contingencies in the home, the child's behavior reverts somewhat to what it was before. It is possible for a child to learn to engage in one pattern of behavior at camp and a quite different pattern of behavior at home. These differences are frequently the result of inconsistent reinforcement contingencies in the two situations.

The use of reinforcement and the goals for which it is used can be completely open. Rickard and Griffin describe how the goal was made perfectly clear in the case of Bill, and it was a goal to which Bill himself subscribed. There is some evidence that indicates that behavior changes will be accomplished more readily if the child knows precisely what behavior he wants to change, what behavior is going to be reinforced, what behavior will not be reinforced, and what the reinforcers are. Although such openness is not necessary to the success of reinforcement techniques, it probably enhances their effectiveness and contributes to an honest and straightforward relationship between the child and his teachers, parents, and counselors.

2

MODIFYING HYPERACTIVE AND AGGRESSIVE BEHAVIOR

Barbara J. Vance
BRIGHAM YOUNG UNIVERSITY

Danny was almost five years old when he entered the summer Head Start class. During the first week he played alone most of the time, usually with finger toys such as puzzles, wooden table trains, beads, and geometric tiles. At the beginning of the second week Danny ventured into the art corner where he eventually dabbled at the easel paints, tried a touch of fingerpaint, wiped a piece of colored chalk across a sheet of paper, or pasted a few colored strips onto a sheet of construction paper. But most of the time Danny just observed life in his new surroundings. At snack time he barely nibbled at his food as he concentrated his gaze on the other children or the teachers. At story time he watched the book or picture from his chair at the snack table some distance away, ignoring encouragement from the teacher aide to join the rest of the children in the story circle.

And then Danny's behavior began to change, subtly but perceptibly. At the snack table he would slowly tip over another child's glass of juice. He would saunter over to the block corner and pull out the bottom block of a tower, turning away as the blocks came tumbling to the floor. The teacher aide would turn around just in time to see the last napkin disappear in the waste basket after she had finished setting the table for a snack. The paint brushes would suddenly turn up in the wrong color of paint, obviously Danny's handiwork. Outdoors Danny would constantly throw the ball outside the fence. When the teacher announced time to go indoors, Danny would engage in such inappropriate behavior only when he had first caught the eye of a teacher. He always received prompt scolding for this behavior.

During staff discussions Danny's teachers expressed frustration in their ability to cope with him. His behavior was destructive, impulsive, and disruptive of group functions. When it was suggested that they might be reinforcing Danny for inappropriate behavior each time they scolded him, the teachers became defensive, arguing that Danny's behavior was so destructive and disruptive that it had to be handled immediately and usually in a punishing manner (that is, by scolding). However, as discussion of Danny's specific behavior continued, it became apparent that most of his inappropriate behavior could be ignored without real danger to persons or property. At the same time the teachers began to recognize appropriate behavior and to give him attention either verbally or nonverbally when Danny engaged in appropriate behaviors.[1]

Later the teachers confessed how difficult it was to ignore Danny's inappropriate behavior, but they stuck to the plan. They had been cautioned that an intermittent schedule of reinforcement would make the inappropriate behavior even more difficult to extinguish. Therefore, even though Danny ran in the opposite direction when the teachers announced time to go indoors, they ignored him and let him run. They wondered if Danny would come back. The first time he ran outside the fence, laughing and yelling in his usual manner to attract the attention of the teacher, one

[1] Editors' Note: Skilled leadership is required to help some teachers try a new approach. Sometimes a useful approach consists of "How about trying it for a week to see what happens?"

of the other children commented, "Look, teacher, there goes Danny again." The teacher simply said, "I wonder what we're going to have for snack today," and continued walking toward the classroom with the other children. Danny watched a few seconds from the other side of the fence, then ran up to the door after the children were seated and yelled, "Teacher, look at me!" Some of the children turned around but the teacher went on talking about the subject at hand as she ate her snack.[2]

The following day Danny came indoors with the other children but was the last to come in. Instead of washing his hands and finding a place at the snack table, he played with the blocks, building high towers and knocking them down, looking at the teacher each time he knocked them down. The teacher ignored him, as did the children by this time.[3]

The third day Danny came in at the tail end of the group and went to the block corner as he had done the day before. However, just before the end of snack time, Danny ran to the table and sat down in an empty chair. All the cookies had been eaten but some juice was left. The teacher said, "Danny, the cookies are all gone, but we'll be glad to give you some juice." A cup of juice was then poured for Danny. All the other children put their napkins and paper cups in the wastebasket as usual. Danny left his on the table. This was ignored.

The fourth day Danny came indoors with the other children, washed his hands, and found a place at the table for snack. The head teacher made a point of sitting by Danny. She didn't make a big point of his coming to the table. She simply included him in the conversation with the rest of the children.[4]

At the same time Danny's behavior in other areas of the curriculum became more constructive. The ball no longer was thrown outside the fence. Instead, the teacher helped Danny find other children who would play ball with him. Danny began to build his own structures with blocks rather than to knock down block structures built by other children. Pinching and hitting behavior stopped as suddenly as it had started. Whenever Danny engaged in painting or other art work, the teacher made a point of giving Danny encouragement by such statements as "I like the colors

[2] Editors' Note: Danny was getting no reinforcement from the teacher following his inappropriate behavior.

[3] Editors' Note: Children will frequently model their own behavior after a respected teacher. Even the behavior for reinforcing or extinguishing a response will be imitated. The combination of both teacher and peer extinction procedures was now in effect for Danny.

[4] Editors' Note: This low-keyed inconspicuous reinforcement may often be more effective than more overt reinforcement, particularly with cases of chronic disruptive behavior. For a contrasting example see Article 7 where conspicuous reinforcement apparently had the reverse effect intended. The "Look-everybody-how-nice-that-Joe-stopped-beating-his-wife" type of reinforcement tends to call more attention to the inappropriate behavior than to the change.

you are using," or "Your picture is very interesting, Danny. Tell me about it." When Danny gave another child a turn on the tricycle, a teacher was available to say "I'm glad you remembered to give Tony a turn." Danny began to smile some, to talk more, and to explore creatively the materials and equipment of the nursery school. The radical change in Danny's behavior from inappropriate to appropriate, destructive to constructive, disruptive to cooperative, non-verbal to verbal was accomplished in less than two weeks and continued throughout the eight-week session of summer Head Start.

3

ASSUMING RESPONSIBILITY FOR APPROPRIATE CLASSROOM BEHAVIOR

Wanda K. Castle
REDWOOD CITY ELEMENTARY SCHOOL DISTRICT (CALIFORNIA)

In the first week of classes several teachers had contacted me regarding the appearance and behavior of Jerry, one of our seventh graders. He had initially attracted attention by wearing unique hats to school, but his teachers were primarily concerned with his continual tardiness to class and lack of materials. Jerry seemed to arrive late to each class during the day with extensive excuses for his tardiness and his lack of books, pencils, and paper. His teachers were also concerned by Jerry's frequent use of baby talk and the making of noises resembling various machines during class. Jerry was reported to be an excellent contributor to class discussions, but now he was creating a disturbance.

Jerry's cumulative folder indicated above average scholastic aptitude test scores throughout elementary school although his grades were consistently below average. Teachers' comments referred to difficulties relating to peers. His records also indicated that Jerry lived with his mother who worked during the afternoon and early evening.

On the following Monday, Jerry and I had our first interview.[1] He

---

[1] Editors' Note: Interviews with the student are not always required in situations like this. Some counselors might ask the teacher for permission to observe classroom behavior; others might work directly with teachers to modify the classroom environment.

was extremely verbal and congenial. We discussed his impressions of the first week of junior high school. When I inquired about his tardiness and apparent disorganization, he said that other people were causing his tardiness and unpreparedness for class. He specified such instances as his locker being jammed, other students being in his way near his locker and in the halls, students taking his pencil from his pocket while in the hall, and other people removing his materials from his desk during class. When he was describing these reasons, he began to use some baby talk. I then asked Jerry how he might improve his organization. He made several suggestions as to what other people might do, suggestions to which I made no response. When he did make a suggestion indicating a change in his own behavior, such as keeping extra pencils in his locker, I remarked, "That's a good idea!" or a similar positive reaction.[2] At the close of our conversation I asked Jerry to review the things he could do to help his preparedness for class during the week, again attempting to reinforce only those statements which referred to his own behaviors. An appointment was made for the following week to discuss his progress.

TEACHER REINFORCEMENT

Following the interview with Jerry I talked for some time with the teacher who had indicated the most concern and willingness to help Jerry improve his behavior.[3] I asked her to try to ignore Jerry when he was late or lacking materials and to make positive remarks when he did arrive before the bell with necessary materials. As this was Jerry's first class each morning, the teacher suggested that when he arrived wearing an unusual hat she would ask him quietly as he entered to place it on her desk and pick it up at the end of the day. No other references would be made to the hat. Occasional positive remarks as to his appearance could be made on those days his head was unadorned.

Two weeks later this teacher reported that Jerry was now arriving to her class on time and with his materials, but I found he was still experiencing difficulties with these behaviors in his other classes. I then talked with his other teachers, asking them to try this reinforcement pattern. We discussed the desirability of reinforcing other behaviors. We planned to comment on Jerry's appearance when Jerry was not wearing a hat or unusual clothing rather than calling attention to any such embellishments. We planned to respond positively to his more mature speech pat-

[2] Editors' Note: The counselor is trying to get Jerry to assume responsibility for his own behavior by extinguishing Jerry's blaming others and reinforcing Jerry's ideas for changing his own behavior.

[3] Editors' Note: Good idea to work first with the teacher already most willing to help.

terns, ignoring his baby talk and noises. Most of Jerry's teachers were quite willing to participate.

COUNSELOR REINFORCEMENT

During this time and in the following weeks Jerry and I met on a one-to-one basis at least once a week. Our first conversations centered on ways to assist Jerry's organization for each class, but our topics broadened to include desired relations with peers, changes in behavior which might be conductive to such relationships, appropriate school attire, and the desirability of good enunciation. The emphasis was upon allowing Jerry to formulate what he felt the desired behavior might be and thinking with him about ways to help his behavior more closely approximate it.[4] I tried at all times to respond positively to remarks indicating some acceptance of responsibility for his own actions.

I inquired informally as to Jerry's progress from his teachers quite often but after about a month felt that a sharing of ideas and experiences might be helpful to all. A conference was scheduled and most of Jerry's teachers were able to attend. All reported improvement, some much more than others. Jerry still reverted to baby talk and had difficulty in establishing positive relationships with others in his class, but the noises and unusual attire seemed to be much diminished. The conference seemed to motivate those involved to continue their efforts.[5]

PARENT REINFORCEMENT

As we felt it would be beneficial to seek cooperation and assistance from the home, I contacted Jerry's mother to arrange an appointment. She was somewhat hesitant but finally agreed to come to the school. Initially she made many excuses for Jerry's behavior and indicated that she regarded him as a small child. When we discussed the importance of learning to accept some responsibility, however, she did indicate that she felt this would be worthwhile and that she would be willing to help. We talked about possible ways to assist Jerry, such as praising him when assignments were completed, making positive remarks when responsibility was shown, and ignoring baby talk. I felt that the conference was

---

[4] Editors' Note: Jerry is being helped to formulate what *he* wants to accomplish. Though the school has certain common goals for all students, the unique role for the counselor is in helping each student state his own goals and devise means of reaching them.

[5] Editors' Note: Those who do the reinforcing need reinforcement too, especially when progress is slow.

valuable in that Jerry's mother realized that the school was interested in Jerry and that we could work together to help him.

Throughout the year I continued to meet with Jerry on a one-to-one basis, talk with his mother periodically, and work with his teachers as much as possible. Jerry seemed to show slow but steady change toward more desirable behavior. Some behaviors seemed to be extinguished, such as wearing bizarre clothing and making machine noises during class. There were still evidences of baby talk and a tendency to blame others for his difficulties, but these appeared to be much less frequent.[6] Jerry's grades had improved, and there was only an occasional instance of tardiness or the forgetting of class materials. He was certainly not a popular member of his class, but he had made some friends. His teachers were generally pleased with his progress and were eager to try reinforcement procedures with other students. I felt that the reinforcement that the faculty members provided was the most important factor in Jerry's improved behavior.

4

REDUCING SOILING BEHAVIOR IN A THERAPEUTIC SUMMER CAMP

Henry C. Rickard and John L. Griffin
UNIVERSITY OF ALABAMA

The amelioration of soiling behavior through reinforcement procedures has been reported by Madsen (1965) and Peterson and Lundon (1965). The latter study is of particular interest because of the authors' emphasis upon cognitive awareness as part of the total treatment plan. As an example they point out that in verbal conditioning experiments, aware subjects produced more plural nouns than did subjects who reported no awareness (Dulaney, 1961, 1962).

The present study stresses both reinforcement for adaptive responses and cognitive awareness. The camper was administered social and candy

---

[6] Editors' Note: One advantage of defining objectives as behavior changes is that one can measure progress by counting the frequency with which a given behavior occurs.

reinforcers for bowel movements under proper stimulus control, the benefits to be derived from bowel control were freely discussed, and attempts were made to help the camper verbalize and be aware of bodily sensations preceding bowel evacuation.

PROBLEM BEHAVIOR

Bill was seven years old when first referred to the therapeutic summer camp. He had a sister one-and-a-half years his senior and a brother one-and-a-half years younger. His father was a graduate student nearing completion of his training; his mother was a housewife and a part-time student in an undergraduate program. Bill had been performing satisfactorily in his school work, but had experienced great difficulty in relating to his peers both at school and in the neighborhood. The parents reported that the primary difficulty was his soiling behavior which had led to rejection by his companions.

When Bill was five a physical condition related to his chronic constipation was diagnosed, operated upon, and presumably corrected. Following the operation Bill was no longer constipated, but his bowel movements failed to come under control as expected. Subsequently, Bill was referred by his physician to a psychologist for a personality evaluation. The results of the psychological tests suggested the possibility of psychogenic causes for the lack of bowel training. The parents were referred to a child guidance center for further evaluation. As a result of the evaluation the youngster was diagnosed as an adjustment reaction of childhood, and play therapy was recommended. Play therapy sessions extended over a period of approximately 16 months. The therapist felt that the child benefited from play therapy but was concerned because the major problem, bowel control, had not responded to treatment. The center felt that the child needed a group living experience and a chance for peer masculine identification. Upon the recommendation of the guidance center the parents referred Bill to the therapeutic summer camp.

THE FIRST CAMP SEASON

Bill's initial behavior at camp was friendly, open, and cooperative. He displayed good verbal skills, reading and conversing easily and intelligently. Initially he responded affectionately with much hugging and "hanging-on" to anyone who attended to him, particularly the counselors and older campers.

He was, however, very resistant to discussing his soiling problem, and it was frequently necessary to remind him to change clothes. During the season the staff agreed that if Bill's soiling behavior was indeed a symptom, the best approach would be an indirect one aimed at building his self-concept and defenses. The plan followed consistently throughout the summer was to place Bill in as many activities as possible where he could obtain a measure of success. The plan was to reinforce adaptive activities with his peers and to minimize failure experiences. He was given special tutoring in games where he was not effective and was encouraged and prompted until he participated in practically all ongoing events. In effect, Bill's treatment during the first camp season was directed toward the development of skills and abilities in numerous areas, particularly the interpersonal, but without a direct emphasis on toilet training.

THE SECOND CAMP SEASON

Following the first camp season the parents reported that Bill had made improvement, particularly in relating to his peers, but that he had shown little progress in bowel control. Prior to accepting Bill for a second camp season a "contract" was mailed to him.[1] In the contract it was pointed out to Bill that his camp experience would have a specific goal—to obtain control of his soiling behavior. It was emphasized to Bill and his parents that, while it was believed that Bill would profit from the total camp program, the main emphasis would be upon direct attempts to modify his soiling behavior. Bill was eager to attend camp and agreed to the contract.

During the first two weeks of camp no treatment procedures were introduced. During this baseline period Bill soiled from two to six times per day and on no occasions successfully used the bathroom. It was observed that he soiled most frequently after the noon meal, during vigorous activity, and at times when he was emotionally upset, for instance, when he was required to take a typhoid shot.

Starting with the third week of camp the group leader, who was working with Bill and seven other boys in a cabin group, began taking every possible opportunity to talk with Bill about his soiling behavior. This counselor had already gained Bill's confidence and respect, having been his cabin counselor during the past season. The counselor concentrated particularly upon trying to help Bill verbalize his feelings about soiling and, more specifically, to help him identify somatic feelings preceding urination and the feelings preceding bowel evacuation. These efforts to talk about the soiling problem and to identify somatic cues continued

---

[1] Editors' Note: Behavor contracts will be described more extensively in Part II, under "Using Behavior Contracts," and illustrated in Articles 15, 16, and 17.

at the rate of about three to four times per week for the remainder of the eight-week camping period.[2]

After the noon meal, at the beginning of the fourth week, the counselor asked Bill to use the toilet. A successful bowel movement was accomplished and Bill was rewarded with chocolate candy. Success was again obtained the following day under the same conditions. On the third day success was obtained but Bill refused to take the chocolate, apparently fearful that the other campers would become aware of the bowel training procedure. During the fifth week the counselor continued sending Bill to the toilet once each day and success was obtained about half of the time. It should be noted that Bill also soiled once or twice a day during this period. During the same period, Bill made his first successful trip to the toilet without reminding or urging from the counselor.

During the sixth week the counselor who had been working with Bill had an accident which took him away from the camp. A second counselor took over supervisory duties and soon reported that Bill was beginning to resist and manipulate. When the counselor set limits or made demands, Bill would soil and become negativistic in other ways. It appeared as if Bill was making efforts at controlling his soiling behavior contingent upon the counselor not setting limits and not making demands.[3] The counselor pointed out what the youngster was doing and stated that Bill must meet his contract to overcome his soiling behavior and at the same time function well with the group.

At the end of the seventh week the senior counselor returned and Bill was sent to the toilet twice a day. He was successful on each occasion and soiled only once during that period. During that time two group sessions of approximately thirty minutes duration were held with both counselors and the entire cabin group of eight boys present, for the specific purpose of allowing each group member to talk about the problems which had brought him to camp. These sessions were designed to desensitize each of the boys, and particularly Bill, to his individual problem. Although Bill feared the group meetings, he had been prepared in advance and was ready to talk about his difficulties. He received a great deal of support from the other group members and was able to describe his soiling behavior more easily than he had anticipated.

During the last ten days of camp Bill was informed that he must be responsible for going to the toilet and that he would not be reminded. During the first three days of this "weaning" period Bill soiled once. During the last seven days of camp he used the toilet without cues from

---

[2] Editors' Note: Exactly how valuable these discussions were is difficult to evaluate in this case.

[3] Editors' Note: Children can and do use reinforcement and extinction procedures also.

the counselors and no further incidents of soiling behavior were identified. At the close of camp an exit interview was held with Bill and his parents in which Bill's soiling behavior was freely discussed. Bill was pleased with the progress he had made, and the counselors and his parents expressed the hope that he would be able to take the progress home with him.

The intervention which appeared most effective was social reinforcement administered by the counselors. The counselors held a high status position with the youngsters and were associated with many reinforcement experiences including guidance on building projects, leadership on hikes and explorations, and providers of food on cook-out days. Approval from the counselors was sought by Bill and the other campers, and presumably served as a powerful social reinforcer.

FOLLOW-UP

Two months after the close of the second season a follow-up study was made. A questionnaire containing specific questions was sent to Bill's parents. In addition, they were invited to make whatever comments they thought were appropriate. The parents indicated that Bill's soiling behavior had decreased but was still evident almost once a day. They stated that he talked about his soiling behavior more easily, although still reluctantly. He was described as having about the same success in obtaining friends. The mother stated that he was still showing greater maturity in the home although he still was not doing well with potential friends in the neighborhood. His school behavior, which had always been acceptable, remained good.

Soiling behavior had been brought under control in the camp situation. The follow-up study suggests that although some improvement was evident in the home situation the newly acquired response did not generalize as well as anticipated. The camper lived at a distance which prohibited direct contact after the camping season. It is possible that a continuing counseling relationship with the parents would have been helpful in transferring to the parents the techniques which were successful at camp.

Identifying Effective
and Ineffective Reinforcers

THE THREE ARTICLES in this section illustrate some interesting features of both effective and ineffective reinforcement. Article 5 by Daley demonstrates how common activities can be used as reinforcers. He describes how a "reinforcement menu" was built by observing the activities in which children ordinarily engage. Then the opportunity to engage in these frequently chosen activities could be used as a reinforcing stimulus. The research was done with mentally retarded children, but the basic idea of using popular activities to reinforce initially more onerous activities is an interesting idea which might well be investigated further by counselors.

Articles 6 and 7 are courageous reports by two secure counselors about their failures in the use of reinforcement in counseling. Article 6 by Korn describes the case of a girl whose standards were so high that praise for her present performance was resented. Article 7 by Varenhorst presents an interesting case of a boy who apparently reverted to undesirable patterns of behavior as the result of a counselor's reinforcement. These two cases clearly point out the complexities involved in the use of reinforcement. The events that are reinforcing for one client may not necessarily be reinforcing for another. It is frequently difficult for a counselor to discover what kinds of events will be reinforcing for any given individual.

It is important to be aware of the fact that individuals do differ in their response to alleged reinforcers so that if one technique does not work, something else can be tried. A great deal of both formal and informal experimentation is needed to discover precisely what kinds of events will be most useful for helping which kinds of clients achieve the changes they desire in their own behavior.

41

5

THE "REINFORCEMENT MENU": FINDING EFFECTIVE REINFORCERS

Marvin F. Daley[1]
UTAH STATE UNIVERSITY

A concept of reinforcement has been developed by Premack which states that "for any pair of responses, the more probable one will reinforce the less probable one (Premack, 1965)." Taking Premack literally, *any* behavior can be used as a reinforcer of *any* other lower probability behavior at the instant that the behavior is a higher probability one. It is not necessary when attempting to modify behavior to depend wholly on candy or trinkets as reinforcers as did early investigators. It is necessary only that the contingency manager be able to identify what students *are doing* most frequently in a given environment.[2]

Homme (1963) observed children in a preschool nursery. The children would run around the room, scream, push a chair across the floor, and play games. All these behaviors were occurring most of the time. As one would expect, the instruction, "come and sit down," would go unnoticed. Applying the Premack principle, the contingency manager allowed the children to engage in their usual behaviors contingent or dependent upon the subjects doing a very small amount of what the experimenters instructed them to do. A typical early contingency required the children briefly to sit quietly in chairs and look at the blackboard. The behavior was followed quickly by the command, "Everybody run and scream now." Immediate control over the situation was obtained. The time spent sitting in chairs was progressively increased and training in school skills was begun. The experimenters reported that they were able to teach the entire first grade repertoire to these students in about one month of training.

In another experiment, Homme (1965a) was able to demonstrate that

---

[1] Mrs. Cheryl Vajanasoontorn played a major role in conducting a part of the research on which the report is based.

[2] Editors' Note: "Contingency manager" as used here stresses the importance of controlling the consequences of certain behaviors, that is, seeing to it that certain things happen when behavior occurs.

preschool Indian children could make substantial improvements in learning English when taught by a contingency management system.

Still another twist for gaining better control over the contingency management has been to develop a kind of "menu" of activities that represent high probability response (Addison and Homme, 1966). The menu has been put in a book form with systematic line drawings or stick figure sketches of the activities. The subject is presented with the menu before executing the task to be learned and is allowed to select from it an event which for him at that moment is a high probability event. Upon completion of the task, he is allowed to go to the reinforcement area and his selection is immediately made available. Homme has suggested that certain reinforcing events could be "daily specials" to be made available on a restricted basis. With contingency management and the Premack principles, the teacher is in a position to deliberately, systematically, and efficiently modify behavior.

One of our first experiments was designed to parallel the regular classroom situation. Five 8- to 11-year-old mentally retarded children from the Cache Valley Day Care and Training Center served as subjects. They were very difficult to motivate and often displayed nonacceptable behavior in the school atmosphere.

Extensive observations were carried out producing 22 items which, because of their high frequency of occurrence, were considered to be high probability behaviors:

a. Talking	i. Dancing	q. Using Colored Pencils
b. Writing	j. Walking	r. Singing
c. Coloring	k. Drawing on Board	s. Swinging on Door
d. Drawing	l. Telephoning	t. Moving Chair
e. Reading	m. Puzzle	u. Erasing Blackboard
f. Swinging feet	n. Blocks	v. Looking out Window
g. Record	o. Jumping	w. RE Book
h. Hugging	p. Drinking	

A menu depicting these activities in color was prepared by an artist and enclosed in a single book with one activity per page. This book indicating the reinforcing events is called an RE menu for short (see accompanying illustration).

The RE menu was introduced to the class by encouraging them to name the activity involved while the RE menu was held before them and the pages turned. The children were then told, "You are going to be able to have time to do what ever you want to do that is in this book. Every time you finish your work, you will get to look at our book and pick what you want to do for four minutes. I will tell you when your time is over to do what you want to do."

REINFORCEMENT MENU

Fig. 1   RE Menu

The lesson activity was presented and upon completion of the exercise the children were told, "Here is the book. Now you can pick what *you* want to do for four minutes . . ." The children were shown the RE materials and were given the next exercise. From here on the children took turns being first to use the menu upon completion of the task.

Lessons were taken directly from the Peabody language development kit (Dunn and Smith, 1965). The stated purpose of the kit is: (1) "to stimulate the over-all oral language facility of the disadvantaged and retarded," (2) "to develop their verbal intelligence through training," and (3) "to enhance their school progress." Each lesson contained an average of three exercises, for example, following directions, identification, classification. In one case, a card is held up and the instruction given to the group to "pick out food eaten for breakfast," "pick out food eaten for snacks." Experimental sessions were 60 minutes long and comparable to a regular class period.

Initially RE activity was made available after every five minutes of work. By the eleventh hour each task was 30 minutes long. The experimenter-instructor was able to gradually shape larger and larger amounts of work to be accomplished before making available the RE menu. Attention span and work output had been increased greatly. After 15 sessions, the children were re-evaluated by means of the Utah verbal language development scale. The range of improvement was 2 years 0 months to 2 years 6 months.[3]

6

REFUSING REINFORCEMENT

Claire V. Korn
STANFORD UNIVERSITY

Most people are happy to receive praise for their actions. It pleases them to know that they have pleased someone else or that they have done well in another's eyes. Simple praise ("You really did a good job," "My, you are good at doing that") and external rewards ("You carried out that

[3] Editors' Note: Subsequent experiments by Daley have shown that low probability school tasks can later become effective items on the RE menu. The children would do units in reading in order to gain the opportunity of solving some arithmetic problems.

job so well that I'm giving you a bonus," "Here's the dime we agreed on for making your bed all this week," "You can have this candy when you've finished cleaning up") are usually valued by the recipients. These minor reinforcements, as any parent knows, can be most useful for keeping things under control around home, and as any teacher knows, can be used in the classroom to keep a child interested in tasks which otherwise might be onerous to him. Both the parent and the teacher will tend to use words of praise and encouragement rather than prizes such as candy and money.

But there are other children and adults who suspect such words, who scorn such blandishments. Sometimes these individuals have set such high standards for themselves that acknowledging they have done well at a more menial level would be a form of self-debasement. Frequently their lack of trust in others' intentions leads them to ruminate about nefarious plots behind the praise or prize. These people are more likely to be seen in guidance clinics, college counseling centers, or graduate schools than in the usual high school counselor's office. Finding suitable rewards for them, helping them lower their unrealistic standards or raise their performances can be a ticklish job. Praise has been questioned as an enjoyable commodity (Farson, 1966). Praise may grease the wheels of social intercourse, praise may grant the praiser status, praise may help maintain interpersonal distance, and praise may generate defensiveness, discomfort, incredibility, and unrealistic aspirations.

Here are a few incidents from the case of Lisa, a very pretty, extremely bright, sensitive, informed nine-year-old, who had come into counseling in a private practice setting. Problems involved family strains (frequent fights and more frequent bad tempers) and school underachievement (she simply could not learn the multiplication tables although she could learn principles of higher mathematics with ease) along with other unstated, but felt, problems. Her own self-estimate was low while her standards were high. In some areas she knew she could function well (for example, playing the piano by ear) but in other areas requiring more application she could not function (for example, reading music). She knew she was bright, but she felt that she could do nothing right. Yet she disparaged others for being "so dumb" and criticizing her when she was right.

The etiology of Lisa's many problems is long and complex. Unraveling the tangled threads of her history might be impossible. It was necessary to accept her as she was each day rather than to probe into her *raison d'être*. The outcomes of her contact with the world were that she mistrusted others, that she looked for multiple motivations behind each statement and usually was accurate in her findings, and that she had established a kind of self-status by playing the role of the misunderstood person. And she often was misunderstood.

Into all this stepped a counselor who was trying to give her a feeling that, indeed, she could do things right—for she often did, but she disparaged the goal she had achieved.[1] Reducing the frequency of family squabbles and increasing academic performance were some of the goals of counseling. Part of the program was to praise her for worthwhile achievements.

The scene to follow is the playroom where the counselor is playing catch with Lisa.

Co: Good, you got it.
Lisa: But I missed the one before.
Co: Sometimes you miss one. It's hard to get them all.
Lisa: I should get them all.

(Later)

Co: Hey! You're doing well. You haven't missed.
Lisa: Why do you always say that I'm doing well? It's not true. I keep missing them.
Co: When you miss some you feel as if you're not doing well at all?
Lisa: Yes, so why do you keep saying I'm doing well?
Co: Uhhhh—
Lisa: Why do you?
Co: Because lots of the times I think you give yourself a bad time when you don't do things perfectly, and I want you to know when I think you are doing well at something. You can still be doing something well without being perfect.
Lisa: Let's do something else.[2]

---

[1] Editors' Note: The response of disparaging one's own performance is easily learned in our society because it is so frequently reinforced (unintentionally): "That's an ugly picture I painted." "No, it's not, dear, it's lovely." Praise occurring after a disparaging remark reinforces disparaging remarks. Some people are seldom praised unless they first engage in self-deprecation.

[2] Editors' Note: Part of the difficulty arises when counselor and client have not yet explicitly agreed on what they wish to accomplish. If the client wishes to be perfect (a goal guaranteed to produce lifetime unhappiness) but the counselor wishes to encourage improvement still short of perfection, the client will naturally resent the counselor's praise. The praise is for a performance the client not only does not desire, but actively rejects. A constructive approach might be to accept the client's desired direction of change but use a different base of comparison. "Sure it would be nice never to miss the ball—always to be perfect in everything you do. Nobody ever is perfect, but it's fun to make progress. You caught the ball three times in a row. Let's see if you can catch it four times in a row now." The path toward perfection runs through the garden of successive improvements.

The scene is now the playroom a year later. The parents had been meeting sporadically during the year with another counselor who had tried to help them recognize and reward desirable behaviors while extinguishing (by ignoring) the undesirable ones which had become family issues. The counselor and Lisa are talking.

Co: How have things been going at home? Have there been any more fights between your mom and you?

Lisa: She's trying to bribe me! She's really trying to bribe me!

Co: What do you mean? What happened?

Lisa: She said she would get me a horse if I'd keep my room clean. And that's bribery. Don't you think it's bribery?

Co: Well, it depends on how you look at it. That room is pretty important to your mom and I guess it's so important that she thinks it would be worth even a horse for your room to be kept clean.[3]

Lisa: But I *do* keep it clean. There's nothing on the floor any more. Of course, the bed's not made. But she's trying to bribe me.

Co: What your mother thinks of as being clean isn't the same thing as what you think of as being clean. Do you think it's fair to get something you want for doing something well?

Lisa: Yes. But it depends on how you do it. If I got a house or room of my own or something for keeping my room clean, or got a horse for taking care of a dog or something like that—but those aren't good examples—that would be fair.

Co: The reward should somehow be related to—connected to—the thing you're being rewarded for?

Lisa: Yes, that's it. A horse doesn't have anything to do with a room.

Co: Maybe your mom meant to tie them together somehow, like with responsibility. If you were responsible enough to take care of your room, you might be responsible enough to take care of a horse.

Lisa: She did say something about that. But I wouldn't have to take care of the horse anyway. It would have to be boarded.

Moral: Good intentions and rewards are not enough. The reward has to mean the same thing to the person receiving it as to the one giving it.[4]

---

[3] Editors' Note: A good answer. Critics of reinforcement techniques sometimes refer to reinforcement as "bribery," a word with negative connotations. Such a reference is incorrect since bribery involves a reward ". . . for perverting the judgment or corrupting the conduct of a person in a position of trust" (Webster's Collegiate Dictionary). Keeping a room clean can scarcely be considered a perverted judgment or corrupt conduct.

[4] Editors' Note: Fitting the reward to the task is highly desirable when possible but not at all necessary for the reward to work. An effort to help Lisa and her mother to agree on certain common goals and specific steps for reaching them would seem prerequisite to the horse trading.

7

REINFORCEMENT THAT BACKFIRED

Barbara B. Varenhorst
PALO ALTO UNIFIED SCHOOL DISTRICT (CALIFORNIA)

Jimmy May was a fast-talking, gum-chewing, motorcycle-riding, happy-go-lucky underachiever. His pudgy face showed evidence of poor eating habits and infrequent use of a razor. His sportshirt was usually clean, but the jacket he always wore looked aged. Although 17 years old he was still trying to complete credits for his sophomore year.

His father had left home when Jim was a baby. He lived with his mother, who ran a beauty parlor and catering service. His sister, of whom he was very fond, lived with them until she married an engineer and moved away. Jim helped his mother and aunt with the catering service and held down a succession of jobs, including digging graves in the cemetery and washing dishes in a restaurant. He even claimed he had his own "band" and he "made plenty on this." He complained of payments on his car, the repair bills on another car, and payments on an expensive stereo he had purchased. He kept busy.

Whenever Jimmy's name was mentioned around school, teachers groaned and the Dean would shake his head and sigh. Jimmy missed classes, never turned in his assignments, couldn't read well, and disturbed classes by frequent interruptions when he came late to class. Case conferences were held, parent conferences were held, and he was "counseled" by counselors, the nurse, and the Dean. Occasionally the principal would give his advice on Jimmy's problems.

Seldom would a day go by that Jimmy was not seen in some area of the office. He frequented the nurse's office most often, complaining of stomachaches, headaches, colds, and pains. At no time was his entire body at rest. As he sat talking, a leg would be thumping and an arm would be shaking while his mouth moved. The family doctor had prescribed tranquilizers to slow him down.

On frequent occasions he would pop into my office with the question, "Can I talk to you a minute, Doc?" If time was available, I would invite him in, and if not, I would ask him to fill out a request slip. The conferences were never long and usually ended with Jimmy jumping up and saying, "Gotta shove off now. See you later." Through such conferences I gradually came to know him well and was looking for a way to help him in areas where he said he needed help.

Then, in the fall, Jimmy became the football manager. He was introduced at the first school assembly and his name and picture appeared in the school paper. He was seen on campus in a white shirt and tie and neat cardigan. When his counselor called a case conference for the "annual planning session" of what to do about his school work, his teachers reported that Jimmy was a new boy. He was no longer missing classes, his assignments, even though still of poor quality, were coming in. He was not disruptive in class and he was not spending as much time in the nurse's office.

As psychologist for the school, I attended this case conference. Finally, I thought, Jimmy has demonstrated some behavior that can be reinforced. This was the breakthrough I'd been looking for.

The following day I had my opportunity. Jimmy popped into my office in his usual manner.

"You know Jimmy, I've heard some wonderful things about you."

"Ya, whad'ya hear?" he asked in a suspicious voice.

"Well, your teachers have commented on how well you're doing in all your work," I said with my brightest smile. "The football coach said how regular you are in your work as manager and what a fine job you're doing."

"Where'd ya hear all this?"

"Well, yesterday the teachers met to discuss your school progress and talk over your academic plans. They couldn't say enough nice things about you," I continued.

"Ya, well it's really nothing. I've been doing 'bout the same. Do teachers meet like that very often?"

"Oh, from time to time they meet to see what they can do to help a student. We call it a case conference. Sometimes we invite parents to attend too."

"Whad'ya know about that. Well, gotta shove off now."

With that he was gone.

A few days later Jimmy's English teacher stopped by my office. He wanted to know what had happened to Jimmy. "Ever since our case conference Jimmy's changed. I haven't seen one paper from him. He's missed a class and the other times he's come late. He seems to have reverted back to what he used to do."

I was dejected. I explained to the teacher what I had done and why I had done it. "I just don't understand what happened."

For days I stewed over the problem, realizing that my attempts to reinforce improved behavior had backfired. From this point on, Jimmy did reverse his behavior. Obviously, I had not helped the situation and perhaps had been the cause of this sudden reversal.

Jimmy continued to stop in for his brief, staccato conferences. He was asked about what had happened, but would not talk about it. Toward the end of the year, when Jimmy was in real academic difficulties (he failed all his classes but one) we talked in more specific terms about the future. He said that he wanted to continue in high school so he could graduate. He even talked of going to summer school. Then, during the last week of school, he told me that his counselor wanted him to go to Continuation High School.[1] He wasn't going to have any part of it. I explained that this might be a way for him to manage to graduate. I said I was sure that he was getting tired of fighting the system and that only students who were serious about completing their education were wanted at Continuation High School. I also said that I had mentioned the possibility to the Continuation teacher. The teacher was a fine person and seemed eager to work with Jimmy.

As Jimmy listened, his face lightened and he said, "It's really like that there? Well, I guess I'm kinda interested. Do you suppose that teacher would take me if you arranged it?" I assured him that would be the case and he left asking me to go ahead and arrange it. This was done and the following year Jimmy enrolled at that school.

What contributed to my ineffective efforts to reinforce Jimmy? Perhaps I did not use what was actually positively reinforcing to him. Perhaps praise from me at the time was not something he wanted. Or perhaps I used too much and this had the opposite effect on his behavior than was intended. Perhaps it was the knowledge that teachers were discussing him and this frightened or angered him, or perhaps his attention was called to what he was doing and he felt he could not live up to the sudden expectation that was presented to him. Maybe he thought he would lose all the other attention he had been getting from the nurse, counselors, the Dean, and myself if he started doing what we wanted him to do.

All of these are possibilities.[2] They suggest and illustrate the complexity of applying reinforcement techniques for behavior change. Much more knowledge will be needed to understand fully the effective use of different kinds of reinforcement for counseling different individuals.

---

[1] A modified and shortened school program for potential school drop-outs. (No work is included in the program.)

[2] Editors' Note: Yes, possible and probable. With the benefit of hindsight we can hypothesize that Jimmy's association with the football team had provided him with models and reinforcement for a different type of behavior. The well-intentioned praise and the information that he was the subject of a case conference notified him that he was in fact different from those he was seeking to emulate.

Structuring and Reinforcement

BEFORE A CLIENT can be appropriately reinforced, he must manifest some behavior that begins to move him toward his goal. At the beginning of counseling, however, few clients even know what their goals are. The counselor must begin by helping the client to formulate his own goals. Some structuring by the counselor is usually necessary before the goals become clearly articulated.

The first step is to allow the client to express his own concerns in his own way. At the very beginning the counselor may be well advised to listen empathically and attentively, making every effort to understand the problem as the client sees it. Frequently the counselor will need to summarize or clarify what the client is saying and how the client is feeling about it in order to make sure that he is perceiving the problem accurately. In this beginning stage the listening, reflecting, and clarifying of feelings are essentially those procedures which have been advocated by Carl Rogers and others.

Once the problem has been accurately perceived and articulated by both client and counselor, however, it is time to do something about it. There are, of course, a few clients for whom listening, reflection, and clarification are sufficient to enable them to identify their own goals and take the required action. For many others, however, the counselor's responsibilities have not ended, but have only begun. The counselor's next responsibility is to help the client formulate his goals and help the client take the necessary actions to accomplish them.

The articles in this section provide illustrations of how the counselor can help a client to structure his goal in terms of desired behavior changes and how a counselor can then use reinforcement to support him as he begins making progress toward these goals. In Article 8 Hoopes and Scoresby describe how it is necessary first of all to have the client agree verbally that he does in fact want to change his behavior. A major goal and specific subgoals are then established with an action program designed to move the client toward the mutually agreed-upon goals. Reinforcement is provided not only by the counselor, but by the client himself and others in the client's environment.

Article 9 provides a detailed case study by Hoopes describing how a college girl was helped to overcome the habit of procrastination with the help of a counselor applying these structuring steps in a series of interviews. Scoresby in Article 10 further elaborates the basic steps in another case study, this one concerned with improving the study habits necessary for successful academic accomplishment.

Structuring in group counseling is illustrated in Article 11 by Ryan. The group consisted of failing college students who wanted to remain in college and achieve successfully. Before inaugurating a program of improved study skills the counselor endeavored to help each student formulate for himself values he wanted to get out of his college education. This brief excerpt presents in capsule form the manner in which the counselor structured the group session in order to help the students articulate their goals.

Working with a population similar to Ryan's, Fuhriman in Article 12 describes the specific steps used to help students implement more successful academic behavior. The basic steps are those previously suggested by Hoopes and Scoresby, but a number of specific action programs are suggested which may be particularly useful with the low-achieving student.

In all of these case studies the counselor begins by clarifying the problem, then helps the client structure behavioral goals that will lead him toward the major goal he wants. Following this the counselor helps design action programs to accomplish the goals, then arranges for the client to be reinforced for any progress, and, finally, assesses the degree to which the procedure and structuring have accomplished the desired results.

8

COMMITMENT TO CHANGE: STRUCTURING THE GOALS AND GROUND RULES FOR COUNSELING

Margaret H. Hoopes and A. Lynn Scoresby
UNIVERSITY OF MINNESOTA

In working with college students in academic difficulty or with behavior problems, we can systematically structure the counseling interview in such a way that behaviors are changed and problems resolved with a consistently high degree of success. By structuring, we do not mean that certain things must take place at certain times or in certain sequences. Rather, we mean that certain elements of the counseling interview are present consistently throughout any or all of a series of counselor-client contacts.

IDENTIFICATION AND CLARIFICATION OF BEHAVIORS

Together the client and counselor investigate, clarify, and specify the present observable behavior of the client which may have created the problem situation. For example, when a probation student is involved, the counselor asks the student to tell him about his present and past study habits, how he takes notes, reads, reviews, studies for tests, how much time he spends studying, under what conditions, and so forth. Any behavior which contributes to the problem is investigated.

The same process occurs with a "problem" involving interpersonal relationships. Behavior which makes the client uncomfortable or unhappy is identified.

A freshman girl wanted to move away from home. Her father was not living and she did not get along with her mother. However, further discussion revealed that she really was not yet willing to leave her mother alone. Consequently the goal finally worked out by the client and counselor was to modify the home situation so that it would be more satisfactory to the girl. The girl and her mother "couldn't communicate." "Life seemed unbearable." When asked to further specify the behavior involved in her relationship with her mother, the girl indicated the following: (1) "I can't seem to share personal feelings with my mother," (2) "We don't do things together," and (3) "Mother seldom shares feelings and thoughts with me." Through exploration and discussion, the problem situation was put in behavioral terms so that the client and counselor could deal with specific behaviors.

COMMITMENT TO CHANGE

Two types of commitment must be obtained: (1) The client must make a verbal commitment to change his behavior; (2) The counselor and client must make a mutual commitment to follow the interview ground rules of *honesty and responsibility.*

A necessary part of the commitment process is for each client to state his problem in terms of a goal which, when achieved, is the resolution of the problem situation. For some students, it may be graduation, improved grades, better personal relationships, or any of many possible alternatives. The goal selected by the client becomes the *major goal* and all interview activities are directed toward attainment of this objective.

A probationary student's goal might be to raise his grade-point average. His counselor might say, "Your way of note-taking, reading, and studying has resulted in your present grade-point average of 1.50. Are you sufficiently interested in raising your grades to make the necessary changes in your study habits?" *A verbal response is required.* The client's response to the counselor's question becomes the verbal commitment to change.

Should the client's reply be negative, reclarification and reidentification of the problem is undertaken. If the client is still unwilling to agree to a change of behavior, or that a change is necessary, it is evident that a basic problem is not being dealt with in the counseling interview. Either the process of identification and clarification must produce a new goal acceptable to client and counselor or the counseling must be referred to another counselor or terminated.

If the answer is affirmative, the counselor outlines the two vital ground rules of honesty and responsibility to be followed in any and all succeeding counselor-client contacts. The client is asked two questions: (1) "Will you agree to be honest even though at times it may be difficult for you to do so?" (2) "Will you agree to be responsible for your behavior when we are together and when you are outside of this interview?" Both of these questions are explored until the client is able to understand some of the implications behind such commitments and definitely commits himself to obey the rules. *Verbal responses are required for both ques-*

tions. Following the client's commitments, the counselor pledges his honesty and his agreement to be responsible for his own behavior throughout the remainder of the counselor-client contacts.

COMMITMENT TO GOAL ATTAINMENT

Once the major goal and the ground rules are agreed upon, the action necessary to attain the goal must be determined. Three steps are necessary. (1) The major goal set by the client is divided into subgoals. A subgoal may be the elimination of a specific observable behavior which blocks or disrupts the client's progress toward the major goal, or it may be the creation of a new specific observable behavior designed to move the client in a desired direction. (2) The counselor and client decide on the action program, the method or process of implementing the subgoals into the client's repertoire of behaviors. (3) The client verbally commits himself to be responsible for fulfilling any or all action programs agreed upon.

In the case of the girl having difficulty in her relationship with her mother, the goal was "somehow to learn to enjoy being together." This major goal was divided into the following subgoals:

1. The daughter would learn to listen to her mother's comments.
2. The daughter would share her feelings and experiences with her mother.
3. The daughter would actively work toward sharing time and activities with her mother.

The action programs used to create the new behaviors were the following:

1. Whenever the mother talked, the daughter would listen and respond in a positive way by asking a question or making a pertinent comment.
2. By the end of each day the daughter would share with her mother at least two specific events or ideas which had occurred that day.
3. During mealtime the daughter would ask at least one question about her mother's current activities and one question concerning her mother's past experiences.
4. During the week the daughter would initiate the planning of some activity with her mother and would carry out at least one activity (for example, movie, church social, party).
5. The daughter would write a capsule summary of her daily efforts to fulfill the action programs and bring these accounts to the next counseling interview.

In succession, the daughter *agreed verbally* to each of the action programs.

Often there are more action programs necessary to reach the major goal than can be simultaneously carried out by the client. In this case, a sequence of action programs is planned beginning with a few, adding others as needed, modifying existing programs as required, and creating new ones if warranted.

By breaking the major goal into smaller parts, the counselor creates an opportunity for the client to enjoy success experiences. The client is given something tangible to do, something which can give evidence of progress.[1]

REINFORCEMENTS

Three sources of reinforcement are available to the client: (1) counselor reinforcement of client behavior, (2) client reinforcement of his own behavior, and (3) reinforcement by the environment outside the counseling relationship.

The counselor reinforces any progress or effort by the client to attain his own goals. Reinforcement would be provided for any existing behavior which may move the client toward his goal, for the successful completion of any step in an action program, for efforts to reinforce himself, and for taking the "risk" of commitment.

Generally the counselor reinforces verbally or visually by nodding his head, smiling, or saying "Good," "That's great," or "I bet you feel better."

The client reinforces himself by following a reinforcement schedule created by the counselor and client which is integrated with the client's action programs. For example, the client might reward himself after an action program of two hours of study with a soft drink, a phone call to his girl friend, or other pleasant activity.

We have found that a change in client behavior often produces a modification of his feelings and attitudes. For example, when the probation student had unproductive study habits he reported dissatisfaction, depression, and discouragement; but as he realized that he could fulfill his action programs and saw himself progressing toward a goal he reported feeling "freer," "happier," and "more enthusiastic." We feel that these changes of affect can become the basis for a well developed intrinsic self-reinforcement system appropriate not only to the present problem situation but adaptable to many problem areas. The counselor can teach the client to control how he feels by what he does. By asking questions like "How do you feel differently now?" and "What do you think are the

[1] Editors' Note: The major goal may seem so unattainable to the client that he might well become discouraged. The subgoals and specific actions, though not representing total satisfaction, do permit progress to be seen and felt by the client, thus encouraging further efforts.

reasons for feeling better or worse?" the counselor helps the client associate feelings with behaviors and to seek the behaviors that elicit the
rewarding positive feelings.

The environment reinforces the client also. Family, friends, teachers,
and employers can support his action programs. The counselor teaches
the client to be sensitive to reinforcing conditions in his environment.[2]

FOLLOW-UP

The follow-up process is part of every counselor-client contact after
the first interview. Its major purposes are: (1) obtaining a factual report
of what the client did in his specific action programs, (2) modifying
existing action programs if needed, (3) implementing new action programs into the client's repertoire of behaviors, (4) enabling the counselor
to reinforce the client's fulfillment of his commitments, and (5) permitting
the counselor to focus on the client's feelings about successful action
programs and to teach him intrinsic rewards for behaving responsibly.

The follow-up process is essentially one of teaching the client that he
can become predictable in his behavior.[3]

9

OVERCOMING PROCRASTINATION

Margaret H. Hoopes
UNIVERSITY OF MINNESOTA

Barbara came into my office for a routine clearance procedure required
of all off-campus transfer students. She was personable, attractive, and
intelligent. She had a B.S. from a small state school and had been admitted to the College of Education to become a teacher.

[2] Editors' Note: Improved behavior will usually be reinforced naturally by those
near the client. Sometimes the client may be willing to describe his goals and action
program to his family or friends and deliberately ask them to tell him when he begins
to improve.

[3] Editors' Note: Having self-control or a "sense of agency" involves the ability to
produce desired consequences by manipulating one's own behavior. People who can
predict and control their own behavior are more free to create desired consequences
for themselves than those whose behavior is unpredictable.

Fall Quarter, her first quarter at the university, was just completed. Near the end of the routine part of the interview I asked her if she was satisfied with her course work and her decision to come to the university. She replied that she liked her classes and the university and that any dissatisfaction she felt was with herself.

IDENTIFICATION AND CLARIFICATION

"What is the problem?"

"I never seem to finish anything or if I do it's at the last minute and it's done poorly. I'm the world's worst procrastinator. I should have done much better in my classes. I crammed at the last minute and got by with C's."

"You seem to have assessed your situation."

"Oh, yes! I recognize my problem and can and have talked about it for hours. That's all I do about it! I can't seem to do anything but talk. I've always gotten by in school, doing just enough to get by. I get by in other things too. My personality gets me by with my family and friends. They forgive me for my goofs."

"You don't like this about yourself?"

"No, I don't! But I don't do anything about it! I have a friend who is a psychologist. We've talked for hours. He tells me that I have some guilt in my past that stops me from finishing things that I start—that won't let me finish things."

"I don't think we can do anything about that guilt theory, Barbara, but if you would like to forget about it I believe that there are some things you can do that will change your behavior and your feelings about yourself."

"Really? Could we forget it? I have spent hours trying to think up something I could feel that guilty about," said Barbara seriously with a great deal of emotion.

COMMITMENT TO CHANGE

"Yes, we can forget it. First, let's investigate a few other areas. You say you have been procrastinating and not doing well or not finishing things all of your life?"

"For as long as I can remember."

"But you have been getting by? You're now 23 and have established patterns of behavior acceptable to your family and friends."

"Yes, but most of the time I don't like me."

"As I see it, here is a decision you must make. Do you really want to change your behavior? It's one thing to say it, another to mean it. It's going to take the kind of effort that will be difficult for an old procrastinator like you. Do you understand what I am saying?" Barbara nodded. "Do you want to make that kind of effort?"

We sat there for five minutes while Barbara stared at her shoes. Finally she looked up at me. "Yes, I do want to change. I'm not sure that I can, but I want to try."

"Good! Together we can work something out I'm sure. Before we do that though let's talk about our relationship. In order for us to accomplish our goal we need to freely exchange feelings and ideas. This implies a trust in each other whereby we can be honest in all that we do. Can you accept that?"

"Yes. I consider myself an honest person. I am surprised though about how much I have told you already."

"The kind of honesty we'll be working with will be quite confrontive at times; that is, I may point out behavior I see that isn't in keeping with your goal. You may not like it. You may feel frustrated and sometimes angry. I want you to share these feelings with me too. Can you do that?"

"Yes."

"The other things we should consider is responsibility. Will you assume full responsibility for your own actions? You look puzzled. Mainly this means that you can't blame other people, events, or things for your actions. You will be making commitments to do certain things here and outside. If you don't fulfill them you may want to blame someone or thing other than yourself. You won't realize all the implications of this now but will you apply it? Will you accept the responsibility of your behavior?"

"I'll try."[1]

"This is a two-way agreement. It applies to me also. I will be honest with you and responsible for my part of our talks together. Feel free to ask questions at any time. As we make plans you should understand what we are doing and why."

COMMITMENT TO GOAL ATTAINMENT

"Now Barbara, what is it that you want to change about yourself?"

"I want to complete the jobs I have to do and stop procrastinating."[2]

---

[1] Editors' Note: Barbara may not know what these two promises really mean for her own behavior at this point. Her assent may be in response to social pressure. A counselor could give examples of the kinds of behavior implied by these two promises to prevent the client from feeling she was signing a blank check.

[2] The major goal.

At this point I handed her a piece of paper. "Let's go to work. Write down two things that you are procrastinating on right now."

"With school out for vacation I'm not worrying about studying, but I don't have my Christmas presents bought or my Christmas cards out. I'll get the Christmas presents but here it is December 21 and I haven't done my cards."[3]

"How important to you is it to get these cards out?"

"Very important."

"Why?"

"These are my good friends. I write to most of them only once or twice a year."

"How will you feel if you can't get them out?"

"Like a dog!"

"All right. Under Christmas cards on that paper write, 'Getting my cards out is the most important thing in my life right now!'" She wrote this and looked up at me expectantly.

"How soon can you work on your cards?"

"I have to work this afternoon so tonight would be the earliest possible time."

"Do you have the cards?"

"No, but I can get them on my way home."[4]

"Good. When is the latest time that you would like to have the cards in the mail?"

"Tomorrow noon."

"That's good! Now what distraction might come along that would stop you from doing your cards tonight?"

Barbara thought for a moment. "If everyone went out to the Green Lantern I'd probably go." Barbara lives in a house with ten girls.

"If everyone went? If one or two stayed home would you stay home and do your cards?"

"Yes."

"But if they all went you'd go and then it would be their fault because you didn't stay home and do your cards?"

At this she began to smile. "So that is what you meant about being responsible for my own action?"[5]

"You're right. I think it might be beneficial for you to note the distractions that you allow to divert you from accomplishing the things you intend to do. See if you are blaming other things and other people. I'm

---

[3] Identification of a subgoal.
[4] Action program.
[5] Editors' Note: Her promise to be responsible now implies a specific behavior—not blaming her house-mates for distracting her.

now referring to all of your activities for the next few weeks. Can you see purpose in doing that? Will you do it?"

"Yes. It interests me already."

"It may help you to write them down. Are there any other distractions that might stop you from writing the cards?"[6]

"TV."

"Then it would be the TV's fault if you didn't get them done?"

Barbara laughed.

"Is there any program on tonight that is more important to you than your friends?"

She shook her head and laughed again.

"Then getting your cards done really is the most important thing to you right now?"

"Yes."

FOLLOW-UP

"Good. I would like you to call me before noon tomorrow and tell me how you feel about what you have done."

"That would not be right. I've got to be responsible for myself. I can't use you."

"That's true, but until you have established some new behavior patterns, I will allow you to use me in that way. Notice that I have asked you to tell me how you feel about what you have done. This implies that I believe that you will succeed. I'm sure that in so doing you are going to find out some interesting things about yourself. I'd like you to share them with me. Will you call?"[7]

"Yes. What else do you want me to do? I can't believe this whole thing."

"You're excited about it?" Barbara nodded. "I'm going to be gone part of the holidays. Why don't you come in the first week of the quarter? At that time I would like to hear about the distractions in your life. I'll also ask you what new things you have learned about yourself. The real test of this is to see how it will influence your study habits and other areas in your life about which you are dissatisfied."

---

[6] Editors' Note: The counselor does a thorough job of helping the client to anticipate the possible obstacles to performing the required action.

[7] Editors' Note: The counselor has wisely left the door open for the client to call whether or not she completes the task on time. Sometimes the action program undertaken by the client is more ambitious than he or she can actually accomplish the first try. The client promises to call and report what happened and how she felt about it, whether success or failure. If a failure occurred, a modified action program could be mutually designed.

"I'm interested in that too. Okay. I'll call you tomorrow. Thank you so much."

First Telephone Call

Barbara called me at 10:15 A.M. the following morning. Her voice rang with elation as she told me that she had just put her cards in the mail. I complimented her on her success and asked her how she felt. She said that she felt wonderful and that she wanted me to know that she had also done her Christmas shopping. It was evident that she was very pleased with herself. I asked her if she had any other action programs going. She laughed at this and said that she was going to answer two letters which required decisions on her part. She had procrastinated six months on these.[8] I told her how pleased I was with her and reminded her that I would see her in January.[9]

Second Telephone Call

My schedule was such that Barbara couldn't see me until the third week of the quarter. We did have one telephone contact during the interim. At this time she reported that applying "nonprocrastination" to everything in her life was not as easy as the Christmas cards had been. She had almost given up several times but had come back to it because of the way she had felt in "outsmarting her procrastinations." She felt she had done this by taking a careful look at her distractions. She also said the success she had had with the cards had taught her to be dissatisfied with her old habits. She had continued to try some alternate plans.

We spent time discussing reinforcement and the meaningfulness of a reward system. I pointed out to her that her "feeling good" had been a reward to her and enough reinforcement to propel her into ensuing action programs. I indicated that immediate planned rewards incorporated into every action program would provide incentive to continue. She immediately grasped the implication of this and said that she would apply this principle.

Subsequent Follow-up

During the second and ensuing interviews, we continued to explore Barbara's behavior, identified those behaviors she wanted to eliminate and replaced them with new ones. Mutually planned action programs

[8] Editors' Note: The successful accomplishment of one small task frequently has a generalization effect.

[9] Editors' Note: The counselor has been reinforcing the client's progress through each step of the total counseling process.

were reinforced by my support of her positive behaviors and by her own reward system.

Barbara often mentioned that changing her behavior was hard work and at times she wanted to revert to her old ways. Though she reported occasional discouragement and actually failed to complete action programs, she was enthusiastic and vigorous in pursuit of her major goal. Each defeat of procrastination by completion of a task was to her a personal victory which made her "feel good." She reported that "getting a task completed, well done, was as heady as wine."

At the time of this writing the case is still in progress. Barbara is establishing new and satisfactory behaviors with fewer contacts with me. An occasional contact appears to be sufficient for her as she reports completion of action programs and initiation of new ones. Her concept of herself and her attitude about what she can do appears to be far different than that displayed in the initial interview. The success of her first action program seemed to give her tremendous impetus to carry her through discouragement. Apparently she is well on her way toward her goal of being the kind of person who completes what she starts, on time, and with a personally satisfying degree of efficiency.

10

IMPROVING ACADEMIC PERFORMANCE

A. Lynn Scoresby
UNIVERSITY OF MINNESOTA

Kathy was a senior, majoring in elementary education. She appeared to be soft-spoken and quiet, but was able to meet people freely and easily. She was fairly attractive in appearance and had a steady boyfriend.

She described her parents as "middle-class people" anxious about her and her education. She felt close to her family and enjoyed being with them.

THE FIRST INTERVIEW

Because of her unsatisfactory grades, Kathy had been placed on academic probation. She had a 1.00 ("D") grade-point average in her major subject area. Since she was five honor points below a required 2.00 grade-point average for all academic credits, she could not enter her student teaching program. If her grades for the current quarter did not improve she would likely discontinue her schooling. She had been on probation for two of the three quarters she had attended the university.

During our discussion of her situation, she appeared quite despondent and frustrated. She often remarked that she "studied hard, but didn't seem to get anywhere," and that perhaps she was "too dumb to make it." She "probably studied an average of 10–12 hours a week, read a lot but had a hard time concentrating, didn't take reading notes, and often didn't understand the lectures." She thought that she had "good" study habits, but that "something else must be wrong."

Major Goal and Commitments

I asked Kathy to describe a goal that I could help her obtain. She stated that she wanted to improve her grades so that she could "get off of probation and into student teaching." I pointed out to her that her present study habits were probably accounting for her academic situation and if she wanted to improve her grades she should consider making some changes. I asked if she was willing to make any change necessary to reach her goal of improved grades. She seemed somewhat hesitant, but finally agreed.[1] I asked her to agree to be honest with me and to accept the responsibility for her behavior. She questioned both commitments. I explained that honesty meant telling the truth even though it might incriminate her, and responsibility meant to do what she agrees to do. She accepted both commitments.

Subgoals

I asked Kathy which of her study habits she would like to work on first. She wanted to learn how to remember what she read. We talked about the role of reading notes in learning. She agreed that reading notes would help her to concentrate on her reading and remember what she had read. She agreed to follow a system of reading where she would survey the section of reading, ask questions about each part of the section, and take notes by answering the questions. She also agreed to recite her notes and review them periodically.

---

[1] Editors' Note: Kathy determined the goal to "get off of probation and into student teaching," but the counselor was largely responsible for recommending the means. Since Kathy believed her study habits were already "good," her hesitancy to adopt the counselor's methods is understandable.

Action Program

I suggested to Kathy that most students do not use their time effectively and she might find it helpful to determine exactly what she did with a week's time. She agreed to make a daily schedule of her planned activities and to record specifically what she did during the time she had set aside for study.

I asked her to designate a 90-minute section each week that would be inviolate to other activities and would be used for a review of her class notes and reading notes. She agreed to do this and stated that her time would be every Saturday morning from 9:00 to 10:30 A.M.

At this point the interview was terminated. Kathy had agreed to take reading notes, make a schedule of her time, and hold a weekly review. She also agreed to bring some of her reading notes and time schedules to the next interview so we could discuss them.

THE SECOND INTERVIEW

Kathy returned in seven days for the second interview. She brought with her some reading notes and daily schedules. We discussed her reading notes and I checked briefly to determine if they were consistent with the text. I asked Kathy if she thought the notes helped her to concentrate and remember what she had read. She thought so, but would like to try them for a longer period of time to make sure.

Reinforcement

I complimented her on her efforts and verbally reinforced the fact that she had been responsible for her behavior. I asked Kathy if she had learned something about herself during the week. She replied that she wasted a lot of time and used some of her time unproductively. Both of her statements were corroborated by the schedules since she had studied only 13 hours and had not accomplished much. I complimented her again for her efforts and pointed out that she was being honest with me by filling out her schedules frankly, even though she knew how it would appear to me.

I asked Kathy if she had reviewed Saturday morning at 9:00 A.M. and she stated that she had done so and found the review helpful in understanding some of her class notes. I indicated to her my pleasure in seeing her accomplish what she had agreed to do.

Self-Reinforcement

After completing the follow-up procedure, I asked if she knew the meaning of the word "reinforcement." She gave a vague definition which permitted a discussion of reinforcement and its role in helping her to change her study habits. I asked if she could see how I had been reinforcing her. She wasn't sure until I pointed out some of my comments about her schedules and reading notes. I also suggested that such reinforcements were part of my being responsible to her and that she could and should learn how to reinforce herself. We discussed her action programs for the following week and considered how to use reinforcement to help her change. She thought that she would reinforce herself for holding the weekly review and for reading a certain number of pages. A new action program of increased study time would be reinforced every additional hour she studied. Some of the reinforcements she thought of were "a ten-minute telephone call, some fruit, just relaxing, or talking with a friend in the dorm." She agreed that for each time she did something which helped her improve her grades, she would give herself a reward.[2]

Preparing for Examinations

The second interview was conducted prior to midterm examinations and Kathy was quite worried about her tests. Two procedures were suggested: (1) increased reviewing and (2) making up her own tests before taking the real one in class. She agreed and wanted to bring a test she would construct to the next interview to see if she had written it properly.

THE THIRD INTERVIEW

Before the third interview, Kathy had taken her midterm examinations and received her scores in all but one course. She received B's in three courses as expected, but an unexpectedly low grade in a fourth course. We discussed her feelings about what she was doing now and if she thought the changes of her study habits had improved her grades. She decided that studying more, reviewing, and taking reading notes had definitely made a difference in three of her five courses. When asked about the two remaining courses, she stated that she didn't study for them as

---

[2] Editors' Note: Helping a client learn how to reinforce himself is in effect teaching him self-control.

much as for the others because she wasn't interested in one and the other had a poor teacher. I suggested that lack of interest or a poor teacher was not a good reason for low achievement because she had agreed to make any change necessary to improve her grades. Studying more for a class she wasn't interested in or which had a teacher she didn't like was obviously part of the necessary changes. She finally agreed to this point but indicated that it would be difficult to work hard at something she didn't like.[3]

The Post-Midterm Slump

Kathy had held a weekly review, had written some sample tests, but had not studied very much since taking her midterm tests. In fact, she had averaged less than eight hours of study time for each of the two weeks between counseling interviews. I encouraged her to continue the weekly review and the reading notes, but pointed out to her that she had been quite irresponsible for her behavior by agreeing to study more each week (until she had reached a goal of 30 hours per week) and not fulfilling her commitments. She replied that she had felt exhausted after taking her tests and needed the time to rest. I asked if she really used her time wisely and she admitted that most of it had been spent with her boy friend. I asked if she thought her behavior was contributing to her goal of improved grades and she thought not but stated her desire to get better grades and to study more. I asked if there was a difference between the way she felt now and the way she felt before the tests. She replied that she felt guilty for not keeping her promises and didn't feel very confident that she would get higher grades. We explored her feelings and I suggested to her that perhaps her present feelings were a result of what she had been doing. If that were the case, she could feel better by doing more.[4]

Kathy had been following a reinforcement program and she indicated that she thought it helpful to her. She agreed to plan to study more each

[3] Editors' Note: Though a poor teacher and "lack of interest" may indeed make learning more difficult, both excuses place the blame for poor performance somewhere else. The commitment to be responsible for one's own behavior is difficult to keep, but the counselor is wise to keep the emphasis on the client's developing the best methods of learning in spite of poor teaching and low initial interest. In helping the client decide on subsequent courses and instructors, the counselor might encourage the client to investigate potential courses and instructors in advance to maximize chances for quality instruction in "interesting" subjects.

[4] Editors' Note: Whenever prolonged efforts precede reinforcement, the efforts immediately following reinforcement are reduced. Politicians vacation after the election is won. Newlyweds have honeymoons. The natural "slump" should be anticipated by both client and counselor. It might have been wise to program deliberately reduced work efforts after mid-term examinations in order to prevent the guilt responses arising from inability to maintain a steadily increasing work schedule.

week and to keep taking reading notes and reviewing. I told her I was encouraged by her commitments and her desire to work harder, and hoped that she would fulfill her commitments.

THE FOURTH INTERVIEW

Most of the fourth interview time was taken by following up Kathy's action programs similarly to previous interviews and by discussing the forthcoming final examinations. We talked about scheduling her time to prepare for each test and to plan a systematic approach to review for each course. She suggested that she wanted to spend more time on the courses she had done poorly in on the mid-term examinations. Together we worked out a schedule where she could have adequate study time for each course. We incorporated a reinforcement program in her study schedule and she agreed to follow it.

She had been taking reading notes since the first interview and had reviewed her class notes each week since that time. Since the third interview she had increased the amount of time she studied each week until she had finally reached her goal of 30 hours per week. She agreed to return and bring the results of her tests as well as her grades for the quarter.

FOLLOW-UP

Kathy returned after the Christmas holidays and reported that she had obtained a 3.0 average in the current quarter's courses. Her grades were high enough to remove her from probation and to permit her to qualify for student teaching. Subsequent contacts with Kathy have revealed that she is progressing toward graduation and has maintained many of the study habits she learned during the series of counseling interviews. She has indicated that it is more difficult without me and would like to drop in periodically so that she could use me to check up on her. To this I agreed.[5]

[5] Editors' Note: We counselors want to feel needed, but eventually we may feel the greatest sense of achievement and satisfaction when clients reinforce us by saying, "I don't need you anymore. I've learned to solve my own problems."

11

FORMULATING EDUCATIONAL GOALS

T. Antoinette Ryan
UNIVERSITY OF HAWAII

Following individual interviews, four male counselees concerned with the problem of school failure entered their first group counseling session. Three were 18-year-old freshmen, and one was a 20-year-old junior. All had indicated a general concern with the problem of potential school failure and had requested to participate in the group counseling sessions. Each had stated that he wanted to achieve the specific objectives of improving his study habits, and increasing his feelings of satisfaction and success in relation to the college experience.

In this first session, the counseling goal was to help the counselees identify values of a college education for themselves. Each client had already expressed a strong desire to remain and succeed in college in spite of his previous unsuccessful performance.[1]

C   1   Tell me, Mike, why do you think fellows go to college?[2]

C1-M   1   Well, I think the reasons vary. I know there are a lot of people that I see around here that seem to have the idea that this is the place to go so you can get a reasonably well paying job, live in a reasonably nice house, and drive a reasonably nice car.

C   2   I see. Good ideas[3] and . . . (interruption)

C1-J   2   And other people, I don't know they seem to be here to learn something about themselves and then a lot of people just don't know why they're here—like me for instance.

[1] Editors' Note: Those clients who wanted to reconsider whether or not they should remain in college were not included in the particular series of group counseling sessions. The groups were formed of individuals all of whom wanted to accomplish the same kinds of goals.

[2] Editors' Note: A cue designed to focus the discussion on the purpose of today's session—identifying values of a college education for each client.

[3] Editors' Note: The ideas were not all that good, but the counselor reinforced the expression of possible values some people might wish from a college education. Counselor approval does not necessarily indicate that the counselor agrees with the substantive ideas expressed but does indicate that the counselor believes the client is moving toward the client's own goal.

C	3	What do you think about this, Sam.[4]
C1-S	3	Well, I agree with Mike. There is some stereotyped idea that everybody has (pause)
C	4	What do you think? How do you feel about this, Terry?
C1-T	4	Well, I think that just about covers it—except for a few people I've noticed around campus who come to college to . . . merely as a status symbol. I never thought of it, but . . . well look at me. I'm a jock. I really am. But, I come to college. So that makes me feel good. I don't know . . . Now another guy . . . I don't know. He comes just so he can think of himself, "I am somebody. I am a little better than average."
C	5	I see. Then you feel that being part of the college gives you a kind of identity.
C1-T	5	Well, I think that one thing is that you're meeting different people and people from different parts of the world and different parts of the United States. You're able to, you know, broaden your horizons. . . .
C	6	Sure. Mm-mmm. And Mike, how do you feel about this?
C1-M	6	Well, in high school where you learn the basics of study you get pretty much a general education. College, now, gives you a wide diversity of opportunities and things to learn about—different places and different subjects. Ya, I guess you could say that's how I feel about it. Ya, that's what I think.
C	7	Sure. I agree with you. Good. And, Jack, what do you think about this? How do you feel?
C1-J	7	I don't know. I really don't. I don't know . . . why did I come? I don't know. I guess when I think of it I always viewed college as a sort of place where I could find myself.
C	8	Find yourself?
C1-J	8	Ya. Find myself. You know . . . in high school . . . I don't know . . . you have an idea of what you want. You come to college and it's just the idea of getting into all of this. What you bring as your talents and what interests you and what you would give. And a lot of guys feel that . . . and, now that I'm here and my major is science. . . . Well, that's it. But that is just self-centered. I thought I'd like to be a doctor . . . but still I want to leave enough leeway so that if I, say, I take a course or so and find out that I'm not cut out to be a doctor . . . enough leeway so I can make it a kind of period where I can actually find out who am I . . . you know . . . how do I fit in . . . never thought of it . . . but yes, guess that is it. I can find out how do I fit.
C	9	Help you make up your mind then, you feel.

[4] Editors' Note: The counselor did not wish to reinforce talk about the absence of goals and so cued one of the other clients. Apparently the counselor did not hear the goal "to learn something about themselves" because later statements of this goal were reinforced.

C1-J   9   Ya, and I don't know. I'm to the point right now, I don't know . . . I don't like the way things are. I don't know. I am thinking about, maybe . . . shall I stay with this or shall I look to something else.

C   10   I see. You feel, then that college is a place for finding yourself. And, Sam, how do you feel about this? What does college mean to you?

C1-S   10   Well, it will mean that I'm more fit to enter into the world of business which is my major.

C   11   Yes

C1-S   11   Then I'll be able to communicate with people on their level. . . .

The session continued with the counselor reinforcing attempts by clients to formulate values to be gained from a college education and ignoring irrelevant remarks. In closing the session the counselor used cueing and positive reinforcing comments to focus on the specific goals set for the session and to make a subcontract with the clients aimed at getting their commitment to translate verbal responses into action during the coming week.

C   42   I see our time is almost up for tonight, fellows. This session certainly went fast. Before you go, let's summarize our session tonight. What were our main feelings and thoughts? What were the main ideas and feelings that related to our goal for tonight—identifying some values of a college education? Jack, what do you feel about this?

C1-J   42   Well, we felt college is worthwhile. We all had the idea that to go anywhere in life we needed a college diploma and that college is a necessary item. It is needed to fill out our lives and to go up the ladder . . . and where a guy can find himself . . . can decide what he wants.

C   43   Hm-mmm. Right. Well, very fine. I think we've gotten off to a good start in expressing our feelings, in talking out these things. I think we've gotten some good ideas and had some thoughts that relate to our goal. I feel we really accomplished something in our group tonight. We'll have a definite goal next session, too, just like tonight we agreed on our goal as thinking about and expressing feelings about, and identifying some of the values of a college education. Now, let's have a kind of agreement for the coming week. How about really keeping in mind the thoughts and feelings we expressed tonight . . . and see if anything comes up during the week that you can point to and say, "This helped me to know myself a little better," or "I see how this course is going to be important in getting me ready for that life of good living, good income, good job, good car," or "This experience was a good one for getting to know more people."[5] First thing when we meet next

[5] Editors' Note: The counselor summarized some of the main values that had been expressed earlier but that Jack had overlooked in his summary.

time we'll talk about these things—what happened this week to each of you that related to our session tonight. O.K.?

Cl   43   (All) O.K.[6]

In subsequent sessions held weekly over an eight-week period, group sessions focused on kinds of study behaviors most likely to be associated with success in scholastic endeavors, for example, note-taking and making time schedules. Specific sub-goals relevant to the clients' major counseling aims were identified for each counseling session, and behaviors consistent with these goals were reinforced.

12

STRUCTURING FOR ACADEMIC SUCCESS

Addie Fuhriman
UNIVERSITY OF UTAH

"I received a letter from the college saying I had been dropped from school and that if I wanted, I could make an appointment with a counselor and discuss the matter. That is why I am here." Other students request help after having been placed on probation or having failed requirements for transfer.

These counselee students were in a college of the university where the main academic goal is a two-year Associate of Arts degree. The majority of these students had completed four quarters of work with grade averages ranging from D— to C—. The college has an open-door policy. The majority of the students are below the 50th percentile on the Minnesota Scholastic Aptitude Test and below the 50th percentile in their high school class rank.

COMMITMENT TO CHANGE

During the first interview the possibility of the student's doing something other than attending school was considered. Also discussed was

[6] Editors' Note: An informal commitment is made to relate the next week's experiences to the goals formulated.

what the counselee would be willing to do if he were permitted to remain in school. If the student decided he wanted to remain in school, he was asked to make two commitments:

(1) See the counselor once a week until the two of them decided differently.
(2) Do during the week what had been decided upon during the short, weekly interviews.

After the student came to this commitment and had stated it, I mentioned my commitment—that if the student were willing to try and would do what had to be done, I would likewise be willing to try and would invest my time and effort in being a resource to the student. The structuring of the commitment was intended to convey an interest in and a positive regard for the client—"You are worth my time." No assurance was given that the student could or would perform better academically.

STRUCTURING THE COUNSELING INTERVIEW

Starting Where the Client Is

It seemed critical to use a definite structure to determine the point where the student was at the present time. Specific questions were asked, for example, "How much studying do you do each day?" One student was studying one-half hour a day while another student was studying one hour a day. The same beginning point was not required for both students. The one student's schedule began on a base of one-half hour a day for each class while the other student's began on a base of one hour of studying a day per class.

Making a Schedule

The structuring of the oncoming week and the duties to be accomplished occupied the majority of the time in each interview. The first task involved drawing up a schedule of the time the student spent in class and the time that would be set aside for studying each day. This was a joint project in which I gave suggestions such as placing the study time close to the class time while the student, for example, suggested staying at the library to study instead of going home where there were distractions like television.

Anticipating Problems

There was a direct attempt made to foresee and discuss the possible distractions and fears for the oncoming week. My typical question was

"What's going to get in your way of studying this hour?" One student came up with the idea that if he didn't read the television guide he would have less of an interest in watching television. Another student said that the least little noise distracted him. He decided to wear ear plugs while he was studying. Another knew that he would be distracted with questions from his family. His decision was to tell his family about his studying and his preference for not being disturbed. He then would use his breaks between studying to talk with his family.

Many of the ideas came from the student. He could gain confidence in his own resourcefulness, realizing that he had some control over the situation.

Planning Some Specifics

Planning for the specific programs came next. For example, one student planned to break up the study time so that he began by reviewing his class notes for the day, then he did the reading assignment, and he finished by reviewing the reading assignment and asking himself questions on the reading.

Another project was to study for half an hour and then take a three minute break and reward himself for having studied. This break could be to exercise, play the guitar, get something to eat, or whatever he wanted to do. After three minutes he was to return to his studying for another half hour.

One project was especially for those who daydreamed while they were reading. I had the student keep a pad of paper by his side and when he would start to daydream he was to write down a word or two describing the content of his daydreaming. He was to bring the daydream sheet the next time he came. I told the student the purpose of doing this was to get the ideas out of his mind so that he could return to his reading. One student came up with the idea that he thought I was having him do this in order not to forget what he was thinking. It appeared that at times daydreaming is concerned with what has to be done. In writing the ideas down one is more able to return to his task because he knows he has a record of it. The daydreaming sheet also proved valuable as it gave a lead as to what occupied the student's mind. It also gave some insights into his study habits as well as some emotional items that were getting in the way of his effectiveness in his academic life.

The student who had the habit of falling asleep while reading was to read aloud, stand up and read, or walk and read until awake again.

To one student I suggested that he choose one new thing he had learned during his day of studying and bring that up for a topic of discussion with his family at supper. In one case this also provided the student an opportunity to interact with his father and to "hold his own" in a discussion.

One student was having particular difficulty in the interpretation of literature, so his assignment was to ask three questions in class during the week. He was to ask the instructor for his interpretation of some point of the literature and then to express his own to check it out.

Another student had particular difficulty in writing essay questions, so he was to sit down and write two essay questions that he would ask on a test if he were the instructor of the class. He was to answer the questions and bring them to the counseling session to discover places where he could increase his essay writing skills.

Each week new projects or additions to the old projects were added. Study time was also increased each week until a maximum plateau was reached. The structure on the projects was an intentional maneuver to increase the possibility of the student's success, thereby insuring the student of being in a position to rightfully receive reinforcement.

USING POSITIVE REINFORCEMENT

Counselor Reward

Reinforcement or reward was a major factor in the interview. There did not seem to be a great need for the punishment or the nonencouraging remarks as many of the variables that would cause the client to fail were discussed *before* they occurred and his awareness of those pitfalls and his skills to combat them were beginning to develop before he stumbled upon them.[1] The structure increased the probability of success.

Counselor verbal reinforcement consisted of such statements as, "That's great!" "I'm proud of you," "You came through again!" These were given only when they were earned and when they were sincerely felt.

Self-Reward

A definite attempt was made to get the counselee to reward himself. For example, a student would take a break and do something he liked to reward himself for his work. One reward involved an additional half hour of study for a student who had been studying for a total of one-half hour each day. The first week on his schedule his study time was for one-half hour on each subject. He was successful during the first week and came in with all of his time checked off and completed. I congratulated him and said, "Good, and because you have done such a good job we'll reward

[1] Editors' Note: The natural environment provides more than enough punishing consequences without a counselor's contribution. The client needs support for even faltering steps forward.

you and *let* you study an extra half hour each day next week." At the present time the counselee is studying an hour a day on each subject and has added fifteen minutes a day for each class to begin his review of the entire quarter in preparation for finals.

Another way to encourage self-reward was to ask the student if what he was doing was making any difference. One student reported that for the first time he knew what the professor was talking about in class, he understood the test questions, he was caught up in his assignments, and school was fun now. This allowed him to see his own benefits and reward himself verbally.

Reward from Others

Getting some external rewards became easier because papers were turned in for the first time and returned with high C's, B's, and A's. Quizzes were taken and perfect scores were received; midquarters came and went with B's and A's and the reinforcement from these began to supplement the counselor's and counselee's own reinforcement.

Other external rewards came from significant others. The student would tell his family each day how much he had studied, report his scores on tests and involve the family in discussions of what he was studying. The family involvement aided his retention and also was a means of putting him in a position where someone had a greater opportunity to say, "That's interesting," or "That's good." I placed the counselee in a position to become aware of what others were thinking of his work by asking: "Are others aware of what you are doing?" "How do they feel about it?" The usual answer was, "They are proud of me," "They just can't believe it," "My girl just can't understand it."

DEVELOPING INTERDEPENDENCY

One risk in structuring is that the client will persist in a dependent relationship with the counselor. Direct attempts were made to lessen the dependency and increase the interdependency by dispersing the sources of reinforcement to (1) the counselee himself, (2) the work as evaluated by the instructors, and (3) significant others in the counselee's environment. More important, the client was encouraged to build mature relationships of an interdependent nature, first with the counselor and then with those in his natural environment.[2]

[2] Editors' Note: The author's stress on interdependence, not independence, is important. In a complex society no one can be truly independent. The task for counselors is to help clients become effectively interdependent—giving and receiving in mutually beneficial relationships.

The significant dependency was one the client formed on himself. For example, one counselee could not help smiling when he walked in because he was so excited with the results of what *he* had been doing. The next week he was scheduled for two tests, one term paper and a theme. On his way out of the door he said, "I probably won't be 'smiling' next week." The counselor replied, "That makes me sad." "Why?" "Because I have come to depend on that smile."[3] The client turned on his heels and said, "I'll come through"—and he did! He moved from probation one quarter to the "Dean's List" the next.

[3] Editors' Note: Possibly the counselor's expressed dependency on the client inspired the client to depend on himself. It seemed to work here for a female counselor with a male client. Would it work as well with other combinations?

Role-Playing and Reinforcement

THE TWO CASE STUDIES in this section illustrate the use of role-playing and reinforcement with the same problem, an inability to speak before a group without severe feelings of anxiety. In Article 13 by Hosford we see what can be done with an elementary school girl; Varenhorst in Article 14 shows how the problem can be treated with a high school girl.

The role-playing technique has many variations. In counseling the technique may consist of a client practicing some behaviors he wants to learn in a situation where any errors he makes will not be ridiculed or punished in any way. Role-playing enables a client to rehearse a new behavior as often as necessary without anxiety about its consequences.

In order for the role-playing technique to be successful, it is essential, of course, that the counselor respond in a positive way to any client improvement (or even an attempt at improvement sometimes). The counselor should not laugh at the client's attempt even if the client tries to be funny by "hamming it up." Neither should the counselor point out faults in the performance at first. The client is usually extremely sensitive to the possibility of appearing ridiculous and is very much aware that his performance is faulty. The client needs encouragement for continued practice and some positive feedback about those specific features of his performance which are showing improvement.

As a client gains confidence in his own ability to improve, the counselor may make suggestions about specific ways to improve the performance even more. For example, in Article 14, Varenhorst asked the client to speak louder. The suggestion was positive since it described specifically how the performance might be improved. The client herself could not have detected the deficiency without help.

For role-playing to have its maximum effect, it should be performed under situations which are as nearly realistic as possible, a "dress rehearsal" so to speak. Hosford, in Article 13, even had his client role-play walking to the front of the room in preparation for giving an oral report. Initial role-playing situations may be performed in a counselor's office. Ideally, later role-playing sessions would be conducted in the same environment where the final performance is to be expected.

Occasionally roles are reversed in counseling so that the counselor plays the part of the client and the client plays the part of some person with whom he may be having difficulty. The counselor may then demonstrate an alternative method of reacting to the problem situation while the client reacts the way he anticipates the other person would act. Role-playing in this way is similar to the modeling techniques which are described and illustrated in more detail in Part III. One difference is that in role-playing the client can get a feeling for how the "other guy" perceives the situation by playing the other person's role in addition to his own.

13

OVERCOMING FEAR OF SPEAKING IN A GROUP

Ray E. Hosford
UNIVERSITY OF WISCONSIN

Mickey was a bright sixth grade girl who was referred to me because she demonstrated acute anxiety when asked to read, give a report, or perform in any manner before her classmates. When asked by her teacher to give a book report, Mickey could barely begin before her voice became almost inaudible because of her tension and anxiety.

After the initial discussion with her teacher, I made arrangements to observe Mickey's behavior in and outside of the classroom. Because many withdrawn children find making oral book reports a painful experience, I was interested in determining which, if any, other behaviors Mickey could or could not perform. By carefully observing her behavior it was evident that she did not manifest the behaviors usually associated with the shy withdrawn child. Mickey was not especially quiet in the classroom. She did participate in class discussions and quite often voiced opinions and advanced ideas during those times in which the teacher or another student led the group. During committee projects Mickey took an active role, sometimes one of leadership. On the playground, I noticed that she appeared to have warm personal relations with others and quite often was the loudest member of her group in the various games played.

In discussing the problem with Mickey, she related that she had "always" been unable to talk before a group. She was rather upset with her teacher because she said that her past teachers had known this and did not ask her to perform such tasks. She explained that she wanted very much to be able to talk in front of the class but, she said, "I just can't."[1]

Because her cumulative record indicated that two years earlier her parents had been concerned about her problem, a conference was soon initiated with them. Discussion of Mickey's problem took place with the father and Mickey present. Her mother was unable to attend. Her father asked how her anxiety toward talking before a group developed. I replied that I really didn't know. One possibility was that Mickey overheard someone else describing fear of public speaking. Or she may have had a bad experience the first time she attempted to talk before a group. Maybe she wasn't prepared, or something might have happened to make the class members laugh at her or in some way make her feel anxious. More important than attempting to determine what caused Mickey's problem, I felt, was to discuss ways in which she could learn how to talk before a group without experiencing this anxiety.[2]

I explained to both Mickey and her father that learning a behavior a little at a time in a relaxed manner is quite often successful in helping

[1] Editors' Note: Mickey did not initiate the request for the counselor's service. If the teacher had not noticed the problem and made the referral, Mickey might well have been content to continue avoiding oral reports whenever possible. However, when given the opportunity to discuss her problem she clearly wanted to change her pattern of behavior. Many remediable problems remain unmentioned and untreated because teachers and counselors do not make available an opportunity for the student to discuss the problem openly.

[2] Editors' Note: Such an approach is quite contrary to therapies which assert that insight into the origin of a problem is sufficient to alleviate the difficulty. Behavioral counselors generally spend little time trying to reconstruct the original cause(s) of the problem (unless a client wants to prevent a similar problem from arising again). Regardless of the origin, the important issue is how to remedy the presently existing difficulty. Only when a counselor had differentially effective treatments for a problem with different origins would an investigation of origins be important.

people perform the same behavior which had previously presented considerable anxiety. The counseling procedures were explained and both Mickey and her father indicated that they would like to try them.

COUNSELING PROCEDURES

In the counseling setting Mickey met with me regularly once a week for six weeks. Here she role-played the behaviors in giving an oral report. The important difference, however, was that she practiced these behaviors under low-stress conditions so she would experience little or no anxiety. For example, during the first session Mickey role-played getting out of her seat and coming to the front of the room. She also read short paragraphs orally but this was done while sitting at her seat. Each week she gradually increased the activities and the length of the presentation. During each session, I reinforced her by saying "very good, Mickey," "Hey, that's great!" and gave other types of approval as she role-played the part of giving a report. I kept pointing out the progress she was making but at the same time encouraged her to role-play the behavior only as long as she experienced little or no anxiety.

I also worked closely with Mickey's classroom teacher in a program designed to gradually increase the degree to which she performed orally before a group. The teacher agreed to include Mickey in a social studies committee which was to give oral presentations each week on various countries which the class was studying.[3] The important point was that she was to participate only to the extent she could perform the behavior without any anxiety. Thus, at first, the extent of her participation was only to stand at a large map and point out the area or region about which some member of the group was talking. Later, members of the group, at the suggestion of the teacher, involved Mickey gradually into more of the discussions. This was promoted by having two students on the committee ask Mickey questions such as, "What's that region called just north of Paris?" She was also asked by the committee if she could point out the major geographical features of the country they were discussing and tell the names as she did so. Members of the group thanked Mickey for helping out and the two co-chairmen of the committee were reinforced for gradually including Mickey into the discussions and for telling her that she had done very well. The seating of the committee, while in front of the room, was a semi-circle in which only the chairman looked directly at the audience. The members of the group were told that they were to discuss their reports as if they were alone in the room. This procedure

---

[3] Editors' Note: Cooperative working relationships with teachers are absolutely essential for effective behavioral counseling.

was done in part to help Mickey remain relaxed but it was found that the other members of the group also interacted more easily when seated in this manner.

The dyadic counseling was terminated when Mickey related that she was taking an active part in the committee discussions. The teacher, however, continued reinforcing Mickey for any improvement that she made.

RESULTS

Mickey gradually became more comfortable while in front of the class and eventually was able to give reports on her own. The committee performed so well that other teachers asked to use the group as a "model" for committee procedures. Thus the group performed for two other classrooms which provided Mickey with a valuable experience of speaking before different groups of people.

At the end of the school year the teacher planned culmination activities for each of the major teaching units. Mickey was among those who volunteered to give an oral presentation on what the class had done in social studies during the year.

14

HELPING A CLIENT TO SPEAK UP IN CLASS

Barbara B. Varenhorst
PALO ALTO UNIFIED SCHOOL DISTRICT (CALIFORNIA)

Cindy hesitantly walked into my office for the conference she had requested. She only sat on part of the chair I offered her and held her arms rigidly against her body as she rubbed her hands together, waiting for me to begin. As I had never met her before, I studied her as I smiled and welcomed her. She was thin and tall, but her big eyes were sad and her mouth drooped. She frequently swallowed and moistened her lips as she waited.

"You said that you wanted to see me, Cindy," I began. "Is there something I can help with?"

"I want to learn to speak up in class," she blurted.

I couldn't believe what I had just heard. I smiled to myself as I rubbed *my* hands together under the desk. This was a classic case for behavioral counseling![1]

"Well, perhaps I can help you then. But before I can I'll need more information. Tell me why you want to learn this. Why do you feel you don't know how?"

"I don't have many friends and the friends I want to have know how to speak up and tell you what they are thinking. I have ideas and want to express them, but when I'm called on, I can't think of what to say or what I do say is real dumb. Sometimes I can't even put up my hand, although I want to say something."

"Is it the same in all your classes, or is it easier to do in some and harder in others?" I asked.

"It's about the same in all of them, but I guess it's easier in social studies because you can prepare ahead of time for that."

As we continued talking, I found that her actual goal was to be able to speak in her art seminar class. She loved art and enjoyed her work, but as a part of the class the students criticized one another's work. Frequently she had ideas about another's art piece but just could not get the courage to say anything. Since she had never contributed to these sessions of criticism, she thought kids believed she didn't have any ideas. She felt they thought she was dull and therefore didn't like her.

Her problem extended into her social life where even in social gatherings she could not say anything. The only place it was different was when she was with two close friends who knew her well. She admitted that she was afraid of what people thought of her if she should say something.

I asked if she had much opportunity to talk at home. She felt that she could, if she wanted to, but there really wasn't much chance. There was always a commotion at home and others in the family did the talking at the dinner table. Actually, she felt, she really didn't talk much to anyone.

Finally, we agreed on a plan. First we made a chart of all her classes with the days of the week across the top. I explained that we would put a check by each class for that particular day whenever she made some contribution in class. If she spoke up twice, she would get two checks. I showed her where I would keep the chart and she could fill in the blanks if I wasn't there.[2]

Then I suggested that we start working on the class where speaking

---

[1] Editors' Note: Seldom is a counseling goal stated so succinctly so early in such explicit behavioral terms.

[2] Editors' Note: An interesting technique for self-reinforcement.

was the easiest, social studies. The next time she had an assignment that was to be discussed in class she was to let me know. Before going to class we would practice by talking through the assignment. This would be in a few days, so I made an appointment for the following day.

When she came, I took the part of the teacher and asked questions as if I were calling on her. She had prepared a speech which she mumbled in a quiet voice. I praised her for what she had done and said, "But we're in class, now Cindy, and I couldn't hear you. Could you speak up?"[3]

She cleared her voice and began again, forgetting parts of what she wanted to say.

"That's much better! It really doesn't matter if you say it exactly the same way each time. Tell me just what are the points you want to get across to the class."

She relaxed and clearly told me what she wanted to say. I then explained that she only needed to remember what she wanted to say, not the exact order of how she was going to say it. I added that when we are nervous we tend to forget things if they have to be said in just the right way. "We just want to concentrate on your saying something and I don't care whether or not it comes out just perfect." Then we went through another role-playing session. Each time we repeated this, I asked her to speak a little louder and to tell me the same material in a different way.

Finally, I said I thought she was ready, but that I wanted her to come in before school to have a final rehearsal before the class. She agreed to do this.

During the day I made a point to see her teacher and carefully explained what we were trying to do. I asked him to call on Cindy as soon as she put her hand up, so she wouldn't back out if she had to wait to recite. He agreed.[4]

After Cindy's rehearsal on the final day I suggested she stop in after school. We could talk about how it had gone and then could put a check in the square by social studies.

I was waiting at the door as soon as school was over and Cindy came

[3] Editors' Note: Role-playing is probably successful in cases such as this primarily because the desired response can be practiced with *no negative consequences* for errors. Anxiety is produced when punishing consequences, real or imagined, are associated with a behavior. The counselor responds by identifying the positive features of the performance for praise before describing how to improve the next try.

[4] Editors' Note: Should the client be told that the counselor conferred with the teacher about her problem? If the client asks, we believe the counselor should describe the steps employed and the reasons for each procedure. It may often be advisable to obtain the client's permission in advance to consult with a teacher about the client's problem. However, if permission was not obtained and if the client does not ask, sometimes more harm than good comes from volunteering too much information. Remember what happened in Article 7 when the counselor told a client about case conferences held about him without his knowledge.

running in. Her face was bright and her words came tumbling out. She had been called on and she was able to say what she wanted. She even had made another contribution on another question. I beamed and told her how pleased I was with her success. I said I was very proud that we could make two check marks for this day and made a great big one for the second contribution.

The next step in our program was to prepare for the next opportunity in social studies and to begin work on English. We set up regular practice sessions, and always the brief meeting before school and the follow-up conference after school.

As the check marks on the chart began increasing, I brought up the subject of art seminar. Since this was not a discussion we could prepare for directly, I asked her to talk about some of the art work being done, including what she herself was doing. She brought in a piece of pottery to show me and we discussed it. Then she told me that a critique session was approaching.

I knew this was a critical session and a test of what she had been learning in her other classes. Since I couldn't role-play effectively for this class, not knowing a great deal about art myself, I decided merely to encourage her. I told her that I thought she had developed a lot of confidence and that her ideas had always been good and other students would appreciate what she would have to say. Needless to say, I too, was nervous, sitting in my office during that period.

Rather than waiting until school was over, she appeared at my door right after the art class. Her face was really beaming then, and I knew that she had been successful. We talked about it as we put the first check on the chart after art seminar.

These sessions continued for a long period of time. Gradually I suggested fewer appointments and she agreed. Then I suggested that she only come when she felt she needed to. By this time we were not filling in the chart, since discussion of the day seemed sufficient.

Eventually Cindy stopped coming. When I would see her on campus I would inquire about her progress which she assured me was continuing. Later, she brought me the pot she had shown me earlier as a thank you for helping her.

Perhaps Cindy had other problems. Or maybe she would have liked to learn other social behaviors. Perhaps later she might come back to talk about these. But she had come with the specific request to learn how to speak up in class. She was now doing this and her need for my counseling services had ended.

Using Behavior Contracts

A COUNSELOR MAY USE reinforcement quite naturally and spontaneously in response to gradual improvements in a client's behavior. A counselor may also deliberately plan the administration of reinforcers. It is clear from a number of studies that whether the reinforcement is spontaneous or planned it can modify client behavior.

But should the client be aware that the counselor is using reinforcement? In our view there is no reason to hide the fact. When the goal of counseling is a mutually agreed upon change in behavior on the part of a client, then both client and counselor take pleasure in seeing improvement. The counselor's expression of that pleasure may well give additional satisfaction to the client and thus encourage him still more.

Since there is nothing secret about the techniques of behavioral counseling, the contingencies of reinforcement may sometimes be made quite explicit in advance. The behavior contract is a logical outgrowth of specifying reinforcement contingencies in advance. Infrahuman animals respond to various reinforcing stimuli in much the same way that human beings do. However, language enables human beings to anticipate changing their behavior on the basis of a verbal promise or agreement that some positive consequences will be forthcoming.

A behavior contract is an agreement between two or more persons specifying what each person will do for a stated period of time. It takes the form, "I'll do _____ for you in exchange for your doing _____ for me." A time limit is usually stated or implied. If the time limit is not specifically stated, the contract should be renegotiable whenever either of the parties to it thinks the terms of the contract are unfair to him.

Explicit written contracts are a relatively recent contribution to counseling and psychotherapy. Some traditionalists are shocked by the explicit terms and incentives in behavior contracts. In one contract, for example, a disadvantaged student contracted to earn a daily salary simply for attending college with bonus payments for good grades. However, the only differences between this type of contract and a traditional scholarship were that the agreement was explicitly stated in advance and the payments were made weekly. Traditional scholarships also pay money for attending school and for getting good grades, but the payments are made annually and the agreement may not have been written in advance.

Many possible contractual arrangements between clients and counselors are possible. The examples in this section represent the application of behavior contract methods to rather extreme types of behavior. In Article 15 Keirsey provides a detailed example of how behavior contracts can be used in the case of severely disruptive classroom behavior. The specific application is termed "systematic exclusion," an agreement under which the child gains the privilege of attending school without teacher or parental nagging in exchange for his adherence to rules about his classroom behavior. Only as long as his behavior does not disturb others will he retain the privilege of remaining in school. The reinforcer for the child in this contract is the privilege of remaining in school. Some people would say this may be a doubtful privilege for the child, but Keirsey maintains that, at least for elementary school children, attending school is indeed a privilege.

A further application of the technique of systematic exclusion is supplied by Shier in Article 16. The problem behavior is bizarre and difficult to control. The advantages of using medical help are evident in this case since it appears that the addition of some drug therapy in combination with the systematic exclusion technique did result in a prolonged, though not yet permanent, remediation of the behavior problem.

Dinoff and Rickard in Article 17 extend the concept of behavior contracts to other kinds of behavior. In a therapeutic summer camp children were given the experience of negotiating contracts in which their behavior would be rewarded by certain kinds of privileges and benefits that the camp could supply. The extension of this concept to contracts at home between a parent and child is also illustrated.

Although most of the behavior problems described in this section are severe, behavior contracts can also be used to good advantage with less severe types of problems. Behavior contracts usually make explicit what is already understood implicitly. Sometimes the very process of arriving at an agreement makes clear understandings that were only dimly perceived.

Counselors themselves need not be a party to many behavior contracts. Frequently the counselor may serve the role only of helping to negotiate a behavior contract between two or more parties who may be having some type of a misunderstanding. The potential benefits of behavior contracts in cases of marital disharmony, conflicts between parents and children, as well as problems between teachers and students have scarcely begun to be realized.

15

SYSTEMATIC EXCLUSION: ELIMINATING CHRONIC CLASSROOM DISRUPTIONS

David W. Keirsey
COVINA-VALLEY UNIFIED SCHOOL DISTRICT (CALIFORNIA)

Jimmy Cyclone makes a shambles of the classroom and of the teacher. Her methods of dealing with him fail. The principal and the parents fail also, no matter how much and in what way they exact penalities, give counsel, or give rewards. Even medical and psychiatric interventions fail. Is there any alternative to expulsion from school? Such an alternative does exist and is described here.

A contract is drawn up. Each person agrees to do his part. The child agrees to do as he pleases. The teacher agrees to send him home immediately when he exceeds any specified limit, such as getting out of his seat without explicit permission, talking without explicit permission, or making a disruptive noise or motion. The teacher also agrees to forego all "commercials" (attempts to sell constructive or conforming behavior to a reluctant buyer), to avoid all attempts to influence him in any manner whatsoever, and never to speak to him about his misbehavior either by reminding or coaxing him. The parents agree not to talk with him about school at all, and not to punish him in any way for school behavior. The principal agrees to supervise the child's leaving class and going home and not to discuss behavior with the child unless the child initiates such discussion. No one talks, each acts.

The first day Jimmy lasts five minutes. He gets up out of his seat, his teacher sees him and immediately gives the signal to leave. He reports to the office and goes home. His mother says nothing to him about it. The next day he stays for ten minutes. This time he leans back in his seat too far so that the chair falls with a loud clatter. His teacher merely signals him to leave. His mother does not discuss it with him when he gets home. However, she becomes very upset and calls the psychologist. The psychologist reassures her that this is precisely what should happen and that he is very pleased with the teacher's cooperation. He predicts that Jimmy will last fifteen minutes the next day and cautions her not to discuss school with Jimmy even if Jimmy tries to draw her into a conversation about it. This pattern continues. Mother has to be reassured twice more that things are going well and that it is important that Jimmy actually be sent home on each occasion that he exceeds a specified limit. Father threatens to go back to spanking him for his misdeeds, even though he has acknowledged that previous attempts to use spanking have ended in obvious failure and even worsening of misbehavior. The teacher admits that when Jimmy is not there the whole class is calmer, more productive. The other children wonder what's going on. They begin to feel sorry for Jimmy because he is sent home for such trivial offenses. Finally, on the ninth day after the contract was made, Jimmy stays all day. He proudly announces this to the principal. The principal is surprised and says so. For the rest of the year, with only two exceptions, Jimmy remains in class without a single disruptive act. He soon begins to do his work. Parents and teacher remark that "he is not the same child." The other children like him now and play with him. He is more relaxed. He likes himself. He smiles now. He is elected class president.

The teacher and the parents want the contract discontinued now that he is controlling himself. This is done. His chronic misbehavior returns immediately and with renewed vigor. The contract is installed again. The misbehavior disappears instantly. The same contract is used the following year. The third year it is used only during the last semester. The following year it is not used at all—he is in charge of himself. It works.

This is not an atypical outcome in the use of systematic exclusion. The method has been used widely in the schools of California since 1957

(Keirsey, 1957). Until then the method had been employed with about 50 cases. Since then, the method has been used perhaps a thousand times, although this is at best a wild guess. But plainly it is used and it pays off.

CHRONIC MISBEHAVIOR

Occasionally one encounters a child whose misbehavior is marked by its chronicity rather than its type or its acuteness. What does this mean? It means that the child never really stops misbehaving. Each act in itself is trivial, something that many of the other children will do one time or another during the day. Thus, it is not what the child does, so much as how frequently he does it. As he comes into the room, he bumps into someone and snickers about it. Five minutes later he falls out of his chair. In another five minutes he yawns loudly. Shortly after this, he breaks his pencil—doubtless on purpose—and strolls to the pencil sharpener. To and from the pencil sharpener he catches the attention of several other children with an interesting repertoire of grimaces and gymnastics. At this juncture the teacher reminds him that he is calling too much attention to himself and that it is best that he get busy with his work. Yet five minutes later he talks to his neighbor and shortly after this he gets out of his seat and wanders over to the nature display, fiddles with and breaks one of the objects. This brings the teacher to him. She scolds him, telling him that he should not handle property of others, should stay in his seat, and should get busy with his work. Thus far, he has done none of his work. By now teacher's temperature is slightly elevated. This pattern of behavior continues throughout the day. Occasionally the teacher intervenes with such measures as scolding, reminding, coaxing, urging, threatening, swatting him, sending him on an errand, sending him to the office "to think it over" and "to see the principal."

There are some rather striking features about this interaction of teacher and pupil that bear examination. First, notice that it doesn't matter what the teacher does, or which method she uses; his misbehavior continues. He may stop for ten minutes—may "miss a beat" or two—but essentially the rhythm of chronicity is kept up as if it were unrelated to the teacher's attempts to stop it.

With a frequency of one disruptive act per five-minute interval, however small these acts—grimacing, shuffling of feet, getting out of seat, yawning loudly—the total day is comprised of an impressive summation of disruptive behavior. The teacher has tried to cope unsuccessfully, with about every fifth or sixth act. Finally, having run through her stock of techniques for stopping misbehavior and inducing productive behavior, she finally allows herself to recognize that she is going through the list the fourth time. Whatever the condition that brings it about, she eventually "blows her stack."

THE TEACHER'S DILEMMA

Why does she blow her stack? Because she hates the child? No, rather because she is blocked in her desire to be a good teacher; because she feels helpless; because her methods that have worked for twenty years— do not work with this child. This child threatens her sense of competence. And it is this that occasions the emotional upsurge. Many teachers justifiably pride themselves on their ability to handle children, misbehaving children included. When such a teacher—experienced, expert, confident—comes up against this sort of child, she cannot quite believe that her methods are ineffective. Consequently, she continues applying these measures long past the point of reason. They have always worked, why don't they work now? She continues, certain that sooner or later the child will "come around." In the meantime, she inexorably and inevitably loses her respect for this child, just as his classmates do, as they should. The end result is unadorned disgust, contempt, and outright hatred. Finally, she appeals to the principal or to the parents or both. They scold, remind, encourage, cajol, bribe, spank, threaten, incarcerate, suspend, lecture, give friendly counsel, use a schedule of positive reinforcement, adjust the curriculum, on and on. Yet the pattern of chronic misbehavior continues. Now the principal begins to think in terms of expulsion—sending the child home for good (suspension is merely temporary exclusion from school).

What is the dilemma? On the one hand no single act of disruption warrants much reaction, but on the other, the cumulative effect of the frequency literally "packs the air" of the classroom with chronic tension. When the child is absent, there is a very noticeable change in classroom atmosphere.

How frequently does one encounter a case of such severity? In suburban schools with middle class parents, the frequency is about one per school or perhaps one per two schools, about one for every 500 children. Obviously this pattern of behavior may exist in degrees. One child may have a frequency or beat of one disturbing act in each five-minute interval while another may do one thing in each thirty minutes (eight disturbances per day versus fifty disturbances). Both are "chronic" misbehavior, but the latter is much less disturbing in that the classroom tension level is not nearly so high. Naturally, there are more cases of the less extreme frequency, but these are more tolerable and more easily dealt with by normal teacher, principal, and parent techniques. The truly chronic misbehavior pattern will take more heroic efforts and methods than those ordinarily used.

CONSEQUENCES OF BEHAVIOR

Experimentation with the systematic exclusion method of dealing with chronic misbehavior was begun in 1952.[1] This method was inspired by the psychology of Harry Stack Sullivan. Oddly enough though, the method is much more coherent with the social field theory of Alfred Adler and his disciple Rudolph Dreikurs. Dreikurs' (1964) concept of logical consequences is more applicable here. Systematic exclusion is easier to understand as a special case of the method of logical consequences. In the interest of conceptualizing the method, we would do well to examine, if only briefly, the distinction between logical and arbitrary consequences.

The method of consequences consists in invoking a system which controls the behavior of the child and people around the child such that a given act on the child's part results in a specified act on the part of those around him. When he does something, others are constrained to react as specified by the system. It is an action-reaction system, where action and reaction are contingent.

Logical and Arbitrary

There are at least four methodologically separate types of consequence available for such a system: (1) penalties, (2) rewards, (3) feedback, and (4) restriction. The first two are arbitrary; the second two are logical.[2] Let us see what the distinction is. An arbitrary consequence, (1) penalties or (2) rewards, is one that cannot be deduced from the act that it is contingent upon. Suppose Jimmy Cyclone sasses the teacher and in consequence his mother won't allow him to watch TV for a week. What is the relation between watching TV and sassing the teacher?

---

[1] Choice of the word "exclusion" was, from a legal standpoint, unfortunate, since exclusion means that the child is barred from the attendance by the Board of Trustees because of some physical or mental condition which presumably is beyond the will of the child. "Expulsion" would have been an equally bad choice in that this too is an action by the Board of Trustees in barring the child from attendance because of willful behavior. From a legal standpoint, the word "exemption" would have been preferable, since this is an action taken by the school authorities to allow the parent to withdraw the child from school temporarily until some physical or mental condition has abated.

[2] Editors' Note: We believe penalties and rewards may or may not be "logical" just as feedback and restriction can sometimes be "arbitrary." See our introductory comments to this section.

Clearly, there may not be any logical relation as viewed by Jimmy. The contingency tends to be arbitrary. This penalty that Jimmy pays is chosen, not because it is logically connected to his asocial act, but because it is deemed the thing most likely to bother him. Such consequences are chosen arbitrarily, since the purpose is related to payment, not logic. Understand now, this does not mean that arbitrarily chosen consequences are ineffective. It means rather that there is a difference between logical and arbitrary consequences which should not be ignored. With certain types of problems, arbitrary consequences are far more effective in modifying behavior than are logical consequences.[3] For example, reward methods have shown themselves to be extremely powerful, not only in starting productive behavior, but also in stopping disruptive behavior.

A logical consequence is one chosen because it should logically follow a given act simply because that is the way things happen in the real world. Unfortunately, with children especially, more because of the tendency of adults to protect them from reality than from children's relative lack of development, reality or logical consequences are too long in coming and/or are not clearly seen. Often consequences are obscured because other things obtrude, such as adult "commercials" about what is going on.

There are two kinds of logical outcomes of negative acts: feedback or knowledge of results, and restriction of freedom. It is the latter that concerns us here.

Restriction

The concept of restriction brings up one of the basic postulates of social field theory. It can be stated as an axiom: Abuse of a freedom limits that freedom—sooner or later, in one way or another. Turning this postulate into a methodological principle would consist in seeing to it that the abuse of freedom does in fact, and immediately, bring about or entail limitation of the freedom involved.

Johnny makes noises with his chair; so in consequence, the teacher takes away the chair for a period of time, say the rest of the day. He is no longer free to use the chair. She does not scold him, or get his mother to spank him, or take away his bicycle—rather she takes away the thing he abused. He misuses his chair, therefore he loses his chair.

Mary is sassy toward her mother. Mother does not slap her or scold her,

---

[3] Editors' Note: The distinction between "logical" and "arbitrary" consequences is not easy to make nor do we ascribe necessarily more effectiveness to one than the other. Possibly more important is the frequency with which the consequence follows the action. Logical consequences always occur (pain after hitting thumb with hammer) but arbitrary consequences require a human agent who may occasionally forget or neglect this duty. This arbitrary consequence may be administered on an intermittent basis while logical consequences are administered continuously.

rather she invokes the logical consequence of removing the child from her presence—or herself from the presence of the child. Mary abuses her mother, therefore she loses her mother—not her bicycle or her dinner or some other irrelevant privilege.

Suppose it doesn't "bother" Mary to be away from her mother for the time being? Suppose she is perfectly happy playing in her room or outside—if that is where mother chooses to send her? Fine! The fact that there is little or no punishment involved in the limitation or restriction of a privilege in no way affects the corrective efficacy of the method. The punishment methods are specifically designed and chosen to bother, to hurt, to arouse feelings, to make the culprit sorry, remorseful, repentant. Not so in the case of the restriction methods. The purpose of restriction methods is to let reality shape behavior. The rule is this, that behavior will take whatever shape reality dictates if nothing interferes. Children, underneath it all, are born pragmatists, which means that they alter their deeds in accord with the consequences that ensue from those deeds.

Unfortunately, in the case of misbehaving children especially, reality (what Dreikurs calls "natural consequences") is interfered with by the well-meaning adult. Usually this interference consists, at first, in a stepped-up program of "commercials" and threats, and later penalties. These usually are quite effective in obscuring the culprit's vision of reality as well as shielding him from the effects of reality, that is, the natural consequences of his deeds.

Penalty methods often change feelings. Restriction methods often change relevant behaviors. Joe talks out in class. His teacher scolds him. This makes him feel bad. He may or may not talk out in class in the next five minutes. Jimmy talks out in class. His teacher sends him home. How he feels is irrelevant. It is impossible for him to talk out in class for the rest of the day because he isn't there. Whatever has happened to his feelings is problematic, but his behavior has altered radically from attending class to going home.

SYSTEMATIC EXCLUSION

Systematic exclusion applies the methodological principle of restriction in a very specific way. Return now to the case of Jimmy Cyclone. He misbehaves, in a small way, within almost every five-minute interval. This constitutes an abuse of the freedom to attend school. The principle of restriction is that whatever freedom is abused must be restricted—temporarily lost. Therefore, since Jimmy abuses the privilege of being at school, it is that privilege he loses.

How does one go about setting up a system to see that this happens without Jimmy construing it as just one more attempt to bother him or to make him feel bad?

First Interview With Teacher

It is important to get a detailed description from the teacher of what is happening in the classroom. Filling out a questionnaire will not do, though it may help focus the interview. One must examine the dialogue which has been going on between the teacher and child. Interview her in the classroom. What does the child do when he first comes into the room? Have the teacher give examples of what he does. See where he is sitting. What does she do when he does what he does? What does he do then? What does she do? Then what does he do? Then she? How is the class when he is gone?

Show her that you understand how difficult it is for her and the rest of the class with such a constant disruptive presence. This can be done by making statements suggesting how she must feel; for example, "I don't see how you can stand him behaving like that day after day, week after week, month after month." "Wouldn't you like to wring his neck sometimes?" "That must be awfully irritating!"

One must avoid giving the impression that one expects the teacher to be able to cope with this kind of behavior. If she feels she ought to be able to, it is up to the psychologist to help her see how unusual this child is, that ordinary reasons do not apply and that therefore ordinary methods will not work.

It is important to elicit from the teacher any ideas of what methods she figures ought to be tried which have not yet been tried. She may have an approach, a card up her sleeve, which she believes would work, but feels that such a method would be unacceptable. For example, she may feel "if the principal would paddle him, he'd straighten out!" As long as she has such a card up her sleeve, she cannot wholeheartedly use *your* method. So this card must be put on the table. Indeed, this might be taken as a general operating rule: *In encountering each participant—principal, teacher, child, parents—make sure that their untried solutions are brought forth and that each admits that the method has been tried and failed or that it would fail if used.* Almost invariably, the "untried solution" of each is some variant of the penalty method, such as spanking, scolding, staying after school, loss of TV, and the like. Usually the untried solution will not have been examined carefully, so that there will not be many details that the teacher or parent will volunteer on just how this could be done. A few questions about the details of how the method would be applied usually lead the person to admit that it has already been tried or that it just would not work if tried. If the method does seem feasible or if the person is convinced that it would work, then it is well to go ahead and use the method just to prove that it will not work. (If it is a penalty method, it probably will not work on such a case.)

Frequently, by the time the teacher has requested help, say after Christmas, the child has made such a shambles of her class and has made her feel so powerless for so long that she dislikes the child with some intensity. If things have gone this far, it is well to find another teacher for the child.

When one intends to shift a child from one class to another, it will be necessary to help the teacher cope with her sense of guilt. This can be done by explaining that no matter what is done, it cannot be done in this class because the child has wrecked his relations with his classmates and with her making an about-face all but impossible. In another class, with systematic exclusion, he would have no chance to destroy his relations. Thus, the teacher needs to be assured that any success in another class will be due not to any greater skill on the part of the other teacher, but to the rigid circumstances under which he will enter the new classroom. Hence, it will be necessary to explain the systematic exclusion procedure to her even though she will not be the one using it. She will have invested, by this time, a tremendous amount of energy and emotion into this case and will not lightly give up the child to someone else, unless reassured that it is best for her class, for the child, and for her, to remove him from the situation that he has created. Her pride must be carefully guarded in such a situation. She must know that you and the principal regard this as a most unusual case which will require a most unusual method, perhaps for years to come.

Interviewing the Child

The order in which one gets involved with the main participants is flexible. There are advantages to each order just as there are disadvantages. But usually, one would want to see first the teacher and then the child.

It would be prudent to avoid giving the child the impression that one's interest in him is administrative. Nothing is lost and much is sometimes gained by indicating to the child that one's job is that of helping those children who have trouble in school at the same time one makes it clear that the reason for the encounter is precisely that the child is, in fact, having trouble. Thus, one does not ask him if he is having difficulties, but announces that it is because he is in difficulty that this interview is occurring. The remainder of the interview might be used to find out what the child thinks is happening. Does he want that to be what is happening? If he sees things as bad for him, ask him if he would like some help to make things go better. Suggest that possibly the teacher and parents are "getting after him," scolding, blaming, and so forth. Would he like them to stop? Ask him what would happen if suddenly the teacher and his parents stopped getting after him to behave himself and do his work. What would he do?

Suggest that perhaps he is unhappy at school. How would he like it if the psychologist were to persuade everybody that it would be OK to let him stay home? Some will say no, don't do that. Others will say they would like that. This gives the psychologist a methodological cue. One child wants people to "get after him," another child wants people to "leave him alone." The child who backs away from the suggestion that adults might no longer try to get him to work in school must be treated in one way, that is, with a "proclamation" approach. The child who eagerly affirms "getting people off my back" is dealt with another way, that is, with a "contract" approach. The distinction between proclamation and contract will be discussed later.

The initial interview need not be lengthy. Its purpose is to establish the psychologist or counselor as one who intends to help the child do better at school, one who is prepared to get others to make unusual concessions and unusual arrangements for the child. In other words, he establishes himself as the child's advocate. He indicates that the teacher and principal are worried about the child and that he will return to the child with some plan of action. As the child's advocate, he leaves the impression: "I'll see what I can do for you."

The Parent Encounter

The next step is more touchy and more crucial—technologically—than any of the others. The parents will be loaded with negative feelings. These must be "drained off" before any other work can be done. By accepting their feelings as natural under the circumstances, it is easier to persuade them that you are indeed concerned, not with defending the school, but with doing something to help the child. And this must be the theme— *what to do.*

The caseworker presents himself as one who is hired by the school to help children do better at school. The focus, in other words, is not on understanding, but on changing behavior. This focus will help the parents turn their vision from trying to find the causes—which to them will constitute blame—to trying to determine what to do. It is well to suggest that the causes of any case of such behavior are so complex that it is fruitless to concern oneself with them. *It is of utmost importance to get the parents to stop playing the game of "who is to blame."* They must see you as one devoted solely to determining what to do to help this child and that you are too intent upon this purpose to bother with such academic questions as whose fault it is or what the causes are! In other words, here is a case where it may even be necessary to belittle the question of causality in the interest of insuring parental cooperation.

This doubtless seems strange and may require some explanation. The premise is this: If one allows one's transaction with the parents to dwell on causes, these causes, once surfaced, become excuses and as such militate against doing much of anything about the problem (Glasser, 1965).

Once trust is established, and it is necessary that the parents trust you, explore the history of the child's behavior. How was he as a baby? Was he always extremely active? When did the hyperactivity begin? Inquire about his behavior in each grade and the correlated behavior at home. This is not a search for causes, but a history of what he has done and what people have done in reaction to his behavior. The focus is not on "why" but on "what." This historic search establishes the tenure and continuity of the child's problem—acknowledges that it did not come out of the blue or because of the incompetence of his last teacher.

These things—blowing off steam, establishing trust, charting the behavioral history—these are enough for the initial interview. The next interview may be devoted to disclosing the plan of treatment.

Interviewing the Principal

One has thus far gotten involved with the teacher, the child, and one or both of the parents. The next step is to return to the principal and propose the use of systematic exclusion. Whether or not he is familiar with the method, it is unwise to neglect a thorough exposition of its theory and procedure.

It is important that the principal—and later, the parent—sees this method as an alternative to expulsion. The method, in other words, is presented as a way of protecting the child from expulsion. It is not "just something else to try to see if it will work." All other known methods have failed. This is "the last ditch stand." It is not whether to send the child home, but how long to send him home, that is, either temporarily or for good. Temporary exclusion is presented as a safeguard against permanent exclusion.

Although the plan is presented as a therapeutic regimen as well as a protective regimen, the emphasis with the principal is better placed on the latter. Thus, this should be seen by him as primarily an administrative way of protecting the class from disruption, the teacher's sanity, and the child's privilege of attending school. Only secondarily is it seen as a way of helping the child get control of himself. In presenting the plan to the parents, it is well to reverse the emphasis—first treatment, then protection.

The principal must be committed to the position that he will no longer allow this child to disrupt the classroom, whatever the causes of such behavior, even if it means expulsion. This commitment places systematic exclusion in the role of a savior and not a villain, or at least as the lesser of two evils. But the counselor does well to emphasize that in his opinion such a program of controls is precisely the kind of counseling the child needs, quite apart from administrative necessities.

It will be important to discuss the legal issues involved in the procedure. Systematic exclusion comes under the exemption law. It is not suspension, nor expulsion, nor exclusion, as these terms are understood in the legal sense. Suspension, expulsion, and exclusion may be executed by the school officials without parental consent or sanction. Exemption allows for dismissal from school only with parental sanction. In systematic exclusion, the child is dismissed at parental request, that is, is released to parental custody.[4]

The task, then, remains that of convincing the parents that in the interest of their child's welfare such a request be made. Thus, on each occasion that the child is dismissed, it is understood by all that the parents had requested such dismissal.

The Second Parent Encounter—Presenting the Plan

It is important to have the parents acknowledge that they do not know what to do to control their child's behavior at school. If either parent proposes some procedure, say spanking, ask him what have been the results of this method to date. Get him to admit that it does not work— that is, it does not control behavior. Ask him, then, if he is proposing that we use a method that clearly has not worked.

Point out that the principal is in the position of having to consider expulsion; that it is his administrative responsibility to do so. Suggest that their child is not doing his work, is not learning, and is making it most difficult for the other children to learn. If he is friendless and disliked, point this out. Describe, in other words, how bad his predicament is, emphasizing that his present attendance at school is not doing him any good, but, on the contrary, is doing him harm. This fact will have to be repeated on a number of occasions because the parents will want to forget it.

---

[4] Nothing in the California Code of Education nor in the Administrative Regulations (Title V) can be construed to limit the *amount* of time that a child is released from attendance or the *frequency* with which such release occurs under the exemption law. Counselors and psychologists in other States might well check the pertinent legal requirements.

SELF-CONTROL

Explain that his major problem is not learning, but rather it is self-control. He does not control himself. He cannot even attend school, not to mention learning, if he cannot control himself. The school cannot control him. The home cannot control him. Can he learn to control himself? That is the question that must be answered. How can the question be answered? How can his need for self-control be fulfilled?

The solution is a system or plan whereby he is given constant practice in self-control as the major education offering. Not academic training, but self-control training. Academic learning will have to wait on learning self-control.

How are we to do this? Simply send him home when he fails to control himself as the immediate and inevitable consequence of that failure. Thus, in order to stay in school, he must practice self-control. There will be no other means provided for him to remain in school. The teacher will be forbidden to influence him in any manner in this regard. The parents will agree—if they buy the plan—to forego any help.

The parents will protest that this is precisely what the child would like. After all, he hates school, as he should, considering his sorry experiences there. He will therefore deliberately break the rules just to get sent home!

One's answer should be: Baloney! He likes school. He wants to be in school.[5] He just has not found out yet that being in school is what he wants. Indeed, much of his problem is that he doesn't really know what he wants because his whole life has been lived negatively, in terms of what others want and don't want. What others wanted and didn't want have furnished him his only motive. With this plan, what others want is removed from his life by radical surgery. He is to do as he pleases! But first he must discover *what* pleases him since he can no longer do what *dis*pleases others. The instant he does that, he is no longer around to continue it.

Thus, one tells the parents, every minute he remains in school is one minute of practice in self-control to fulfill his wish to be in school. Where before a whole day in school gave him nothing, now five minutes in school is curative of his most basic problem. Ask the parent, Can self-control be achieved without practice? And how can he practice self-control now, having relinquished his responsibility to his teacher and his parents?

[5] The instances in elementary school (middle class) of a child who truly does not want to go to school are so rare that methodologically one must assert that no such case exists, that is, the burden of proof must rest on one who asserts the presence of such a case.

It is now possible to say to the parents that this method has been used on hundreds of children for almost two decades with a high percentage of success. A successful case is defined as one where, after from one to four weeks of being sent home every day, the child ceases to break rules and stays in school thereafter every day, all day.

The parent will object that he won't learn anything if he is not at school. One answers this by reminding them that he is not now learning anything—not doing his work—and that therefore he can scarcely lose something he does not already have. But, one can add, after from one to four weeks he *will* be in school in a position to learn if he so desires. Here one reminds them that the gaining of self-control is a necessary prerequisite to learning, as they well know, but will choose to forget.

To whatever degree the parents understand the plan, the primary reason for explaining it is to get them to accept it. It is not prudent to count on their continued understanding of the program. Nor is it prudent to assume that once the parents have agreed to it they will continue to agree after it is started. Some parents can verbalize the methodological theory with seemingly accurate understanding and three days later act as if they had never heard of these ideas. Some will also forget what they agreed to. But be not dismayed. The important thing is that they did agree and that the plan was installed. From there on, one must, as before, use one's wits to keep things going for that first crucial two weeks. After that, with the child behaving himself, parental understanding and acceptance become largely irrelevant.

The Staging Conference

The contingency that each disruptive act enjoins the teacher to send the child home is hard to establish. The teacher will find it very difficult to actually dismiss Jimmy when all he did was whisper to his neighbor or get out of his seat. She is not only going to need the sanction of the administration and parents, but this sanction must be very official and out in the open. Even better than a sanction for such rigidity, she is more comfortable in being ordered to so behave.

The teacher is not the only one who needs the reassurance of common sanction for this strange procedure. All parties concerned need it. All must see with their own eyes and hear with their own ears this agreement on what is to happen. The child must see that his parent is actually committing himself to this plan with others as witness. The only way that this can be done is by an open confrontation of all parties. This is the function of the Staging Conference. The teacher, principal, child, parent, and counselor or psychologist meet together to discuss the plan.

Twenty to forty minutes will suffice. It is best, though not necessary, to hold the conference in the morning just before school. This gives the child an immediate opportunity to test the alleged contingency between limits and consequences.

CONTRACT OR PROCLAMATION

The structure of the conference may vary with the personalities involved. The principal may take the lead or the counselor, whichever one plays the role best and depending on whether a contract or a proclamation is to be used. A *contract* is a written agreement where each party promises to do something in exchange for the acts of the other party. Thus, in the contract the child agrees to play his part, namely, to do as he pleases and take the credit or blame for what ensues. A *proclamation* does not ask the child to agree to anything. It is simply proclaimed that the persons involved will act as stipulated. What the child does is his business. Generally, the contract is used for compulsive misbehavior, while the proclamation is more appropriate for impulsive misbehavior. If one is in doubt about the basic personality structure of the child, it is safest to use the contract approach. Unfortunately, on the surface the compulsive and impulsive types look pretty much alike in the way they act as children. A contract doesn't bother an impulsive but a proclamation does bother a compulsive.[6]

BRIEFING CONFERENCES

Although many variations are possible, essentially the conference should consist in specifying the role that each person is to play. Usually one should brief each participant before the meeting. This preconference briefing of child, parent, teacher, and principal emphasizes that each is not the sole target of the conference nor a mere passive bystander.

CHILD

One can suggest to the child that as his counselor, one is acting in his behalf and will be telling each person what is expected of him. One does well also to warn the child that he will not understand everything being said, but not to worry about it (this forestalls a ploy often used by children in which they contrive not to understand). Also indicate that he will

---

[6] Many impulsives are mistaken for brain injury cases. Hopefully, the bandwagon for finding "brain-injured children" and giving them pills will some day run out of fuel or off the rails, as it deserves to.

be asked some questions about the classroom rules that are to apply solely to him.

TEACHER

In briefing the teacher, one should warn her that she will be asked to agree to exclude the child for the slightest infraction and that things are going to be said in a rather unusual way to create a dramatization of the conference on setting the specific rules and mentioning what would constitute a breach of these rules.

PARENT

Briefing the mother is the most important of all four briefings and must not, therefore, be omitted should time augur against some omissions. It is imperative, especially in such a group confrontation, that she feel the counselor is on her side, truly advocating the welfare of her child rather than the protection of the class. She will have a tendency to speak for the child, ask him if he understands, prompt him to pay attention, put words in his mouth, warn him that he must try or he'll be sorry, give him a pep talk to the effect that "I know you can do it . . . ," and so forth. That is, the symptoms of her inability to disentangle herself from her child will likely become painfully evident in the stress of the conference. One must specifically enjoin her not to do these things and warn her that if she does, the counselor will openly contradict her and ask her to discontinue speaking for or to the child. Despite this, she is likely to, at least, give him a pep talk, in which case the counselor must say he doubts precisely what mother is sure about. If she says, for example, "Oh, I'm sure Johnny will be able to stay in his seat . . . ," the counselor cuts in and says, "On the contrary, it will be very difficult for Johnny to remember to stay in his seat, even if he wants to; I predict he won't be able to for a long time, maybe even a month of being sent home every day for getting out of his seat!" Again it is prudent to warn mother that this is what she can expect and that we will be doing it so Johnny will get full credit if he stays in his seat. We do not want to taint his achievement with encouragement.

PRINCIPAL

In briefing the principal, one establishes who is to conduct the conference, the counselor (psychologist) or the principal. Either one can appropriately chair the conference while the other asks clarifying questions.

CONDUCTING THE STAGING CONFERENCE

After everyone is seated, the counselor explains why the conference is being held, namely, in order to agree on what each person is to do so that the child will know what to expect of each adult. The reason for this should be mentioned rather bluntly; namely, that the child is doing things that bother the class and that no one knows how to stop this behavior. For example, the counselor might say:

"We are meeting here because Jimmy is in a lot of trouble and there isn't one of us here who knows how to help him. We've decided that the best thing we can do for Jimmy is just let him alone. Jimmy, I want you to meet Mrs. Smith. She is your new teacher. What I want you to know about Mrs. Smith is that she is not going to try to get you to do anything at all. In fact, she promises you right now, don't you Mrs. Smith? that she will never try to get you to do or not do anything. She will never remind you, she will never coax you, she will never encourage you, she will never urge you, she just won't try to get you to do anything or not do anything. She promises this. If she breaks her promise, she will be letting you down, failing you, going back on her word, doing you harm. Mrs. Smith, do you promise never to give Jimmy a second chance? If she breaks her promise, you let me know and I'll scold her. Now, Mrs. Smith will be very friendly with you, and she'll help you if you want help. If you don't want help, don't ask for it. If you do want help, ask for it. She'll give you help, but she won't try to get you to do anything. If you don't want to do your school work, that's your business. You don't have to. In fact, if you want to, you can sleep all day as long as that doesn't bother anybody. From now on you can be your own boss. You can do anything you choose to do. It is your choice. If you don't choose to do your work, don't do it. If you don't choose to study, don't study. If you choose to hit somebody, go on and hit him. If you choose to make a noise, make the noise. If you choose to get up out of your seat, get up out of your seat. You can choose to do anything you wish.

"When what you do bothers somebody else, then you can't stay anymore. You can do *one* thing each day that bothers somebody, after that you won't be there. When you do something that bothers somebody else in any way, Mrs. Smith is supposed to send you home. She is supposed to say something to you or make some kind of signal which tells you to go home. You may not come back until the next day. That's all that will happen to you. When you do something that bothers somebody, you can't stay. So, if you ever want a vacation, here is the way to get it. Now remember, Mrs. Smith can't try to get you to do anything, so that means that when she tells you to go home and you don't want to go, she can't try to make you go. She can't even talk to you about it because that would be trying to get you to do something.

"Now, there may come a time when you have been trying hard to stay in school all day long, and one of the rules is that you can't get up out of your seat without permission, and you are working on something that you're interested in and you forget and you get up out of your seat without permission and then suddenly you remember and catch yourself, but in the meantime Mrs. Smith saw you. It's too late. Because she saw you, she has to send you home. Now you are going to feel bad about this today because maybe some of the other kids got up out of their seats without permission. Why shouldn't you be able to? Well, remember I said before, the reason you can't is because you are your own boss. They aren't. They have to be reminded. They have to be scolded. They have to be encouraged. You don't. So, when you get up out of your seat without permission, Mrs. Smith has to send you home.

"Now this is going to make you mad, and you are going to sit there and think, 'They're picking on me, none of the other kids have to leave. I won't go.' Since Mrs. Smith can't try to get you to go except to give a signal, all she can do then is to call the principal and the principal will come and carry you out, if necessary. This is a lot of bother and these people don't want this to happen every day, so whenever this happens, you can't come back for three days. So, if you ever want a three day vacation, all you have to do is break one of the rules, for example, get up out of your seat without permission, and when the teacher tells you to go, just sit there, act like you didn't hear her, and the principal will come down and you can walk out with him, go home, and stay home for three days.

"You may be thinking, 'Well, heck, I don't want to go home for three days, because my mother will get mad at me and scold me and maybe even punish me.' This isn't true. You can have fun when you get home. It'll be just like Saturday because your mother, right here, right now, is going to promise you, aren't you Mrs. Jones?, that after you have broken a rule and have been sent home, it will be just like Saturday. No punishment, no scolding, in fact, Mrs. Jones promises you right now that she won't even ask you why you are home. She won't even talk to you about it unless you want her to talk to you about it. But she promises you that she won't punish you or scold you in any way.

"The reason for this is that we don't want you to feel bad. Mrs. Smith won't be sending you home to make you feel bad, but because you broke the rule and that is the only reason. If you can have fun at home, that's fine. We don't want you to feel bad. We want you to feel good. In fact, it might be a good idea if your mother would have some games for you to play at home. When you are home, you have to stay in the yard because it is against the law for you to be off your premises during school hours. After school is over, you can go wherever you usually do go after school.

"Now, let's figure out what rules we should have in the classroom. Your last teacher told me that one thing you do that bothers the other kids is that you get up out of your seat often and wander around. So, one of the rules should be that when you get up out of your seat without asking permission of the teacher, you have to go home for the rest of the day. Your teacher also told me that one of the things you do that bothers the other kids is that you are talking out a lot and making noises, so I think another rule should be that whenever you talk out without permission or make unusual noises, the teacher will send you home for the rest of the day. Another thing that the teacher told me that you do a lot of is hit and push and pinch and that sort of thing. So, we might make the rule that anytime you hurt somebody else in any way, the teacher will send you home.

"I should say at this point that the teacher won't send you home for something she doesn't know you did, but if she is pretty sure you did something, then she *must* send you home. Whenever she is in doubt as to whether or not you did something, she is supposed to guess that you did do it and send you home. Now, lots of times this will be unfair because you may not have done it. But if she suspects that you did something, that means that you get sent home, because, remember, you're different from the other kids. You get into trouble more than they do and it's just as if there were a spotlight on you. And in order to stay in class, if you want to, you have to be better than all the other kids.

"But I imagine lots of times you won't want to stay in school, so all you have to do is break one of these rules or let the teacher suspect that you have broken one of these rules. You may think that it is going to be easy for you to keep from breaking these rules. It won't be. It's going to be rough. In fact, I think you are going to find that it is much harder than you thought, you're going to find that if you want to stay in school, you have to practice, actually practice, on how to keep from breaking the rules. Here's the reason why. All your life you've had people there to remind you. Now, no one will be reminding you. Not even once. So it's going to be hard, and I doubt if you'll be able to stay in school very much for the first couple of weeks. You'll probably be sent home every day. Every day, even after just a few minutes in the classroom, you'll probably have to go home, but that's all right. It takes a lot of practice to be able to remind yourself.

"I think it would be wise for you to try this teacher out. She may not be able to actually send you home just for breaking these little rules. So you might be able to get away with a lot of things. I think you ought to try her out and see, because you probably know by now that a lot of the times grownups don't really mean what they say. These grownups may not mean to carry out what I say. It's going to be very hard for Mrs. Smith to do what I am asking her to do because all her life she has been doing the opposite. She has been reminding, she has been encouraging, she has been coaxing, she has been scolding, she's been doing all the things that teachers usually do, and I am asking her to do the opposite. To leave you alone. To let you be your own boss. To let you remind yourself if you want to be reminded. She's going to find it almost impossible to keep from reminding you. She's going to find it almost impossible to send you home just for talking out without permission.

"But I'm asking her to do this. I'm asking everybody here to let you alone; to let you be your own boss; to let you fail if you want to; to let you succeed if you want to. And the reason I'm asking everybody to do this, is because nobody here knows how to help you. Maybe you can help yourself. If you do, you get all the credit. Every minute you stay in that classroom will be one minute that you yourself, all by yourself, decided that you would stay in that classroom. Everything that you do in that classroom will be because you decided you would do it for your own reasons and not for somebody else's reasons. Everything you do, good or bad, right or wrong, will be your own doing for your own reasons. No one else gets the credit.

"It may happen that you will be able to find something else to do besides breaking those rules that will bother somebody. When this happens, we can talk about it again and figure out a new rule and add it to the list that we have. Before we break up, I want to warn everybody here, Jimmy will probably be coming home every day for two or three or maybe four weeks, perhaps even two or three months. This is all right. It takes a long time to learn to be your own boss, with nobody to remind, nobody to encourage, nobody to scold.

"If the kids ask you what is going on, my suggestion is that you tell them, 'This is a deal between Mrs. Smith and me.' They'll respect this. Anytime you want to talk to me, let Mrs. Smith know, and she'll get in touch with me and I'll come down and we can talk."

THE CONTRACT

Another approach is simply to read a written contract, such as the one accompanying this paper, and get each person to state that he understands the rule described and will act as stipulated. With some cases it may be wise to role-play how it would happen that the child would break a rule and how the teacher would signal him to go home.

At the end of the conference, each person signs the contract or proclamation. With the proclamation, the child does not sign. If there is no printed contract, the counselor records what the rules are to be and indicates he will draft a contract for all to sign. The contract should contain a clause indicating that the parents agree that it is inadvisable for the child to attend school on such days as he breaks a stipulated rule, they request that on such a day he be dismissed from school and released to the parents, and they understand that the child is thereby declared exempt from compulsory attendance at school.

The Follow-Up

Since most children under these circumstances break a rule almost immediately—probably to test the limits—it is advisable to suggest to the mother that one hopes he'll break a rule immediately to reassure himself that the teacher will do her part. One should also explain that it is quite necessary that the child actually build up a history of instances where he breaks a rule and the teacher immediately sends him home. This, one explains, is the only way he can really believe in the actuality of the machinery.

After two or three days of the child coming home shortly after he gets to school, the mother is likely to blow her cork. One must be ready to reassure her that things are going as planned and that it is best that they go that way. Careful surveillance of the procedures must be maintained until the child has started to stay most of the time without breaking rules. It will also be wise to check on the teacher to make sure she is not overlooking rather obvious disruptive acts. Occasionally, one might confer with the child to determine whether his teacher or mother is breaking the contract. Children under such circumstances are very much aware of adult lapses and will readily disclose this to the counselor.

If one finds that the mother is threatening, bribing, or punishing the child for being sent home, it may be necessary to confront the child and mother and perhaps father all at once and get them to agree to honor the contract. This still may not get the mother to stop because the child knows how to manipulate her into such behavior. Even so, it tends to interfere with the game somewhat and minimize the power the child has in controlling his mother. Generally speaking, despite the almost inevitable lapses of mother and teacher, the child will usually get enough intrinsic payoff from being in school on his own to make him want more of it. There is no choice but to sweat it out, counting on the effects of natural consequences.

Special Problems

If after three weeks there has been no steady increase in the amount of time that the child is staying in school, it is well to assume that something is wrong. The most frequent sources are those mentioned above; the teacher is overlooking the child's first few disruptive acts or the parent is punishing the child for being sent home and/or bribing him to stay in school.

THE PSYCHOPATH

Occasionally, one finds a child for whom having an impact on others is more important than any other motive. This is the psychopath or sociopath. Ruesch (1957) calls them "the persons of action." The author has yet to find a case in which systematic exclusion works with the psychopath. Happily, such cases are fairly rare, at least in middle class schools.

THE "MARTYR"

Another type of case which now and then will defeat the method is the martyr. On the surface the martyr and the psychopath may look alike in that both tend to dramatize themselves for the benefit of onlookers. The difference, usually, must be determined by examination. The martyr will show complexity of personality structure, while the psychopath will show simplicity and lack of imagination. It is important to detect the difference because systematic exclusion will work on the martyr but will not work on the psychopath.

However, use of the method on the martyr requires a variation of the method. Thus far, two ways of installing the system have been presented: proclamation and contract. Yet a third is required for the martyr, namely, direct installation. The martyr—with his basic hysteroid character structure—plays games with words. He oversymbolizes. The staging conference plays right into his hands, making it possible for him to dramatize the situation, where he goes "on stage" as a martyred person. Confront him, however, with automatic exclusion, without explanation, without fanfare, without trying to help him understand, and he has no choice but to drop his neurotic symptoms—at school at least.

The Rules

During the first several years of the use of the method, the author believed that the rules should be made up specifically to fit the behavior pattern of the child. For example, if the child frequently knocked over his chair, then a proper rule would be that whenever he knocks over his chair, he is sent home. Lately, it has been proven that such specificity is not at all necessary. Three rules cover any possible disturbance that a child might devise. Thus, any act of *disruption, aggression,* or *destruction* results in dismissal. In explaining the rules to the child, teacher, and parent, one can give examples of, say, disruption. Since the act of getting out of the seat, talking, and motioning are the most frequent abuses, these might well be the examples that the counselor cites. But these general rules allow the system to cover any particular form of misbehavior the child might care to invent once the system has gone into effect, making it unnecessary to alter the contract or proclamation.

Rationale

The essence of the method is not the contingency of limit and consequence as some behaviorists would appear to claim. No, the reason it works is not because there is now a bond between breaking a rule and getting kicked out of school, but because the child is finally convinced that no one is going to intercede, that no one is going to try to stop him, that no one is going to give him a "commercial." There's the essence, his growing conviction that he's on his own to face the logical consequence of his deeds.[7] Automatic consequences are not enough, by themselves, to do the job. Put a commercial in between his deeds and their so-called consequences and just see how much effect they have.[8] He will make a shambles of the classroom! Why? Because the commercial and not "the consequence" is what he sees as the consequence of his deeds. And that's what he wants, involvement of the adult, control over her feelings and behavior—power, service, revenge (Dreikurs, 1964)! Therefore, the solution is to remove that which he seeks, the commercial, the "sell job" which signifies to him that the adult is occupied with him.

In milder cases it is enough just to discontinue the commercials. The misbehavior stops because it is not getting what it was designed to get. In these tougher cases of truly chronic disruption, however, an immediate natural, logical consequence has to be tacked on. But failure to recognize the central place occupied by the radical surgery on commercials almost guarantees failure of the method.

It is because the child faces a logical consequence that teacher and parent are able to forego their commercials. If one uses an arbitrary con-

---

[7] Editors' Note: Whether the reason for success is in the new consequences or is due to the child's new convictions cannot be tested. The action taken by the counselor was in establishing the new contingencies for remaining in school, an action necessary to change the child's convictions. The effects of alternative actions can be compared. But an action cannot be compared with the subject's internal convictions especially when the only method of producing the required convictions is the one specified action. Keirsey's fine detailed description of the technique may suggest alternative procedures that may produce the same or even improved results.

[8] Editors' Note: An interesting alternative!

sequence, say spanking, the adult cannot quite bring himself to forego the attempt to get the child's sanction. Thus, in offering the adult consequences in lieu of commercials, consequences which are self-evident and require no explanation to the child, one relieves the adult's doubts. It is this feature that enables the adult to forego his verbal ministrations and it is this feature that is the methodological essence of systematic exclusion.

Results of Systematic Exclusion

Depending on the degree of one's skill and conviction, which may increase skill, the method should work in from 75 percent to 90 percent of the cases, judging from the author's own experience and from reports of others who have used the method. But what is meant by "it works"? Although, of necessity all disruptive behavior disappears, does this mean that the child is cured? Certainly not. Removal of the system of consequences brings back the disruptive behavior immediately. No, the cure, if any, is long in coming. Doubtless there are curative effects in the constant practice in self-control and in the enforced detachment from adult reactions. If there are such effects, they can only be regarded as a bonus and byproduct. The real cure, if any, comes from having a normal school experience, however enforced such experience may be. Doing ordinary things—sitting at a desk, doing school work, making friends, playing at recess, and so forth—has enormous intrinsic and corrective worth. After months, and sometimes years of such enforced experience, it is difficult for the child to maintain his neurotic system.[9]

[9] One case required the method from first grade through half of the eighth grade, that is, for eight years, after which he fared well, despite his psychotic mother.

EDUCATIONAL CONTRACT

PARTICIPANTS _____Pupil

_____Teacher

_____Principal

_____Guardian

_____Guardian

_____Attendance
Officer
_____Witness

LIMITS   On violation of any stated limit, the pupil is under suspension from School for _____ day(s).

Aggression: _____

_____

Destruction: _____

_____

Disruption: _____

_____

ROLES   Each signatory agrees to play the role specified, as follows:

TEACHER   On detection of limit violation the teacher will signal the pupil to leave the class. He will on no occasion try to influence the pupil to do or not to do anything (no urging, reminding, coaxing, encouraging, or scolding). He agrees to respect the pupil's *right to fail* or succeed on his own and to acknowledge that he is not responsible for the success or failure of this pupil.

PRINCIPAL   On notification or detection of a limit violation the principal will see to it that the pupil leaves the school. He agrees to see to it that the pupil leaves the class when the signal given by the teacher is not acted on by the pupil. When this happens the pupil will be suspended for 3 days including the day of suspension. He agrees to see to it that the parent is notified of the suspension at the earliest possible moment. He agrees that he will not discuss with the pupil in any way the pupil's behavior. (There is to be no persuasion, encouragement, "pep talks," reminders, or scoldings.) He agrees that he is not responsible for the success or failure of this pupil. He agrees to see to it that the attendance officer is notified of all suspensions, absences, and tardinesses, and of the reasons therefore.

PARENT   The parents agree that they are not responsible for the success or failure of the pupil at school. They agree that they are fully responsible for the pupil when he is not on school grounds. They absolve the school district of any responsibility whatsoever for this pupil when he is not on school grounds. They agree not to scold or punish the pupil for school behavior or to discuss school behavior with the pupil unless the pupil so desires. They agree that they will not seek explanations for suspensions from any person other than the attendance officer.

ATTENDANCE OFFICER   The attendance officer agrees that he is responsible for supervising breaches of contract and for revising the contract as needed. He agrees to be responsible for processing all absences, suspensions, and tardinesses. He agrees that he is fully responsible for the success or failure of the pupil in school and that he hereby delegates this responsibility to the pupil.

PUPIL   The pupil agrees that he is fully responsible for himself and that everything he does and does not do is done or not done *by his own choice.* He agrees to take credit for his failure as well as his success *regardless of how people treat him.*

Dated _____

Pupil	
Parent	
Parent	
Principal	
Teacher	
Attendance Officer	
Witness	

16
APPLYING SYSTEMATIC EXCLUSION TO A CASE OF BIZARRE BEHAVIOR

David A. Shier

PALO ALTO UNIFIED SCHOOL DISTRICT (CALIFORNIA)

J.F. was a new student. He was registered in the neighborhood elementary school third grade shortly before school opened in the fall. His father, who came to school to register him, commented in passing that the school would "probably see me quite a bit in the very near future." Apparently he expected J.F. to have some difficulty adjusting to the new school situation.

PROBLEM BEHAVIOR

At the end of the first day of school J.F.'s teacher conferred with the school psychologist about a "very strange child" in her class. She described him as a source of constant disruption. His behavior consisted of inappropriate and strange laughter, talking out, and persistent moving around the room. Arrangements were made for an observation in two days.

A series of observations were made beginning on the third day of school. J.F. was a thin, hyperactive and generally disorganized child. He seemed to be constantly talking, out of his seat, flitting around the room touching people and things, and laughing in a high pitch at times that were unrelated to any class activity. He was highly distractible with an apparent inability to concentrate on a task for more than a few minutes. He gave the appearance of living in a world of his own. When at his seat and not actively disrupting the class, he frequently rocked, chewed on any available object, and made grimaces.

Upon arrival at school in the morning, J.F.'s high pitched laughter would begin, frequently interspersed with the words "wiener," "penis," and "gaucho." He appeared to be unable to stand still in line outside the classroom. He frequently derided other class members, calling names and punching, frequently in the genital area.

Upon entering the classroom, he usually would run around, touch things and ask in a loud voice, "What am I supposed to do now?" He often stood at his desk, rather than sitting, for as long as the first ten or fifteen minutes.

J.F. had difficulty with all academic subjects. Although the *Gilmore Oral Reading Test* placed him at fourth grade level, functionally in the classroom he read close to the second grade level. Even at this level, he was unable to sustain attention to a reading task for more than a few minutes. Any assignment that required reading was done in a hurried superficial way. His greatest academic difficulty was in arithmetic. He could not equate 10 ones and 1 ten.

J.F. had great difficulty following the simplest directions. He often asked many questions but seldom waited for an answer or seemed aware of the answer.

J.F. did appear to enjoy art work and drawing. He repetitiously drew pictures of monsters and deformed people and was an excellent draftsman for his age. His handwriting was described as "beautiful." His letters were almost perfectly formed.

A more objective representative behavior sample for a 40-minute time period is as follows:

Out of seat and wandering around room, 5 times.
General disruptive noise, 4 times.
Talked out, 15 times.
Laughed, 5 times.
Interacted with observer, 2 times.

Outdoor behavior was as deviant as that in the classroom. It consisted of frequent fighting with other students, complaints to the teacher about other students, apparent confusion, inability to follow game rules, and occasional refusal to come back into the classroom without coaxing.

BACKGROUND AND FAMILY DATA

J.F. was adopted by his present parents at six months of age. Data on his natural parents are unknown. He was born approximately one month prematurely. He lived in foster homes until adopted.[1] His mother reports that he was a very "anxious" infant when he entered the present household. He did not want Mrs. F. ever to be out of sight during waking hours. The grandfather is quoted as having thought there was something "different" about J.F.

Early in life J.F. developed "many allergic reactions" and had received medical treatment. The parents reported no difficulty in this area at the present time. Also, early in life he became very prone to motion sickness, a problem that continues to persist. Some of his own most vivid memories relate to his difficulty in traveling.

When J.F. was three years old, his parents adopted another boy under one year of age. The younger brother has been the antithesis of every aspect of J.F. He is described as a model child, both at school and at home. He qualified as mentally gifted in the California program. The younger brother has been and continues to be the object of both envy and hostility on the part of J.F. The mother quoted J.F. as asking one time, "Why does K. always do things right and I wrong?"

J.F. began school in Michigan. From the beginning he had difficulty adjusting to the school environment. By mutual school and parental agreement, J.F. spent a second year in kindergarten to "give him more time to grow up." The parents evaluated the second year as "much more successful."

The first grade year was a poor one. J.F. was referred for school psychological services. He had difficulty with all academic endeavors and was unable to do seat work "without individual help." His classroom behavior was described as follows: "For no apparent reason he will hit, punch and scratch his classmates. At one point during reading he will laugh and after every word he reads he looks to see if all are watching him."

The psychological report contained group mental maturity test scores (low nineties), and numerous phrases, such as, "poor reality testing," and "emotional difficulties." The final recommendation was a strong plea for

---

[1] Editors' Note: We do not know what kind of an environment J.F. had during the first six months of his life, but it is quite likely that emotional and physical deprivation occurring then could contribute to a pattern of persistent maladaptive behavior which might be very difficult to overcome fully by later treatment. Would J.F.'s problem have been prevented if he had been adopted six months earlier?

The school's task now is to help J.F. with his present behavior problems. Whose problem is it to prevent future children from developing behavior problems like this?

J.F. to "be seen by a psychiatrist or someone competent to work with youngsters who have emotional difficulties." The father later reported his conference with the psychologist as "the most unpleasant fifteen minutes I have ever spent in my life." The father said J.F. was described as "severely emotionally disturbed."[2] The psychologist strongly recommended psychiatric help.

J.F.'s year in the second grade appears to have been relatively uneventful. At the end of the year he transferred to his present school.

J.F.'s father and mother are upper middle class in terms of socioeconomic status. The father has had four years of college and is a self-employed businessman. He is able to come to school when asked. The mother has had two years of college and is a full-time housewife. Shortly after J.F. entered third grade, she was briefly hospitalized but appears to have been in good health during the past year.

At the first parent conference, only the father was able to attend. He was initially tense and somewhat defensive. However, as the conference progressed, he became much more relaxed and volunteered considerable background information. His description of home behavior was consistent with that seen at school. He said J.F. was hyperactive and highly distractible: "He can't even sit through *Batman.*" J.F. was described as expressing constant concern about monsters and about his younger brother's ability. He looked upon himself as being "the bad one." From a very early age he had had a fear of the dark. J.F. seemed to be a real concern to his father. Mr. F. appeared interested and anxious to cooperate in any way he could.

Three proposals were made: (1) the psychologist would do further testing to gather more information, (2) a program of systematic exclusion was outlined for the father's consideration, and (3) the father was asked to seriously consider getting some medical opinions, particularly the possibility of a neurological evaluation.

The systematic exclusion was intended to help J.F. make an immediately more satisfactory adjustment to the school environment and to help him enter into the activities of the classroom in a more acceptable manner. The father agreed to these three points. A second conference was scheduled when both parents could meet with the school to begin the program.

PSYCHOLOGICAL TESTING

Wechsler scores were as follows: Verbal IQ, 79; Performance IQ, 71; Full Scale IQ, 72. The Verbal Scaled Scores ranged from 4 (Comprehen-

---

[2] Editors' Note: Merely labeling behavior does not seem to help much.

sive) to 9 (Vocabulary). The Performance Scaled Scores ranged from 3 (Block Design) to 8 (Object Assembly).

Wide Range Reading Vocabulary was 3.8. J.F. read words rapidly and in song. Binet, Form L-M, IQ was 76. Wepman Auditory Discrimination, 2 X errors. For his age level, this was very strong. Peabody Picture Vocabulary, IQ, 96. On the Bender-Gestalt, his Koppitz Score was 8. "Normal" range for his age group is 0–3.3 with higher scores indicating greater distortion. There was considerable amount of rotation during Bender design reproduction. Drawings were done quickly and carelessly.

The general behavior pattern during testing was characterized by constant physical activity, restlessness, inattentiveness, and explosive guessing. Constant urging was necessary. Test patterns suggest that J.F. has little concept of cause and effect or logical sequencing of events. They also suggest the possibility of some perceptual difficulty, particularly evident in the reproduction of block designs, but such problems are not particularly reflected in classroom performance. J.F.'s observed problems may be caused by his inability to attend and organize, rather than by any perceptual disability. Test results also indicate that J.F. can understand spoken language. The total scores probably do not reflect intellectual potential but rather present attitudes, difficulties, and level of functioning.[3]

THE TREATMENT

A second parent conference was held with the school principal, teacher, and psychologist. Both mother and father were present. Both were extremely co-operative. Both agreed to follow any recommendations the school made. Test results were discussed; however, the psychologist stressed that it was difficult to draw any definite conclusions from them because of inconsistent patterns and performances. The father stated that he greatly appreciated this attitude of not being given pat answers.

Detailed mechanics of the program of systematic exclusion were discussed. The role of the parents, that is, of not reacting to J.F.'s being sent home, was emphasized. The role of the teacher, that is, of being as consistent as possible, was stressed. Although such a program would be very restrictive to the mother (she would have to stay home every day), the

---

[3] Editors' Note: Though testing has traditionally been the stock-in-trade of the school psychologist, its actual benefit to the child must be assessed frankly and critically. Does the information gained by testing add to our knowledge of what we might do to help J.F.? Would the teacher or psychologist do anything differently if the test scores had been markedly different? If the test scores make no difference in what is done, then the time required to administer tests might be better spent. Designing optimum learning environments for individual children is an alternative activity which began in this case by helping J.F. gain control over his own hyperactive behavior.

parents expressed their appreciation and desire to co-operate and agreed to do what was necessary. If the mother did have to be away from home during the day, she would notify the school in the morning. This occurred twice during the school year. Arrangements were made to inaugurate the program the following late afternoon with J.F. present.

Medical evaluation was again recommended. The parents had already made an appointment with their pediatrician.

Structuring Systematic Exclusion

The following day the initiating conference was held. An effort was made to make it as impressive, serious, and dramatic as possible. All persons involved sat at a round table. J.F. sat between his parents. His teacher, the psychologist, and the principal were present. The psychologist did most of the talking, which was primarily directed to J.F., in a "firm and friendly" manner.

The conference began with a few remarks about the interest everyone present had in J.F., as illustrated by the fact that we were all there "for him." We all were interested in him and wanted to help him. The conference then proceeded along the following lines:

"In order to help you, J.F., we have made three rules for you. You are to follow these rules whenever you are in class. The rules are: One, no talking. This means talking out in class, with neighbors, laughing, or making any noise with your voice or mouth. How do you get permission to say something?"

"Raising my hand."

"Absolutely right! What will you do if you wish to say something to anyone?"

"Raise my hand."

"Good. Do you understand this rule?"

"Yes."

"Very good. Do you have any questions about this rule?"

"No."

"Two, you are not to move out of your seat without permission. This means standing up or moving your desk or chair outside a line around them. Tomorrow morning you will find a line on the floor around your desk. No part of your desk or chair is to be outside this line. If any part of your desk or chair is outside the line, it will be the same as if you got out of your seat. (His seat had already been semi-isolated in the back of the room. Masking tape was placed on the floor around his chair and table delimiting his area.) You may move the direction of your desk, but no part is to be outside the line. How do you get permission to get out of your seat?"

"Raise my hand."

"Right! Do you understand this rule?"

"Yes."

"Do you have any questions?"

"No."

"What do you do if you want permission to talk or move, and Mrs. A. does not immediately answer your raised hand?"

"Wait."

"Very good." [To the whole group] "I think J.F. understands these two rules very well."

"The third rule is no throwing of anything. By this I mean no propelling. You know what I mean by this?

[nod, yes]

"No propelling through space of any object by any means—no throwing, no snapping of rubber bands, no blowing through straws, nothing. Do you understand this rule?"

"Yes."

"Is this rule completely clear to you?"

"Yes."

"Do you have any questions about this rule?"

"No."

"Now, J.F., will you tell us these three rules?" He named them, without hesitation, in reverse order given. "Excellent work. Now, we all know that boys your age forget rules. To help you remember, each time you forget your teacher will give you one of these." J.F. was shown a half sheet of paper that had blanks for date and time and the statement "To the office: Please call Mrs. F. [phone number] and tell her that J.F. is on his way home." There was space for numerical indication of Rule 1, 2, or 3 and the teacher's initials. "This means that, when you forget, to help you remember, you will go home for the rest of the day. You will come back the next morning and try again. When you go home, you are to stay at home until the usual time you get home from school. When you come back to school the next morning, we start fresh. We don't worry or talk about what happened yesterday. This is being done to help you remember the rules. Do you understand what I've been saying?"

"Yes."

"Why might you be sent home?"

"When I forget a rule."

"To help you remember the rules. What are the three rules again?"

He named them with hesitation on number two.

"We want you here in school with us. It is up to you whether you are here or not. This is your responsibility. Do you understand what I mean by this?"

"Yes."

"We all hope you remember the rules. This is up to you. We can't remember them for you. We can only help *you* remember them. It is up to you, J.F. Do you understand?"

"Yes."

The psychologist then went around the table asking each person by name, including J.F., if there were any questions or comments. There were none.

It was after dark when the conference adjourned. The school personnel felt that they had successfully communicated with—had "gotten through" to—J.F. During the entire conference there was not a single instance of unusual behavior by J.F. He sat poised and attentive during the entire time.

Necessary Conditions

All of the necessary ingredients for a program of systematic exclusion were present:

1. Cooperative parents. They understood the program and agreed to do their part. They would receive J.F. when he was sent home but would avoid any further recognition for his having to come home. There would be no punishment—he was "just there" (at home) until the usual school dismissal time. His coming home was not to be discussed, and minimal response would be made to his discussion of his homecoming. On the other hand, when J.F. stayed at school all day, the parents would express their pleasure at his being able to do this.[4]

2. Unambiguous rules. It was necessary to have rules, a maximum of three, which he either did or did not break. There could be no question. Rules that involve value judgment, such as, "too much" noise, must be avoided.

3. A competent teacher. The teacher's role involved the ability to be consistent. She must be able to overcome the temptation to "not notice." She must also be able to give positive support and recognition to expected behavior, in this case, raising his hand. She also would give recognition to "full days."

4. The initial impact. It was important to make the impression that everyone understood and was in complete agreement and that the program was a consistent and serious matter.

Effect

It was anticipated that J.F. would "test the program" first thing the following morning. It would be surprising if he lasted ten minutes. This is a typical pattern for children beginning a program of systematic exclusion—the time in school becoming longer and longer each day. However,

[4] Editors' Note: The parents are encouraged to reinforce positive behavior but refrain from making negative remarks about lapses.

as usual, J.F. did not do the expected. Instead, he got within six minutes of staying all day.

An analysis of his dismissal pattern for the next five months showed the following characteristics:

1) Between November 16, 1966 and April 7, 1967—83 days of school—sent home 26 times.
2) Longest period he was in school the total day—11 days. This period included both Lincoln's and Washington's birthday holidays.
3) No favored days of the week—was sent home 4 Mondays, 7 Tuesdays, 6 Wednesdays, 5 Thursdays, and 4 Fridays.
4) He was sent home 15 times for breaking the talking rule, 8 times for breaking the out of seat rule, and 3 times for breaking the throwing rule.
5) Of the 26 days he was sent home, only 5 were single days (3 times on Friday). There was only one incidence of 3 days in a row. All other times were 2 consecutive days. In other words, if he were sent home on one day the probability of his being sent home the following day was quite high.
6) He was sent home 17 mornings and 9 afternoons.
7) Thirteen out of the 26 times he was sent home were either within 10 minutes of a break bell or within 10 minutes after a recess or lunch break.

By analyzing this pattern, care could be taken to give him extra support just before or after a class break, although this was not always possible.

Observations showed that the program of systematic exclusion did result in behavior modification. J.F. talked or was out of his seat only with permission, or he wasn't in class. While in his seat, he frequently did not attend to the task at hand, but he was not being disruptive. The probability of his doing the learning task assigned was greatly increased; however, he frequently needed individual attention from the teacher to "get him started." He frequently sat at his desk and played with various "toys," but this was "acceptable" behavior.

On the playground he continued his same behavior pattern—noisy, uncooperative, wild, and disorganized—but, here again, this was not a part of the program. Playground misbehavior was controlled primarily by temporary isolation.

A follow-up conference was held four months later. It included both parents, the principal, the teacher, and the school psychologist. The school personnel summarized J.F.'s progress and dismissal pattern. They expressed appreciation to the parents for cooperation in the project.

The parents reported that at first J.F. seemed dejected when he had to come home and expressed an eagerness to stay in school. However, during the last month, "he did not seem to care." A suggestion was made to reward full days at school with some little token or treat; however, a reward should not be given for every full day, nor should it be given if J.F. asked for a treat. The parents agreed to try this.

The parents reported that J.F. had had a neurological evaluation and that they had requested a copy of the neurologist's report be sent to the school. The neurologist had prescribed a program of Dexedrine medication which would be started in three days. The parents indicated that they wanted to start treatment on a Saturday so they would have an opportunity to observe, first hand, any reactive behavior.

The neurologist's report included a brief medical and educational history and an essentially negative report concerning any demonstrable physiological or structural abnormality. However, the report did note: "I certainly feel that he has an organic problem with attention span." The summary impression was, "minimal cerebral dysfunction syndrome without dyslexic components . . ."

Following the initiation of the Dexedrine therapy program, it was necessary to send J.F. home three times in the third week, then once more the following week. From that time on, J.F. remained in school for the full day for the rest of the year, 47 days.

ONE YEAR LATER

The following year (1967–1968), J.F. was in a new room with a new teacher. About half the students were new classmates.

J.F. began school without any special program or consideration. He has been taken off the Dexedrine therapy program during the summer.

The first day of school his behavior pattern did not differentiate him from any other student. Gradually, during the second day, he began sliding into the old behavior pattern of one year ago. By the end of the fourth day, it was a repetition of the previous year.

In order to assess any residual effect of the previous drug therapy, the neurologist delayed resumption of Dexedrine treatment until the seventh day of school. The fifth, sixth, and seventh days, J.F. was routinely sent home at noon on a shortened day basis. During the morning attendance period constant teacher interaction with him was necessary.

In summary, the program of systematic exclusion was effective in modifying classroom behavior for a period of five months. However, behavior outside the classroom was unchanged. Drug therapy in addition to systematic exclusion resulted in total behavior modification in the classroom during the last three months of the school year. Apparently, neither the medication nor the systematic exclusion program had any residual effect. The question remains: Will the resumption of drug therapy alone result in a satisfactory behavior change, or will a combination of the two programs be needed?

17

LEARNING THAT PRIVILEGES ENTAIL RESPONSIBILITIES

Michael Dinoff and Henry C. Rickard
UNIVERSITY OF ALABAMA

In 1958 Karl Menninger described psychotherapy as a transaction or "contract" between two people. He argued that as in all contracts, the activities of both parties are defined relative to the end goals of the contract. A contract implies that each party desires something from the other, and, that there is agreement upon an equitable exchange. Each individual gives, or loses something and gains or obtains something of perceived equivalence. In business the exchange is of goods or skills for money, and the process is called *bartering*. In politics, the exchange is of services or action for influence and the process is called *negotiation*. In friendship the exchange is of time, interest, and affection, and the process is called *caring*. In still another relationship, one person exchanges his own time and money for the time, kindness, and skill of another in the hope of changing his own life style. This latter process, for want of a better word, is called *psychotherapy* or *counseling*.

More recently Sulzer (1962) discussed the concept of the therapeutic contract as it related to measuring psychotherapy success. He said that "the assessment of 'successful' psychotherapy must be looked at in a different way than has been typical in the past. *Fulfillment of the psychotherapeutic contract is the sole criterion of success, and since each contract is unique, success may be determined only by study of the individual case.*"

CHARACTERISTICS OF A SUCCESSFUL CONTRACT

Behavior can be changed in a two-person interaction if both parties are agreed as to what is expected of each. Menninger felt that the details of the contract must be specified. In the authors' own work with emotionally disturbed children at Camp Ponderosa, a therapeutic summer camp, it seems clear that the neurotic child cannot specify what is expected of him (Rickard & Dinoff, 1965). He can often state the end goal correctly and clearly but he cannot label the means. He can clearly tell you what is *not* expected of him. The first requirement is that all expectations be described explicitly.

Secondly, the contract must be fair in that either member in the therapeutic interaction does not feel abused. An initially fair contract may not be fair at a later date. As a result a therapeutic contract needs to be periodically assessed or renegotiated or both.

Thirdly, the contract must have a goal which is mutually agreed upon. There are occasions when a contract may be met although the end goals of each party are different. Both may be satisfied if their individual goals are met simultaneously.

Fourth, the contract must be reasonable and feasible. Many behavior contracts fail, or, more correctly can never succeed, because the "terms of the contract" are impossible. We all know how many times a parent or a teacher makes an unreasonable one-sided contract with a youngster which cannot be met. For example, the statement "If you ever do that again, you can never watch television again" is totally unreasonable because it is impossible to enforce.

Lastly, a therapeutic contract must be concluded with mutual satisfaction and an assessment of the total contractual agreement. It then becomes the paradigm for future and hopefully successful contracts in other settings.

There is a decided difference between contracts and rules. Rules define what is expected of an individual and what punishments are associated with rule violation. Rules are made by one individual or group to be applied to persons who did not have any direct part in structuring the rules. Contracts must involve at least two persons and define for each what reinforcements and what penalties are contingent upon the behavior of each. In a contract each party must agree to each provision in advance.

CONTRACTS AT CAMP PONDEROSA

Within the Ponderosa camping program, the staff had from time to time experimented with contractual agreements with individual youngsters on a limited basis. No real effort was made to tie the concept into the total treatment program either for the child or the camp. In 1965, however, because of a focus upon problem-solving groups, a technique adopted from Loughmiller's (1965) program, increasing use of specified contractual agreements was made. In the use of the techniques of group problem-solving, each participating member is obliged to stop whatever action is going on and deal with problems as they arise (Rickard, 1966). The obligation to participate in problem-solving was in and of itself a contractual arrangement. Since the new treatment orientation of the camp was to use problem-solving as a device and give it a fair and complete test, one might view this as a "demand" contract in that the campers had little choice but to participate if they attended the treatment camp. If they did not participate, action was prohibited until the problem was resolved at some level satisfactory to the total group. While this is a dictatorial contract, it is often the only choice an adult has for the moment in the management of a disturbed youngster's behavior.[1]

The therapeutic contracts discussed in this paper are the logical end result of problem-solving sessions. When a problem is worked through, a new arrangement has to be formed. The old contract is no longer usable. In each case after a problem was "solved," some sort of new agreement was necessary or it was likely that the problem would be repeated.

Achievable Written Contracts

Written agreements seemed far more successful than verbal agreements, particularly at first. Experimentation with the contract approach included even the youngest children in camp (seven to nine years). At first all groups arranged only small, easily and rapidly met written contracts. It was important for the youngsters to control the "terms of the contract" to a large degree although there had to be agreement as to the end goal.

The campers' contracts were always more demanding than the staff's agreements would have been. The counselors and directors tried to make them "softer" whenever possible, but if the youngsters would not agree, an attempt was made to assist them in keeping their "tough" contract. Impossible contracts were not approved. For example, one group trying to reduce its extensive cursing behavior offered to make a contract that they would never again curse. At that moment there was good group feeling and it seemed reasonable to them. However, the staff only asked them for a slight improvement in their present behavior and for the contract to be re-evaluated and restated from time to time. A series of contracts was proposed instead of an all-or-none contract that probably would fail.

Implied Contracts

As the summer progressed it was pointed out to all the groups that written contracts were not always possible and that all people live in a

---

[1] Editors' Note: In negotiating a contract the adult usually has more "bargaining power" than the child. When the adult has control of the food, housing, money, daily activities, and transportation, the child has little room to maneuver. The adult has a tremendous opportunity and responsibility to exercise this power for the educational welfare of each child.

world of implied contracts. They were asked to move toward implied as opposed to written contracts. Without this next step there could be little generalization to the real world which operated on a handshake or friendship basis. Toward the latter part of the summer the techniques of understanding implied contracts were discussed as were methods of recognizing what was expected of an individual in an interpersonal relationship. The youngsters' ability to accept, understand and use implied contracts when their roles and responsibilities were clearly labeled for them was most gratifying.

Sample Contract

Written contracts have become a permanent part of the Ponderosa program. Specifically, the camp requires written contracts whenever a group of campers leave the site. For example, once each week every cabin group "owns" the camp bus and can plan a trip. They are allowed to requisition money from their cabin bank account. They can travel anywhere the group plans, as long as they have enough money, can return in one day, and deliver a reasonable contract. The following is a specimen contract for a trip during the summer of 1967 between the Cherokees (the oldest group of boys) and the camp. This contract was read aloud by one of the boys in the presence of one of the co-directors who then shook hands with each Cherokee and their counselors after the written formalities of the contract had been concluded.

TRIP TO DESOTO FALLS

We the Cherokees will not buy any cigarettes, fireworks, and so forth. We will need 30¢ for drinks. There will be no cussing (cursing) or shouting out of the bus. If something should come up, we will then call a problem (actually a problem-solving) session. We will wash and clean the bus when we get back. The lunch will (be) furnished by the lunch hall. We can participate in fishing and swimming if (it is) desired while (we are) at the falls. After we get back and wash the bus, we will talk over the contract.

> (Signed by all of the Cherokees, their counselors, and one camp co-director.)

The above contract, written by one of the campers, is a good one in that it clearly states what is expected by all parties and underscores that a contract implies a contribution by each party. These youngsters wanted to go on a trip. They needed consent to leave, money, transportation, and food. The money for the trip would be taken from the group's bank account (implied). They would adhere to the camp policies of calling a problem-solving session if difficulties arose, evaluate the contract when they returned, and wash the bus so that the next group could have its use.

Upon returning, the Cherokees immediately washed the bus and then met with one of the co-directors to assess the contract. This particular contract was kept well as this group had had considerable practice in keeping written agreements. At the end of the evaluation, the co-director again shook hands with each Cherokee and their counselors in an effort to associate handshaking and similar behavior with keeping one's word. The intention, of course, is to promote generalization to the real world.

GENERALIZATION TO HOME SITUATION

The rationale of contracts was discussed with several of the camper's parents who were having difficulty in managing their children. During counseling sessions they were helped to establish a small but hopefully functional contract with their youngster in the staff's presence. It helped, apparently, to label their part of the contract and to realize that they could not attribute all the responsibility to their child for his behavior, but that he needed their participation as much as their concern.

Just recently, a youngster who completed the summer at Ponderosa developed a contract at home with his parents. The youngster, an exceptionally bright twelve-year-old boy, had motivational difficulties. His parents were concerned about his ability to accept responsibilities as well at home as he had demonstrated he could at camp. The boy and his father decided that both should contribute and determine the contract terms. At the follow-up meeting both were enthusiastic about their effort. With their consent, a copy of their contract follows.

CONTRACT

Between (Son's Name), and (Father's Name).

Son agrees to:
1. Carry out garbage pail each day.
2. Work six hours on Saturday every week. Work will consist of anything that he is capable of doing, such as hoeing, weeding, washing the car, or helping father and so forth.

Father agrees to:
1. Pay four dollars ($4.00) per week for above work each week (Saturday).

Both parties agree to the following conditions:
1. Penalty for failing to carry out garbage after being reminded will be reduction of 25¢ for each failure.

2. Penalty for not working on Saturday when work is available will be 40¢ per hour unless condition is covered by another condition.
3. When no work is available due to bad weather or father unable to supervise, $1.00 per Saturday will be paid.
4. Re-evaluation after a trial period of three weeks.
5. If son is sick there will be no penalty reduction on garbage detail, and $1.00 will be paid for Saturday. A total of $2.00 will be paid under this condition.

Signed:_____

Father

Signed:_____

Son

The techniques of therapeutic contracts seem quite compatible with the techniques of behavior modification appearing in the clinical literature. The contract enables responses to occur that are incompatible with the expression of maladaptive behavior. Not only does it specify the responses which are desired, but it presents an opportunity to label how and when reinforcement is dispensed. The youngster can come to recognize that his own responses determine what and how much reinforcement he shall receive. The preparation and assessing of the contract clearly helps the child to develop mediating processes and to learn the occasional benefits of delayed gratification.

Teaching Others To Use Reinforcement

IN SOME RESPECTS the counselor or school psychologist is the one person least favorably situated to make effective use of reinforcement himself. Parents and teachers are in a much better position to use reinforcement because they are with the child for longer periods of time and therefore have many more opportunities to reinforce the child as he improves his behavior.

For the counselor to be optimally effective for the benefit of the client, it is frequently necessary that the counselor spend more time with the client's parents and teachers than with the client himself. The counselor can use this time to help teachers and parents learn how to apply reinforcement contingent upon the improving behavior of the child. When parents and teachers begin to see how reinforcement can be effectively employed, they will generalize the process to other problem cases, and so the counselor's effectiveness will be multiplied many times over.

A counselor needs the co-operative efforts of parents, teachers, administrators, and other school personnel if he is to do this job right. But how exactly does a counselor teach others to employ reinforcement in educating children? The three articles in this section give some specific guidelines as to how it can be done.

Article 18 by Sanborn and Schuster describes the evolution of a reinforcement program from the time the counselors first heard about it until they developed and assessed a rather elaborate program in several classrooms. Several case studies are presented and the authors close with a list of guidelines that the counselors found effective in that particular school.

Hosford, in Article 19, provides a case study illustrating how he worked with a teacher to provide reinforcement contingencies in the classroom while he, serving as counselor, provided additional role-playing training.

Patterson describes in Article 20 how parents can be taught reinforcement techniques and can even co-operate with the teacher in reinforcing work habits in the classroom. Patterson describes the steps used in teaching parents, tells what happened to two boys who were trained to concentrate with the help of their mothers, and closes with some suggestions for those who want to investigate other problems of parent training.

The experiences represented in these three articles are only a beginning point. More experimentation will be required to develop effective ways of helping parents and teachers learn how to educate children. The rather dramatic successes presented here provide some promise that the search may be a useful one.

18

ESTABLISHING REINFORCEMENT TECHNIQUES IN THE CLASSROOM

Barbara Sanborn and William Schuster
SANTA CLARA UNIFIED SCHOOL DISTRICT (CALIFORNIA)

The "problem child" in the classroom is a constant concern of the classroom teacher. These students often have social difficulties, emotional problems, and physical problems. They lack academic motivation. Having extensive information on why the student is a problem doesn't help. The teacher needs information on *what to do.*

The concept of changing behavior by use of candy M & M's as a positive reinforcer was introduced to us by Dr. Stewart Nixon. He showed a film portraying the success that had been achieved by using an electronic device with a first grade, hyperactive child in the classroom. Hyperactive behavior was reduced by positively reinforcing attentive behavior with M & M candy.[1]

[1] Editors' Note: See Article 25 for a detailed description of the procedure.

USING REINFORCERS IN A REMEDIAL READING CLASS

The project was begun in a remedial reading class. This class was made up of six boys, four eighth graders and two seventh graders, who came from their regular reading class one period per day. Before initiating the program the teacher and counselor discussed each individual student's behavior in order to determine what behavior could be rewarded. In some cases it was a struggle to find any good behavior to reward.

The teacher was concerned about the class because two or three of the six boys were creating such problems that it was almost impossible for her to teach. If one or two became disruptive, the others also misbehaved. She had the option of sending them back to their regular class, but because they needed the reading she was willing to try anything before resorting to sending them out of the class. We decided to try M & M's as positive reinforcers for desirable behaviors.

Students

Andy, a seventh grader, was already identified through psychological referral as "educationally handicapped" (E.H.) and would have been in a special class if there had been room. Ricky G., an eighth grader, was almost a nonreader and had been identified in his previous school as E.H. because of a neurological handicap. David, an eighth grader, was living in a foster home because neither his parents nor his relatives wanted him. He could be described as defiant and suspicious. He had already been suspended for fighting and had served other school detentions. Gary, an eighth grader, had been a severe discipline problem the previous year, but was much better this year although he still had a discipline record in the office and was on probation from juvenile hall. He frequently talked back, wasted time and spoke out, disturbing the class. Ramon, a seventh grader, was extremely quiet. He worked well and had no difficulty in the class since he stayed to himself. He rarely spoke, even to the teacher, and never smiled. Henry, an eighth grader, had a discipline record and was capable of being very outspoken and hostile. He said he had one brother in prison for murder and that he lived with another brother. Just before we started with the program in this class, Henry had told his English teacher to "shut up" and had stormed out of the room.

Specifying Desired Behavior

Discussing each student with the teacher served two purposes: first, the behavior to be rewarded was identified and, secondly, the teacher had an opportunity to think in terms of how she would deal with each student and thus would be more oriented to the behaviors of each individual.

It was decided that all but Ramon could be rewarded initially for taking their seats when they entered the class, and they would also be rewarded for bringing a pencil since they rarely did either. If it was impossible to immediately reward all six, the teacher was to reward those who had been the biggest problems.[2] Ramon, who always took his seat when he entered class, was to be rewarded when convenient. In a classroom situation it was impossible for the teacher to dash around rewarding precisely at the moment the desired behavior was shown, so the teacher was asked to do what she could and not worry about "purchasing track shoes."

Administering Candy Reinforcers

The first day when the student entered the class the first boy to sit down was rewarded with two M & M's and his behavior was verbally acknowledged; for example, "This is for taking your seat," or "You sat at your desk, that's great." No negative comments were to be given such as, "It's nice to see you finally found your desk," or "It's about time you . . ." or "This is for not wandering around the room." Other students who sat down were also rewarded as were those who brought a pencil. If they did both, they were rewarded twice. We felt it was important to give verbal acknowledgement as well as M & M's, hoping later the verbal praise would sustain the behavior if M & M's were discontinued. It also gets the teacher into the habit of praising desirable behaviors when they occur rather than reproaching students.

The students were given no indication that they would receive candy. They were not prepared for the reward and were not told what they had to do to get it, why they were getting it, or how long it would last.[3] As the class progressed students were rewarded for specific behaviors. If Gary raised his hand, he was rewarded; if Andy completed two sentences, he was rewarded. The students' reactions to the initiation of rewards was interesting. Not one word was spoken to the teacher or to the other students, and in almost every case the student immediately put the candy

---

[2] Editors' Note: It might seem self-defeating to reinforce the biggest trouble-makers first on the grounds that we are thus encouraging big trouble-makers. However, it is *improvement* that is being reinforced, not trouble-making. Each child needs to be rewarded for making improvement over *his own* past behavior, not for acting better than someone else.

[3] Editors' Note: Note the difference between this and the behavior contract method where contingencies are spelled out in advance. Which method is superior? Are there certain types of students for whom a contract approach gets better results than a simple reinforcement approach? Grist for some experimental studies.

in his shirt pocket and ate it at the end of class.[4] Whatever the reason for the reaction, we stopped worrying, because the behavior rewarded improved immediately. The next day all the students came in and sat down and brought their pencils. They worked better with a minimum need for disciplining.

This pattern of rewarding was continued for two weeks. Within this time behavior and productivity had improved. At this point the teacher and counselor felt the students were ready for the next step which was to reward them for sustained good behavior. Since the object is not to addict students to M & M's, but rather to help them learn proper behavior, they were rewarded less often for good behavior. Their behavior had changed in several ways in this short period of time. They were all entering the classroom in a desirable fashion, taking their seats, bringing their equipment, and actually taking out their books to study. Some were even asking what else they could work on after they had completed an assigned task. They were more polite to one another, and Ramon often smiled. Some ate their M & M's immediately and others lined them up on their desks. One boy dropped his pencil and in an attempt to retrieve it lost four or five M & M's out of his pocket. The teacher said she would replace them but he said, "No, that's all right." None of the students were reported to have eaten candy on the playground or in another class. They apparently never said anything to anyone in their classes, since other students never asked about what was going on in the reading class, nor did teachers hear comments on it. It was still never discussed in the class.

In addition to giving the reward as soon as possible, another basic rule was established: Do not reward if the student asks for it. This is easy to handle if the student comes right out with a request; however, sometimes the request can be disguised. In the reading class the teacher became concerned about Andy. After completing a number of sentences he would raise his hand to get her attention, then point out to her what he had accomplished. She would then reward him for his work; but after this reward he would stop working. Andy also had a very short concentration span. He would work for a maximum of five minutes, daydream, work and daydream. The problem was that his daydream span was about fifteen minutes as compared to his five-minute work span. We decided to attack both situations at once. Since he only worked for a maximum of five minutes, it would be unwise to reward at the end of five minutes

---

[4] Why didn't the students eat the candy immediately? We tried to put ourselves in their place to understand the phenomenon: "I am in a seventh- or eighth-grade class and the teacher unexpectedly passes out candy. Is the teacher experiencing a moment of insanity? Don't breathe, don't move because she might at any moment realize what she is doing and the spell might be broken. I'll put the candy in my pocket so she won't see me eating it and so she won't take it back."

since the goal was to reinforce him while still attending. It was decided to reward Andy every two minutes, and if he called her attention to his work, she was to praise him, but not give M & M's.[5] Within a week his work and daydream periods were in better balance.

The teacher who had Henry and David in one class remarked that both boys were "different people." Henry, who had told her to "shut up" and stormed from the room two weeks before, was polite, co-operative, and even asked if he could make up work he was missing by being in the remedial reading class. David also had displayed these behaviors. Both boys asked if they could be in an additional period of reading. Although M & M's were not used with them in their additional reading class, they displayed good work habits in this situation suggesting some transfer effects from their remedial class.

One of the fears we had was that the students would tire of the M & M's, the "game," or both. We carried on with this program for four-and-a-half months, until the end of school, with no apparent M & M saturation and with no regression in work habits, attitude, or behavior.

Using Token Reinforcers

About one month before school ended we switched from M & M's to tokens in this class. We purchased small poker chips about the size of a quarter, to be given as a reward instead of M & M's. They were to be given less frequently, perhaps one or two a day, three if something spectacular happened. By accumulating tokens, various items from the school store could be obtained. For example, a school notebook costing 29 cents could be obtained with 29 tokens. They could also trade in ten tokens for a ticket with which to get ice cream that was sold after school by the student government. A list of the items and their value in tokens was made available to the students.

This phase of the program was initiated by simply telling the students, "Today you will be getting tokens for the things for which you got M & M's." It was then explained how they could be used. It had been decided previously that in Andy's case he would get both tokens and M & M's since he needs more frequent rewards to sustain his behavior. The teacher, Mrs. S., said that Andy "immediately responded to tokens, whereas he had never *really* gotten down to it with M & M's." Two of the boys asked if they could trade tokens for M & M's, so we decided to add to the list five M & M's for one token. To make it as smooth running as

---

[5] Editors' Note: A traditional teacher would possibly disapprove of rewarding a behavior consisting of such short attention to the task and so much daydreaming. However, the key to success is in rewarding the desirable behavior when it occurs, not in upholding a high standard of performance that cannot be reached.

possible, it was decided that the tokens could only be exchanged at the end of the period. The teacher had an envelope available for each student who wanted to accumulate his tokens. At the end of the period Mrs. S. distributed the envelopes so that students could add the tokens earned that day to their savings. We felt that the tokens would serve a number of functions:

1. The student would have the choice of items he could purchase with them.
2. He could choose how often he would be rewarded, either by exchanging them at the end of each class period for M&M's or waiting for a longer time and exchanging them for a "higher priced" item.
3. He would have a chance to see his rewards for behavior grow, and he would have some experience in managing his "income."
4. Last, but not least, the students no longer had "M&M breath."

Some of the students traded their tokens for M & M's and some got ice cream. Ramon and David decided to save all their tokens until the end of the year. We were very pleased when both boys, after looking over items in the book store, decided to get a book. Andy traded in his tokens three times for M & M's.

EXTENSION TO LARGER CLASSES

As our progress in the remedial program was discussed with other teachers, interest grew and the two eighth-grade teachers who had below level classes expressed a desire to try it in their classes. Miss K. had 21 students and Mrs. B. had 20 students. Both classes were very difficult to teach. In Miss K.'s class four of the 22 students had been referred to the school psychologist and had psychological reports on file, and three of the boys in the class had been in juvenile hall on charges of breaking and entering. Gary, who was also in the reading class, was in this class. In Mrs. B.'s class four of the 20 had psychological reports on file. Ricky, David, and Henry were in this class.

We started the same way with these classes as with the remedial class. The counselor and each teacher discussed the individual students to determine for what behavior each one would be rewarded. After determining this, both teachers initiated the program in the same manner as the reading class; the students were not primed, they were simply rewarded upon entering the class. In both classes it was decided that most students would get rewards for taking their seats upon entering the class and for bringing their equipment. Some were to be rewarded for participating in class, for raising their hands instead of calling out, and for not following the teacher around to ask questions. Arguments and talking by students when they should be quiet was to be handled in this way: any quiet student who was sitting in the area of the talkers, who ignored provocation, or one who tried not to be drawn into conversation was rewarded with M & M's and a comment was made, such as "This is for trying to work," "I know it's hard to concentrate with others talking." These comments were to be directed to the student behaving himself and were not to be used as backhanded sarcasm to the talkers. Immediate reward was considered essential, so at the beginning the teachers were kept busy.

"It really keeps you on your toes. . . ."

"Have to pace the aisles all the time, to see if they're just opening a book when you give a page number."

It should be mentioned here that while the mechanics of initiating this program were not difficult, there seemed to be emotional strain on the teachers. In beginning the program in the reading class and the two eighth-grade classes, both counselor and teachers were apprehensive. We never knew how the students were going to react. Would eighth graders accept this or would they think the whole idea ridiculous and childlike? If they did not accept it, what would be their reaction? We had visions of M & M's being thrown around the room. We were all greatly relieved and surprised when the reaction was minimal in all cases. These are the comments made by Miss K., Mrs. B., and Mrs. S. as transcribed from the tape recording made of the final evaluation session.

Mrs. B.: You know, I didn't get any (reaction at the beginning of the program), that was the strangest thing. And I waited and waited to hear something about "Why are we getting these M&M's?" and I never did, and do you think they talked about it outside of class? To their friends, in at-level and above-level. . . .

Mrs. S.: Well, they didn't from my class (remedial reading) to your class. They never said a word . . . I've had kids from my other classes walk in and see me do this, and they kind of look—but they never say anything either.

Mrs. B.: It's really weird, I can't understand it, because *nobody* eats candy in school. It's the school rule, and for the teacher to *give* them candy—you'd think it would be the talk of the school, wouldn't you?

Miss K.: Eddie R. asked me, and Eddie was an exception. He was the one that was really concerned and asked, "Why, why, why?" And I just didn't answer his question. He was very distrustful and probably had a reason to be. (His father had shaved Eddie's head when he got a bad report last year, and Eddie was very suspicious of everything.) About two or three days later he decided to take them. I'd go up to him and ask, "Do you want them?" when it was time for him to be rewarded, and he said, "Yeh, I asked my Mom, and as long as everyone else is getting candy, I might as well eat too."

Mrs. S.: I think they're afraid it will go away if they discuss it too much, and yet no one has told them they shouldn't. That's the funny part of it.

Both Miss K. and Mrs. B. maintained the policy of being positive with the students and deliberately ignored responding to poor behavior as much as possible. In both cases the teachers reported definite improvement in work and behavior. Shortly after the program was started progress reports were due to be sent home. A majority of students in both classes were usually involved because of their poor work and behavior; however, it was decided that no reports would be sent home since we felt this would be in conflict with the idea of rewarding positive accomplishments.[6]

The teachers wanted to allow the students to start fresh, so they disregarded any of the students' bad grades before the program was started. When the program began each teacher began to change her lessons so that the students could be progressively more successful.[7]

Miss K.: I started out giving really easy tests, the kind of test they were always consistently failing, and I gave them open-book. Now I give almost exclusively open-book tests to them. Recall isn't that important. It's a rereading kind of situation to find the answers in the book. Then when they take the test, they know exactly how to take the test and how to read for a test. The tests have gotten progressively harder until they're up to the standards I think that level of class should be working on. And it's amazing when I look at their grades for this quarter. Last quarter I threw out the previous (before M&M's) grades, and gave them a report card grade on what they had done since M&M's. This quarter I won't have to do it. They're all at least getting C's, most of them are in the B's. Five kids in that class turned in extra credit book reports, and there were no book reports assigned unless you want to.

Mrs. B.: I've had maps turned in, and history reports that they've done on their own for extra credit. The first two or three weeks after I started the M&M program I didn't give a letter grade, just a remark— "Good" or "Showing improvement" or something that seemed to

[6] Editors' Note: If "progress reports" were truly reports of progress and not reports of lack of progress, there would be no conflict. A useful progress report to parents would describe actual accomplishments and behavior improvements, for example, "now takes his seat without reminding," "remembers to put periods at the end of his sentences."

[7] Editors' Note: Excellent idea! The policy of grading on a curve, thereby automatically giving low grades to a selected percentage of the class, probably is the cause of more truancy, drop-outs, vandalism, heartbreak, discouragement, and waste than any other outmoded policy. Giving high grades regardless of performance is almost as bad. Arranging lessons so each child is challenged but can succeed is a most promising development. Every child who achieves an objective could get an A for his accomplishment.

encourage them. Maybe I should have kept it up, but eventually I guess, we do have to go back, I mean *I* have, to the letter grade.

Miss K.: I just gave tests so that they'd all get A's and B's.

Mrs. B.: That would be discouraging if you started them and *they* tried and they were getting nothing but F's. There's no point in that.

Our concern about the lasting influence of M & M's and whether the students would tire of them was unwarranted. The program in both classes went from mid-February to the end of the school year with no substantial let-up in response. There were some students in the two classes who often did not respond to the M & M's, but their behavior was still improved considerably. Since students were rewarded on the basis of their individual accomplishments, they seemed to work more individually, and thus were less apt to be influenced by disturbances caused by other members of the class.

Neither of the two classes were switched to tokens because of the cost. The counselor and teachers were financing the program.

One primary consideration in initiating the program had to do with lesson plans for that day. Since the first day is extremely important for setting up the pattern, the teachers arranged their class time so that the students had an assignment to work on during the first period M & M's were to be given. This allowed the teacher the freedom to get around the class.

Effects on Students and Parents

The program in these two classes was in effect for about four months. After two months both teachers said that the students had improved enough so that they were able to work up to the standards the teachers felt were acceptable. By the end of the year the students were working up to standard, but instead of receiving poor grades they were getting good grades and were working much better.

Miss K. periodically had the students work together on various reports or help one another with homework. Before the onset of the program it was almost impossible, since there was talking and arguments. One of the boys was so disliked that the other students refused to work with him. M & M's were used to reward working well together in groups and cooperating with one another. As a result students who formerly argued were helpful and worked well with others, and the "outcast" was no longer rejected. One reason for this was that he had become much less obnoxious; he no longer wandered around the room, tagged after the teacher, spoke out in class, or pestered students as consistently as he had.

Don, one of the boys in Miss K.'s eighth grade class, had repeated sixth grade. He had been doing so poorly, we were afraid he might extend his stay another year. Don's spelling was something to behold; at the beginning of the year the teacher asked the class how to spell "say." Don volunteered "s-e-y, no, s-y-e." About a month before school was out his teacher came running into the counseling office elated. Don had made only one error on a spelling test and had actually spelled "constitution" correctly. Although his over-all progress was something less than outstanding, he had improved considerably in spelling and in actually handing in assignments. His general "attitude" in class was much more positive.

Three of the students in this below-level class had improved to such a degree that the teacher told them that she would recommend placement in an at-level class if they sustained their good work and behavior. All of these students did very well, and the recommendation was made and honored.

Miss K.:   Some people are trying to improve their report grades. They're so phenomenally better. The last time it was really exciting when they saw their grades. And some people saw that instead of getting N's (Needs improvement) in deportment, they were up to "Satisfactory," and I had some boys that were really terrors, and I thought if I gagged them, it would be nice during class—and they're working for E's (Excellent) now—and they're getting them. And they're turning into gentlemen. There are so many more "pleases" and "thank you's." There's just a day and night difference. I think I've had about 70 percent success. Where I noticed it was at Parents' Night. I've never had a low class that was practically dragging their parents, grandmothers, aunts and uncles into the room to see what *they had done* and how good their folders were—they're so proud of what they're doing, and they don't realize that maybe the reason they can be proud of their work is that they've settled down and done some work for a change. Some of them are 15 years old in there.

Mrs. B.:   I had a much better turnout of parents than I've ever had from a slow group.

Miss K.:   One mother said about a month and a half ago or so . . . "All of a sudden my daughter started improving at home, and she suddenly wants to come to school." I mentioned something about her attendance having improved, and she said, "She doesn't have these headaches before she goes to school in the morning and she doesn't come home in the middle of the afternoon." And I think part of this was that they were getting rewarded at school. A lot of their sickness, I think, is psychologically based or they just don't want to do something and they play sick that day. And they (parents) also said they noticed the children were happier at home, and they would ask their parents more things. We discussed more things at school.

Mrs. B.: I think the change is in the teacher's attitude, too. . . . It's more of a pleasure working with these kids. Because their attitude changes; therefore our attitude changes.

An Attempt That Failed

We tried the program in an "at-level" class of 34 students in sixth grade that did not respond as the others had. The teacher, Miss T., had the type of class that periodically pops up in a school—the students should be like any others, but when they are all put together, "a monster emerges." The program was initiated as in the other classes, and for two weeks worked beautifully; then following a four-day holiday, it went steadily downhill. The counselor and Miss T. decided to find the reason for this by asking the students themselves. The counselor went into the class and talked with the students for two periods. Some students felt it was "bribery" and "kindergarten stuff"; some felt it helped them, some felt it had not. When asked how many felt their grades had improved, about 60 percent of the class raised their hands. By the end of the session the students had decided that they did not want Miss T. wasting her money on them, and that they unfortunately took advantage of her when she was nice to them.[8] They felt she should be ultrastrict, set down rigid rules, and give office detentions if these rules were broken. When the teacher returned to the class, they asked her if they could discuss the program with her. They told her what they had decided. The next day she dittoed a list of rules and regulations and the punishment to be given if broken. This continued until the end of school. Even though the program did not work, the teacher felt it had potential since some of the students had responded very well and had maintained their improvement even after the change in classroom policy.

Miss T.: Something that I thought was so interesting about the kids' own attitude about the M&M's; we only had them for about two weeks, but when we first started they ate them immediately, bang, they were popped right in their mouths. And about the second day, I think, that's all the longer it took, they were no longer eating them, they were lining them up on their desk, so everyone could see how many M&M's they were getting. It wasn't a matter of eating candy anymore, but showing off a little bit. They compared notes—"I've got eight. How many did you get?"

[8] Editors' Note: Though we cannot be certain exactly what happened in Miss T.'s class, one frequent misinterpretation of a positive reinforcement approach is that the teacher should be "nice" no matter how the children perform. In an effective program the teacher is "nice" (administers positive reinforcers and gives attention) only to those children who are showing improvement or are engaged in desirable behavior.

At first they responded beautifully. It was just great. And then it just went. And I'm sorry that it did because not just troublemakers, but a lot of kids in there who weren't doing work responded beautifully. They aren't really discipline problems, they just never did anything, and when I was giving M&M's they were working. And it was kind of a shame when I had to stop.[9]

CARD CARRIERS

In order to deal with individual students who were problems in the classroom, we set up another program. We made up a card on which there were 20 squares. At the top of the card was a line for the student's name and the date. Instead of receiving candy as a reward in the classroom, the student would get the card initialed by the teacher each time he did something right, or improved. For each signature he would receive three M & M's at the end of the day from the counselor. The student was discussed by the teacher and counselor to determine when he could be rewarded. The counselor then talked to the student about specific problems he was having in the classroom.

The card idea was presented to the student in words to this effect: "Since you're having a hard time settling down in class, let's try something. I've talked to your teacher and she is concerned and wants to help. Here's a card. Your name goes at the top. You take this into class and put it on your desk. Whenever you do something right or improve, your teacher will write her initials in one of the squares. The object is to get as many signatures as you can throughout the day. At the end of the day, you come back to see me. Do you like candy? Well, for each signature you get I'll give you three M & M's." The student then would take the card back to class, and it would be signed by the teacher at appropriate times. Along with each signature the teacher would give verbal praise or encouragement. Approximately 20 students were included in this program. There was immediate improvement in all cases; however, not all of these students maintained improvement.

All of the individual "card carriers," a term that was originally used

[9] Editors' Note: There are many possible reasons why a reinforcement program like this might fail. It may work best with students who have long been deprived of much positive reinforcement. Those satiated with reinforcers may find it juvenile and patronizing and react with hostility. The nature of the reinforcer may have to be varied with different groups. The personality of the reinforcing agent may have an effect. The tasks to be reinforced may be so inherently aversive or irrelevant that virtually no reinforcer could make them palatable. Variables such as these need to be investigated experimentally to determine the combination of conditions under which a given technique is most effective.

jokingly but became common usage, began in the core classes, but soon other teachers also started signing the cards, and students were getting their cards signed in art, music, math, and science classes.

Each day the students picked up new cards before class in the counselor's office and returned them after school. Along with rewarding the students, the counselor praised and encouraged them.

Problem Students

Fern was a tiny, below-level sixth grader who had a lisp. She was the epitome of innocence when she stood before you, wringing her tiny hands and looking up with big brown eyes, explaining that her brother had beaten her up again. She was one of four children, her father was not in the home, and her mother worked. With all her seeming innocence Fern was the most accomplished thief in the school. She stole from stores, lockers, teachers' desks, and her mother. She had come in to see the counselor about her stealing, because she was afraid she would get into serious trouble when she got older. Since she was a friend of some other girls who were suspected of stealing, she was asked by the counselor if any of her friends wanted to stop stealing, and if they did, to bring them in and perhaps they could help each other change. In all, ten girls came in to "stop stealing." These ten girls—all sixth graders—were members of a group in which it was prestigeful to steal. The object then was to change the situation so that honesty and resisting the temptation to steal would be the badge of honor. Fern was the most severe problem since her reputation was widespread in the school to the point that other students actually gave her lists of items to steal. She felt that this was a way to keep friends. All the girls came into the counselor's office twice a week, before and after the weekend (when most stealing occurred) and were rewarded with a candy bar for not stealing, admitting they stole, or, especially in Fern's case, stealing less often. As a protection against lying, the "fink system" was used. If the girls were serious about stopping their stealing activities, there had to be a check system, and so they all agreed that "finking" or informing on one of the group who stole would help them. Since Fern responded so well to the candy, and since she was in need of extra attention, the counselor and Fern's teacher, Mrs. N., decided to give Fern a card. Because her attendance was a problem as was homework and her incessant talking, she would be rewarded for work handed in, as well as cooperation in class. The counselor would give a "bonus" for being in school.

Albert and Ronald were likeable below-level sixth graders who were full of energy, talk, and had at their command an unbelievable repertoire of ways to get under the teacher's skin. Ronald was quite capable if he could be settled down, although he did not show his capabilities often. Albert was fairly slow, but could certainly do better work when he attended to the task at hand. The core teacher who had these boys agreed to put them "on the card," and after talking with the counselor individually, they went to class with their cards. Their behavior improved immediately, and as the art teacher and math and science teacher started signing their cards, grades began to improve. By the end of the year, Ronald was in a position to be recommended for an "at-level" class. Albert came in to get his card one morning, and after getting back to class tore it up and told the teacher he was going to try it on his own. He couldn't make it and came back for a card the next day. Following is a letter Albert wrote for an assignment in his English class at the end of the year:

Dear John:
I like school becaus of a card.
The card has made me shape up a lot. It has also done a
lot for me I don't get eny more delention like I had it
cepts me out of the offece more. And I am solo glad that
school is out

Your brother,
Albert

Morris, a below-level sixth grader, with learning difficulties was "put on the card" for a boost in morale. Morris had extreme difficulty retaining information; he was in remedial reading and the teacher said he could not remember the word "they" from one day to the next. His math teacher said one day he could work a problem with no difficulty, and the next day it was completely gone. He had the same difficulty in his core classes, having great difficulty remembering from one day to the next. Morris also daydreamed, sometimes rolled his head on the desk and made gestures and noises as if he were exploding atomic bombs. His teachers were very concerned about his work slipping because despite his difficulties Morris was a very likeable boy who usually tried very hard. Morris was referred for psychological testing for possible neurological handicap, with the hope that the psychologist could give us some indication of how this boy could be taught. Morris was identified as neurologically handicapped but a method of teaching him was not known.[10] We finally decided to reward him with M & M's, so that if nothing else we might be able to keep him from giving up. The result was surprising, the rewards helped Morris remember.

[10] Editors' Note: What good does it do to label someone "neurologically handicapped" if no additional help can be made available as a result of the label?

Teacher Comments

Mrs. S. (Rem. Read.): Almost all of them, *immediately* upon receiving their cards, just improved 100 percent in my class. Like Morris, who needed a little extra push, right at that moment, it seemed to come right back, and he's done *so* much better since that time. And Fern and Raychel, who could absolutely do nothing, immediately were ready to do *anything* at *all* if I would just sign their cards. They didn't say that, but you could tell as soon as they had that card there on their desks, that any assignment that I gave was beautifully done and done in a hurry, and without a lot of sitting around and talking, which was done previously. . . . Cards are every bit as good for these particular children. I got just as good a reaction from signing cards with them as I did from giving M&M's to the ones that I gave those to.

Mrs. N. (Lang. Arts): I think Fern's case is interesting, too, in that she had her card for stealing, and now when anything's missing, she's the first to get really riled up. She wants to know "Who took it?" and they'd better get it back.

Miss F. (Lang. Arts): He's (Morris) not really concerned about the signature . . . he's rather pleased with his progress. Albert's work has improved because of the card . . . his grades have come up. . . . Ronald has shaped up, and Albert has shaped up so much. Albert's work has improved because he has settled down.

Mrs. N. (Lang. Arts): Last Friday we had done a language assignment and we were going to check it Wednesday when we came back after vacation (a four-day weekend). Probably 50 percent of the class completely forgot that the Friday before they'd had the assignment, but three people (Morris, Ron, and Albert) who were in there, that were on the cards—they all three had their assignments ready. Besides their discipline improving their grades, it's all-round study habits. And there's sort of a competition to see who can get the most signatures.

Mr. A. (Art): Oh yes, definitely. The whole classroom is much, much more organized and they get out their materials and work hard. I would say it's been an over-all success for them . . . especially when it's clean-up time . . . I think just the card carriers, they all rush to a sink and do the job, and the others, like Ernie or anyone else in the class who doesn't carry a card, has followed the rest of the card carriers and they also do their jobs. What's also surprising is none of the other kids in class say anything about, "Why don't I have a card?" or "Why don't I get M&M's?" When they first walked in I was surprised, because I thought they'd all start griping that they didn't have a card.

Mrs. L. (Math. Science): Morris is retaining and asking questions if he doesn't understand . . . whereas before he would just sit and make noises and explode bombs.

Mrs. S. (Rem. Read.): I think I noticed this about Morris more than anybody else, too, the fact that he's actually remembering things from day to day, which for him is just *fantastic!*

Mr. A. (Art): I've noticed that in art. He doesn't come up to ask instructions. I give them once. I think those four, especially, are the four who now lead the class in telling them the instructions if they didn't get it themselves. Because they are a slow group. Even Ron, who really had a problem with instructions. He would constantly be coming up to ask me. Now he knows the instructions. He still comes up to ask my evaluation . . . but there's none of this, "Well, I just wasn't listening." They *are* listening now.

Miss F. (Lang. Arts): The nice thing about it is I'm not fighting the whole group anymore. In the beginning they were just one great big discipline problem. The whole class seemed to hate each other and now we're getting along better.

Mr. A. (Art): I look forward to that class coming in now, whereas before I absolutely dreaded it . . . I had to go through instructions over and over and over on simple things. They may not be the most creative class I have, but they're fun, they're exciting, and they listen, and they do try now, which is something sometimes far above some of my other classes.

The teachers felt there was a change in their own attitudes toward their classes.

Miss F. (Lang. Arts): It's because we're not constantly scolding, the other students don't hear this negative approach all the time. They feel better about it. It's not constant nagging.

Mr. A. (Art):   That, and I've noticed their social interaction in the class. They talk much nicer to each other, whereas before it was constant bickering. Now they are polite to each other and really respect each other.

The teachers were asked about the students for whom the card seemed to make little difference. What about the failures? There were four students carrying cards in an "at-level" class. One, Brian, was a card carrier for about two months. Then he decided he would do his work without a card. The teachers felt he had improved. Two other students improved while "on the card," but stopped using it and slipped back, and one did not respond at all. It was felt that perhaps the difference was that if the student felt he had the ability, it was harder for him to improve with the card carrying program because he had a choice. A student who did not feel he had the ability would try. Here are some teacher comments about the "at-level" students:

Miss M. (Lang. Arts):   Brian, he *really* tried and his behavior has really improved, and now he doesn't have the card anymore and he's still pretty good. Sometimes he's a little bit boisterous and plays around too much, but other than that he does a pretty good job.

Miss T. (Math. Science):   Ricky decided on his own to stop using the card. He has stopped working for me which he was doing when he was carrying the card. He worked, and he doesn't anymore; but something that has held over is behavior (he doesn't misbehave). This has been great.

Teachers were asked if they have changed the way they sign the cards since they started.

Mrs. N. (Lang. Arts):   Initially when I started out, whenever they did something that I felt should be rewarded, I'd sign it then, but I find that I'm not doing that now at all. I'm waiting until the end of the period, and because of it *they* remember the things, and we'll discuss it, the two of us . . . at least they're coming to me and discussing what they're doing in a class, whereas before they didn't at all.

Mr. A. (Art):   They like to recall what they did that was right.

The teachers were asked what the disadvantages of the program were and whether it took too much time.

Mrs. N. (Lang. Arts):   It took more time, but I think I should really give the kids more individual attention. It made me give them more attention.

Miss F. (Lang. Arts):   It paid off in that we didn't have to get up in front of the class and say, "Albert, settle down. . . ." The first few days, I found myself with extra time at the end of the period, and I said, "What happened!" We figured out it must be the time I used to spend griping at them.

The teacher who felt that only one of the four card carriers she had in class had improved commented:

Miss M. (Lang. Arts):   I found it hard to get around to everybody and give them signatures when they needed it, and I'd think after everyone was settled down working, "Well, he should have gotten one back then," but I didn't give it to him.[11] I think maybe if I could have gone all the time and been able to give them right when they needed it, all the time, they might have been able to do better.

Student Perceptions

One day four boys were sitting in the office, three of whom were waiting for the counselor to see their cards. The three boys were comparing the number of signatures they had accumulated throughout the day. The fourth boy's curiosity was too much for him and he asked, "Why do you have those cards?" "Because we're bad," answered one of the card carriers without hesitation, and turned back to continue the original conversation. The fourth boy seemed satisfied and did not question further. After school one day two boys came in to see the counselor, just to talk. One was a card carrier, the other was not. The conversation got around to the card and the card carrier's friend asked him why he had one. His answer was, "Because I mess around in class, and this helps me keep out of the office."

The counselor asked two of the card carriers what they liked about the card. One said, "It's nice to hear the teacher say nice things." They also commented that it kept them out of trouble.

Three or four boys and two girls came in individually to see the counselor to ask if they could have a card. The counselor asked why they wanted it, but told them that the teacher would have to be consulted. The teacher, counselor and student all worked together, and a card would

[11] Editors' Note: Good intentions are insufficient.

be given only if the teacher felt that the student needed it. If the teacher or the counselor or both felt that the student should try to correct his behavior on his own, he was not given a card. Alternative ways to improve were discussed. There was never any adverse reaction by a student at being denied a card.[12]

Effects on Grades

The academic, deportment, and effort grades of the grading period before the initiation of the program were compared with those given at the end of the school year. These three categories of grades in six subject areas were used to tabulate improvement of the 33 students who finished out the year. The percentage of improvement by the two eighth-grade classes in the subject areas where M & M's were given was 78.8 percent, 18.3 percent had no change, and 2.9 percent dropped in grades. In science and math where M & M's were not given, 60.6 percent improved, 23.9 percent had no change, and 15.5 percent dropped. Since this was not a randomized well-controlled study, changes are only suggestive.

The card carriers as a group, although their teachers considered them improved, did not show improvement in the three grade categories on the report card even though certain individuals did. The classroom environment had not been changed as much for the card carriers as it was for the M & M classes. In the classes where M & M's were given to all students, the student was rewarded, not only with positive comments from the teacher and M & M's, but also with better grades on tests and homework. In these classes the teacher changed her approach with subject matter as well as her grading system in order to have each student be successful as the change in behavior occurred and work habits improved. However, the subject matter and grading scale remained the same in the card carriers' classrooms, and they were not rewarded automatically with better grades as were the students in the M & M classes. The card carrier did become less of a discipline problem or stealing problem, or less obnoxious, depending on the specific reason for which he was carrying the card.

Staff Relationships

A very important part of this program is the availability of the counselor. In all cases described in this paper the counselor worked closely

[12] Editors' Note: Further questions that need investigation are: What would be the effect of granting cards to some or all of those who "apply" for them? Would it be possible to structure the environment so that the granting of card carrying status was perceived as a privilege signifying that the grantee was considered worthy of the additional time and effort required?

with the teacher for the first few days, during her preparation period. A teacher trying this program in her classes is concerned and apprehensive about its working properly. The counselor made a point of seeing every day those teachers who started their entire class on M & M's. They discussed what had happened, clarified procedures, and worked out problems.

All of the teachers in this program were willing to try because they thought it might help the student. Not all were sold on the idea of using M & M's, but they were at least willing to give it a good try.

The principal and vice-principal at our school had almost identical reactions to the idea of starting the programs. Although they were asked individually, both said in effect, "Try it. You can even give them cigarettes if it will help these kids learn!" The co-operation of both men was constant and reassuring.

When the nurse was told of the program, she was concerned about these students eating candy all day long and the effect it would have on their teeth. She felt it was not wise to have candy given to the students all day and preferred the card carrier program since these students were rewarded at the end of the school day. However, at the end of the school year, she said that the progress of the students on the program was so outstanding that she felt the social and academic progress made by the students was much more important than the possible small effect that it might have on their teeth.

GUIDELINES FOR INITIATING A REINFORCEMENT PROGRAM

The implementation of a reinforcement program is fairly simple. However, we would make the following suggestions on the basis of our experience:

1. Identify specifically what behaviors need to be improved, and set up reasonable goals to be rewarded.

The teacher and counselor together talk over the behavior of the student to determine which behaviors can be rewarded. It is essential that the rewarding be based on improvements in the student's *present* behavior and not on what the teacher feels he should be doing.

2. There must be an immediate response by the teacher to any improvement.
3. Accompany any reward of M&M's or, in the case of the card carriers, a signature, with verbal praise.

Verbal acknowledgement with the reward is valuable for two main reasons: (1) The student often hears the teacher tell him what he's doing wrong, so he usually knows how to be bad. By hearing compliments and positive comments, he will be as knowledgeable about being good. (2) The teacher develops the habit of finding merit, not fault. The teachers found that their attitude changed and they liked themselves better, for instead of criticizing, they were praising.

4. There is no need to explain the M&M program to the student.

When we initiated the program, the teacher did not give the class an explanation for two reasons: (1) We felt explanation would be difficult and would perhaps invite questions not easy to answer. (2) We felt that part of the intrigue would be for the student to try to figure out why he and the others were getting rewarded. This approach proved to be practical.[13]

5. Reward consistently—especially at first.

At the beginning of the program it is important not only to reward immediately, but to reward the same behavior over and over until it becomes a habit. On the other hand, in the classroom situation it is sometimes extremely difficult, if not impossible, to reward everyone that should be rewarded at the same time. After the student realizes the teacher is truly willing to help him, inconsistency of reward may be better tolerated.[14]

6. Ignore negative behavior as much as possible.

The student should discover that good behavior reaps reward and poor behavior is worth nothing, not even the attention of the teacher.

7. Increase standards as the student progresses.

After behavior changed it was not necessary to reward as often. Students were sustaining their improved behavior for an entire class period or longer before being rewarded. In the M & M classes, the teachers were able to systematically raise their grading standards as the classes improved until the students were working at the level of difficulty the teachers desired. The M & M's in effect created motivated students who tried harder. The resulting praise from teachers, the improved grades, the positive comments from parents, the lack of detentions and trouble

---

[13] Editors' Note: Although explanations were not necessary here, perhaps in some instances they would help. Experimentation with and without explanations is needed.

[14] Editors' Note: Some later "inconsistency" may even be desirable. Intermittent reinforcement after the new response is once established has been found more effective in maintaining a response than continuous reinforcement.

with the office, and in some cases even the new respect from classmates became powerful rewards in themselves. The aim of the program is not to addict students to candy, but to give them the feeling and experience of success in contributing to their own education and welfare.[15]

19

TEACHING TEACHERS TO REINFORCE STUDENT PARTICIPATION

Ray E. Hosford
UNIVERSITY OF WISCONSIN

Four seventh-grade social studies teachers discussed with me students who never enter into class discussions. Some students had made no voluntary oral contributions for the two-and-one-half months that school had been in session. Although the instructors had requested individual counseling for these students, I pointed out that problems of this nature can often be treated best in the classroom where the behavior is desired.

PROCEDURES

Because there is increasing evidence that behavior can be modified by operant conditioning procedures, I suggested to the teachers that we try such a program with these students. The rationale and principles of modifying behavior by systematic reinforcement procedures were explained and the teachers indicated that they wished to participate in the project. Because of the considerable interest generated, it was decided to turn the project into a controlled research study. By so doing, it was thought that we would determine better whether our procedures were effective.

Each teacher was asked to identify, for each of the two classes he taught, three students who seldom participated in class discussions and

[15] We would like to acknowledge the following teachers and administrators whose efforts, co-operation, enthusiasm, and trust enabled the program to develop and grow: Charles Ackerman, Lynn Van Winkle, Jeanette Simmons, Betty Brashear, Sue (Koch) Suiter, Betty Strantz, Jerry Andresen, Linda Baity, Louella Bourgerie, Margaret Frazier, June Fujikawa, Joyce Fullerton, William Gordon, Martha Hamlow, Margaret Jackson, Toni-Sue McMahon, Joan Nelson, Herm Neufeld, and Donald Phillips.

who would benefit by learning to participate more. Students being seen by a counselor or other guidance personnel were excluded.

For the first week of the project, the teachers met as a group with me to learn how and when to apply the reinforcement procedures. Mimeographed literature on the principles of positive reinforcement and numerous examples of employing this technique were distributed. The teachers also practiced role-playing the parts of student and teacher while utilizing verbal reinforcement procedures. Other reinforcers, for example, smiles and pats on back, were also used. Instructions were given to reinforce the student immediately *after* he asked any question, answered any question, or entered verbally into any class discussion. Because the goal of our "counseling"[1] was to increase the frequency with which these students entered into class discussions, the teachers were also asked to reinforce negative verbal responses emitted by these students. Such responses as "Mrs. Jones, you gave us too much homework last night," were to be verbally reinforced with something similar to "Thanks, Joe, for bringing that up. You know, teachers would never know just how much homework to assign if students didn't let us know from time to time whether the assignments are too long."

During this first week the teachers were asked also to tally any verbal response made by each of the three students selected in each of their two classes. To be tallied, the verbal response had to be emitted in the classroom. Questions were included. Responses to questions specifically directed to the student by the teacher were not included. During this week the teachers systematically did not reinforce verbal responses more than usual.

From among the three names selected for each class, one student was randomly chosen to receive the reinforcement procedures. A second student was chosen to serve as a control but his name was not given to the teacher.

During the next three weeks each teacher employed the reinforcement procedures with the one experimental student chosen. Each teacher also met individually with me to discuss any particular problems.

In addition to the classroom procedures, every experimental student was seen by me during the third and fourth weeks for two 20-minute interviews. For the first interview, the student was told that the counselors were seeing many students picked on a random basis to discuss their program and plans for the future.

As the student discussed what he was doing in the various subjects,

[1] Editors' Note: Who is the client in this "counseling"? Certainly not the three students in each classroom. They did not request help and probably did not know a program for them was in progress. The clients were the four teachers. They requested help with a teaching problem and co-operated with the counselor in an effort to alter their own behavior to solve it. Hopefully, the students will be the beneficiaries of this program, but they are not the counselor's clients at the moment.

all responses related to "discussing in class" were reinforced with such reinforcers as "Good," "Gee, that's swell, tell me about it." At the conclusion of the first interview the student was encouraged to look through a large assortment of vocational pamphlets and take one along with him. He was further encouraged to discuss the information with his teacher and class.

The second interview continued along the same line as the first with one major addition. At least one positive comment was passed along to the student which had been obtained previously from his teacher participating in the project. A typical comment was, "Mrs. Jones happened to mention to me how pleased she was in the greater interest you have shown in class lately."

During the fifth and final week the teachers were asked again to keep an accurate account of the number of times the students responded verbally in the classroom. This procedure was done also for those students originally referred but who had not received the reinforcement procedures.

RESULTS

The results of the project were highly favorable. The reinforced students increased the frequency with which they entered into class discussions significantly more than the control students.

The teachers were pleased with the procedures for helping students learn to participate in class discussions. They began using reinforcement procedures to promote other behaviors as well. One teacher pointed out that after she saw definite improvement on the part of the students with whom she was working, she decided to try his technique to improve classroom discipline. Her problem was one of getting the students to quiet down when they came into the room so that she could immediately begin class rather than to take the time to "shout them down." The use of threatening consequences, she related, often got the class off on a "sour note." She waited until the desired behavior occurred, that is, the students came in a little more quietly, and then she reinforced them. One reinforcer was ending instruction a little early so that the students were ready to leave for brunch period (a break that they had often previously missed). She commented, "Learning to use this technique completely revolutionized my teaching. I no longer have to shout at the class to get them to quiet down and begin to work."[2]

[2] Editors' Note: If reinforcement techniques make teaching more effective and pleasant, teachers will use them. If not, they won't. The counselor's best strategy is to help the teacher select a specific workable behavior problem where results can be observable within a short period of time. The teacher can then generalize the techniques to other problems.

20

TEACHING PARENTS TO BE BEHAVIOR MODIFIERS IN THE CLASSROOM [1]

G. R. Patterson
SCHOOL OF EDUCATION, UNIVERSITY OF OREGON
AND OREGON RESEARCH INSTITUTE

A procedure will be described in which mothers were briefly trained in the application of behavior modification procedures. They then reinforced certain behaviors of their own children in the classroom.

Recently extensive efforts have also been made to train parents to alter the behavior of their own children in the home. These efforts have focused upon the parents of autistic children (Wolf, Mees, & Risley, 1964; Ray, 1965), the parents of retarded children (Lindsley, 1966), and parents of children referred to out-patient facilities for "disturbed children" (Hawkins, Peterson, Schweid & Bijou, 1966; Wahler, Winkel, Peterson, 1965; Patterson & Brodsky, 1966; Patterson, Hawkins, McNeal, & Phelps, 1967; Zeilberger, Sampen, & Sloane, 1968). These single case studies indicate a promising beginning in the development of both intervention procedures and in the training of nonprofessional *social engineers.*

This emphasis upon training the parent is partially based upon the general assumption that both adaptive and deviant forms of child behavior are maintained as a function of the consequences which they elicit from the social environment (Skinner, 1953). Research findings (Patterson, 1968) suggest that the final outcomes of intervention are, in large part, a function of changes produced in the reinforcement schedules of the *parents,* the members of the *peer* group, or the *teacher.* If these social agents continue to reinforce the deviant behaviors or "forget" to reinforce the newly strengthened adaptive behaviors, then the outcome of intervention efforts will be short-lived at best. The parent, members of the

[1] The writer wishes to acknowledge the assistance of the school counselor for the Willakenzie School, Ronald Little, who actually carried out the contracts with the parents. Lynn Long, Elizabeth Gullion, and Richard Lewis served in the dual role of consultants and observers. The writer also wishes to thank the principal, H. Rice, and teacher, Mrs. Johnson, for the aplomb with which they reacted to rather unorthodox propositions. The preparation of the manuscript was carried out under the auspices of OEG 4–6–061308–0571.

peer group, and/or the teacher should be the primary focus of intervention efforts.

HELPING TWO "POORLY MOTIVATED" BOYS LEARN TO WORK

George and Andy were in the first grade of a public school classroom. The available test scores indicated that both of them had average ability. However, the teacher and school counselor doubted that they were ready for second grade. The teacher described their behavior as "immature," "disruptive," and "poorly motivated." Observation in the classroom showed them to be alternating between daydreaming and bursts of disruptive activity. Little time seemed to be spent in work-oriented activities. While other children were working they tended to be out of their seats and moving about the room; these behaviors seemed to produce a rich supply of social reinforcers (for example, peer attention, laughter). When they did work it was only for short periods of time; even then, the intervals were heavily laced with pressing discussions with a neighbor, sliding across the room or just staring out the window. Previous discussions with the parents about the imminent academic failures had not produced any noteworthy changes in their boys' classroom behavior.

Both of the mothers of these children had received some high school education. When contacted by the school counselor they readily agreed to participate in an experiment designed to help their children.

Observing the Behaviors

Six categories of behavior which had been shown in previous studies to be coded at high levels of reliability (Anderson, 1964; Ebner, 1967) were tabulated: (1) movements in chair, fiddling, wiggling, (2) walking about room, (3) not attending to teacher or class discussion, (4) talking (out of turn) to other children, (5) acting silly, clowning, (6) negativistic, refusing to comply with teacher requests. Although reliability data were not collected for this study, over half of the observers had participated in previous studies and had been shown to be able to code such data reliably.

Three baseline observation sessions were made in the classroom prior to conditioning. These sessions were spaced over a two-week interval. Data were also collected immediately prior to each of the three conditioning trials and over a two-week follow-up period. When any one of six behaviors occurred during a 15-second interval, it was recorded on the check sheet. The observer was signaled at the beginning of each 15-second interval by a portable interval timing device which dispensed visual and auditory signals. On receiving such a signal, the observer moved down one line on the check sheet. A specific response was recorded only once during a 15-second interval; however, several different responses could be recorded in a single interval.

Training the Mothers

After the initial telephone contact with the mothers, the school counselor and the classroom teacher met with them in a series of two one-hour group sessions. In the first meeting the teacher and the counselor briefly described the classroom behavior of the child and indicated again to the parent that the probable outcome of such behaviors was extremely inefficient learning and school failure. The counselor then described the specific behaviors that he noted when observing in the classroom, that is, "George is spending a lot of time just walking around and talking to other kids when he is supposed to be carrying out his desk assignment." "Andy is kind of a dreamer. He really means well and he is smart enough, but he spends a lot of time just staring out the window. You can see on this graph just how often he does that."

It was then proposed that the counselor would teach them a "way of helping your own child" and that they would use that in the classroom. He then gave them copies of a programmed textbook on social learning that presented the main concepts of positive reinforcement, negative reinforcement and extinction. In addition, there were accompanying chapters on certain kinds of deviant child behaviors such as negativism, aggression, hyperactivity, and withdrawal. Each of these chapters contained actual examples observed in homes of how these behaviors might be shaped in the home and also outlined the programs used to alter them. A pilot study had shown that reading the text had produced significant changes in the reinforcement contingencies observed by some mothers in their interactions with their children (Patterson & Gullion, 1968). The book had also seemed useful as a "catalyst" in accelerating behavior modification procedures used in the home with a family who had produced an extremely deviant child (Patterson et al., 1966).

The two mothers returned on the following week after having completed their responses to the programmed textbook. The group, including the teacher, discussed the general principles presented in the book and then talked about how to apply them to specific problem behaviors which occurred at home. For example, it was noted that the family was most likely to reinforce George when he acted silly; inadvertently, he had been trained to become the family clown. These behaviors were also in evidence in the classroom and produce similar reinforcements from his peers. For Andy, it was noted that the mother seemed ready to reinforce him when he complained or indicated that he was not able to complete the task. However, she tended to ignore him when he did complete a task.

It was suggested to the mothers that they could fulfill a valuable function by coming to the classroom and helping the child to practice work-oriented behaviors. Both mothers (and the teacher) indicated a willingness to try; it was agreed that the experiment would last only so long as required to produce a change in the behaviors. At such time, a token program handled by the teacher would be introduced and then gradually faded out.

In the token program the child was presented with a card listing the criterion behaviors, for example, "listened," "participated in group," "recited," "sat still and worked," "completed his assignment." At the end of some substantial period of time, for example, 20 or 30 minutes (or 60 minutes after the program has been in effect for some time) the teacher placed a mark next to those behaviors which characterized the child's performance.[2] Such token programs have been used with marked efficiency in controlling the behavior of groups of deviant children (Birnhauer, Bijou, Wolf, & Kidder, 1965; Haring & Hayden, 1966; Walker & Mattson, 1967).

The child brought his card home each night and the mother paid him his wages earned in M & M candies. The token program was continued for several weeks following the termination of the classroom conditioning procedures. The intervals gradually increased to where the child worked a full day before receiving his points.

The mothers arrived at the classroom, one at a time, shortly after recess. Immediately prior to the first session, the counselor had taken each of the boys to his office and introduced the child to the apparatus with instructions somewhat as follows:[3]

> You have been having a little trouble learning this year and I think it is mainly because you really haven't learned how to work. This is a "how-to-work-box" that will help you to practice working at your desk. Everytime you are able to sit still for a little while and really work, the box lights up and the counter clicks; the counter keeps score. Every time it clicks it means you have earned one M&M candy. Like this. Let's see you work for a minute and I'll show you.

The child was given a book to look at. After five seconds of steady attending to the book, the light flashed, the counter clicked, and one M & M was dropped into his cup.

> "That's it. Good. Now if you talk, look around the room, or walk around— anything like that—the box won't go off. O.K., go ahead let's practice some more."

[2] Editors' Note: A similar token program for "card carriers" is described by Sanborn and Schuster in Article 18.

[3] Editors' Note: A similar apparatus is described by Nixon in Article 25.

Each child was given a ten-minute adaptation period and earned approximately 20–30 M & M's for himself on a variable interval schedule ranging from five to 20 seconds.[4] He was then told that they would try the same thing in the classroom; he would earn candy both for himself and for the other children.

When the children had returned from recess they found the counselor and one of the mothers already seated. After she and the counselor had spent ten or fifteen minutes collecting observation data, the counselor made the following announcement to the class:

> George does not learn as much as he can because he has really not learned how to sit still and work. This is a "how-to-work-box" that will help him to practice working. When he sits still, and works, the light flashes up here like this (demonstrates) and the counter clicks. When that happens it means that George has earned one M&M candy. When he is all done working today, we will take all of the candy he earns and divide it up among all of you. If you want George to earn a lot of candy, then don't pay any attention to him if he acts silly, talks to you, or gets up out of his seat.[5] O.K.? Now George's mother is here to help him to learn to work. Now, let's see how much candy George can earn.

After the mother had observed the counselor using the apparatus for a few minutes she was given the control switch. Each session lasted from 15 to 25 minutes; there were three sessions for each child. The M & M candies earned ranged from 50 to 120. Following each session the announcement of the score was greeted with a good deal of interest and enthusiasm.

Effects

The observation data for the six categories were combined to form a single class of "academically inefficient" behaviors.[6] The rates described refer to the proportion of 15-second time intervals in which the deviant

---

[4] Editors' Note: After the child had been reinforced, an interval of time ranging from as few as five to as many as 20 seconds would have to elapse before he would be eligible for another reinforcement.

[5] Montrose Wolf (personal communication) has recently completed a study which demonstrated that involving the members of the peer group in this fashion accelerated the control over the child's behavior provided by the conditioning programs.

[6] Data from several studies have demonstrated that it is necessary to obtain 20-minute samplings of behavior over a period of several days before it can be assumed that a stable estimate has been obtained (Ebner, 1967; Krumboltz & Goodwin, 1966). The finding of wide day to day and hour by hour fluctuation in rates of social behavior is an extremely interesting finding. It suggests, for example, the importance of stimulus control (situational components) as a major determinant of the occurrence of social behaviors. Probably our future advances in understanding deviant and adaptive child behaviors will be in large part a function of our ability to conceptualize the problem of stimulus control.

behaviors were observed. A reduction of 50 to 70 percent in the occurrence of the deviant behavior took place when the training was in progress. However, the effect was considerably reduced two weeks later. At that time, the data showed only a 25 to 30 percent reduction from baseline levels in the occurrence of academically inefficient behaviors. However, even this seems like a substantial return for an investment of only five or six hours of the school counselor's time. Earlier studies required 10–15 conditioning sessions in order to produce changes of this magnitude.

Even such a modest reduction in the rate of deviant behaviors as reported in these data may produce a significant change in academic achievement as suggested by the teacher's reports several months after termination of the study. The teacher reported that immediately following termination of the project there was a good deal of fluctuation in classroom behavior. However, following this both boys seemed to be working very well. They were, for example, handing in assignments for the first time that year. Follow-up telephone calls in September of the following year indicated that both boys had been passed on to a combined first-second grade group and that they were performing well. The teacher of the class had not noted any particular problem during the first three weeks of school.

IDEAS FOR FURTHER STUDY

The data suggests that other investigators would probably find it reinforcing to proceed with the task of developing procedures for training mothers to work with their own children in the classroom. Hopefully, such replications would provide more stable estimates of classroom behavior and behavior changes. It would also be important to provide data which demonstrate the relation between these behaviors and academic achievement. Because of the implied claim that the mothers also use these procedures in their home, data should also be provided which investigate the possibility of such a "bonus effect."

As there is some interest in replicating this pilot study in our own laboratory, it might be helpful to list the alterations which are being proposed by members of our own group. In terms of efficiency it would seem that a larger group of parents might participate in the group sessions. These sessions should probably also include the fathers as they also provide an important source of reinforcement for the child. Probably it would also be wise to sequence the training program in a contingent fashion. For example, before the parents can be trained to observe they must first respond to the programmed book. Then before intervention procedures are introduced, require that the parent learn to observe his child. For example, each parent must bring in a tabulation of the frequency of occurrence of the deviant behaviors and both the occurrence of the (competing) adaptive responses and the contingencies supplied for these behaviors in the home. How often did the child say something negative, or something positive about school? What was the consequence supplied for these behaviors by members of the family? Such an observation schedule could be tailored for each child in each of the families. The parents must learn to first attend to these events and their contingencies before they can expect to alter them.

It is likely that such groups would be more effective if they contained parents whose children displayed somewhat similar problems. In constructing the groups in this fashion contingencies and programs provided for one child and one family would be more likely to transfer to affect the behavior of other members of the group.

It also seems likely that the teacher who co-operated in the present report was an unusually flexible and patient person. The school counselor who wishes to apply these procedures will undoubtedly find that he will first have to provide some training and support for the teachers who are to participate. Recently, there have been several such programs designed to train teachers in the use of behavior modification procedures. The initial results look very promising. (Lindsley, 1966; Krumboltz & Goodwin, 1966; Becker, Madson, Arnold, & Thomas, 1967.) Undoubtedly, it is the teacher and the parent who will determine the success of such a program. These are the two agents who will provide the social reinforcers necessary to maintain the academic-adaptive behavior "conditioned" by the mother in the classroom. Unless the social environment provides these kinds of support it is doubtful that the alterations in deviant behavior would persist more than a few days following the withdrawal of the systematic intervention. The eventual outcome of the program is a function of how effective the counselor is in training the parent and teacher to dispense social reinforcers.

PART III
Social Modeling Techniques

IMITATION PLAYS A CRUCIAL role in acquiring and regulating all kinds of social behavior. It is difficult to imagine how much of what we do and say could be learned without observing the behavior of others. Almost daily the young child demonstrates his powers of imitative learning—sometimes embarrassing his parents with a minor image of their behavior. The influence of social models consistently points out that "actions speak louder than words," that individuals, often inadvertently, do teach by example. Parents, for instance, do not teach courtesy and politeness to their children by shouting and screaming orders to be polite. A courteous example is far more eloquent and effective.

Social modeling is sometimes called imitative, vicarious, or observational learning. There are several theories of imitative learning. Some contend that the observer must actually exhibit the behavior observed and then be positively reinforced for matching the model's behavior. Other theories maintain that learning can occur simply by allowing the observer an opportunity to observe the model. Whether the observer will then behave as the model depends on a number of environmental circumstances, for example, the availability of reinforcement.

Counselors can deliberately make use of modeling procedures even though much remains to be learned about the process involved. Social modeling techniques have relevancy and promise for all problems confronting counselors. Often a "live picture is worth thousands of counselor words." Creating an opportunity for a client to observe the behavior of another person similar to himself, for example, can have dramatic results. Many times a client may understand his problem but

163

not know how to behave in new ways. The shy, withdrawn adolescent girl can learn new patterns of behavior by having an opportunity to observe others behave in outgoing, socially oriented ways. The overbearing antagonistic adult can acquire new behaviors by observing the socially appropriate behavior of others.

The counselor is in a position to deliberately and systematically develop and use social modeling techniques. Several questions, however, do arise for such a counselor. Which clients might be most effectively helped by using modeling techniques (observer characteristics)? How should a particular modeling technique be presented (mode of presentation)? What kind of model would be best (model characteristics)? With what problems would modeling techniques be most effective (situational factors)?

To date there is something known about each of these questions but much work needs to be done. Social models that are prestigious, competent, knowledgeable, attractive, and powerful should probably be selected. Further, there is some indication that clients may be more influenced when the social model they view is similar to them in some characteristics. However, it isn't clear which similarity characteristics are crucial. But counselors can find out what their clients consider admirable and prestigious and then choose models with these characteristics.

Modeling techniques, of course, can be presented in a variety of formats. The live model is probably the most familiar prototype. The counselor himself can deliberately use himself as a live social model to demonstrate certain behaviors to clients. Or peers of the client may be employed as models in small group settings. Live models do present one problem for the counselor. He has less control over the behavior of the model than he does with symbolic models. A person used in a small group setting as a model may not demonstrate the relevant behavior to the desired extent. The live model is also susceptible to being influenced by the observers and their responsiveness to him. These limitations, however, may be more than compensated for by the highly motivating and arousing effect of using a live social model. Symbolic models, by contrast, do offer the counselor a great deal of control in terms of timing, format, and content. A video-taped social model, for example, can be developed and refined in advance of its actual use in a counseling setting. A written manual or an audio tape can be created and evaluated to accomplish a specific goal. Clients can be exposed to such a model more than once at strategic points in counseling. Furthermore, relationship factors between counselor and client may not be impaired using a symbolic procedure.

The consequences of the model's behavior for the model are crucial. Television commercials exploit this fact. The male model with but a dab of the right hair dressing wins the beautiful girl. The model who demonstrates that what he does produces negative consequences for himself is much less likely to be imitated. If the observer is to imitate the model, he must see the model benefit from the desired activity.

Part III offers a variety of articles describing the use of live and symbolic models. These articles offer encouraging results and raise interesting questions. Should modeling techniques be used in combination with other procedures such as reinforcement or cognitive techniques? Which types of clients with which kinds of problems are most effectively helped with which kinds of modeling techniques? Interested counselors have much work to do in making real the promise of social modeling techniques.

Live Models

MANY COUNSELORS HAVE TRIED to behave as "living examples" for their clients. Parents, too, have often been admonished to practice what they preach. Teachers have been encouraged to teach by example. A good teacher teaches citizenship behavior by handling certain classroom problems by means of "democratic" methods. Pointing out the exemplary behavior of others is a common practice usually accompanied by the admonishment, "Why don't you do it like that?" or "If you could only behave like him."

Often such efforts go awry because of the sometimes inadvertent and unsystematic use of such models. Live models can be an extremely influential way of providing individuals with examples of how to behave in complex situations. Social conversation skills, for example, may be effectively learned by observation. Effective interpersonal behaviors are sometimes best learned through observational experiences with live social models.

Counselors, as well as teachers and parents, can deliberately employ live modeling techniques to demonstrate behaviors. And counselors need not continue to think of themselves as live models to the exclusion of using others in the client's environment. Many times the behavior of a peer or another adult is far more appropriate to the client's problem than that of the counselor himself.

Some problems, however, arise in using live modeling techniques. One problem discussed earlier is the difficulty of exercising control over just what behaviors are modeled. Sometimes, for example, the counselor himself acts in a way that in retrospect he wished he had not. Another problem is that a live modeling experience can be overwhelming for the client. The client as an observer may be presented with too many cues at one time, or the client may be attending to irrelevant cues. Whether or not live models should be used instead of symbolic procedures remains essentially an empirical question.

Ritter, in Article 21, demonstrates how a counselor can serve as a live model in the client's environment rather than in the counseling office. Working with a middle-aged, extremely anxious woman, the counselor served as a model in demonstrating relevant behaviors. Immediately following these demonstrations the client rehearsed what was just observed. Much of the counseling took place in the client's everyday environment, her home and the neighboring streets.

In Article 22 Sarason and Ganzer describe a project in which live, college-age male models were used to demonstrate a variety of behaviors to high-school-age juvenile delinquents. A number of concrete situations such as how to act during an interview for a job, how to interact with a policeman, how to carry on a friendly social conversation, and how to handle a hostile and argumentative father were presented in small group situations by two live models. A great deal of attention was given to selecting models, writing scripts, and rehearsing.

Stilwell, in Article 23, describes his successful use of peers as live models for an autistic boy. These peers, in demonstrating how to play and to verbally interact, were instrumental in helping the client reduce his isolated, extremely withdrawn behavior.

In all of these articles live modeling was combined with other techniques such as positive reinforcement and simulation in helping clients. Many questions arise about specifics of employing live modeling procedures. Answers to such questions will begin to emerge from efforts by counselors to use live modeling in their work.

21

ELIMINATING EXCESSIVE FEARS OF THE ENVIRONMENT THROUGH CONTACT DESENSITIZATION

Brunhilde Ritter
STANFORD UNIVERSITY

This report describes the use of a new counseling procedure called contact desensitization (CD). This technique was initially devised for treating a college undergraduate biology student (Ritter, 1965) who suffered from an extreme fear of dissecting animals. The effectiveness of group contact desensitization (Ritter, 1968a, 1968b, in press) as well as individual contact desensitization (Bandura, Blanchard, & Ritter, 1968; Ritter, 1968c) has been experimentally demonstrated with both snake-avoidant and acrophobic subjects.[1] The foregoing studies, in which preadolescent, adolescent, and adult populations were treated, indicate that the contact desensitization procedure is suitable for use with a wide age range.

When using *in vivo* contact desensitization, the counselor acts as a live social model in the presence of the client. In addition to demonstrating (modeling) certain relevant behaviors, the counselor uses physical contact with the client while shaping his performance. For example, in the initial case (Ritter, 1965) involving the biology student, the counselor at one point had the student place her hand on the counselor's while a dissection was carried out. Coupled with actual demonstrations of appropriate behavior and guided practice the counselor also makes use of nonverbal and verbal positive reinforcers such as smiling, nodding, "fine," and "very good."

The primary steps in contact desensitization are as follows:

1. Modeling or demonstrating behaviors by the counselor which the counselee and counselor have mutually decided are relevant to the problem.

[1] Editors' Note: In the Bandura, Blanchard, and Ritter (1968) study, contact desensitization was compared with two other treatments, systematic desensitization (see Emery, Article 31) and symbolic modeling via a film. Live modeling by the counselor coupled with guided practice involving physical contact (contact desensitization) was found to be significantly more effective and efficient.

2. Assisting the client in repeating the behavior which has been modeled by using behavioral prompts such as placing the client's hand on the counselor's while the counselor touches a feared object or holding the client's arm while walking in a crowded area.
3. Gradual fading out of counselor prompts with a concomitant fading in of independent behavioral rehearsal by the client.

The client is introduced to the least difficult behavior at the preliminary stages of treatment and gradually more difficult responses are shaped as proficiency in the less demanding ones develops.

The relative contributions of the three main components of contact desensitization, that is, demonstration, counselor-contact, and client participation, have been investigated. Results indicated the following: (1) that treatment which includes all three elements is significantly more effective than a procedure in which the counselor demonstrates and then guides the client's participation without using physical contact (Ritter 1968c, in press); and (2) that both the foregoing treatments are superior to demonstration alone (Ritter, 1968c).

The following case illustrates the use of contact desensitization.

MRS. SLOAN AND HER FEAR OF STREETS

Mrs. Sloan was a 49-year-old widow whose fear of street-crossing began approximately ten years ago. She reported that "it came upon me gradually" about a year following the death of her husband. At first she noted that she found herself "clutching" her companions when attempting to cross a busy street. Eventually she became physically unable to step off a curb when alone and thereafter it became impossible for her to cross streets independently. Street-crossing was also extremely difficult and aversive when she was being assisted. Mrs. S. stated that in time the phobia resulted in her withdrawing almost completely from employment, recreational, and community service activities. She wrote that she avoided the foregoing because she was continually fearful a situation would occur in which street-crossing would become a necessity and that her phobia would then become apparent. When attending the few activities in which she had maintained participation, Mrs. S. made great efforts to park at a location which made street-crossing unnecessary. On occasions when this was not possible she was forced to hire a cab to transport her across any intervening streets.

Mrs. S. had been receiving various forms of both individual and group psychotherapy during the ten-year duration of the street-crossing phobia. Mrs. S. wrote that none of the insights she gained during therapy had assisted her in overcoming this fear. Shortly before the onset of contact desensitization treatment Mrs. S. was hospitalized following the consumption of an overdose of sleeping medication. She reported that "despair" resulting from her inability to overcome the street-crossing inhibition motivated this event. Mrs. S. had made three previous suicidal attempts. These had also led to hospitalization.

Because of the target phobia's intensity and the severe restrictions it was placing on Mrs. S.'s life, it was decided to deviate from a conventional once or twice weekly treatment routine. Instead, almost daily sessions were scheduled at the beginning of counseling and a gradual lengthening of the interval between sessions followed.

The First Session

The counselor began treatment at Mrs. S.'s residence for the first six sessions. These arrangements were made both because of Mrs. S.'s limited mobility and the counselor's desire to begin treatment at the location in which it was of major importance to increase this mobility, that is, the area around Mrs. S.'s residence. From the seventh session on Mrs. S. met the therapist at her office, or other designated location, except when treatment plans made it more convenient to meet at Mrs. S.'s home.

At the beginning of the first session the counselor informed Mrs. S. that the approach to be used was essentially nonintellectual. Mrs. S. was told that no attempts would be made to discover how or why her fear had developed but, rather, that all efforts would be focused on eliminating the fear.[2]

A discussion of counseling goals took place. First, a number of streets in Mrs. S.'s immediate neighborhood were selected as treatment streets. They were ranked according to difficulty. Then in an effort to maximize the practical and incentive value of the treatment, Mrs. S. was asked to list the locations of activities she would like to participate in but avoided because of her fear. Arrangements were made to plan walking tours around these locations in the future.

The initial desensitization session was subsequently held in an area adjacent to Mrs. S.'s home. A low traffic location in which a narrow street intersected with a moderately wide street was chosen. The counselor walked across the narrow street for about one minute while Mrs. S. watched. Then the counselor firmly placed her arm around Mrs. S.'s waist and walked across with her.[3] This was repeated a number of times until

---

[2] Editors' Note: In general, a primary characteristic of a behavioral approach is this prime attention to altering the behavior in question rather than a chief concern for the history and speculative interpretations about the problem.

[3] Editors' Note: Contact desensitization is illustrated here. First, the counselor models the appropriate behavior and then assists the client, using physical contact, to practice the behavior just observed.

Mrs. S. reported she was fairly comfortable at performing the task. (It is often not necessary to wait until a client is completely relaxed before moving on to the next step in a CD counseling program. Earlier tasks are frequently repeated during the course of treatment; opportunities are then presented for further desensitization. Often upon moving back to the earlier task, after work with a more difficult one, no anxiety is experienced on the first reattempt of the easier response.) Street-crossing was then continued while the physical contact between counselor and Mrs. S. was gradually reduced until the counselor only lightly touched the back of Mrs. S.'s arm as she walked slightly behind her. Contact was then eliminated completely with the counselor first walking alongside Mrs. S. as the street was crossed and then slightly behind her. The counselor subsequently followed Mrs. S. approximately three-fourths of the way across the street and allowed her to go the remaining distance alone. Gradually the counselor reduced the distance she accompanied Mrs. S. until eventually Mrs. S. was able to cross the street entirely alone.

At this point in the treatment program whenever Mrs. S. had successfully crossed independently, the counselor subsequently also crossed the street. The foregoing sequence was then repeated from the opposite corner, that is, Mrs. S. crossed while the counselor watched; then the counselor crossed.

After several repetitions the counselor deviated from the pattern by not following Mrs. S. after she had successfully crossed. Instead, she waited at the starting position while Mrs. S. stood across the street and asked Mrs. S. to cross again independently. Mrs. S. attempted this but after a few steps into the road returned to the curb stating she could not accomplish the task. The counselor therefore shaped "returning to the starting position" (SP) as follows: The counselor left SP and walked approximately three-fourths of the way across the street toward Mrs. S.; she then asked Mrs. S. to walk to her which she did. The counselor accompanied her back to SP while supporting her arm. This additional physical contact was provided in an attempt to dissipate any anxiety which may have been aroused by Mrs. S.'s recent inability to perform the counselor's request. This step was repeated with no physical contact. Next, the counselor walked to the middle of the street, waited for Mrs. S. to come to her and accompanied her back to SP—again without physical contact. The distance the counselor required Mrs. S. to walk unaccompanied was gradually increased until Mrs. S. was able to cross the street two ways independently with the counselor remaining at SP. In order to facilitate two-way independent street-crossing, both corners were used as starting positions during this phase of treatment. After approximately 21 minutes of treatment, Mrs. S. was able to perform two-way unaccompanied street crossing starting from either corner with moderate ease.

Mrs. S. was still somewhat apprehensive when cars were attempting to make turns into the street while she was crossing.

Since there were no traffic lights at this intersection, the wider street at this location was not considered a suitable treatment site. Therefore, desensitization was continued at a broad and more heavily trafficked intersection where there was a traffic light. Again the counselor demonstrated crossing first. Then Mrs. S. and the counselor crossed the street a number of times with Mrs. S.'s arm being supported by the counselor. Following this, the counselor and Mrs. S. walked across the street along side each other but with no physical contact. After a little more than 30 minutes the first session was terminated.

Next Few Sessions

The basic procedure followed in session one was repeated with increasingly wider and more heavily trafficked intersections during succeeding sessions. Each session was begun with a task Mrs. S. was able to accomplish with relative ease during the preceding meeting. Sessions were scheduled at varying times to insure opportunities for evening as well as daylight desensitization. In the course of treatment Mrs. S. frequently mentioned that contact with the counselor was very reassuring. To use the reinforcement value of counselor contact for goal achievement, the counselor occasionally rewarded independent performance with contact when contact as a behavioral prompt had been withdrawn. For example, when Mrs. S. successfully crossed a difficult intersection independently, the counselor accompanied a verbal congratulation with an arm around Mrs. S.'s waist or a pat on the arm. Cigarette breaks after a subgoal had been achieved were also used as reinforcers.

Changing Procedures and Achieving a Goal

At the outset of the sixth session the headquarters of a community service group to which Mrs. S. wished to donate volunteer services but avoided because of its location was selected as a goal. The service group was situated in the main shopping area of Mrs. S.'s community. A tour was mapped out beginning at a parking lot which necessitated crossing several streets.

At this point the counselor was not using modeling or physical contact as a preliminary step in promoting street-crossing at new locations (the exception to this was when Mrs. S. needed help with a particular street). The counselor instead was merely walking alongside her. Initially the counselor and Mrs. S. walked the length of the tour to the service group building and back to the parking lot side-by-side with no physical contact.

This tour was repeated with the counselor waiting at each street corner until she crossed alone. The counselor subsequently followed. Then Mrs. S. completed the last part of the tour which required crossing three streets—all of which could be seen from one observation point. The counselor remained at this location as she walked to the target point and back alone. The counselor then went into a building where she could observe Mrs. S. but could not be seen herself. Mrs. S. repeated her walk. This event marked the first time Mrs. S. had crossed any streets alone without having the counselor in view. The experience represented a very reinforcing occasion for both members of the walking team! A few days later she traveled to the headquarters by herself in order to volunteer her services. She reported being only slightly apprehensive when crossing the necessary streets.[4]

Establishing and Achieving Specific Goals

At the ninth session terminal goals were discussed. The counselor and Mrs. S. decided on four goals, which were referred to as two "tour" goals and two "site" goals. Tour One goal involved crossing 15 streets of varying widths in the vicinity of Mrs. S.'s residence. Tour Two goal required crossing eight streets in the main shopping area of the community. Site One and Two were both located at busy intersections. Mrs. S. was to walk successively to each of the four corners of the intersections thereby crossing four streets before returning to the starting point. A goal was to be considered successfully completed when two successive performances were achieved without the counselor being in view. Both performances were not to occur on the same day.[5]

After this discussion Tour One was begun. The counselor crossed the first three streets with Mrs. S. with no physical contact. Thereafter, the counselor waited at each corner until Mrs. S. had crossed first. Forty-eight minutes were required to complete the tour.

Working toward a Second Goal—"Site One"

During the same session the counselor and Mrs. S. drove to the location of Site One. A corner was selected as a starting point. The counselor and Mrs. S. walked through the four corners of the intersection together with

---

[4] Editors' Note: Notice how the counselor had the client successively practice, with positive results each time in the relevant real-life setting, closer and closer approximations to the goal behavior and how the counselor literally faded out of the situation, leaving the client to perform successfully alone.

[5] Editors' Note: By specifying the objectives of the counseling in this way both the counselor and client know clearly where they are going and when they have arrived. How to get there also tends to be clarified and facilitated.

no physical contact. Mrs. S. was then asked to attempt the four crossings herself. She was somewhat apprehensive and feared she might become frightened while attempting to complete the circuit and would therefore be unable to return to starting point. The counselor suggested that Mrs. S. signal with a slight arm movement if she became too anxious to continue at any point. It was agreed that at the signal the counselor would come to Mrs. S.'s assistance. The hand signaling arrangements allayed Mrs. S.'s fears and she proceeded to cross the intersection. When Mrs. S. reached the corner which was diagonally opposite SP, she signaled. The counselor crossed over to Mrs. S. as prearranged.

Mrs. S. began voicing dejection over her inability to complete the task and her consequent feelings of failure. The counselor halted this recitation since she did not wish to reinforce what was considered nonproductive self-criticism. The counselor mentioned that this failure was no cause for self-criticism and that energy which would be used in self-deprecation could be more productively expended in further street-crossing practice.[6] The counselor suggested that Mrs. S. continue transversing only two of the four crossings until these could be managed comfortably. After the half circuit was repeated two times, Mrs. S. again attempted a complete circuit and succeeded. The session terminated with Mrs. S. having moved closer to her goal: two independent crossings on separate days without the counselor in view.

ACCOMPLISHING "TOUR TWO"

Session 10 was begun at Tour Two. On the first trial the counselor accompanied Mrs. S. but waited at each street corner and allowed her to cross alone. On the second trial the counselor waited at the parking lot starting point while Mrs. S. completed the tour independently. The counselor and Mrs. S. then drove to Site Two. The counselor asked Mrs. S. if she felt she could cross the intersection four ways on the first attempt. She said she would try; and she succeeded. The counselor then went into a shop several yards away which allowed her to observe Mrs. S. without being visible herself. Mrs. S. was again successful in performing the four-way crossing.

Session 11 was also begun at the location of Tour Two. For the second time the counselor waited at the parking lot starting point while Mrs. S. completed the arranged walk; once again she was successful. The Tour Two goal was thus achieved.

---

[6] Editors' Note: A good point. Often counselors inadvertently encourage negative feelings and depressing thoughts in their efforts to be empathic and understanding of what clients say.

REQUIRING THE CLIENT TO BE MORE RESPONSIBLE

The intersection at Site Two was subsequently reattempted during Session 11. The counselor went into the shop which provided one-way viewing while Mrs. S. proceeded to the designated intersection. Shortly thereafter Mrs. S. joined the counselor and stated that while attempting to cross the intersection she had become frightened. She was certain she couldn't perform the task independently and again felt like a failure. She simply could not believe she had actually crossed the intersection alone. Further, she pointed out that when she first began treatment she had no intention of trying to learn to cross major intersections. She was quite satisfied with lesser goals and wanted to give up on this task.

The counselor reminded Mrs. S. that they had in effect made a contract when goals were mutually set up during the previous session. It was pointed out that fulfillment of this contract was the responsibility of both members involved. If Mrs. S. had not had a ten-year history of involvement in therapy and had not given evidence of extreme dependency in her other relationships, the counselor would have now assumed responsibility for directly helping her handle Site Two. However, the counselor felt it was important to shift the major control of the therapeutic program to Mrs. S. at this point in order to facilitate the fading out of therapist support. She had become familiar with the procedures being employed and had made considerable progress. It was the counselor's judgment that Mrs. S. could now design her own program.[7]

The counselor therefore told Mrs. S. that she would have to decide whether or not she wished to break the contract. She could do so thereby terminating the therapeutic program. The counselor additionally pointed out that she had made considerable progress, was familiar with the procedures, and could devise her own treatment plan. It was made clear that Mrs. S. could determine the amount of treatment time required and that assistance from the counselor would be available when necessary.

Mrs. S. was told that she would essentially be taking on the role of the counselor while the counselor would take on the role of consultant and assistant. Mrs. S. was asked to think about the alternatives and let the counselor know what her choice was the following day by phone. The counselor suggested that before the present session was terminated Mrs. S. again go to the intersection and try to do as much as she could, even if it was just to step off the curb.

She left but returned in a few minutes stating she had not made any

[7] Editors' Note: Too often counselors fail to "teach" their clients how to design strategies to change their own problem behaviors.

progress. The counselor said that she was only expected to do her best and was pleased that she had tried again. The counselor concluded by saying that she would await her decision. As requested, Mrs. S. telephoned the counselor on the following day. She stated that she was again in a state of despair, that she felt everything was lost, and that she had failed. Upon the counselor's inquiry she replied that she had not been able to make any steps toward planning a counseling program.

TAKING THE RESPONSIBILITY AND BEING SUCCESSFUL

The counselor suggested that as a first step in her treatment plan she might map out a tour which included some streets she could already cross comfortably and some untried streets.[8] Mrs. S. accepted this recommendation. Finally, the counselor asked her to keep careful records of activities because this information would be useful to her in future planning. She also asked Mrs. S. to report how things went via a telephone call that evening. The phone call revealed that her despair had been dispelled and that she had managed to cross some moderately wide streets which she had never crossed previously. The counselor expressed her approval and suggested that Mrs. S. continue her efforts. She also suggested that Mrs. S. repeat Tour One. A telephone call from Mrs. S. indicated that she had followed the latter suggestion. Mrs. S. also proposed a plan which required the counselor's assistance at an intersection similar in difficulty to Site Two.

The counselor and Mrs. S. met at this intersection for Session 12. The counselor reminded Mrs. S. that she was to determine how long she wished her assistance. She accompanied Mrs. S. (without contact) during street-crossing for approximately ten minutes. Mrs. S. then decided to begin independent crossing and continued this for another ten minutes. Next, the counselor and Mrs. S. went to the Site Two location where Mrs. S. successfully achieved independent four-way crossing on the first attempt. At this session Tour One was completed independently without the counselor in view. This marked the achievement of terminal behavior on another goal. At the close of the session the counselor asked Mrs. S. to continue practicing and to develop a plan for achieving the Site One goal.

Mrs. S. continued to make telephone reports of her practice activities. During one of these calls she suggested that Site One practice begin with the counselor accompanying her. The counselor said, speaking as a consultant, she would advise working at an intersection somewhat less diffi-

---

[8] Editors' Note: The counselor deliberately did not make reflective and "empathic" responses here to avoid reinforcing and encouraging the client's feelings and thoughts of failure. Instead, the counselor suggested a goal-relevant behavior.

cult than Site One as a preliminary goal. She added that since Mrs. S. previously could not believe she had performed independently at this site after doing so and had difficulty imagining herself being able to repeat this success, it might be more meaningful and convincing if she mastered that particular site herself. Mrs. S. agreed somewhat reluctantly.

On the thirteenth session the counselor merely observed while Mrs. S. made eight independent crossings at the practice intersection she had chosen. Mrs. S. then stated she was ready to attempt Site One independently while the counselor was in view. The counselor observed 28 crossings before Mrs. S. indicated she was ready to attempt four-way transversing without the counselor in view. She was successful but commented that while she was now beginning to believe that she was actually able to make the crossing, it was still quite difficult for her. Work was therefore continued. The counselor observed Mrs. S. make twelve additional crossings. Thereafter she again crossed four ways with the counselor not in sight. However, since both performances at Site One occurred in the same day, this did not represent goal achievement. During the final session terminal behavior at both sites was repeated. The final two goals were achieved.

TO CONCLUDE

The counseling described above extended over a period of 47 days. During this interval Mrs. Sloan's street-crossing inhibition was successfully treated in terms of the goals jointly set by the client and counselor. It may be that with clients as pervasively fearful as Mrs. Sloan, combining deep muscle relaxation training with contact desensitization would accelerate progress.[9]

Information from investigations such as those previously cited in which the relative efficacy of components of contact desensitization were studied, and from reports on the therapeutic use of demonstration alone and demonstration combined with reinforcement (for example, Jones, 1924a; Sherman, 1965; Wilson and Walters, 1966; Bandura, Grusec, & Menlove, 1967; Bandura & Menlove, 1968; Ritter, 1968c), should be helpful in adapting contact desensitization to the treatment of problems involving deficit and avoidance behaviors.[10] The theoretical discussion

[9] Editors' Note: The potential applications of contact desensitization procedures to counseling problems are many. Problems involving excessive interpersonal anxiety and stress, for example, might be effectively treated by variations of this procedure.

[10] Editors' Note: Blanchard (1968) for example, recently found that live modeling coupled with physical contact and client participation was generally most effective in reducing snake phobias. For some subjects, however, modeling alone (demonstration) was quite effective. The question arises as to which types of clients are best helped with what combinations of treatment.

by Sheffield (1961) of learning from demonstration and practice is also relevant.

In order to explore the clinical application of contact desensitization further, Mrs. Sloan's fear of criticism will be treated with contact desensitization procedures. Currently a follow-up study is under way to assess the stability of Mrs. Sloan's behavioral changes.[11]

22

DEVELOPING APPROPRIATE SOCIAL BEHAVIORS OF JUVENILE DELINQUENTS[1]

Irwin G. Sarason and Victor J. Ganzer
UNIVERSITY OF WASHINGTON

We will describe briefly the rationale, development, and procedures employed in a current research and demonstration project concerning the rehabilitation of the male juvenile offender. The project has not yet been completed. However, we do have some preliminary data, and our approach to the problem and the procedures employed are sufficiently well defined to permit description.[2]

This research is an outgrowth of social learning theory and research dealing with the processes of observational learning, and of sociological

[11] Editors' Note: It will also be interesting to find out how Mrs. Sloan's newly acquired behavior in now being able to travel about more freely will influence her behavior in other areas of daily living.

[1] This research has been supported by grants from the Social and Rehabilitation Service, the National Science Foundation, and the National Institute of Mental Health.

Robert Tropp, Supervisor of Institutional Services; Superintendent William Callahan and Assistant Superintendent James Gibbons of Cascadia Juvenile Reception-Diagnostic Center; and Cottage supervisors Lawrence Castleman and John Sanguinetti and their staffs have contributed importantly to the conduct of the research reported in this paper.

The cooperation and consultation of staff psychologists, Sarah Sloat, Theodore Sterling, and V. M. Tye is gratefully acknowledged.

The following assistants have contributed importantly to this research: David Barrett, Peter Carlson, Duane Dahlum, Douglas Denney, Richard Erickson, Robert Howenstine, Robert Kirk, David Snow.

[2] Editors' Note: See Sarason (1968) for a more complete report of the rationale and development of this project.

and clinical evidence relating to the behavior of crime and delinquency. Our present work with delinquents is also related to work on the relationship between anxiety and observational learning.

OBSERVATIONAL LEARNING AND DELINQUENCY

Delinquency is clearly an enormous social problem. The social and vocational behavior of delinquents is a major part of that problem. The basic question is how to change certain behaviors of delinquents. Delinquency need not be viewed in terms of a "mental illness" conception. An assumption underlying our research is that much of juvenile delinquency may be seen as a reflection of inadequate learning experiences. The delinquent is someone who has fallen out of the mainstream of his culture. He is someone who is deficient in socially acceptable and adaptive behaviors. His deviant behavior may be viewed as part of a rebellion against societal norms and as a failure to have acquired socially useful ways of responding. Much of this failure may be due to inadequate opportunities to observe and display socially useful behavior. This interpretation is consistent with empirical evidence (Bandura & Walters, 1963), sociological theories, such as those dealing with differential association (Sutherland, 1955), and clinical observations.

In this project, adolescent delinquent boys are being provided opportunities to observe special modeling situations. These situations emphasize concern with (1) vocational planning, (2) motivations and interests, (3) attitudes toward work and education, and (4) the utility of socially appropriate behavior. A major aim of this project is to demonstrate that when juvenile delinquents are given an opportunity to observe socially acceptable behavior in healthy, accepting persons, and also to imitate this type of behavior, a strengthening of planning ability together with an increased likelihood for socially acceptable responses will occur. The strengthening of both planning ability and the tendency to think in socially positive terms are viewed by us as building blocks upon which realistic social and vocational development can be based.

The justification for focusing on modeling effects in the vocational-educational area is that this area is so crucial to the development of the teenager. Some persons may profit ultimately from lengthy introspection and theorizing about the multiple ramifications of having had certain types of interpersonal experiences. But for the juvenile delinquent, insight-oriented exploration may be completely impractical. Unless he can find a useful and satisfying niche for himself within complex modern society, attempts to modify his behavior in broad, nonvocational areas may, in all likelihood, come to naught. What can be done to direct the young offender onto a socially appropriate vocational course? While this project is not aimed at training these youngsters to perform particular types of jobs, it is hoped that its procedure will contribute significantly in providing a healthy impetus for their vocational and concomitant social and educational development.

Cascadia

Cascadia is part of the Division of Juvenile Rehabilitation of the State of Washington Department of Institutions. The center, located in Tacoma, serves all delinquent children between the ages of eight and 18 who are committed to the Department of Institutions by the juvenile courts. Children are admitted directly to Cascadia. The length of stay is approximately six weeks for new commitments and about three weeks for parole violators and recommitments.

A diagnostic formulation of each child's problem is carried out as follows: psychologists administer a selected battery of psychological tests; caseworkers interview each child and combine this information with other material, such as the juvenile court worker's report, into a psychiatric social history; teachers test each child to determine his level of academic achievement and report on his classroom behavior and attitudes; cottage counselors and recreation leaders report their observations of behavior; a psychiatric examination is given in selected cases; a regular medical examination is conducted shortly after admission and reported for inclusion in the case file; and the chaplain reports on religious background and attitudes.[3]

Cascadia's nine cottages are each staffed by a Supervising Group Life Counselor, Assistant Supervisor, and four staff counselors. Each cottage houses 20 to 25 children. Six persons staff each cottage in shifts around the clock. Two of the cottages serve as the location of the project. The population of these cottages consists primarily of male first offenders, aged 15 to 18 years.

Training the Social Models and Developing Procedures

Two ingredients were needed for modeling opportunities to be effective: (1) an objectively describable modeling situation and (2) good rapport between models and subjects—the models must be liked by the subjects and must be persons with whom boys would want to identify. Early preliminary studies led us to the conclusion that, while the models

[3] Editors' Note: A question which might be asked is whether all this psychological testing actually results in significant improvements in the problem behaviors of the delinquent boys.

should interact informally with subjects of Cascadia's cottages, modeling sessions should be clearly labeled and easily identified situations. We have spent much time working on these situations and training our research assistants to be effective models and empathic reinforcing individuals.

The four clinical psychology graduate students who were initially to serve as the models began preliminary work on the project by meeting informally with groups of boys in order to get generally acquainted.

The series of informal chats that were conducted over a period of several weeks were tape recorded. The focus of the discussions, in which two of the models participated, was generally on the boys' problems, their perceptions of the adult and peer world, their needs, desires and goals, and their feelings about themselves and their identities in general. We spent considerable time listening to these tapes in order to make a rough content analysis of major problem and interest areas as discussed by the boys. These areas were noted and subsequent groups of boys were asked to spontaneously role-play some of the problems. For example, the problem that teen-agers have in dealing with authoritarian adults served as one topic around which spontaneous role-playing behavior was elicited. That is, one boy or one of the assistants would play the role of an authoritarian teacher and another boy would act the role of a teen-ager who was being disciplined by the teacher, or two boys would role-play a dialogue in which one boy tried to convince the other not to experiment with narcotics. These and many other areas of importance to adolescents were also tape recorded. Further study of the boys' spontaneous behavior in these situations resulted in a series of revised and expanded dialogues which were typed up in script form, not unlike the scripts used by actors when learning various parts for plays or movies. Depending upon the content and situations, the roles included in these scripts were written out containing "parts" for two to four people.

To date we have developed from 16 to 20 of these scripts which may be roughly categorized into three or four content areas.[4] Some deal with the problems teen-agers have in coping with authority, which involve various aspects of the control of impulsive behavior. For example, we have a script dealing with how to appropriately interact with police officers, and another concerning the question of how to behave during a job interview. A related area concerns the importance of planning ahead, a behavior in which delinquent youths are notoriously deficient. Other areas of importance concern the problem of negative peer pressure, how to recognize it, what it means, and various ways to cope with it. Another general topic has been that of making a good impression, not in the sense

[4] Editors' Note: Copies of these scripts are available from the authors, Department of Psychology, University of Washington, Seattle, Washington 98105.

of "conning" somebody or manipulating, but concerned with various aspects of dealing with others in a positive sociable manner.

The four models practiced and repracticed the various roles included in these scripts. These practice efforts were tape recorded, replayed, and the behavior of the models as well as the content of the scenes were further modified through discussion. Most of the scripts were actually tried out, using the boys as an audience. Their reactions to and opinions of the material regarding its realism and appropriateness were obtained. It was during this time that we became increasingly aware of several common problems which other authors have noted as being particularly characteristic of delinquent youth. These problems generally concerned the boys' motivations to work in groups and their often very poor attention span. An obvious prerequisite for learning via the direct observation of a model's behavior involves these two important variables.

We initially estimated that the boys' general level of attention could be maintained for approximately 20 to 30 minutes. We then instituted several procedures to maintain better control of this short and fluctuating attention span. One "gimmick" which evolved was the provision of a soft drink for each boy about midway through a one-hour session. While initially perceived as a "bribe" by many of the boys, the soft drinks were soon readily accepted as something that the group leaders wanted to share with them.

Another, and perhaps the most important method of maintaining attention, is the actual amount of physical activity which the modeling situations require. Rather than sitting passively in a chair, the models and boys are on their feet and actually moving about the room a great deal during the session. This physical activity, combined with the heavy emphasis on affect and nonverbal expressive gestures, has done a great deal to facilitate motivation and attention to the content and purpose of the dialogues as used in the groups. Since many delinquent boys are primarily action- and movement-oriented, and rely considerably less on verbal skills, the nonverbal focus has proved to be very important.[5] The third procedure for maintaining interest has been the replay of the audio tapes in the groups after the boys have played the various roles. This "feedback" has proved to be of considerable interest to the boys since it affords them the opportunity to actually hear and correct elements of their own behavior. A fourth procedure of maintaining attention has been to ask one of the boys in the group to summarize what has gone on in the scene or situation that has just been enacted. Since the boys do not know beforehand who is going to be asked, it is necessary for them to be very attentive during the sessions in order to answer the questions satisfac-

[5] Editors' Note: It is for this reason that many efforts to use "traditional" counseling groups, that is, verbal interaction exclusively, with atypical students have failed.

torily. Similarly, the fact that each boy knows that he is expected to imitate the model's behavior promotes increased attentiveness. It is estimated that our current procedures are able to hold the boys' attention and interest for an hour or more.

New models have been added to our staff. First, they were given an orientation concerning the purposes and procedures followed in the groups. Then they had the opportunity to read over and begin memorizing the existing scripts. Concurrently, they were engaged in the writing of new scenes and practicing the various roles themselves. They were also able to observe several group sessions conducted by the experienced models from behind a one-way mirror in the group rooms. Finally, a new model would then begin working with an experienced model in the groups themselves. In general, the experienced model's behavior in itself served as an effective model on which the new model's behavior could be based.

The introduction of closed-circuit television equipment as a technical aid has had considerable impact, both with respect to increasing the sensitivity and self-awareness of the models as well as its probable effect on the subjects. The models video-taped all of their role-playing sessions just as they had been doing them in the groups. These tapes were then watched and evaluated by the models and staff, especially with regard to affective and expressive behavior. From observations of the tapes it was possible to point out to the models some of their habitual behaviors which were then either eliminated or emphasized in order to maximize their effectiveness in the group. It was felt that this immediate audio-visual feedback provided a much clearer objective picture of the model's behavior as it was seen by the boys.

THE ORIENTATION SESSION

In all of our work with delinquent boys we have tried to foster a practical, problem-solving atmosphere. The following is an excerpt taken from the first day's orientation given to experimental subjects.

"First, let's all introduce ourselves, starting with me. I'm Mr. _____ and this is Mr. _____ (boys introduce themselves). We are working with small groups of boys here at Cascadia. We are doing something new to show you some different ways of handling common situations and problems that will happen in your lives. The situations we'll work with and emphasize are often particularly important for fellows like yourselves. We say this because just the fact that you're going through an institution will have important effects on your lives, and we want to work with you to teach you better ways of handling some of these effects. In other words, we want to work together with you to teach you new ways to handle problem situations. These are situations which we feel will be of importance to you in the future. They are things that probably all of you will run into from time to time and we think that you can benefit from learning and practicing different ways to act in these situations.[6]

"The way we want to do this isn't by lecturing or advising you. Having people watch others doing things and then discussing what has been done is a very important way and a useful way to learn. It is easy to learn how to do something just by observing someone else doing it first. Often times, just explaining something to someone isn't nearly as effective as actually doing it first while the other person watches. For example, it is easier to learn to swim, or repair a car if you have a chance to watch someone else doing it first.

"We think that small groups, working together, can learn a lot about appropriate ways of doing things just by playing different roles and watching others play roles. By role, we mean the particular part a person acts or plays in a particular situation—kind of like the parts actors play in a movie scene, only this will be more realistic. These roles will be based on actual situations that many young people have trouble with, like how to control your anger, or resist being pressured into doing destructive things by friends. Other roles are directly related to fellows like yourselves who have been in an institution. These are situations such as your review board, or the ways you can best use the special skills of your parole counselor to help you after you leave here. Things like this are things that not everyone can do well. We want to emphasize better ways of doing these things and coping with similar problems which will be important in the future for most of you. Everyone in the group will both play the roles for themselves and watch others playing the same roles. This is like acting, only it is realistic because it involves situations in which you might really find yourselves. We feel that the situations are realistic because they are based on the real experiences of a lot of fellows who have gone through Cascadia.

"There are seven of us here at Cascadia who are working in these small groups. We are not on the Cascadia staff. We are here because we are interested in working with fellows like yourselves and in helping you improve your skills in how you approach the situations I've just described. Since we are not on the Cascadia staff, we do not have anything to do with the decisions made concerning you or where you will go after leaving here. We do not share any of our information with the regular staff. Everything this group does or talks about is kept strictly confidential and isn't available to or used by the staff in any way at all.

[6] Editors' Note: Notice the explicit focus on teaching and learning from the beginning.

"This group is one of several we have been working with here on _____ Cottage. Each group meets three times a week for about 40 minutes at a time. This same group will meet together each week during the time you are all here at Cascadia, but different ones of us will be with this group on different days. We will be playing different roles in different situations on each day. We want you to watch us and then take turns in pairs, playing the same roles yourselves. We will also discuss how everyone does, what is important about the particular roles or situations and how they may be related to your lives. We will want you to stick closely to the roles as we play them but also add your own personal touch to your role. As you will see, it is important that we all get involved in this as much as we can. The more you put yourself into the role you play, the more realistic it will be to you and to the rest of the group. We see these scenes as examples of real situations that you will all find yourselves in sometime, and it is important to play them as realistically as possible. We will outline each scene as we go along.

"Also, each meeting will be (tape recorded or TV taped). We use these tape recordings for our own records of how each group proceeds. These tapes are identified by code numbers, and no one's name actually appears in the tape. The tapes are confidential too, and will be used only by us. As we said, none of this information is used by the regular staff.

"Before going any further, we want to give you an example of what we're talking about. Mr. _____ and I will play two roles which involve a scene that has really gone on right here in your cottage. This scene is based on information we got from a cottage counselor and other boys who have been on this cottage. This situation involves a common cottage problem and we will show you some things that can be done about it."

A SOCIAL MODEL SESSION—THE "JOB INTERVIEW"

Each session has a particular theme, for example, applying for a job, resisting temptations by peers to engage in antisocial acts, taking a problem to a teacher or parole counselor, or foregoing immediate gratifications in order to lay the groundwork for more significant gratifications in the future. In each situation emphasis is placed on the generality of the appropriate behaviors being modeled in order to emphasize their potential usefulness.

An example of one session is the Job Interview in which roles are played by an interviewer and a job applicant. The dialogue emphasizes the kinds of questions an interviewer might ask and the various positive, coping responses an interviewee is expected to make. Also, such factors as proper appearance, mannerisms, honesty, and interests are stressed.

One of the models verbally introduces each scene at the beginning of a meeting. The Job Interview scene introduction is a general example.

Introduction

Having a job can be very important. It is a way that we can get money for things we want to buy. It is a way we can feel important because we are able to earn something for ourselves through our own efforts. For this same reason, a job can make us feel more independent. Getting a job may not always be easy. This is especially true of jobs that pay more money and of full-time jobs. A job may be important to guys like you who have been in an institution because it gives you a chance to show other people that you can be trusted, that you can do things on your own, that you are more than just a punk kid. However, because you've been in trouble, you may have more trouble than most people getting a job. In the scene today you'll have a chance to practice applying for a job and being interviewed by the man you want to work for. Being interviewed makes most people tense and anxious because interviewers often ask questions which are hard to answer. After each of you has been interviewed, we'll talk about the way it felt and about what to do about the special problems that parolees may face in getting jobs.

Scene One

A boy who is on parole from Cascadia is applying for a job at a small factory in his home town. He is 18 and has not finished high school but hopes to do so by going to school at night. Obviously the boy has a record. This will come up during the interview. Pay careful attention to how he handles this problem. This is a two part scene; first, we'll act out the job interview, then a part about another way of convincing an employer that you want a job.

(Mr. Howell is seated at his desk when George knocks on the door.)
Howell: Hello. I'm Mr. Howell, and your name?
(Mr. Howell rises—shakes hands)
George: George Smith.
Howell: Have a seat, George.
(Both sit down)

                Oh yes, I have your application right here. There are a few questions I'd like to ask you. I see that you have had some jobs before; tell me about them.

George: They were just for the summer because I've been going to school. I've worked on some small construction jobs and in a food processing plant.

Howell: Did you ever have any trouble at work, or ever get fired?

George: No trouble, except getting used to the work the first couple of weeks. I did quit one job—I didn't like it.

Howell: I see that you have only finished half your senior year in high school. You don't intend to graduate?

George: (Showing some anxiety) Yes, I do. I intend to go to night school while I'm working. It may take me a year or so, but I intend to get my diploma.

Howell: How did you get a year behind?

George: I've been out of school for awhile because I've been in some trouble. Nothing really serious.

Howell: I'd like to know just what kind of trouble you've had, serious or not.

George: Well, I was sent to Cascadia for six weeks, but I'm out on parole now. I just got out a couple of weeks ago. One of the reasons I want a job is to help keep me out of trouble.

Howell: What kind of trouble were you involved in?

George: A friend and I stole some car parts off an engine. I guess we were pretty wild. I'm not running around like that any more though.

Howell: You sound like you think you can stay out of trouble now. Why do you think so?

George: In those six weeks at Cascadia I thought about myself and my future a whole lot, and realized it was time to get serious about life and stop goofing off. I know I haven't been out very long yet, but my parole counselor is helping me with the problems that come up. I'm trying to stay away from the guys I got into trouble with. I really think that if I could get a job and be more on my own, it would help a lot.

Howell: Yes, I think you're probably right—but, I'm afraid we don't have any openings right now. I'll put your application on file though and let you know if anything turns up. I have several other applications too, so don't be too optimistic.

George: All right. Thank you.

(George stands and starts to leave as he says this line.)

Scene Two

It is now two weeks later. George has called back several times to see if an opening has occurred. He now stops by to check again.

(George knocks on Mr. Howell's door.)

Howell: Come in.

George: (Enters room while speaking) I stopped by to see whether you had an opening yet.

Howell: You certainly don't want me to forget you, do you?

George: No sir, I don't. I really want a job; I think it's the best thing for me to do now.

Howell: You know, I believe you. I wasn't so sure at first. It's pretty easy for a guy who has been in trouble to say that he's going to change and then do nothing about it. But the way you've been coming here and checking with me so often, I think you're really serious about it.

George: Yes sir, I am. I started night school this week. I think I'll be able to get my diploma in a year. So, if I had a job now I'd be all set.

Howell: Well, I've got some good news for you, George. I have an opening for a man in the warehouse, and I think you can handle the job if you want it.

George: Yes, very much. When do you want me to start?

Howell: Tomorrow morning at 7:30.

George: O.K.

Howell: I'll take you out there now and introduce you to Mr. Jones who will be your supervisor.

Scene Three

This is the same setting as Scene Two, but somewhat different.
(George knocks on Mr. Howell's door.)

Howell: Come in.

George: I stopped by to see whether you had an opening yet.

(Enters room while speaking)

Howell: You sure are persistent. Have you tried other places?

George: Sure, I'm checking back on them too. Getting a good job isn't easy.

Howell: (uncomfortably) Ah, well, look. We're not going to have a place for you here. I wouldn't want you to waste your time coming back again. We can't use you.

George: (Rises to go) Well, (pause) O.K. Thanks for your trouble. Look, what's up? I know that your company is hiring other fellows like me right now.

Howell: Er . . . that's true. Uh, I'm afraid that we have a company policy not to hire anyone with a record.

George: How come? That doesn't seem fair to me.

Howell: Well, er, ahem . . . that's just the company's policy. I'm sorry, but my hands are tied. There's nothing I can do about it.

George: Well, I would have appreciated knowing that right away.

Howell: I'm really sorry. I can see you're trying. . . . I hope you get a job.

George: Well, do you know of a place that could use me? Since you're in personnel, maybe you've heard of something.

After these scenes were played by the two models, each boy played George's role. At the end of the session, these discussion points were emphasized:

1. Importance of presenting oneself well. Getting a job is "selling yourself" too. In both scenes the boy takes the initiative instead of waiting around passively for things to happen.

2. How to deal with the fact that one has a record. Here, the boy had to admit to having a record because of the time in school gap. If he had lied, the interviewer would have caught this and formed the impression of dishonesty. Discussing the possibility of cases when telling about a record might be unnecessary. Situational factors are very important.

3. It is understandable to feel anxious when being interviewed because getting a job is important.

4. Persistence is a trait employers like. In this case, it is an important reason why he got the job.

TOPICS FOR OTHER MODELING SESSIONS

The other scenes which we have developed and used in the modeling groups follow a similar format and may be roughly categorized into several content areas and described as follows:

1. Scenes dealing with the problem of self-control: planning ahead, delay of impulsive action such as aggressive or flight behavior, and so forth. (a) One scene in this category involves a dialogue between an institutionalized boy and his caseworker, based around the importance of using time in the institution wisely to plan and prepare for the future. (b) A home problem scene concerning a fight between a father and son over compliance with rules, with the boy controlling his anger enough not to run away, which usually leads to more trouble. (c) A scene contrasting two ways to deal with peer criticism, one based on an appropriate way and the other which leads to a fight. (d) Two scenes based on the importance of controlling anger: recognizing it, labeling it, and emphasizing the often undesirable consequence of impulsive aggressive behavior, especially when directed toward authority figures.

2. Common situations involving negative peer influence: several scenes based on resisting pressures to conform to delinquent standards and behaviors. (a) Two situations illustrating ways and reasons for not showing off in typical situations, one involving street drag racing, the other, disruptive classroom behavior. (b) A script illustrating the importance of regular school attendance, the "vicious circle" aspects of truancy, and the related problems it generates. (c) A group scene with four roles in which a parolee must resist his peers' spontaneous plan to steal a car, touching also on the fallacy of "if you don't go along with the crowd, you'll lose friends." (d) A related scene dealing with adolescent drinking parties and some of the things an adolescent must consider before getting involved.

3. The third content area focuses on appropriate social-interpersonal behavior and the impressions one makes on others. (a) The Job Interview Scene is an example of this concept. (b) Examples of dialogues

involving a boy being "tested" for acceptance into a group or clique of his peers, including both appropriate and inappropriate ways to behave.

4. Aspects of the concept of taking responsibility and the consequences of not doing so. (a) A scene concerning a boy's prompt solicitation of help with school problems in order not to fall behind and perhaps drop out. (b) The difficult but frequently necessary task of apologizing to another and accepting responsibility for correcting a misdemeanor.

THE SEQUENCE FOR EACH SESSION

The following procedures were developed for presenting and working with this material within the group sessions. Each session is attended by six persons, two models and four boys. One complete scene is used for each meeting. Each meeting follows a sequence: (a) One model introduces and describes the scene for the day; (b) models role-play the scripts while the boys observe; (c) one boy is called upon to summarize and explain the content and outcome of the situation; (d) models comment and discuss the scene, then replay the recording; (e) pairs of boys imitate and rehearse the roles and behaviors; (f) a short "break" is taken, while soft drinks are served and one of the two role-playing imitations is replayed; (g) the remaining boys act out the scene; (h) one of these two performances is replayed; and, finally (i) final summaries and comments concerning the scene, aspects of its importance, and general applicability are emphasized.

SOME RESULTS

To assess the effect of these group modeling sessions, self-report and observer ratings were used. The self-report measures involved a semantic differential scale and the Wahler Self-Description Inventory (Wahler, in press). The Self-Description Inventory contains an assortment of positive and negative items, such as "has a good sense of humor" and "am often depressed or unhappy." Each item is rated on a nine-point scale from "very much like me" to "not at all like me." The observer ratings, made by cottage staff workers, involved a seven-point, ten item Behavior Rating Scale, including such items as "lies regularly—always tells the truth" and "often hits and pushes—never hits and pushes," and a Weekly Behavior Summary. This Summary has seven categories such as Relationship with Peers, Work Detail Performance, and Personal Habits.

Experimental and control groups were matched for (1) age, (2) intelligence level, and (3) severity and chronicity of previous delinquency. There has been a consistent tendency for experimental boys to show less discrepancy between "me as I would like to be" and "me as I am now," from pre- to post-testing than control boys. One of the most suggestive findings is that boys who have received the modeling conditions become more personally *dissatisfied* with themselves as their stay at Cascadia proceeds. Control boys, on the other hand, become more *satisfied* with themselves as their stay in Cascadia proceeds. These changes are reflected in pre- and post-differences in mean Self-Description Inventory scores in which experimental boys consistently increased endorsement of negative and decreased endorsement of positive items. The reverse was true for the control boys. At this point the meaning of these results is not immediately obvious. However, one possibility is that untreated delinquents in an institution are initially anxious because of the strangeness of being in the institutional environment for the first time. As they adapt and "rest up," their anxiety level goes down and they therefore become more self-satisfied. If this is true, it may be that the experimental procedures we have been employing have been successful in stirring up the treated boys at Cascadia. Our results concerning self-satisfaction suggest that lessened defensiveness and greater willingness to admit to having problems and difficulties have characterized the responses of the experimental, but not the control boys.

In general, the findings showed that boys who were members of our experimental groups showed more change in their behavior and attitudes than did matched control groups of boys who did not participate. Overall, the experimental subjects were rated by cottage staff as showing more positive behavior change and more over-all change on the Behavior Rating Scale than did control boys. While the Weekly Behavior Summary data were incomplete, the available findings were consistent with those derived from other measures, that is, experimental boys showed more positive behavior change than did their matched controls.

In addition to the self-reports and staff ratings of attitudes and behavior, we were interested in the boys' subjective evaluations of the meaning of the modeling experiences, and in what ways they had been or will be personally useful. One boy in particular felt that the Review Board Scene, one of the modeling situations based on a re-enactment of the staff meeting at Cascadia which determines the placement of the boy, was very useful in that it reduced his anxiety and furnished information as to what to expect when he went before the Board. In addition, he felt that it increased his trust in the Cascadia staff and offered some proof that the staff were concerned and based their decisions on information and other considerations which enabled them to make a valid placement. This boy had previously expressed very strong feelings that decisions regarding his future were more or less left up to chance. In addition, several members of the cottage staff had felt that this boy had gained appreciably in trust and cooperation, largely as a result of his participation in the modeling groups.

Another boy evaluated the modeling experiences as beneficial primarily in that they gave him the opportunity to "put myself in somebody else's shoes" and thus better understand how and why people react differently to different situations. He believed that these new perceptions had helped him increase his ability to accept others. Other boys have felt that practice in imitating various roles had increased their skill in communicating with each other and also facilitated their willingness to relate to adult authority figures. Both the Cascadia and the Research staffs have frequently observed that group participation increased the quality and frequency of interactions on the part of some of the more shy and withdrawn boys. A withdrawn boy often becomes the cottage scapegoat, and we have had several in our groups. These boys have required extra initial support and protection, but in most cases have responded quickly to the well-structured procedures and have become better accepted, especially within the group, but on the cottage as well.

The project staff visited two of the State Department of Institutions forestry camps several months after completion of the studies for follow-up informal contact with group boys. It was somewhat surprising to discover how much of the material in the group sessions the boys still remembered. Many of them were able to describe accurately many of the modeling scenes virtually point by point. Two of the boys who were having some difficulty adjusting to forestry camp life commented that they could "stick it out" and related this decision to some of the lessons they had learned from scenes which had dealt with the theme of emotional control. In general, these boys felt that their participation in the groups would have greater value once they were released from the institution. This may be largely true because most of the scenes focus on readjustment and coping behaviors and situations of the kind which most probably will be encountered by the boys after their return to their communities.

An example of the value of the modeling procedures was derived from an interview with a parolee taken some three months after his release from Cascadia. This example involves the usefulness of one scene, the Job Interview Scene. The boy was applying for a job. He had been seated in a company waiting room for several minutes and had begun thinking about the Job Interview Scene and the previous modeling group. He reviewed to himself the dialogue in the scene, how the scene was handled, and the types of questions he had been asked. He felt that this procedure had greatly reduced his anxiety prior to actually being interviewed by the personnel manager. He looked at this as a very positive and practical experience and felt that it had greatly enhanced his ability to make a good impression and be honest with the interviewer, which subsequently resulted in his being hired for the job. It would, obviously, be of interest to know how this boy functioned in a variety of real life situations besides that of the job interview, for example, arguments with parents and peers, and temptations to act antisocially.

CONCLUSION

Persons behave as they do and adhere to particular constellations of attitudes and beliefs, in part, because of their past history of modeling experiences. A modeling experience is one in which a developing individual takes on characteristics of a significant other, termed a "model", in his environment. This imitative-like acquisition of responses may be for good or ill, and may have conscious and unconscious components in varying degrees.

It is generally recognized that juvenile delinquents are handicapped by a history of inadequate and unfortunate modeling experiences, often concurrent with extensive interactions with antisocial models. Can juvenile offenders between the ages of 15 and 18 benefit from concentrated exposure to healthy significant others? Can this exposure lead to observable and quantifiable changes in behavior? Our research has been based on the assumption that both of these questions can be answered affirmatively.

23

USING BEHAVIORAL TECHNIQUES WITH AUTISTIC CHILDREN

William E. Stilwell
AMERICAN INSTITUTES FOR RESEARCH

Techniques based on principles of social learning have been successfully used to develop new behaviors and eliminate undesirable behaviors (Bandura & Walters, 1963). The head-banger, for example, has stopped banging (Lovass, Freitag, Gold, & Kassorla, 1965), the near-blind has been helped to see (Wolf, Risley, & Mees, 1964) and the nonvocal has learned to vocalize (Kerr, Meyerson, & Michaels, 1965). These changes have been brought about, in part, through the use of encouraging "successive approximations" of desired behaviors by means of positive reinforcement and through providing observational learning experiences. The changes have been dramatic, rapid, and encouraging.

The study reported here was conducted at Napa State Hospital. This hospitalized autistic child is similar to those described by Kanner (1943) and Rimland (1964), who exhibit a narrow range of behaviors, particularly in social skills. This child was a complete social isolate who also exhibited self-destructive behavior such as biting and clawing himself.

Peers were employed as social models to provide examples of appropriate social behaviors. As a result the child learned to play in close proximity to his peers. For this child, and others with whom I have worked, developing a specific behavioral goal represents an important step in the sequential development of social behaviors. This case illustrates how the following steps can be used to accomplish a specific counseling goal.

STEPS IN TRAINING

The fundamental procedure in the training program used incorporated five interdependent and interrelated steps: (1) problem assessment, (2) goal selection, (3) contingency analysis, (4) stimulus control development, and (5) actual sequential training. Briefly, these steps will be described.

Assessing the Problem

First, problem assessment focused on the determination of behavioral base levels. That is, the focus was on finding out what are the child's current patterns of behavior. Information from a variety of sources was employed: medical and social histories, interviews with staff members, and the actual observations of the child's behavior on the ward. These data were synthesized into statements about the child's modal or characteristic behavior such as "He hits two sticks together," "He shies away from fast moving peers," "He does not speak more than one word," and "He slaps peers." Other behaviors which were not "problem-oriented" were also noted in this synthesis. The emphasis was on gathering specific information, primarily through observation as to what the child does.

Selecting Behavioral Goals

The selection of a behavioral goal is the second step. The counselor must consider each behavior in terms of its potential for training and modification.[1] Four guidelines for goal selection were employed: (1) the behavior to be reduced or eliminated is either antisocial or asocial; (2) some form of the desired behavior is already part of the child's behavior; (3) the selected goal was observable; (4) the behavior to be modified relates to the child's prosocial development.

Analyzing the Contingencies

The third step is contingency analysis. That is, what are the consequences of the child's behaviors and what responses function as positive reinforcers? The investigator must specify what reinforcers are to be used for the particular child. In this study rapid behavioral changes were desired. Hence, M & M candies were selected as an often powerful, but quickly satiating reinforcer. However, other reinforcers, sometimes called "natural reinforcers," may be discovered and used by observing the consequences of responses in the child's present environment. What is maintaining present behaviors? Can these consequences be used to encourage the desired behaviors which are not occurring with much frequency at present?

In addition to the primary reinforcer, M & M candies, strong social reinforcers such as "That's good," "Keep it up," "You are doing well," and a smiling face were employed. A distinction was made in the application of these reinforcers. A social reinforcer such as smiling was provided immediately after an increase of behavior took place. The food reinforcer, M & M's, were used intermittently when the child completed a chain of behavior, such as sliding down the slide or saying something to a peer.

Establishing Control

The fourth step is the establishment of stimulus control. This is essential before the actual sequential training program is initiated. The child was trained to reduce the competing behaviors and to "pay attention" to the counselor. The length of stimulus control training depends on the intensity and complexity of the established behavioral repertoire. Usually certain criterion behaviors such as compliance with statements such as, "Put

---

[1] Editors' Note: Here is an instance where the "client" does not select the goal of counseling. Stated differently, the client in this case is society.

your hands down" and "Sit back in the chair" can be used as indicators that stimulus control has been established.

Developing a Sequence

The fifth step involves the actual training program based on hypotheses and data generated during the four previous steps. In the problem assessment step a kind of base rate of the problem behavior is obtained. This information becomes a standard against which changes in behavior can be compared. The direction of these changes is derived from the degree the behaviors appear to be atypical. For example, the chattering child might learn the discrimination of when to chatter. Or the silent child might learn to speak a few words. In the third step the crucial relationships between the child's behavior and some externally available objects such as toys or a word receive attention. Is it the fact of talking or what is said that influences the child? Is the child looking at a comparatively complex talking-clock or the bright red block? Answers to these questions lead to the hypotheses about what might be used as effective reinforcers.[2] In the fourth step of building a training program the agent of change (a ward technician, a counselor, or a teacher) becomes active in attempting to influence directly the child's behavior. This step is usually taken after the counselor has gathered enough information to be able to successfully promote the desired behavioral change.

In the fifth step the sequences for mastery can be laid out. Goals can be specified and procedures can be described. In this manner each step within the training program can be evaluated. When too many failures to reach the next step occur, a change in the sequence can be implemented.

At first many different strategies might be attempted, evaluated and discarded. However, each different program can feed into the next so that a "best" technique is developed for the particular problem. This technique, which is developed from some grossly defined problem through a series of steps toward a readily observable goal, becomes the child's sequential training program. The over-all fundamental procedure is demonstrated in the following case study.

THE CASE OF CURT—USING MODELS TO COUNTERCONDITION

A behavioral chain which began with isolated walking and ended with self-destructive activity dominated this 12-year-old boy's repertoire. His operant level was an isolated, ambient walking through groups of quiet

---

[2] Editors' Note: Article 5 by Marvin Daley illustrates the value of finding out what are the "natural reinforcers."

peers and around clusters of highly mobile and verbal peers. This behavior was often accompanied by crying. When an adult or peer approached the boy, the intensity of his crying increased. The boy clamped his teeth onto his right foreknuckle. This gnawing had occurred so frequently that a thick tooth-marked callous had developed on his hand. The task for the counselor was to develop a prosocial repertoire which included approaching peers. The focus for behavioral modification was on the first element of the behavioral chain, the isolated walking. This change would reduce the probability for the remainder of the chain to occur.

The training program for this boy represents a departure from reported laboratory training programs in that after the development of stimulus control in the training room the child was trained in the open ward (Bijou, 1966). Within the open ward situation the sequential development of "playing on the slide" and "sitting with peers" was incorporated to focus on the behavioral goal. Two techniques were used.

Using Peers as Models

First of all, peer models were employed. The procedure in establishing "playing on the slide" followed these steps: (1) the investigator stood near the base of the ladder and said, "Curt, come here." The approach by the boy was reinforced with an M & M. (2) Then, in succession, he climbed to the top of the ladder, sat down and was rewarded. (3) He slid to the bottom of the slide and received food and social reinforcement (smiling face). This behavioral chain occurred three times over a 15-minute period. Then a peer approached the investigator. Mark, a peer, had been watching Curt perform on the slide. Apparently he had also seen the M & M's. The boy reached for the candy-pocket:

Mark: Give me some candy!
Counselor: You have to earn it, Mark. Curtis is working for his candy.
Mark: I want some M & M's.
Counselor: Do you want to work? You have to earn your M & M's.
Mark: Give me M & M.
Counselor: I will hire you to work for me, Mark. We can have a contract and shake hands and you can get paid.
           Silence.
Counselor: I want Curt to slide down the slide. Will you help me?
Mark: Alright.
Counselor: For every trip down the slide that Curt makes after you, I will give you one M & M.
Mark: Two.

Counselor: Mark, I'll run out of candy. One.
Mark: OK.

In this way Mark agreed to become a model for the behavior of "playing on the slide." In later sessions other peers asked to make contracts with the counselor. Several times in this study six boys including Curt were playing on the slide.

An important change occurred in Curt's behavior. Less and less M & M's were required to reinforce his behavior on the slide. Finally, Curt caught up with his models and made a complete trip for only one M & M. It must be pointed out that the investigator used almost continuous verbal and nonverbal social reinforcement while the boy was completing each trip down the slide.

Interfering with Avoidance Behavior

Secondly, Curt's behavior of avoiding other boys on the ward was directly confronted. A type of counterconditioning approach was used. That is, a positive stimuli, M & M's, was presented at the same time as was a negative stimuli, the physical presence of the peers.[3] Generally the boys who became the models were also those who had been the more "aggressive" members of the ward. Curt had avoided their rapid movements whenever possible. In this aspect of the study both on the slide and later around a picnic bench Curt was rewarded for remaining near these boys. The candy was paired with being near the boys. Curt was able to sit with these boys for up to five minutes. During this time he was prompted to give objects to the peers and to receive candy and toys from them. The purpose of these exchanges was to begin working on a behavior similar to sharing.

Changes in Curt's Behavior

The models facilitated Curt's acquiring of the desired behavior. Before the introduction of peer models and later during one session in which the models were absent, the boy rarely engaged in the "playing on the slide." In the early sessions Curt completed a trip down the slide about one time in five minutes. This rate was increased to almost one trip per two minutes as the number of models was increased. One day when the model peers were absent Curt completed the trip down the slide only twice in

---

[3] Editors' Note: Counterconditioning, as a principle, generally involves the elimination of a response by eliciting a strong incompatible response in the presence of cues that usually bring about the undesired behavior. Whether the M&M's operated in this fashion is debatable.

thirty minutes. On the following day, with the models present, Curt and his peers resumed the same frequency as before their absence: one complete trip in two minutes. He also sat with the group at the end of "playing on the slide." In effect, the peer models became the agents supporting Curt's changes in behavior. He performed in their presence and did not in their absence.

At the end of these sessions with Curt two changes were observed. First of all he was observed to approach several of the less active boys much more often. This usually precipitated his isolated walking. Secondly, on the less desirable side, he was observed to frequently stand near the slide, but not to climb on it. Once when the counselor entered the ward, Curt immediately climbed on the slide. This behavior suggested a problem in using peer models: How to develop some sort of rewarding system which would encourage peers to maintain a program once it was started? In the absence of the peer influences Curt apparently was unable to maintain his newly acquired behaviors. Clearly, a next step would have been to explore ways of sustaining this new sequence of behaviors by Curt. The study did demonstrate, however, that it was possible to significantly change the behavior of this institutionalized autistic boy through the use in part of modeling techniques.

Filmed Models

SOCIAL MODELS CAN be presented to the observer in a variety of ways. Much of what may be called observational learning occurs through the observation of live models in our natural environment. Parents, teachers, and peers often serve as influential social models.

However, live observational experiences have some disadvantages, one of which is the problem of controlling the model's behavior. Even with practice and rehearsal the model may not comprehensively demonstrate the desired behavior, especially certain subtleties and nuances of behavior. Furthermore, many situations do not lend themselves readily to having a model physically present. The most appropriate and influential model may simply not be physically available. Then, too, bringing in a live model might be socially disruptive as, for example, in a small counseling group.

Much of what is offered by a live modeling experience can be reproduced on film. Films can present to the observer many important auditory and visual cues as well as contextual ones which are deemed important for learning to occur. A decided advantage in using a filmed procedure is the ability to structure and determine just what is to be modeled. In the natural environment observer-learners are provided many observational experiences but many are of inappropriate and undesirable behaviors. Through the use of filmed presentation, such as 8mm film or a video tape, the observer can be presented with a highly controlled, planned observational experience. In addition, the use of filmed media often serves to focus the attention of the observer and minimizes distractions. Careful and close attention to the model is essential. A final advantage of filmed models is their flexibility and utility. Once developed the same filmed model procedure, or parts of it, can be used over again in a variety of settings.

The two articles presented here involve problems of elementary school students in the classroom setting. In Article 24 Hosford and Sorenson describe a social model film for use with fourth, fifth, and sixth graders with problems of being unable to speak up in class. Assuming that many of these children did not know how to participate in class, they created a film which presented a shy, elementary school student talking with a counselor. The film presents concrete examples of how a student might participate more in the classroom. The filmed model can be used with students in a classroom setting, not merely in one-to-one counseling. The initial time and effort necessary to develop and evaluate effective and efficient modeling procedures may in the long run prove itself to be an economical and effective counselor activity. Large numbers of students might be enabled to identify potential problems early and take constructive steps in time.

Article 25 by Nixon presents an ingenious effort to use a filmed social model to reduce hyperactive behaviors in a classroom setting. Nixon's study highlights an important point in using social model procedures: the observer often needs to be trained in what to observe. Providing an example of a complex type of behavior for an observer does not guarantee that the observer will notice it. Does he know what to look for? To better insure that the student did observe, Nixon provided a type of "discrimination training." He gave the observer examples of a model student who demonstrated task-oriented behavior as well as inappropriate nontask behaviors in a classroom setting. The observer was asked to identify, while watching a model film, the behaviors which were task-oriented and was positively reinforced for making a correct identification.

Another important feature of Nixon's investigation was combining the film model procedure with reinforcement for attentive behaviors in the classroom. Once the student tried out behaviors that had been observed, the consequences would be positive.

Both articles are suggestive of the great potentiality of using modeling techniques via films. Although both articles present work done in the elementary classroom, many other settings, educational and otherwise, are appropriate for using filmed modeling procedures. Both articles also imply that classroom teachers can work cooperatively with counselors in assisting individuals with problem behaviors.

24

PARTICIPATING IN CLASSROOM DISCUSSIONS

Ray E. Hosford and Don L. Sorenson
UNIVERSITY OF WISCONSIN

How can shy students be assisted to take part more readily in classroom discussions? This study explored one way, that of providing students with examples and suggestions of what they could do to participate more effectively in class discussions.

Most of us can learn a great deal by observing others. Research studies in counseling (for example, Krumboltz & Thoresen, 1964; Krumboltz & Schroeder, 1965; Krumboltz, Varenhorst, & Thoresen, 1967; Thoresen & Krumboltz, 1968) have demonstrated that providing students with social models who present examples of how to behave does help these students.

Bandura and Huston (1961, p. 312) have pointed out, "children not having the habit of responding independently are apt to be more dependent on, and therefore more attentive to cues produced by the behavior of others." It seemed reasonable to us that starting to explore how modeling techniques might be used with elementary students would provide information useful to classroom teachers and elementary school counselors.

We were interested in finding out if a social model could be developed with shy elementary school children. In particular we wanted to find out if such a social model could be presented as a film in a regular elementary classroom. Also, would presenting the model on film or on audio tape make any difference?

We started out by surveying 20 fourth, fifth, and sixth grade classes to determine how prevalent the problem of being unable to speak up in class was with this age group. About 25 percent of the students in these classes stated that they had identified themselves as having the problem of being unable to participate in class discussions. We assumed that many of these students avoid entering into class discussions because they did not know how or where to begin.

MAKING A SOCIAL MODEL

We began with a student, Steve, who was identified by his teachers and parents as being unable to speak up in class and who had indicated that he would like help with this problem. The counselor made a tape recording of the interview with Steve, the "model student." Basically the counseling session consisted of verbal interchanges between Steve and the counselor in which Steve responded to cues and questions as to what he might do to begin speaking up in class. Often the cues were such that Steve had little difficulty responding with a "good" question. Whenever he suggested, for example, "I could begin by asking a question," he was reinforced with, "That's an excellent way in which to begin." The interview was terminated after Steve had made several suggestions of things he might do. From this audio tape a film script was constructed and the model counseling session was put on 16mm film. The same student, Steve, was used as the model client and a doctoral student in counseling at the University of Wisconsin was employed as the model counselor. The film when completed was eight minutes long. An audio tape was also made from the film soundtrack.

The Social Model Film

The following is an excerpt from the social modeling film:

Counselor: Good Good. Now that's one way to start, isn't it?
Steve: Yeah.
Counselor: You know—would you like to practice this now so that tomorrow you'll know what you're going to do?
Steve: Uh huh. Okay.
Counselor: Now why don't I pretend that I'm your teacher? Now, that's Mrs. Jones, isn't it?
Steve: Uh huh.
Counselor: Okay, class, it's time for science and we've been studying the stars. Now is there anyone in here who has read anything about the stars?
Steve: I have.
Counselor: Oh you have, Steve, good. What have you read about the stars that you would like to tell us?
Steve: Well . . . the earth circles the sun every year.
Counselor: Right! Now, is the sun a star?
Steve: Uh huh.

Counselor:	Good. Now do you think maybe you could try this tomorrow in Mrs. Jones' class?
Steve:	Uh huh. Okay. Suppose so.
Counselor:	All right. Now, how else could you speak up in class?
Steve:	Well, I guess I could ask some questions.
Counselor:	Asking a question is a very good idea, and it's a good way, I think, to begin speaking up.
Steve:	Yeah.
Counselor:	Have you found it difficult to ask questions before?
Steve:	Yeah. I'm sort of shy about asking things.
Counselor:	Okay now, let's see. Tomorrow you have science, reading, and spelling. Do you think you could begin by asking one question in science and one question in reading?
Steve:	Okay.
Counselor:	All right. How about trying one now? What question could you ask in reading?
Steve:	Well, there is a kind of page in our workbook that I don't quite know what it means. We're supposed to write down the main topic—yeah, the main topic, and I don't know what a main topic is.
Counselor:	That's a good question, very good. So you could ask your teacher —what, now? Pretend I'm your teacher. Ask me a question about the main topic.
Steve:	Well . . . what is the main topic on . . . well, what is the main topic.
Counselor:	What do we mean by main topic?
Steve:	Yeah.
Counselor:	Excellent. Okay. Now let's try it once more. I'm Mrs. Jones, okay? And I'll say, All right, students, now you all have the assignment. But now, are there any questions? Steve, do you have a question?
Steve:	Uh huh. I don't quite know what the main topic is.

How the Model Was Used

The filmed social model was shown in 20 fourth, fifth, and sixth grade classrooms. The students were told that since many of them had expressed difficulty in speaking up in class a film had been made to provide suggestions on learning how to participate. The film, it was explained, featured a fifth grade boy who had the same problem, not being able to participate in class. After talking with a counselor this boy, Steve, was able to speak up more often. The students were instructed to listen for the suggestions of how to participate more successfully.

In some of these classes the audio taped social model was played instead of the filmed model. The teacher was present in the classroom during the film or audio tape playing.

Some Results

At this point we were basically interested in finding out if elementary students at this age level would watch and listen to the model. We were also concerned about the classroom teachers. Would they think that such a procedure was helpful and meaningful? We developed a questionnaire which assessed the recall of students. Would they be able to remember the specific suggestions offered by Steve and the model counselor? This would let us know whether the students had attended to the behaviors of the social model. Besides wanting to know this, and whether showing a film or playing an audio tape was really feasible and workable we sought answers to these questions: (1) Would students be more predisposed to use the model's suggestions if presented on film compared to audio tape? (2) Would a greater number of students perceive the social model interview to be "real" rather than staged if they saw the film compared to the tape? (3) Would the film model promote a greater amount of student identification with his problem as compared to the audio tape? and (4) Would having students experience the social modeling twice significantly improve their recall of suggestions for participation?

We also asked the classroom teachers to write down their comments immediately after they either viewed the film or listened to the audio tape.

FINDINGS

Analysis of the questionnaires revealed that:

1. Girls recalled a significantly greater number of the model's behaviors and suggestions when they watched the film model than when they listened to the audio model. This was not true, however, for the boys.

2. The type of model, audio or film, did not significantly affect the degree to which students indicated they would use the model's suggestions if they had such a problem. Over 90 percent of the boys and girls indicated that they would use some of Steve's ideas.[1]

3. Girls thought the film model was much more "real" than the audio model. This was not true for the boys.

4. More girls than boys identified with the filmed model as to stating they had a similar problem. This difference, however, was not found between girls and boys for the audio tape.

5. Having students watch the film model twice, one week apart, did significantly improve their recall of what was modeled. Listening to the audio tape again, however, did not improve recall.

[1] Editors' Note: The critical question of course is whether the audio or film model causes students to actually participate in class discussions. Even the best of intentions. . . .

6. When asked "What was the most important thing that you learned from Steve's story?", about 50 percent stated they had learned something about what is counseling.

The comments of teachers were very favorable and positive. Most thought it was worthwhile and relevant. Here are excerpts from their written comments:

Teacher I: Making children aware of going to someone when problems arise seems excellent therapy. Perhaps the shy children will benefit from this suggestion, if any transfer occurs from the presentation. . . .

Teacher II: . . . should give room for thought on the problems Steve had . . . maybe the children will recognize a way to take care of an individual worry.

Teacher III: Very good. The use of it in a group doesn't isolate specific children.

Teacher IV: Summary, excellent (for helping such students).

Teacher V: Very good . . . it will perhaps help the child to identify his problem and in so doing he can help solve his problem. . . .

Teacher VI: I think this should be of help to those who have this problem. In fact, it should be a benefit to all. Perhaps a boy and girl could have been used. I think the use of the boy, Steve, was a good idea. I think the students could identify with Steve.

Teacher VII: . . . The film should help children to do some self-analysis.

Teacher VIII: . . . An appropriate and useful problem was considered.

IN CONCLUSION

The study had encouraging results. It seems feasible to develop and use modeling procedures in the classroom setting with elementary age students. Of course, the next step is to find out if shy students, who are given an opportunity to observe a model, actually do increase their participation in class. Do they enact the observed suggestions and behaviors? Should the results of the present study support the effectiveness of these procedures for decreasing anxiety associated with such problems, it is anticipated that film prints will be made available for use by school counselors to help students learn how to solve this and other problems.[2] It is further anticipated that 8mm versions of the films could be supplied in film cartridges ready for use in individual automatic viewers. Thus all a student with such a problem needs to do is to insert the cartridge, turn

[2] Editors' Note: Several studies have recently demonstrated that social modeling procedures are very effective in reducing fear and stress (avoidance behaviors) to certain situations. See Bandura, Grusec & Menlove (1967); Bandura & Menlove (1968); and Ritter (1968).

ɔn the machine and he has an individual screening, in private, of a
nodel-counseling interview. It may be that there are certain types of
;tudents and problems for which social modeling techniques would be
»specially effective. These and other questions need our attention. Coun-
ɩelors and other school personnel need to start providing some answers.

25

INCREASING TASK-ORIENTED BEHAVIOR

Stewart B. Nixon
SANTA CLARA COUNTY HEALTH DEPARTMENT (CALIFORNIA)

Teachers, counselors, and others generally have as their goal changes
in a youngster's behavior. This may be spoken of directly, "Johnny should
stay in his seat during reading time," or in a more indirect manner, "I
hope Johnny can improve his attitude toward learning." Within the
school setting, there is general agreement that certain behaviors are more
acceptable than others. For example, few would question that a child
should learn basic subject material, that excessive conflict with school
personnel or peers or both is undesirable, and that antisocial behavior is
less desirable than law-abiding activity.

Can a filmed social model be used to reduce hyperactive classroom
behaviors and at the same time increase task-oriented behavior? Although still in a formative stage, principles of social learning, such as
social modeling, provide the beginnings of powerful procedures to
bring about changed behavior in a short period of time. Traditional
procedures need to be re-evaluated. Patterson (1968) has suggested,
for example, that the traditional procedure of seeing youngsters once or
twice a week within a counseling setting should be seriously questioned.
He and others have gathered evidence that dealing directly with the
peers, family, and classroom teachers of a student who manifests inappropriate behavior can be very effective in changing the student's behavior.[1]
Where this may not be possible, direct conditioning procedures with the
student can measurably increase task-oriented behavior and decrease
inappropriate behaviors (Patterson, 1965; Nixon, 1965).

[1] Editors' Note: Patterson and others in Articles 18–20 describe how to work
directly with parents and teachers. See also Articles 29 and 30.

REDUCING INATTENTIVE BEHAVIORS

In this study I was concerned with how to reduce the distractible behaviors of students in an elementary classroom. The study involved second grade students who had been identified by their teachers as "hyperactive," that is, as being inattentive, seldom listening, fidgeting and frequently attracting the attention of others by grimacing, striking, or poking.

Identifying Hyperactives

Over thirty elementary classrooms were visited in a school district which serves a predominently Negro community. The classroom behaviors of students nominated by teachers as being highly distractible were observed and rated for several days. From these observations a group of twenty-four students, one per classroom, were selected, all of whom were Negro except for one Mexican-American student.

Discrimination-Modeling Procedure

One of the problems of these young, highly distractible students was their inability to stay with a task. It was reasoned that many of them might not know what paying attention really involved. Therefore, a social modeling procedure was developed to help these students learn the difference between task-oriented behavior and distractible hyperactive behaviors. The student was taken from his classroom and told he would see a movie. A film featuring a student much like himself was used. Ten scenes of youngsters in task-oriented situations and five scenes of distractible hyperactive behavior were shown. The hyperactive sequences were interspersed between the task-oriented scenes.

The movie was shown by using an 8mm projector flashed into a ground-glass screen so that total darkness was not required. When a given task-oriented scene was on the screen, the projector was stopped and the subject was asked, "What is this boy doing?" When the subject had identified the youngster in the movie as writing, studying, or otherwise involved in a task-oriented behavior, the experimenter would activate a small light by the screen, give the subject a candy M & M or penny alternately, and comment further on the many good things that happened to the youngster in the movie because he was studying so hard, for example, "I'll bet other youngsters really want to play ball with him because he was working so hard;" "His parents were very pleased and happy because he was paying attention;" "He probably got lots of prizes for doing what the teacher asked him to." When a nontask-oriented sequence was shown, there was only a comment to signify that the subject had correctly identified the scene. No praise, enthusiasm, or material reinforcers were given for describing nontask-oriented scenes. The contingencies of the experiment were not explained during this first session. The counselor did point out that the light went on when the subject identified the task-oriented scenes in the movie. The student was further told that from time to time a person would place on his desk a box with a counter and light similar to the one next to the screen. The student viewed this model film on two occasions outside the classroom.

The Reinforcement Box

Showing students examples of task-oriented behavior was considered the first step. Now the student "knew" the difference between paying attention and not focusing on the task at hand. The next step was to encourage task-oriented behavior in the classroom. A remote controlled "reinforcement box" was developed. The box permitted immediate reinforcement of task-oriented behaviors when they occurred.

After the modeling-discrimination treatment (movie), the counselor went into the classroom and placed a conditioning apparatus housing a counter and light on the subject's desk. This apparatus was operated on a remote-control basis, similar to a one way "walkie-talkie." Specifically, the device consisted of a receiver ($9'' \times 6\frac{1}{4}'' \times 2''$) containing batteries and electronic parts to operate the light and counter. The transmitting mechanism ($4'' \times 6\frac{1}{4}'' \times 2''$) was small enough to be strapped to one's belt or fit in a woman's handbag. A small push-button switch was connected to the transmitter. This switch could easily fit into one's pocket. Hence, the entire transmitting mechanism was not visible. By pushing the button on the switch, the light and the counter in the receiver were activated.

To help the student learn how the reinforcing box worked, the counselor would sit in the back of the room, in good view of the student, for intervals of ten to fifteen minutes and reinforce the youngster approximately every minute if he was engaged in task-oriented activity. Activation of the light and counter constituted the initial reinforcement. At the end of the session, the experimenter would go to the subject and praise him for having earned the number of M & M's and pennies that the counter tallied. (Half of the total would be M&M's and the other half pennies.) The envelope containing these reinforcers was shown to the subject and he was told that at recess or noon (whichever came next in the day's schedule) the teacher would give him the envelope. After the first two operant conditioning sessions in the classroom, the youngster was told the contingencies of the experiment, that is, that the light and counter would go on when he was attentive and doing what the teacher had assigned. Likewise the subject was told that he should continue working hard, even when the machine was not on his desk. After the third or fourth conditioning session in the classroom, the subject was exposed to the model-discrimination movie treatment for the second time.

SOME CHANGES

Teachers and other school personnel noted marked changes in the behavior of certain youngsters. These changes were in the predicted direction. Hence, it is possible that the procedure is effective for certain youngsters. A striking example of behavior change toward more task-orientation involved Gordon. Movies were taken of Gordon before treatment had commenced. The films clearly illustrated this seven-year-old's excessive hyperactivity. A typical scene in the movie showed Gordon running up and down the aisles, yelling across the room, making faces and wildly gesticulating at his neighbors. The teacher noted that this was very typical behavior for this youngster. Five weeks after completion of the conditioning treatment, films were again taken of Gordon's behavior. Sustained attention spans of ten minutes could be noted. During these periods of task-orientation, Gordon would ignore other children who were talking to him or moving by his desk. One boy stood for a time with his hand on Gordon's desk, then touseled his hair. Another youngster tossed an eraser on Gordon's desk. Gordon appeared to pay no attention to this activity, but continued to copy an assignment from the board.

Some students unlike Gordon showed no appreciable change although no one became more hyperactive. This failure to show significant improvement might have been the result of several factors. Not providing the student enough exposure time to the modeling film and not sufficiently reinforcing him in the classroom when he was behaving in appropriate ways could be factors.[2]

The study did establish the feasibility of using a filmed social model procedure with elementary students. The filmed social model used in this study represents only a beginning. A great variety of filmed models can be developed and evaluated as to their effectiveness in assisting students with many different problems.

[2] Editors' Note: Patterson (1968), in discussing this study, points out that better results might have occurred if the students were positively reinforced more often during viewing the model film and in the classroom. If the "reinforcement box" could have been permanently located on each student's desk and activated intermittently, more positive results could be expected.

Audio Tape Recorded Models

USING SOCIAL MODELS to demonstrate behavior is not limited to live or pictorially presented social models such as on film or television. Clients can learn new patterns of behavior or be assisted in making use of behaviors already learned by listening to others who are not physically or visually present. Oral instructions, for example, constitute one type of audio model. In many real-life situations oral instructions are presented simultaneously with visual and physical cues.

In assisting some clients with problems it may be crucial for the counselor to provide examples of appropriate behavior which present visual as well as auditory cues. The client may need to actually see and hear another person behaving in a certain way, especially if nonverbal behaviors are important. However, filmed or live models may present too many cues, some of which are confusing and contradictory to the observer. Audio presentation limits the number of cues and may facilitate the observer's attending to the desired behavior.

We do not yet have research data which would enable us to predict when an audio model is more (or less) effective than a live or filmed model. Audio models do offer some advantages to the user, however. First, audio recording equipment is relatively inexpensive. Second, the procedure of making audio models is fairly quick and easy. Third, it is relatively easy to use an audio model with clients, either individually or in groups. Clients can even be trained to operate audio tape recorders so that a counselor need not be physically present.

Individuals may tend to be differentially responsive to auditory or visual cues. Eventually research studies may show that certain types of clients can be more effectively helped when

211

presented with audio modeling procedures while other types of clients are much more responsive to visually and pictorially presented modeling procedures.

The following three articles describe how audio-taped group social models have been developed and used. The small groups of students are able to model, not only specific suggestions about problems, but also how to communicate with each other and the counselor. In all three studies verbal and nonverbal reinforcement accompanied the group modeling procedure, though modeling may also be used effectively alone.

In Article 26 Stewart employed four high school students to provide examples of how to identify career alternatives, how to seek information relevant to alternatives and how to start making use of information relevant to post high school plans. To supplement information conveyed in the social modeling procedure, Stewart developed a series of structured materials to be used by students who listened to the tapes in small counseling groups. These materials serve to focus the attention of the students on many of the points mentioned on the audio tapes. The use of these materials suggests the possibility of creating a series of printed materials which could be used in conjunction with a series of audio model tapes without the need to have a professionally trained counselor physically present. Some students may benefit more from a combination of audio and written materials than from a typical face-to-face counseling interview. The article provides detailed information on how the audio taped social models were developed with typical high school students, and it suggests that the students who served as social models benefited considerably from the experience. Perhaps the most effective way of helping some clients is to ask them to play the role of model, not client.

In Article 27 Smith used a group audio tape to encourage students to use their unscheduled time more constructively. A distinguishing feature of Smith's study is the training of classroom teachers to serve as group discussion leaders. Smith presents detailed information on how teachers were trained to use the audio tape model and to use verbal and nonverbal reinforcement procedures in the small group setting. The study demonstrates how teachers may be selected and trained to counsel successfully with certain problem students.

Beach, in Article 28, presents an ambitious project on underachieving junior high school students. Using a series of audio tape group models, Beach attempted to assist eighth grade students to change their behavior in such areas as participating in class discussions, doing homework more efficiently, improving study methods, and increasing reading comprehension. Verbal and nonverbal reinforcement by the group leader supplemented the tapes. An important feature of this study was that full-time school counselors were trained in a relatively short period of time to assist in the development and use of the social models.

26

EXPLORING AND PROCESSING INFORMATION ABOUT EDUCATIONAL AND VOCATIONAL OPPORTUNITIES IN GROUPS

Norman R. Stewart
MICHIGAN STATE UNIVERSITY

Confusion or uncertainty about future plans is a central concern of most students. This does not suggest however that students respond to this concern in a common manner. Some gather cues from their environment and seem to map their future with ease. Others struggle from decision to decision. Many, perhaps most, rely more upon the element of chance as they think and worry about the future but take few steps to learn about the world they soon will enter. Levels of intelligence, dependency, and motivation are interwoven factors that account, in part, for individual differences in career planning.

For counselors, helping students consider and inquire about future possibilities represents one of their principal tasks. The results of their efforts are often disappointing, however. Counselors frequently feel that they are working with uninterested or unmotivated students. They believe students need more than to talk occasionally about future plans. Career days and business—industry—education days are attempts to close the communication links and get information from informed sources. But the infrequent and occasional nature of such activities does not suffice.

Counselors can point to sources of information. Many are within the counselor's office. Others are available within the community or for the price of a postcard. If only there were some way to get students more concerned, to have them explore and question, say counselors, then students would finally discover some facts that might be relevant and useful. But how to do it? The sources are so impersonal, the print so small, and the task is so unappealing.

One might ask, "What would motivate students? If the task is unappealing, what could we do to maximize the student's motivation?" Two possibilities, in combination, were used in this and other projects conducted at Michigan State University between 1965–1967.[1] First, we believed that people motivate each other through working on a common task. We recognized peer influence as an important determinant of adolescent behavior and reasoned that the enthusiasm of one might spread to others. We decided, therefore, to use small groups rather than an individual approach to counseling. Second, we sought an outside stimulus both to motivate the group and to give them an example of how a group much like themselves might behave and approach the task of career exploration. Frequently group members wonder just what is expected of them and seek a concrete example of how others might approach a task such as theirs.

CREATING THE GROUP SOCIAL MODELS

Encouraged by previous research using social models in career planning we decided to develop a series of models. However, we decided to create a group social model which to our knowledge had never been used in a counseling setting. We would make audio tapes of a "model" group that illustrated good group procedures and use these as a catalyst for activity within some 60 other groups which we termed "project" groups.

Earlier we had reasoned that the spring term of the eleventh grade was a critical point in future planning and so our study was focused upon eleventh graders. We wanted our "models" to be as much like those involved in the project as possible and planned to seek typical eleventh graders as models.

One of our first concerns was number and sex of the students to be involved in the model group and in each project group. Four seemed like a reasonable number. More could have been involved, but we planned to have only three sessions and thought the smaller number would allow each member to be more active in the group. Our initial project was designed for two males and two females in each group. The second project used only males because we wanted to see whether males, who seem typically less responsive to adult-arranged activities, would become involved.

[1] Carl E. Thoresen was the principal investigator of these projects while at Michigan State University.

The Beginning Steps

A high school counselor arranged for us to meet with the two male and two female students who were to be our social models. It seemed that we should seek students who were outgoing, persevering, cooperative, and imaginative, yet who would be perceived as "genuine" and somewhat "typical" by our project group members.[2] We met with the four eleventh graders and talked candidly with them about our purposes. We explained that we wanted to make a "stacked" tape in that it was to be filled with concrete ideas about how one might explore future possibilities. We stressed that about two hundred students would be listening to the model tapes as a way of getting suggestions of how to seek and use information. The model tapes would also be used to demonstrate (model) how a group could work together and how members could provide each other with ideas and encouragement. The success of the project, we pointed out, might well rest with their ability to convey enthusiasm and creative ideas to the listeners.

Initially, we talked for a few minutes about career planning and how a hypothetical student might go about it. Each model student had a form, "Possible Interests after High School," before him to encourage a systematic recording of his thoughts and plans for career exploration. Conversation was informal and humor frequently intervened. Information sources were bantered about and, as the conversation shifted, we noted that each was compiling a list of sources and ways of seeking sources. A humorous misunderstanding may illustrate this. One of the model students was talking about the work of a nuclear scientist. Another lamented, "If only there were a TV program called 'Men of Science,' this might be used as a source." As we talked, the "Men of Science" illustration was mentioned by one member after another. Weeks later, while making the third model tape, a member volunteered that anyone interested in a scientific career should certainly be watching "Men of Science" each week.

Frequently, we returned to a discussion of our basic purpose: Helping the unseen audience to become involved through the activity of the model group. Our informal discussions helped members of the model group to candidly discuss how they might sharpen examples of where they might find further sources of information.

Three "blue-sky" sessions were held, each about 20 minutes in length, and followed by soft drinks and cookies. We wanted them refreshed and motivated for the task ahead! Next, a model tape itself was made. This audio tape was then critiqued with suggestions for how it could be improved.

[2] Editors' Note: The problem of model characteristics is an important one. The particular characteristics to be used often depend on the particular problem and clients involved.

NAME: _____

POSSIBLE INTERESTS AFTER HIGH SCHOOL

1. _____   2. _____   3. _____

SOURCES OF INFORMATION THAT WOULD HELP ME CLARIFY MY THINKING:

WRITE	WRITE	WRITE
_____	_____	_____
_____	_____	_____
_____	_____	_____

OBSERVE	OBSERVE	OBSERVE
_____	_____	_____
_____	_____	_____
_____	_____	_____

READ	READ	READ
_____	_____	_____
_____	_____	_____
_____	_____	_____

LISTEN	LISTEN	LISTEN
_____	_____	_____
_____	_____	_____
_____	_____	_____

VISIT	VISIT	VISIT
_____	_____	_____
_____	_____	_____
_____	_____	_____

TALK	TALK	TALK
_____	_____	_____
_____	_____	_____
_____	_____	_____

Rather than working with all four model group members, we decided to concentrate for purposes of making the model tape on only one student. We urged the group to collectively assist him to work through his concerns about the future. To provide some cues for sources of information-seeking we had signs marked *Read, Write, Listen, Observe, Talk, Visit,* before each member. Several sources in each area had been discussed during our "blue-sky" sessions and the words served only as a stimulus to insure a mentioning of a variety of information-seeking. The model tape was about ten minutes in length. At the end of the tape was a brief summary of each activity which the model student planned to undertake. As they left the session, each member was given a handout, "Examples of Information Sources," to assist him in seeking a wider range of information.

Three model tapes were made with the four model students at two-week intervals. To insure realism the model students considered their own plans and ideas. The first model concentrated upon the wide range of information sources that might be used in the early stages of career exploration. It was anticipated that students would experience difficulty in using sources appropriately even though they had been identified. Therefore, the second model tape was directed at a more discriminant use of information sources. We stressed that all sources could not be used in a similar manner. A policeman probably would know neither the number of policemen in the United States nor the projected need for officers during the decade ahead. However, he could reveal some satisfactions and dissatisfactions of police work that he had experienced. Conversely, the *Occupational Outlook Handbook* would be a more accurate source for facts and statistics than for impressions.

At the beginning of the second session each member was given the model "Activity and Outcome Review" concerning Herbie Tobz' interest in dentistry. They also received two or three blanks so that they could record their activity, its outcome, and the meaning to them. They were handed "Getting Helpful Information," to review between the second and third meetings. This form presents suggestions as to how information sources can be used appropriately.

Finally, it was reasoned that gathered information is of little use to the student unless he is able to separate what is important, useful, and meaningful, from that which is not, and then is able to apply it to his immediate situation. The third model tape, therefore, was directed at the "sifting and sorting" process. The model group worked with "An Occupation and I" as they made the third tape.[3] It should be noted that each group made use of the same materials as they listened to each model tape.

[3] Editors' Note: Having certain clients function in a "social modeling role," that of trying to help others by giving examples of appropriate behaviors, may itself be a very powerful counseling technique. The author is currently investigating this possibility.

EXAMPLES OF INFORMATION SOURCES

Do you know what you want to do after high school? Are you really sure that what you "think" you'd like to do is *really* what you *want* to do? Many students who aren't really sure of their future plans never do anything concrete to help themselves decide. And many students who think they know what they'd like to do have never really investigated their choice thoroughly.

> The best way to find out about occupations and schools in which you're interested is to get information about them. Really, it's not such a big job. A good way to go about it would be to break the job down into small steps. Each step should be a different way of getting information about occupations and colleges which you think you might like. Some of the best steps to use are: observing; listening; reading; visiting; talking; and writing.

You've already started to compile a list of information sources. Perhaps you will get added ideas from the examples given below. If so, add them to your list and check them out.

OBSERVE: . . . . a secretary at work

. . a doctor making his office rounds

. . . . a TV program on plant biology

LISTEN: to a speaker on the foreign service

. . . . to a Navy recruiting officer

. . . to a college admissions officer

VISIT: . . . . a college campus

. . . . . a law firm

. . . . a retailing store

TALK: . . . to your family doctor

. . . . to your chemistry teacher

. . . . . . to your neighbor in the Air Force

WRITE: . . . . to the engineering society

to the Defense Department about service opportunities

. . . . to your aunt who is an elementary teacher

ACTIVITY AND OUTCOME REVIEW

INTEREST: Dentistry

NAME: Herbie Tobz

		OUTCOME	MEANING TO ME	
	ACTIVITY	(WHAT I FOUND OUT)	ADVANTAGES	DISADVANTAGES
READ:	Occupational Outlook Handbook on dentistry	That dentistry is a growing profession but getting into dental school is difficult.	If I went into this, it would have a good future.	I might not be accepted for dental school.
VISIT:	MSU Campus	They don't have a Dental School, only Pre-Dental courses.	Could enroll in Pre-Dental program because campus is close to home.	Would have to transfer schools later.
WRITE:	American Dental Association	Requirements for occupation (academic).	I fulfill many of the academic standards.	My manual dexterity is not that high.
TALK:	To Dr. Jones, our dentist.	Dental work is hard physically, must stand on feet all day, work with reluctant patients.	I am strong and enjoy working. Don't mind standing.	I hate screaming kids.
LISTEN:				
OBSERVE:	A filmstrip on dentistry.	There are many related fields which support the dental profession.	If I can't make dental school, I might look into these related fields.	I'm not sure I would like these types of jobs.

GETTING HELPFUL INFORMATION

Now that you are somewhat familiar with the six basic information resources (talk, listen, read, write, visit, and observe), it would be worthwhile to give you some tips about how best to use them. Here are some suggestions. Don't limit yourself to these only.

TALKING
In talking with a person:

1. Attempt to ask specific questions:

   NOT: "What is electrical engineering like?"

   BUT: "I dislike reading. Would I have to do much reading as an engineer on the job?"

2. Ask questions that allow the person to answer freely and don't bias his answers because of his embarrassment for you or himself.

   NOT: "I believe that I am very intelligent and could easily succeed as a lawyer, don't you?"

   BUT: "What single trait or skill must a person have if he is to succeed in your job?"

3. Attempt to seek from the person information that is not contained in books.

   NOT: "About how many petroleum engineers are there in the United States today?"

   BUT: "What, for you, is the most rewarding aspect of your job?"

LISTENING

Listening is one of the best ways to gain information . . . Be alert!

1. Listen to the job information with an unbiased attitude.

   NOT: "All secretarial jobs are alike, I don't want to sit behind a typewriter all day."

   BUT: "What is it about this occupation that I would like and what wouldn't I like?"

2. Listen carefully to the information given so that you may ask questions on things not covered that interest you.

   NOT: "I am interested in electronics, but is it true that it is one of the most highly paid professions?"

   BUT: "What courses should I take if I want to become an electrical engineer?"

3. Be alert to what the person has to say about working conditions, qualifications, and other things that *you* are interested in.

READING

You should try to get the most out of what you read. Reading a catalogue, for example, is not like reading a novel. You must look for specific information.

1. Reading the literature that concerns *you*.

   NOT: "This looks like it might be fun to read although I'd never consider being a pilot."

   BUT: "I'm looking for a list of Dental Colleges. Is this where I can find it?"

2. Get the most up-to-date information you can.

NOT: "This old book sure has weird ideas about advertising."

BUT: "Advertising is a fast moving and challenging profession according to the latest issue of *Life*. Is this what *I* want to do?"

WRITE

1. Don't write for materials just because they are available.

NOT: "Let's send out for all of this information."

BUT: "H-mm, I'm interested in becoming a mechanic. Where would I write to get information on this job?"

2. Write for literature that is up-to-date and represents your needs and desires.

NOT: "Gee, they have all sorts of information about farming in the United States."

BUT: "Where could I write to get the materials I want about being a rancher?"

3. How does the information you write for make a difference in what you need to know now?

NOT: "I'd like to know about the teachers' retirement plans."

BUT: "What kinds of courses would I have to take in college to become a teacher?"

VISIT

When visiting a job site or college, it is important to have some idea of what you are trying to find out.

1. Don't go to a place without first knowing something about it.

2. Ask specific questions about things that interest *you*. Prepare some of these ahead of time.

NOT: "I could look around, I guess."

BUT: "Is it possible for me to visit the history department, since that is what I want to go into?"

3. Check on the facilities that would affect you.

NOT: "I could see if they have a large auditorium on campus."

BUT: "I'm interested in music as a career. What is your music department like and what are the qualifications for getting in?"

"I like to study in a quiet place. Does the library here offer study rooms, or is there some place else I could go?"

OBSERVING

You may find that you will learn more about a job by observing than by reading about it.

1. When observing a job try to imagine what it would be like to be a "part of it." (Put yourself in their "shoes".)

NOT: "Gee, that looks like fun."

BUT: "I wonder what skills are involved here. Do I have them?"

2. Observe the working conditions and demands of the job.

NOT: "Is it air conditioned in here?"

BUT: "Will I enjoy working in here? Do I like the social conditions? Can I meet the physical demands?"

AN OCCUPATION AND I

INTEREST:_____   NAME:_____

SCHOOL:_____

REQUIREMENTS	AMOUNT OF REQUIREMENT (Circle)	IS THIS I? (Check)		
		O.K. for me	Not sure ??	Not I Doesn't fit
ACADEMIC				
1. Years of preparation beyond high school	none, two, four, six, eight, more, don't know	____	____	____
2. Place in graduating class	upper third, middle third, not a factor, don't know	____	____	____
3. Amount of reading as part of job	little, some, a great deal, don't know	____	____	____
4. Creativity and imagination	great, considerable, little, don't know	____	____	____
5. Ability to remember details and think logically	little, considerable, great, don't know	____	____	____
PHYSICAL				
1. Body size	large, normal, not a factor, don't know	____	____	____
2. Physical strength	great, normal, not a factor, don't know	____	____	____
3. Concentration or coordination	great, normal, not a factor, don't know	____	____	____
4. Number of hours demanded per week	many, normal, not a factor, don't know	____	____	____
5. Stress or anxiety involved	great, normal, not a factor, don't know	____	____	____

INTEREST

A person in this occupation would be expected to require . . .

1. . . . mechanic skill and dexterity	seldom, occasionally, frequently	____	____	____

REQUIREMENTS	AMOUNT OF REQUIREMENT (Circle)	IS THIS I? (Check)		
		O.K. for me	Not sure ??	Not I Doesn't fit
2. . . . logical thought, reasoning, and solution	frequently, occasionally, seldom	____	____	____
3. . . . an artistic flair or expression of mood and thought	occasionally, frequently, seldom	____	____	____
4. . . . a high degree of accuracy while doing routine kinds of work	seldom, occasionally, frequently	____	____	____
5. . . . working with people in order to sell them something or convince them of your viewpoint	occasionally, frequently, seldom	____	____	____
6. . . . working with people in order to assist them, help them, or provide service for them	seldom, occasionally, frequently	____	____	____

PERSONAL TRAITS

A person in this occupation would be expected to . . .

1. . . . *not* demonstrate a very aggressive attitude in his work and in meeting people	usually, occasionally, seldom	____	____	____
2. . . . act with great enthusiasm and lots of drive	seldom, occasionally, usually	____	____	____
3. . . . complete difficult tasks which require both physical and emotional control	usually, occasionally, seldom	____	____	____
4. . . . *not* demonstrate fluctuations in mood and be neither gloomy nor excitable	usually, occasionally, seldom	____	____	____
5. . . . be willing to take orders and carry them out as told	usually, seldom, occasionally	____	____	____
6. . . . be outgoing and pleasant in order to form many friendships	seldom, occasionally, usually	____	____	____

From what I have learned so far:	Good	Fair	Poor	Don't Know
1. My chances of getting into the program of preparation for this occupation are....	_____	_____	_____	_____
2. My chances of completing successfully the preparational program are....	_____	_____	_____	_____
3. My chances for moving upward after getting in this field are....	_____	_____	_____	_____
4. My chances of liking the work and life that are demanded by this job are....	_____	_____	_____	_____

SUMMARY:

_____ 1. After my investigation, I'm really not interested in this occupation.

_____ 2. *No decision!* I need more facts. Before I can go further I need to know specifically:

      a. _____

      b. _____

      c. _____

      d. _____

_____ 3. I'm interested! Before planning further, however, I need to consider fully these factors:

      a. _____

      b. _____

      c. _____

      d. _____

_____ 4. This seems to be the *best* choice I have considered. I now plan to take these steps to test my decision further:

      a. _____

      b. _____

      c. _____

      d. _____

USING THE SOCIAL MODEL TAPES

Project groups were randomly selected from interested eleventh graders in 20 high schools in the Michigan State University area. Students were asked if they were interested in exploring career possibilities with a counselor. At the beginning of the first session the counselor explained the basic purpose of the group and indicated that the group would be listening to a group of students much like themselves and then would function as a group in attempting to identify specific sources of information and suggest ways of using these sources. Stimulus materials in the form of handouts were used in the same manner and sequence as with the model group.

The model tape was played. After listening to the tape the counselor again defined the group's purpose, that of listening to a series of tapes of students presenting ways of getting and using information about future plans. The counselor then suggested that the group discuss their reactions. At the end of about 25 minutes of discussion, the three-minute summary segment of the model tape was played to the project group. The counselor then focused the group members' attention upon their purpose, and they summarized activities and goals they had set for themselves and emphasized things they would do during the week before the next session.

The enthusiasm and innovative thinking of the "models" was picked up by the project groups, although some may have been unaware of the process. In some cases students directly quoted sources from the model tape with comments such as "Like the guy on the tape said, you could find. . . ." In other instances, much like the "Men of Science" incident, project group members offered suggestions taken directly from the model tapes as though they had not heard the tape. One said, "I never thought of this before, but I suppose you could always call a vet or somebody like that and ask him if you could ride around with him for a day."

The First Model

The following is an excerpt taken from the first model tape, followed by an excerpt taken from a project group session. As the model group discussion progresses, the counselor focuses upon writing as a source of information. Members of the model group assist John, the student model, to identify sources of information in the various fields he is considering. The counselor reinforces John's enthusiasm and encourages the group to consider other sources that might help him.

Counselor: Well, if we kind of started in terms of ideas about writing to different places, I'm wondering, as a group what we might be able to come up with here.

John: Well, the first thing that I, uh, would do is be to write the medical school that I'm familiar with—uh, U of M [University of Michigan]—has an excellent medical school. And WSU [Wayne State University] has a medical school and beside that . . . someone . . . I . . . could write to the American Medical Association.

Counselor: Right.

Rose: Well, John, along with writing to the med school of your choice, why don't you write to the school of education, too . . . I mean. . . .

John: Yeah, well, uh, yeah, I forgot about that. I'm interested in the Navy, also, and could write to the Department of the Navy, uh, or the Naval Reserve in town here.

Counselor: Good. Do you know just what would be available at this place right in town?

John: Um, yes, there's the Naval Reserve right over here on the corner and you can get literature and information from there and also from the University which has NROTC . . . uh, Naval Reserve training. . . .

Members of the project groups also had the *Read, Write, Listen, Observe, Talk, Visit* signs before them and were encouraged to keep these general sources in mind as each member discussed planning. On one tape a project group member focused upon writing in much the same way that the model counselor had done on the model tape. The counselor assisted him in making the suggestion a specific one. Others contributed also, and the counselor reinforced their behavior.

Jack: Yeah, but Al, you ought to be able to find out a lot about vet medicine by writing, too, you know. . . .

Counselor: Could you be specific, Jack? What, specifically could Al do in the area of writing?

Jack: Well, he could write any university that has a vet school, although I'm not sure where . . . yeah, and then the AMA is for people doctors (laughter) and there must be some outfit like that for vets.

Al: Sure . . . Doc Brennan ought to know about that . . . he probably belongs or something and . . . there must be something locally like the SPCA or something. . . .

Irv: No, no . . . you could visit them, but you could get a lot of pamphlets and stuff right in the Counseling Office, uh . . . and maybe find out from the pamphlets whether there are other outfits to write to.

Counselor: Right. Al, some of their suggestions are excellent. But I'm wondering about other sources of. . . .

Some project group members were at a loss as to where to start. They were not ready to seek information and needed assistance from the group and the counselor as to how to identify their interests at a more elementary level. As in the excerpt that follows, the counselor and group attempt to assist the member in identifying his interest or goal.[4]

Ed: I'm as anxious about the future as the rest . . . anyone else, but that doesn't help much. I guess I just need direction or something.

Counselor: Are you saying that you'd like to do something, but just can't think where to begin?

[4] Editors' Note: This suggests the possibility of selecting students on some explicit basis other than just interest in considering future plans. Perhaps a separate type of social model could be used initially to prepare students for the kind of modeling used here.

Ed: Yeah.
Counselor: Have you an idea of some occupations you'd at least like to con-
               sider seriously?
Ed: Sure. Electronics and stuff like that.
Sam: Electronics seems too broad. I mean . . . well, just what do you
               mean by electronics? Can you, you know, get at an actual job?
Ed: All I know is I like electronics . . . to fool with. . . .
Brad: How about starting with job level? You could be a worker that
               just puts the same circuits together or a guy that's thinking of uses
               for ComSat fifty years from now. Both are electronics people.
Jerry: Well, Ed, I mean, you're a good math student, well, I just can't
               imagine you not going to college. Routine stuff doesn't fit . . . it
               seems like. . . .
Counselor: When you first mentioned electronics, were you thinking of some-
               one or a type of person or something you'd read?
Ed: Yeah. Well, not really. For example, I always have thought of
               myself as being in electronics, but I don't even know what that
               really means. . . .

The Second Model

The second model tape focused on how to be more discriminating and
careful in seeking information (see the Getting Helpful Information
form). In the next excerpt from the second model tape, Jim helps John,
the student model, to ask questions of his doctor that are more likely to
produce the personal perceptions that would not be found in source
books. Other members then suggest that John follow a similar procedure
as he explores his second career possibility, teaching.

John: I secured an appointment with my family doctor, to, um, pos-
               sibly be with him in his office.
Counselor: To go down and visit him?
John: Yeah, to go down and talk to him about what's going on in his
               office and I hope to ask him some questions that will pertain to
               what I want, like—not a question he can't answer freely like, "Do
               you think that I'd make a good doctor?" or I think I'd ask him
               something like, "Do you like your work?" or. . . .
Jim: No, why don't you ask, "What do you like about your work?" He
               might answer [to "Do you like your work?"], "Yes, I like my work."
               Most doctors do.
John: You mean, what specifically he likes about it?
Jim: Yeah, what he likes about his job and what he doesn't like. And
               that way you can probably get more about the job itself than his
               participation in it.
John: Like you mean, what he personally looks for in a doctor or some-
               thing like this?

Jim: Right, and, well, what he would suggest for qualifications of a
              doctor, or something like this?
John: Well, what about a teacher? I mean, how could I find out what
              somebody expects in a teacher and what they see in a teacher . . .
              what they would like to see in a teacher?
Paula: Well, why don't you go to a principal of a school and ask him?
              You know, he's the one who hires and fires the teachers—ask him
              what he would look for in a good teacher.
John: You mean you'd think he'd have definite ideas?
Paula: Oh, yes, for a principal!
Rose: He might be able to tell you some things about teacher-to-teacher
              relationships in the school and how the other teachers react not
              only to the students but to each other.
Counselor: Excellent. Talking to the principal should. . . .

Jim and the counselor also suggest that when one seeks information, he
must be aware of his biases. As he explores, he must attempt to be as
objective as possible. Continued effort was made throughout the second
model tape to stress objective exploration, appropriate use of sources,
and specific goals in information-seeking.

Counselor: John, what would you be looking for if you were to see a film or
              go over and talk to them?
John: I . . . I think I'd look for the things that I'd personally want like
              a . . . well. . . .
Jim: Or that might be wrong, because, I mean, sometimes when we go
              in to look at something, you know, we're looking for just what
              you want. Ah, you might miss an idea or two that never came
              along. I mean you have to go into it open-mindedly and not just
              look for specific things. . . .
Counselor: That's good, you know, in terms of the biases we all have about
              some things and sometimes if we don't really acknowledge the
              bias we kind of see and hear what we want to and not what is
              really there.
Jim: Yeah, yeah, you can go into a film, say about teaching, and go in
              with the attitude that, well, the teacher's got to be around pound-
              ing on the kids all day, you know, and so you'll find that in the
              film, but if you go in open-mindedly you might see that that's only
              brief periods of time. . . .

The Third Model

The final model interview proved the most difficult. This model tape
focused on what we termed the "sifting and sorting" process. In the
following excerpt from the third model tape the counselor is explaining

how to complete the form entitled "An Occupation and I." Later on the group is interacting with John.

Counselor:	Let me make a comment about the summary here. As you think about this occupation, Jim, staying with engineering, what does it look like? Either "I am really not interested," "no decision, I really do not know enough yet," "I am interested but I am going to try and find out more," or "I am definitely interested, this seems to be the best choice that I've considered so far." The idea is to put down what you'd now like to find out in terms of some of the things you circled like "I don't know" or "I'm not sure," but here we are going to be much less vague. We're going to be more specific about very concrete things that you can put down to do. So rather than say, "Talk to someone who was in engineering," you might want to put down "Talk to an engineer about number of hours I would have to work" or "Talk to an engineer about the amount of time I'd have to spend on detail and routine"—very specific kinds of questions. Why don't you take a few minutes now and go through one of these for each of your areas. So, Jim, you've been thinking of either going into business or engineering so you'd fill out two. . . . John, what other kinds of things do you feel you should be doing now in terms of trying to clarify some of these things?
John:	Well, I was wondering about the competition in college, you know, what I have to—how would I have to, uh, what sort of courses would I have to take. How would I succeed in college. I had a chance to look at the freshman class profiles and, um, there was given for U of M the, um, high school averages, grade-point averages, and the STEP averages and, um, I think maybe this would be a guideline, I don't know.
Paula:	I don't know, would that really tell you whether you're going to succeed or not? Whether you have to maintain that average?
Jim:	No, it would just kind of show you that, uh, you'll be working with people that are more or less in their specialty so that if they have a higher grade-point average so you know if you know kids around here who carry that grade point, you know what your competition. . . .
Counselor:	Well, how is John going to start kind of sifting and sorting here? You've mentioned a couple of things. He's also thought about teaching.
Jim:	Yah, what kind of stuff have you got down for teaching? to compare, to see which one. . . .
John:	One of the factors I'm considering in both fields, um, is the years of preparation once you get out of high school, I mean how many years?
Jim:	They're both quite high so that wouldn't really make any difference between the two.

John: There was one point in here, uh, I feel that I could communicate with adults and be pleasant and outgoing with adults and I was wondering if in teaching how would I be able to, uh, what sort of relationship would I have with somebody that was younger than me. Would I have a tendency to look down on this person or would I have a tendency to have little patience with this person? . . .

Jim: You have to come into contact with children sometimes in general practice, but if you did go into medicine and specialize you could, you know, wouldn't have to worry about this, so that might be one good point in favor of medicine.

Rose: You know one thing, John, you're talking about teaching. That was my major interest, teaching. I had the opportunity to teach in a sixth grade class, but it threw a completely different light on the whole thing and, uh, I found myself having a lot more prob-lems than I had ever anticipated. You know, I felt I was baby-sitting and not teaching. And that is a major problem and it gave me second thoughts about teaching—whether I could stand that for 52 weeks.

Project group members were frequently at a loss as to how to handle the information they had gathered. The counselor tried to assist the students in examining specific facts and behavioral observations they had gathered. The temptation to generalize was great and the counselor was forced to continually restructure in order that group focus be kept on that which might be useful to a member. An excerpt from a project group tape points this out:

Counselor: George, how could the information your neighbor gave you be of help here?

George: Well (chuckle) the thing that surprised me more than anything else was that he was so anxious, well, glad that I had talked with him about it. That really kind of encouraged me because he was . . . seemed so interested in what I was interested in and I think he was. . . .

Counselor: What are some of the things that you found out from him? I mean, some of the specific. . . .

George: Oh, I think . . . well, first of all the profession is politics and so I think one of the biggest considerations to me anyway, would be just the physical . . . well, could I take the job physically. I'll go to bed at 2:00 A.M. and he'll have his lights on still and I don't know whether I can take that kind of stuff. And then also, how I would get into something like politics. I just don't know. But I really think that I'd like it, but. . . .

Counselor: What have you observed? Or what have any of you observed? . . .

George, you mentioned the hours a politician keeps, but what else have you observed? What can you relate this to?

Dave: A lot of it comes down to just how you are with other people. You can talk about dentistry or politics, but a lot of it depends on how you can get along with them.

Counselor: Okay, but we're wandering. Let's get back to George and some specific. . . .

George: I think Steve had a good point earlier when he said there are two things you have to look at when you go into a profession. One is if you like the profession and if you can get along with it for the rest of your life. The other thing is how well qualified you are to get in. Like, there may be some professions that you are very well qualified for but you can't stand . . . and there are other things that you would love to be in, but you can't meet the qualifications so it looks like you'd maybe have to compromise in some way.

Counselor: Right. The decision is two-pronged. Our purpose is to attempt to determine. . . .

Counselor Using Verbal Reinforcement

The counselor frequently provided the initial structure and encouraged group participation. He then reinforced responses that were of an information-seeking variety. Counselors working with project groups tended to modify their behavior as they listened to the model counselor, also. That is, the model counselor served as an example for the counselor as to how to conduct the group session after listening to the tapes. In one group, Richard was interested in becoming a draftsman and had thought of a draftsman he might visit. However, he really didn't know how to approach the task. The counselor put the problem in perspective, encouraged group suggestions, and reinforced information-seeking responses.

Counselor: Okay, how could we help Richard a little here? Specifically, what might he ask his father's friend that would tell him something of the work of the draftsman that he couldn't pick up in a book?

Bruce: How about, "Is work tiresome, monotonous, boring?"

Scott: Or, "What would it be like after I got into it?" "What would the hours be?" "How much are you involved with those around you that you work with and how much do you have to associate with people that come in and work with other people?" In other words, "Can I work alone as an individual, or with others?"

Counselor: That would be a good thing to find out. If you don't like interacting with people too much that would be a pretty important aspect. What would be one of the best ways to find something like that out?

Richard: Oh, probably talk or write to the people who are in the occupation.

Counselor: How else? Can you think of another way that you could find out what goes on there?

Richard: I could observe, maybe, the place where the person works and watch him work for a couple of hours or so and find out if he mingles around or just stays in one location of the office and doesn't work actually with others.

Counselor: Right. By observing you could tell if you keyed on exactly what he did and with whom he associated if you watched carefully, as Bruce said, whether he worked alone or spent much of his day intermingling with other workers. So, you could determine this not only by the question you phrased, but also by the way you keyed your observation.

Richard: I'll have to think just how I might do that, but I think I could get a lot more information by planning something like this.

EFFECTS OF THE MODELING EXPERIENCE

Two weeks after the third and final session a follow-up was done. Each student who had participated was individually seen by a trained interviewer to determine such things as how much and what kinds of information he had sought and what he was now planning to do.

From the audio tapes of project group sessions those of one group were chosen. The fact that all group members had professional goals, however, marks this group as atypical. Nonetheless, it demonstrates the exploratory behavior of the four eleventh graders during the course of the project.

Joe

Joe had identified dentistry and accounting as career possibilities at the initial meeting of the group. He made an appointment with his dentist, but it was scheduled to occur after the interview with the evaluator. However, he had talked at some length with the dentist on the telephone. Also, he had read pamphlets concerning dentistry at both the school and county library, written for pamphlets from three agencies or associations, and written to five medical associations and asked for information they might have available concerning dentistry. Further, he had spent a morning sitting in the inner office of a second dentist and watched him work. Joe also had been active in seeking information about accounting. He visited a neighbor in his accounting office, read three pamphlets and a book in the school library, and talked at length with his father about the pros and cons of accounting. His father, although not an accountant, was knowledgeable in the area.

Stan

Stan, interested in medicine and law, visited his family doctor at the office and attended a career day program concerning new trends in medicine that featured a doctor, two nurses, and an X-ray technician. He had talked with his father, who was a lawyer, about entering the profession, visited his office, and observed him working with clients. At his father's suggestion he had twice attended court during the course of the group project.

Fred

Fred visited a lawyer, also, and read the log of activities that the lawyer kept daily as well as discussed various law schools. He found the pamphlets he read in the school library too broad and learned more by visiting the office of a neighbor who was a lawyer and asking him specific questions. Fred had written to four law schools, a bar association, and a nonprofit organization for occupational information. He also was interested in becoming a psychiatrist. He was surprised to learn from pamphlets in the school library that one must first become a medical doctor and was rather discouraged because of the long years of preparation. However, he visited a general practitioner who was a neighbor and had received two pamphlets and the promise of more from the American Medical Association.

Loren

Loren first read a number of pamphlets and books about medicine and discussed the chances, financially, of attempting to become a doctor with his parents. He wrote for and received an undergraduate catalog, a pamphlet on medicine as a career, and a medical school catalog from the state university and attended medical career day at the hospital. Finally, he visited his family doctor and concentrated his conversation on questions that other sources had been unable to answer. The doctor reviewed office procedures with him and told him of his work on a typical day. Also, the doctor explained the relationship of the general practitioner to specialized branches of medicine. Loren's second interest was law. His information-seeking in this area was admittedly negligent. He had done some reading, but said that he had learned most about law from hearing Fred discuss it within his group counseling sessions.[5]

[5] Editors' Note: Relevant and meaningful data need not be obtained firsthand by each person. Quite possibly the use of small groups composed of students with comparable interests and goals could significantly increase the availability of data beyond what one student could do on his own.

CAREER DEVELOPMENT REMAINS AS A PRINCIPAL TASK OF THE SCHOOL COUNSELOR

Despite the abundant supply of attractive reference books and pamphlets some catalyst is needed to help students to become involved in exploratory activity. In addition, concrete techniques are needed to help counselors work with students on problems of career and training. Students and counselors are inspired frequently by knowing how others handle similar tasks. The tape excerpts have suggested that student behavior and response patterns were altered by the model tapes. Counselors, also, followed the lead of the counselor on the model tape and stressed the value in seeking specific information. While much needs to be learned about what types of modeling procedures work best with what kinds of students, the results of this project were encouraging enough to continue exploring the use of modeling techniques in career counseling.

27

ENCOURAGING CONSTRUCTIVE USE OF TIME

James E. Smith
NOVA SCHOOLS, FORT LAUDERDALE, FLORIDA

I was interested in finding out how students could be encouraged to spend more of their unscheduled time in doing school work. The situation involved a flexible scheduled high school in which one third of the student's time was not specifically scheduled, that is, the student was not assigned to a specific area of the school, but attended any one of several resource centers, open classrooms, or went to the school cafeteria. Use of unscheduled time became a problem when it was determined that about 75 percent of the students spent their unscheduled time in the cafeteria. It was felt that this amount of unscheduled time in the cafeteria was excessive. Something needed to be done to encourage students to spend more of their unscheduled time in work-oriented areas.

I decided to use what has been termed a social modeling-reinforcement procedure to influence students in how to use their unscheduled time. (See Krumboltz and Thoresen, 1964) If students were given the opportunity to hear how other students, much like themselves, used their unscheduled time, and discussed how they could make use of these ideas, then these students might spend less time in the cafeteria. I reasoned that providing students with such examples of how to use their time and giving them positive encouragement during discussion might be very influential. I also thought that working with students in small groups might enhance the effectiveness of the modeling experience (See Smith, 1965, for a complete report).

SELECTING STUDENTS AND TRAINING TEACHERS

Two schools were selected for this study: Roy Martin Junior High School in Las Vegas, Nevada, and Ridgewood High School in Norridge, Illinois. Roy Martin and Ridgewood appeared similar in at least two ways: (1) the schools were composed primarily of students of lower-middle socioeconomic status and (2) they were similar to national norms on intelligence and achievement test results. In addition administrators of each school had developed a similar form of flexible scheduling, that is, class periods that vary from 20 to 140 minutes in length, class groups that vary in size from 10 to 300 students, and courses that are taught by teaching teams composed of two to six teachers.

Approximately 300 ninth-grade students at each of the two schools were invited to participate in special small group discussions on how they might use their unscheduled time more effectively. Individual invitations were given by means of a letter. The letter and attached reply sheet were distributed and collected during a home room period. Students who desired clarification of the program were referred to me. Students who volunteered were requested to indicate the number of periods of their unscheduled time that were spent in schoolwork-oriented areas and the cafeteria the previous two days. From the list of ninth-grade volunteers, the 80 students from each school who spent the greatest percentage of their unscheduled time in the cafeteria constituted the students to be seen.

Training Teachers as Group Leaders

In each school two senior teachers were selected to be group discussion leaders. A senior teacher was defined as one with a minimum of five years of experience, a Master's degree, and credits for at least two graduate guidance courses. Two teachers, one male and one female, each with the above qualifications, were selected at each school.

The four teacher discussion leaders were trained in principles of social learning, with emphasis on social modeling and positive reinforcement.

Material was used from previously published work (Krumboltz and Thoresen, 1964) to demonstrate how to use a social model tape in a small group and how to use verbal and nonverbal positive reinforcement. I explained the purposes of the study and trained the teachers by emphasizing the following information:

1. Increasing his desire to use unscheduled time effectively
2. Helping him make specific plans for using the time effectively
3. Providing approval for his experiences indicating effective use of unscheduled time.

MODEL REINFORCEMENT TREATMENT

I pointed out to the discussion leaders that to accomplish these purposes in the brief amount of time available to work with students it was necessary for the discussion leader to give thought to the following points:

1. What are the verbal statements that should be positively reinforced?
2. How can these best be elicited from the group members?
3. What are the reinforcing actions which he can provide?
4. How can the resources of the group, particularly those pertaining to contributing helpful suggestions and providing peer reinforcement, best be utilized?

The following suggestions were used to aid the group discussion leader in planning and carrying out the discussion. They served as general guidelines, and the group discussion leader modified and expanded upon them as needed:

Defining Verbal Statements To Be Reinforced Positively

In general these would be statements by students indicating understanding, agreement, and planning appropriate to the purposes for which the unscheduled time is provided. More specifically it would include such types of statements as:

a. Indicating the value of using unscheduled time effectively
b. Indicating specific plans for improving the use of this time
c. Indicating specific instances of having used the time effectively.

To maximize these types of statements occurring, the focus of the discussion should be carefully structured. The discussion should maintain a positive frame of reference and be aimed at discovering more productive uses of the time and making plans accordingly. It should not focus mostly upon the problems and difficulties the students have encountered in the past. The discussion can easily become dominated by talking of past difficulties, reasons why it isn't easy to use the time effectively, and informal testimonials regarding lack of self-discipline. These should be carefully handled by the group leader in such a way as to move quickly toward possible solutions, rather than dwelling simply on gaining insight into why the time hasn't been used effectively in the past.

Negative, or problem-centered statements should not be highly reinforced. They should be simply accepted as valid and used as a starting point for bringing positive suggestions as to solutions to these problems. The focus should immediately move to possible courses of action which can be taken to overcome the stated problem.[1]

Eliciting the Desired Statements

Taking steps to bring about the behaviors which were to be reinforced was crucial. The group leader should take an active role in this by selective questioning or "cueing." These leads should be designed to influence the direction of the discussion, and to encourage all of the group members to participate.[2] The following types of questions or leads may be useful:

1. "I would appreciate it if someone would explain . . . (or clarify) . . ."
2. "I have been wondering. . . ."
3. "Does anyone know of instances where. . . ."
4. "Several times I have heard students state that . . . Does this seem to be something that you have experienced . . . (or would agree with)?"

TO DRAW OUT OTHER MEMBERS:

5. "I am wondering how others who haven't spoken up view this."
6. "Mary brought up an interesting point . . . I am wondering how this would be viewed by some of the rest of us."
7. "As I thought about this it seemed to me that . . . Now I'm wondering if anyone else looked at it, or thought about it, that way."
8. "I think your point is interesting, John, and I'm wondering how it relates to. . . ."

TO SYNTHESIZE AND CLARIFY:

9. "Several of you have brought out interesting points on this. Mary indicated. . . . Bill stated that he. . . . Now would it seem that . . . ?"

[1] Editors' Note: An excellent point! Too often as counselors, teachers, and parents we inadvertently encourage and maintain negative, self-depreciating talk which does little to really change the problem behaviors in desired ways. Perhaps the positive and the constructive, stated in terms of specific behavior, needs more accentuating by us.

[2] Editors' Note: Everyone uses a variety of "cues," sometimes unknowingly, in talking with others. Here the group leader, deliberately and specifically uses cues to elicit responses relevant to the group's objectives.

10. "Several of you have mentioned a number of useful things. Now I'm wondering just what each of you might plan to try differently this coming week."

Types of Reinforcing Statements

In general, reinforcing actions are those which signify approval, recognition, and encouragement. The group leader can draw from his own natural repertoire of both verbal statements and nonverbal actions. Examples of these will include such things as:

"That sounds like a very good idea."
"I'm sure a lot of students would agree with that."
"That's a very good point."
"Right." "Good." (and so forth.)

The leader can give careful attention and indicate interest in what the student is saying by:

Leaning forward as the person speaks.
Keeping your eyes on person while he is speaking.
Nodding your head up and down.
Smiling.

Some General Suggestions

The following points were suggested to the group leaders:

1. Provide encouragement by being continually optimistic, enthusiastic, and positive about the students learning to be in better control of their use of time, and gaining from using the time effectively.

2. Encourage the students to explore new uses for their unscheduled time in keeping with their interests and curiosity.

3. Near the close of the first session, encourage the students to make some specific plans, and to return to the following meeting prepared to discuss what they observed regarding their own use of time and that of others, as well as how well their own plans worked out.

Group leaders were asked to think in advance of the main ideas for the opening statements for each group meeting. Leaders were told that the following would be good beginning comments:

The purpose of our getting together is to help you decide how you might go about getting the very most out of your unscheduled time.

To do this we will need to think about what you would like to accomplish during that time . . . some of the things you could do to accomplish what you wish to. . . . I'm sure some of you have some valuable ideas and experiences already along these lines. Through sharing these, maybe we can all discover some more useful things you would like to try. . . . Why don't you tell us about the thoughts you've already had as to what you would like to accomplish during your unscheduled time.

THE MODEL REINFORCEMENT DISCUSSION SESSIONS

After the discussion leader greeted the students, he stated,

> I suggest we begin to talk quite specifically about the reason why we all met here today. All of you have indicated some interest in thinking about how you might use this unscheduled time that you have throughout the week here in school. By getting together and sharing our ideas, finding what sort of problems you have been experiencing in using this time, as well as some of the things you have found very helpful, maybe we can learn and come up with some things each person will want to try on his own in the next few weeks.
>
> Before we start our own discussion, I thought you might be interested in listening to a tape recording of a group of students in another school who met to discuss this topic. These students were much like yourselves, and they found that through sharing ideas and making plans together they were able to learn how to use their time effectively. Let's listen for specific ideas and then we can discuss them along with our own . . .

After the students listened to the model tape the discussion leader asked the students about their own ideas on using time and whether they had heard any helpful suggestions. The discussion session continued with the counselor carefully listening for any response which he judged to be concerned with the effective use of unscheduled time. The counselor reinforced verbally any indication that the students had in the past, or intended in the future, to utilize their unscheduled time in an effective manner. He also reinforced any student who emitted any information-seeking response that was concerned with effective use of unscheduled time. Examples of the behaviors that were reinforced are:

1. "I use 20-minute periods to review for my next class."
2. "You know, if I did my homework during any free time, I would have more time to myself at home in the evening."
3. "Perhaps I should investigate each area and find out what each has to offer."
4. "Perhaps I could get a friend to go with me to the _____ area."
5. "Perhaps I could talk to my _____ teacher about the _____ resource center."

The discussion leader reinforced the desired verbal behavior with the following type of responses:

What John pointed out earlier in our conversation regarding exploring things is a good way of meeting your interests.

Several have indicated, and correctly so, that this is a way of becoming more responsible for one's own time.

Mm-Hmmm.

That's a very good idea, Mark.

That should be interesting, I bet there are a number of others interested in that same thing.

I certainly agree with you.

The session was terminated with the counselor asking each student, "What do you think you might wish to do between now and the next time we meet, to learn more about the resource centers and make some plans?" The students volunteered to make a daily or weekly plan of things to do with the free periods and to find out if a plan can be followed, see what other resource centers are like and make a list of all the resource areas and what is available in them.

The discussion leader verbally reinforced each of these statements.

The second session began with the discussion leader stating, "I am glad we are all able to be back together again today and talk further about this. When we talked last time, many questions came up that were interesting to me and I'm wondering how you solved them and what you found since we talked last." The session continued with the counselor reinforcing desired verbal behavior.

SOME RESULTS

Presenting students with an audio tape social model did significantly increase the amount of unscheduled time spent in school work-oriented areas. Students completed a daily reporting form for one week following their two model discussion sessions. When compared with other students, those who met in the model reinforcement discussion session spent considerably more time in work areas than in the cafeteria. The results have these implications:

1. Students can be helped to identify certain behaviors they wish to change and such behavior can be stated in observable terms. In this study, the students indicated they desired assistance in utilizing more effectively their unscheduled time. The behavior was defined in terms of time students were spending in work related areas.

2. Teachers can learn, while on the job and with relatively little difficulty, how to employ counseling techniques to assist students.[3]

3. Symbolic modeling of desired student behavior is an effective procedure,

[3] Editors' Note: Much can be done in training teachers to employ several techniques in working with students in a variety of settings, as this study illustrates. See Articles 18, 19, 20, 29, and 30 for examples of teacher training procedures.

a means to assist students in changing their behavior. In this study an audio tape of a small group of students discussing how they might utilize their unscheduled time more effectively with their teacher was used as a symbolic model. Modeling is a procedure which may require little time to administer, but when used in conjunction with other techniques can influence the relevant behaviors of students.

28
OVERCOMING UNDERACHIEVEMENT

Alice L. Beach
SANTA CLARA UNIFIED SCHOOL DISTRICT (CALIFORNIA)

This report illustrates how social models may be developed and used effectively by counselors in intermediate school settings in helping seventh and eighth grade underachievers. The records of more than 2,000 seventh and eighth graders in four intermediate schools were used in order to obtain data on students' scholastic ability and grade point averages.[1] These data were converted into normalized standard scores with a mean of 50 and a standard deviation of 10. Underachievers were defined as students whose grade point average was 10 or more points below their scholastic ability scores. Students were randomly selected from these underachievers and placed in counseling groups. Each group consisted of four students of the same sex, and was led by one of the regular staff counselors of the same sex from that school.

TRAINING THE SCHOOL COUNSELORS

To prepare counselors for the project a consultant experienced in developing and using social models conducted twelve training sessions with the counselors. The first six of these training sessions focused on principles of social learning. Counselors read several case studies which illustrated use of a variety of social learning techniques and also listened to several social models tapes. The next six meetings consisted of individual and group criticism and discussion of audio tape-recorded practice group

[1] The project was conducted in 1964–1965 in the Jefferson Union School District, Santa Clara, California.

counseling sessions.[2] Between sessions each counselor practiced using an audio tape social model with groups of underachieving students who had been identified but were not scheduled to participate in the project.

MAKING THE SOCIAL MODEL TAPES

Seven model tapes about six minutes in length each were prepared. Scripts were written for the first six of the model counseling sessions. Three eighth grade girls and three eighth grade boys who attended a junior high school in another city were selected as student models.[3] The author and a male counselor from a local junior college played the roles of the model counselors.

Model Tape 1

The first model tape introduced three underachieving students:

1. A student who was doing poorly and was indifferent about his performance.
2. A student who was doing poorly but was concerned about his difficulty.
3. A student who was doing average work and who didn't understand why anyone should be concerned about his mediocre performance.

It was assumed that these three model students would represent at least some of the most important attitudes held by underachievers. By hearing different types of students, therefore, students would be more likely to identify with at least one of the model students.

Model Tape 2

This tape included discussion about the values of education, and what can be done to improve participation in class discussions. Suggestions included: (1) speaking up in class when one has something to contribute; (2) asking for clarification of a point; and (3) the importance of knowing how to ask a sensible question.

Model Tape 3

This tape presented specific suggestions on how to ask good questions. Suggestions included: (1) asking the question seriously without trying

[2] Editors' Note: It's not clear that 12 sessions were actually needed to train the school counselors.

[3] Editors' Note: Knowing just what criteria to use in selecting students to perform as social models is a complex problem. At present it seems best to select persons who are of high status, prestigious and competent, as perceived by the clients to be counseled.

to be funny; (2) using good English in asking a question; and (3) making the question specific, so that the teacher will know what part of the topic the student understands and what he does not understand.

Model Tape 4

Here the focus was on suggestions of how to do homework more efficiently. Examples included: (1) asking for clarification of assignments which are not understood; (2) writing down homework assignments in a particular place; (3) writing down dates when things are due; (4) having a separate place for homework assignments in each subject; and (5) having a regular time and place to study, when all members of the family will leave him alone.

Model Tape 5

The theme of this session was on suggestions for improving study methods. Topics were: (1) talking over study problems with parents can gain cooperation in keeping younger siblings out of the way; (2) scheduling study time helps concentration; (3) using TV viewings as a reward; (4) usefulness of books on how to study; (5) surveying or skimming a reading assignment before going over it carefully; and (6) where to find books with study suggestions.

Model Tape 6

This tape presented more ideas on study methods, with such suggestions as: (1) it is better to get accustomed to one new technique before working on the next; (2) surveying a reading assignment before careful study; (3) making up questions to ask oneself about the assignment, as a way of getting ready to look for answers; (4) periodically stopping in studying in order to recite to oneself; (5) going over class notes to make better outlines; (6) filling in class notes with notes from the textbook; and (7) reading assignments with the positive intention of remembering.

Model Tape 7

The final model tape contained a general summary of ideas and suggestions covered in the first six model tapes. Each model student recopied the particular suggestions and ideas that he or she planned to act on.

The seven model counseling sessions represented successive meetings with the same students. On all of the model tapes the model counselor verbally reinforced the student's achievement-oriented responses, and led the students to consider ways in which school work could be improved and the possible future outcome of high academic achievement. An achievement-oriented response was defined as a verbal statement by the student indicating that he would like to improve his school work, that he felt education had specific value to the individual or that he had thought of specific steps in improving his study efficiency. Examples of achievement-oriented responses are: "I'm going to start writing down important things the teacher says;" "You can get better jobs if you get good grades in school;" "I'm going to try to figure out ways of studying better."

TRANSCRIPT OF A MODEL TAPE

The complete script for one model tape is presented. This is the male model tape for the fifth session. The same script was used for the fifth female model tape with minor changes in phrasing.

Paul:	At first it didn't work out too well, because my sister, well, she kept coming in to bother me even after my Mom told her to leave me alone. But now she's sort of got the idea.
Co:	Good, Paul. After talking it over with your folks, they helped you to set up a study schedule.
Paul:	Yeah—well, I think what really did it was showing Mom I'd really keep my sister out of her hair at certain times.
Co:	Um hmm, fine.
Paul:	And I'm sort of trying—well, to decide how to divide up my time— I mean, well, you know—when I sit down to study, I look to see what I have to do for the next day, or something, and decide how much time I can work on, I can spend on, say, math, and I know that I have only a certain length of time before I have to study the history assignment, or something, and—well, it seems like that makes me concentrate better. Because I know I have to quit working on math at a certain time, so I'd better get it done.
Co:	Um hmm. That sounds like a good idea—budgeting your study time.
Gordon:	I tried that—in a way.
Co:	Good—
Gordon:	Well, I mean, it wasn't exactly like that. But the other night—well, I decided I had to get my work done by a certain time no matter what. See, my favorite TV program was going to come on, so I sort of used it as a reward. I just thought, well, decided to do a certain amount before the program came on, and if I didn't finish that part of my homework, then I couldn't see the program.
Co:	Fine, Gordon. It sounds as though both you and Paul have hit on something that can help. Budgeting your study time is good, and

then you can include other things you want to do in the schedule—give yourself a reward.

Gordon: Another thing, you know—I kind of enjoyed the program even more than I usually do. I didn't have to feel guilty about goofing off.

Co: Um hmm. You worked hard, so you knew you had earned a break . . . Ted—have you tried any of the ideas we've talked about?

Ted: Well, I was going to tell you—I found a book about how to study, and so I tried some of the things it said.

Paul: Gosh, I'd like a book like that. Does it have stuff in it that's any good?

Ted: It tells about a lot of things. For one thing, it tells about what you're trying to do—figuring out a study schedule. And there was something else I tried.

Co: Books about study methods can be a big help.

Ted: Well, I don't know how it'll work out, because I haven't gone to my science class yet. But I think I know the lesson better than I usually do—

Co: Good—

Gordon: Don't make such a big secret out of it—what did the book say?

Ted: I'm not making a secret out of it—what you do, see—I don't know if it would work for all my courses—anyhow, we had to read a chapter in the textbook. So the first thing you're supposed to do is just *look* at the chapter instead of reading it.

Paul: Just look at it! How do you do that? I mean, you—well, I don't get it—

Ted: Yeah—you look at it real fast. You read a little—you know, there's a kind of introduction at the beginning of each chapter. So you *read* that. But then you go through the chapter and just read the various headings and subheadings.

Co: That sounds good—

Ted: —and when you get to the end of the chapter there's a summary, so you read that. And you read the captions under pictures, too.

Gordon: You mean you learn what's in the chapter just by—

Ted: Wait a minute. I'm trying to tell you. *After* you go over the chapter fast—after you survey it, see, then you go back to the beginning and really read it.

Paul: Well, I don't get that. What's the point of going over it fast like that if you just have to go back to the beginning and read it anyhow, the way you're supposed to do in the first place?

Ted: It gives you a general idea of what it's all about, and then when you go over it slowly it's easier to see how details fit in.

Paul: I don't know—that sounds—

Ted: No kidding! I mean, you know, maybe it won't work out when I get to class. But—I'll bet it does, though, because I sure feel that I got a lot more out of that assignment than I usually do.

Co: I think you've found something that could really work for you, Ted.

Ted: The funny thing is—well, I'm not saying that I'm going to be perfect now, or anything. But, anyhow, somehow it was more interesting to me.

Co: Fine—

Ted: It seems to me that even if I do forget a lot of the details, I got a better idea of the whole thing.

Co: You probably did, Ted, and you'll probably remember it better, too.

Ted: I've only read part of the book about studying, so maybe I'll find out some other good ideas too.

Gordon: Where did you get a book like that?

Ted: In that paperback bookstore on the highway—Kepler's. I was in there looking at all the books—they've got a lot of different kinds of books there, about almost everything, I guess. And I just happened to see this one, so I bought it.

Paul: Oh—I don't—I mean, I'd like to get one, I think, but I don't have the money—

Co: You think a book with study hints would be helpful—that's a good idea, Paul. But if you can't afford to buy a book like that, what can you do about it?

Gordon: He could look for it in the library, I should think. That's what I think I'll do. And if they don't have it at school, you can always go to the public library.

Co: Um hmm, that's a good idea, Gordon. Why don't you and Paul see if you can find a book on study techniques, and then we can discuss some of the ideas about studying better.[4]

USING THE MODEL TAPES

The counselor began by saying, in effect, "You have been called in because we feel that you have the ability to do a lot better in school than you have been doing in the past. It has often been found that getting together in groups like this one and talking about the reasons we don't do as well as we might can be very helpful. As you know, students often have the same kinds of problems and may be able to suggest things to each other as to possible ways to improve their school achievement. But before discussing this, I thought you'd be interested in hearing a tape recording of other youngsters who had a similar problem."

Following this introduction, the first model tape was played. The counselor then switched the tape recorder to the record position and asked the group members to discuss their own schoolwork, and to relate what they had heard and their reactions to it. The counseling session continued with the counselor reinforcing any achievement-oriented verbal responses. It was assumed that the following types of counselor responses would be

---

[4] Editors' Note: Notice that the counselor on this model tape often verbally reinforced student responses.

positively reinforcing: "Yes, that sounds like a good idea;" "Right, that's a good point;" "Mm-hmm;" "Very good. That would be a good thing to try." The counselor also used nonverbal behavior assumed to be reinforcing, such as nodding, leaning forward, smiling, and other gestures. Seven sessions were held once a week for seven weeks. A model tape was played at the beginning of each session.

TERESA MORALES

Teresa, who participated in the project, was a Mexican-American girl whose IQ was 111 as measured by the California Test of Mental Maturity.[5] She was a large girl whose appearance was very sloppy, and she wore her hair in a wildly exaggerated "teased" style. Throughout the previous year her attention to schoolwork and her grades had been consistently low and dropping. Teresa's parents had never visited the school, even to attend a PTA meeting.

Teresa was one of a group of eighth grade Mexican-American girls whose primary interest appeared to be to frighten their classmates. They went about as a group, and frequently cornered other girls to threaten them. This led to her being detained in the county juvenile hall for a brief time.

Toward the end of the series of social model counseling sessions Teresa's father began to come to the school to see the counselor. He became interested in the school, and both parents helped with preparations for the eighth grade dance at the end of the school year. Teresa became much neater in appearance, and began to have more friendly contacts with her classmates, while at the same time she was able to maintain relationships with the Mexican-American girls. Although her grade point average was only slightly better by the end of the school year (1.67) than it had been previously (1.61), she did earn one A, which previously she had been unable to do.[6]

The following year, in high school, Teresa continued to improve. Only one of her high school grades was as low as C and her grade point average was 2.08. Nevertheless, this was a noticeable improvement, and seems to be significant in comparison with fifteen comparable underachieving 8th grade girls who had not had counseling. Their combined average had dropped from 2.374 to 1.983 in high school.

Following a visit to the high school, the intermediate school principal,

---

[5] Name has been changed to protect student's anonymity.

[6] Editors' Note: Grades are influenced by a variety of factors. Perhaps the important thing for Teresa at this point was that she was still in school and that her grades had not continued to decline.

who had seen Teresa by chance, said to the counselor, "If you could have seen Teresa—she has bloomed. You should be very proud. The time you have spent with her has certainly been worthwhile."

During Teresa's freshman year at high school her sister, Conchine, was in the seventh grade in the intermediate school Teresa had attended. Conchine's attitude toward school was very poor, as were her grades. Teresa made several visits to her former counselor to discuss her sister, as well as to talk of her own progress. The father also continued his contacts with the school, and on one occasion said to the counselor, "Anything the school says I will back." According to the counselor, it was only through the efforts of Teresa and her father that Conchine was kept in school.

TO CONCLUDE

It cannot be proved, of course, that the changes in Teresa were the result of the social model counseling alone.[7] Nevertheless, the changes were real and did follow the counseling. Other counselors also reported changes in students. For example, although one boy indicated to the group that the counseling sessions were of little interest to him, one of his teachers told the counselor that the boy had been coming in early to do makeup work, while another teacher said he had started doing his homework.

Another counselor had a call from the mother of a counselee. The mother said that she was delighted that her daughter was finally doing her homework, and added that the girl was using TV as a reward when she had completed portions of her work. A number of other parents telephoned to express their pleasure over their children's improvement at home. Many of the students themselves stated that they felt the counseling was helpful, and that they wished the meetings could continue.

[7] Editors' Note: This points up the need to use a variety of outcome criteria as evidence of change. It may be more appropriate to find out if Teresa changed those specific behaviors which were modeled on tapes such as speaking up in class, reading skills, organizing time, and study habits. Perhaps too much was undertaken at once in this study. Several studies are needed which explore more comprehensively the use of modeling procedures to alter each different behavior.

Modeling Behavioral Methods
with Teachers

WHAT IS THE BEST WAY to consult with a teacher or parent about the problems of a student? The answer depends on the purpose of the consultation. Counselors typically are not trained in consultation techniques with parents and teachers. Counselors are sometimes advised, however, to be warm and friendly conversationalists, "Show that you're concerned." Such concern frequently does little to alter the client's behavior. In some situations it may even create new problems for the client as well as the counselor.

Counselors can assist students by working in certain ways with the significant persons in the student's everyday environment, for example, the student's parents and teachers. At times significant changes can only come about if these persons modify their own behavior toward the students. To help these significant persons make crucial changes the counselor can demonstrate how to behave. He can show how to identify certain behaviors, how to form tentative hypotheses, how to gather and organize data. The counselor can instruct parents and teachers how to approach problems behaviorally. And the counselor can best do this by modeling the methods of a behavioral approach as he consults with the teacher, the administrator, and the parent.

A major objective of modeling behavioral methods is to enable clients to learn how to exercise greater control over their own behavior. The counselor has a dual purpose in consulting with others. He may assist in solving a particular problem, and he may teach another person a general method for solving similar problems in the future. Learning better teaching and child-rearing methods gives parents and teachers better control of their own behavior.

In Article 29 Moore and Sanner present the details of two cases to illustrate behavioral consultation. Prime focus is on assisting the teacher, as client, in identifying the antecedents and consequences of problem behaviors, in generating hypotheses and in defining problem situations in terms of what are the desired behaviors. Techniques include selectively reinforcing teacher responses as well as deliberately modeling certain ways of describing problem situations.

In Article 30 Goodwin describes how to use behavioral analysis with a teacher concerned with a disruptive and socially isolated sixth grade boy. This article demonstrates that the counselor can effectively instruct teachers in analyzing complex problems in the classroom.

A major implication of both articles is that counseling needs to be conceptualized broadly to include working with significant persons in the student's environment. The counselor has an instructional task in helping clients and those in their environments to understand and utilize principles and techniques based on human learning.

29

HELPING TEACHERS ANALYZE AND REMEDY PROBLEMS

Rosemarie Moore and Kenneth Sanner
PALO ALTO UNIFIED SCHOOL DISTRICT (CALIFORNIA)

Guidance consultants in the elementary school serve the adults who have significant influence upon the behavior of children. Consultation topics include the total educational program, and consultation services are not restricted to "problem" behaviors of children. Consultants work principally in two ways: by systematic consultation procedures and by modeling. This process of consultation involves seven steps: (1) problem identification in terms of specific behaviors and educational objectives,

(2) identification of desired behaviors, (3) tentative hypothesis-making about causes of the behaviors under consideration, (4) observation and data collection, (5) organization and integration of data, (6) program development, and (7) evaluation of outcomes, including further planning.

This approach is described in several illustrations of school service provided to teachers. The same procedures are followed with other school personnel, and with parents.

A CRYING CHILD

Sybil was a second grade child who was referred by the teacher for crying at inappropriate times. Observations showed that when Sybil raised her hand to volunteer an answer, she cried if she was not called upon. The teacher would ask a question, Sybil would raise her hand, and when the teacher called on another child, Sybil would begin to whimper. Whenever Sybil cried, the teacher gave her attention. It was further noted that similar behavior occurred on the playground. For example, if Sybil did not get the ball, she would cry. Her peers responded to such crying with sympathy and attention as the teacher had done in the classroom. If Sybil was given the ball, she stopped crying.

It seemed reasonable to hypothesize that Sybil's crying was being positively reinforced by her teacher and peers. A program was devised with the teacher to alter this sequence of responses to Sybil's crying. First, when Sybil raised her hand initially, the teacher would call on her. The lesson would continue. The next time, the teacher would call on some other child. If Sybil cried, the teacher would ignore it. The lesson would go on. The next time, if Sybil's hand was raised and if she was *not* crying, the teacher would call on her. The teacher also would offer cues, such as, "Yes, Sybil, now that you are not crying, please tell us what you have to say." Receiving the teacher's overt attention then became contingent for Sybil upon not crying. Later the consultant observed that Sybil's crying in the classroom had ceased. Also, her peers' responses to Sybil's crying on the playground followed closely their teacher's handling of it in the classroom and her crying diminished there as well.

BEHAVIORAL CONSULTATION—THE PROCESS

Let us consider how the process of consultation provides for application of the principles of social learning theory.

Guidance consultation seems to involve three dimensions. One dimension is direct aid in planning with teachers or parents, to solve specific problems of educational development. The request for consultation is usually related to some such problem. A second dimension is teaching the teachers and parents, through modeling, specifically how to identify problems, observe and gather data, make tentative hypotheses, and so on. A third dimension, perhaps the most difficult and surely the most crucial, is helping the consultee to translate thought into action (Bruner, 1966), that is, to put a plan into operation.

Each of these dimensions is being affected at any given time during consultation. The guidance consultant's behavior serves as a model of how to identify a problem, form hypotheses, and gather data. This occurs while the consultant is working directly with a teacher on a particular problem. The consultant also responds differentially to what teachers say and do, ignoring some responses and encouraging others. This approach influences their behavior toward the goals of the consulting interview. Putting the plan into action depends in part on what behaviors the consultees have available *and* the anticipated consequences for them. The consultant can help maximize positive consequences which will be encouraging for the teacher or parent in continuing a plan which is under way.

The general sequence that is usually followed is as follows:

1. The consultee's presentation of the problem
2. The relationship of the problem as presented to specific educational goals
3. A restatement of the problem in terms of behavior, usually seen as undesirable behavior
4. An exploration for relevant variables, including investigation of what is maintaining the undesirable behavior, how it is being rewarded (data gathering, hypothesizing)
5. A decision as to an alternate, desired behavior (behavioral objective)
6. A plan for eliciting and maintaining the alternate behavior
7. Plans for how to evaluate attainment of behavioral objectives and the methods used.[1]

Teachers are concerned about children's behavior, and usually they can describe undesirable behavior. Rarely, however, do they view children's undesirable behavior as part of a sequence of interactions, even in the classroom. The question, therefore, is how to demonstrate to the teacher the usefulness of behavior descriptions and analyses.

These steps are used by the consultant beginning to work with a teacher.

1. Accept the problem which the teacher brings.
2. Determine the behavior to be modified by assisting the teacher in giving descriptions of current undesirable behavior and descriptions of desirable behavior.

[1] Editors' Note: There is a strong flavor of the "applied behavioral scientist" here working co-operatively in a tentative, inquiring manner.

3. Hypothesize with the teacher about what maintains the present undesirable behavior and what influences are available to her to develop or increase the desirable behavior.

"WHAT CAN I DO?"

In the case presented in the following dialogue, the guidance consultant had previously worked with the kindergarten teacher. This contact is, however, the first concerning this specific problem. The dialogue was recreated from case notes and tapes.

T: My class was previously good, but lately it's just falling apart. I don't know why . . .

C: What has been happening to make you say that?

T: Well, several of the children just seem to be disturbing any group activity lately. They're often beyond the limits of any participation with the class—oh—running in the room when it's time to be changing activities and ignoring my requests and suggestions a lot of the time . . . as for coming into the group, there's Tim, Sue, and Larry, and of course Donny.

C: You said recently more children have behaviors you're concerned about —how recently?

T: Oh, let's see. Before Thanksgiving vacation, only Donny was acting as if he didn't like to do anything I asked or suggested when he was part of the group. Now, three others behave more as Donny has always done. But they know better—they used to be much more willing to go with the group.

C: Let's take Donny—whose behavior has concerned you since early in the year. Tell me about what he would do, for example.[2]

T: First, he stood, instead of sitting, at floor circles, and he distracted the others by sliding or walking in the room when they were sharing something, or listening to me, or getting ready to sing. And he often interrupted different other children during their indoor activity periods in a teasing kind of way. When outdoors at play time, he'd pull away from me when I tried to intervene in his unsafe use of play equipment and tried to take him to one side.

C: Those are behaviors you'd probably have to respond to. What would you be apt to do—say at group time indoors, or on the play yard?

T: I didn't want the other children to reject him—and so—well, in the circle I'd ask him to sit down, saying it quietly. Then if he didn't, I led him over with me to stand by my chair or kneel there, so he would be less conspicuous and less apt to begin disturbing other children. He was near me during group circle, most of the time! On the playground if he was in the way, or hurt, or had been retaliated against for teasing

[2] Editors' Note: Note that the consultant quickly gets the teacher to focus on identifying the problem in terms of specific behaviors.

someone, I held him and talked to him aside—to let him and the other children know definitely that I still liked him and only disliked some of the things he did.[3]

C: Let's see—you wanted mainly to change Donny's behavior toward group participation. Yet, at the same time, you wanted to model friendliness and regard for Donny to the other children. Both in class and outside in the yard Donny was getting a great deal of your attention and concern. But, he wasn't changing his behavior?

T: Yes . . . I treated him warmly and always told him *why* I wanted him to stop doing each thing.

C: How about the rest of the children—those behaving more as you wished and expected? What was happening for them?

T: I tried not to disrupt their ongoing experiences any more than necessary. Their things—activities—went right on.

C: And how about recently—when the several other children have begun to behave similarly to Donny—have you given *more* attention to them— more than before, when they were doing what you wanted them to do?

T: Why, yes. That's probably a big part of my problem. I can't help four or five of those children at once. I try not to get angry, but I don't know what to do. Something is wrong!

C: Let's look more closely at what sequence of behavior you've described. What has happened to Donny and the other three children just after their own actions may help us to look at the consequences for them. Sometimes children aren't learning what we want to teach them.

T: I suppose the other children in the class have learned more than Donny has . . . because they surely don't reject him. It almost seems they copy him!

C: Yes. For several months Donny has behaved in a way to ignore your instructions about group behavior. What do you suppose he'd *lose* if he changed? Or, what good and desirable effects accompany his present behavior?

T: I guess you think it's my attention and special efforts with him that he gets.

C: In both class and playground situations—after Donny did something his teacher did not want, he received more attention and concern from her than before.

T: It's hard to believe my special interest and help are so important . . . especially when I used it to tell him what else to do. But it all makes sense looked at that way. That might make sense too—about why more children seem to do what Donny does, than earlier in the year.

C: From the description—when the few other children recently began to behave in similar ways to Donny in class-group situations—their teacher

[3]Editors' Note: Sincere efforts to "approve of the person as a person but disapprove of some of the things he does" often go awry because the objectionable behaviors are inadvertently reinforced.

has given more attention to *un*desirable behaviors than to their former and more desirable actions.

T: Now—I really have some work to do—maybe if I give my attention and interest differently with Donny, the other three children will be influenced too. Where do I start with Donny?

C: What exactly would you like to have Donny do differently? There are probably several changes you'd like to see . . .

T: I'd like him to be more responsible—more sensitive to my requests and others' needs.

C: What could he *do*—say, in classroom or on the playground—that you would interpret as "responsible" or "sensitive"?

T: Well, he should

1. Sit down with others at storytime (he stands and moves now).
2. Stop talking or poking others when I ask him, also without my having to ask.
3. Wait his turn on play equipment and not begin before others are through and out of the way.

C: Good! It's important to decide just what behaviors you want him to develop. That helps you know exactly what you want to pay attention to. Could you start with, say, the first one—sitting down when other children do—at story or song time?[4]

T: Let's see. I'd need to pay attention to him when he sits down—and maybe even ignore when he doesn't? But he *never* sits down at group time—how can I get him to do it?

C: Yes—paying attention to his sitting down while others are is what you'd want to notice and praise. But just now he probably only sits at other times during the day. When does he sit now?

T: Oh, he does sit often and works lots of times, like during art work with materials. I see I can notice and praise all the times when he sits and works with the group as I meant. And ignore the times he doesn't?

C: Yes! If you pay attention to the behavior you want him to *increase* and at the same time ignore those you want him to *decrease*, the behavior change should be more rapid.

T: This is going to be interesting to try, I mean—if it's useful, I will try this, maybe with his talking out too . . . I have often just answered him, even though I probably should just not answer, so he'll quit. Anyway, I'll try with Donny's sitting.

C: The technique could be helpful in a number of similar situations. Let's discuss how things are going with Donny in two weeks.

T: Thanks. I will see how the idea works—it's kind of interesting.

[4] Editors' Note: Describing words like "responsible" and "sensitive" in terms of actual behaviors is a crucial and sometimes difficult task for many persons. Note that the consultant reinforced the teacher for specifying what she meant by these terms.

This excerpt highlights two procedures in consultation:

First, the contingencies for the consultant to respond to the teacher are her behavior descriptions about herself or others. The consultant responds verbally and nonverbally in order to reinforce the teacher's descriptive statements of behavior. For example, the guidance consultant did not reinforce the rather general behavior characteristics of "positive" and "sensitive" which the teacher originally stated to be desirable alternative behaviors for the child. Instead, the guidance consultant questioned the teacher further to elicit statements of behavior and reinforced those statements.

Second, the consultant models the behavioral approach by responding with questions and comments in behavioral terms and related to situational variables which might influence behavior. For example, the teacher listed three specific behaviors that she wanted to help Donny change. The consultant responded positively, and immediately. The same technique, that is immediate positive response, is one which the teacher can use toward a child's desired behavior.

JOHN, THE "EMOTIONALLY DISTURBED CHILD"

This case involved John and a third grade teacher who asked the consultant to test a boy in her classroom because she thought he was "emotionally disturbed." (The magical powers of testing!) He said that he would be glad to do what he could to help her and that they should make an appointment to discuss it. The goals of the first interview were: (1) identification of the problem in behavioral terms, (2) a consideration of relevant variables, and (3) identification of which variables could be altered.

Another goal of the first interview involved the teacher's perception of the consultant. If the consultant expects to influence the behavior of the teacher, the consultant must be viewed by the teacher as a rewarding, prestigious figure. The implication that the consultant believes that the teacher is capable of handling the problem, as well as the rewarding comments made to her during the interview, should help establish that the consultant is a rewarding figure or at least not a punitive or indifferent one.

Describing Behaviors

The consultant's initial goal with Johnny's teacher was to have her talk in terms of behavior and events. He started out by asking her in what way she thought he could be helpful to her. She reiterated that she thought Johnny was emotionally disturbed because of some of the things he did and because she had been unable to stop his misbehaviors over several months. The consultant agreed that the situation must be discouraging and asked her to describe how Johnny behaved that made her feel that he was emotionally disturbed. The consultant attempted to be sympathetic to her problem and directed the discussion to actual behavior.

The teacher began to describe things Johnny did that made the consultant wonder how she had managed to cope with him at all. Johnny was constantly "bantering," as she put it, with her or the other children. He never completed his work and frequently screamed in defiance of her or of the other children. She then went on to describe her unsatisfactory contacts with Johnny's parents who vacillated between punitiveness toward Johnny, which the teacher did not want (for example, "We give you permission to whip him in school, because we do at home; it's the only way to handle him."), and protection of him and implied criticism of the teacher (for example, "He doesn't do *that* at home; maybe he needs a more *experienced* teacher."). The teacher said that the parents seemed pretty disturbed themselves.

While the teacher spoke, the consultant tried to respond in a way that reflected his interest in school events and specific behaviors. For example, he asked the teacher to describe a "bantering" episode in behavioral terms. During the talk about the parents he did not respond at all. As she began to talk about Johnny in school (for example, "I can tell when he's had trouble at home."), he became more active and interested and soon they were talking only about his behavior in school. Even when the teacher was able to mention her own anger at Johnny and that maybe her own "permissive atmosphere" within the classroom was the fault, the consultant responded by asking what she did when she felt angry and asked her to describe what she meant by "permissive atmosphere."

This approach seemed to make possible the achievement of the consultant's first goal: a discussion of the actions of Johnny, his peers, and the teacher. It could be reasoned that this occurred because the consultant deliberately cued and responded only to statements which focused on behavior and events.

Desired Behaviors

The next phase of the interview concerned desired behavior rather than a description of misbehaviors. The consultant made the transition by commenting that the teacher's responses to Johnny seemed understandable, and that what she called "permissive atmosphere" appeared educationally sound and that she apparently had evidence of its effectiveness from her other pupils through their educational growth.

The consultant then asked the teacher if Johnny ever acted otherwise. She assented by saying he didn't always act like this. In fact, his behavior seemed unpredictable. She gave some examples of desired behavior. Her comments implied that he was "good" whenever he was intensely interested in something. Also, he apparently was bright, and he was not deficient in any of the basic skill areas, such as reading and math. Further questioning revealed that Johnny behaved desirably only in solo activities or alone with the teacher. This phase of the discussion identified areas of strength upon which the teacher could build.[5]

The next phase of the discussion had to do with Johnny's reward system: what kinds of things seemed to please him? Aside from the possible pleasure attained occasionally in just the act of learning, Johnny loved receiving compliments from the teacher; these compliments unfortunately were rare because of his frequent misbehaviors. The consultant asked what Johnny got out of misbehaviors, that is, in what ways were they rewarding or pleasing to him? The teacher replied she did not know, unless they were attention-getting. The consultant said that was a reasonable hypothesis—did the behavior stop when he got attention? She replied that it did not, but became worse. This sequence was important in that the teacher was encouraged while hypothesizing to look immediately for evidence to support or reject the hypothesis. Further information seemed necessary, such as what the teacher wanted Johnny to do in class, whether he could do it, and under what circumstances.

In this phase of the interview, the teacher focused on desired behaviors, not just the absence of an undesired behavior, and upon the varying circumstances surrounding these occasional desired behaviors. The teacher was becoming aware of the possibility that some of the significant influences that affected Johnny's behavior were under her control (such as her compliments to him).

Next, it seemed appropriate to the consultant to talk with the teacher about learning, in nontechnical terms. He suggested that it was useful to think of behavior, good or bad, as having been learned and therefore able to be unlearned. In the light of the reported child-rearing practices of the parents, it could be that Johnny had not learned appropriate classroom or social behavior, or was confused about it. Perhaps he had always been told what *not* to do, and had been inconsistently rewarded for a variety of behaviors.

---

[5] Editors' Note: Identifying positive behaviors and exploring what seems to cause them is an important step that is often ignored in concentrating only on the "problem."

It was decided that since Johnny had given evidence during class of knowing how to behave appropriately, the task for the teacher was to help him generalize this response category to additional classroom situations, some of which probably were frustrating to him already. Since Johnny responded positively to the teacher's approval, she was asked to think of ways that her approval could be made to depend upon his desired behavior; further, could circumstances be arranged so that Johnny would be assured of receiving approval when he showed the behavior? In other words, the consultant emphasized there must be a payoff to the child for performing the desired behavior, if it is to increase in frequency.

Parental handling of Johnny was considered to be a significant variable by both the teacher and consultant. They agreed that the teacher would work with the student as described above, and that the consultant would work with the parents to assess their interest in the school's approach and to enlist their participation. This plan emphasized for the teacher that home co-operation presumably expedites progress in changing a child's behavior, but teachers still do influence a child's behavior in the school setting of classrooms.

The goals of the interview at this point seemed to have been met: the teacher had some plan on which to proceed with realistic goals for Johnny and for herself. Testing by the consultant was not mentioned, although the teacher did request that the consultant observe in the classroom to help assess her responses to Johnny's behaviors.

In summary, the general goal of the conference was to have the teacher look at specific behavior by Johnny, in the context of what was happening during his behavior, before, and after it. Further, the teacher's attention was directed toward Johnny's reward system, and upon those rewarding events which were under her influence in the classroom. When sufficient information was obtained, hypothesizing could occur and behavioral objectives be planned. The technique used by the consultant was primarily differential responding to the teacher's comments, while at the same time modeling an approach to child study based upon principles of learning. Planning could occur when the consultant and teacher were using the same principles to analyze behavior and how behavior is influenced when it occurs.

The outcome was gratifying; the teacher developed her own hypotheses and plans of action, plans which were consistent with her own style and her acquaintance with Johnny in her classroom. And, finally, she had an investment in putting the plan into action, because it was her own, and she had requested follow-up observations to provide for her evaluation of the effectiveness of her plan while it was under way.

30

CONSULTING WITH THE CLASSROOM TEACHER

Dwight L. Goodwin
SAN JOSE STATE COLLEGE

John was a sixth grader who had few friends and who performed poorly as a student. He would frequently stare at his hands while sitting in class, holding them up to the light and blowing on them. John's behavior had started to disrupt the class, especially the teacher, who consulted with me about how John might be helped. The case illustrates how a counselor or psychologist can work with a classroom teacher in eliminating undesirable behavior and developing appropriate behaviors. In effect, the counselor can model a strategy, in his work with the teacher, which serves as an example of how the teacher, in turn, can behave when problems arise.[1]

USING BEHAVIORAL ANALYSIS

Analysis of the student's behavior is the starting point. To assist in analyzing the problem situation, a chart called the Behavior Analysis Chart was used. The chart, which accompanies this article, is divided into three parts. From the array of problems John presented, the teacher was first asked to select a single target behavior as a starting point for the analysis. Under Part B, the behavior selected by the teacher is stated. Part A involves what happened *before* the behavior in question occurred, that is, what usually happened before John held up his hands to the light. Part C asks for information about what happened right *after* the behavior occurred. For example, what did the teacher and students do when John stared at his hands.

In terms of the problem behavior—John's prolonged staring at his hands—the charting of contingencies is now complete. That is, some of

[1] Appreciation is expressed to Beverly Swanson, John's teacher, whose interest and imagination contributed to the success of this consultation.

TABLE 1

Behavior Analysis Chart		
A (Antecedents)	B (Behavior)	C (Consequents)
Independent work was assigned	John holds his hands to the light and blows on them	Peers comment on behavior and call him names
No direct teacher instruction was given	Stares at his hands for prolonged periods	Peers imitate behavior
Other pupils worked by themselves		Teacher asks "Why?"

the stimulus events which appear to trigger the deviant behavior are listed under A and events which seem positively to reinforce the behavior are listed under C.[2]

Changing the Consequences and Observing Results

The first step in reducing the frequency of the deviant behavior is to eliminate the chances for reinforcement of the behavior, such as that given by his peers or teacher. In this case, the teacher and psychologist decided to eliminate completely reinforcement following hand-staring. This implies that reinforcers will be withheld immediately following the deviant behavior, but this step requires a knowledge of what is reinforcing for the child. John was observed to be especially responsive to grades received for his assignments and to verbal recognition by the teacher in class for his performance. The approval or disapproval of his peers, however, had little predictable effect on John's behavior.

It was reasoned that John could be rewarded only as long as he could remain in the classroom. The psychologist and teacher agreed to have John leave the classroom to go to the library for filing duties when the teacher observed John staring at his hands. The following procedures were set into motion:

1. The teacher asked John to remain after school and explained the steps to be followed. He was told that his spending long periods of time looking at and blowing on his hand was becoming more noticeable and this was distracting other students as well as the teacher. In order to help him overcome this habit, the teacher explained that she had worked out a

[2] Editors' Note: Making such observations of behaviors in the actual setting is a crucial first step. Too often labels are prematurely attached to a behavior ("John is neurotic . . .") without carefully determining how the person and others act before and after the behavior occurs.

plan so that he could learn to stop doing this before it really got started. In this way he wouldn't have to tolerate the teasing and name-calling of the other students.

2. John and the teacher agreed that she would tap John on the shoulder as soon as she spotted the behavior starting. John would then leave the room and go to the library. The purpose of the signal was to avoid the possibility of further peer recognition stemming from the teacher's having to ask John to leave the classroom.

3. Following the signal, John would leave the room quietly and go to the library (across a corridor) where arrangements had been made for him to file returned library cards for a 15-minute period. The length of the "time-out" period was kept short so that John could return to the classroom, thereby increasing the opportunity for John to receive reinforcements for acting in socially adaptive ways.[3]

4. At the end of the 15 minutes, John was to return to the classroom and resume his work.

This procedure was designed to accomplish two main objectives: (1) prevent the deviant response from being reinforced by John or by others, and (2) promote the development of anticipatory responses (cues) so that John would experience some of the unpleasantness of leaving the room when he began to stare or blow upon his hands.

If this analysis were correct, John would learn to respond to anticipatory cues and thereby gain greater self-control over this behavior.

This plan was begun and a record kept of the frequency with which John had to leave the classroom for blowing and staring at his hands. During the first two weeks, John had to leave eight times. Beginning with the third week, John's leaving the room gradually decreased to an average of once a week. By the seventh week, the deviant behavior had been virtually eliminated.

Not Working on Assignments

The teacher and counselor decided to further examine what events might contribute to hand-staring. The teacher observed that this behavior increased when John appeared frustrated and was unable to proceed with an assignment. A behavioral analysis was completed by the teacher. Antecedents of the behavior in question, not working on assignments, included ambiguity about doing the assignments in terms of length, degree of thoroughness, quality. Consequences of this behavior were unfavorable grades and hand-staring. John was uncertain about what factors determined grades. In order to bring John's behavior under con-

---

[3] Editors' Note: Often procedures, such as suspension, exclude the person from the environment for long periods of time, thereby preventing the person from observing and demonstrating appropriate behaviors for which he can be reinforced.

trol, the teacher was asked to make very explicit the conditions under which John could expect a certain grade. Mathematics, because of its general explicitness, was agreed upon as the starting point for setting definite criteria for grading. The teacher explained to John the number of math problems to be completed for a particular grade on each day.

Although matters of neatness, accuracy, and need for showing computations were regarded as important, the first step was to specify the number of problems to be completed. For example, doing two pages of problems resulted in a grade of A. The teacher stated *each day* how many problems must be completed to receive a grade of A, B, and so on.

After two weeks the teacher reported that John regularly met standards for receiving A's for the number of problems accomplished and John's grades showed a consistent rise and fewer instances were noted when his work came to a halt.

Improving Social Behaviors

Although John ceased his hand staring behaviors and improved his study habits, he was without friends in the classroom.

Again the problem behavior in terms of antecedents and consequences was charted. The completed diagram indicated that only when an assignment demanded contact with other pupils did John associate with his peers. He showed few if any approach responses and usually greeted the attempts of other pupils with anger and rebuffs. The presence of other pupils often resulted in his complaining to the teacher about their being near his desk and that they interfered with his work.

Discussion with John's parents and a review of the cumulative record showed that John had been observed to be aloof and detached for several years. Recalling the improvement in John's performance when he understood the basis on which grades were assigned, a plan was devised to help John acquire social skills, beginning with his participation in structured group activities within the class. The teacher discussed the importance of being able to work together with the class, suggesting that children would need to learn techniques for group collaboration and planning. Naturally, grades would be awarded according to their performance within the group. Criterion behaviors of co-operativeness, listening to each other's suggestions, clarifying objectives, and others, were enumerated. Six students were invited to test their skills in solving a "class problem" suggested by the teacher. After five minutes, the teacher stopped the group and assigned a grade to each student and gave her reasons in terms of the criteria explained at the outset, somewhat as follows. "Alice, you've listened carefully to the suggestions of others but didn't say anything yourself so your grade is a B minus. Bob, you get a

B plus because you did have a suggestion to make and you paid attention to what others were saying, and Roger, I'm sorry but a C is the highest grade you can receive because although you did have some suggestions, you interrupted others on two occasions."

John's group was called after two others had participated. Throughout earlier demonstrations, John was observed to be watching carefully. He received a B minus for his first performance.

This procedure was repeated several times in the ensuing weeks. John's grades for social interaction in these groups improved. More importantly, however, the percent of time he engaged in social behavior with his peers increased. He was observed, for example, on several occasions in the cafeteria to take his tray over to the table where several other members of his class were eating. Once there, he was observed to interact freely with them.

TO CONCLUDE

A follow-up conducted a year later showed John to be making good academic progress and maintaining the friendship of a few other boys in his class. His hand-staring behavior had been eliminated and he had shown significant improvement in being socially responsive to many of his peers.

The aim of the foregoing assessment and treatment program was to eliminate disruptive behavior, encourage more efficient task performance, and develop needed social behaviors. This procedure required some 12 to 15 hours of the counselor's time in consulting with the teacher and parents plus as many hours of the teacher's time in making observations, recording John's behavior, and planning with John individually. Considering the observed student's progress, both academically and socially, such an investment seems warranted.[4]

[4] Editors' Note: The time spent by the counselor with the teacher relative to John's problem may seem excessive. However, such an investment should be viewed more broadly in terms of the ability of this teacher to handle other current and future problem situations more effectively.

Counterconditioning

"THE TROUBLE WITH YOU is that you're too tense, all tied up. You've got to relax, calm down."

"Go in there and tell him just what you think. Demand your rights! It'll make you feel better."

"Whenever I get tense, I head for the refrigerator and get something to eat."

In counterconditioning certain responses occur which are incompatible and antagonistic to other responses. This notion of incompatible behavior is reflected in the comments above. To eat, or to be assertive, or to relax physically in situations that usually cause tension can reduce anxiety. Eating, being assertive, and feeling relaxed are all behaviors which may be incompatible with anxiety for some individuals. It is like replacing old responses with new ones. Of course to do this the new competing response must be stronger than the old. Creating situations in which new, more adaptive behaviors can successfully replace the old problem responses is one of the counselor's crucial tasks.

The first reported systematic application of counterconditioning occurred when the extreme fears of animals of a young boy, Peter, were eliminated through feeding the boy in the presence of a caged rabbit (Jones, 1924b). Each day the caged rabbit was brought closer to the table where Peter was eating. Eating in the presence of the rabbit (aversive stimuli) had a neutralizing effect in that the sight and presence of the animal no longer caused the boy to be anxious. The key to counterconditioning is to produce responses which are incompatible with fears and anxieties.

In helping clients with problems involving fears and

anxieties counselors cannot always introduce the actual fear-causing object. Wolpe (1958) devised a way which greatly increased the possible uses of counterconditioning in counseling. This form of counterconditioning, which he termed "systematic desensitization," utilizes the client's imagination as a way of introducing the fear-arousing stimuli. By having the client imagine anxiety-provoking situations and, at the same time, eliciting in the client responses that are antagonistic to anxiety, usually relaxation, Wolpe demonstrated that clients behave in more calm and socially appropriate ways to stressful life situations. In systematic desensitization Peter, instead of eating in the physical presence of the rabbit, would have imagined being in situations with rabbits while, at the same time, being physically relaxed.

Most client problems contain stress and anxiety behaviors. Counselors can effectively design specific counterconditioning experiences for their clients in helping to eliminate anxiety problems. Physical relaxation has been the most common response used to eliminate anxiety. Several methods are available to teach clients how to relax physically, for example, progressive relaxation exercises. Music and other sounds, such as recorded sounds of waves at the ocean beach, can be effective in helping some clients to relax. And of course a large comfortable recliner chair helps considerably.

However, relaxation is not the only response incompatible and antagonistic to anxiety. Assertive behaviors, in the form of a polite refusal, a genuine expression of praise, an exclamation of joy or irritation, may serve to inhibit anxiety in interpersonal situations (see Neuman, Article 39). Certain sexual behaviors, eating, some drugs, and carbon dioxide may be used in certain situations to interfere with anxiety.

Counselors need to determine in detail with their clients the circumstances in which problems occur. It is for this reason that telling someone to have something to eat, to assert himself, or to calm down and relax seldom does any good. The crucial ingredient is missing, namely, the specific *pairing* of the relaxation, for example, with the specific anxiety-provoking situation. Techniques of behavioral analysis (see Articles 29 and 30) can be of help in assisting clients to identify specific life situations causing stress and anxiety.

Much needs to be learned about counterconditioning methods. Emery in Article 31 presents in considerable detail the techniques of the most commonly used counterconditioning procedure: systematic desensitization. To illustrate the use of this procedure Emery presents the case of a test-anxious college sophomore, closely following the procedure developed by Wolpe. Variations, however, are possible. Items from the anxiety hierarchy may sometimes be experienced directly in real life, *in vivo*, rather than through imagination (see Articles 21 and 41). Sometimes desensitization may be employed in a small group setting (Articles 42 and 43). Some clients, given relaxation training and help in identifying specific anxiety producing situations, can use desensitization techniques on their own in real-life situations. Combinations of desensitization, reinforcement, and modeling procedures can be very effective (Article 21). Sometimes a client may experience a great number of problems each requiring specific counterconditioning (see Article 42).

The principle of counterconditioning offers a very promising foundation that counselors may build upon in creating other effective techniques.

31

SYSTEMATIC DESENSITIZATION: REDUCING TEST ANXIETY

John R. Emery
HUMAN RESOURCES INSTITUTE, LA JOLLA, CALIFORNIA

Systematic desensitization is a technique which counselors are using to help clients who experience unpleasant emotional reactions. Basically, this procedure consists of describing situations which are increasingly anxiety producing (an "anxiety hierarchy") to a deeply relaxed client until he is able to visualize the most stressful scenes on this list without anxiety.

Desensitization can be conceptualized in terms of the psychological principle of counterconditioning. Extinction of the unpleasant emotional reactions occurs because the usual anxiety responses cannot take place when the client is experiencing more pleasant stimuli (for example, deep relaxation). Since one cannot be relaxed and anxious at the same time, the anxiety can be systematically reduced by pairing the eliciting stimuli with deep relaxation.

Wolpe (1952) was the first to publish an account of the desensitization technique. Wolpe's subsequent writings on the subject (1958, 1961, 1962, 1964) show further clinical evidence for the efficacy of the techniques for eliminating inappropriate fears in human beings.

Other investigators (Ashem, 1963; Bond & Hutchinson, 1960; Clark, 1963; Cowden & Ford, 1962; Geer, 1964; Kushner, 1965; Lang & Lazovik, 1963; Lang, Lazovik & Reynolds, 1965; Lazarus, 1961, 1963, 1965; Wolpe & Lazarus, 1966; Paul, 1966; Paul & Shannon, 1966; Rachman, 1959) have also found desensitization to be an effective technique in treating a wide variety of fears and related problems.

THE TECHNIQUE OF DESENSITIZATION

When To Use It

Desensitization is not a "cure-all" technique. Criteria for selection of desensitization as a counseling technique have yet to be developed. At present the decision to use desensitization is primarily up to the counselor. The nature of one's clientele may be a determining factor as to how often desensitization is utilized. The author has found that he uses the technique with approximately 7 percent of the students seen at a university counselling center, while in private practice he uses it with approximately 15 percent of his clients. If a client wants to rid himself of some anxiety-response habits, then the desensitization technique is selected as appropriate. For the majority of clients desensitization is one of several techniques used in combination to accomplish a change in behavior.

Explanation to Client

Once desensitization tentatively has been chosen as an appropriate technique it is important that each client understand and accept the treatment process. Both the theory and course of treatment should be explained briefly. It should be made clear that the anxiety is the result of learning and that the treatment is a learning process. The explanation (adapted from Paul, 1966) approximates the following:

> The emotional reactions that you experience as a result of your previous experiences with _____ situations often lead to feelings of anxiety or tenseness that are really inappropriate. As long as you can recall how you've felt in these situations, it is possible to work with your reactions

right here in this office by having you imagine yourself in these situations as vividly as possible.

The specific technique we will be using is one called desensitization. This technique utilizes two main procedures—relaxation and counter-conditioning—to reduce your anxiety. The relaxation procedure is based upon years of work which was started in the 1930s by Dr. Jacobsen. He developed a method of inducing relaxation which can be learned quickly and which will allow you to become more deeply relaxed than ever before.

The real advantage of relaxation is that the muscle systems in your body cannot be both tense and relaxed at the same time; therefore, once you have learned the relaxation technique it can be used to counter anxiety, tenseness, and the feelings like those which you experience in the _____ situation.

Relaxation alone can be used to reduce anxiety and tension, and I'll be asking you to practice relaxation between our meetings. Often, however, relaxation is inconvenient to use, and really doesn't permanently overcome anxiety. Therefore, we combine the relaxation technique with the psychological principle of counterconditioning to actually desensitize situations such that the anxiety no longer occurs.

The way in which we will do this is to first determine the situations in which you become progressively more anxious—building a hierachy from least anxious to most anxious situations with regard to _____ .
Then I will teach you the technique of progressive relaxation, and have you practice this. You will see how this operates shortly when we actually start training. After you are more relaxed than ever before, we will then start counterconditioning. This will be done by having you repeatedly imagine the specific situations from the anxiety hierarchy while under relaxation. By having you visualize very briefly the situations which normally arouse anxiety, while you are deeply relaxed, those situations are gradually desensitized, such that they no longer make you anxious. We start with those situations which bother you the least, and gradually work up to those which bother you the most.

Once questions have been cleared up as to the theory and course of treatment and the client affirms he is willing to begin, treatment can commence.

Training in Muscular Relaxation

The client is given a one-page outline of the relaxation procedures that are most often used with desensitization:

Relaxation is a skill which can be improved with practice. At first, it will take approximately 20 to 30 minutes to go through the entire procedure properly, but eventually you will be able to become quite relaxed in 10 to 15 minutes. The basic principle is that when muscles are tensed, and then released, they go into a deeper state of relaxation. It is important to focus your thinking on the muscle system you are relaxing.

The procedure is: Tense the muscle group. Say *"relax."* (It may be helpful for you to count up to 5 as you are tensing a particular muscle group, for example, 1 . . . 2 . . . 3 . . . 4 . . . *relax*).   Then relax that muscle group *immediately*. At first, exercise each muscle group at least twice. With practice, you will find which muscle groups are most effective in helping you to relax.

The client should be seated in a comfortable chair preferably a reclining one that is capable of being adjusted to whatever position the client finds most relaxing. In the nearly horizontal position (which most clients prefer), the head should be resting on the back of the chair with legs extended and arms resting on the arms of the chair. In this way none of the body muscles are used to support the body—the support is given by the chair.

Before beginning the actual tensing and relaxing of the muscle groups named on the outline it has been found helpful for the counselor to demonstrate the tensing and relaxing of each muscle group to the client. The client is encouraged to try any exercises he is uncertain of doing correctly. Once the client has closed his eyes (any contact lenses removed), the room darkened and any outside noises neutralized (airconditioners, fans and "white noise generators" are helpful here), relaxation training is ready to begin.

A partial transcript from an audio tape recording of a relaxation session with a client who had tried relaxation four times previously (once in the counselor's office and three times in the privacy of his room) is presented below. An ellipsis (. . .) denotes an interval of 5 to 15 seconds.

> O.K. just settle back in the chair and relax as best as possible. Take a few deep breaths and begin to feel yourself let go . . . . Now, extending both arms straight out clench your fists more and more tightly as I count up toward 5 . . . 1 . . . 2 . . . 3 . . . Good . . . 4 . . . Relax. Just let your arms drop wherever they will and begin to appreciate the difference between the feelings of tension, which you felt a few seconds ago, and the feelings of relaxation in your hands and arms now. . . . Now let's concentrate on the muscles in your forearms, extending both arms straight out once again only this time push forward with your hand . . . 1 . . . 2 . . . 3 . . . 4 . . . hold it . . . now, relax. Just let your arms go up and concentrate on the warm, tingling feelings of relaxation spreading throughout your forearms . . . O.K., fine, let's concentrate now on the muscles in your upper arms. To do this bend both arms at the elbow and flex your biceps, more and more as I count toward five . . . 1 . . . 2 . . . 3 . . . 4 . . . Relax. Attend to the heavy, warm feelings associated with relaxation as they spread downward throughout your arms right

to the tips of your fingers. . . . Let's concentrate now on the muscles in your forehead. Wrinkle up your forehead (or frown) by raising your eyebrows . . . 1 . . . 2 . . . more and more . . . 3 . . . 4 . . ., now do the opposite of tension and relax . . . . Just let all the muscles in your forehead smooth out and become smoother and smoother . . . O.K. Let's work on the area surrounding your eyes and nose. Close your eyes more and more tightly as I count up toward five . . . 1 . . . 2 . . . 3 . . . feel the tension . . . 4 . . . Relax . . . . While keeping your eyes closed, just enjoy the soothing calm feeling in your eyes, similar perhaps to that which you feel when closing your eyes after reading for a long period of time. . . . Now, let's work on the area surrounding your lips, cheeks and jaw . . . just draw the corners of your mouth back further and further, try and get that ear to ear grin . . . 1 . . . 2 . . . 3 . . . 4 . . . Relax, just let your jaw hang loose . . . appreciate the feeling of relaxation . . . . Now, grit your teeth and feel the tenseness in your throat muscles get greater and greater as I count up toward five . . . 1 . . . 2 . . . 3 . . . 4 . . . Relax. . . . Just let your neck hang loose, let it relax at whatever position it feels most comfortable . . . as you continue to relax further and further notice how your breathing has become more and more regular . . . . Good . . . . now, let's concentrate on your shoulder muscles, go ahead and shrug your shoulders and try and touch your ears . . . 1 . . . 2 . . . 3 . . . Good . . . 4 . . . Relax, let your shoulders slump and attend to the warm, tingling feelings as they spread throughout your shoulders and connect up with the relaxation in your arms . . . let the tingling feeling spread throughout your arms right to the tips of your fingers . . . . Now, go ahead and arch your back more and more as I count up toward five . . . 1 . . . 2 . . . 3 . . . 4 . . . hold it . . . now, relax, let your whole body just slump back into the chair . . . let the chair support the weight of your body, just let your whole body relax further and further . . . O.K. let's concentrate now on your stomach muscles more and more as I count up to five . . . 1 . . . 2 . . . 3 . . . 4 . . . hold it . . . now relax, just let your stomach muscles go . . . remember, each time you breathe out your stomach muscles relax . . . and each time you breathe in this relaxation begins to spread throughout your entire body . . . further and further . . . notice how you're breathing freely and deeply, freely and deeply. . . . Let's shift our attention now to the muscles in your thighs . . . straighten out both your legs and bend both your legs and bend your toes back toward your head, feeling the tension in your thighs . . . 1 . . . 2 . . . 3 . . . more and more . . . 4 . . . Relax, let your legs drop and attend to the difference in this large muscle group between the feelings of tension and now the feelings of relaxation . . . a warm, tingling feeling spreading throughout your legs. . . . Once again, go ahead and straighten out both your legs only this time bend your toes away from your head, tensing your calf muscles . . . 1 . . . 2 . . . 3 . . . 4 . . . now, relax . . . no more tension at all now, nothing but relaxation . . . enjoy the calm, soothing feeling of relaxation as it spreads right to the tip of your toes. . . . In order to help you relax even further I'm going to mention the various muscle groups you've been tensing and relaxing, only this time don't tense them, simply relax them further and further . . . try and get that extra bit of relaxation in each muscle group as I mention it . . . your forehead . . . the area around your eyes and nose . . . your lips, cheeks and jaw . . . just begin to feel a wave of relaxation spreading downward across your facial muscles . . . let this wave continue to spread downward through your neck muscles . . . across your shoulders . . . down through your arms right to the tips of your fingers . . . across your chest and down your back . . . into your stomach muscles . . . notice how your breathing becomes more and more regular as the waves of relaxation continue downward through your thighs . . . and calves . . . right to the tips of your toes.

Upon completion of the relaxation or desensitization session, the following is used to help the client emerge from the relaxed state:

You have been relaxing very well . . . . In order to help you replace some of that tired heavy feeling in your body with some fresh energy I'm going to count backwards from five to one . . . and when I reach the count of one you will open your eyes and feel quite refreshed and calm . . . 5 . . . 4 . . . 3 . . . you may begin to stretch if you wish . . . 2 . . . 1.

Note should be made here that the first few times a client practices relaxation he is encouraged to tense and relax each muscle group twice. Total time for this procedure takes approximately 25 minutes. However, in the preceding taped example about 13 minutes were required to have the client become fully relaxed. Each client is encouraged to practice relaxation once per day in the privacy of his own room until he gets a "feeling" for relaxation (usually one to two weeks).

After every session where relaxation is used, an inquiry is made of the client to determine which exercises are most beneficial to the relaxation process. After about five sessions with a client the relaxation is usually individualized to allow the client to emphasize those muscle groups found to be the most effective in aiding relaxation and to disregard those muscle groups not enhancing the relaxation process.

Constructing Anxiety Hierarchies

An anxiety hierarchy is a list of situations the client is asked to imagine while relaxed. These situations are ranked from those only slightly anxiety producing to those which raise extreme anxiety.

Construction of the hierarchy begins at the same time relaxation training does. Quite often the first few sessions spent with the client, after desensitization has been selected as an appropriate technique, are equally divided between practice in relaxation and in identifying situations for the hierarchy.

It has been found useful to have the client list as many anxiety producing situations as he can think of before discussing them with the counselor. Besides saving precious interview time, the list serves as an excellent base for discussion. By discussing this list and the client's past learning history, the counselor and client attempt to determine the stimuli which elicit the anxiety. This behavioral analysis of the client's behavior is often the most difficult procedure in the desensitization technique. Some of the common stimuli or themes (for example, fear of dogs, fear of heights) are quite easily identified with the relevant stimuli. Others (for example, guilt feelings, fear of social situations) are not as easily identified with the precipitating stimuli and more discussion is usually needed before the actual sources can be discovered.

In the course of constructing the hierarchy the client may mention several objective fears (for example, petting a rabid dog, flying in an airplane with one engine dead). These types of situations need not be included in the hierarchy since they are indeed rational fears.

Once all relevant items have been listed, they are then ranked by the client, from most anxiety producing to least anxiety producing. An example selected from the author's file was the hierarchy of a 27-year-old law student who wished to rid himself of his fear of eating in public places.

SUDS	ITEM
(95)	1. Having dinner at a girlfriend's house with her parents present
(85)	2. Having dinner out with a girl
(80)	3. Having breakfast out with a girl
(70)	4. Having dinner out with your parents
(60)	5. Having dinner alone at an unfamiliar restaurant
(50)	6. Having dinner at the university cafeteria with some classmates
(45)	7. Having dinner at the university cafeteria by yourself
(40)	8. Having dinner alone in a familiar restaurant
(35)	9. Having dinner at an old friend's house
(30)	10. Having lunch at the cafeteria
(25)	11. Having breakfast at the cafeteria
(15)	12. Having breakfast at a familiar restaurant on Saturday morning
(10)	13. Having lunch with a long-time friend
(5)	14. Having lunch in your apartment

In order to help the client evenly space the intervals between situations, each item on the hierarchy is assigned a number, by the client, between 0 and 100. The figure 100 represents a situation that would be severely anxiety producing while 0 represents a situation that would be free from anxiety. Wolpe and Lazarus (1966) call the unit of this method of ranking a "sud" (subjective unit of disturbance) and feel that as long as items are more than 10 suds apart the spacing is satisfactory. Additional items may be added to the hierarchy at any time and, as often happens, items may be reranked at any time within the hierarchy.

If the client has more than one set of anxiety-producing stimuli a different hierarchy is constructed for each theme. Frequently multiple dimensions will occur within a hierarchy. For example, with a client being treated for a fear of driving more than two miles from her home, six variables controlled the intensity of her reactions:

1. Heaviness of the traffic
2. Time of day (or night)
3. Distance traveled from home
4. Seat belt fastened
5. Another couple in the car
6. Weather conditions

The various combinations of dimensions within the hierarchy led to construction of a hierarchy with 135 items. The most important criteria here seem to be that (a) the lowest item on the hierarchy does not create undue anxiety and (b) the spacing between items is neither too large nor too small.

Working through the Hierarchy while Relaxed

Before actual desensitization can begin the client's "imagination" must be assessed. During the last relaxation practice session, when the client has become relaxed, he is asked to imagine himself in a few "neutral" scenes. For instance, for the previously mentioned law student, the following situations were used to assess his imagination:

> Just continue to relax as you are, appreciating that warm, heavy feeling spreading throughout your body. Now, while you're relaxing I'd like you to imagine yourself in the following situation as vividly as possible. . . . You're standing in the middle of a forest . . . by a brook . . . here comes a crumpled piece of paper floating downstream . . . watch it as it floats by you . . . and continue to watch it float downstream until it's out of sight . . . good, now stop imagining that and imagine yourself as realistically as possible in the following situation . . . you're riding your bike across campus . . . on the way to play tennis with a friend . . . O.K., fine, now stop imagining that . . . next, I'd like you to imagine yourself in a different type of situation . . . one I'll call a personal form of relaxation . . . this personal form of relaxation is some thing, some place or event or happening, past, present, or future that you can imagine yourself in. . . . It must be a very pleasant and enjoyable situation to imagine yourself in and as the name indicates whatever you do imagine will be something personal . . . therefore I will not ask you to tell me what it is you are

imagining . . . O.K., go ahead and imagine yourself in a personal form of relaxation for a minute or so. . . .

The client is then reawakened in the usual manner. Immediately upon reawaking, the client is questioned as to the efficacy of the following:

1. Relaxation
2. Neutral scenes
3. Personal form of relaxation

If the relaxation was satisfactory, if imagination of the neutral scenes was adequate and if the personal form of relaxation was found to be worthwhile, desensitization is almost ready to begin.

However, occasional roadblocks are found. The author has found that about 95 percent of his clients using the desensitization techniques have been able to relax satisfactorily using the aforementioned relaxation training. For those not able to successfully use the relaxation training, hypnosis has been effective. The hand-levitation method of Wolberg (1948) or the eye-target method of Hilgard (1965) are most often used. In contrast Wolpe and Lazarus (1966) have used hypnosis with one third of their clients. They originally thought that hypnosis speeded up the desensitization but since have found little evidence to support this supposition.

For those students who have trouble projecting themselves into the imagined situation, one of the following solutions may alleviate the problem. The situation may be described in minute detail, the client may be asked to repeat in detail himself the situation as he is viewing it, or the client may indeed be confronted with real anxiety-producing auditory stimuli. For instance, a student with an intense fear of high-pitched noises (especially a dentist's drill) is presented with tape recorded drill sounds from a local dentist's office.

Occasionally, clients say they find it hard to force themselves into imagining an anxiety-producing situation after one of pleasant relaxation. It has been found useful to have the client imagine himself first in a neutral scene (for example, sitting in a movie theatre and looking at a blank, white screen) and then to have him imagine the anxiety-producing situation.

Rarely does a client have any trouble picturing a personal form of relaxation. Most clients have four or five favorite situations to picture themselves in, and, although they are not asked what they are imagining, many voluntarily tell the counselor. The following examples are frequently used:

1. Lying on the beach feeling the sun soaking into your body
2. Watching a beautiful sunset
3. Soaking in a tub of hot water

All that now needs to be accomplished before desensitization can begin is to set up a satisfactory signaling system so that the client can communicate with the counselor during the desensitization session with as little speech and movement as possible. Most clients find that raising the index finger of one hand will suffice to let the counselor know of any anxiety. It must be emphasized to the client that the least bit of anxiety is worth signaling.

Desensitization is now ready to begin. The following example is drawn from the first session with the 27-year-old law student, whose anxiety hierarchy was previously presented. After the client had been appropriately relaxed, he was addressed as follows:

Now I'm going to ask you to imagine yourself as vividly as possible in a number of situations. Remember, if you feel the *least* bit anxious while you're imagining yourself in any of these situations be sure and let me know by signaling immediately. First, I'd like you to imagine as vividly as possible that you are having lunch in your apartment (pause of 5 seconds—no signal). Stop imagining that and continue relaxing, just enjoying the calm, soothing feelings associated with relaxation (pause of 10 seconds). O.K., once again, imagine yourself as realistically as possible having lunch in your apartment (pause of 10 seconds—no signal). Stop imagining that and now imagine yourself in one of your personal forms of relaxation just letting yourself relax further and further (pause of about 20 seconds). Now, stop imagining that and imagine yourself as vividly as possible in the following situation . . . you are having lunch with a long-time friend (pause of 3 seconds—no signal). Stop imagining that and continue relaxing while concentrating on the looseness and heaviness of your body (pause of 10 seconds). O.K., once again, imagine yourself eating lunch in your apartment (pause of 20 seconds— no signal). Stop imagining that now and switch over to one of your personal forms of relaxation while you continue to relax and enjoy yourself (pause of 20 seconds). O.K., stop picturing that and imagine yourself as vividly as possible having lunch with a long-time friend (pause of 8 seconds—client signals). Stop imagining that; in order to help you relax even further I am going to count from 1 to 10 and with each count you'll feel yourself sinking into a deeper, more complete state of relaxation, further and further, so that when I reach the count of 10 you'll feel completely relaxed . . . completely relaxed . . . 1 . . . 2 . . . just let yourself go further and further . . . begin to feel yourself slipping more and more . . . 3 . . . 4 . . . more and more, sinking into a deeper and more pleasant state of relaxation . . . 5 . . . 6 . . . notice how your breathing has become more regular and how you're breathing freely and deeply, freely and deeply . . . 7 . . . 8 . . . deeper and deeper . . . more and more relaxed . . . 9 . . . 10 . . . completely relaxed, completely relaxed (pause of 10 seconds). Now, once again, I'd like you to imagine yourself as vividly as possible having lunch with a long-time friend. . . .

(pause of 5 seconds—no signal). Stop picturing that and go back to a personal form of relaxation, just letting yourself go further and further (pause of 20 seconds). Stop picturing yourself in that situation and visualize yourself as realistically as possible having lunch with a long-time friend (pause of 10 seconds—no signal). Stop imagining that and continue to concentrate on those loose and heavy feelings of deep relaxation as they spread throughout your entire body (pause of 20 seconds). You have been relaxing very well . . . In order to help you replace some of that tired, heavy feeling in your body with some fresh energy, I'm going to count backwards from 5 to 1 . . . and when I reach the count of 1 you will open your eyes and feel quite refreshed and calm . . . 5 . . . 4 . . . 3 you may begin to stretch if you wish . . . 2 . . . 1.

After the session described above, the client opened his eyes and after about 15 seconds began to stretch slowly, yawn, and smile contentedly. This typifies the usual situation. He was immediately questioned as to the efficacy of the relaxation (which he reported to be very good) and to the clarity of the situation he was asked to imagine (which he reported to be clear). He stated that he had felt moderately anxious the second time he had imagined having lunch with an old friend—yet that he had felt no anxiety whatsoever with the last two presentations of the identical scene.

As usual, the scenes of this client (14 in all) were listed on separate pieces of 2″ × 4″ paper, kept in the client's folder. The following notations made by the counselor indicate what transpired during the previous session.

Having lunch in your apartment 11/3 +5, +10, +20	Having lunch with a long-time friend 11/3 +5, −8, +5, +10

Beneath each situation, the date and length of time (in seconds) imagined are recorded by the counselor. A (+) before the time indicates the client did not signal anxiety, a (−) indicates that the client signaled that he felt anxiety.

The author has found the following plan to work effectively with a majority of clients. If the client does not signal anxiety, he imagines each scene for first 5 seconds, then 10 seconds, then 20 seconds. Between scene presentations the client's relaxation is enhanced as much as possible by suggestions of warmth, relaxation, lack of tension, heaviness, numbness, or imagining a personal form of relaxation for approximately 20 seconds. Each situation in the hierarchy is presented at least three times. If the client does not signal anxiety and the counselor does not detect any anxiety during the three presentations of an item, the next item on the hierarchy is begun. Often, however, in the interest of variety, higher ranked situations on the hierarchy are introduced before a lower ranked situation has been successfully presented for 20 seconds.

If, on the other hand, the client signals anxiety, or the counselor detects anxiety in the client, the latter is immediately asked to "stop imagining that." Suggestions of relaxation are then presented for approximately one minute or as long as needed until the client appears to have rerelaxed adequately. Occasionally, prearranged hand signals are used to aid the counselor in knowing when the client is ready to begin the imagining process again. After this rerelaxing the identical situation is presented for a shorter period of time. Gradually the client is exposed to longer periods of visualizing until he can imagine the situation for 20 seconds without signaling any anxiety. If the client repeatedly signals upon presentation of a new situation, yet does not signal at all when presented with the situation immediately lower on the anxiety hierarchy, new situations need to be added to the hierarchy and placed between these two situations. Hopefully, the use of "suds" will prevent this from occurring.

In the previously described session, seven presentations were made of two different situations. The typical desensitization session involves five to ten presentations of two to three different situations. The criterion for how much is accomplished each session appears to rest with how comfortable the client feels in proceeding. It should also be noted that a session always ends on a successfully completed item (that is, one where the client does not signal anxiety). Normally, each session begins with a single presentation of the last successfully completed item. In the preceding example, the young man would be asked to imagine himself having lunch with a long-time friend for a period of 10 seconds.

Occasionally, special hand signals need to be set up between client and counselor for the following reasons:

1. The client continually falls asleep. The frequency of this problem occurring seems to increase if a session is held early in the morning or late in the afternoon.
2. The client takes an unusually long period of time to picture himself in the situation.
3. The client, after relaxation, does not feel well enough relaxed to begin imagining himself in situations.

Problems (1) and (2) can be alleviated by simply having the client signal (with another finger than that used to indicate anxiety) when he has the scene to be imagined in mind. This forces his attention to be directed toward the situation he has been asked to imagine, away from a pleasant (and often sleep-inducing) scene and lets the counselor know when to keep track of the length of time the scene is imagined. Problem (3) is similarly eliminated by asking the client to signal if he does not feel relaxed enough to begin imagining situations from the hierarchy. If he signals, further relaxation is in order.

The average number of sessions required to complete the usual hierarchy seems to be between 10 and 15, as shown by Wolpe and Lazarus (1966) and confirmed by Emery (1966). However, this may vary widely depending on the particular problem and client. Most clients can effectively eliminate unwanted anxieties by meeting once a week for about three months, or, as the author has found in working with college students, by meeting twice a week for one quarter of college work.

THE CASE OF JIM

A pilot study in desensitization was carried out during the Spring of 1965 with 15 college students. The common problem that all the students presented was one of test anxiety. Results of this pilot study led to a more sophisticated, experimentally controlled study (Emery and Krumboltz, 1967) which showed that desensitization appears to be an effective method of reducing test anxiety. The following case is that of a young man selected from the pilot study.

Jim, a 19-year-old sophomore, answered the advertisement in the daily college newspaper which offered to help students overcome "clutching" or "freezing-up" on examinations. Jim was a history major who had recently transferred to Stanford after a year at a smaller college where he had obtained a 3.4 (B+) grade-point average. Stanford had been his original college preference, but he had been denied admission as a freshman. When, after his first year elsewhere, he had reapplied to Stanford and been accepted he was overjoyed since he was an only child whose parents were both Stanford graduates. Upon arriving on campus, he found that his roommate in the dormitory was a National Merit Scholar who had a 4.0 grade-point average, did little studying (at least Jim never saw him studying), and spent the majority of his time playing bridge in the dormitory lounge. As far as scholastic ability went, Jim himself was no slouch since his College Board SAT scores totaled 1324. His high school grade average was 3.6.

Since his arrival at Stanford his grades had slipped far below what he was accustomed to, but he had managed to get a 2.4 average. The competition he had feared had materialized and he had become quite nervous, worrying about his chances of graduate school, as well as just being able to graduate from Stanford. It was here, then, at the beginning of Winter Quarter that he presented himself for help.

First Session (1/11/65)

After obtaining the background material previously mentioned, Jim was asked to describe in detail how he felt at that time about taking exams. He said that he always had been able to do well in all his courses, with the exception of scientific courses (especially biology, chemistry, and physics). He related that his parents had never done well in any of their scientific pursuits during their academic careers and that consequently they had warned him of possible trouble in any science courses during his junior high school years. By the time he reached high school, some of his parents' forewarnings had become self-fulfilling, and he found that he generally received B's and C's in his science courses as opposed to A's in his other courses. He recalled that he had felt more anxious while studying for and taking his high school science exams than his other high school exams.

During his freshman year at college he had carefully avoided taking any science courses in order to keep up his average and qualify for transfer. Having successfully accomplished this he found himself faced with the unpleasant prospect of having to take science courses at Stanford in order to fulfill his natural sciences requirement for graduation. During his first quarter, therefore, he had taken Biology 1 and Psychology. His biology professor was an international expert in the field of biology and an excellent and prolific writer. His textbook was five inches thick. The tests had been fair but very difficult. Consequently he had ended up with D in biology; in a somewhat similar situation, although not to the extreme that it had been in biology, he had received a C in psychology. Jim stated that his biggest problem in both courses had been his "rotten" performance on midterm and final exams. As he related, "If I hadn't done well in my biology lab section, I'd have flunked for sure."

Jim gave the impression of being an enthusiastic yet somewhat nervous student whose anxiety seemed to be heightened by the possibility of having his goals thwarted. When questioned as to how many other situations aroused a comparable amount of anxiety within him, he replied that calling a girl for a first date came pretty close to bothering him as badly, but that this had changed for the better within the past year.

Jim seemed to be a likely candidate for desensitization, so the technique and rationale behind it were described to him. His reaction was that it sounded logical but too easy; he was skeptical, yet he was willing to give it a try. I assured him that it would not be too easy and that he would have to concentrate on learning to relax and on imagining the relevant situations which produced his anxiety. He replied, "Let's go."

Before leaving, Jim completed a copy of the Test Anxiety Scale (see Emery, 1966). His score was 62 which when compared with norms for 1078 Stanford undergraduates placed him at about the 95th percentile (Mean = 43, Standard Deviation = 11).

Second Session (1/13/65)

This session was devoted entirely to demonstration and practice of the relaxation technique. The counselor modeled the method of tensing and then relaxing each of the muscle groups in the usual order (that is, hands, forearms, upper arm, forehead, eyes and nose, lips, cheeks and jaw, throat, shoulders, chest and upper back, stomach, thighs, and calves). After it was ascertained that Jim understood the various tension-relaxation exercises, he proceeded to do each of the exercises twice. It took approximately 35 minutes for Jim to complete the exercises. He expressed great satisfaction with the results, the benefits of which were somewhat diminished during the thigh exercises by a cramp in his right leg. He was cautioned not to overdo the tension at first and to practice these exercises once a day in the privacy of his room.

Third Session (1/18/65)

Jim reported that his attempts at relaxation had been successful although not quite as good as when he had attempted them the previous time in the counselor's office. (The author has found that the large majority of clients find the relaxation exercises to be more effective in the counselor's darkened office while in a reclining chair. They report that it is easier for them to relax if someone else is telling them what to do.) The entire session was spent questioning and probing Jim as to the specific situations which bothered him with regard to the testing situation. At the close of the session, ten situations had been listed and Jim was asked to give some thought to other situations which might be included on his anxiety hierarchy before the next session.

Fourth Session (1/20/65)

Jim brought in a list of five more situations which bothered him with regard to testing situations. After further probing and discussion he ranked the total of 15 situations in the following order:

(95) Noticing that 30 minutes remain on the biology final and that you have an hour's worth of work to do

(90) While taking the biology final you come to a question you do not know the answer to

(80) While trying to think of an answer to an exam question you notice everyone around you writing very rapidly
(70) Walking into the room where the biology final is given
(65) Walking with a group of friends to the biology final
(60) The biology final is being handed out—you receive a copy
(50) It is the day of the biology final—one hour left until exam time
(50) Talking with a good student the night before the biology final
(40) Studying the night before the biology final
(30) Discussing the biology professor and how brilliant he is with some friends
(25) Studying for the biology final that is next week
(20) Copying someone's long and complete notes for a missed biology lecture
(15) Thinking of the biology lab and its weekly quiz
(10) Professor announcing that the biology midterm is one-and-a-half weeks away
 (5) Walking to a biology lecture

The "suds" scale was then explained to him, with the resulting levels shown in the parentheses to the left of each item. He was reminded that he should feel free to add, delete, or switch the position of an item on the hierarchy whenever he deemed it necessary. (Jim was taking only one science course this quarter.)

Fifth Session (1/25/65)

The entire session was spent in further practice of the relaxation procedure. Jim's enthusiasm spurred him into tensing his muscles with great vigor (no cramps this time, though) with the resulting relaxation being deeper than he had ever experienced before. While relaxed he was asked to imagine himself in (1) a neutral scene and (2) a personal form of relaxation.

Upon emerging from the relaxed state, he described his feelings as very pleasurable and calm. He reported that he had indeed felt a warm, tingling feeling as it had spread throughout his body and that he had been quite aware of the heaviness and looseness in his body. He also stated that he had imagined both the neutral scene and a personal form of relaxation with clarity.

Upon further questioning he reported that he didn't find any of the muscle-group exercises more beneficial than any other. It was agreed then to continue the present relaxation procedure which consisted of relaxing each of the muscle groups once and required about 15 minutes. Jim was reminded that he could revise the relaxation procedure at any time during our sessions if he found that certain exercises were becoming more effective than others. It was agreed that regular desensitization would begin next time and that Jim would signal with his index finger if he felt the least bit anxious.

Sixth Session (1/27/65)

The first regular desensitization proceeded without incident. Jim relaxed well and imagined the two least anxiety producing situations without signaling any anxiety. Notations made by the counselor were as follows:

(5) Walking to a biology lecture   1/27   +5, +10, +20
(10) Professor announcing that the biology midterm is 1½ weeks way 1/27 +5

After awakening, Jim stated that he had relaxed well and imagined both scenes clearly.

Seventh Session (2/1/65)

Once again the relaxation and imagining of scenes appeared to go without any difficulties. Jim relaxed very well and made no attempt to signal anxiety at all. Notations made by the counselor were as follows:

(10) Professor announcing that the biology midterm is 1½ weeks away 2/1 +5, +10, +20
(15) Thinking of the biology lab and its quiz   2/1 +5, (+10, +20)— asleep

Questioning upon his awakening revealed that he had been so relaxed that he had fallen asleep. He could remember vividly imagining himself in the first four situations, but didn't remember hearing anything beyond that except my counting backwards from 5 to 0, as part of the awakening procedure. Further notation was made and in order to prevent reoccurrence of this situation, a new signaling procedure was instituted. The new signaling arrangements were as follows:

(a) Signaling with index finger of left hand to indicate anxiety
(b) Signaling with index finger of right hand to indicate that the presented scene was being imagined

Before leaving, Jim stated that all his coursework was proceeding smoothly, that his weekly biology lab quizzes were "O.K., but no better than last quarter," and that his biology midterm was scheduled for 2/23/65, about three weeks hence.

Eighth Session (2/3/65)

The new signaling procedure was reviewed, Jim was relaxed and again imagined the scenes without signaling anxiety. The following notations were made by the counselor:

(15) Thinking of the biology lab and its quiz   2/3 +5, +10, +20
(20) Copying someone's long and complete notes for a missed biology lecture   2/3 +5, (+10, +20)—not vivid

Upon awakening, Jim reported that he had relaxed well and that there had been no problem with his falling asleep. The new signaling system seemed to have worked well, but further questioning of Jim as to the vividness of his imagining the scenes presented divulged a new problem area. Jim said that his biggest difficulty here was in having to force himself to imagine himself in a slightly unpleasant situation as opposed to imagining himself in an enjoyable and relaxing situation (for example, his personal form of relaxation). He stated further that during the last two presentations he had been asked to imagine, he had continually flitted back and forth between pleasant and unpleasant scenes.

At this point the counselor was not sure what to do since he had not been faced with this situation previously. Further discussion and some mutual counselor-client ingenuity led to the following (and hopefully final!) set of signals:

(a) Signaling with index finger of left hand to indicate anxiety
(b) Signaling with index finger of right hand to indicate that the presented scene was being imagined
(c) Signaling with small finger of right hand to indicate that the neutral scene was being imagined

The rationale here was to have Jim imagine himself in a neutral scene as an intermediate step between pleasant and unpleasant scenes. The neutral scene which Jim imagined was sitting in a lighted movie theater by himself, looking at the blank white screen. It was agreed to incorporate this within the desensitization procedure starting with the next session.

Ninth Session (2/8/65)

Regular desensitization, incorporating the transitional neutral scene, continued without any difficulties. Jim relaxed well and made no attempt to signal any anxiety. The neutral scenes were handled as shown below.

With Jim relaxing (for example, imagining a personal form of relaxation) the counselor began as follows:

> Now, stop imagining that and come up to your neutral scene . . . when you have the neutral scene in mind let me know by signaling . . .

(pause of 5 to 15 seconds—client signals) . . . O.K., fine, now I'd like you to imagine yourself as vividly as possible in the following situation (for example, the next situation on the hierarchy).

Jim reported that the neutral scene worked well, that he had no trouble switching his imagination from pleasant to unpleasant as long as the transitional scene was used, and that he had imagined all scenes quite vividly. The counselor made the following notations:

(20) Copying someone's long and complete notes for a missed biology lecture
2/8 +5, +10, +20
(25) Studying for the biology final that is next week   2/8 +5, +10

Tenth Session (2/10/65)

Regular desensitization continued as usual. During the second scene presented, Jim signaled anxiety for the first time. Further presentation of the scene, after some rerelaxation, did not evoke any noticeable anxiety. Questioning of Jim following his awakening indicated that he had felt anxious while imagining the second scene presented, but not while imagining it in further presentations.

(25) Studying for the biology final that is next week   2/10 +10, −14, +10, +15, +20
(30) Discussing the biology professor and how brilliant he is with some friends   2/10 +5, +10

Eleventh Session (2/15/65)

Another regular desensitization session was held without any problems. Jim relaxed well, as usual, and did not signal that he felt anxious while imagining any of the situations. Notations made by the counselor were as follows:

(30) Discussing the biology professor and how brilliant he is with some friends   2/15 +10, +20
(40) Studying the night before the final   2/15 +5, +10, +20
(50) Talking with a good student the night before the biology final   2/15 +5, +10, +20

Twelfth Session (2/17/65)

Regular desensitization took place until repeated signaling by Jim on one situation brought progress through the hierarchy to a halt. About half of the session was then spent discussing possible reasons for his repeated signaling. It was concluded that the situation, "The biology final is being handed out—you receive a copy"—should be relocated higher on the hierarchy with an approximate value of 75 suds. The following notations were made by the counselor:

(50) It is the day of the biology final—one hour left until exam time   2/17
    +5, +10, +10, +20
(60) The biology final is handed out—you receive a copy   2/17   —4,—2

Thirteenth Session (2/19/65)

Regular desensitization took place once again. Jim was not as relaxed as usual and reported that his upcoming biology midterm was beginning to bother him somewhat. He signaled that he felt anxious on the second presentation but was later able to imagine the identical situation for longer periods of time. The counselor made the following notations:

(50) It is the day of the biology final—one hour left until exam time   2/19
    +20, +20
(65) Walking with a group of friends to the biology final   2/10   —4, +3,
    +5, +10

(Before the next regularly scheduled meeting Jim called to cancel the next session due to his grandfather's sudden death. He also reported that he felt he had done better than usual on his biology midterm exam and looked forward to continuing our sessions as soon as possible.)

Fourteenth Session (3/1/65)

Before starting desensitization, Jim expressed great enthusiasm over the fact that, "this stuff may really work!" He stated that he had received a C on his biology midterm (as compared to a D and F the previous quarter) and was further encouraged by the fact that he had not felt "anywhere near as tense and choked-up" as he had on last quarter's biology exams. Further questioning revealed that he had felt anxious prior to the exam, yet once he had become engrossed in the exam his anxiety had somehow decreased. (Jim's enthusiasm and progress at this time were also very encouraging to the counselor.)

Regular desensitization was continued in the usual manner with Jim relaxing very well, imagining the scenes very vividly and not signaling any anxiety. The following notations were made by the counselor:

(65) Walking with a group of friends to the biology final   3/1 +10, +20
(70) Walking into the room where the biology final is given   3/1 +5,
    +10, +20
(75) The biology final is being handed out—you receive a copy   3/1 +3,
    +5

Fifteenth Session (3/3/65)

Regular desensitization session with no difficulties. Jim relaxed well and imagined the scenes vividly. The following notations were made by the counselor:

(75) The biology final is being handed out—you receive a copy 3/3 +5, +10, +20

(80) While trying to think of an answer to an exam question you notice everyone around you writing very rapidly 3/3 +5, +10, +20

(90) While taking the biology final you read a question to which you do not know the answer 3/3 +5, +10

Sixteenth Session (3/8/65)

This final desensitization session was carried out without any difficulty. Counselor notations were made as follows:

(90) While taking the biology final you read a question to which you do not know the answer 3/8 +10, +20, +20

(95) Noticing that 30 minutes remain on the biology final and that you have an hour's worth of work to do 3/8 +5, +10, +20, +20

Jim relaxed very well, imagined the scenes vividly and reported to his amazement that he felt no anxiety at all. He felt the sessions had been very useful and was looking forward to being able to demonstrate just how useful they had been during his biology final to be held in two weeks. He was reminded that he should feel free to contact the counselor at any time before finals week. Before leaving he again took the test anxiety scale (TAS) given to him during the first session. This time his score was 42, which was one point below the mean score for Stanford undergraduates and markedly lower than his first score of 62.

Summary and Follow-up

In many ways, Jim represents the typical student in desensitization. Sixteen meetings took place over a period of eight weeks, during which the first five meetings were used to help prepare the client for desensitization; the final eleven meetings in carrying through the actual desensitization process. During those final eleven sessions a total of 70 scene presentations were made to Jim. On 62 of these presentations he felt no anxiety, on two presentations he fell asleep, on two presentations he did not imagine the situations vividly and on four presentations signaled that he felt anxiety. These difficulties were overcome, respectively, by having the client signal when he had the scene in mind, by having the client imagine himself in a transitional neutral scene, and by rearranging the order of items on the anxiety hierarchy.

A 20 month follow-up has been rigorously carried out to determine the efficacy of the desensitization treatment for Jim. Inquiries were made of Jim by phone or letter at the following times:

(1) At the beginning of the quarter following his treatment, Jim related his quarter GPA had risen from 2.4 (Fall Quarter) to 3.0 (Winter Quarter). Most important was that he reported not "tensing" or "blocking" on the biology final and that his course grade had risen to a C (from a D the previous quarter).

(2) Twelve months after concluding the desensitization treatment, Jim reported that his overall GPA at Stanford had risen to 3.0. In three science courses he had taken since his last report (Biology 3, Geology 1 and 10) he had received two B's and one C.

(3) Twenty months (January, 1967) after concluding his desensitization treatment, Jim reported his overall GPA had risen to 3.2 and that he was looking forward to entering law school. Completion of another TAS at that time showed a score of 40, almost identical to what he scored immediately upon conclusion of desensitization.

PART V

Cognitive Techniques

BEHAVIORAL COUNSELING HAS sometimes been charged with deriving its principles from animal studies and not taking into account the complexities of human behavior. Although it is true that some basic principles have been derived from animal research, it should be clear to the reader who has inspected the preceding four sections that behavioral counseling has gone considerably beyond what the animals can tell us.

The techniques described in this part are termed cognitive techniques. In some ways, however, the techniques described in the preceding four parts are also cognitive techniques. Formulating the goals of counseling, reinforcing and modeling responses, and counterconditioning emotional reactions all involve verbal concepts, thoughts, plans, and the ability to express one's observations and reactions.

Cognition refers to the process of knowing. Knowing is one of those internal constructs which cannot be directly observed. We infer that another person knows if he emits certain verbal symbols or if he acts appropriately in a given set of circumstances. Cognitive techniques in counseling are techniques designed to help the client know himself and his environment so that he might act more appropriately in future problem situations.

Cognitive techniques differ from reinforcement techniques, for example, in that the precise response desired cannot be stated in advance. For example, in simulation techniques we want the client to know what it is like to solve an accounting problem. We do not necessarily want the client to become an accountant; neither do we necessarily want him not to become an accountant. We want him to know what solving accounting problems feels like so that he can decide for himself whether or not he wishes to explore the profession of accounting further.

We want clients to know how to plan and make independent decisions for themselves. We want them to know the process, but we do not and cannot determine what decisions they will make as a result of using this process.

Confrontation techniques are designed to let a client know exactly how he behaves, what he looks like, and how he affects other people. We cannot be sure to what use the client will put this information. He may decide that he likes the kind of impact he makes on other people and wants to continue unchanged. He may decide that his own behavior is self-defeating and therefore will look for some alternatives that will produce more desirable results for him.

The purpose of counseling is to help people become self-sufficient and effective problem solvers. Part V contains several illustrations of methods that can be used to train people to become self-sufficient problem solvers. Accurate knowledge of one's self and one's environment is a prerequisite to effective problem solving. If the counselor applies these techniques well, the client will not only be able to solve his immediate problem but will have learned some techniques for better solving his future problems.

Simulation

A JET PILOT DOES not learn his profession merely by reading books and hearing lectures before he is turned loose to pilot a jet airplane. He spends many hours in a simulated trainer learning how to manipulate the controls and respond appropriately to emergency conditions. The advantages of simulation are obvious. If the jet pilot makes a mistake in his simulated trainer, the error is called to his attention. He is given appropriate instructions as to how he should have reacted and he is allowed to try again. If he were to make the same mistake in a real aircraft, the consequences might be so disastrous that he would never be able to make any kind of a mistake again.

Simulation might also be used to arouse interest. Imagine that a high school student was allowed to operate a simulated jet plane and that he was quickly able to master a simple problem. Wouldn't he be likely to want to find out more about his chances of becoming a jet pilot? And once he started exploring, wouldn't he want to find out about other occupations?

Many students find it difficult to choose among different career possibilities because they simply do not know what it is like to experience the work of different occupations. If counselors had available simulation kits for different careers, they could provide work samples derived from a variety of different occupations and thereby give students an opportunity to feel what it is like to solve problems in any given occupation. Problem-solving career kits have been under development at Stanford University, and part of a sample kit in accounting by Krumboltz and Sheppard is included in Article 32.

Simulation techniques can also be useful for counseling clients to practice responses under conditions that will not be disastrous if mistakes are made. Varenhorst in Article 33 describes the *Life Career Game*, a simulation technique designed to help students anticipate the consequences of many of life's decisions. In this game students can plan the way in which hypothetical persons spend their time and can see probable consequences of these decisions. The way in which one decides to spend the next hour seems to be a trivial decision to most people, yet the sum total of hourly decisions produces either a satisfying life or a life compounded with various degrees of misery. Students can practice making decisions for other people and can see the consequences of a series of decisions. Varenhorst reports that students become quite involved in the decision process and transfer it to their own life decisions.

Simulation can be real, or it can be imaginary. Davison, in Article 34, provides a fascinating description of imaginary simulation. In order for a boy to learn self-control in the face of unreasonable authority, he learns with the help of a counselor to imagine that his father is in an extremely angry mood. The boy must simulate in his imagination the only condition which will permit him to exercise self-control. This unusual technique raises a number of interesting problems both ethical and practical.

The development of appropriate simulation activities for a variety of social, emotional, personal, and occupational problems is an exciting challenge for any counselor. The examples cited in this section are only beginning illustrative steps.

32
VOCATIONAL PROBLEM-SOLVING EXPERIENCES

John D. Krumboltz
STANFORD UNIVERSITY
Lawrence E. Sheppard
EMERY UNIFIED SCHOOL DISTRICT
EMERYVILLE (CALIFORNIA)

Many young people would like to decide on some occupational goal, but their knowledge and experience are so limited that they cannot make even a tentative decision. Others do make firm career commitments but often on the basis of inaccurate or unrealistic expectations of the type of work that will be required of them. Almost all have doubts about what they themselves are capable of accomplishing.

Young people seldom have the opportunity to solve the types of problems faced by people in many occupations. Young people may observe employed persons at their work, but even then they see only the outward manifestations of the job, not the problem-solving process itself. An adolescent may have virtually no idea of the problems and responsibilities faced on the job by his own father. Even though he may see his father at work on some occasions, he sees only the superficial aspects of the job. He may see his father signing his name, punching a calculator, talking to a secretary, or adjusting machinery. But the youth has no conception as to what is being accomplished, what problems must be solved, and how this job fits into the total process. Most of all he has no idea whether he himself could do the job.

Problem-solving materials have been designed to give young people the opportunity to solve simple but realistic problems similar to those solved by members of various occupations.[1]

The problem-solving materials were prepared in accordance with the following guidelines: (1) the problem should be realistic and representa-

[1] A package of problem-solving career kits which simulate the activities of 20 different occupations is available from Science Research Associates, Inc., 259 East Erie Street, Chicago, Illinois 60611.

tive of the type of problems faced by members of the occupation; (2) 95 percent of the target population (high school students) should have no difficulty in reading the problem; (3) the problem should be considered intrinsically interesting by the majority of the target population; (4) at least 75 percent of the target population should be able to read the material and solve the problem successfully within 50 minutes; (5) the problem should be completely self-contained and self-administered.[2]

AN EXAMPLE: THE ACCOUNTANT'S KIT

The accountant's kit begins by explaining briefly the valuable services performed by accountants. It then asks the student to imagine that he is an accountant who has been consulted by the owner of a small sport shop about diminishing profits. Since it was assumed that the subjects had no prior experience with accounting or banking procedures, a brief explanation of how a check is written, endorsed, and cleared is provided. The student is then asked to remove a packet of canceled checks from an envelope and compare them with the records kept by the bookkeeper. A detailed comparison would reveal a number of discrepancies involving forged signatures, overpayments, possible kickbacks and misappropriated funds. The student is then asked to pick which of three letters he would write to the owner of the sport shop. Any student discovering four of the eight possible discrepancies is told that he successfully mastered some tasks like those performed by accountants.

The canceled checks, the accountant's letters and the other forms were constructed to be nearly identical to the corresponding documents used in business. The complete kit was examined and approved for accuracy and representativeness by two certified public accountants prior to the preliminary testing. Slightly more than 90 percent of the high school students who tried the kit attained "success" in solving the problem.

---

[2] A counselor should not have to get involved in administrative trivia. A student perplexed by vocational uncertainty could try 1, 3, 10, or 20 kits before discussing with a counselor which experiences appealed to him. A student already "certain" of his career choice could try related kits to confirm (or upset) his conviction. The counselor need only say, "Here, take this, follow the directions, and then let's discuss your reactions."

THE ACCOUNTANT'S KIT

Would you like to be an ACCOUNTANT?

Before you can decide you probably would like to know more about the job. What does an ACCOUNTANT do?

Here is one kind of problem which ACCOUNTANTS must solve.

See if you can solve it.

Read the following material carefully and follow the instructions.

WHY ARE ACCOUNTANTS NECESSARY?

Millions of dollars are stolen each year by dishonest employees. They may write false statements on business records, write incorrect checks, or forge signatures.

One job of an ACCOUNTANT is to check these business records to correct errors and prevent possible theft.

YOUR PROBLEM . . . . . .

Imagine now that you are an ACCOUNTANT.

You receive a telephone call from Mr. E. Z. Mark, owner of the Mark Sport Shop.

He wants to hire you to go over his records to make sure everything is in order.

He is worried that his business does not seem to be making as much money as it should.

You inform him that your fee for inspecting his books is $25.00 per hour and he agrees to pay you on that basis.

**BEFORE YOU CAN EARN YOUR PAY, HERE ARE A FEW FACTS
YOU MUST KNOW. . . .**

1. WHAT IS A CHECK?

- Some people pay for things with cash. Another way is to pay by check.
- If you deposit your money in a bank you may arrange to
  ask the bank to pay money out of your account.
- A check is simply your request to the bank to pay a certain
  amount of money to whomever you say.

2. HOW IS A CHECK FILLED OUT?

- Suppose you wanted to pay $1.58 to your friend, Jack Martin. Your
  bank would supply you with the blank check forms.

Notice that the name and address of your bank appear here.
Your name may be printed by the bank here.

Your checks are numbered here (this is the 255th check in the series given you
by the bank).

WELLS FARGO BANK   №. 255

August 21 19 64

PAY TO THE ORDER OF Jack Martin $ 1.58

One and 58/100   DOLLARS

MY NAME

My Signature

You would fill out the rest like this:

You write the name of the person who would receive the money here.

You write the amount in dollars and cents here.

You spell out the amount of money here to make certain it is clear.

You write the date here.

You sign your own name here.

3. WHAT HAPPENS TO A CHECK AFTER IT IS WRITTEN?

- Jack takes the check to the bank and endorses it. This means he writes his name on the back of the check so the bank will have written proof that Jack has received the $1.58 from the bank. The bank will accept Jack's signature only since the check was made out to Jack.

- Only the payee (person to whom the check is written) is to endorse the check. Some companies use a special stamp instead of a signature. No one other than the person or company you wish should endorse the check and receive the money.

- The bank takes the check that Jack has endorsed and gives him the $1.58.

- The bank subtracts $1.58 from money you gave to the bank.

- The bank stamps the check as paid and the date it was paid.

- The bank returns the check (which is called a "cancelled" check now that the bank has put its stamp on it) to you along with a statement as to how much money you have left in your bank account.

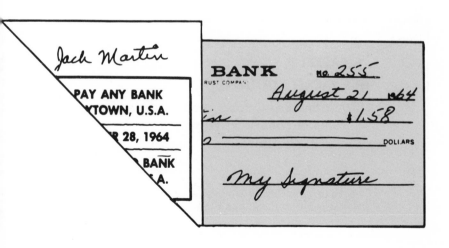

NOW TO EARN YOUR $25.00 PER HOUR

- You go to see Mr. Mark. He introduces you to his bookkeeper, Mr. Robert Baron, a clean-cut young man who he says is very honest and dependable.

- Mr. Mark gives you the following information:
  1. The owner, Mr. Mark, is the only person allowed to sign a check.

  2. He has only one employee, Mr. Baron, who does all the office work and helps with the sales since Mr. Mark is away from the store much of the time.

  3. Samples of his and his bookkeeper's signatures are as follows:

E. Z. Mark	Robert Baron

  4. Open *PACKET A*, below. It should include (1) Mr. Baron's Record of Checks Written for October, (2) The cancelled checks for October, which have been cashed and returned to Mr. Mark by his bank, and (3) your Report Form.

  5. Now, look at the instructions for your job on the next page.

PACKET A
THIS PACKET CONTAINS:

1. Cancelled October checks received from bank
2. Record of Checks Written
3. Report Form

Checks used in this kit are courtesy of:
Wells Fargo Bank, San Francisco, California

YOUR JOB

- Take the cancelled checks, the Record of Checks Written, and your Report Form out of *PACKET A*.

- Inspect each check carefully on both sides and compare it with the Record of Checks Written for October 1964, which was kept by Mr. Baron.

- List on your Report Form, Part I, anything you feel is incorrect in these records. Take as much time as you need.

- You have been hired by Mr. Mark and now must report to him exactly what you discovered to be incorrect.

- Take the three letters out of *PACKET B,* below. Which one letter will you send to Mr. Mark?

- Circle Letter A or B or C in Part II of your Report Form.

PACKET B

THIS PACKET CONTAINS:

1. Letter A
2. Letter B
3. Letter C

NO. 291

October 3, 19 64

PAY TO THE ORDER OF ___ A & B Football Supply ___ $ 100.00

One Hundred and ———————— NO / 100 ___ DOLLARS

WELLS FARGO BANK

MARK SPORT SHOP
1234 STADIUM RD.
ANYTOWN, U.S.A.

E. Z. Mark

FOR DEPOSIT ONLY
A & B FOOTBALL SUPPLY

PAY ANY BANK
ANYTOWN, U.S.A.

OCTOBER 28, 1964

WELLS FARGO BANK
ANYTOWN, U.S.A.

SAMPLE CHECK

NO. 292

October 7, 19 64

PAY TO THE ORDER OF ___ Robert Baron ___ $ 350.00

Three Hundred Fifty and ———— NO / 100 ___ DOLLARS

WELLS FARGO BANK

MARK SPORT SHOP
1234 STADIUM RD.
ANYTOWN, U.S.A.

E. Z. Mark

Robert Baron

PAY ANY BANK
ANYTOWN, U.S.A.

OCTOBER 28, 1964

WELLS FARGO BANK
ANYTOWN, U.S.A.

SAMPLE CHECK

NO. 293

October 15, 19 64

PAY TO THE ORDER OF ___ Joe's Bicycle Parts ___ $ 200.00

Two Hundred and ———————— NO / 100 ___ DOLLARS

WELLS FARGO BANK

MARK SPORT SHOP
1234 STADIUM RD.
ANYTOWN, U.S.A.

E. Z. Mark

Robert Baron

PAY ANY BANK
ANYTOWN, U.S.A.

OCTOBER 28, 1964

WELLS FARGO BANK
ANYTOWN, U.S.A.

SAMPLE CHECK

NO. 294

October 16, 19 64

PAY TO THE ORDER OF ___ Art's Camping Store ___ $ 100.00

One Hundred and ———————— NO / 100 ___ DOLLARS

WELLS FARGO BANK

MARK SPORT SHOP
1234 STADIUM RD.
ANYTOWN, U.S.A.

E. Z. Mark

FOR DEPOSIT ONLY
ART'S CAMPING STORE

PAY ANY BANK
ANYTOWN, U.S.A.

OCTOBER 28, 1964

WELLS FARGO BANK
ANYTOWN, U.S.A.

SAMPLE CHECK

NO. 295

October 18, 19 64

PAY TO THE ORDER OF ___ Robert Baron ___ $ 350.00

Three Hundred Fifty and ———— NO / 100 ___ DOLLARS

WELLS FARGO BANK

MARK SPORT SHOP
1234 STADIUM RD.
ANYTOWN, U.S.A.

E. Z. Mark

Robert Baron

PAY ANY BANK
ANYTOWN, U.S.A.

OCTOBER 28, 1964

WELLS FARGO BANK
ANYTOWN, U.S.A.

SAMPLE CHECK

NO. 296

October 25, 19 64

PAY TO THE
ORDER OF _____ . _____ Baron Real Estate Co. _____ , 300.00 _____

Three Hundred and _____ NO / 100 _____ DOLLARS

WELLS FARGO BANK

MARK SPORT SHOP
1234 STADIUM RD.
ANYTOWN, U.S.A.

E. Z. Mark

Robert Baron

| PAY ANY BANK ANYTOWN, U.S.A. | OCTOBER 28, 1964 | WELLS FARGO BANK ANYTOWN, U.S.A. |

SAMPLE CHECK

NO. 297

October 5, 19 64

PAY TO THE
ORDER OF _____ Brown Real Estate Co. _____ , 300.00 _____

Three Hundred and _____ NO / 100 _____ DOLLARS

WELLS FARGO BANK

MARIE'S DRESS SHOP
1234 PETTICOAT LANE
ANYTOWN, U.S.A.

Marie Marketer

| FOR DEPOSIT ONLY BROWN REAL ESTATE CO. | PAY ANY BANK ANYTOWN, U.S.A. | OCTOBER 28, 1964 | WELLS FARGO BANK ANYTOWN, U.S.A. |

SAMPLE CHECK

RECORD OF CHECKS WRITTEN

OCTOBER 1964

MARK SPORT SHOP

DATE OF CHECK	PERSON TO WHOM CHECK IS WRITTEN	CHECK NUMBER	CHECK AMOUNT	REASON THE CHECK WAS WRITTEN
Oct. 3	A & B Football Supply	291	$ 50.00	To pay for 8 footballs
Oct. 7	Robert Baron	292	350.00	Wages for last month
Oct. 15	Joe's Bicycle Parts	293	200.00	To pay for bicycle parts
Oct. 16	Art's Camping Store	294	100.00	To pay for 3 pen flashlights
Oct. 18	—	295	—	Check destroyed, made wrong
Oct. 25	Brown Real Estate Co.	296	300.00	To pay for month's rent
	Total October 1964 Checks		$1,405.00	

REPORT FORM

Print your name here_____

First   Last

PART I   LIST OF ERRORS FOUND.

PART II   Which letter will you send to Mr. Mark?

A   B   C   (circle one)

PART III   Did you find the number of errors for a successful job?

YES   NO   (circle one)

NOTE: When you have completed the job *please replace all the material* except this Report Form in the proper packets.

LETTER A

Mr. E. Z. Mark, Owner
Mark Sport Shop

Dear Mr. Mark:

I have examined the Record of Checks Written and the cancelled checks for the month of October 1964, in accordance with generally accepted accounting standards.

In my opinion the above records present fairly and accurately the bank expenses of the Mark Sport Shop for the month of October 1964, and represent good business methods for the month under review.

Very truly yours,

Certified Public Accountant

LETTER B

Mr. E. Z. Mark, Owner
Mark Sport Shop

Dear Mr. Mark:

I have examined the Record of Checks Written and the cancelled checks for the month of October 1964, in accordance with generally accepted accounting standards.

In my opinion the above records present fairly the bank expenses of the Mark Sport Shop for the month of October 1964, with some minor exceptions which I shall list separately on my Report Form.

Very truly yours,

Certified Public Accountant

LETTER C

Mr. E. Z. Mark, Owner
Mark Sport Shop

Dear Mr. Mark:

I have examined the Record of Checks Written and the cancelled checks for the month of October 1964, in accordance with generally accepted accounting standards.

In my opinion the above records do not present fairly or accurately the bank expenses of the Mark Sport Shop for the month of October 1964. A list of minor and major errors is enclosed on my Report Form.

Very truly yours,

Certified Public Accountant

- You should have circled Letter C in Part II of your Report Form.

- You should have listed at least *four* errors in Part I of your Report Form. (There are more than four, but if you found four, you have the right idea.)

- If you did not find four errors, go over your work once again to see what you may have missed.

- Now perhaps you would like to see if you correctly found four of the possible errors.

- Open *PACKET C*, below, and remove the Correct Answers, and compare your answers with them.

- Did you successfully find four errors that were among those listed on the Correct Answers?

- Circle either *YES* or *NO* in Part III of your Report Form.

- If you said *YES*, you have successfully solved one of the types of problems faced by *ACCOUNTANTS*.

Of course you realize that *ACCOUNTANTS* help solve many other types of problems also. Perhaps you would be interested in discovering more about *ACCOUNTING* as a *possible career* for you.

PACKET C

THIS PACKET CONTAINS:

Correct Answers
(Do not open until you have
finished the problem)

CORRECT ANSWERS

1. **CHECK 291:** Amount of check ($100.00) different from Record of Checks Written ($50.00).

2. **CHECK 292:** Signature forged (see sample signatures).

3. **CHECK 293:** Wrong person endorsed check (see back of check).

4. **CHECK 294:** Nothing wrong with check *but* $100.00 appears to be too much to pay for three small flashlights.

5. **CHECK 295:** Despite indication that this check was destroyed, it was actually cashed by Mr. Baron who appears to have forged Mr. Mark's signature.

6. **CHECK 296:** Check made out to a different company than shown on the Record of Checks Written. Possibly so Mr. Baron could endorse and cash the check himself.

7. **CHECK 397:** This check was incorrectly charged to Mr. Mark's account by the bank. The bank should be notified of this error and the check charged against the account of Marie's Dress Shop. (Note lower left hand corner of check.)

8. **RECORD OF CHECKS WRITTEN:** The total for October checks showing $1,405.00 is incorrect. The correct total is $1,000.00.

EVALUATION

Criterion instruments were designed to assess the extent to which students developed an interest in activities and occupations related to accounting and the extent to which they engaged in exploratory activities relevant to their career choice.[3]

The problem-solving experience stimulated relatively more information-seeking behaviors for some individuals than others. Perhaps such a problem-solving experience would be a significant event at one crucial time in an individual's career development but insignificant before he was ready or after he had made other commitments. The fact that some subgroups were affected more than others suggests that further research is needed on the timing of problem-solving within the sequence of career decision making.[4]

[3] The purpose of the kits is to stimulate interest in career exploration, not to "sell" a particular occupation and not to serve as a psychometric interest or aptitude test. Desired behaviors involve curiosity arousal followed by occupational-educational planning and information-seeking.

[4] Detailed reports of research on this and other kits are reported in J. D. Krumboltz, L. E. Sheppard, G. B. Jones, R. G. Johnson, and R. D. Baker. *Vocational Problem-Solving Experiences for Stimulating Career Exploration and Interest.* Stanford, Calif.: School of Education, Stanford University. Final Report of Project No. 5–0070, Contract No. OE 5–85–059, U.S. Office of Education, 1967.

It is hoped that the provision of simulated job experiences will enable persons to better determine for themselves whether a certain type of work will enable them to receive the kind of reinforcers they seek from life.

33

LEARNING THE CONSEQUENCES OF LIFE'S DECISIONS

Barbara B. Varenhorst
PALO ALTO UNIFIED SCHOOL DISTRICT (CALIFORNIA)

Most of us would enjoy gazing into a crystal ball for a glimpse of the future. For if one knew what the future would be like, and how one would have to adapt to the future, or what problems would have to be faced, one might behave very differently in the present.

Because we are human we can affect the future and change it to create different environments and experiences. And because we are human we can change ourselves to live in that future. But lacking the crystal ball and knowing little about the future, we do not usually know in what ways we would like to change and how to plan for an unknown that may be different when we "arrive." That which we do know we only know in bits and pieces which are heavily influenced by past experiences and interpretations. A more objective method of anticipating future consequences of present decisions is needed.

Counselors tired of merely giving interest tests and dispensing occupational information, are searching for more effective ways of vocational counseling. Over a period of years I have investigated ways to assist students in effectively planning their lives. In searching, I have experimented with a simulation approach that seems to provide many of the necessary conditions for significant vocational guidance.

The core of vocational planning, of course, is utilizing the process of decision-making: the sorting through of possible alternatives, the identifying of consequences, and the choosing one or several based on an individual's desire to acquire some of society's rewards or to experience personal satisfaction for achieving valued goals. The objective of vocational guidance should be the assisting of students to become independent decision-makers. To do this certain conditions must be met.

SOME NECESSARY DECISION-MAKING CONDITIONS

Involvement

Students must feel the need to make decisions and must be aware that they are in a decision-making bind. If students are not concerned or emotionally involved in a need for assistance, what is done for or with them will have little effect. Some students may find the immediacy of the present sufficiently demanding and satisfying to have little active concern for future planning. Or some may feel so defeated by what they have experienced to date that they feel powerless to affect the future in any way. A counselor may have to help students realize that what one does and chooses has some affect on outcomes and goals.

Relevant Facts

Students must gain some sense of the context of the future against which they can weigh alternatives open to them. They need some understanding of the operating principles of the society in which they will live. To know this they may have to be provided with data and information which differ from what we usually provide them.

Clarification of Values

Students need assistance in understanding what is now rewarding to them and what may be rewarding to them in the future. What do they value and in what order do they value these things? Perhaps they need a variety of social models from which they can select and define their values. An opportunity to observe these models could help them differentiate what behaviors seem associated with consequences students find personally desirable.

Practice in Making Decisions

Students need meaningful practice in making decisions. Decision-making is a behavioral skill that must be learned. It is learned gradually by first making simple decisions, experiencing the consequences, and trying again on increasingly complex decisions. Some students are asked to make the complex decisions regarding the planning of their lives with very little previous experience in decision-making.

THE LIFE CAREER GAME

The Life Career Game, a simulation technique, is one approach that when used effectively can assist students to learn decision-making by providing these four conditions. To do this, the game extensively uses social learning principles of modeling, reinforcement, successive approximation, discrimination learning, and skill development. The game was developed by Dr. Sarane Boocock (1967) of the Johns Hopkins University. I have adapted it as a counseling tool to be used in educational settings and have used it over the past three years, in various settings, particularly at Gunn Senior High School and Wilbur Junior High School in Palo Alto, California.

Life Career is a decision-making game. Students who play the game are able to span eight to ten years in the future as the decision-maker of a fictitious person presented to them in the form of a profile, that is, a written case history. Students play in teams, working with the same profile person, attempting to plan the most satisfying life for that person over the eight-year period. Teams plan this life by making decisions as to how the person will allocate a certain amount of time (84 hours) to doing different activities during a typical week for each of the eight years. Players are then fed back the consequences of these decisions in the form of scores or game points which are indications of the relative satisfaction of the life being planned. Thus the decision for each succeeding year must take into consideration the consequences of decisions made in the preceding years. Scoring of the game is based on probability tables and data that have been compiled from analysis of current national statistics related to career planning. Thus, through the scoring, students are introduced to facts regarding operating principles of our society.

Through the use of equipment and routine of the game, attempts are made to simulate the job, education, and marriage opportunities as they exist in American society today. By participating in the game, students experience the necessity to behave in certain ways to achieve desired rewards or goals. Therefore, if players wish their student to get a job, for example, they must take some action, such as leaving their seat and going to the job table where they experience job hunting, filling out a job application, and being interviewed for that job. There is no attempt to approve or disapprove of these operating principles in American society; they are presented in such a way that they can be better understood and dealt with by young people who may confront them in reality as they plan their own lives.

Physical Arrangement

The room is set up so that students can work in teams of two, with room to write and spread out necessary materials needed for the playing of the game. In addition, a job table, an education table, a marriage and family table, and a score table are designated at some place in the room. Students come to these tables at appropriate times, seeking service or counsel. If the group of students is small, the counselor or teacher can manage to run all of these tables herself. For larger groups, assistants may be necessary and these can be either adults or other students.

Player Materials

Each team of students is given materials needed to play the game. These consist of: (1) the written profile of the hypothetical student (for example, see Figure 1), (2) a list of courses offered in the school where the profile student is enrolled, (3) a transcript sheet on which teams record the grades their students earn, (4) the planning sheet on which they will record how their student spends his time and (5) a summary sheet on which scores are recorded (Figure 2).

The planning sheet is marked off in hour blocks beginning with 8:00 A.M. Monday morning and ending 9:30 P.M. for each day of the week. Teams of students write in each square what the profile student is doing, even if the student is talking on the telephone to a friend, watching TV or doing dishes. When all 84 squares have been filled in, teams add up the amount of time they have assigned to the four categories: education, job, family life, and leisure. On the basis of these hours, scores are given for this particular round of the game.

Playing of the Game

To introduce the game, the counselor explains the purpose of it, indicating through such a discussion the possibilities this may have for assisting them in their own personal planning of their lives. They are then told that the object of the game is to plan the most satisfying life for this student. It is pointed out that everyone may have different definitions of life satisfaction, although many people seek similar goals such as education, a good salary, a job with some recognition, a home and family. In this game, however, there is no hidden biased definition of satisfaction

MARY

Mary, age 16, is an extremely intelligent and creative girl. In junior high and first year high school she was placed in gifted classes and advanced placement classes. She has demonstrated talent in creative writing and has done some outstanding art pieces, particularly with watercolors. She loves to do studies of faces.

In junior high, Mary got all A's and B's. During her sophomore year a dramatic change took place. She was absent frequently from school, failed to meet class assignments, and eventually withdrew from school to attend a private school. As a result, she only earned one unit of credit in the tenth grade, getting a D in Painting and a D in Girls P.E. However, she was reenrolled in the public high school, and would like to take classes with her own classmates. She still seems lost, and questions the purpose of school, college, society's values, etc.

Mary has an older brother who lives at home, but is attending a nearby state college as a freshman. Her father is a librarian at the state college, earning $8,000 per year. Mary's mother also works, in an office at a nearby private university. She makes $4200 per year. Both parents are college graduates.

When Mary is not at school, she meets with close friends for "discussions" about life and society and other problems. She sometimes stays up all night, either painting or writing poetry. She has dated college and graduate students, and is allowed quite a bit of freedom regarding what she does.

She has no idea what her future plans might be. She is under a great deal of pressure from her parents to go to college. Since she reads a great deal, she feels that much of her education can be acquired this way. She is not opposed to learning, but to requirements of school. The tension at home has added to her problems in making some important decisions.

GRADES

	9	10
English	A	F
Social Studies	A	F
Math	B	F
French	A	F
Biology	B	
Girls P.E.	B	D
Exp. Art	B	
Painting		D

COPY THESE GRADES ON TO THE LIFE BOARD GRADE TRANSCRIPT.

V = AA;   Q = AA;   Electives = AA

FIG. 1.   *Profile of the Hypothetical Student*

HIGH SCHOOL YEARS

SCORING SUMMARY FOR ROUND_____TEAM NO._____

I. EDUCATION

Name of Class	Hours in Class (per week) (must be at least 30)	TOTAL HOURS	Hours of Study	Grade Rec'd (from chart)	Points Rec'd (from chart)	TOTAL POINTS
1. _____	_____		_____	_____	_____
2. _____	_____		_____	_____	_____
3. _____	_____		_____	_____	_____
4. _____	_____		_____	_____	_____
5. _____	_____		_____	_____	_____
6. _____	_____		_____	_____	_____
7. _____	_____		_____	_____	_____
	TOTAL _____				Education—TOTAL _____

II. WORK
Name of Job

_____

TOTAL _____   Work—TOTAL _____

III. LEISURE

	Hours		Points
1. Athletic Team	_____	(must be at least	
2. Club, church	_____	12 to score)	_____
3. Hobby	_____	(must be at least	_____
4. Fun with friends	_____	6 to score)	_____
5. Relax at home	_____		_____
		Leisure—TOTAL	_____

IV. FAMILY

	Hours		Points
1. Hours spent in housework		(must be at least	
	TOTAL _____	7 to score)	_____
2. Marriage score			
Total weekly hours	84	Family—TOTAL	_____

TOTAL TEAM SCORE _____

Add Bonus upon Graduation from High School   10

TOTAL TEAM SCORE (after Senior Year) _____

FIG. 2. *Summary Sheet of Scores*

that must be discovered in order to win. But, just as in life where we take into consideration our own personal likes and dislikes and characteristics in defining what we want from life, so must teams consider carefully the characteristics of the profile student as presented in the case history in order to increase their chances for winning. Following this preliminary presentation, the playing can begin.

Throughout the playing of the game before a team can have their student engage in certain activities they have to arrange for this by utilizing the services at one of the tables. For example, a student cannot spend time working at a job until the team has secured a job for him at the job table. If a team is going to have their student receive any post high school education, they must apply for admission at the education table. If they want their student to get married or have children, they make application for this at the family table.

Additional rules are included in the process of the playing for the purpose of increasing playability and introducing other realities of life. To do this, each team picks an "unplanned event" card at the end of each round. An unplanned event may tell the team that their student lost his job, or was drafted, or was promoted, or had a divorce, or an unexpected child. Such events, when they occur, must be handled in the future planning the team does with their student. Likewise, when a student gets married, he is required to provide a certain minimum income for himself and family, and he must spend a required number of hours doing household chores, which change as the family picture changes.

At frequent intervals the playing is stopped for group critiques and discussion. This can become the significant part of this learning experience because it provides opportunities to reinforce learning, to utilize peer modeling and to emphasize certain concepts. To do this the leading team is asked to explain the strategy they have used in planning the student's life. This may be followed by asking the teams with the lowest score to explain their strategy. From such explanations, other teams may question why a team did one thing and why another team did something else. Some teams may question the fairness of the scoring system which may start a discussion on aspects of society as it functions with respect to work, or education, or family life.

HOW THE GAME FULFILLS DECISION-MAKING CONDITIONS

Involvement

Immediately on beginning the game, students become involved in decision-making since they recognize that for the playing to continue, they must make decisions. Furthermore, the decision-making field prescribed for them is in terms of deciding how to effectively and wisely divide up a quantity of time in order to win game points. Further involvement is motivated by the presentation of a hypothetical student upon whom they can exercise autonomy and power. To do this they are confronted with the immediate need to consider alternatives open to this person. These alternatives can be emphasized by a group discussion of all possible alternatives before the playing starts. Which of these factors are the most powerful in creating involvement on the part of players has not been determined. However, observation of teams at work will testify to this involvement as they play undisturbed even when 30 adults may be in the room watching them. Additional evidence of a type of involvement is the fact that teams sometimes identify their student with a last name or give names to the children of the student. Such human aspects of life have appeal to students and seem to indicate the success of the simulation.

Relevant Facts

Throughout the playing of the game, students soon realize that they need facts before they can make a decision. Not only must they have facts but they must know where to get these facts and how to weigh them regarding possible consequences of their decisions. For example, when students begin considering what courses the profile student should take in school, they begin asking about graduation and college requirements. During one session a student asked if biology met the lab requirement for the University of California. Although I thought most students must know this by this time, I suggested that he check the catalog of the university that I happened to have in the room. Both he and his partner immediately picked it up and went in search of the answer. Soon the team was back frustrated because they couldn't find what they wanted in the maze of information spread throughout the catalog. Together we went through it, finding other bits of data the team thought might be valuable later on in the game.

Alternative use of time becomes a real issue following the first round of the playing. At this time, grades for each of the classes the student has taken are determined. Grading is based on the ability of the student, which is stated in the profile, the amount of time the student spends studying each of these subjects, and the throw of a die which simulates the more subjective variables affecting grades. As soon as a team gets these grades for their student they realize that the amount of time studied is the one variable over which they have some control. They begin considering whether they should take more time from some other activity to increase the amount of time spent studying or whether they will live with the grades the student earned. This usually requires finding out how important grades will be to the future plans they may have for their student. In some cases, in order to find this out they have to check at the school table about grade-point entrance requirements for different schools. Some students have said that they had not previously appreciated the extent to which grade-point averages discriminate between college entrance possibilities.

Clarification of Values

Discussions have frequently led into debates about values. Students become aware that they must know what they value before they can decide what they want to do. During one such debate the following conversation took place:

"There's a big difference between what I *should* do and what I *will* do. I know I should spend more time studying, but I don't know that I actually will."

"Who do you think determines the 'should' in your life, Gretchen?" I asked. "And what determines the 'will' in what you do?"

Other students broke in with the idea that society says what we should do, and our own desires determine what we actually do, although many students do not really decide this. They just live.

"But don't we value most what we choose to do at the time we decide to do it?" I asked.

"No," Mike said. "Because we may really want something different later on but don't know it now. Some kids, for example, don't know how much they want to go to college in order to work hard now for good grades."

"If you did know this, would the 'should' and 'would' be pretty much the same, Mike?"

Mike and others nodded agreement and then said that it is really hard for a person to know what he wants so that he does not make mistakes.

After this conversation, as students went back to work, some teams decided to have their student do more studying, saying that although they did not think he really would spend that much time doing it, because of the kind of person he was, they were going to have him do it because of future plans *they* had for him.

This same issue comes up over another matter in the game. Teams will ask if they can start over since they see where they have made their mistakes and would now like to change what they have done. Each time this is asked they are told that since in life we cannot start over, they cannot either. They will have to decide what they can do from here to make the best of these past decisions.

Another incident occurred when a girl was looking over the chart of hour requirements for family chores. She came across the fact that when a girl marries she must spend a minimum of 25 hours doing housework. Although teams were working on the life of a boy at the time, and this piece of information did not apply to the student, she announced to the group assembled with an incredulous voice, "Twenty-five hours doing housework each week? Boy, *I'm* not getting married if that's the case! I don't want to do that much housework." Apparently marriage, at this point, was viewed in a different value context from that of merely a desirable romantic adventure.

Practice in Making Decisions

The first decisions that students have to make in the game seem fairly easy since they are more familiar, for example, what courses to take, whether to spend this hour in study or leisure. Gradually, however, teams become involved in more complex, difficult decisions, requiring skill that they may have learned from these more simple ones.

A group of girls were planning the life of a low-ability girl, Ann, who had a poor family situation and limited vocational skills. After one team managed to get Ann graduated from high school they came to the marriage table to get her married. After using the first spinner for this, I told the team that she did not have the opportunity to get married this year. With that, Judy, the spokesman for her team said,

"But she's got to get married. She's pregnant!"

"Then you really do have a decision-making problem," I said. "What are her alternatives?"

Judy suggested marriage was a possibility, but eliminated that because she did not think Ann really liked the guy and besides that was not a good solution. Her partner suggested adoption. Judy stated that Ann could have the child and keep it while she lived at home. Finally they decided on that alternative. Later when I came around to the team I saw that they were not having Ann make enough money to support herself and the child according to the minimum income rule. So I suggested that she would have to get a different job to earn more money.

"No, she doesn't want to change her job since she likes it and the boss is good to her and the hours are good," Judy said.

"Then how are you going to handle the problem?" I asked.

They didn't know.

Finally, after a period of time, I looked up at the wall score chart and saw written under "special events" for their team the words, "The baby died." I explained to the two girls that I did not think that was any solution to the problem and certainly they did not want Ann's baby to die.

"Yes we do," said Judy. "She would become too attached to it and since she can't support it, the baby has to die."

"Well, Judy, I'm making an arbitrary rule for the game and saying that the baby can't die and that you and your teammate will have to find some other way to deal with the problem." Then I took a look at Judy's face and added, "Why don't you come in to talk to me about this privately, since you seem so concerned about it?" She agreed to do this.

During the conference she revealed that she herself was pregnant and was facing the exact same problem of not wanting to marry the father, not wanting to give up her job, and not wanting her parents to know of her problem. Consequently, she was considering ways to "have the baby die," feeling this was the only alternative open to her. In this context a direct confrontation with consequences related to her problem were discussed.

Students who play this game do apply what they are doing to their own life. Conflicts sometimes arise between team partners, since individuals do have different ideas about a life. This is an opportunity to practice joint decision-making that may be necessary in later life, such as in marriage. At one point in a game, one team partner threw his paper down on the table and announced to his female partner in a loud voice, "I just can't work with you!" With that he got up and walked out of the room. Eventually he did return to continue the game.

APPLICATION OF LEARNING PRINCIPLES

Learning through Social Modeling

Obviously, a great deal of modeling of varieties of decision-making takes place during the game. The potential for learning through imitative behavior is especially great since powerful peer models are the ones doing the modeling. By selective reinforcement of some of these models, such learning can be encouraged. Sometimes students themselves positively reinforce certain behaviors.

One day I was walking around the room helping individual teams when I overheard the following conversation:

"Do you plan how you're going to spend *your* time each week?"

"Naw. I never give it a thought. I just do what I want to do at the moment," his partner said.

"Ya, but listen to those guys over there talking about how they plan. Do you really think they do?"

"No. I just think they're doing it for the game."

Later, when the group was talking about the current round of scores, I found an opportunity to bring up whether students actually planned their time. One student said, "I didn't realize until I started playing this game how carefully you have to plan in order to work into a week everything you want to do. It's really hard." Another student spoke up and said, "I've noticed in this game that the team that gets the highest scores are those that have a strategy for their student's life and that takes planning." With that, a third student said, "But I bet it's that way in life, too, and those people who plan actually get more out of life." Finally, a girl said, "You know, after I played this game last week, I took home one of the plan sheets and worked out a plan for *my* week. You know what? I found I got three times as much done with much less struggle than I've ever had before."

As she was saying this, I was watching the team that had had the previous debate. Both boys were listening intently and squirming somewhat as the conversation continued.

Discrimination Learning through Selective Reinforcement

Part of the power of this game is that immediate feedback is provided constantly throughout the playing. Because students respond to competition, the scores themselves provide reinforcement, encouraging teams to continue making certain decisions, or discouraging other decisions. Arguments have been raised regarding the use of scores in this way, since it is claimed that students merely play for the score and do not attend to any learning about decision-making. However, learning concepts are incorporated into the scoring system itself, and it is necessary to acquire some of these principles to "play for the score." When this question is raised by students, I have asked them if they would like to eliminate the scoring. Each time the students have decided that life is competitive and therefore it is good practice to experience what it will be like through the score system.

It has been observed, though, that after four or five rounds of the game, students tend to lose interest in the scoring itself and begin concentrating more on what is actually happening to their student. Their comments after playing several rounds center far more on issues related to life planning than on the scores they are getting.

The scores do provide a type of reinforcement that affects behavior, however. One team that had shown little interest in the game began to win. As their scores got higher other teams began asking them questions and they began to participate in group discussions. Eventually they became animated and involved in the debates that were taking place.

Skill Building

The counselor does take an active role in teaching skills by what she says and does. Actual activities in the game are designed to teach students to do certain things, such as filling out a job application, applying for a scholarship, seeking information, and learning to go through a job interview. The counselor can appropriately praise students when they do a good job at these tasks, or can call attention to teams who have demonstrated particularly good skill in finding something or have been successful in some attempt. An effective means of teaching some skills is for the counselor to role-play with teams when they come to the various tables for services. She can take the part of an admission counselor, a marriage counselor, or an employer. If she really is imaginative, students soon get into the spirit of the role-playing.

SOME OBSERVABLE OUTCOMES

Carefully designed studies to examine the long-term effects still need to be conducted. However, some observations have been made that give indications of the potential of this activity.

1. One student came to me following the game to talk about a problem she faced with her mother. During the conference she said that she had transferred out of math because she was having problems with her teacher. She had talked this over with her counselor, who had given her the transfer. Then she said she began thinking about Mary, the student used in the game, and said that she had decided she did not want her life to turn out to be the mess that Mary's was. She also had thought that the reason Mary's was a mess was that she did not stick with things. This student went in to see her counselor again, telling her that she had changed her mind, and returned to the math class to face her problem.

2. At the conclusion of school a student from a class that had used the game told me she wanted me to know that as a result of her game experience she had changed her college choice. Before starting the game she had been accepted at two colleges and had chosen College A. During the playing of the game and due to a consideration of new factors brought out in the game, she had decided College A was not a good choice and had since decided on College B. She felt much better for her decision.

3. Following the use of the game in a social studies class, students were asked by their teacher to evaluate it and its worth to them. The teacher reported that one student had said, "At first I didn't like the game. It wasn't fun and making decisions was hard work. Then I became involved and I now feel it was the most valuable experience I have had in high school. Although I'm a senior, I feel that all sophomores should be required to go through this and it might make a big difference in their whole high school life."

4. The student who was the prototype of Mary, a profile student, was asked to come back to high school and meet with the group that had planned her life. I asked each team to tell Mary what they had done with her life. Although a bit embarrassed about their ideas, they did tell her. She was flat-

tered by some and amazed at others. Then she told them what had happened to her and said, "I wish I had a chance to play this game when I was having all my problems in school. I think it would have helped me to see some things no person—my counselor, my teachers, or parents—could get me to see because I wouldn't listen." When she finished, one member of the group said, "I would like my life to be used in the game and I will come back next year to meet with another group of students who use it."

Such evidence suggests the possibilities of this approach as an influential counseling technique. Its use is being continued and evaluated to determine the extent of its effectiveness as a tool for counselors.

34

SELF-CONTROL THROUGH "IMAGINAL AVERSIVE CONTINGENCY" AND "ONE-DOWNSMANSHIP": ENABLING THE POWERLESS TO ACCOMMODATE UNREASONABLENESS[1]

Gerald C. Davison
STATE UNIVERSITY OF NEW YORK AT STONY BROOK

Deliberate attempts to apply principles from general experimental psychology to the modification of human behavior in clinical settings go back at least 40 years, to the pioneering work of Mary Cover Jones (1924a, 1924b) and to Smith and Guthrie's (1921) folksy prescriptions for breaking children's bad habits, as well as those of horses. Since Lazarus' (1958) and Eysenck's (1959) independent coining of the phrase "behavior therapy," there has been an interesting shift in the approaches and techniques devised. Wolpe's work, which certainly occupies a central position in the history of this field, exemplifies this trend. As he presents the evolution of "psychotherapy by reciprocal inhibition," we see experimental work with cats (Wolpe, 1948) being extrapolated and applied

[1] I wish to thank my wife, Carol, for her critical comments on earlier drafts of this paper.

to the elimination of neurotic fears in human beings (Wolpe, 1952, 1958). Aside from differences in technique that one might expect in moving from cats to humans (it is unlikely that one would toss a cat-biscuit at a fearful human client), Wolpe introduced a variation which added immeasurably to the scope of his several presumably counterconditioning procedures: aversive stimuli were presented to the *imagination* of the client in addition to, or instead of, confronting him with the real-life stimulus. That the range of neurotic disorders was immensely extended by this not-so-simple step can be seen by inspecting some of the case reports of clinical behavior therapists (for example, Lazarus, 1963; Lazarus & Davison, in press; Wolpe, 1958, 1964; Wolpe & Lazarus, 1966). The dimensions of fear that are amenable to desensitization in imagination are considerably more complex and subtle than could be feasibly handled with real-life exposures.

This trend, from the actual to the symbolic, can be seen in yet another area of behavior modification, namely the positive counterconditioning of inappropriate sexual responses. For example, Freund (1960) showed male homosexuals pictures of nude women during increased sexual arousal; Thorpe, Schmidt, and Castell (1963) presented *words* like "heterosexual" during periods of relief in an aversive counterconditioning regime; and Davison (1968) paired culture-appropriate female *images* with sexual arousal in the elimination of sadistic fantasies.

In the area of aversive counterconditioning, we can likewise see a shift from reliance on actual stimulus situations (for example, Lavin *et al.*, 1961) to the use of verbally presented aversive stimuli in imagination as a means of supplanting undesirably pleasant feeling-responses with more appropriate negatively toned reactions. The first published account of this is to be found in the aforementioned article by Lazarus (1958), in which he suggested to the client that he begin to feel very anxious when imagining himself perform a maladaptive anxiety-reducing compulsive behavior and to feel calm and relaxed when resisting the tendency to perform the compulsive act. More recently, Cautela (1966) has reported several cases illustrating ingenious variations on this procedure, which he calls "covert sensitization." With a case conducted independently of Cautela's work, Davison (1968) supplemented imaginal positive counterconditioning with one session of intensive covert sensitization.

While the trend seems to go from real life to imaginal, it should not be forgotten that one of the earliest attempts to bring personality development and psychotherapy into general experimental psychology paid considerable attention to thoughts and feelings. Dollard and Miller (1950) made the central assumption that these "inner states" obeyed the same laws as overt responses. Thus, it may be that behavior counselors and therapists have come full circle. It should, therefore, come as no surprise to those familiar with the literature that the client's verbal reports of his own inner feelings and ideations are used extensively by clinical as well as experimental behavior therapists.

There is a considerable body of evidence which demonstrates the applicability of simple operant conditioning principles to human behaviors labeled "abnormal" (for example, Lindsley & Skinner, 1954; Ferster, 1961; Ayllon & Michael, 1959; Davison, 1964, in press). These studies, and many like them, have in common the following: in each instance the therapist-experimenter, or his agent, applies or withdraws certain reinforcing or punishing stimuli *contingent on* the emission of a particular overt behavior. Upon reflection, one is not surprised to find these earliest reports restricted to institutional settings, where the therapist can exercise the degree of environmental control which appears necessary for techniques based on this conditioning paradigm.

Of what value, however, is the operant paradigm to the clinician working for only a very limited period of time with a client whose extra-consulting room environment cannot be manipulated to the extent possible in an institution? Indeed, if for various reasons important reinforcing agents, like spouses or parents, are not accessible to the therapist as trainees, is the operant approach of any relevance at all, except perhaps for enabling the clinician to increase the relative frequency of various classes of verbal behavior in the consulting room (Krasner, 1962)? The case reported below seems to this writer of heuristic value in re-examining the fruitfulness of approaching certain outpatient problems within what reasonably appears to be an operant model. As with virtually every case study, it is impossible to isolate the "active ingredients" with any degree of certainty. Moreover, possibly relevant variables will be introduced which can only with much strain be fitted into a behavior modification framework. The report will hopefully suggest a useful new direction, however, that might be explored by other workers faced with similar problems.

A REBELLIOUS BOY

The client was an 11½-year-old boy, referred to me for handling a "big crisis" at home. The boy was constantly clashing with his parents, refusing even to eat meals with them, and most recently not even talking with them. The boy had been seen in therapy the previous year by a female psychologist who, however, doubted that he had been frank with her.

Discriminating When "Good" Behavior Occurred

This good-looking husky boy, appearing at least 16 years of age, entered the interview situation with numerous complaints about his poor treatment at home. The therapist let him ventilate for several minutes, for it seemed unlikely that the boy could concentrate on specific questions while so agitated. Information had been obtained prior to this interview indicating that his recent obstreperousness was in sharp contrast with his reportedly good behavior at summer camp the month before, as well as with his reasonable deportment at school. This difference in behavior immediately suggested to the therapist an important difference in contingencies, and this area was the first to be explored. When the boy had simmered down, the therapist asked him directly why he had behaved so well at summer camp. The boy replied that it had been very clear to him at the outset that bad behavior was severely and immediately punished by the counselors, with interesting activities made contingent on good behavior. The school situation was described in similar fashion. Asked to contrast these situations with what held at home, the boy stated that he behaved obediently only when he felt that his father was angry; the father, according to the boy, was fairly oblivious to misbehavior except when in a sour mood, a discrimination which the naturally rambunctious and intelligent fellow had learned to make.

Learning To Imagine Aversive Consequences

Faced with the necessity of effecting rapid improvement (the father was ready to send him off to a boarding school, and the boy was ready to run away), and feeling that a "big brother" type of relationship was rapidly developing, the therapist enlisted the boy's co-operation in the following "experiment." Since most of the current flare-ups with the father followed upon the boy disobeying him or disagreeing with him, and since, moreover, the boy never crossed the father when he adjudged him to be feeling angry or unhappy, the boy was instructed to watch for situations in which he could conceivably disobey his father and then to imagine, as hard as he could, that his father was extremely sour—so sour, in fact, that he was just about ready to attack him both verbally and physically. As the boy quickly realized, this bit of imagination was designed to create for him the same subjective situation that made for obedient behavior on his part. It was also explained to him that if we could control his behavior by "creating" an angry father, we might be able to avoid his having to face an *actual* angry father. The session closed with several minutes' practice in imagining his father being very angry; the boy was able to generate considerable apprehension, as well as the hoped-for reluctance to cross him.

The second session, nine days later, revealed that the home situation had improved dramatically. The boy reported spontaneously that he had used the "little trick" anywhere from 10 to 25 times; he was able to describe several of these incidents in great detail. The relationship had improved so much, in fact, that the father had taken him the day before to an automobile show where the two of them spent a fairly enjoyable day together.

Recognizing the "One-Down" Position

A possible consequence of the apparent effectiveness of this strategy, however, was of considerable concern to both therapist and client. It was clear to both (and was verified by independent reports from another therapist who had been seeing the parents) that the father was often extremely unreasonable, especially when he had been drinking heavily. Since he was, in point of fact, a rather heavy drinker, the objective home situation was a difficult one, and to train the boy to make himself uneasy in order to avoid arguments and heated flare-ups presented both ethical and therapeutic problems (assuming for the moment that the two can be separated).[2] The therapist's reservations were all the greater in view of the boy's charming naturalness and spontaneity. Consequently, in this second session, another important theme was opened, namely, discussions about social games (compare Leary, 1957; Berne, 1964). For example, after listening to agitated complaints about his father's unreasonableness, the therapist pointed out that an 11-year-old boy is, by the nature of our social system, in a very poor "one-down" position in respect to his elders. While one was free to object to this, it was best to view the situation in perspective. Indeed, by allowing his freedom to be limited by his father in certain trivial areas, he would be able to increase his over-all freedom —a smiling reinforcing agent is more likely to reinforce than is a grouchy one. Another fruitful way to view this would perhaps be that the therapist pointed out that greater rewards could be enjoyed if the boy suffered himself to delay his gratification (Mischel, 1965).

[2] Editors' Note: The possible ethical danger is in teaching a person to be subservient to tyranny. The "one-downsmanship" game seems to be a particularly interesting technique since it helps the boy to survive the current period of injustice the better to avoid or overcome it in the future. It certainly does not condone the father's actions by reinforcing temporary obedience to unreasonable authority. If the father's behavior does not improve, the time will undoubtedly come when the boy will openly rebel or leave home permanently. Such defiance may be well justified, but it needs to be successful when it does occur. Only victorious rebels are heroes.

One might label this as "training to psychopathy"; however, it appears unnecessary to describe the behavior with a pejorative term that denotes an underlying disease. What seems important here is that the therapist suggested to the boy (who tested out at about 140 on the WISC) a new orientation to an admittedly undesirable and apparently unchangeable home situation in the hope that this would neutralize any possible adverse consequences of the self-controlled "imaginal aversive contingency" training which looked promising as a technique for creating and maintaining peace. This philosophical aspect of therapy, moreover, entered in also to help the boy understand and even forgive some of his father's excesses, namely, his father's work was probably so aggravating and frustrating that, in the absence of more adaptive behaviors, drinking himself into a semistupor every evening represented his best solution to relieve the tensions built up during the day.

The third session, a week later, revealed that the improvement was being maintained. Of course, the therapist responded to such reports with sincere approval, stressing that the boy was exhibiting magnificent self-control in the face of a difficult situation. Being himself quite skeptical about the "trick," however, the therapist played Devil's advocate several times, suggesting other reasons for the improvement, for example, trying to please him. The boy, on his part, insisted that it was indeed the "trick" that was behind the change, and he buttressed his conviction with several examples. The boy was also beginning to initiate additional beneficial changes in his behavior at home, for example, turning down the volume on his record player so as not to disturb the father.

The fourth session revolved about a recent altercation at home. As the boy described it, his father had become so abusive and unreasonable the previous evening that the boy was unwilling, or unable, to play the one-down game, and voiced some disagreement with his father—quite legitimately. The ensuing argument grew to such proportions that, in tears while relating the incident, the boy felt that he could not return home after the day's session. The therapist, therefore, decided for the first time to intercede with the father by requesting that the parents' therapist[3] telephone immediately to urge the father to stay away from the boy at all costs until things quieted down. An appointment was made for the following day. Peace had been restored, and therapy proceeded as usual.

Perceiving Effects of Behavior

A third element became evident at this time: pointing out to the boy the consequences of his behavior. As is often the case even with "healthy"

---

[3] Editors' Note: Wonder how the father's therapist was trying to help the father.

people, the effects which we have on significant others are oftentimes unknown to us—except insofar as we may get ourselves into serious trouble. Considerable time was devoted, therefore, to telling the boy that some of his well-meant joking was probably very irritating to teachers, peers, and, of course, his parents.[4] The intent was to teach him to discriminate between situations when particular kinds of behaviors would meet with disapproval as opposed to those in which the same behaviors would stand a good chance of favorable reception. At all times this endorsement of social conformity was presented in the context of creating larger areas of really meaningful personal freedom.

Termination of Therapy

In addition to continued improvement in relations with his father, other happy changes began to appear over the remaining seven sessions, not the least of which was an increase in the freedom which the boy was allowed. For example, his father finally consented to his chumming around with a particular boy who he had earlier felt would be a bad influence. Moreover, the boy was reporting decreasing need to use the "imaginal aversive contingency" technique, for at least two reasons: his father was becoming more reasonable, and he himself somehow felt it less pressing to disagree with him on the trivia that had been the basis of the referral problems.

Many of these last sessions were extremely short, sometimes only 15 minutes long, and they were devoted essentially to reinforcing the strategies that had been operating, as well as providing an opportunity to apply them to different kinds of situations. When therapy was terminated, there had been no domestic fights for six weeks—something of a record for the household.

RATIONALE

If there is such a thing as "the real description" of an event, it must not be thought that the foregoing is presented as a faithful and inexorably accurate reproduction of a therapy which extended over five months.

---

[4] Editors' Note: It is difficult for a person to learn when and what kind of joking is appropriate because other people usually laugh (but for different reasons) whether the joke is appropriate or not. Laughter is usually reinforcing to the joker. The inappropriate joker's victims put up a jolly front to avoid the serious charge of lacking a sense of humor. They counterattack, however, or shun the joker in subtle ways only dimly perceived by the joker who therefore tries all the harder to amuse them. A sensitive and skillful counselor would be needed to teach the discriminations required to break this vicious circle.

Although copious notes were typed immediately following each interview, it is obvious that the data were filtered through the therapist's own set. All one can honestly do with the fantastically complicated therapy situation is attempt to convey some of the highlights and suggest possibly fruitful areas for others to examine. Case studies make for good heuristics, but woefully inadequate proofs.

Three themes have been depicted in the foregoing: (1) the use of an "imaginal aversive contingency" technique; (2) the discussion of social games; and (3) exercise in examining carefully the consequences of one's own behavior. There is probably a fourth relevant variable underlying the other three: (4) rather quickly the therapist became an important figure in the boy's life, someone, in simplest terms, whose approval and suggestions meant something. One can describe this relationship in any number of ways. The writer's own bias leads him to construe it in terms of the therapist acquiring working control over the boy's behavior for a limited period of time. Through his status, the therapist was able to insure that his instructions for instigating change would probably be followed. No doubt his approval for improvement on the boy's part played an important role in consolidating the gains.

Let us examine more closely that aspect of the therapy which seems the most interesting, namely, the use of "imaginal aversive contingency." Important to note is the functional analysis on which this rested. The therapist, concerned with getting the boy to behave well, was attentive to situations in which such desirable behavior had recently occurred. These were readily available in the form of summer camp and school. The next step was to explore with him the characteristics of these situations which he felt accounted for his good behavior, and then to contrast them with situations in which he misbehaved. Then contacts with the father were examined for circumstances in which there was obedience or disobedience. Tying all these bits of information together, it was possible in the very first session to suggest a reasonable tactic to the boy for helping him control his own behavior. If you will, the boy generated his own discriminative stimuli (S^D's) so as to change the very nature of the psychological situation: by pretending that his father was angry, he was able to signal to himself that disobedient behaviors on his part would likely lead to highly aversive consequences. One can only speculate on the boy's perception of himself following successful use of the procedure, but there seems little doubt that being able to exercise such self-control made a profoundly favorable impression on him. Being in effective control is desirable within almost any theoretical framework (for example, Mandler & Watson, 1966; Mowrer & Viek, 1948; White, 1959).

The technique appears to relate fruitfully to Goldiamond's (1963) interesting analysis of self-control in terms of the organism's setting the conditions for certain responses to occur. Seen in this way, the boy created the conditions under which obedient, nonrebellious behavior occurred— namely, an angry father about to explode if an infraction occurs. In this fashion, the control of the boy's own behavior was vested *in himself*, for he did not need to rely on the environment for setting the conditions which control the most adaptive behavior. Of course, it must be kept in mind that the stimulus situation being created here for the control of behavior is within the boy's mind (pardon the expression), that is, entails the generation of *covert* response-produced discriminative stimuli.

This technique seems similar to Homme's (1965b) "control of coverants." Assuming, as this present writer does, that "inner states" are important for behavior modification and that, furthermore, they can be handled in the same manner functionally as overt behaviors (as Dollard and Miller pointed out some years ago), Homme outlines regimes that are designed to eliminate overt behavior by making incompatible covert behaviors interfere with them. Thus, for example, in eliminating smoking behavior, the first step would be to find situations in which the person does not feel like smoking, for example, immediately following a frightening film on cancer of the lung. The next step would be to encourage this kind of incompatible thought in situations which tend to elicit smoking. Following the occurrence of the thought, positive reinforcement of some kind would be arranged in order to strengthen this "coverant" at the expense of the overt behavior of smoking.

Although this brief outline of Homme's clever notions barely suggests the complexity and potential power of the approach, the similarity with the imaginal aversive contingency technique should be clear. From relevant case history material the therapist discovered conditions under which the undesirable behavior did not occur. The next step was to create those conditions in imagination, maximizing the probability that the target behavior would, in fact, not occur. The final step was to see to it that this "coverant," to use Homme's term, was reinforced. If I had been familiar with Homme's work prior to this case, I would probably have paid closer attention to insuring that some kind of reinforcement followed quickly upon occurrence of the coverant aside from the expected avoidance of an argument with the father. As it turned out, the boy did enjoy considerable reinforcement for use of the trick—a terrible home situation improved considerably and speedily.

Planning

MANY PEOPLE HAVE NEVER learned to solve their problems in a wise and rational way. Their decisions tend to be impulsive, based on whims, stereotypes, and inadequate information, and made without knowledge of alternative courses of action which could bring more satisfying consequences. Perhaps some decisions in life should be made impulsively. However, other decisions have such far-reaching consequences that it would pay any person to spend some additional time and effort in engaging in a more thoughtful and logical decision-making process.

The two articles in this section describe methods for helping young people learn a more effective method of making decisions. Article 35 by Yabroff outlines a method that has been tried successfully with junior and senior high school students. Magoon, in Article 36, describes the methods and materials developed originally for college students but which have also been adapted for other groups. The specific materials and procedures differ considerably in these two articles, but the basic purpose and rationale are consistent.

When a client asks a counselor for specific advice, for example, "What college should I go to?" or "What occupation am I best suited for?" how should a counselor reply? Both articles make clear that the counselor is not in a position to give a direct answer. He cannot say, "You should go to Yale" or "You should be a plumber." The best reply that a counselor can give to such value-laden questions would be, "I do not know what you should do, but I do know how you can decide for yourself. Would you like me to help you learn how?"

The process of learning how to make wise decisions is outlined in these two articles. Yabroff is concerned with how students can be helped in the process of choosing a college.

Magoon's concern is with choosing a curriculum and an occupation after being admitted to college. The basic process first involves deciding that a problem exists and defining exactly what the problem is. Then alternatives must be generated so that the client can see possible directions. The client must obtain information about the feasible alternatives including any information that would help him to estimate his probable success or satisfaction in each alternative under consideration. His own values, standards, and interests have to be considered along with his abilities, aptitudes, and experiences.

The end result of this process is not a solitary conclusion. It is more likely to be a hierarchy of plans constructed so that if the first alternative does not work out as expected, several other alternatives are available. A wise plan is one best suited to achieve the client's desires under presently anticipated conditions but flexible enough to take advantage of new opportunities and changing circumstances.

35

LEARNING DECISION-MAKING[1]

William Yabroff
UNIVERSITY OF SANTA CLARA

How might counselors train students to be better decision-makers? What kind of information *is* personally meaningful for the immediate choices these students must make?

In this article a decision-training program which was developed to help answer these two questions will be discussed. It is hoped that others with similar concerns will be encouraged by this discussion to develop programs appropriate for their own students and schools. The decision-train-

[1] The decision-training program was developed through six years of research in the Palo Alto Unified School District and supported by NDEA Title V funds. Among those making major contributions to the project were Dr. Richard Carey, Dr. Robert Clarke, Dr. H. B. Gelatt, and Dr. Murray Tondow.
   Recently, a system for collecting and reporting local probability data for individual schools was developed by Instructional Systems Corporation. Those wishing further information should write to ISC, 3997 Bibbits Drive, Palo Alto, Calif. 94303.

ing program is not a substitute for those activities that characterize high school guidance today. It complements these activities, as it helps the students take fuller advantage of educational planning sessions currently provided by counselors.

The goals of the decision-training program are:

1. To help the student learn *how* to choose rather than *what* to choose
2. To provide specific facts for his immediate choices based on the experiences of recent graduates from his school whose classroom performance was similar

BEGINNING WITH STUDENT CONCERNS

Before the student is ready to take decision-making seriously, he must be assured that specific long-range goals need not be set before he can deal with immediate choices. Most ninth graders have been continually asked by parents, teachers, and other adults about what they want to do in life. Since they are not ready to answer this question, they often have the notion that until they know for sure "where they are headed," they are just marking time. Some are discouraged about looking ahead at all because they think everyone else really "knows where he is going except me!" It is helpful first to let students discuss their own plans and feelings about the future.

Mr. Jones, a ninth-grade counselor, might begin the decision-training program like this:

"Good morning, students. Soon you will be planning your high school program. The story of what happened to students like you in this school as they went through high school and beyond is part of the information you need to know at this time.

"In the next four days, I will not question what you choose. I will only help you learn how to choose. I will not ask you what you want to do in life. You do not have to select an occupation, a college, or make specific decisions now. So don't turn me off before we begin. And a good place to begin is with you. . . ."

Early that fall each student completed a planning questionnaire. The results of this questionnaire provide his class with their first group discussion—and their first local information. The class will see that at least three out of ten have no idea at all of what they want to do in life! Another four out of ten have a vague idea, and only a few students are certain about their long-range goals. Even these will change their minds two or three times before high school graduation. Mr. Jones will point out that many seniors and students in college have no more idea of what they want to do than his present ninth graders today. The students begin to realize they are not alone in their confusion about the future.

The questionnaire also reveals that nine out of every ten students plan to go to college. Six out of ten plan to enter a prestige college! Local follow-up studies show that only *one out of every ten* former graduates entered a prestige college.

Personal Values

At this point it is tempting for Mr. Jones to give a short lecture on the necessity of being "realistic" about goals. However, he knows that the success of the program rests with his own willingness to let students explore the meaning of the local data themselves. Instead, he asks what going to a prestige college might mean. Where did they learn to value this? Are there other ways of defining "success"? He will help the students come to terms with their *own* values by showing them the contrast between present aspirations and what actually happened to former students like them from their school. This is illustrated in Figure 1 taken from the student workbook.

Good Decisions

Decisions are nothing new to the ninth grader. He has made many before, most of them somewhat automatically. He knew what to expect since he had made similar ones in the past and experienced the consequences of his choices. Decisions about the future require a different approach. The student does not know what to expect—he has not experienced the results. Therefore, the ninth-grade student needs to fill in the experience void by seeing what happened to former students like him when they made similar choices. The more specific this information is, the more likely the student will make a wise choice.

Recently psychologists and social scientists have made extensive studies in the field of decision-making. Students are informed of three prerequisites to good decision-making. These are (1) specific facts about the choice, (2) a knowledge of other available alternatives, and (3) some estimation of the possible consequences. Other factors such as risk-taking and strategy are also involved but are not essential to the beginning decision-maker.

EXPLAINING GRADES

Each student is given the decision-training booklet along with his own grade-point average earned in the ninth grade.[2] This grade average will

---

[2] The ninth-grade academic average was found to be the best single predictor of success in high school courses and performance in the first year of college (along with the total high school grade average).

Ninth Graders Plan for College

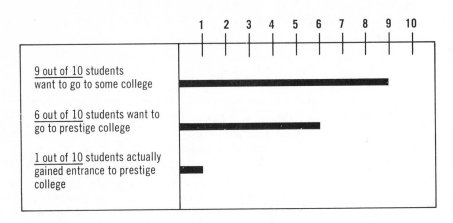

Suppose the class you are now in has thirty ninth graders. About twenty-seven out of the thirty in your classroom plan on going to some kind of college. If 60% are planning on a prestige college, how many students in your classroom would this represent?_____ If only 10% might enter a prestige college, how many students in your classroom will this represent?_____ Since only a few students entered the kind of college which they aspired to in the ninth grade, what about the rest? Were they in a sense, failures? Did their directions go sour, prove a blind alley?

What does a prestige college mean to ninth graders like yourself?_____

Why do so many ninth graders aspire to this goal? _____

Where do you think they learned to value the "prestige college" goal? _____

If entrance to Stanford or Harvard symbolized "success," was there really anything wrong with the goal of trying to be successful? Think about this. Are there other ways for you to be successful besides going to a prestige college?

By now you probably have an uneasy feeling that some of your own long range goals and aspirations may not be achieved. Though this booklet will not tell you what to strive for, you will probably begin to question some of your present ideas and values. If you are stout at heart, want a bit of adventure and can take some honest bare facts about the choices facing you in the next three years, read on.

FIG. 1.   *Aspiration and Actuality Chart*

play an important part in helping the student use information on former graduates from his school. With it he will be able to enter any of the number of experience tables found in the booklet.[3] Since most of the experience tables report grade averages, the counselor must be sure that students understand precisely what grades mean and do not mean.

[3] Throughout the article, selected portions and experience tables will be taken from *Invitation to Decision*, the instructional group guidance booklet published by the Palo Alto Unified School District in 1966 and written by William Yabroff.

It is easy to talk about grades with students who are good grade-getters (the top 17 percent). For most, however, grades have not been very rewarding. To many they are discouraging. Generally, students are confused about what grades mean. It is helpful to be very specific about how students are graded. In essence, grades are given for: (1) homework assignments turned in, (2) correct answers on classroom tests, and (3) physical behavior in the classroom, that is, paying attention, listening, participating in class discussions, and so forth. Being specific about the behaviors on which students are graded will help them in the event they choose to raise their grades.

It is equally important to be specific about what grades do not mean. They say little about success outside the classroom, talents and interests, goals and aspirations, or how worthwhile the student is to himself and to others. Only when grades are thoroughly discussed and placed in their proper perspective is the student ready to enter the experience tables.

EXPERIENCE TABLES

Let's return to Mr. Jones as he introduces experience tables to his ninth-grade class.

"A research team has been at work gathering facts about former students in our school. These are students who:

sat at your desks in this classroom
took the same courses which you will choose
graduated from the same high school
entered the kind of colleges or jobs you will consider
came from the same kinds of homes
had similar hopes and fears
were faced with choices like yours today

"They are also like you in that they entered high school with the same grade average that you have at this moment. Their story will provide you with some of the alternatives and consequences which you need for your own planning today."

Data for the experience tables[4] came primarily from two sources: (1) the high school transcript of the preceding graduating classes, and (2) simplified follow-up studies of these same graduates. Follow-up studies gathered information on where the student was, his record of performance in his first year of college, and selected thoughts made by

---

[4] We chose the name "experience table" in place of the more common term expectancy or probability table, because we did not want students to feel that these tables were a definite forecast of their own futures. Since they reported the performance of former students, the term "experience tables" was also a more accurate description.

graduates about their high school days. These thoughts were in response
to the question, "If you could talk with a ninth-grade class today, what
are some of the things you would tell them?"

Former students were grouped into five categories according to their
ninth-grade averages. These categories were below C (below 2.0), C (2.0
to 2.4), C+ (2.5 to 2.9), B (3.0 to 3.4), and A (3.5 to 4.0). We were
then able to construct experience tables on the major high school course
areas, posthigh school activities entered, and performance in the first year
or two of college. In this manner, present ninth-grade students, knowing
their own grade-point average, could see what had happened to students
like themselves as they went through high school and beyond. The experience tables reported data rounded to the nearest decimal.

Estimating High School Grades

An experience table showing the relationship of ninth-grade grades to
total high school grades earned by former students is given in Figure 2.

Each student is asked to find his appropriate grade column and record
how many out of every ten former graduates like him earned various
high school grades. Thus, a student who presently has a C average in the
ninth grade was able to see that in the past, two out of every ten dropped
below C in high school, five out of ten maintained a C average, and three
out of ten earned a C+. He could further see that, up to this time, no
former student who entered high school with a C average jumped to a
B or an A in their over-all high school grades.

Such facts come as a surprise to many ninth-grade students. Although
the information given in such an experience table applies to all in this
particular school, each student interprets the data differently, according
to his own values and goals. Some are encouraged to see that former
students similar to them successfully completed high school. Others, who
might have assumed they magically would raise their grades if they
buckled down in the junior or senior year, were rather shocked to find
that few if any students in the past had managed to do this.

Anticipating Activities After High School

An experience table showing what former graduates did after high
school is given in Figure 3. With this experience table, each ninth grader
could find how many out of every ten former students entered various
activities after high school graduation *from his school.*

Figure 3 shows that some students from every grade group chose
further education and some from every grade group chose immediate
employment after high school. These data explode the myth of clear

GRADES EARNED IN HIGH SCHOOL

High School Grades (Total Average)	(The Average For All Courses)				

	Below C	C	C+	B	A
A	0	0	0	–	6
B	0	0	2	5	3
C+	0	3	5	4	1
C	3	5	3	1	0
Below C	7	2	–	0	0

Below C	C	C+	B	A
(Below 2.0)	(2.0-2.4)	(2.5-2.9)	(3.0-3.4)	(3.5-4.0)

My 9th Grade Average

" ▬ " minus sign means less than one out of ten.

FIG. 2.   *Relationship between Ninth-Grade and Total High School Grade Point Averages*

distinctions between college and noncollege bound students at the ninth-grade level. Even students whose present average is below C can see that some former graduates like them entered college!

Other experience tables show the performance of former graduates in a number of key high school courses. It would be possible to generate tables for all the major course areas, including nonacademic subjects.

1st Year Activities

	Below C	C	C+	B	A
IV—Colleges of Highest Entrance Requirements	0	0	—	1	3
III—Colleges of High Entrance Requirements	—	1	2	3	5
II—Colleges of Medium Entrance Requirements	—	2	3	3	1
I—Junior College	5	5	4	3	1
Technical School	—	—	—	—	—
Military Service	1	1	—	0	—
Employed	2	—	1	—	—
Married, Seeking Work	2	1	—	—	—

My 9th Grade Average

— = Less than 1 out of 10

FIG. 3. *Relationship between Ninth-Grade Average and Activities After High School Graduation*

336

These would be helpful to students who might not choose further education after high school.

Anticipating Types of First Year Jobs

Not all experience tables predict grades. Figure 4 shows the kinds of jobs obtained by former students immediately after graduation.

1ST YEAR EMPLOYMENT OF 1963 GRADUATES

HIGH SCHOOL GRADE AVERAGE

Below C (29 Students)	C to B (42 Students)	B to A (5 Students)
Delivery Boy	Telephone Operator	Sales Clerk
Donut Fryer	Secretary	Credit Clerk
Assembly Worker	Bank Teller	Telegram Messenger
Production Worker	Mechanic	Secretary
Bank Teller	IBM Verifier	
Sales Clerk	Keypunch Operator	
Secretary	Shipping Clerk	
Mechanic	Fireman	
Typist	Sales Clerk	
Stock Clerk	Dental Assistant	
Draftsman	Waitress	
Cook	Shipfitter Apprentice	
Gas Station Attendant	Laboratory Technician	
Woodworker Apprentice	Stage Technician	
Printer	Typist	
Record Keeper	Cashier	
	Truck Driver	
	Semi-conductor Tester	

FIG. 4.   *An Experience Table Showing Jobs Obtained After High School*

Study the experience table on the top of the page. Do you notice a difference in jobs obtained by students with various high school grade averages? Probably not. Why do you think this is so?

_____

_____

Please remember that these are beginning jobs. Do you think this experience table will forecast what jobs the students will have five or ten years from now?

The Use and Abuse of Experience Tables

The role of the counselor in helping students use the probability data is critical to the success of the decision-training program. This role can best be described as that of a co-pilot alerting the student to the kind of terrain over which he has chosen to fly, but reserving the destination of the flight to the student himself. The experience tables give some indication of what the student is up against in the pursuit of any given high school program or posthigh school goal. They point to realistic alternatives which the student may consider, but they do not solve problems or make decisions. The following is an example of how Mr. Jones might help his students use experience tables constructively.

"Suppose Pat today was a C-average ninth-grade student. Can anyone here predict what Pat's grades might be three years from now?"

Some students respond, "Yes, her grade will be C because five out of ten students in the past earned such a grade." Others might reply, "No, we can't predict Pat's grades because the table does not apply to anyone today. Things are different from what they were two or three years ago." Neither answer is satisfactory. Mr. Jones asks other questions to elicit a more thoughtful approach. "Will Pat raise her grades? If so, what do you think is the difference between former students who raised or lowered their grades? Now suppose Pat wants to go to a college that requires an A or B average? No one in the past with grades like hers entered such a college. What now? Should Pat change her college plans?"[5]

The prediction of weather provides an excellent contrast to the use of experience tables in predicting classroom performance. When the weatherman forecasts a five out of ten chance of rain, he compares the past records of atmospheric conditions to those of today. If conditions today are like those in the past when there was a 50-50 chance of rain, he has some basis for his prediction. Pat, the C-average ninth-grade student, has a record of the past also. The experience tables tell her the average grades former students earned. The conditions are similar, because they, like her, began high school with the same grades. However, there is an important difference between Pat and the weatherman. Pat has some control over her conditions in school. She can make choices that will determine how similar or different her performance will be from previous students.

When students see the proper use of experience tables, they avoid either predicting from or rejecting the data. They begin to use the tables as a source of alternatives and a record of past consequences. How similar or different their own experience will be depends upon a number of choices which they will make.

---

[5] Editors' Note: These thought-provoking questions are well suited to stimulating group discussion. The modern counselor is not content with only the one-to-one counseling model. Instead he asks how he can best use his time to help all students in the school become better decision-makers. Working with groups is one way to reach more students.

COLLEGES GROUPED FOR EARLY PLANNING

There are many ways to group colleges, but for the purpose of early planning we found it helpful to group them by the kinds of courses they require for entrance. Extensive examinations of catalogs reveal that colleges can be grouped according to the number of "special unit" courses required. Special unit courses are those in foreign language, mathematics, laboratory science, and fourth-year senior English. For all practical purposes, colleges were found to fall into four categories: Group 1—those that required no special unit courses and accepted whatever grades the students had earned; Group 2—colleges requiring up to two special units, with a strong C or better grade average; Group 3—colleges requiring two to five special units, with college-recommending grades of B or better; and Group 4—the highly selective colleges that required more than six special units and very high grades. Examples of colleges grouped by special units and grades are given in Figure 5.

GROUP IV COLLEGES
Highest entrance requirements
Requires more than 6 special units
Strong "B" or "A" grade average
    Carnegie Tech
    Mills
    Pomona
    Stanford
    Harvard

GROUP II COLLEGES
Medium entrance requirements
Requires 0 to 2 special units
    (may recommend more)
Strong "C" or better grade average
    Linfield
    Oregon State
    *All California state colleges
    Pacific University
    Whitworth

TECHNICAL SCHOOLS
No special units required
Your best grade average
    Sullivan Beauty School
    Curtis Institute of Music
    Automation Institute of San
        Francisco
    Academy of Stenographic Arts
    Bay City College of Dental
        Medical Assistants

GROUP III COLLEGES
High entrance requirements
Requires up to 6 special units
"B" to "A" grade average
    Carleton
    Colorado College
    Oberlin
    Univ. of Southern California
    Washington Univ.

GROUP I COLLEGES
Junior colleges
No special units required
Your best grade average

    Menlo College
    San Jose City College
    Foothill College
    College of San Mateo
    San Francisco City College

EMPLOYMENT

    Sales Clerk
    Telephone Operator
    Truck Driver
    Secretary
    Postman

FIG. 5.   *An Example of Colleges Grouped by Special Unit Courses Required for Entrance*

When colleges are grouped in this manner, the ninth-grade student can see several things. First, of course, he can see that whatever high school program he selects, the opportunity to go on for more training after graduation is available. Many ninth graders are under the mistaken impression that unless they are in the traditional "college prep program," a college education will be denied. More than 50 percent of the colleges do not require courses traditionally associated with a college prep program.

To be more specific, a listing is made of each college or job obtained by former students with any given ninth-grade average. Such a listing, as illustrated in Figure 6 portrays to the ninth-grade student the wide number of alternatives open to former students like him in any of the college group categories.

C+ (2.5-2.9) 9TH GRADE AVERAGE

SCHOOL (396 STUDENTS)

GROUP I

School	Students # of	School	Students # of
Biola College	1	Ambassador College	1
Crippled Childrens School	1	Casper	1
Don's Beauty School	2	Foothill Junior College	159
Millard School	1	Marin College	1
Mt. View Beauty School	1	Menlo College	7
Palo Alto Beauty School	1	Monterey Peninsula College	2
Providence Nursing College	1	Morton Junior College	1
Radiology School	1	San Francisco City College	1
San Francisco Art Institution	1	San Mateo College	3
Sunnyvale Beauty School	1	Stephens College	1
		Valley Junior College	1

GROUP II

School	Students # of	School	Students # of
Arizona State	1	Nevada Univ.	3
Brigham Young	2	Oregon State Univ.	1
California Lutheran	1	Oregon Univ.	8
California State Poly	13	Pacific Lutheran	1
California Western Univ.	2	Puget Sound Univ.	2
Chico State College	7	San Diego State	8
Citadel Military College	1	San Francisco State	8
Colorado State College	3	San Jose State	47
Colorado Univ.	7	Southern Oregon State	1
Iowa State Univ.	1	Univ. of Pacific	5
Linfield College	3	Utah Univ.	2
Montana State Univ.	1	Whitworth Univ.	2

(cont.)

SCHOOL (396 STUDENTS)

GROUP III

	Students # of		Students # of
Arizona State Univ.	1	Saint Lawrence College	1
Arizona Univ.	3	San Francisco Univ.	1
Baylor Univ.	1	Santa Clara Univ.	3
California Univ. Berkeley	11	Shimer College	1
California Univ. Davis	7	Southern California Univ.	1
California Univ. Los Angeles	2	Tampa Univ.	1
California Univ. Riverside	1	Utah State Univ.	1
California Univ. Santa Barbara	7	Washington Univ.	4
Colorado College	1	Westminster College	2
Connecticut Univ.	1	Wheaton College	1
Gonzaga Univ.	1	Whitman	1
Idaho Univ.	1	Whittier	2
Michigan Univ.	1	Willamette Univ.	3
Northwestern Univ.	1	Wisconsin Univ.	1
Notre Dame College	1	Worcester Academy	1
Pacific Univ.	1		

GROUP IV

Cornell Univ.	1	Pomona	1
Middlebury	1	Stanford Univ.	7
Mills College	1	Williams College	1
Occidental College	1		

WORK (33 STUDENTS)

TYPES OF JOBS

Credit Clerk	Stage Technician
Fireman	Stock Clerk
Sales Clerk	Telegram Messenger
Secretary	Telephone Operator
Semiconductor Tester	Typist

FIG. 6. *An Example of Specific College Listings for C+ Ninth Grade Students*

Mr. Jones illustrates the use of these alternatives by citing the example of a pilot charting his flight course. Prior to take-off, he selects alternative landing fields in the event he cannot reach his original destination. Thus the list of colleges entered by former students provide one of the indispensable steps in good decision-making, namely, to know likely alternatives.

EFFECTS OF TRAINING IN DECISION-MAKING

A "good" decision is one made with knowledge of facts, alternatives, and possible consequences. Thus, counselors can help students judge *how* the choice was made. A "realistic" decision is one in which the student has a likely chance of success. In the final analysis, this can only be judged *by the student himself*. He has the key to those motivations and efforts which might considerably alter the probabilities of success based on the accomplishments of former graduates.

Realistic Decisions

In practice, we have found that when students are given specific information, most make choices that are judged to be more realistic by counselors. Evaluations show that such students selected high school courses and posthigh school plans more commensurate with their abilities than students who did not receive the information. However, as many raised their aspirations as lowered them, depending on what they felt would be a successful course of action to follow.

Experience tables of students in their first two years of college, along with summary follow-up studies and interviews with former graduates, help the young decision-maker re-examine his purposes in school. The local data go far beyond grades, high school courses, and college entrance requirements at this point. The students see that although many former graduates were successful in the colleges they chose or the jobs they entered, a large number were not. For the most part, those who dropped out or failed in their first year of college were both academically prepared and mentally capable of completing their educational plans. Why did they fail? What other facts are important in educational decision-making? Such questions lead the students into discussions about the importance of early planning and of taking the matter of choice-making seriously in personal as well as educational areas.

Parent Reactions

Ninth-grade students are reluctant to discuss their high school plans with parents. Even though counselors urged students to share the local data with their families at home during the guidance program, less than half were willing to do so. Parents were then invited to evening meetings to view the data and discuss its implications for their own sons and daughters. After such meetings parents reported that home discussions took place frequently, and students seemed willing to talk about the "experiences of former students like themselves."

Most parents were enthusiastic in their response to the local data. They studied the information and found it personally applicable to high school and college planning. It was particularly helpful in selecting a number of posthigh school alternatives to consider with their sons and daughters. A few parents, primarily of low-ability students, felt threatened and discouraged. They accused the counselors of trying to predict what would happen to their children, and such predictions were gloomy at best. They misunderstood the use and purpose of the experience tables, and an evening meeting was too brief to clear up this kind of misunderstanding. With the exception just noted, parents seemed grateful and relieved to receive such specific data about future alternatives and consequences.

36

DEVELOPING SKILLS FOR SOLVING EDUCATIONAL AND VOCATIONAL PROBLEMS

Thomas M. Magoon
UNIVERSITY OF MARYLAND

The Effective Problem Solving (EPS) counseling model grew out of several related problems.[1] First, traditional counseling practices are very expensive in terms of time, in professional manpower needed, and in the considerable demands placed upon the motivation level of clients seeking counseling assistance. Second, educational and vocational counseling needs to be thorough. Third, counseling services need to meet relatively large numbers of clients and to do so quickly. Fourth, vocational-educational uncertainty problems are very frequent and lend themselves to a problem-solving approach.

[1] The first use of this counseling model was with the students of the Precollege Summer Session of the University of Maryland during the summer of 1964. The model has since been revised six times and the application presented in detail is an edition used with college-level clients seeking counseling about their vocational-educational indecision.

CHARACTERISTICS OF THE EFFECTIVE PROBLEM SOLVING (EPS) PROCESS

The model, which accompanies this article, is best described as a type of self-directed learning program. The program teaches the individual the steps to be taken in effective problem-solving. The client then applies these steps to a particular problem, namely his own educational-vocational uncertainty. He considers the relevant data about the problem, integrates such data, and evolves several alternative plans of action in terms of the relevant information he has gathered and evaluated.

The model is quite structured in sequence and in format. The sequence follows six steps in problem solving. The format is that of mimeographed parts each consisting of a carefully arranged sequence of questions. The questions are not formal or "stiff." Rather they are cast in conversational form. Their content is really a transposition of the kinds of inquiries counselors frequently employ in enabling clients to resolve such uncertainties.

The client responds to these inquiries largely in writing—item by item. The counselor reviews the client's work as each part is completed and contributes further written or oral questions or statements which are tailored to the relatively unique nature of each client.

The counselor's role in the EPS process includes several functions. He serves as consultant to the client in his problem-solving work. He also brings his particular training and skills to bear on making the EPS process move optimally for each client, that is, maintain the client's involvement in the task. In contrast to usual counseling practices, the counselor can work with from one to five clients at a time. The clients, however, typically work individually rather than as a group.

The structured nature of the EPS materials means that in one sense the content is limited. To deal with this limitation frequent inquiries of the client are made as to other data which warrant inclusion. The structure also carries with it a heavy cognitive emphasis. Although this is intentional there are still both structured inquiries regarding the affective state of the client and opportunity for counselor inquiries regarding affective components of the client. The emphasis upon writing is an integral part of bringing coherence and sequence into the client's problem solving behavior. Typically, six to eight sessions are needed to complete the program.

The model is quite individualized in several ways. First, the client works through the model at his own pace. Second, as the client finishes parts of the material and is given the next set, the counselor reads over what the client has done and, whenever appropriate, raises further questions which are tailored to the unique complex of characteristics the client has revealed up to that point. Third, although there may be several clients at work in the same room at the same time, the counselor is able physically to move about among the clients responding to them differentially as the need may arise.

Introduction to Clients at the First Session

"You are perhaps surprised that there are several other students here as well as you and I. This is because I have found that I can work with several students at the same time.

"You may also notice that I have introduced myself to each of you, but not introduced you to each other.[2] This is because whether or not you know each other is irrelevant to your interest in being here and making plans. You may become acquainted with one another during the times you and I are working together and if so it will come about by your own choice rather than any necessary condition for making effective plans.

"You have come to the Counseling Center because you were undecided in some way about your educational and vocational plans. You have explained your uncertainty when you met one of our counselors in your preliminary interview. The counselor judged that the counseling method we call Effective Problem Solving would be of the most help to you and this is why we are here."

SEQUENCE OF USE

The EPS content is arranged in 13 parts, typically two or three mimeographed colored pages to a part.

Part I: Base-Rate Information and Introduction

OVERVIEW

Part I (Figure 1) asks the client to make as explicit as possible his current views regarding his occupational planning and calls for the client's judgment as to the three occupations for which he would be best

---

[2] Editors' Note: Other counselors might elect to have the group work together.

suited and the three educational plans for which he would be best suited. The base-rate inquiry ends with a probing question for any "don't know" responses which the client may have made. Part I ends with seven statements descriptive of "What do you do in this self-directed learning program?"

COUNSELOR FUNCTION

The counselor distributes Part I with the instructions to provide the base-rate information as explicitly as possible and to find any questions that the last section may raise. The counselor also indicates he will answer any questions and will (a) exchange Part I for Part II whenever a client is ready to do so; and (b) study the client's Part I and on the sheet will write any questions that seem relevant for the client to resolve.

These questions are a form of counselor feedback. Some client responses are often ambiguous or generalized, such as "teaching." The counselor's intervening question may be, "What ideas do you have as to the level or subject?" Another example is "civil service." The counselor's intervening question may be, "This covers all kinds of occupations— what kind did you have in mind?" The theme of the feedback is to teach the client to make explicit his views and to make such expressions specific enough so that they may be used and evaluated by him and by the counselor subsequently in the process.

The counselor returns Part I (open to the questions he has raised) for the client's study and responses. Subsequently, the counselor reviews how the client has coped with the issues raised.

PROBLEMS

Some clients perceive the object of the task as "filling out forms." Signs of this perception warrant intervention by the counselor to structure again the nature of the process.

Since Part I offers the first response material from the client, it is particularly important for the counselor to respond in ways which will teach the client the necessity of explicit and articulate responses as opposed to those of an implicit or ambiguous nature. This response style is a prerequisite in each succeeding part, hence the need to establish the style at the outset.

There are many temptations to the counselor to respond to the client's responses to this part in terms of why, how long, how does one plan relate to another, and so forth. These counselor interventions are not relevant to the base rate nature of Part I, and premature for this stage of the EPS process.

Part II: Effective Problem-solving

OVERVIEW

Part II (Figure 2) describes the process of problem-solving. The client is asked to write down the six steps.

COUNSELOR FUNCTION

The primary function here is to clarify any questions or misunderstandings—in short, to ascertain that the clients understand that this counseling model involves applying the EPS process to their own educational-vocational indecision. Responses to client questions at this stage usually are applicable to each client present and hence are usually discussed orally for the benefit of all clients.

While clients are learning this material, the counselor may be reviewing the clients' Part I's or related materials regarding the clients.

As each client finishes with this part, the counselor provides Parts IIA & IX, *Occupations for Investigation*.

PROBLEMS

Some students may read the material superficially. There is a potential for a "let's-get-on-with-it" attitude. The counselor can often reward this expression of intent and use it to illustrate the importance of the first stage, that of definition. That is, at this moment the problem or task at hand is not "how to get to the next step," but rather, "how to get ready for the next step."

Parts IIA and IX: Occupations for Investigation

OVERVIEW

This is a single sheet (Figure 3) which provides a convenient means for the client to list the names of occupations which occur to him already or at any time during the subsequent eight stages of the EPS. The part carries the "& IX" label also to indicate that Part IX will also involve identification of an array of occupations for investigation by the client.

COUNSELOR FUNCTION

The counselor periodically may review this part primarily to encourage the client's use of it as a time-saver as he moves through the process. The counselor's review will offer the chance to provide clarifying questions to the client in the event that his occupational entries are too generalized to be useful in the subsequent stage of consulting occupational-educational information.

The counselor may also note the degree to which the client puts his occupational eggs in one or more baskets. (For example, an array of physician, veterinarian, psychologist, psychiatrist, dentist all have in common not only a baccalaureate education but graduate or professional school education as well, and a substantial to strong curriculum requirement of biological science.)

PROBLEMS

Clients sometimes delay responses until at or near Part IX, thus requiring either (1) more time to go back over work they have already done, or (2) on the spot creation of an array of occupations.

The suggestion of balancing occupational alternatives between those which do and those which do not require a college education has varying relevance for each client. For those clients for whom it is a realistic consideration, avoidance of the suggestion presents clinically significant material for counselor inquiries.

Part III: Taking Stock of Your Study Time and Efficiency

OVERVIEW

Part III (Figure 4) initiates the client's self-study and does so in a domain of daily behavior that is most open to his own observation as to his typical behavior, the forces affecting it, and the changes which occur in it. The content questions concern amounts of study time, the client's evaluation as to any insufficiency, alternative causes, and motivation for change.

COUNSELOR FUNCTION

This part provides the counselor with first indications as to the investment the client is making in study behavior, its result for him, the degree of openness with which he evaluates antecedent conditions and prognosis for change. Counselor inquiries are tailored to impressions gained along these dimensions. The client is informed that his future behavior is best predicted by his past behavior. If he wants to change, action more strenuous than making New Year's resolutions will be required.

The counselor can contribute to more client change by keeping aspirations realistic. Often a small change in study time may lead to more reinforcement for the client than a large amount proposed but not accomplished.

The counselor's review of the client's evaluation of antecedent conditions can reveal cues as to client realism, psychopathology, or experience of unusual environmental conditions. These cues may warrant alternatives in treatment plans for some clients (that is, the client whose emotional life is so disrupted that he is unable to profit from the EPS model at this time).

PROBLEMS

Proneness of some clients to produce superficial analyses of past and present study behavior is sometimes very evident. A more common problem, however, is sensitizing the client to the fact that his daily study behavior represents a mainstream of habitual actions, so habitual and personalized that the client may accept them as "givens," not readily open for evaluation, and hence for alteration.

Inconsistencies in client response are not uncommon. When these can be observed, they represent a strong stimulus to the client's problem-solving (that is, "You say you need to study more hours, are willing to do so, yet doubt you can do so; How can this be?").

Part IV: Taking Stock of Your Achievement and Ability

OVERVIEW

Part IV (Figure 5) is one of the longest sections and also calls for introduction of test data in the form of a measure of academic ability, the American College Test (ACT). The counselor provides the local percentile equivalents for the client's ACT subscores and composite score, and the client continues from that point. The stimulus material concerns subject fields in which the client did his best and poorest work (and why). Next the client's relative academic standing in high school (HSR) and in college (GPA) are presented and their implications posed. Similar inquiries are made regarding academic ability. Questions are then raised as to the degree of congruity between the client's ability and achievement and any trends in the client's achievement. Part IV concludes with an inquiry as to the fields of study the client finds most attractive and how suitable these appear in light of the client's ability and achievement to date.

COUNSELOR FUNCTION

The counselor provides the ACT test data and also provides (via a plastic-covered sheet) self-interpreting charts whereby the client can evaluate both his high school achievement and his college achievement in terms of those students with whom he is competing. Adjectival descriptions are provided for bands of relative achievement ("well above average" to "well below average"). In the case of grade-point averages, the client also can see the noticeable trend in college achievement from freshman to senior years, a most relevant piece of data for the planning of many clients.

Interventions of the counselor in this part sometimes are occasioned by client inconsistencies or by seeming errors in client evaluation of the data.

PROBLEMS

Part IV is perhaps too long. It is a potentially discouraging part for clients of limited ability and achievement, and in some cases it promotes client preoccupation with trivial differences in test scores, that is, a client may lay stress on his best ability area, for example, English (24th percentile), as opposed to his weakest area, mathematics (20th percentile).

Part V: Taking Stock of Your Work Experience

OVERVIEW

Part V (Figure 6) calls for exploration of past and present work experience in the jobs of most relevance to the client's planning. The client describes each job, the most and least attractive features of the work to him, and what he learned.

COUNSELOR FUNCTION

The client responses offer the counselor quite clear indications as to the degree to which the client has been open to, and observant of, his involvement in work. When there is evidence of little impact from such experiences, the counselor's inquiries can stimulate some reconsideration by the client. For example, to a client response of "Wouldn't want to do that job for my life's work," the counselor's review might lead to asking, "What is there about *you* that leads you to conclude this?"

PROBLEMS

A common situation is for some clients to lack any paid job experience. Volunteer work is included here partly to cope with this.

The vocational relevance of past work experience is a complex matter that seems to rest less on the job duties per se than upon the context of the work and the incidental learnings that the individual acquires. A number of clients do not discriminate sufficiently among the questions raised regarding each job experience. Some clients observe that the different questions ask the same things.

Part VI: Taking Stock of Your Leisure Experiences

OVERVIEW

Part VI (Figure 7) is designed to elicit description and evaluation of three uses of leisure that may have the most relevance for educational-vocational planning.

COUNSELOR FUNCTION

Common types of counselor inquiry in this part involve the client's omissions (only two of three leisure activity items completed), over-looking themes common to the various activities (all involving socially isolated activities), or such literal interpretations of leisure uses that the client cannot identify any vocational implications among them.

PROBLEMS

Not infrequently clients indicate unstructured uses of their leisure (bull sessions, talking) or unstructured social events (dates, movies, TV-viewing).

This is another part in which the client is apt to lose his involvement with the task as an integral part of the EPS process of evolving plans.

Part VII: Taking Stock of Your Interests

OVERVIEW

Part VII (Figure 8) deals with both expressed and inventoried vocational interests. The client is asked to identify three occupations of most interest to him presently and what there is about himself that would make the occupations attractive to *him* whereas they might not be so for someone else.

Interests are then categorized in terms of the Strong Vocational Interest Blank (SVIB) groupings. The groups are described briefly and then illustrative occupations for each group are cited. The client indicates by a plus sign (+), zero (0), or minus sign (−) his degree of interest in each of the occupational groups. The client then transfers these to a chart. The counselor adds correspondingly +, 0, and −, entries for the client's degree of inventoried interest similarity with each occupational group. The client then uses this chart to deal with the subsequent questions of those occupational groups for which he has both expressed and inventoried interest (the ++ cells of the chart). These are followed by the other combinations (that is, + with 0 or —, and 0 or — with +). The client is asked to explore possible reasons for the differences and their implications for his vocational planning.

The counselor introduces test data, an interpretation of the SVIB in terms of +, 0, or —, symbols. The symbols approximate the meanings of primary, indeterminant, and reject interest patterns. In addition the counselor designates the names of any occupations among the 0 or — occupational groups for which the client reveals a primary degree of interest similarity.

A common problem is that of flat SVIB profiles. A related problem is that of the relatively less valuable women's form for use with female clients. The women's form is treated in the same manner, that is, coding the same occupational groups as for men.

The printed inquiry concerning differences between expressed and inventoried interests (the + with 0 or —, or the 0 or — with +) frequently causes confusion among clients. Several revisions have reduced the confusion, but it still presents a problem in delayed client understanding. The difficulty is not only in the item wording but in the implications with which the client needs to wrestle.

Part VIII: Taking Stock of the Opinions of Others

Part VIII (Figure 9) attempts to sensitize the client to the interpersonal context of his plans. The stimulus items ask for the identification of three persons whose opinions are most important to him regarding his planning. Then, first for vocational and next for educational plans the client is confronted with questions as to their expectations, the congruity of their expectations with his own, and the ramifications of following plans at variance with those such others might expect.

It is in response to the stimuli of Part VIII that the climate of the client's familial relationships is often revealed (for example, nonlisting of any relatives among significant others, indicating of "I want whatever they want for me," or 'What they expect doesn't make any difference."). Such client responses often warrant counselor responses promoting more elaboration, clarification, or integration of the client's particular response with responses to previous parts.

PROBLEMS

In spite of revision to minimize it, there are still instances of client difficulty in perceiving either the role of environmental expectations or just what the nature of those may be. Another issue lies in the fact that while two to three significant others are requested initially, the subsequent items deal with "them" thus creating problems for the client whose significant others may hold quite varying expectations. Rather than being organized into vocational and educational parts perhaps it would be more relevant to subsume these under each significant other.

Review of Parts IIA & IX: Occupations for Investigation

OVERVIEW

Parts IIA & IX (Figure 3) were described previously. The client and counselor do additional work with these parts here.

At this stage the client should have built an array of occupational possibilities warranting investigation. The second column is one in which he is asked to conceptualize these in group (SVIB) terms. The rationale for this is that such conceptualization may stimulate other occupational possibilities of the same class, may reduce stereotypic views of specific occupations, and should enable the client and counselor to note the degree of concentration or spread among the fields and levels of work selected.

It is from this array that the client then moves to investigation of occupational and educational information.

COUNSELOR FUNCTION

Since the client responses to this part define the extent of the occupational environment he will investigate, the adequacy of his responses are critical. The counselor's role here is, via review, to insure that the array is sufficient in number, diversity, and level for the client as the counselor understands him. Naturally, the necessary characteristics of the array will vary greatly from client to client. The counselor's review also insures that there is sufficient specificity in the occupations listed so that the client's information search will be fruitful.

PROBLEMS

Not infrequently clients overlook maintaining this log as they proceed through the EPS. At this point, some clients rather quickly attempt to free associate an array without consideration of their work up to that point—the antithesis of the EPS model.

Part X: Occupational Facts

OVERVIEW

Part X (Figure 10) consists of an introductory message, a list of the 80 odd possible major fields of study within the University of Maryland,[3] and then six to ten copies of the Occupational Facts Chart—one for each of the occupations to be investigated by the client.

The stimulus material is quite delimited, asking only eight questions, three of which are answerable by multiple-choice responses. The client searches for the kind of work performed, its main involvement (things/ data-ideas/people), needed educational skills and interests, the client's main strengths and weaknesses for the work, and concludes with multiple-choice judgments of the client's suitability for the work and similar suitability for the requisite education and training.

The *Occupational Outlook Handbook* is a primary source of information here in addition to other occupational briefs and educational and training materials.

COUNSELOR FUNCTION

There is less need for counselor review and comment on this part than upon most of the other parts in the EPS process. Given an adequate array of occupations to investigate and given assurance of information being available for the client's investigation, the counselor's primary function involves review of the first sheet completed and occasional questioning as to the consistency of the client's suitability judgments with prior data the client has recorded. (For example, poor ability or achievement in mathematics and science, no relevant work or leisure experience, yet evaluates himself for the work and training of the engineer as "fairly well suited.")

---

[3] Editors' Note: Counselors at other schools could easily generate a corresponding list.

PROBLEMS

Pursuit of the EPS model is put to considerable test here since the habitual stereotypic views of occupations plus the cultural prestige values of such occupations can easily interfere with the client's analyses. Part X often is time consuming, and as such is viewed as taxing by clients with relatively mild degrees of motivation.

Part XI: Summary and Integration

OVERVIEW

Part XI (Figure 11) brings together the client's complete EPS efforts. The client is asked to make absolute and relative evaluations of the various occupational possibilities.

COUNSELOR FUNCTION

Part XI is perhaps the most difficult for the counselor. It represents the integration of the considerable amount of data by the client and each portion is assigned a value by the client. The counselor assesses the client's objectivity in evaluating his selected occupational possibilities. To facilitate the counselor's feedback, a number of the most likely comments are printed in the corner of the chart and hence the number(s) of the statement can be inserted on the chart wherever the counselor judges the comment to be most appropriate. (For example: "5"—How realistic an evaluation is this?)

PROBLEMS

Part XI is both clerically and intellectually the most demanding of the EPS stages. Some clients relapse into impulsive or occasionally distorted evaluations of their attributes. The counselor's role is a critical safety valve in these instances encouraging the client to take a "second look" at the data. Valuable as this intervention may be, it is, of course, not a uniformly successful response. The problem, made obvious by the written nature of the material, is that of unrealistic evaluations by the client. At times it has been meaningful to clients to relate the computer programming observation of "garbage in—garbage out."

The counselor's responsiveness in providing feedback may be lessened here—perhaps as a function of the amount of stimuli confronting him, perhaps as a function of the material having been considered before, albeit in a part-by-part fashion.

Part XII: Choice of Plans and Taking Action on Them

OVERVIEW

Part XII (Figure 12) is fashioned to stimulate the client to convert evaluations into a hierarchy of suitable occupational and educational plans (in some ways akin to the base-rate material gathered at the beginning of the EPS process).

COUNSELOR FUNCTION

The counselor needs to review the client's hierarchy of plans for clarity to insure that the client knows what specific actions to take if he decides upon one or more of these plans.

PROBLEMS

Some clients need further reinforcement by the time they have completed Parts X or XI. The possibility of reconsidering earlier inadequate plans places heavy demands on the client's motivation level. Some clients persist in their first plan even when it is far less realistic than their second or third. Counseling efforts focusing upon the alternative courses of action may be helpful since these alternatives will be ready when and if the client may have need of them.[4]

ADMINISTRATION

Forms have been developed for collecting student evaluations of the EPS process (Part XIII) and for summarizing the results.

Settings

The EPS model has been tried in several different settings: (1) a precollege summer session for marginally achieving high school students who wish to try the college experience, (2) regular college undergraduates self-referred for educational-vocational counseling, (3) junior college

---

[4] Editors' Note: A wise policy in our estimation! Sometimes highly motivated individuals achieve their "unrealistic" plans. A counselor who would have talked them out of their aspirations would have been guilty of premeditated obstructionism. Counseling about alternative plans is like discussing parachutes with a pilot flying a biplane to the moon.

students, (4) high school students, and (5) junior high school students. Appropriate modifications in the materials must be made for each population.

Group Size

The EPS model can be employed with from one to five clients concurrently. Once the counselor is accomplished with the model, the group size can be tailored to the number that demands optimum use of his time. I have found four to be best when the model is implemented as described in this article.

Rate of Work

Initially, in the precollege summer session groups our interest was to structure the sessions (and client work outside the sessions), so that in a given session the clients tended to be at about the same stage in their problem-solving. The main advantage of this was that any counselor observations or group discussions or both would be relevant to all clients in the group. However, clients tend to move progressively farther apart as their EPS work continues. They tend to complete the process over a varying number of sessions. Typically this means that the counselor works with a decreasing number of students per session. To some extent this enables the counselor to invest more time with the more complex cases.

One possible arrangement to balance out the number of clients per session over several EPS cycles involves introduction of new clients into EPS "groups" as clients terminate. Although it presents several casework management problems, this suggestion offers to make the most efficient use of limited professional counseling time.

Distribution of Materials

Clients are confronted with only one task at a time and the magnitude of each task is quite limited. In contrast, to confront clients with the complete set of parts at the outset would have a deterring effect on their commitment to the task at hand.

There are, of course, numerous variations in distribution of the parts. We have made distribution of several parts (I, II, and III) to clients on the waiting list *prior* to their first counseling appointment. Similarly, we have arranged for clients to work with some parts at home, returning them before or at their next counseling session, for example, clients who were motivated to move at a faster rate, or those whose counseling may be interrupted for a period of time, or those who have to travel considerable distance per counseling session.

Length of Sessions

In good, tradition-bound fashion, our greatest experience has been with 50-minute sessions. There have been occasions for use of briefer time periods after initial sessions. I have also employed one-and-a-half- to two-hour sessions as well as sessions on successive days. There appears to be no general advantage to any variation.

Written or Oral Interactions

The printed statements and questions are largely taken from commonly emitted counselor responses during typical interviews. The client can be told to read the statements as if the counselor was speaking to him.

The client's responses are elicited in writing following each question. The counselor can add subsequent questions or statements in either written or oral form, whichever may motivate the client to clearer analyses.

The counselor will interact orally with clients more at the beginning and end of sessions and typically more on some parts of the EPS than on others. There is more counselor talk in the initial session and on the last two parts than on many in the middle.

Variations in Usage among Counselors within the Same Setting

Although the EPS stimulus materials are quite structured, they have engendered much variability among counselors' use of them. I would guess that for those clients for whom the model is appropriate there is more variability in counselor behavior under the EPS model than within our traditional vocational counseling practices.

Some counselors devote more time to group discussions when the group seems to need motivation to continue. Clients seemed reassured that they were not alone in their doubt and indecision, and that areas of common difficulty in university life existed and were amenable to constructive efforts at change. Hearing others face up to, and deal with, related, but not the same, problems allowed clients to try out different solutions and alternatives themselves.

Variations in grouping different types of students are possible. Clients with different basic orientations to education and occupation seemed more ready to comment upon others' responses to EPS issues, and to listen to comments by others with different orientations. When considerable homogeneity exists among clients, feelings of competition and insecurity are apt to arise, inhibiting mutual interaction.

Certain sections of the materials may not be assigned. The study habits section and occasionally the aptitude-achievement section may be omitted, particularly for nonstudents or students on the verge of graduation.

Sometimes severe emotional or social problems appear. The educational-vocational planning may then be held in abeyance. Counseling is restructured and directed at different objectives.

THE EPS MODEL: PRO AND CON

Advantages

MORE SYSTEMATIC AND THOROUGH

The structured nature of EPS insures that the involved client deals at some length with all of the relevant areas of the problem-solving process.

COUNSELING IN GROUPS WITHOUT GROUP COUNSELING CONSTRAINTS

The model offers the flexibility for each client to be proceeding at his own rate.

A BETTER GRASP OF THE PROCESS

Clients can identify the sequence of stages and anticipate a finite end point. The rate at which they can accomplish the end point is under their own control.

BRINGING FURTHER ORDER INTO THE COUNSELING PROCESS

As a result of creating one ordering (as illustrated by the first form of the EPS model), subsequent orderings are easier and simpler to generate. Future models can benefit from the present experience.

MAKING INDECISION AND ITS SOLUTION A COHERENT PROCESS

Where the client experiences a coherent process of problem-solving from the stage of problem definition to subsequent periodic review, it appears most probable that the counseling experience will generalize to future events of concern to the client.

A FUTURE RESOURCE FOR THE CLIENT

By virtue of the written nature of the EPS materials the counselor can insure that the client obtains copies of whatever parts (from none to all) of his problem-solving work he anticipates use for in the future. For some clients this prospect serves as an additional incentive for their problem-solving efforts.

EXPLICITNESS OF FUTURE ACTIONS

The model encourages clear planfulness up to whatever level of specificity the client can attain at the time. The provision for periodic review is clear recognition of the continuous nature of vocational planning.

MULTIPLE PLANS IN PRIORITY

The EPS model calls for evolving more than "a plan." In fact it calls for up to three alternative plans varying in degree of appropriateness to the client.

COMMUNICATING TO OTHERS

The EPS structure has proven to be one which is easily communicable to prospective clients, parents, and faculty members. It is also a valuable addition to counseling and clinical training. It has had the effect of making the trainees' subsequent traditional counseling proceed in a more goal-directed manner.

EMPHASIS ON CLIENT RESPONSIBILITY

The focus of responsibility for problem-solving rests with the client. The dependent client, the manipulative client, the minimally motivated client are, in our experience, more likely to be mobilized to problem-solving behavior as a function of this particular model. Furthermore, the counselor's time is more efficiently utilized with such clients.

Disadvantages

ALTERATION IN COUNSELOR BEHAVIOR

The counselor will experience an unusual degree of silence—that is, clients engaged in thought and writing. This can be quite vivid and for some counselors uncomfortable. Writing is slower and more demanding, in a way, than oral responding.

RIGID NATURE OF EPS

Although it is an empirical question ultimately, I believe it unlikely that only a few parts could be employed with the same result as if the total set was employed.

WRITTEN FORM OF EPS IS IMPERSONAL

There tends to be less oral interaction and more structured interaction. The degree of oral interaction is one of the variables the counselor can adjust to what may be optimal for a given client.[5]

INSENSITIVITY OF THE MATERIALS TO INDIVIDUAL DIFFERENCES

A brief form of intake interview appears most relevant for refining judgments as to which clients would appear most appropriate for this form of counseling assistance.

INAPPROPRIATE FOR SOME CLIENTS WITH EMOTIONAL PROBLEMS

Some clients may not be able to profit from continued EPS work, at least at the time, and referral to another counseling mode may be warranted. It is clearly more cumbersome to refer such clients to another counselor or another counseling time than under traditional counseling practices.

MISPERCEPTIONS FROM WRITTEN MATERIALS

Some clients view EPS work as "filling out forms." Disengagement from personal involvement in problem-solving is the antithesis of the model's purpose. The alert counselor can engage the client in resolution of this problem as a preproblem.

MINIMIZED PROBLEM DEFINITION

The definition stage is underemphasized in the process itself, possibly deterring generalization of the client's problem-solving habits to other problems. The intake process with the client actually represents the stage of problem definition.

[5] Editors' Note: Efforts would need to be taken to insure that this EPS process does not become a lonely burden for the client (or the counselor). One could, for example, experiment with clients mutually administering the steps to each other and then consulting a counselor together.

CONTENT SPECIFIC TO SETTING AND CLIENTELE

The change of clientele from a precollege summer session clientele to that of academic year clients appearing at our counseling center warranted far more revision of the materials than we had anticipated. A substantial investment of time and thought is needed in adapting the model to new situations.[6]

OMISSIONS AND COMPROMISES

There is no stimulus material explicitly dealing with disabilities. Test score data are cast into a relatively small number of adjectival categories. Omissions and compromises such as these appear to be at least a temporary part of any venture into a further ordering of the counseling process.

[6] Editors' Note: A counselor wishing to adapt this model for another school would need to have local test norms and accurate information on local curricula. Some changes in wording would also be required. Counselors might also wish to experiment with other changes in procedure or format. However, the most difficult part of the task has already been accomplished by Dr. Magoon and his staff of counselors at the University of Maryland. Our inclusion of all parts of the EPS process in this book testifies to our belief that the technique would be generalizable to many settings and useful for many clients.

MODEL OF THE EPS PROCESS
Figure 1 (1)

NAME_____   DATE_____

Before moving into the Problem Solving Process, it is important to record your current thinking on several questions. Your answers will provide a background from which to start. Only you can provide this background.

These questions may be difficult to answer, but do the best you can. Be as specific as you can. If you are *completely unable* to answer these questions, indicate "Do not know."

1. For what *occupation* would you say you are *best suited?*

2. For what *occupation* would you say you are *next best suited?*

3. For what *occupation* would you say you are *next best suited?*

4. *How much education* do you expect to get and *what kind?* (College degree, technical or business school, graduate or professional school, apprenticeship, etc.)

5. *In what field of study* do you expect to concentrate?

6. If you have indicated you "Do not know" to Nos. 1, 2, or 3 above, why do you suppose this is?

MODEL OF THE EPS PROCESS (*cont.*)

Figure 1 (2)

WHAT DO YOU DO IN THIS SELF-DIRECTED LEARNING PROGRAM?

1. You learn the steps in Problem Solving and then apply the Problem Solving Process to your own vocational and educational planning.

2. The program is largely in written form. Your success depends on the seriousness and thoroughness of your written responses. Many questions are asked and much effort on your part will be required to arrive at the answers. Finding these answers and writing them down is a concrete way of really involving yourself in Problem Solving.

3. You will need to be on guard against reaching quick, vague, or superficial answers to the many questions that will be raised for your consideration. To do *yourself justice*, you will need to give careful and serious thought to *all* the questions.

4. The materials are arranged in a sequence. Your work on one part is necessary for the later steps to be of value to you. For the soundest planning you need to work through these materials step by step.

5. You may find that there are some things missing which you regard as important to consider in your planning. There are places to add these into your planning as you go along.

6. The Counselor's part in this process is to assist you in this work by:
   a. providing the materials which are designed to stimulate your thinking and planning.
   b. clarifying things you do not understand in the process.
   c. acting as a consultant and catalyst to your Problem Solving efforts.

7. Now turn to Part II and find out what this Effective Problem Solving Process is all about.

NAME_____   DATE_____

EFFECTIVE PROBLEM SOLVING

WHAT IS IT?

A name for a systematic process of coping with matters of concern to you. Following the process offers the greatest chance for resolving many problems—that is, producing results that you will find most satisfying and successful.

The process is quite straightforward, and it can be applied to many kinds of problems which you encounter.

STEPS IN PROBLEM SOLVING:

We can describe a number of steps involved in the process. By understanding these, you can apply them yourself to the task at hand *now* and to problems which confront you in the *future*.

The steps are:
1. Define the problem
2. Gather relevant information
3. Weigh the evidence gathered
4. Choose among alternative plans or goals
5. Take action on your plans
6. Review your plan periodically

Now for a closer look at these:

1. DEFINE THE PROBLEM:

You have to know *what* the problem is in order to be able to solve it.

You must begin by defining the problem or task in very clear fashion.

The clearer it is the easier it will be to solve and the better will be the solution.

A common error is to believe symptoms are the problems. Symptoms are usually only signs of some problem. For example, an inability to study is really a symptom or sign of a problem. The problem may be a lack of ability or weak study methods, difficulty in giving up immediate satisfactions for the sake of long range goals, distractions over relationships with other people, etc. To solve a problem you must attack *it*, and not some surface symptoms.

The problem which you will work on in these meetings is one shared by many students. This is the problem of planning your career, i.e., making vocational plans and usually educational plans as well. You will work toward arriving at well-considered answers to the following questions:

VOCATIONAL
    a. For *what kind of vocation* am I best suited?
    b. For *what kind of alternative vocations* am I best suited?

MODEL OF THE EPS PROCESS *(cont.)*
Figure 2 (2)

EDUCATIONAL
a. For *what kind of education or training* am I best suited?
b. For what kind of *alternative education or training* am I best suited?

How important is vocational and educational planning?
You will spend more of your adult life in your career than in *any other single activity*. You will be living with your solutions for years to come. Effective solutions are satisfying to live with. Ineffective solutions are hard to live with and hard to overcome.

Now the problem is defined. What is the next step?

2. GATHER RELEVANT INFORMATION

a. First, you need to identify what kinds of information are relevant. For the educational-vocational problems concerning you, here are some of the most important areas to consider:
(1) Study—the amount of time and the efficiency of your studying
(2) Academic ability
(3) Academic achievement
(4) Work experiences
(5) Leisure experiences
(6) Interests
(7) Others' expectations of you
(8) Occupational and educational facts (information about occupations, requirements of different kinds of education, etc.).

b. Second, you need to gather these kinds of information about yourself, that is, find out the facts regarding yourself in each of these areas.

3. WEIGH THE EVIDENCE

This step refers to considering each bit of information you have gathered about yourself.

Where do you stand on each of the areas listed above? How do you evaluate yourself in terms of each?

4. CHOOSE FIRST AND ALTERNATE PLANS OR GOALS

a. Here is the step where you *combine* your evaluations covering all the information you have gathered and weighed.

b. Keep in mind that some of this information is more important and should be weighted more heavily than other information.

MODEL OF THE EPS PROCESS (*cont.*)
Figure 2(3)

   c. What first plan and what alternative plans best fit all of the information you have gathered and weighed?

   d. A good check on the soundness of your plans is to determine whether your plans follow consistently from the definition of the problem and the information you have gathered and weighed. If they do, fine. If they don't, revise your work and try to make them do so.

5. TAKING ACTION ON YOUR PLANS

   a. What can you do *now* to further these plans?

   b. What can you do *subsequently* to further them?

6. PERIODIC REVIEWING

   a. Your plan or goal should be the best one possible *at this time*. But as you gather additional experience, these plans should be reviewed in light of your accumulating experience.

   b. If you find you need to alter your plans or shift to an alternate plan—fine. If not—fine. In general, if you have been thorough and careful in the first five steps, the modifications will be minor ones, but any plan should be reviewed periodically and updated as needed.

   c. There is considerable comfort for anyone in having a plan for his educational and vocational future.

   d. More importantly, by following this process of problem solving, you not only have *sound plans,* but you can feel assured you have some *sound reasons* as to *why* you are pursuing them.

As a summary, to get these steps in mind look back at the material above and then write down the six steps here:
   1.
   2.
   3.
   4.
   5.
   6.

Is everything clear so far? If not, check back to clarify your thinking or ask the Counselor about anything that is unclear so far. You can use the space below to jot down any questions you might have about the Problem Solving Process. If there are no further questions, you should be set to put the Effective Problem Solving Process to work for you.

MODEL OF THE EPS PROCESS *(cont.)*
Figure 3

NAME_____   DATE_____

OCCUPATIONS FOR INVESTIGATION

NOTE: This sheet is for your use as you work through the Problem Solving Process. In the upper right hand corner is marked "IIA and IX". This means you may start making use of the sheet from Part II on and will use it specifically as Part IX a little later on.

In a number of places, as you work along you will be meeting questions about yourself and occupations. When this happens various occupations will likely come to mind. When they do, this sheet is to be used to write down the names of any such occupations that seem to be worth your learning more about.

Then later on when you reach the stage of analyzing a number of occupations you will have a number of them already jotted down. You should have *at least six* occupations by that time, and since about 50% of college students do not graduate, you should probably have some occupations which do and some which do not require a college education.

LIST OF OCCUPATIONS

	OCCUPATIONS	OCCUPATIONAL GROUP TITLES (omit this column until you have finished Part VIII, then refer to Part VII, page 3 for the Group Titles)
1.		
2.		
3.		
4.		
5.		
6.		
7.		
8.		
9.		
10.		

MODEL OF THE EPS PROCESS *(cont.)*
Figure 4 (1)

NAME_____   DATE_____

TAKING STOCK OF YOUR STUDY TIME AND EFFICIENCY

NOTE: Now you are going to start to gather and organize information about yourself. You will recall that this is the second step in the Problem Solving Process.

_____ 1.   How many *hours a day* did you devote to studying while in high school?

_____ 2.   a.   How many *hours a day* are you devoting to study in college?

b.   This amount is _____ more, _____ the same, _____ less than your college studying last year.

3.   A college student should be prepared to spend 5 or more hours a day in study outside of class, in order to be reasonably assured of having devoted enough study time in college.
a.   In this sense, how similar are you to the typical student?
(Check one of the following)

_____ I am similar to the college student in this regard.

_____ Not similar and I need to spend more than that amount of time studying.

_____ Not similar, but I don't need to spend that much time studying.

b.   If you have checked the third alternative, explain why:

4.   How does the amount of time you spent in (a) high school and (b) college so far compare with 5 hours per day? (Enter the difference in hours and circle 'more' or 'less'.)

a.   High School:
        (more)
_____ hours   (circle one)
        (less)

b.   College:
        (more)
_____ hours   (circle one)
        (less)

5.   The chances are that there is a discrepancy between your high school (and perhaps your college) study time, *and* the amount you may need in college.

MODEL OF THE EPS PROCESS (*cont.*)

Figure 4 (2)

Even if you indicated willingness to change, you are used to spending the amount of time daily that you listed in No. 2 on the previous page.

Your study time is a habit and *likely a very strong habit* at that, regardless of whether your study is efficient or inefficient. Habits are difficult to change partly because they are automatic, partly because they are comfortable. Good habits are useful and time-saving; bad habits need to be and can be changed.

6. Are you willing to spend 5 hours a day in study, if necessary?
_____yes _____no _____uncertain
If not, why not:

7. Now you have the opportunity to consider the *meaning* of some of this information for you. Here are some questions to work on:

8. If you say in answer to 4b, that you have been studying *more than 5 hours daily*, you should carefully consider these questions:

a. How efficiently do you study?

b. How well do your learning and your grades reflect the amount of time you are spending in study? If they don't match, what are the possible reasons for this?

c. Has there been any marked shift in your pattern of study? Yes_____ No_____ If yes, when did the shift take place? Why did you change? What effect did it have? Have you maintained the changes? If not, why not?

d. Is any change needed *now* in your study habits?
_____Yes _____No _____Uncertain
If you checked yes:
(1) What changes do you think you should make?

(2) How will you make them?

MODEL OF THE EPS PROCESS (*cont.*)
Figure 4 (3)

9. If you say in answer to 4b that you have been studying *less than 5 hours daily,* you may well need to study that much more per day. For good problem solving, you need to figure out *why* you have studied less in the past. Here are some of the conditions which might account for this (check as many as apply to you).

_____ a. Insufficient interest in studying and school work.
_____ b. Insufficient academic ability which leads to frustration in attempting to learn.
_____ c. Poor study habits reducing how much you learn and/or remember.
_____ d. Concern with other interests.
_____ e. Preoccupation with other problems.
_____ f. Other (fill in) _____

If you checked No. 9:
(1) Why do you think these conditions have persisted? That is, what has prevented you from successfully coping with each of them?

(2) What are you going to give up or do differenty in order to invest this added study time? (That is, if you have filled up your time in some way in the past, what will you give up *now* in order to spend more time in study?)

(3) How confident are you that you can alter these conditions? (Keep in mind that real changes in habits are not made by just making New Year's resolutions.)
_____Very confident   _____Quite confident   _____Not confident

(4) What steps can you take to aid in making the changes?

MODEL OF THE EPS PROCESS (cont.)

Figure 4 (4)

10. *Efficiency of Your Reading and Study Skills*
    a. Now either you have some intentions about changing your study time, or perhaps you feel you study a sufficient amount right now.
    b. Apart from study *time*, what about the *efficiency* of your reading and study skills?
    c. Here is a checklist that will help you organize your thinking about the efficiency of your skills.

	EFFICIENT	SO-SO	INEFFICIENT	
(1)	_____	_____	_____	Methods or habits of study
(2)	_____	_____	_____	Listening to lectures and note-taking
(3)	_____	_____	_____	Reading speed and comprehension
(4)	_____	_____	_____	Vocabulary
(5)	_____	_____	_____	Spelling

    d. If you are motivated to improve your skills, you should consider entering the Reading and Study Skills Laboratory, a program which offers individualized help in any or all of the areas listed above. In the Reception Area of the Counseling Center is a 6-minute tape recording which describes the offerings of the Lab and the procedures for entry into the program. See the Receptionist if you wish to listen to the recording.
       (1) Have you listened to the tape recording already?
           Yes_____ No_____
       (2) Do you intend to listen to it?
           Yes_____ No_____ Uncertain_____
       (3) Do you intend to enter the Lab?
           Yes_____ No_____ Uncertain_____

MODEL OF THE EPS PROCESS (cont.)

NAME_____   DATE_____

Figure 5 (1)

NOTE: Now you are about to gather and organize a different kind of information about yourself, namely your *academic ability and achievement*.

TAKING STOCK OF YOUR ABILITY AND ACHIEVEMENT

1. **DIRECTIONS:** The first question is divided up to best indicate different areas of academic work.

    For each area you may enter indications of your academic ability (from ACT or other ability test scores) and of your achievement.

		ENGLISH	MATH	SOCIAL SCIENCE	NATURAL SCIENCE	TOTAL (Average)
a.	Your ACT scores	_____	_____	_____	_____	_____
*b.	% of Md. students you exceeded on ACT	_____	_____	_____	_____	_____
c.	Your typical *high school* grades	_____	_____	_____	_____	_____
d.	Your typical *college* grades	_____	_____	_____	_____	_____

    *From a sheet which Counselor has.
    e. What has been your grade point average each semester in college?
    _____First Sem.   _____Third Sem.   _____Fifth Sem.   _____Seventh Sem.
    _____Second Sem.   _____Fourth Sem.   _____Sixth Sem.   _____Eighth Sem.

    HIGH SCHOOL ACHIEVEMENT

2. Look at '1.c.' above. In which of the four areas of course work in high school did you do your *best* work generally?

3. Why do you think this was so? (Be specific):

4. Look at '1.c.' above. In which of the four areas of course work in high school did you do your *poorest* work, generally?

MODEL OF THE EPS PROCESS (*cont.*)
Figure 5 (2)

5. Why do you think this was so? (Be specific):

6. a. Your percentile rank* in your high school class was _____.
   *(This means the percent of students you exceeded.)
   b. However, when compared with the high school ranks of University of Maryland students, what percent of University students do you exceed? _____
   c. Why is your rank in '6.b' less than your rank in '6.a'?

   d. How would you describe your rank in '6.b'?
      well
   _____above   _____above   _____average   _____below   _____don't
        average   average   average   know

COLLEGE ACHIEVEMENT

7. Look at '1.d' on the previous page. In which of the four areas of college coursework have you done your *best* work generally?

8. Why do you think this has been so? (Be specific):

9. Look at '1.d' on the previous page. In which of the four areas of college coursework have you done your *poorest* work generally?

10. Why do you think this has been so? (Be specific):

11. If there are discrepancies between your high-school and college grades in particular areas, how do you account for them? Inasmuch as one's past achievement is the best index of one's future achievement in a given area (and a better index than ability test scores), these questions warrant your very careful consideration.

12. a. What is your cumulative grade point average in college?_____
    b. How does your grade point average (college achievement) compare with that of other Maryland students in your class? (See Table 2 or ask the counselor for information on this.)
       ___Well above average   ___Average   ___Below average   ___Don't know

MODEL OF THE EPS PROCESS *(cont.)*
Figure 5 (3)

ACADEMIC ABILITY

13. Look at '1.b' on the previous page. In which of the four areas of coursework do you have the *strongest* ability?

14. Look at '1.b' on the previous page. In which of the four areas of coursework is your *weakest* ability?

15. Combining Information about Achievement and Ability.
   a. It often happens that a student with a certain level of ability in a particular area (as indicated by a score on the ACT or another ability test) will achieve lower grades than would be predicted on the basis of ability test scores. On the other hand, it sometimes happens that a student will earn better grades in a particular area than would be predicted on the basis of an ability test score in that area. As you examine your grades and test scores in the four areas, in what field or fields do you find such discrepancies? What might be their cause? Give careful consideration to this question.

   b. Do you notice any general tendency for your grades to be lower than might be predicted on the basis of your test scores, irrespective of area?
   _____Yes   _____No
   If yes, you should think very carefully about possibe reasons for your under-achievement. What explanations occur to you?

   What do you think would be necessary in order to bring your achievement into line with your abilities?

Figure 5 (4)

16. *Your Present Thinking in the Light of Your Achievement and Ability*
   a. Although you may be unready to commit yourself to an academic major and/or a vocation, you have surely given thought to various possibilities. What fields of study are most attractive to you?
   (1)
   (2)
   (3)
   b. Think about these fields of study in relation to the information you have gained about your abilities and achievement. On the basis of this information, do these fields seem suitable or unsuitable for you? (Check each)

	SUITABLE	UNSUITABLE	DON'T KNOW
(1) First field (16a(1))	_____	_____	_____
(2) Second field (16a(2))	_____	_____	_____
(3) Third field (16a(3))	_____	_____	_____

   c. If you are uncertain, what further information do you think you need?

MODEL OF THE EPS PROCESS *(cont.)*
Figure 6 (1)

NAME_____   DATE_____

TAKING STOCK OF YOUR WORK EXPERIENCE

NOTE: Another kind of relevant information to gather and organize is your work experience. This experience can tell you more about yourself than you may think. For example, how much money you made from a job is usually less important here than what you can learn about yourself and the world of work from the job or jobs which you have had.

Recall what job or jobs you have held. Your thoughtful reactions to these experiences are very significant for your planning. Consider as jobs any part-time, summer, or full-time employment as well as any volunteer work you may have done.

First, what jobs have you had? Describe the two which might have the most significance for your vocational planning (put one on this page and one on the next page).

1. a. *Job title* and three main duties:

  b. What did you like *most* about the work?

  c. What did you like *least* about the work?

  d. What did you *learn about yourself* from this job?

  e. What did you *learn about jobs and working* from this job?

  f. What do your answers above suggest for your vocational and educational planning?

MODEL OF THE EPS PROCESS *(cont.)*
Figure 6 (2)

2. a. *Job title* and three main duties:

b. What did you like *most* about the work?

c. What did you like *least* about the work?

d. What did you *learn about yourself* from this job?

e. What did you *learn about jobs and working* from this job?

f. What do your answers above suggest for your vocational and educational planning?

3. If you have had no work experience, consider these three questions:
    a. Why not?

b. Do you have any feelings about this?

c. Does this tell you anything about yourself?

Figure 6 (3)

4. In looking for work, what steps have you taken?

a. What other steps might have been taken?

b. Does this behavior tell you anything about yourself?

MODEL OF THE EPS PROCESS (cont.)

Figure 7 (1)

NAME_____   DATE_____

TAKING STOCK OF YOUR LEISURE EXPERIENCES

NOTE: Another relevant kind of information to gather and organize concerns how you have used your leisure time.

Everyone has a certain amount of leisure time (that is, time not devoted to study, sleep, eating, family responsibilities, or a job). How you have chosen to spend this time is important information about the kind of person you are.

The uses of leisure time that are important here are the ones that may tell you something about yourself useful in your planning. Consider particularly the kinds of things that, compared with others, you have done more of, spent more time at, become more knowledgeable or skillful at, etc. In other words, consider the kinds of things that help to make you a different person from someone else.

LEISURE

1.   Leisure time activities: (Think of school, church or community activities, special talents or skills, crafts, hobbies, etc.)

2.   Write down below *three* of these uses of your leisure time. Try to select ones which may have some relevance for educational and vocational planning. Under each one, try to explain what you have gained from it.

a.   (1)   Activity:

(2)   What have you learned about yourself that may be of value in your planning?

b.   (1)   Activity:

(2)   What have you learned about yourself that may be of value in your planning?

MODEL OF THE EPS PROCESS *(cont.)*
Figure 7 (2)

c.   (1)   Activity:

(2)   What have you learned about yourself that may be of value in your planning?

3.   Now look back over your description of these uses of your leisure time.
a.   Is it a pretty accurate and complete picture?

b.   If not, describe what is missing below:

c.   Looking over *all* of these uses of your leisure, try to fill out the following:

(1)   Among your uses of leisure, what achievement or accomplishment are you *most proud of or satisfied with?*

(2)   What do your uses of your leisure time have in common?

(3)   What do your leisure time experiences suggest about *job activities* which you might find satisfying?

NAME_____   DATE_____

TAKING STOCK OF YOUR INTERESTS

NOTE: Just as information about abilities and academic achievement is an important
kind of information to gather and weigh, so too is information about your
interests. Remember that interests and abilities are *not* the same thing—you may
have interests in a field, or interests in common with people in it, but you may
lack the abilities necessary to prepare yourself for this field or to succeed in it.

Similarly, you may have the ability to do a number of things in which you
have little interest, or little interest in common with those who are in the field.
Keep this difference in mind as you consider now the area of your interests.
It is another important kind of information about yourself.

Your interests can be studied from two standpoints:

(a)   *Your expressed interests* (that is, what occupations interest you?)
(b)   *Your measured interests* (that is, how similar are your interests to those
of successful people in different kinds of occupations?)

Sometimes these two ways of viewing interests will coincide, but sometimes
there are differences. Your careful consideration of the following information
and your answers to the questions below should help you clarify and understand your interests and what they mean in planning.

PART A—YOUR EXPRESSED INTERESTS:

1.   In the past (college and/or high school), what occupations do you recall considering
most seriously as possible occupations for yourself? List them here:

a. _____   d. _____
b. _____   e. _____
c. _____   f. _____

2.   a.   *Presently*, what occupation do you feel would be your *first choice* for a career?

_____

b.   What attracts you to this choice? (Again, avoid quick or superficial answers—
think hard about what there is about yourself that would make the occupation
attract you where it might not attract someone else.)

MODEL OF THE EPS PROCESS (*cont.*)

Figure 8 (2)

3. a. What occupation would be your *second* choice? _____
    b. What attracts you to this choice?

4. a. What occupation would be your *third* choice? _____
    b. What attracts you to this choice?

5. What other occupations are you presently considering?
    a. _____   c. _____
    b. _____   d. _____

6. Now look at the occupations and reasons for being attracted to them which you have listed in 2.a&b, 3.a&b, and 4.a&b. Can you see *any common elements here*— that is, do the occupations which attract you seem to be related in any way?

7. OCCUPATIONAL GROUPS:

Occupations can be grouped in ways that may help you think about them in relation to yourself. A convenient classification is given below. Read over the description of each of the groups below as well as those on the next sheet (which includes more occupations in each group). Then indicate your degree of interest beside each group on this page by marking:

+ for "Like"
0 for "Indifferent" or "Neutral"
— for "Dislike"

I. _____ BIOLOGICAL SCIENCE OCCUPATIONS: Occupations involved in discovery and application of science to humans and animals. (Such occupations as physician, psychologist, dentist, veterinarian, etc.)

II. _____ PHYSICAL SCIENCE OCCUPATIONS: Occupations involved in discovery of scientific knowledge. (Such occupations as physicist, engineer, mathematician, etc.)

IV. _____ TECHNICAL, APPLIED, AND OUTDOOR OCCUPATIONS: Occupations involving less training or emphasis upon theory and discovery of principles and more emphasis on applying knowledge and skills. (Such occupations as skilled trades, protective jobs, other technical and outdoor work, etc.)

V. _____ SOCIAL SERVICE OCCUPATIONS: Occupations involved in helping others to learn new information, attitudes or skills. (Such occupations as teacher, personnel worker, minister, social worker, etc.)

VI. _____ ESTHETIC OCCUPATIONS: Occupations involved with artistic or musical performance. (Such occupations as musician, artist, etc.)

VIII. _____ BUSINESS ADMINISTRATION OCCUPATIONS: Occupations which involve the internal workings of any business organization. (Such occupations as accountant, office manager, purchasing agent, etc.)

IX. _____ PUBLIC CONTACT OCCUPATIONS: Occupations in which the work involves dealing with people and involves trying to influence or persuade them. (Such occupations as salesman, etc.)

X. _____ VERBAL-LINGUISTIC OCCUPATIONS: Occupations dealing with words, spoken or written. (Such occupations as advertiser, lawyer, journalist, etc.)

MODEL OF THE EPS PROCESS (cont.)

ILLUSTRATIVE OCCUPATIONS

Figure 8 (4)

I. BIOLOGICAL SCIENCES

Dentist
Physician
Veterinarian
Psychologist
Optometrist
Lab Technician
Dental Assistant
Lab Assistant
Nurse
Osteopath
Psychiatrist
Biologist

II. PHYSICAL SCIENCES

Architect
Engineer
Chemist
Meteorologist
Dietitian
Physicist
Astronomer
Mathematician
Weather Observer
Lab Technician
Lab Assistant
Programmer
  (Computer)

IV. TECH—APPLIED— OUTDOOR

Military Officer
Agriculture Agent
Forest Ranger
Vocational Training
  Teacher
Production Manager
Tree Surgeon
Fish & Game
  Warden
Aviator
Radio Operator
Farmer
Animal Breeder
Nurseryman
Contractor
Business Education
  Teacher
Policeman
Fire Protection
Surveyor

Draftsman
Technician
Machinist
Plumber
Mechanic
Computer
  Operator
Data Processing
  Equip. Spec.
Math-Science
  Teacher
Phys. Ed. Teacher
Surveyor
Painter
Carpenter
Electrician
Printer
Broadcasting
  Technician

V. SOCIAL SERVICE

Elem. Sch. Teacher
Home Ec. Teacher
Clergyman
Social Worker
Welfare Worker
Nurse
Counselor
Personnel Worker
Employment
  Interviewer
Library Asst.
Practical Nurse
Recreation Worker
Occupational
  Therapist
Physical Therapist
Social Sci. Teacher
Public
  Administrator
YMCA-YWCA Secretary
Urban Planner
Speech Therapist

VI. ESTHETIC

Art Teacher
Artist
Decorator
Commercial
  Artist
Designer
Draftsman
Photographer
Baker
Beautician
Dressmaker
Tailor
Musician
Actor
Dancer
Music Teacher
Dance Teacher
Librarian

VIII. BUSINESS ADMINISTRATION

Auditor
Accountant
Actuary
Business Teacher
Publishing Agent
Cashier
Office Machine
  Operator
Office Manager
Executive
Secretary
Office Worker
Statistical Clerk
Bookkeeper
Paymaster
Secretary
Stenographer
Typist
Pharmacist
Certified Public
  Accountant
Purchasing Agent
Banker
Mortician
Credit Manager
Keypunch
  Operator

IX. PUBLIC CONTACT

Sales Manager
Salesman
Public Relations Worker
Buyer
Advertising Agent
Bill Collector
Radio, TV Announcer
Sales Clerk
Airline Stewardess
Receptionist

X. VERBAL- LINGUISTIC

Author
Reporter
Lawyer
Teacher of English
  and Languages
Proofreader
Literary Agent
Translator
Interpreter
Advertiser

MODEL OF THE EPS PROCESS (*cont.*)
Figure 8 (5)

PART B—YOUR MEASURED INTERESTS:

1. In working on the last few questions you have been considering your expressed or felt interests. Now you are to gather some information about your interests as measured by the Strong Vocational Interest Blank.

    What will this information be like? It has been found that people who are successfully employed in an occupation tend to be similar to one another in many interests, and different in their interests from people in other occupations. The Strong Vocational Interest Blank enables you to compare your *interests* with those of successful people in a number of different fields.

    The assumption here is that, *other things being equal*, you are likely to find satisfaction and success in those fields where your interests are similar to those of successful persons already employed in the work.

MODEL OF THE EPS PROCESS *(cont.)*

Figure 8 (6)

2. INTEREST CHART:

This sheet is divided into two parts. In the upper part you should copy in your marks ($+$, $-$, or 0) from question No. 7—that is, your expressed interests in each of the occupational groups. The lower part (the row underneath your expressed interests) gives you a condensed picture of how similar your likes and dislikes are to those of successful people in broad groups of occupations. (The Counselor will provide this information). The Counselor will indicate this by entering marks for your measured interests from the interest inventory which you have taken.

OCCUPATIONAL GROUPS

	I. BIOLOGI-CAL SCIENCES	II. PHYSICAL SCIENCES	IV. TECH-NICAL—APPLIED—OUTDOOR	V. SOCIAL SERVICE	VI. ESTHETIC	VIII. BUSINESS ADMINIS-TRATION	IX. PUBLIC CONTACT	X. VERBAL—LIN-GUISTIC
a. Your Expressed Interests (from No. 7)								
b. Your Measured Interests								
Your interests are also similar to:								

MODEL OF THE EPS PROCESS *(cont.)*
Figure 8 (7)

3. In No. 2, you have now summarized, for each group of occupations, your expressed interests in that broad area of work and the similarity of your interests to those of successful people in that broad area of work.

   a. MEASURED INTERESTS +, EXPRESSED INTERESTS +
   Comparing No. 2.a and No. 2.b, consider those groups for which you have both + marks. Enter below the names of the occupational group or groups that are "++."

   (1) Occupational Group: _____
   What occupations within this group warrant the most consideration in developing your vocational plans?

   (2) Occupational Group: _____
   What occupations within this group warrant the most consideration in developing your vocational plans?

   (3) Occupational Group: _____
   What occupations within this group warrant the most consideration in developing your vocational plans?

Figure 8 (8)

4. Now consider the groups for which you have one +, but the other mark is 0 or —. These groups are harder to interpret in your planning because there are many possible explanations. Here are questions to work on concerning these groups:

   a. MEASURED INTEREST +, EXPRESSED INTEREST 0 OR —
   List these groups below and after each one consider the question which follows:

   (1) Occupational Group: _____
   Why do you think your measured interests are similar to those of people in this group of occupations?

   (2) Occupational Group: _____
   Why do you think your measured interests are similar to those of people in this group of occupations?

   (3) Occupational Group: _____
   Why do you think your measured interests are similar to those of people in this group of occupations?

MODEL OF THE EPS PROCESS (*cont.*)
Figure 8 (9)

b. MEASURED INTERESTS 0 OR —, EXPRESSED INTEREST +
List these groups below and after each one consider the question which follows:

(1) Occupational Group: _____
Why do you think your measured interests are different from those of people in this occupational group?

What effect (if any) should this difference have on your planning?

(2) Occupational Group: _____
Why do you think your measured interests are different from those of people in this occupational group?

What effect (if any) should this difference have on your planning?

(3) Occupational Group: _____
Why do you think your measured interests are different from those of people in this occupational group?

What effect (if any) should this difference have on your planning?

11. a. How thoroughly do you feel your answers cover these questions?
_____Very thoroughly   _____Somewhat thoroughly
_____Thoroughly   _____Not thoroughly at all

b. If you feel your answers are not thorough or omit important aspects of interests and your evaluation of them, what can you add to make your answers more thorough?

MODEL OF THE EPS PROCESS (*cont.*)
Figure 9 (1)

NAME_____   DATE_____

TAKING STOCK OF THE OPINIONS OF OTHERS

NOTE: Here is another kind of information to gather and organize. No one lives in isolation from others. You constantly influence and are influenced by others. Certain persons' opinions and expectations are more important to you than are others. Sometimes others' opinions are clearly conveyed to you. Often these opinions may be expressed very indirectly, but may still be influential.

OTHERS' OPINIONS

1. What two or three persons' opinions are most important to you with regard to your educational and vocational planning (such as, father, mother, other relative, teacher, friend, etc.)?

    a.
    b.
    c.

2. EDUCATION:

    a. What kind and how much education do you feel *they* expect of you? Be careful here. Don't say something vague like, "Whatever is best for me." Go beyond this and consider what education you think they regard as best for you.

        (1) What kind and how much?

        (2) What alternative education might they like to see you get?

    b. In what way are these similar or different from your expectations?

    c. How would they react if you did *something else*, that is, did not achieve this education? Again, be thoughtful in your answer.

    d. How would you feel about their reaction?

    e. How would you deal with these feelings?

MODEL OF THE EPS PROCESS (cont.)
Figure 9 (2)

3. VOCATION: Be careful here. Again don't say something vague like, "whatever is best for me." Go beyond this and consider what vocation you think they regard as best for you.

   a.   What *vocation* do you think they would like to see you enter?

   b.   What *alternative vocation* do you think they would like to see you enter?

   c.   In what ways are these similar or different from *your* expectations?

   d.   How would they react if you entered some *other* occupation?

   e.   How would you feel about their reaction?

   f.   How would you deal with these feelings?

Figure 10 (1)

NAME_____   DATE_____

OCCUPATIONAL FACTS

NOTE: By this time you should be getting some clearer impressions about *your own characteristics*. You have now gathered and organized materials related to your study habits, academic ability, achievement, work and leisure experiences, and your interests. Gathering and weighing this information should be giving you some ideas as to the kinds of information you need about occupations, as well as about the education and training required for them.

   On the back of this page is a list of all possible college majors within the University.

   How many occupations and kinds of education should you investigate? Enough so that you have at least 6 of the attached sheets filled in—one for each occupation.

   The occupations to work on are *those which you have listed on the last part*, Part IX "Occupations for Investigation."

   Look over the questions on the chart *before* you start reading about the occupations in order to have a guide in mind as to what to be looking for in your reading.

   Note especially how you rate yourself for each occupation (Nos. 7 & 8 on the attached charts). You will be using these ratings in the next Problem Solving step.

MODEL OF THE EPS PROCESS (*cont.*)

Figure 10 (2)

MAJOR FIELDS OF STUDY—UNIVERSITY OF MARYLAND

AGRICULTURAL

Agricultural Economics
Agricultural Engineering
Agricultural & Extension Education
Agronomy
Animal Science
Botany
Dairy Science
Entomology
General Agriculture
Horticulture
Poultry Science
Pre-Veterinary Science
Pre-Forestry
Pre-Theology

EDUCATION

Academic Education
  (Secondary Schools)
Agricultural Education
Art Education
Business Education
Early Childhood Education
Elementary Education
Home Economics Education
Industrial Education
Education for Industry
  (A non-teaching program which
  prepares students for
  supervisory positions
  in industry)
Library Science
Music Education
Physical Education & Health Educ.
Special Education

ARTS & SCIENCES

American Studies
Art
Astronomy
Botany
Chemistry
Comparative Literature
Economics
English
Foreign Area Studies
  (French, German, Latin
  American, Russian, Spanish)
French
General Biological Sciences
General Physical Sciences
Geography
German
Government & Politics
Greek
History
Latin
Mathematics
Microbiology
Music
Philosophy
Physics
Pre-Dentistry
Pre-Law
Pre-Medical
Psychology
Russian
Sociology
Spanish
Speech
Zoology

BUSINESS & PUBLIC ADMINISTRATION

Accounting
Finance
Economics
General Business Administration
Geography
  General Geography
  Cartography
  Urban Geography
Government & Politics
  General G & P
  International Affairs
  Public Administration
Information Systems Management
Journalism
Public Relations
Pre-Law
Marketing
Personnel & Industrial Relations
Production Management
Statistics
Transportation

ENGINEERING

Aeronautical Engineering
Chemical Engineering
Civil Engineering
Electrical Engineering
Mechanical Engineering
Fire Protection

PHYSICAL EDUCATION, RECREATION, & HEALTH

Recreation
Dance
Health Education
Physical Education

HOME ECONOMICS

Applied and Practical Art
Food
General and Family Life
Home Economics Education & Extension
Institution Management
Nutrition
Textiles/Clothing

PHARMACY

Pharmacy

UNIVERSITY COLLEGE

General Studies

NURSING

Nursing

MODEL OF THE EPS PROCESS (cont.)

Figure 10 (3)

OCCUPATIONAL FACTS CHART

NAME _____   DATE _____

1. Name of occupation investigated:

2. What kind of work is done?

3. Which does the work mainly involve?   ( ) Things   ( ) Data or ideas   ( ) People

4. What does the work require?
   a. Education needed (kind & amount)   a. _____
   b. Skills needed   b. _____
   c. Attitudes or interests needed   c. _____
   d. Other (fill in)   d. _____

5. Your main strengths for this occupation:

6. Your main weakness for this occupation:

7. How suitable would the job be for you?
   ( ) *Not suited* (don't have the same abilities or skills required)   ( ) *Fairly well suited* (would be an average member of the occupation)
   ( ) *Doubtful suitability* (would be a below-average member of the occupation)   ( ) *Well suited* (would be a better than average member of the occupation)

8. How suitable would the required education be for you?
   ( ) *Not suited* (would be a failing or uninterested student in)   ( ) *Fairly well suited* (would be an average student in this education)
   ( ) *Doubtful suitability* (would be a barely passing, mediocre student in this education)   ( ) *Well suited* (would be a superior student in this education)

MODEL OF THE EPS PROCESS (*cont.*)

Figure 11 (1)

SUMMARY AND EVALUATION

NOTE: Up to this point, you have been considering one kind of information at a time. Now is the time to consider each bit of information in terms of different occupational groups and occupations. That is, by this time you have some ideas as to your standing on each of the kinds of information that are relevant to consider in planning. Now, how does your knowledge add up for each of several alternative occupational plans?

What you have completed so far lays the foundation for this next step in the Problem Solving Process. This step is very critical since it involves pulling together all of your information. This is essential to converting your understandings into plans for the future.

DIRECTIONS FOR COMPLETING PAGE 2 OF THIS SECTION:

COLUMN 1—OCCUPATIONAL GROUPS: List the occupational groups that seem most appropriate for you.

COLUMN 2—OCCUPATIONS: List several of the occupations which you have investigated for each group—occupations which seem appropriate from your study of them. Some may require college education, some should not. *Caution:* Avoid general labels like "Government" or "Business"—such labels are too general for you to evaluate yourself on.

COLUMN 3—REQUIRED EDUCATION OR TRAINING: Note the kind and level of education or training required for each of the occupations you have listed. To save space, you may put code numbers in the summary to represent the kind of education or training needed; the code is listed at the top left of the summary table.

COLUMN 4—RELEVANT INFORMATION: This is where you *evaluate yourself* for each of these occupational plans *in terms of each of the kinds of information you have been gathering and weighing.* This is hard work requiring your best thinking, and you are now approaching the "payoff" for your Problem Solving.

First, review Section III of the Effective Problem Solving Process, *(Taking Stock of Your Study Time and Efficiency).* As you look over your answers in that section, consider your evaluation ($+$, $-$, 0, or ?) for *Study Time* as it relates to the specific occupations you have listed. Enter that evaluation on the lines corresponding to these occupations.

Next, enter your evaluation of your *Study Efficiency* as it relates to the various occupations on the corresponding lines.

Then review Section IV, *(Taking Stock of Your Academic Achievement and Ability).* Again, record your evaluations of these factors related to the several occupations you have listed.

Continue the same type of evaluations of Sections V, VI, VII, etc.—through Section X, *Occupational Facts.*

If this process has omitted any factor which seems important to you in your planning, enter that factor in the section marked "Other," and evaluate it in the same manner for each occupation considered.

NOTE: Throughout this process, remember that any kind of relevant information may warrant different ratings for different occupations.

COLUMN 5—TENTATIVE FINAL EVALUATION: To make similar $+$, $-$, or 0 ratings for your Tentative Final Evaluation, you must carefully weigh your evaluations of all the relevant information in order to make a decision regarding each occupation. This evaluation would be easy if it were simply a matter of adding pluses and minuses; but the process is not that simple, for some kinds of relevant information are more important than are others in determining realistic occupational plans for yourself.

Enter in this column your Tentative Final Evaluation for each occupation—*the best evaluation you can make with the information you have available at the present time.*

COLUMN 6—COUNSELOR COMMENT: In this column are listed several statements and questions which your counselor might make in response to your evaluations. He will designate his responses to various parts of your Summary and Evaluation by using the numbers corresponding to these statements.

You can write your responses alongside his comments or on the blank parts of this sheet.

NAME _____   DATE _____

SUMMARY AND EVALUATION SHEET FOR VOCATIONAL PLANNING

NOTE: Pulling together all of the information for planning is a hard job, but this sheet will be of considerable assistance to you in doing so.

CODE FOR COLUMN 3:

(1) Graduate or Professional school degree beyond college.
(2) College degree.
(3) Two year college (academic or vocational program).
(4) Technical, business, or specialized school.
(5) Military services schooling.
(6) Apprenticeship or on-the-job training.
(7) No particular educational requirements.
(8) Other (explain).

COLUMN 4

RELEVANT INFORMATION

How do you evaluate yourself regarding each of these kinds of information you have gathered for each of the occupations listed?

Use these ratings:
$+$ supports this plan
0 neutral or indeterminant
$-$ contradicts this plan
$?$ need more information

COLUMN 1	COLUMN 2	COLUMN 3	Study Time	Study Efficiency	Achievement, High School	Achievement, College	Work Experience	Leisure Experience	Other's Opinions	Measured Interests	Expressed Interests	Occupational & Educ. Facts	Other
OCCUPATIONAL GROUPS	OCCUPATIONS WITHIN EACH GROUP	REQUIRED EDUCATION OR TRAINING											
(Refer to Groups on Your Interest Sheets)	(Be Specific Enough to Evaluate Each)	(Use the Codes from Upper Left Corner of This Sheet)											

MODEL OF THE EPS PROCESS (cont.)

Figure 11 (3)

COLUMN 6

COUNSELOR COMMENT

1. Occupational groups seem confused; check Section VIII.
2. This title is too general to evaluate accurately; try to be more specific.
3. Is this the only type of education that will permit you to enter this occupation?
4. What college majors would be appropriate for this field?
5. Is this a realistic evaluation?
6. This doesn't follow from your earlier evaluation, does it?
7. How might the discrepancy between your measured and expressed interest affect your success in this field?

8. What further information do you need?
9. Why have you evaluated these occupations differently?
10. How realistic is this occupation for you?
11. What would be a beginning or entry job that would prepare you for this occupation?
12. This looks like a sound evaluation.
13.

COLUMN 5
TENTATIVE
FINAL
EVALUATION
(+, 0, ?, -)

MODEL OF THE EPS PROCESS (*cont.*)
Figure 12 (1)

NAME_____   DATE_____

CHOICE OF PLANS AND TAKING ACTION ON THEM

NOTE: On your Summary and Evaluation Sheet (the fold-out form) you have made your best evaluations of the educational and vocational plans which you have analyzed through this Problem Solving Process.

The next step in the process is to *convert your evaluations into actions*. Analysis and evaluation are of little benefit unless they can be converted into action.

Looking at the occupations which you have evaluated in your Summary and Evaluation Sheet, which three do you regard as realistic plans for yourself?

1.   For which occupational plan are you *best suited*?

2.   For which occupational plan are you *next best suited*?

3.   For which occupational plan are you *next best suited*?

4.   *What steps can you take* to prepare yourself further for your No. 1 plan? (education, summer experiences, part-time job, etc.)

5.   *What steps can you take* to prepare yourself further for your No. 2 plan? (education, summer experiences, part-time job, etc.)

6.   *What steps can you take* to prepare yourself further for your No. 3 plan? (education, summer experiences, part-time job, etc.)

MODEL OF THE EPS PROCESS *(cont.)*
Figure 12 (2)

7. *Possibility of not completing college:* More than 50% of university students do not graduate. If this should become the case with you, what effect would this have on:

    a.   Your No. 1 plan (and your education or training for it)?

    b.   Your No. 2 plan (and your education or training for it)?

    c.   Your No. 3 plan (and your education or training for it)?

8. You have now gone through the Problem Solving Steps by applying them to your own vocational and educational planning.

9. Is there anything missing at this time that you need to consider and add into your planning? If so, what?

10. If there is, what can you do to consider it in the same way and incorporate it into your planning?

11. Is it accurate to say that your next steps are to pursue your No. 1 plan with No. 2 and No. 3 plans respectively in reserve should you need them?

    _____Yes   _____No   _____Uncertain

12. If you indicate "No" or "Uncertain", how would you describe your next steps?

MODEL OF THE EPS PROCESS (*cont.*)
Figure 12 (3)

13. Remember that your evaluations and planning should be regarded as *the best plan that can be made at this time*. As you accumulate more experience—such as through taking action on the plans, receiving grades from another completed semester, etc., your plans should be reviewed in light of your added experience. If your plans need to be changed, fine—*you have learned a process* for reconsidering them.

    If they do not need to be changed, fine. Then you have that much more assurance that your earlier plan was a sound one. But this periodic test of your plans is important.

14. Are you satisfied with the outcome of your Problem Solving Process?

    _____Yes   _____No   _____Other   If not, why not?

    What further efforts can you make at this point to deal with this?

Confrontation

THE TRADITIONAL WELL-TRAINED counselor learns to understand the world as it is seen through his client's eyes. If he understands that world correctly, he is able to describe the thoughts and feelings of his client in ways congruent with the client's perceptions. The ability to understand a client and to communicate that understanding to the client is an extremely important skill for any counselor to learn. It is the logical first step of many counseling encounters.

For the benefit of the client, however, there come times when it is not sufficient to continue viewing the world from the client's frame of reference. There are times when the client needs to see himself from some other vantage point. The view of one's own behavior from the inside looking out is quite different than it is from the outside looking in. Having the advantage of both points of view can benefit the client's cognitive structuring of his own behavior and the environment in which he operates.

Confrontation methods are purposefully designed to give the client an alternative point of view. They enable him to see himself and his own behavior from the point of view of other people with whom he comes in contact. Some confrontation methods appear to be rude and unmannerly. Members of a group may tell each other exactly why they do not like one another. If the group has been prepared for this kind of revelation and if it is held within a context where alternative responses can be learned and supported, then it is possible for such unmannerly confrontation to have a rather quick and beneficial effect.

Without adequate preparation and without an opportunity

for alternative learning and positive reinforcement, however, rude confrontations may degenerate into a series of insults arousing hostility, defensiveness, and resistance to change. Confrontation can be either extremely beneficial or extremely harmful depending upon how well it is handled by the counselor.

Confrontation is particularly beneficial in situations where the client does not know that his behavior is inadequate. The client may think that his own behavior is as good as it can possibly be and that his troubles can be attributed to other factors over which he has no control. More frequently the client is simply ignorant about the consequences of his own behavior because he has never had an opportunity to observe himself as others see him. The two articles in this section offer some intriguing solutions to these problems.

Walker, in Article 37, describes a technique called "Pounce," a method of helping clients learn that they are not only responsible for their own employment problems, but that they can do something constructive about them. "Pounce" takes the form of group counseling in which the group confronts each member with the fact that he is giving rationalizations for his lack of employment. The group members reinforce each other for being able to describe their difficulties in terms of behavior they can take to overcome the problems.

Prazak, in Article 38, describes how clients can learn specific job-seeking skills once they have been "pounced upon" sufficiently to desire employment interviews. The confrontation methods include not only frank evaluations by other clients in group sessions, but the use of video tape and Polaroid cameras. The use of television and photography to provide accurate feedback of appearance, behavior, and mannerisms is a refreshing innovation. The eloquent objectivity of the method itself can break through the hardened defenses of some of the most obstinate clients. The confrontation methods are followed by specific training in substitute behaviors and liberal doses of positive reinforcement for the improvements that take place.

Confrontation methods offer one hopeful step in answer to Robert Burns' famous plea:

> Oh wad some power the giftie gie us
> To see oursels as others see us!
> It wad fra monie a blunder free us,
> An' foolish notion.

37

"POUNCE": LEARNING TO TAKE RESPONSIBILITY FOR ONE'S OWN EMPLOYMENT PROBLEMS

Robert A. Walker[1]
MINNEAPOLIS REHABILITATION CENTER

At the Minneapolis Rehabilitation Center we see many people who have been out of work for a long time. Such people often have adopted a variety of socially acceptable explanations of why they are not working. While these reasons may not be accurate, they are necessary for maintaining self-esteem since some explanation has to be given to neighbors and friends who daily march to work. Some of the more common rationalizations promoted by our clients and supported by others are that "there are no jobs" and that "no one hires you without work experience." Other clients mention a variety of discriminatory ploys such as race, age, or a physical handicap. Over a period of time these reasons are so well supported by others that they become part of a client's repertoire of responses to the question, "Why aren't you working?"

REPLACING INSOLVABLE PROBLEMS WITH ACHIEVABLE GOALS

Although it is true that the excuses clients give are often indirectly related to getting a job, it is distressingly apparent that many of the problems listed are insolvable, even by the most imaginative of counseling approaches. Concentration on these problems not only wastes both counselor and client time, but also deflects the counseling program away from critical and treatable problems which are directly related to why the client is unemployed. A common result is that the counseling interviews lack any real content since both the defensive client and the relationship-sensitive counselor are reluctant to grapple with some of the client's more

---

[1] Appropriate credit must be given to Janice Arndt Prazak and Neal Rogat, both accomplished Pouncers and co-developers of the system.

unappetizing but critical behavior. Such a situation allows the client to sail blissfully through counseling services, talking about insolvable problems, and later to lose the job because neither counselor nor client was willing to face the fact that the client could not take orders from bosses without blowing up.

Experienced counselors have long relied on confrontation as the technique of choice for raising problems which clients find difficult to face. However, this technique requires the counselor to be aware of just what the problem is, to be able to state the problem so that the client can understand it, and to be willing to confront the client with problems that may jeopardize the treasured "relationship."[2]

From the client's viewpoint, agencies too often assume that the counselor is an effective social reinforcer, and that the client sees and accepts him as a person of some consequence. The latter requirement has become more apparent and less attainable as government-sponsored counseling programs reach out for clients whose acceptance of the counselor's opinions is minimal. Because these clients often see the counselor as a representative of the establishment, his reinforcing capabilities and subsequent effect on client behavior are limited.

A final factor which makes it difficult for professional staff to use confrontation is the dedication counselors have for trying to understand unemployment in psychological or medical terms. Both terms are of limited use since they do not explain why people do not work, nor are the problems readily treated. The psychological model produces an endless number of insightful statements. Many of these may not be at all related to not working (for example, "this client has tenuous relationships") and, furthermore, the conditions as stated are incredibly resistant to treatment. Another favorite gambit of rehabilitation counselors is to use the medical model to describe their clients' unemployment. The use of this diagnostic construct neatly restricts the counselor's service by insisting that the client is unemployed because he is a paraplegic. If one accepts this statement as a proper vocational diagnosis, then his only recourse as a counselor is to counsel away the damaged spinal cord, as that is the reason which described why the paraplegic is not working.

In summary then, the problems that stimulated the development of the technique called Pounce were: (1) the tendency of our clients to give insolvable problems as reasons for their unemployment, thereby avoiding the real reasons, (2) the hesitancy of counselors to initiate realistic con-

[2] Editors' Note: The "relationship" advocated by Carl Rogers and others is built by the counselor's understanding the client's problems from the client's point of view. If, however, the client's point of view is constructed of elaborate rationalizations for not taking any constructive action, some alternative technique is needed. A helpful relationship can be built in more than one way.

frontation, (3) the failure of clients to accept counselor information when it was unpleasant, and (4) the absence of any system that operationally explains why it is that people are unemployed.

In correcting such a wide range of problems, staff members of the Minneapolis Rehabilitation Center first developed a list of those vocational problems which were felt to be critical to both getting and keeping a job. Two criteria had to be met before any problem was included on this list: First, by consensual agreement the problem had to be of such importance that unemployment would persist if it remained unsolved. Second, the terms used to label the problem could be used independently by various staff members on the same client with virtually perfect agreement. This second criterion demanded that the problems be defined operationally and that specific behaviors be used whenever possible. The result of employing these two criteria was that the center's staff reviewed and tested hundreds of items through a variety of procedures. Finally, a list of 12 problems was agreed on which, when used in a patterned interview, would describe operationally what changes were necessary if a client was to obtain and keep a job. These critical vocational behaviors and the frequency with which each was encountered in a sample of 60 clients were as follows:

1. Inappropriate job objective—25 percent
2. No job objective—50 percent
3. Does not look for work frequently enough—80 percent
4. Cannot explain skills to an employer—85 percent
5. Poor personal appearance (grooming and clothing) and inappropriate interview mannerisms—40 percent
6. Inability to explain problems such as age, disability, lengthy unemployment, and so forth, in the job interview—90 percent
7. Excessive tardiness—25 percent
8. High absenteeism rate—25 percent
9. Inability to get along with supervisors—35 percent
10. Inability to get along with co-workers—30 percent
11. Does not produce enough work (primarily consistency of effort)—15 percent
12. Does not produce quality work—15 percent

CLIENTELE

The list of employment behaviors felt to be critical to successful employment by our staff and stated in operational terms enabled the center to find out quickly why a person was not working. The next difficulty was finding a process which would extinguish the client's tendency to offer insolvable problems as reasons for not working and to get him to state (prior to his receiving any service) one or more of the 12 treatable reasons why he was not employed.

Types of Clients

The ages of the clients surveyed showed a bimodal distribution with peaks occurring at ages 20 and 40. About one third were being supported by welfare, and their socioeconomic level was generally low. Almost half had a physical disability which had some effect on vocational planning. The primary problems met in this population were in the psychological and social areas. Almost half of the group had had a psychiatric diagnosis and slightly less than half had received prior services for emotional problems, mostly with poor results. Lack of family support, drinking problems, and criminality (33 percent) were often seen. Personality testing with the MMPI showed deviant scores on scale four (psychopathic deviate) at a rate of eight times the expected frequency. Poor work references and a history of many jobs of short duration with long periods of unemployment between jobs were frequent. The average client had been out of work six months, even though there was a surplus of jobs in the community. Although almost all our clients had been through counseling programs of one kind or another, their self-defeating behaviors and unemployment had persisted; their commitment to employment was minimal and few of them saw themselves as having to go through an agency program just to get a job. Thus, teasing out the correct problems from clients and getting the client to accept them were not simple matters.

As might be predicted in this population, when confronted with traditional techniques concerning the real reasons they were out of work, our clients continued to insist that their problems could be attributed to, for instance, lack of a high school diploma, despite assurances that the average person in the labor force has less than 12 years of schooling. The solution to these many problems was the development of a three-component program lasting three days. The program was run by carefully selected staff members who: (1) systematically diagnosed clients' problems, (2) presented certain types of agency information, and (3) relied on other clients to prepare the subject for the services available in the agency. The use of clients to prepare other clients was based on the simple premise that clients would have more impact on each other than professional persons would have on them. Pounce is only one dimension of the preparation component, but it is the key program in producing acceptable reasons from the client as to why he is not working. Acceptable reasons are those which the client can understand and which the agency can realistically treat. The treatment services for these treatable problems usually last from two to six weeks and begin immediately after the three-day program.

Selection of Clients

Two procedures are used to select clients for Pounce, and all clients selected must meet both criteria. First, one has to find out how the client explains his unemployment. Clients who provide nontreatable problems or inappropriate reasons to explain unemployment or say they don't know why they are unemployed are considered prime candidates. Some of the unacceptable reasons include the following: "There are no jobs," "Employers won't hire me because I have a physical disability," "I am a Negro," "I am too young, too old," and so forth; "I have been in a state hospital, penal institution," and so forth; "I don't know what kind of work I can do" (not always an incorrect statement); "I can't seem to find a job I like," "I can't get a job because I have no work experience, no high school diploma," and so forth. Approximately 90 percent of all clients state one or more untreatable problems as the primary reason they are not working.

The second selection criterion involves ability to profit from Pounce. Shortly after beginning Pounce, it was felt that the severely retarded, brain-injured, mentally ill, and psychopathic personalities were poor candidates. In the confusion of scheduling for the program, a number of clients entered Pounce who, the staff felt, could not gain from the program. Surprisingly, many of these clients were able to make considerable use of the program, and it was found that the staff could vary the degree of Pounce ("light" versus "traumatic" Pounce) and protect clients who are usually seen as being fragile. The term "fragile" deserves some explanation. Because of the hard-nosed characteristic of the staff used in Pounce, it was originally felt that anxious clients would literally collapse when "Pounced" upon, and the staff would end up treating more problems than they had originally expected. As experience grew and staff capabilities increased, rejection of clients for Pounce was primarily due to their inability to learn because of mental confusion or severe retardation (those with an IQ below 70). In effect, clients who can listen and learn facts about working and not working are good candidates. Clients with psychopathic personalities, although very difficult to Pounce upon because they often lie, are excellent "Pouncelors" and can often assess with surprising accuracy, better than many counselors, why a person is not working. However, until some experience has been gained in Pounce, clients with approximately average learning ability and those who are obviously in touch with reality make the best trial group. Approximately 75 percent of all clients seen at the center enter Pounce.

THE POUNCE PROGRAM

In order to use Pounce effectively, it is necessary to understand the entire format, since other program systems are all carefully sequenced and inter-related. The program is run with groups of six to eight clients who have been selected for the reasons described earlier. Selection takes place at the intake interview which occurs two or three weeks prior to Pounce.

First Day

The key for a successful Pounce session depends almost entirely on how well the clients are prepared on the first day. The times given for each unit will vary to some extent. It is important that each topic be mastered by the group even if more time is needed before moving on to another subject.

HALF HOUR

The general purpose is to help the clients understand that they are meeting in a group so that they will be able to help each other in the program. Acceptance of this idea provides a partial rationale for Pounce on the second day.

HALF HOUR

Members introduce themselves and talk about such things as families, hobbies, hometown, and so forth. The first hour should help the clients see that they will help each other "solve" their problems and that they are very much like one another. The purpose is to make them feel relaxed and to develop some group bonds.

45 MINUTES

There is a presentation of reasons for being unemployed which are unacceptable to the center and a discussion of these reasons. Blackboards, handouts, and other visual aids are very helpful. Clients are rather surprised to find out that their commonly stated reasons are considered by the center to be incorrect.

45 MINUTES

Reasons are presented which are acceptable to the center and discussion of these reasons takes place. This list is similar to the 12 critical vocational behaviors listed earlier except that the problems are stated as personal questions (for example, "Do you look for work?"). The first two questions are broken down as follows: Do you know what skills you have? What kind of job can you learn to do? How good are your basic skills (reading, arithmetic, and so forth)? Do you know about what kinds of jobs there are? What kinds of jobs do you like to do? Do you understand your physical capacities? This procedure enables the client to choose a good reason that explains his unemployment. Clients usually pick problems such as not being able to explain skills and are not willing to admit such problems as a personal appearance that is blatantly grubby.

THREE HOURS

Clients are informed of services available in the center—what they are, what they do, and types of problems they work on. Discussion of topics such as tests, teams, emphasis on the fact that "you are the one who is unemployed," training versus direct job placement, how to get the best service from the staff, this is what a vocational counselor and social worker does, this is how the workshop operates, and so forth. Much effort is directed toward personalizing this information for the clients since they generalize poorly and have difficulty applying factual information to their particular problems.

Apart from specific information, general themes are also established and interjected throughout the day. Two of the most common themes are the importance of asking questions and giving information. Clients sent to the center are often quite passive and fail to seek and use feedback from the staff. Since information is essential in life planning, clients are continually confronted with the necessity to do things such as asking questions and giving the staff information. A final theme involves action instead of talk. Since many of our referrals have already been through many community services without any benefits, they have learned to play the "great insight–no action" game with great skill. Indeed, their verbal psychological insights are accurate and penetrating, but it is quite clear that the insight has not translated itself into behavior. In its simplest form the staff continually states, "Quit talking and do something."

ONE HOUR

Why aren't you working? Group discussion, some minimal confrontation, and continual referring back to good versus bad reasons and agency resources.

At the end of the first day the client should begin to feel comfortable in the group and recognize that his problems are quite similar to those of other group members. He should have tentatively begun to understand that his problems are different from what he first thought they were, and that saying what the "real problems" are is important. As yet, he is still not willing to admit certain types of problems (for example, "I drink too much and get fired because of it."). Good responses are selectively reinforced throughout the session.[3] Typically, bad reasons are ignored but never supported. Finally, the client should have a good understanding of what the center services are for and should begin to see that getting back to work is his own personal responsibility and not that of the center.

Many clients are poor learners and fail to understand that "new think" is a necessity. Constant repetition and manipulation of other clients so that they extinguish bad responses and support good responses goes on continually. Group techniques which force the clients to respond and to come up with "good" answers and which explain how agency services will help "good" problems but not "bad" problems are an absolute necessity. A straight lecture of factual information works poorly.

Toward the end of the first day it usually is necessary to raise the group's anxiety level to promote more intensive and personal participation. One method is to ask a question concerning how many in the group think they will be going to work after leaving the center. Universally, all clients say they will be working. After a long and deadly silence the staff person announces with dramatic effect that half of the group will not work and of the few that will go to work, at least one person will lose his job within 30 days. Clients are typically stunned at these agency base-rate statistics and stare at each other in disbelief. Finally, one or more clients ask why it is that everyone will not go back to work. The staff person, using a precise tone of voice coupled with a withering stare, announces that those who will remain unemployed will do so because they will not admit their problems nor use the agency services to help themselves. Clients often retort that they do want to work on their problems but they are not sure what they are. This subject usually is terminated by the staff person saying with an air of mystery that by this time tomorrow each of you will know what his problem is. No further discussion is held on this topic and the group is either terminated for the day or switched to another subject.

Second Day

As mentioned earlier, the ideal size of a group is from six to eight clients. Fewer than five clients is difficult, because the clients do not play the game quite as well in a small group. More than eight clients creates

[3] Editors' Note: In this setting the goal of counseling is to obtain employment for the client. Both client and counselor give verbal assent to the same goal although the client may have mental reservations and believe the goal is unattainable. A "good response" is now defined by the counselor, not necessarily the client, as a response likely to move the client toward the goal. The client may not at first see the relationship between a "good response" and the goal.

time problems and places a good deal of personal stress on the staff person running the program. Pounce begins early on the second day by a quick review of the first day's main points.

The main points to review prior to Pounce are that the agency can help good problems but not bad ones, that each client has to help one another to see what the real problem is and finally, that half will not go to work because of failure to admit what the real problem is and to be willing to do something about it.

INTRODUCTION

"We are going to play a game today which we think will help you. The game is called Pounce. I will be the Pouncer and one of you at a time will come to the front of the group and be the Pouncelee. I will be asking each of you some questions about why you aren't working (remember the good and bad reasons why people don't work?), and what you are going to do about it while you are here in the agency. The rest of you will be Pouncelors. (Explain similarity between Counselor and Pouncelor.) When I finish asking one of you questions, I want each of you Pouncelors to tell the Pouncelee what's wrong—why he's not working and what he has to do about it before he can go back to work."

Careful selection of the first Pouncelee is important to get the game off to a good start. Clients who glibly state a number of obviously inappropriate reasons for not working and whom the group feels comfortable in pouncing on are ideal. The session is tape recorded so that the clients can listen to their performance on the third day if necessary.

SAMPLE DIALOGUE

The client sits in a special chair close to the Pouncer (staff person). For 10 to 20 minutes, the Pouncer asks the client a number of specific questions based primarily on the last 10 of the 12 "good reasons" for not working. A good general first question is "Why aren't you working?" or "What are you going to do while you're here?" A brief sample of some questions which occur during Pounce and typical client and staff responses follows:

Question: Why aren't you working?
Client (A): I have a medical problem.
Staff   : We can't fix it here. You better see your doctor.
Client (B): I have a bad back.
Staff   : Fifteen percent of people now working have bad backs. How did they get jobs?

Client (C): I can't find a job I'm interested in.
Staff   : Do you think everyone who is working likes their job?
Client (D): No one hires you without work experience.
Staff   : If that were true, no one would ever work.
Client (E): No one will hire me because I'm too old.
Staff   : Do you think we can make you young again? Maybe we can change your birth certificate and that will take care of the problem.
Client (F): There are no jobs.
Staff   : That's right. All those jobs in the want ads are phony.
Client (G): I don't know where to look.
Staff   : (Hand him the phone book)—Check the Yellow Pages and away you go—we like simple problems like that.
Client (H): I don't know what I can do with my bad arm.
Staff   : All day long you reach, grab, and lift things, but you say you don't know what you can do?
Client (I): No one will hire me because I'm Negro.
Staff   : Just how do you think we can handle that problem?

Question: Have you been looking for work?
Client (A): Yes.
Staff   : Then I'm sure you can give me the names of three places you went to last week.
Client (B): No.
Staff   : How do you expect to get a job if you never look?

Question: How would you explain to an employer that you could work as a (provide client with a job title)?
Client   : I'd tell them I could do a good job.
Staff   : Well, Pouncelors, would you hire him?

Question: Do you think the way you're dressed anyone would hire you?
Client   : I suppose they would.
Staff   : Ask the Pouncelors about that one.

Question: Do you always fidget that much in a job interview?
Client   : Yes, I get nervous.
Staff   : Do you think employers like to hire nervous people?

Question: How would you explain the fact that you have been in a state hospital for six years?
Client   : I would tell them that I was sick.
Staff   : Employers won't hire sick people. Everybody knows they can't work.

Question: Have you had any trouble in getting to work on time, or miss-
ing days?
Client   : No.
Staff   : With those qualities what are you doing in a rehabilitation center?

Question: How do you get along with bosses or co-workers?
Client   : Fine.
Staff   : Then how come you lost so many jobs?

Question: Are you a hard worker? Get a lot done and good quality stuff
too when you're working?
Client   : Oh, yes.
Staff   : If you're that great, how come you're not working?

GROUP INVOLVEMENT

These brief examples of client questions and staff responses show the
directness of the confrontation technique. During the course of the interview, it is usually a good idea to bring in other clients for comments and
to give them a chance to ask questions. The essential ingredient in the
procedure is that the staff member must ask questions and respond in a
way that makes bad responses obvious to the Pouncelors. If the staff
member is overly subtle, clients will fail to see the real reasons why the
Pouncelee is not working and therefore be unable to Pounce. Once the
"interview" is over, other clients are asked "Why isn't he working?" If
the technique has been handled well, other clients will be able to state
with surprising accuracy why the Pouncelee isn't working. They also ask
the Pouncelee other questions to develop other "pounceable" issues and
candidly offer him suggestions as to what to do about it. Some of the
more common statements raised by Pouncelors are as follows: "He never
looks for a job; that's what's wrong." "He uses his bad back as a crutch."
"He don't want to work—he's a lazy guy." "She looks so sloppy, I wouldn't
ever hire her." "If he doesn't stop drinking he'll never work." A sample of
suggestions offered by other clients is: "He ought to get out and find out
about jobs." "He shouldn't start the program because he doesn't want to
work." "Spend less time watching TV." "Quit feeling sorry for yourself
and do something." The rapid give and take and the participation rate of
clients are a continual surprise. Clients who have been pounced usually
are the best Pouncelors and are quite aggressive in confronting other
clients. The point of view expressed by the statement (made on the first
day), "You're in a group to help each other," provides a rational basis
for much of the Pounce session. Clients seem to enjoy the game, and a

great deal of laughing and joking takes place. They are reluctant to take coffee breaks and are unaccountably eager to sit in the "hot seat."

In order that other clients clearly see that the Pouncelee has made a mistake in explaining his unemployment, a number of simple ploys are used. When the client has made a bad response such as, "There are no jobs," the Pounce staff member can reply in a variety of ways like: "He's right; no one who lives in St. Paul works"; or "As a matter of fact no one ever quits a job who lives in that town." The technique is one of expanding the statement to the point of absurdity so that the other clients can see it clearly. Simply repeating the statement with appropriate dramatic pauses also highlights the problem for the clients. The Bela Lugosi ploy works well. Inappropriate client responses are met with raised eyebrows, a slight leer, and a glance toward other clients that clearly indicates the jugular vein has been reached. Throwing it back to the group with comments, stated in acid tones, like: "Well, what do you think of that one?" or "I hope you Pouncelors heard that one," also works well. Anxiety-producing quotations of statistics such as "80 percent of those people now working don't like their jobs," usually are quite unsettling. Repeating agency base-rate statistics such as "Only one of you will go back to school for training" (many clients see training as a panacea for unemployment) are helpful. A question commonly used, which never fails to bring out a variety of group responses, is, "Will he be one of the people in here who won't go to work?"

Somewhere in the process a discussion is usually held on "why work?" During this time, the staff member presents an airtight argument which clearly proves that one does not have to work and that, freed of such an odious responsibility, one can really enjoy a number of life pleasures. The staff member then gives advice about how to get along without a job and how to get on high-payment welfare programs. This discussion typically ends with the staff member commenting that it is certainly gracious of those who will be working ("only half of those in this room") to support those who will not work. Clients who have no intention of working and have been found out usually earn hostile glances from other clients.

The second day is completed when every client has been through Pounce. In some cases, if the client persists in responding with the wrong reasons, his portion of the tape recording is played back in front of the group. One method used when this occurs is to write down the real reason offered by other clients on a blackboard. At this point the group is highly verbal and quite adept at pouncing on a client who has not played the game well. The Pouncelee has almost no recourse, and he will usually produce appropriate verbal behavior because of the pressures of the group.

Third Day

The last day has less structured content and is developed for the most part to pick up and review those problems that the group has not handled well. A technique called "True Confessions," a session conducted like an Alcoholics Anonymous meeting in which the client must admit to his personal failures, has been used on occasion. Task assignments to demonstrate one's willingness to go to work are sometimes given. An example would be telling a client to get information about a specific job. Replaying the tape recording for each client when alone or in front of the group has also been done.

"MY SERVICE CONTRACT"

The primary task for the client on the last day is to write his service contract. This form, filled out by the client, requires him to state with precision why he is not working and what services in the center he needs to use. The contract is a mimeographed form titled "My Contract with the Minneapolis Rehabilitation Center." It contains questions which the client must answer. The questions are designed to find out whether the client can state his problems and select the right staff person to work with on the problem. Some of the questions in the contract are: "What are the *real* reasons you are not working?" "What problems will your vocational counselor help you with?" "What problems might you have in keeping a job?" Following this are several statements to the effect that when the contract is signed, the client has decided to go to work and to co-operate with the center in his program.

Each contract is reviewed by a staff person with the client for corrections, some of which are inevitable. Clients are able to say their problems much better than they can write them. The contract is then given to the staff member who will be working with the client with additional comments written on it by the Pounce staff. This procedure insures that the client and the treatment staff are fully aware of what the task is, what services are going to be needed, and what problems still have not been accepted by the client.[4]

PROBLEMS AND POSSIBILITIES

Regardless of the close structure and the simplicity of the concepts involved, learning is a difficult task for most clients. It is not unusual

[4] Editors' Note: For other examples of behavior contracts see Articles 15, 16, and 17.

to get excellent group participation and accurate statements of the problem and still have clients write their service contracts in an inappropriate fashion. The results of the program are unquestionably variable, and Pounce is no panacea for every client. Some comfort can be gained from the truism that if clients responded quickly, they would not be in the center in the first place. Professional counselors and caseworkers who refer a client to the center are sometimes shocked to hear that he is handled in such an apparently rude fashion. When interpreting the program, one has to emphasize the results gained from the program rather than the process itself. It is also helpful to have referring sources watch a Pounce session since it is obvious that many clients do enjoy the game and see it as helping them.

Applicability for Other Programs

Although the format might have to be modified to some extent because of the ways in which clients are referred and the objective of this agency, the Pounce technique can be used in many settings. State rehabilitation programs, rehabilitation centers, sheltered workshops, Youth Opportunity Centers, Job Corps Camps, Title V Work-Training Programs under the Economic Opportunity Act, and a variety of employment-oriented Community Action Programs are all potential users. Further use of the technique might reveal possibilities for mental health settings and institutional programs for criminal offenders and the mentally ill. The primary prerequisite is to define operationally what behaviors you want from the client. Administrators will be pleased to hear that the program is one of high volume and low cost which can utilize staff members with bachelor degrees and conserve personnel at the master's-degree level.

Staff

A most apt description of a person who can run Pounce is someone who can look a Negro squarely in the eye and say, "We can't change the color of your skin—what's the real reason why you're not working?" The technique is not temperamentally suited for many professional staff. Other desirable personal qualities include someone who can resist behaving in a sympathetic or accepting manner and yet whom clients will see as eager to help them get back to work. The staff person has to have the instincts of a barracuda and be willing aggressively to strip the client of the rationalizations that prevent him from working on the actual reasons for his not being employed. Originally the program was manned by counselors and caseworkers with master's degrees who were selected for their ability to be objective and to criticize clients openly. Since the program content is now structured to the point that it is more science than art, people with only a bachelor's degree are being employed. Having a master's degree offers no clear advantage in providing a good program. It should also be mentioned that Pounce tends to be physically exhausting because the staff person needs to be with the clients almost full time for three days. Responses to clients' statements are programmed to the point where monotony sets in, and it may be necessary to rotate staff to maintain an atmosphere of spontaneity. Early efforts tend to be somewhat discouraging until the technique is mastered.

EVALUATION

The primary purpose of Pounce is to get the client to produce appropriate verbal and written responses about why he is not working.[5] The underlying assumption is that clients will tend to work with staff on these problems if they are admitted and that a good outcome will result if both client and counselor are clearly aware of what needs to be done and are concerned with realistic and critical client goals.

A primary source of concern for the staff was the possible harmful effect to a client from an often unpleasant and uncomfortable experience. However, predictions that clients would clam up or leave the program have not been borne out. As a matter of fact, most clients are fascinated by the program and are almost reluctant to leave at the end of a good day of Pouncing. The clients frequently continue after hours and it is not uncommon to hear clients repeating an attack on a client who refuses to acknowledge that he has not been seeking work. Some clients have been so eager to demonstrate their willingness to seek work after being pounced on that they have gone right out and gotten a job and have never begun the program. Only two out of 250 clients have failed to start the service program because of anger or lack of interest. This frequency is actually less than the drop-out rate which occurred during the first three days of the center's program prior to using Pounce.

Evaluation of the Pounce portion of the three-day program at the center primarily involves a pre- and post-test of the reasons the client gives for unemployment. This form is filled out by the clients. These written statements are compared with the staff's judgment as to why the person is not working. This system enables the Pounce staff to identify the people who did not use the program well and to modify the technique accordingly.

[5] Editors' Note: Actually this is only the immediate goal, but the long-range goal is for the client to take effective action in seeking employment so as to obtain and hold a satisfying position. Ultimately Pounce must be evaluated by assessing the number of satisfactorily employed clients.

One of the benefits noted from the Pounce program was a decline in drop-outs in the service phase. This was especially true for those who drop out because of lack of involvement in the program or because of misunderstanding about what services are available. A reduction of client time (20 percent) in the treatment service phase was felt to be another indicator of client readiness to work on significant problems and of the success of the preparation program. An unusual but rewarding gain was that some clients aggressively sought staff interviews and insisted that the staff member help them with their problems.

As the program matures and as other types of client benefits are more clearly seen, it is likely that a systematic evaluation procedure will be adopted in the hopes of demonstrating that clients profit from services when they know what their problems really are.[6]

38

LEARNING JOB-SEEKING INTERVIEW SKILLS

Janice Arndt Prazak
MINNEAPOLIS REHABILITATION CENTER

One of the first questions asked by many clients who come to the Minneapolis Rehabilitation Center for help with their unemployment problems is, "Will my counselor get me a job?" Most of those who ask this question have been through the revolving door of rehabilitation services several times before. Other counselors have placed them on jobs—jobs which they promptly lost—and they have come to expect direct job placement as an established service of every agency that works with unemployed people. They look surprised and very skeptical when they are told, "We will help you find out what your skills are, and help you to decide what kind of work to look for; but, instead of placing you directly on a job, we will teach you how to look for work on your own."

The center subscribes to the philosophy that providing a temporary solution to alleviate a chronic problem is not good rehabilitation. Instead,

---

[6] Editors' Note: As described here Pounce has much in common with the Synanon Game, a group procedure used by a self-help group called Synanon to treat problems of drug addiction and alcoholism.

the client must be taught more effective ways of solving his own problems so that he can be independent in the future.

Today's unemployed client, plugged into a job through no effort of his own will often be back warming the doorstep tomorrow. If, instead, he is taught to find his own job, he has an investment in keeping it because he involved himself in getting hired. If he loses the job, he then has the ability to find another one independently. It is especially important for clients seen in a rehabilitation setting to learn job-seeking skills because their job turnover rate is twice as high as that of the general working population. Half of the clients who find jobs will lose them or want to change within a few months. Most of the other half will stay on the job less than two years. Even those clients who need direct intervention with the employer by the counselor must be able to represent themselves adequately in a job interview. Job-seeking skills are, therefore, of value to the client all of his working life.

Some clients expect that they will never be able to learn to look for work on their own even though they would like to become independent job seekers. Others, who have enjoyed the luxury of being able to explain away their chronic unemployment by saying, "I went down to that agency, but they didn't get me a job," suddenly realize, when confronted with the idea of independent job seeking, that their comfortable rationalization is about to be taken away from them. They are going to be expected to interview for their own jobs, and if they fail, they have no one to blame but themselves.

Individual counselors do not have the time available that it takes to thoroughly teach a client all he needs to know to produce a good job interview. Even if they did have the time to modify the client's interview behaviors, few counselors are able to objectively assess and identify the specific behaviors that made an interview good, and those which make it poor. Even employers and personnel workers have a difficult time specifying what it is about an individual that makes them want to hire him. From a group of ten applicants with highly similar qualifications for a job one may be chosen because he had something special which impressed the employer. Yet, it is unlikely that the employer could articulate what the chosen applicant said or did that convinced him this one should be hired.

The reason that counselors are unable to critically evaluate the practice, or mock, interviews they have with clients is that they lack an assessment model of appropriate interview behaviors by which to measure the client's performance. Relying on some general guide lines of his own judgment, the counselor's criticism may be a statement to the effect that a client "doesn't talk enough" in the interview, but he is not able to specify just what statements the client should have made. The client can understand that he should talk more but cannot determine for himself what to talk about. The ambiguous suggestion to "talk more" may be interpreted by the client to mean that he should talk about his problems and why he needs a job to support his family. In trying to improve his interviews he may produce more words, but then the counselor tells him that he took too much time and talked about things that were irrelevant. More mock interviews result in some accidental improvement and the client now "sounds right" to the counselor so he is sent out to find a job. Or, the counselor tires of listening to the client's interviews and decides to let him get more practice by visiting employers. Many counselors believe that a client really needs to experience several actual job interviews before he can learn to improve his interviewing skills—that it is impossible to really teach the client to interview in a simulated situation. The result is that the client may use up all the prime job leads in his field while he is bumbling through interviews "for experience." When he finally masters some interviewing skills by trial-and-error learning, he has to resort to less desirable job leads. Being continually rejected he builds up a series of failure experiences which make it increasingly difficult for him to persist in looking for work.[1] The time he spends not getting hired further decreases his chances of ever being hired since the longer he has been on the labor market, the more suspicious employers become, and the less likely they are to offer him a job. It is likely that employers make the decision of whether or not to hire an applicant within the first five minutes of the interview. Therefore, in order to utilize those five minutes effectively the client must either already have developed interviewing abilities, or be taught exactly what to say and when to say it.

IDENTIFYING CRITICAL INTERVIEW BEHAVIORS

Identifying the critical behaviors in employment interviews was a difficult process. Experienced counselors were in disagreement concerning what was appropriate interview behavior. Some counselors, for example, felt that the client should appear for all job interviews dressed in a suit and tie while other counselors maintained that the clients who were applying for unskilled and semiskilled jobs should dress more casually. Some counselors felt that the client should discuss an obvious physical problem only if questioned by the employer; some felt that direct intervention was needed for all individuals with major handicaps. Most of the counselors had difficulty in deciding what a client should say in response to questions about negative factors in his history. Observing employment

---

[1] Editors' Note: Reinforcement and extinction processes operate in job-seeking too. Interviewing without success eventually extinguishes interviewing behaviors.

interviews in industry was of minimal benefit since employers were unable to specify why they hired one individual rather than another. The assessment model was finally constructed by compiling a variety of opinions from counselor and employers and selecting out those specifics which best answered the question, "What behaviors must be presented in an interview in order for an individual to be hired?"[2]

The following assessment model consists of five critical areas of interview behavior which are specifically defined. Using this model, a client's performance can be objectively rated, and the areas where improvement is needed are easily discernible.

1. Ability To Explain Skills

The interviewee must be able to describe his work skills using names of machines or other technical terminology appropriate to the job for which he is applying. He must be able to describe related experiences of training which he has had, and be able to answer the question, "Why should we hire you?" by referring to his skills. He must supply this information within the first five minutes of the interview. He must respond to such ambiguous questions as "Tell me a little about yourself," by citing his work skills and related abilities.

2. Ability To Answer Problem Questions

The interviewee must be able to explain his answers to all questions on the application blank. He must be able to respond to the employer regarding any "negatives" such as hospitalization for physical or emotional illness, prison record, poor job history, little education, age, no experience in job for which he is applying, and so forth. His answers to questions in these areas must end with a positive statement about his being able to do the work despite the problem. If he has an obvious physical handicap, he must mention it within the first two minutes of the interview and state why it does not affect his ability to do the work.

3. Appropriate Appearance and Mannerisms

He must be neat and clean, wearing clothes similar to those worn by people who do the kind of work for which he is applying. He must maintain good eye contact with the interviewer, must refrain from exhibiting nervous mannerisms which distract the interviewer.

[2] Editors' Note: The question lends itself to experimentation. The compilation of opinions may yield some useful approximations, but it would be possible to design a series of experiments to test empirically what kind of applicant responses made favorable impressions with which types of employers.

4. Enthusiasm

This psychological concept is operationally defined as stating sometime during the interview that he wants to work; asking whether there is a possibility of working overtime; or asking whether there is anything special he can do to learn more about the company or about the job while his application is being considered.

5. Fine Points of Interview

He must walk in and out of the interview situation briskly, must have a firm handshake, must ask specific questions about the job, and must use a "call-back" closing ("Would it be all right if I called you on Wednesday to find out about the job?").

TRAINING PROGRAM

The two-day intensive program to teach clients these behaviors uses a behavioral model and multiple delivery systems. One staff person has responsibility for the group. Three to eight clients are referred each week by their counselors. These clients have undergone a workshop evaluation and are ready to enter the labor market.

The major prerequisite for a client starting the job-seeking skills program is that he have a job objective established with the help of his counselor. Much of the content which the client must master in the group is focused around his job objective. He must be able to substantiate his skills by referring to past work experience, experience in a rehabilitation workshop, or training. Knowledge of the job objective enables the staff to individualize the information which the client is provided.

The group begins with the staff helping the clients to discover what kinds of help they are going to need in job seeking. Most of them have had a number of unsuccessful experiences in job interviewing prior to coming to the Center and can identify a major problem that they have had in an interview. Usually it is explaining a physical disability, hospitalization for emotional problems, or incarceration. Rarely do they request help in explaining their skills, improving their appearance, or in general interview techniques. Some participants readily admit the need for help and are eager to get started. Others are more resistive and tend to deny that they need or can use improvement in interviewing.

Most clients have never seen a job interview and have little knowledge of expected interview behavior. Simply telling the client about his mistakes after he has presented a poor interview not only leaves the client on the defensive, but, more important, he may feel the counselor's criticisms are unjust.

Modeling a Desirable Interview

To help the clients in the job-seeking skills group see that they are being dealt a fair game, a video tape of a good model interview is played before they are asked to present an interview. This allows them an opportunity to compare privately what they know of their own skills with the quality interview presented in the video tape.

On the model tape a staff member acts the part of an individual applying for a job as a punch press operator. Demonstrating each of the critical interview behaviors, he explains his skills to the employer, documenting them with past work experience and rehabilitation-center evaluation results. He shows the employer that he is dexterous despite his handicap by taking a book of matches out of his pocket and holding the match in his impaired hand while he lights it. He wears clothing appropriate to the job, looks directly at the interviewer, and refrains from nervous mannerisms. He states that he is interested in working, asks about overtime possibilities, uses a handshake and "call back closing" correctly. Although the interviewee on the tape performs everything correctly, his behavior is not so highly polished that the clients would have difficulty identifying with him, or become frustrated because he was modeling a standard far above their ability to perform.

Playing the video tape gains the immediate attention of even the disinterested group members. Professionals observing the group never cease to be amazed at the amount of information clients are able to learn from a ten-minute model tape.

Time is allowed following the video tape for the group to react to the model. This gives the clients an opportunity to ask questions about what they saw and to make comments. The staff member draws the client's attention to the important interview behaviors illustrated in the model by asking questions relative to the critical areas in the assessment model. Such questions might be: "Did you see how quickly the interviewee told the employer about his skills?" "Did you see how he showed the employer that he could use his artificial hand?" "Did you notice that he asked to call the employer back?"

Clients frequently comment, "I've got to explain some of the same problems he has—if I could learn to do it that well, I'd sure get hired." "I never thought of asking an employer if I could call him back—I think I'll try that next time."

Verbal and nonverbal reinforcement is offered for answers which suggest that the clients are beginning to pick up verbal and motor behaviors from the model which they can use in their own interviews.

Roleplaying and Reinforcement in a Mock Interview

Following the tape discussion the group participants each try a five-minute mock interview on video tape. This allows them an immediate opportunity to practice some of the new behaviors they saw on the model. Condensed job application forms which their counselors have helped them complete provide the basis for interview questions. Taking the role of an employer the group leader asks about their skills for the job and requests additional information about problem areas. Questions are purposefully made difficult to help the client find out what he will need to work on in the group.

Some typical questions are these:

"I see here you didn't work for the last three years, why was that?"

"I notice that you didn't finish high school—we rarely hire people without a high school diploma."

"You put down that you received Workmen's Compensation—my insurance might go up if I hire someone who was injured before on a job."

"I see here you have had emotional problems—we don't hire people who are not in good mental health."

The clients discover that there are many questions which they do not know how to answer, and their anxiety level soars as their answers fall short of the model. At this point even the last doubting Thomas concedes that he needs help in learning how to interview.

Aware of the discrepancies between their interview and the model tape, most clients are highly self-critical. Left for more than a few minutes with this anxiety the embarrassed client would begin building his wall of defensiveness; however, the staff member steps in immediately and verbally reinforces the good portions of the client's interview since most clients demonstrate some techniques which they saw in the model interview tape.[3] The group watches as each member is interviewed, and the staff encourages the group to respond immediately after each interview.

The group has much greater reinforcement value for the client than a professional staff member would have. Members begin to model the good behaviors presented by other clients. Selective reinforcement—for good behaviors only—whets the appetite of the group members, and they become eager to correct poor responses in order to gain more approval.

---

[3] Editors' Note: Positive reinforcement for the good parts is probably as important as getting the client to identify his inadequacies. A little success provides the motivation to overcome the remaining deficiencies.

Teaching Specific Responses

EXPLAINING SKILLS

In the game of "Explaining Skills" the job applicant is holding an ace if he can cite previous work experience in the job goal area. Education or special training is his next highest card, followed by rehabilitation-center training or experience. His poorest suit is having only an aptitude based on information secured from aptitude or intelligence testing. Although weak, this is better than describing no assets at all. Few clients are aware of which cards they hold until they are offered some clues by the staff in the form of questions about skills related to their job goal. A machine operator, for example, would be asked: "Have you ever operated any kinds of machines before?" "Did you ever read blueprints other than at the center?" "Did you take high school drafting?" "Do you have any hobbies where you work with machines?" "Did you work with machines when you were in military service?" "Have you taken any tests where people said you had a good aptitude for mechanical things?"

Sometimes a model tape is shown which illustrates an individual being questioned by staff to find his assets. Each group member is helped to find four or five assets that he can use. These are recorded by him in a special notebook which he uses throughout the group and keeps for later reference. The staff member helps him to assign priorities to the assets and to state the assets in sentence form so it will be easier for him to learn them. His notebook would then contain statements such as these:

"I worked as a mechanic for a year when I was in the Army."

"I operated a Bridgeport Upright Milling Machine at the Rehabilitation Center."

"I do most of the repair work on my car—always have."

Use of sentences helps the client to structure exactly what he must learn to say in the interview. The more specific information he has, such as names of machines and technical terms, the better able is he to convince an employer that he knows something about the job.

An indirect advantage of the game of Explaining Skills is that the counselor and client are forced to choose a job objective which can be well documented in terms of the client's skills and physical abilities and which will not be affected by his limitations. Inappropriate job objectives are, therefore, easily identified and the referring counselor is requested to reconsider the job choice with the client if a rationale for the job objective cannot be established.

Sometimes clients enter the group with two possible job objectives. Rather than forcing these clients arbitrarily to choose one of the possibilities, the group leader helps the individual list the assets he would be able to present for each one, and the choice becomes clear when the client sees which list of assets is longer and would give him more selling power in an interview. A client may still insist on the job choice which is least appropriate for him. He is then asked to select which job he wishes to be interviewed for in the group. Naturally he selects the one for which he has the most assets because this is the easier one for him to present in a mock interview. Invariably, he becomes so committed to this choice that he seeks work in this area when he completes the group. In the process of learning how to convince an employer that he has the best work skills in this particular area, he sells himself as well. He is then no longer held back from job hunting by indecision.

Too often clients fail to understand the value of their assets when job hunting. For many of them a disability has been the ticket which purchased things they needed in the past, for example, eligibility for vocational services. Current publicity encouraging businesses to "hire the handicapped" further deludes the client into thinking that his disability ticket is equally valid when he goes to apply for a job. "Employers hire skills, not handicaps," the group is advised. "No employer will hire you just because you are disabled, but an employer will hire you *in spite of* your disability if you convince him that you have the skills to do the job. It is important for you to learn your skills and talk about them, not your problems."

EXPLAINING PROBLEMS

Having built a foundation of salable assets gives each individual a cushion of dignity, and the group can then proceed to work on Explaining Problems without fearing that any of the clients will be terribly threatened. A completed application blank is used to determine what questions employers may ask which would be difficult for the client to answer because most employers also use the application blank as a basis for the interview. Clients are most vulnerable on questions in the areas of physical or emotional illnesses, imprisonment, age (older or younger than most people in the job), education (much more or less education than most people doing that kind of work), work history (none, gaps, no experience in the job for which he is applying, having been fired), and selective service classification. The client is helped to complete his sample application form at this time in a way that is consistent with his answers to problem questions. He is helped to decide what information must be revealed on the form and what factors are unimportant and need not be recorded. Several general guide lines have been developed by the staff to determine how the client should answer problem questions on the application and in the interview:

(1) Keep answers short, and always end with a postive statement. ("Yes, I have had a little trouble with my back, but the doctor says I can go to work, and I know I can handle this job without any problems.")

(2) If the problem is obvious to the employer, for example, physical handicap or age, introduce it early in the interview without waiting for the employer to ask about it.

   a. "I suppose you are wondering whether my artificial hand affects my work. I lost my hand several years ago so I have had to learn how to do things with it. (Puts coin on table while he talks) As you can see I have no trouble picking up small objects."

   b. "I know you might wonder whether a person my age can do the work. As you can see on the application, I'm 52, but I'm in good health and can work an eight-hour day easily. If I'm hired, I plan to stay on this job—I'm not like the young kids, always looking for greener pastures!"

The object of the game is to turn a problem such as age into an asset. A person who is younger than most people on the job would advertise himself by saying, "I realize I'm young, but I'm anxious to get into a job where I can use my skills and work myself up in the company."

(3) If the individual has a physical problem that is not obvious, or has been in a mental or penal institution, he is usually instructed to leave questions in those areas blank on the application and respond only if asked about them. ("I had some problems with my nerves so my doctor and I decided I should go to a hospital for some help. I'm glad I went—everything's cleared up and I feel fine now.") Other decision rules involve such things as: Never use medical or psychiatric labels—they tend to frighten employers away. Never have the client say he "was sent" to a hospital—it sounds less serious if he participated in the decision.

   If the client has a penal record his only alternative is to admit the mistake. ("I ran around with some bad kids when I was younger and we got into some trouble. I've grown up since then, and I know I won't do anything dumb like that again.")

(4) Too little education: ("I left school to go to work. I wish now that I'd finished; but I'm planning to go to night school to get my diploma. I can read and write, and I know I won't have any trouble doing the work on this job.")

   Too much education (often seen in people with emotional problems who have to downgrade themselves vocationally because they are incapable of utilizing their full intellectual potential): These individuals may choose to omit information about their education beyond high school. If they choose to include the information, they may defend their occupational choice by saying, "I did take some college courses, but I found out that I really didn't like intellectual jobs. I've decided that I would do much better at a job like this.")

(5) Selective Service Classification: ("I have a little problem with my eyes

(or whatever it is). The army didn't want to take a chance on putting me through combat training, but for regular work I am fine.")

(6) Work History: Sometimes a client who has periods of unemployment in his history has worked at part-time jobs during this time and can use this information in the interview to help him sound less chronically unemployed. Self-employment may also be indicated to fill gaps—even if he was only fixing radios in his basement. Women can usually justify periods of unemployment by saying that they were needed at home. The client who was fired or laid off is encouraged to indicate more acceptable reasons for leaving the job such as "Seasonal or temporary work, better hours, better pay, better location, and so forth." If he has to use as a reference a job where he didn't do very well he should forewarn the interviewer by saying, for example, "If you call Mr. Jones at ABC Trucking he will probably tell you that my work wasn't very good; but if you'll check some of my other references, I'm sure you'll find that other employers were well-satisfied with my work."

Each answer is carefully worked out to fit the individual client's situation. The staff always asks the client first whether he knows what he would say in the interview about a certain problem. If his explanation is acceptable, he is encouraged to use it. If not, the staff helps him modify the answer or offers suggestions if the client has no answer. The clients practice their answers to problem questions and their asset explanations in the group, and also in pairs, outside of the group. Verbal repetition is essential since most of them learn poorly when studying written materials by themselves.

MAKING AN ATTRACTIVE APPEARANCE

A major problem was anticipated in getting the client to dress and groom himself appropriately. Cleanliness, neatly pressed clothing, and freshly trimmed hair are not characteristic of the general client population in a rehabilitation center. The grand scheme originally developed to correct the client's behavior in the area of personal appearance included use of a color Polaroid camera to take "before" and "after" pictures. In the first two experimental groups, pictures were taken of each individual in the group on the first day. They were then asked to compare their pictures with the standards of dress outlined in their notebooks according to job area. (Work clothes are described for men and women going into janitorial or factory work. Casual dress is outlined for individuals seeking jobs such as stock clerk, orderly, or entry level clerical. Office clothes are recommended for clerk-typist, receptionist, or retail-sales applicants. Grooming standards and suggestions are also provided in the notebook.) Individuals in the group were requested to return the following day dressed as they would for an interview with the understanding that they would also be video taped. A second picture revealed a remarkable change.

Initially, it was hypothesized that the group was responding to the Polaroid pictures. However, video tape alone was used in subsequent groups to reflect appearance, and except for an occasional problem, group members, who are always aware that they will be on video tape, evidence quality appearance in the group. Viewing the results of their grooming efforts on the television screen is sufficient reinforcement for them to maintain this standard of appearance when they begin looking for work.

The wonders of video tape were further demonstrated when it came to dealing with the problem of mannerisms. Correcting these behaviors is nearly impossible for a counselor using a mock interview in his office. Verbally informing the client of his unnecessary motor movements does not readily correct the behavior since the client himself does not realize he is doing anything out of the ordinary and is unable to see the necessity for correcting the behavior. Even if the inappropriate mannerisms are extinguished the only reinforcement the counselor is able to offer is praise. This reward is seldom sufficient to insure that the new behavior will be strengthened. Under the tension of a real interview situation the client's nervous mannerisms are likely to reappear.

The anxiety of being video taped during a mock interview in the job-seeking group elicits all types of extramotor behaviors from clients. The video monitor is turned so that the client cannot see what is being taped; the camera zooms in to focus on close-ups of wringing hands, jiggling knees, facial grimaces, and use of pencils, jewelry, papers, and so forth as playthings. Skirts that are too revealing, bad posture, and flyaway hair are all appraised by the critical eye of the zoom lens. When these are played back on the video screen, they are greeted by the "star" with disbelief: "Did I really do that?" "Do I really look like that?" Frequently, the individual whose mannerisms were caught by the camera will sit through the replay without saying a word, and no comment is necessary from the staff or the group.[4] However, in the final taping on graduation day the individual, aware that his behaviors fall short of the standard presented in the model, has corrected his own behavior and is rewarded by personal satisfaction with his own image as well as by comments from the group on how much "more confident" he looked.

Surprising behavior changes occur in large numbers of clients seen in the Job Seeking Skills Group. Counselors are amazed to see change take

---

[4] Editors' Note: Confrontation methods are designed to give an individual accurate feedback about himself and his impact on other people. Walker, in Article 37, described ways a counselor could lead a group to give accurate feedback. The use of video tape is in some ways even more powerful since it records faithfully exactly what happened and is undistorted by human bias and misperception.

place in their clients that had not occurred in four weeks of working with them. Many a counselor comments that his client's verbalization of interest in working and willingness to look for work increases substantially after he has been in the group.

EFFECTS OF TRAINING: A CASE STUDY

When Homer entered the group his counselor said, "I doubt that much is going to change with this guy. He has a Workmen's Compensation claim pending, and although he has work skills, I doubt that he is going to go to work until the claim is settled—maybe not even then. He just doesn't have any interest in finding a job."

The "Before" Interview

Interviewer: Good morning, sir, what can we do for you today?
Client: (hesitantly, with downcast eyes, and monotonous voice): I came in to see about a job.
I.: Which job are you interested in; we are hiring for several openings.
C.: Machine operator.
I.: Have you ever done this kind of work before?
C.: No.
I.: What kinds of abilities do you have that would qualify you for this job?
C.: (long pause) I have run a punch press at the rehab center.
I.: You were at a rehabilitation center? Why?
C.: I had a back disease and needed some help in finding a job.
I.: We don't hire people with bad backs—bad for our insurance rates.
C.: Well, I don't think I would have any problems with the back. If you will give me a chance, I'll really work hard.
I.: Do you have any questions for me?
C.: No.
I.: I'll have to see several other applicants, but we'll keep your application on file, and I'll call you.
C.: Thank you. Good-bye.

Homer participated in the two-day job-seeking skills group, had an opportunity to pick up more specific information about his skills, received help in answering problem questions, and was able to practice the total interview and receive positive reinforcement from the group and the worker for learning the right things to say and do in an interview.

The "After" Interview

Interviewer: Good morning, sir, can I help you?

Client: Yes. I'm here to apply for the job of punch-press operator which you advertised in this morning's paper.

I.: Yes . . . Tell me a little about yourself.

C.: I have been a construction worker for several years, and now I want to get into machine work. I had some experience repairing machines while I was in the army. I also went to the Minneapolis Rehabilitation Center where they evaluated my skills, and I found out I am better than average on the punch press.

I.: Why did you go to the rehabilitation center? Do you have a physical problem?

C.: I had a little trouble with my back, but it's all taken care of now and I'm ready to go to work. The rehabilitation center helped me decide what kind of work I wanted to do since I wanted to get out of construction work and into a year-round job.

I.: I don't know if we can hire you—our insurance company might raise our rates if we hired somebody who had received Workmen's Compensation.

C.: I'm registered with the Industrial Commission because of my injury, under the Second Injury Law. This means that if I should hurt my back again, it is likely that this would be paid for out of a special fund and not affect you at all. You can check with the Industrial Commission if you want more information about that.

I.: I might do that—guess I'm not too familiar with the new laws. I see here you didn't work during 1960—what were you doing?

C.: I was upset over some big problems in my family and got real nervous. My doctor and I decided I could use some help for my nerves, so I went to a hospital for a while. They really helped a lot. I don't have any family problem now and haven't needed any pills for my nerves for several years. I feel the best when I'm busy working.

I.: What else can you tell me about yourself?

C.: I operated a 5-ton and a 14-ton punch press at the center. I also can read simple blueprints and use a micrometer so I can do some of my own set up. I am sure that after I've been here for a while I could learn to do most of my own set-up work.

I.: Do you have any questions about the job?

C.: (Client asks and receives answers to such questions as "What shifts are there? Could you tell me a little more about the kind of work you do here? Is there a possibility of working overtime? What is the starting pay? How good are chances for advancement?")

I.:   Thank you for coming in. I have several others to see, and I will call you by the end of the week to let you know.

C.:   Is there a possibility that I could call you? I have some other interviews scheduled and may not be home much during the daytime.

I.:   Yes, you may call me on Friday if you like.

C.:   Thank you. I'll plan to call on Friday.

Homer received much recognition from the group, his counselor, and the staff member for the remarkable behavior change which was evidenced when his first and final interviews were replayed on video tape on "graduation" day. He became so impressed with his newly developed interviewing skills that he decided not to wait for the compensation claim to be settled. Instead, he moved into the job market and was promptly hired as a punch-press operator at a better-than-average salary.

PART **VI**

Multiple Techniques

JOHN MUIR, THE FAMED conservationist, once said that when we "try to pick out anything by itself we inevitably find it hitched to everything else in the universe." Human problems are that way, complex and confounding, influenced by a host of factors known and unknown.

Because of this the behavioral counselor is not hitched to any one technique. To the contrary, the most salient feature of the behavioral approach is the emphasis on a multiplicity of techniques for the multiplicity of client problems. Real and meaningful problems of individuals are multiple. What a person says, what he does, how he thinks, and what he feels interact with his environment, with what others say and think and feel. Problems of clients are expressed covertly and internally as well as overtly and externally. The extremely anxious and shy adolescent, for example, confronted with the situation of having to speak out, reacts internally in terms of physical and thought processes, externally through motor responses and verbalizations (or lack of them). Sometimes the counselor must first reduce the physical stress before the client can effectively deal with thoughts and other feelings. And sometimes the counselor must simultaneously work on altering thoughts, physiological reactions, motor behaviors, and verbalizations. To be effective and efficient in helping clients, the behavioral counselor must draw upon a wide array of techniques. He has no one counseling method, even for clients with the same general problem.

In this respect the behavioral counselor has much in common with a systems analyst who may be helping to explore a complex problem such as training astronauts or designing

429

model cities. Such an analyst continually asks himself, given these objectives and these resources, what are the different methods that can be developed and used in the most effective and efficient way. To do this requires a willingness to behave in very creative ways. One must be able to tolerate some ambiguity, tentativeness, and uncertainty since there is not the security of having one answer, one methodology for all clients and problems. Rather, there is the challenge of making decisions about how best to employ which techniques with which clients.

The behavioral counselor cannot escape simply by proclaiming that the "client is just not ready for counseling." The burden, in fact, is on the counselor to tailor techniques to the particular client. And the "quality of fit and fineness of trim" will depend on the counselor's knowledge and understanding of complex human behavior. The behavioral counselor has occasionally been falsely described as someone who only administers simple reinforcers. Instead, the behavioral counselor must be concerned with continually trying out combinations of promising techniques and observing what actual changes result. These techniques cannot be applied in any mechanical fashion. Great sensitivity, wisdom and emotional stability are needed to adapt flexibly to the client's often changing needs.

This section presents articles in which combinations of the techniques described in previous sections are used. Considerable ingenuity and creativity is demonstrated by counselors in these articles in selecting and then tailoring a variety of techniques for particular client problems. In using multiple techniques counselors do not always select the most appropriate technique. Sometimes a procedure is better used at a different time in counseling. Sometimes the sequence of techniques could be better arranged. Even though the behavioral counselor may sometimes stumble and fall, he usually falls forward. With specifically stated objectives and with concrete criteria upon which to evaluate effectiveness, a counselor can learn from his success and failure experiences.

Interpersonal Problems

INTERPERSONAL PROBLEMS INCLUDE problems in sexual relationships, responses to authority figures, the ability to develop friendships, the ability to supervise or be supervised, children's problems with parents, parents' problems with children, marital disharmonies—in short, any situation in which two or more persons have an unsatisfactory relationship. To speak of interpersonal problems is to speak of a host of overt and covert response patterns of the individual person. These complex behavioral patterns involve a variety of responses: words spoken in particular ways involving tone, inflection, syntax; gestures, glances, postures, and facial expressions of many types and kinds; thoughts and "internal" sentences on many themes; and somatic responses affecting heart rate, blood flow, respiration, and skin conductivity. This complexity is stressed here because the way problems are conceptualized in counseling has a marked influence on the way counselors seek to treat interpersonal problems.

Traditionally counseling theories and practices have viewed interpersonal problems from a verbal perspective. Within this view individuals who have difficulties in their relationships with others have been judged to suffer from a lack of clarity and understanding of their situation. Such clients supposedly need to have their actions clarified and to gain insight into why they act as they do. This has led to interview strategies which focus primarily on the exchange of verbal and nonverbal responses between counselor and client, exchanges seeking to clarify, reflect, and interpret. Coupled with this has been the belief that the counselor, being a certain kind of person, was the necessary and sufficient ingredient in helping

431

clients with their interpersonal problems. His warmth, genuineness, and regard, as manifested in his interview behavior, would suffice. Very recently, however, interpersonal problems have been conceptualized from a broader perspective, one that views such problems as complex social-psychological phenomena which have been acquired as a result of environmental experiences. Because they involve learned patterns of behavior, interpersonal problems lend themselves to analyses and treatments that focus on discovering those factors in the client's environment which currently are contributing to and maintaining the behaviors in question. What specific experiences might produce relevant changes in the client's behavior?

One important implication is that the counselor, in working with interpersonal problems, must give critical attention to analyzing and assessing the client's present environment. What is really going on in the client's life? He must consider strategies of change relevant to the client's particular environment. Such a counselor must engage in a great variety of activities as he works with clients in encouraging a variety of specific changes. And to do this the counselor needs access to techniques that go far beyond the spoken word and the interview situation. In one view, the counselor must engage the client in approximations of real-life situations if he is to effect significant changes in the real-life behavior of the client.

In Article 39 Neuman presents a case in which a variety of techniques were used to assist a young man to interact more effectively with girls and with his parents. Social modeling, behavioral rehearsal, verbal and nonverbal reinforcement, notetaking, and assignments were used to counsel the client. Neuman focused consistently on the client's actions, that is, on what the client was *doing* in the current situation and what the client could do specifically to bring about desired changes. No effort was made to explore the historical dynamics of the client's problem. The focus was pinpointed on specific behaviors and on using the interview as well as outside assignments to generate more adaptive behaviors. It is interesting to note that a strong positive relationship between counselor and client seems to have emerged as a consequence of the tangible successes in changed behavior that the client experienced.

D'Zurilla in Article 40 offers cases of two male college students who suffered from extreme anxiety and nausea relative to dating girls. Both cases focused on training the clients to use self-control techniques in real-life situations. The article illustrates the point that counselors, in order to help clients with interpersonal problems, must focus much more on situations that closely approximate the actual problem settings of clients. D'Zurilla trained the clients themselves to eliminate excessive anxiety responses through self-administered desensitization techniques, calling attention to the need to explore how counselors can help clients develop skills of self-control.

Geisinger in Article 41 demonstrates a wide array of techniques to help a young woman overcome problems of sexual anxiety, nonassertiveness, and excessive jealousy. The case demonstrates that the counselor can simultaneously employ different techniques in working with the same client on several problems. Geisinger's approach stands out in sharp contrast to the traditional practices of many counselors who typically have but one procedure for the many problems of a client. A broad-spectrum approach to techniques is of high priority in dealing with the complexities of interpersonal behaviors.

39
USING ASSERTIVE TRAINING

Donald Neuman
SAN DIEGO STATE COLLEGE

When a client walks into a counselor's office and complains, "People seem to take advantage of me . . . I don't know why . . . ," assertive training needs to be considered as a way of effecting behavioral change. This method, discussed at length by Wolpe and Lazarus (1966), consists of arranging environmental situations with the client so that certain impulses previously inhibited by anxiety can be expressed in overt behavior. Assertive behavior that tends to replace the anxiety raised by certain situations can result in positive consequences, such as feelings of control and dominance. The old anxiety-producing situations thereby gain new meaning for the individual.[1]

Salter (1961) first categorized unassertive people as "inhibitory personalities." These passive clients often find it difficult to do such things as initiate a conversation with others, return faulty merchandise, acknowledge praise or compliments, retaliate when verbally abused, or ask people to do things for them. They usually are either colorless, frightened people who avoid social contact and thus often lose much of the enjoyment and satisfaction in life, or they are the pity-seekers who relate how dreadfully they have been exploited in life and how they have not been able to do anything about it. Somatic symptoms such as headaches, asthma, and ulcers frequently may be related to a person's inability to discharge appropriate impulses.

One of the crucial requirements of treating unassertive clients is to identify and isolate specific target behaviors. For example, when a client relates that he feels "depressed," the traditional question "why" ought not to be asked. Instead, inquiries should be made such as: "In what situations do you feel this way?" "What measures have you taken to combat your depression?" "What exactly happens when you feel this way?" Ullmann (1967) has suggested that the counselor begin by asking "what" rather than the traditional "why." To identify the distinct behaviors needed to elicit change, the counselor must know what the client is doing, what the consequences of certain behaviors are, and what must be done to change the behavior.[2]

Historically, an assertive response or feeling that is frequently punished results in learned inhibitions of normal assertive behaviors. For example, a mother might upbraid her son as follows: "The only way for you to deal with your father when he is in these bad moods is to ignore him. . . . He really doesn't *mean* what he says . . . above all don't talk back to him because that will only aggravate him . . . *understand* him." The son then learns to suppress his legitimate urge to fight back in some way because the aversive guilt feelings elicited by his mother are paired with the consideration of an assertive act.[3]

---

[1] Editors' Note: Precisely how these assertive responses actually "replace" those called anxiety and how certain mediating processes are involved is at present unclear. What is clear is that clients can be assisted in overtly expressing their real feelings and thoughts without experiencing great anxiety.

[2] Editors' Note: Excellent point! Counselors need to give much more critical attention to what specifically and concretely is going on in the client's pattern of daily living. See Articles 29 and 30 on behavioral analysis.

[3] Editors' Note: Much of what Berne (1964), Ginott (1965), and others have been saying recently about parent-child interactions is pertinent to this—parents often create environments which offer strong negative consequences for justified and genuine "assertions" by children.

THE CASE OF TOM

To illustrate the specific techniques involved in asseru.
the case of Tom will be presented. Tom, a rather slim, handsome .
came to me initially complaining that he was unable to control his
frequency of masturbation. Further exploration and discussion of his
concern revealed that there was an absence of heterosexual activity,
that he lived at home, and that he avoided "direct" confrontations with
people, including his father. His older brother manifested essentially the
same pattern until he married and moved out of the house. Apparently,
the masturbatory behavior was evidence of a wish to experience anxiety-
free social relations with females. In reality, this wish was carried out
only in daydreaming and fantasy. I decided to focus on increasing the
frequency of "real-live" female contact, rather than working directly on
decreasing guilt-eliciting masturbatory activity. In doing so I avoided
dealing directly with a very anxiety-arousing activity and started the
counseling with a more positive emphasis.

Goals and Techniques

The following goals were co-operatively established by Tom and me:
(1) Increase heterosexual behaviors such as asking girls for dates,
holding their hands, kissing them, and carrying on interesting conversations.
(2) Increase assertive behavior with peers and parents such as initiating interpersonal contact with other students; avoid short replies to
questions but rather expand on verbal responses; tell his father that he
did not like his lack of consideration for other members of the family.

SOCIAL MODELING

Assertive people known to the client can often be used to provide an
example to follow. For example, a client might be asked about an
acquaintance he admires. The counselor can discuss with him the assertive
behaviors that distinguish this person from others. The client may then
attempt to try out these behaviors with other people.

In this case I inquired as to the availability of a peer who might provide a "dating-behavior" model to follow. A fellow classmate was
chosen who dated frequently and studied occasionally with Tom. He was
to observe closely his friend's verbal and nonverbal behaviors that
seemed to work. He was then to try out the ones he felt comfortable
using. Between classes, Tom was to approach a girl sitting alone in the
crowded student union and ask if the vacant seat next to her was taken.

.f she invited him to sit down, he was to do so with a smile. The conversation might then take the form of "Hey, I see you're taking sociology . . . are you in Smith's section?" or "What did you think of the game the other night?"

To give him confidence in putting his arm around a girl or holding her hand on dates, he was to select a movie that had several love scenes in it. During these "arousing" scenes, I suggested that he pattern his behavior after the male model on the screen. Discretion and feedback, however, was the watchword. Tom and I discussed these and he reported successful experiences in trying them out.

BEHAVIORAL REHEARSAL

The counselor can play the part of the client to illustrate the effect of certain behaviors. He also can provide an opportunity for the client to practice safely various interpersonal verbal responses and ways of reacting to people. The counselor can play the role of an overbearing acquaintance in the client's life and can have the client practice exactly what he would say to that person during an aggressive interchange. Just saying the words, followed by positive consequences, often allays many unwarranted fears the client may have.[4]

With Tom, I enacted several anticipated responses of a girl in various situations. One situation involved telephoning a girl for a date.

Tom: Hi Sally. This is Tom. . . . What 'ch doin'?

Counselor Oh, hi, Tom. I'm studying for my English test Friday.
(as girl):

Tom: Yeah, I've got a history test coming up, too, next week . . . but I'm really not too worried about it now . . . but I will be the night before the exam, I guess. Say . . . do you think you could go to the game Saturday night . . .?

Counselor: Gee. I don't know . . . let me tell you tomorrow in class . . . my folks are planning on coming up this weekend. . . .

Tom: Fine. I'll look forward to seeing you in class tomorrow.

Counselor: Sure. See you tomorrow.

Tom: Right. Bye now.

Various alternatives were discussed depending on the content of the conversation such as graceful ways to accept a "rejection" or handle a

---

[4] Editors' Note: Role-playing can be a very effective and efficient procedure. One of its significant advantages is that it permits the counselor and client (or clients if a group is involved) to simulate reality in a controlled manner, gradually introducing more factors found in real life environments. See Articles 13 and 14 for other examples of role-playing.

pause in the dialogue. In other words Tom practiced ways to respond to conversation shifts. He found that this helped him to decide quickly on alternative statements.

This method consisted of having Tom record his extra-interview episodes in a notebook. Data were collected and cues were provided to discuss significant interpersonal situations. For example, after his first date, Tom wrote down what he thought were the important happenings that evening. He described what took place when he held her hand during the movie, how he attempted to kiss her goodnight and other successes and failures during the evening. In fact, it was only the second time he had kissed a girl and he felt quite ecstatic about his success. The only failures came in the area of conversation when he felt uncomfortable during awkward moments of silence. It was suggested that he survey the environment for conversation cues such as "Doesn't that guy over there remind you of Ed Sullivan?" In short, note-taking provided data on specific behaviors and their consequences. With these kinds of data we discussed constructive suggestions on how to remedy ineffective responses.

The Third Interview

To illustrate some of the above an excerpt of my third interview with Tom follows:

Counselor: Well . . . what's been happening?

Tom: Not much . . . I called up this girl . . . or I was going to . . . and I called her up . . . there was no one home. . . .

Counselor: Oh . . . you did call her up eh? . . . good. . . .

Tom: After that though . . . I just really felt . . . that I really didn't want to go out that bad.

Counselor: You did make that attempt though. . . .

Tom: Yeah . . . and I figure I'll try again for this weekend.

Counselor: Like you'll call somebody up tonight?

Tom: Yeah. I could but it seems like I'm just not enthusiastic about asking a girl out. . . .

Counselor: When you called her up . . . were you a little bit anxious . . . or tense? . . .

Tom: A little. I tried not to be . . . practiced the deep-breathing and muscle exercises. . . .

Counselor: Good . . . good . . . Do you think you could try it again? Perhaps you could call her tonight.

Tom: OK . . . I'll try . . . I think that would be all right. . . .

(Later in the same interview some notes Tom had taken were discussed.)

Counselor: This situation . . . "Upon reaching the destination, you don't know whether to hold her hand or not" . . . What would you have liked to have done?

Tom: To hold her hand . . . casually. . . .

Counselor: Well . . . Let's see . . . could you ease into the situation . . . like after opening the door for her . . . say . . . "Come on . . . let's go" as you grab her hand firmly?

Tom: Hmm . . . I . . . maybe. . . .

Counselor: If you could think of a reason for holding her hand . . . besides the fact that it feels good . . . like an image of leading the way . . . or something. . . .

Tom: Hey . . . (smiles) . . .

Counselor: Reach out and take her hand . . . I really doubt that any girl would withdraw her hand when you offer yours to her . . . upon getting out of the car. . . .

Tom: Yeah . . . you're right . . . I don't think any girl would draw her hand away . . . but then . . . I . . . never held a girl's hand before . . . uh . . . uh . . . I haven't been out that much . . . ah . . . that sounds like a good procedure . . . but what would she think?

Counselor: If you know where you're going to take her, you firmly take her by the hand . . . cause she's just a girl . . . she needs you to help her . . . to show her around . . .

Tom: Yeah . . . you're probably right . . . but . . . it seems . . . maybe . . . when I put . . . want to put my arm around her . . . how would I go about it? . . . you know . . . I'd probably stretch (stretches with arms in air) . . . like this . . . and . . . relax . . . same time . . . and come down with my . . . uh . . . arm around her like this. . . .

Counselor: Yeah . . . That's right . . . perfect! . . . very good . . . You relaxed and at the same time put your arm around her . . . Great.

Tom: Maybe . . . I ah . . . could see how she responded . . . you know . . . whether she moves away . . . or something . . . and then know if she likes it ah . . . maybe it'd be OK if you came right out with it . . . "Why don't cha move over here a little closer?" . . .

Counselor: That's it . . . that's right!

Tom: I was wondering about that.

Counselor: Good idea . . .

Tom: (laugh) ah . . . yeah . . . (smiles broadly)

Counselor: You know, girls like to be touched too . . . you could be doing them a favor too you know . . . really . . . have you ever seen it that way?

Tom: Yeah. I . . . I . . . can see it that way . . . they want to go through all of this . . . but I guess what it comes down to . . .

is . . . that I'm afraid I'll make a fool of myself . . . if I try it and . . . I usually do . . . and . . . I guess I don't realize that they like the physical contact too . . . (voice quivers).

Counselor: Well, they do!

Tom: I don't know . . . I guess I'm just afraid I'll make a fool out of myself.

Counselor: You're afraid you'll make a mistake . . .

Tom: Uh huh . . .

Counselor: Well, what makes you think that they will dislike you if you try something . . . something rather normal like holding hands . . . with a girl?

Tom: I dunno . . . I guess . . . it's my general attitude . . . ah . . . you know . . . women . . . maybe they like the groovy type of guy . . . and you know I'm not free and easy . . . with them . . . they're going to like the type that isn't going to have any trouble . . . ah . . .

Counselor: The thing is . . . Tom . . . the more you practice the assertive stuff . . . the more you'll be groovy . . . you need to learn and get used to the groovy stuff . . . then they'll see you that way . . . the thing you have to do is act . . . on the impulses you feel. You know . . . do it.

Tom: Well . . . I'll try . . .

(Later in the same interview)

Counselor: Do you have some guys . . . that sit next to you in class . . . or that you hang around with . . . after class?

Tom: I usually . . . don't want . . . to . . . I don't really know anyone . . . I don't want to.

Counselor: Why not?

Tom: I don't know . . . I guess I feel I'll be wasting my time . . . I don't think they would want to . . . maybe I really want to but . . . don't know how . . . I dunno.

Counselor: How about this week . . . you know . . . strike up a conversation with some guy you see regularly . . . like in class . . . maybe ask him about an assignment or just walk along with him wherever he might be going. . . .

Tom: Yeah . . . I think I know of one guy that sits near me in my English class . . . He did say hi to me the other day . . . I'll try that. . . .

Counselor: Again, I'd like to have you record what happens when . . . you ah . . . try to initiate a conversation with him . . . If you get a little nervous . . . work some of these muscle exercises . . . or yawn and stretch . . . or something . . . that'll be a goal for this week, OK?

Tom: Fine . . . I think I could do it. . . .

(Last five minutes of the interview)

Tom: Sometimes . . . I wish I could tell my dad . . . how I feel sometimes . . . the reason I don't tell him off . . . is just to avoid an argument. I don't want to stir things up . . . 'cause I don't like 'em stirred up that much . . . once in awhile OK . . . but it's too much.

Counselor: What happens when you stir things up and say what's on your mind? . . .

Tom: It's really not when you argue . . . actually . . . it's the after effects. . . .

Counselor: What are they?

Tom: It's really not that much . . . he hollers for a while . . . then deadly silence. . . .

Counselor: I see. So you're afraid that if you do something, the consequences will result in deadly and painful silence . . . pouting behavior on his part . . . What do you think you could do about this?

Tom: Well . . . I was thinking . . . actually . . . I could move into an apartment next semester . . . but my mother and father, I think, wouldn't like it . . . They'd think something was wrong. They don't want to lose me, I guess.

Counselor: Well, it could be because they don't see you as an independent man . . . and feel that you still need them . . . but how are you going to convince them otherwise? You're going to have to show them . . . by your actions . . . that you are grown up.

Tom: Yes . . . but I think if I move out now . . . it will be like my older brother who moved out because he wanted to be independent . . . and my dad will think I'd be doing the same thing . . . that is, moving out because I want to get away from him . . .

Counselor: Oh . . . I see . . . What do you think your alternatives are? . . . Really . . .

Tom: I'd really like to move out . . . but I'm worried about what he would think . . . afraid to go against his wishes . . . It's tough . . . I guess I'd choose to move out . . . though.

SOME OBSERVATIONS AND RESULTS

A pattern often emerges when counseling with the unassertive person. At first he becomes aware of his lack of assertiveness and experiences distaste and regret. This encourages the client to embark on tentative attempts at assertive behaviors. Support from the counselor and, if possible, solicited assistance from other significant people in the client's life, help considerably. It is crucial that the consequences be carefully considered before assertive attempts are made by the client. Successive approximations can aid in treatment by initially arranging small or easily attained goals so that positive consequences are certain to be identified with the assertive act. The client may be overassertive at times but the pendulum is easily reversed to achieve an adaptive balance. He then becomes indifferent to petty frustrations and learns to react properly to the real injustices in his life.

Gradual approximations of the ultimate behaviors desired are needed. Agreement on an easily attained goal for the week might be an initial assignment. For example, to ask a friend for a piece of paper usually meets with success even though it may represent a significant accomplishment for the client. Weekly goals, successively more difficult, can be set up during the interview. It goes without saying that support and encouragement by the counselor is crucial.

One goal that Tom selected was to tell his father, that week, to stop changing the TV channel while he was watching it. Various outbursts of anger were anticipated and ways of responding to this anger were discussed. Subsequent goals ranged from telling his father where he was going at night rather than asking his permission, to informing him that he was going to move out of the house and live in an apartment.

Tom demonstrated some real changes. He smiled more with girls, sustained flirtatious glances, and interacted with considerable confidence. And the more he interacted, the more he wanted to because the consequences were so positive. This assertiveness also tended to generalize to instructors, club members, parents, and peers. His frequency of dating increased and he noticed that girls were even giving him "come-hither" looks in the library! After eight sessions, Tom and I decided to terminate counseling. He parted with this comment: "I might be back to see you . . . but hell! I really don't need to."

Several months later Tom reported that he had really worked on being more assertive with his father, culminating with his decision, announced to his father one evening, that he was moving to an apartment. (Since then he decided to move to a dormitory because apartment living was too lonely!) He also reported that he had been dating girls regularly, especially one girl but after several weeks had decided not to date her. "She really has little to say. . . . I think I can do better." Finally he commented that during this time his pronounced fear of driving a car in freeway traffic had disappeared. Tom observed that he felt like a "new man."[5]

[5] Editors' Note: While these changes are most encouraging, it is difficult to pinpoint the many factors which actually caused them. Perhaps one major factor was the counselor's consistent focus on "actions"—what Tom could specifically do here and now.

40

REDUCING HETEROSEXUAL ANXIETY[1]

Thomas J. D'Zurilla
STATE UNIVERSITY OF NEW YORK AT STONY BROOK

Behavioral counseling techniques may be extended well beyond the traditional interview sessions to include *in vivo* or in-real-life procedures if those experiences are appropriately used to facilitate desired changes in behavior. One possible method in this regard is instructing the client to manipulate and control certain aspects of his own behavior and experiences, over which he currently has good control, to produce favorable changes in other, poorly controlled aspects of his behavior. The deliberate and systematic use of this procedure should lead to the self-control of the problem behavior; that is, control of the problem behavior primarily by stimuli produced by other responses of the same individual (Bijou & Baer, 1961; Goldiamond, 1965; Skinner, 1953). This self-control procedure should facilitate independent problem-solving ability and add considerably to the effects produced by other techniques in the interview setting. In some cases, it may be an effective treatment in its own right.

Using *in vivo* "homework assignments" with clients is a practice of long standing. Too often, however, very little planning goes into these *in vivo* assignments for clients, along with scant regard for factors governing behavior change and self-control. For example, a client may be asked to perform a pattern of behavior over which he has little control at the time, or he may be asked to perform a response in a situation where an incompatible response tendency is much stronger. As a result, the client often fails to respond and the counselor simply concludes that he is not yet "ready" or "motivated" to carry out *in vivo* assignments. Rarely have comprehensive, systematic programs been planned and prescribed, as the primary treatment method, for progressive self-control and elimination of problem behaviors.[2]

---

[1] The author wishes to express his appreciation to Marvin R. Goldfried and Gerald C. Davison for their suggestions and criticisms.

[2] Notable exceptions to this have been the work of Salter (1949), Wolpe (1958), and Wolpe and Lazarus (1966), using *in vivo* assertive and sexual responses by clients to gradually eliminate certain fears.

Recently, however, the concept of self-control has been receiving more attention in the research and theoretical literature (Aronfreed, 1964; Aronfreed & Reber, 1965; Bandura & Walters, 1963; Goldiamond, 1965; Homme, 1966; Kanfer & Goldfoot, 1966), and there have been promising results in counseling settings.[3]

COUNSELING FOR SELF-CONTROL

These two case reports illustrate the self-manipulation of certain behaviors and experiences, notably differential relaxation, by male clients to help control and overcome chronic anxiety and gastric distress related to females. The first case, that of Frank, describes the use of *in vivo* self-controlled procedures to supplement the primary treatment of systematic desensitization. Although similar procedures have been encouraged in most systematic desensitization cases, counselors rarely have attempted to maximize their effects by explicitly training the client in their use and checking on their application during the course of counseling. Most counselors assume that the major effects of counseling will result directly from what goes on in the interview setting.[4]

The second case, Steve, is unique in that after several initial assessment and training sessions the entire treatment program was carried out by the client himself without any contact with the counselor.

FRANK'S ANXIETY AND NAUSEA WITH GIRLS

Frank was a 21-year-old student in his senior year at the State University of New York at Stony Brook. He came to Psychological Services complaining of disturbing anxiety and nausea (with occasional vomiting) in social situations with girls, especially when the contact was close and personal, such as on a date. Anxiety and nausea occurred on every date with varying severity depending upon time since the last meal, type of food eaten, and the nature of the activity. The reaction was usually the strongest when the client arrived at the residence of his date and continued at a high level of intensity on the way to the planned activity. In most instances, the reaction gradually became less disturbing during the date and occasionally disappeared, especially if considerable activity was

---

[3] For examples, see Cautela (1966a, 1966b); Davison's Article 34 in this book; Ferster, Nurnberger, and Levitt (1962); Goldiamond (1965); and Gray, England, and Mahoney (1965).

[4] Editors' Note: It is very difficult for most counselors to accept the notion that their face-to-face, personal contact with clients may *not* be the most important and crucial factor in promoting changes in their client's behavior.

involved, such as playing tennis or going swimming. Because of this problem, Frank had avoided frequent dating. For approximately three months prior to counseling he had been dating only one girl, Alice, a student at Smith College.

Frank's anxiety-nausea on dates had been a problem for approximately six years. Before the problem developed, he had dated girls without special difficulty, although he reported that he had always felt somewhat uncomfortable with girls. The client also reported that the problem had been getting worse in the past few years. He first sought help from his family doctor soon after the reaction became a problem. He was told that he was merely experiencing "growing pains" and that the reaction would soon disappear. About six months prior to seeing me, Frank consulted a private psychiatrist. He received psychoanalytically-oriented psychotherapy for about three months but terminated because he could see no evidence of progress.

Other difficulties reported by Frank included frequent mood swings, irritability, chronic dissatisfaction, feelings of inferiority, and lack of self-confidence. He recalled that these difficulties seem to have developed during the six years in which the anxiety-nausea problem had been in existence.

Starting Systematic Desensitization

After several assessment sessions the decision was made to use systematic desensitization along with *in vivo* "assignments."[5] The first four treatment sessions were used for training in deep muscle relaxation, construction of the initial anxiety-hierarchy, and instructions for *in vivo* self-control. During relaxation training, the client was also instructed to practice the method at home at least once per day. In the initial hierarchy, it was decided to focus upon Frank's girlfriend, Alice, since she was the only girl with whom he had been having regular personal contacts. The casual contacts which he had been having with girls on campus presented no disturbing problems. At first, several themes involving mediating or internal variables (for example, anticipation of rejection and disapproval and sexual feelings) were considered but were discarded as being less appropriate, at least initially, than the simple dimension of proximity to Alice in terms of time and space. Frank reported that his next personal contact with Alice would be at the time of the Thanksgiving vacation when he planned to drive to Smith College and bring her home for the vacation. Before this time, only contacts by telephone and letter were anticipated, which also tended to elicit the anxiety-nausea responses.

---

[5] Editors' Note: See Emery, Article 31, for details of systematic desensitization.

Preparing for Contact with Alice at Smith

The following anxiety hierarchy was constructed:

1. Relaxing in comfortable chair in room at home, thinking only of relaxing
2. Talking with friends on campus, someone mentions the name "Alice"
3. Relaxing in comfortable chair in room at home, thinking of Alice
4. Writing a letter to Alice in room at home
5. Eating dinner at home with parents, talking about going to pick up Alice
6. Driving in car on the way to Smith College
7. Reading a letter from Alice in room at home
8. Talking with Alice on the telephone
9. Driving in car at Smith College, seeing Alice standing in the distance
10. Driving in car with Alice on the way to go sailing
11. Driving up to Alice's dormitory, seeing her coming out and walking toward you
12. Walking around the campus with Alice
13. Talking to Alice in her dormitory room

When Frank became efficient in being able to relax himself, he was given specific instructions to begin anticipating tension-provoking situations in his daily activities, recognizing tension at the first sign of its appearance, and relaxing it away using covert verbal cues such as saying "relax, let go completely" to himself and tension-release exercises. The situations discussed corresponded to the items of the anxiety-hierarchy.

Frank was also instructed to manipulate his eating behavior and activities related to the items of the hierarchy. To begin with, he was to avoid food-intake for several hours prior to initiating any phone, letter, or personal contact with Alice with the exception of certain liquids, such as water and coffee. Moreover, the last meal before a contact was to include only easily digestible foods. A typical "ulcer diet" was referred to for this program.

Frank was also instructed to expose himself to situations and experiences of low anxiety-provoking potential, such as talking to a friend and mentioning Alice's name (see hierarchy), and to avoid experiences of medium and high anxiety potential. The above factors were to be manipulated by the client according to a "graded tasks" procedure where steps toward experiences with a higher potential for disturbance are taken only when the lower step is accomplished without disturbance. Thus, he was instructed *gradually* to bring the time of food-intake closer to the time of contacts with Alice, to eat a greater variety of foods, and to initiate contacts higher up in the anxiety-hierarchy.

Counseling sessions involved working up the hierarchy according to the usual systematic-desensitization procedures and checking on progress regarding the self-control procedures. One modification was made to facilitate *in vivo* self-control. For the first six items, Frank was instructed to signal when he experienced tension, stop imagining the scene, and to relax away the tension. No further relaxation suggestions were given by the counselor during this procedure unless the client was unable to relax away the tension using self-produced cues, such as "relax, let go completely," in about 30 seconds. The next item was presented only when the client signaled a return to his previous, relaxed state. For the remaining items, the client was asked to relax away the tension *while maintaining the image*. He was instructed to stop imagining the item only if it appeared that anxiety was increasing or if he was unable to relax away the tension in about 30 seconds.[6]

In the fifteenth session the first anxiety-hierarchy was completed in systematic desensitization. According to Frank, it appeared that the combination of systematic desensitization and the *in vivo* procedures had enabled him to overcome all disturbance associated with life experiences up to and including item 8 on the anxiety-hierarchy.[7] The remaining situations were not experienced in real life since Alice had changed her Thanksgiving vacation plans and decided to spend the time with relatives who lived near Smith College. However, Frank reported that he was planning to drive to Smith the following week to bring Alice home for the Christmas holidays.

At this time Frank reported a successful experience with another girl at Stony Brook the week before the fifteenth session. The girl had invited him to visit her in her off-campus apartment and he accepted. He experienced no nausea during the entire visit. Some anxiety and tension were felt, however, which he successfully controlled and eliminated by employing self-induced differential relaxation. It is interesting to note that this successful experience occurred before the personal contact items of the anxiety-hierarchy were worked through in systematic desensitization.[8]

[6] Editors' Note: Details of procedures in "usual" systematic desensitization, as described by Emery in Article 31, should be considered tentative as this variation suggests. Some clients may be more effectively helped by multiple exposure to hierarchy items, involving such combinations as verbalizing the item, rehearsing the scene with the counselor (simulation), imagining the scene, and experiencing the item *in vivo*.

[7] Progress in systematic desensitization did not proceed without difficulty, although smooth progress has often been suggested in case reports. Difficulties occurred in relaxation. On several occasions the client was faced with conflicts and difficult decisions in the life situation which tended to disrupt desensitization treatment temporarily. However, space limitations prevent a more detailed description of these difficulties here. The main objective at this time is to focus upon those procedures and experiences which are directly related to the self-control aspect of treatment.

[8] Editors' Note: This nicely illustrates the generalizing effect of counseling to problem-related situations. It also points up the value of focusing on client self-control techniques from the very beginning of treatment.

Successfully Dating Alice and Giving a Speech

In the fifteenth session, the following short hierarchy was constructed to help Frank handle any disturbance that might be associated with activities leading up to a date with Alice during the Christmas vacation:

1. Dressing in room before leaving for a date with Alice
2. Driving in car on the way to Alice's home for a date
3. Walking up to the front door of Alice's home
4. Standing in the doorway as Alice opens the door and invites you in
5. Sitting in the living room talking to Alice and her mother

This hierarchy was completed in the seventeenth session. At this point, Frank reported that he had become more generally relaxed and confident in all interpersonal situations.

He reported success in controlling and significantly reducing anxiety in a speech-making situation using the self-control method. The experience involved delivering a talk before the class in a psychology course. In the past he had always experienced considerable anxiety and distress prior to and throughout such an experience. This time he employed differential relaxation at the first appearance of tension and successfully completed the talk without any disturbing anxiety.

The seventeenth session was the last before the Christmas vacation, when the client would be driving to Smith College to bring Alice home. He was instructed to employ differential relaxation on the trip as he did in connection with the speech-making experience.

Reducing Nausea

In the eighteenth session, the first following the Christmas holidays, he reported that he had experienced anxiety on the way to Smith but had successfully controlled and relaxed it away. At one point he was unable to reduce anxiety through differential relaxation while driving so he pulled over to the side of the road and relaxed more deeply. Frank also reported that there was no vomiting and no significant anxiety during several dates with Alice during the vacation period. However, on one occasion he experienced nausea. This occurred during a Christmas party when he ate and drank much more than was appropriate. This was the first time since the beginning of counseling that the taking of any kind of food or drink had been attempted in a dating situation.

At this point the possibility was considered that a nausea response might have been developed in this client as an independent conditioned response to a stimulus complex involving the presence and consumption of food and drink within the context of a date with a girl. An attempt was made to deal directly with this possibility through the use of a modified desensitization approach. First, the following dinner-date hierarchy was prepared:

1. Lying in bed the morning of the dinner date
2. Eating breakfast the same day
3. Eating lunch the same day
4. Dressing just before leaving for the date
5. Driving in car on the way to the date
6. Walking up to the door of Alice's home
7. Sitting in the living room, talking to Alice and her mother
8. Sitting in the living room, seeing plates, glasses, and so forth on the dining table
9. Sitting in the living room, seeing Alice and her mother putting food on the table—vegetables, turkey, and so forth
10. Getting up and walking to the dining room, looking at the food
11. Sitting at the table next to Alice, looking at the food
12. Putting food on your plate
13. Putting food in your mouth
14. Drinking milk and eating cake following the meal

The modification in usual desensitization procedures involved the placing of one of the client's favorite peppermint candies on his tongue following relaxation and just prior to imagining the items from the hierarchy. The client was instructed to let the candy dissolve in his mouth during the desensitization procedure. He was asked to signal whenever he felt either nausea or anxiety. It was hypothesized that the candies might help to counteract and eliminate the nausea response to the hierarchy situations. The client was also instructed to use the same peppermint candy in the life situation prior to any eating situation with a girl.[9]

After two more sessions the dinner-date hierarchy was completed. During this time Frank reported that he had dated two girls from Stony Brook. On one of the dates he ate food with no disturbing reactions. He used peppermint candies with apparent success. Two weeks later he reported that he had again dated the same two girls. This time food was eaten on both dates with no anxiety or nausea. He indicated that the dates were quite pleasant and satisfying. On neither of these dates was it necessary to use the candies.

[9] Editors' Note: Very interesting hypothesis. The eating of peppermint candy while actually feeling very calm and relaxed and at the same time imagining scenes of eating with a girl might have become a conditioned stimulus. As such, eating peppermints in real life situations would tend to elicit responses associated with feeling calm and relaxed.

Some Results

In the twenty-eighth and final session, Frank reported greater self-confidence, more satisfaction with life in general, greater stability in mood, and less general anxiety. There was no longer any disturbing anxiety or nausea during heterosexual contacts. A very important step forward was the fact that he had just accepted an invitation to go to a "Sadie Hawkins" dance with a girl with whom he was only slightly acquainted. He said that he definitely would have refused only a few months ago.

A follow-up interview three months later revealed that there had been no setbacks and no substitute "symptoms" or additional problems. In fact, he had continued to improve in most areas, especially frequency of and satisfaction with dating, self-confidence, and feelings of adequacy.

STEVE'S FEAR OF GIRLS

Steve was a 21-year-old student in his junior year at Stony Brook. He came in complaining of anxiety and nausea associated with personal contacts with girls. Again, the problem was especially disturbing on dates. Steve was not dating at all at the time of treatment because of this reaction.

This problem dated back about ten years. When he was about 11 years old he began to feel anxious and nauseous when he talked to or thought about a pretty girl that he liked. If he had recently eaten, the reaction would be particularly intense and vomiting would usually occur. The client soon learned to avoid eating for several hours prior to any expected social contacts with attractive girls to prevent vomiting.[10] However, anxiety and nausea continued. In the case of any unexpected contacts soon after food intake, the reaction again occurred to the degree that the client was forced to remove himself from the situation to avoid vomiting.

Because of this disturbing problem the client had done very little dating until about two years before he came in for counseling when he had tried "going steady." He had attempted to cope with the situation by controlling eating and using "self-hypnosis." The latter involved lying down on a bed, trying to relax, and giving himself hypnotic suggestions taken from a book on hypnotic induction. He had also given himself

---

[10] Editors' Note: An unusual example of the process of negative reinforcement in operation: the termination of an aversive stimulus (vomiting) strengthened certain behaviors (avoiding food before seeing girls).

suggestions to the effect that the anxiety-nausea reaction would not occur. The client employed this procedure before each date for about one month. When this method failed to produce significant improvement, the client gave it up and relied primarily on the procedure of controlling eating.[11]

After about six months of going steady, Steve finally had ended the relationship because of the difficulties involved, even though the steady dating resulted in some reduction in the frequency and intensity of the reaction. During the year and a half before treatment the client never dated the same girl more than three times. He felt that the reaction had greatly interfered with his heterosexual development during adolescence and had resulted in a lack of self-confidence in social relationships and feelings of inadequacy. Other problems reported by the client were anxiety associated with taking examinations and disturbing thoughts about possible illness and disease.

Starting Desensitization

After Steve and I explored details of his problem, three problem categories were identified: formal date, telephone conversation, and informal meetings, such as meeting a girl in a bar and "picking her up." As in the case of Frank, the presence and consumption of food and drink tended to aggravate the anxiety-nausea reaction in these situations. Since Steve was interested in a particular girl, Ellen, she was used in the anxiety hierarchies. The one concerning a date was as follows:

1. Lying in bed in the morning on the day of a date with Ellen
2. Getting out of bed in the morning on the day of the date
3. Eating breakfast on the day of the date
4. Driving home from school for dinner on the day of the date
5. Eating dinner with parents on the day of the date
6. Getting out of the car at Ellen's home
7. Walking up to the door of Ellen's home
8. Meeting Ellen at the door
9. Driving in car with Ellen on the way to a restaurant
10. Sitting at a table with Ellen in the restaurant waiting to be served
11. Eating with Ellen in the restaurant
12. Sitting in the car with Ellen—you attempt to kiss her
13. You attempt to kiss Ellen, she turns away without saying anything
14. You attempt to kiss Ellen, she verbally rejects your advances

---

[11] Editors' Note: A possible key to Steve's lack of success involved his failure to pair explicitly and concretely his self-induced relaxation with specifics of the problem situation. Being relaxed per se in nonrelevant stimulus situations does little to alter reactions in relevant situations.

Self-administered Counseling

At this point the academic semester ended after eight counseling sessions. It was not possible to continue counseling through the summer as planned since Steve had decided to take a job in his home town. It was agreed that he would attempt to apply desensitization principles on his own during the summer and return in the fall to begin formal desensitization treatment.

He was enthusiastic about desensitization treatment and well-motivated to try out a self-control program. First, the client decided that he must try to arrange as many "treatment trials" as possible during the summer. He contacted a girl, Carol, who lived in his neighborhood, and began to see her regularly, nearly every day. His "procedure" was based upon the self-manipulation of three behavioral variables: (1) eating, (2) relaxation, and (3) activities associated with the anxiety hierarchies.

EATING TREATMENT

With regard to eating behavior, he started by setting up a three-hour minimum time period between eating a meal and contacts (both phone and personal) with Carol. Gradually, with each success experience, that is, contacts without disturbing anxiety or nausea, he moved the meal-time closer to the time of the contact until he was able to eat a meal with Carol on a date without disturbance. In addition to manipulating time of eating, he also manipulated the amount of food. He began by eating very small portions and gradually increased the amount until he was eating an average portion before and during a date.

RELAXATION TREATMENT

In regard to the use of relaxation, Steve started by practicing deep muscle relaxation, following the procedures used during relaxation training in counseling, in his home before each date with Carol. He initiated the procedure each time at the first sign of anxiety. In employing this procedure, Steve patterned his self-produced cues after the verbalizations of the counselor during relaxation training; that is, he talked to himself in such terms as "Tense the muscles of your arms," "Relax," "Let go completely," "Notice the contrast," and so forth. In addition to employing complete deep relaxation in this manner, the client used differential relaxation to relax away any tension he experienced during activities just prior to and on the date. After a few weeks of successful dating without a major reaction, the client began to rely entirely upon the latter procedure to maintain control over anxiety.

Confronting Actual Situations

With the regular and systematic use of these procedures, Steve reported that he had completely eliminated the problem with telephone contacts in about two or three weeks. In regard to personal contacts with Carol, progress occurred more slowly but steadily. After about six weeks, he felt that he had the reaction completely under control.

Then a setback occurred. On several occasions he became anxious and experienced nausea at Carol's home. He relaxed himself somewhat in the situation by using differential relaxation with tension-release exercises. Then he moved his mealtime before a date back about 20 minutes, gradually decreasing the time period again on future dates. The client reported being surprised about the effectiveness of a 20-minute change in mealtime. At this point he also returned to practicing complete deep relaxation before a date. He reported that this procedure eliminated the reaction again in a few days. There were a few subsequent relapses following periods of several days when Steve was unable to see Carol for various reasons. In each case he coped successfully with the problem in the same manner as reported above.

After three months the client was able to eat a meal immediately before a date without experiencing disturbing anxiety or nausea and without subsequent relapse. After five months he was eating meals with Carol on a date without any anxiety or nausea.

DEALING WITH A FAILURE

The first setback reported above appeared to be related, at least in part, to considerable anxiety associated with the client's sexual experiences with Carol. At the time of this setback, the client had attempted sexual intercourse with Carol for the first time. This was his first attempt at sexual relations with any girl. Although Carol was co-operative, he became highly anxious and could not maintain an erection. In co-operation with Carol, the client postponed intercourse at this time and began systematically to employ Wolpe's (Wolpe & Lazarus, 1966) self-control procedure for using sexual responses to overcome anxiety and inhibition associated with sexual behavior. (He had become acquainted with this procedure in his abnormal psychology course.) He also used differential relaxation as an aid in the procedure. For one week, sexual intercourse was not attempted. Instead, he and Carol engaged in various kinds of precoital sexual behavior which had lower anxiety-provoking potential until he was getting aroused with a strong erection and anxiety was virtually eliminated. Then intercourse was again attempted with much greater success this time. The procedure was repeated until the problem was completely overcome.

Effects of Counseling

When the client returned in the fall, he described the above procedures and results and expressed confidence in his ability to continue on his own. Therefore, no formal counseling was initiated at that time. In a follow-up interview in January, Steve reported that the problem had been completely eliminated since October and that there had been no further relapses. At the time of the interview he was still going steady with Carol. There was no evidence of substitute "symptoms" or new problems. The client reported feeling much happier in general, more satisfied with life, and more adequate as a person. However, the client's other two problems—that is, test anxiety and disturbing thoughts about illness—remained essentially unchanged even though he made some attempt to deal with these situations on his own as well. This failure could be interpreted as reflecting the need for a careful and thorough assessment of the major determinants of the problem behavior before a self-control program is planned and prescribed.[12]

OBSERVATIONS ON THE CASES OF FRANK AND STEVE

These case illustrations suggest what a client is capable of doing, independently, in the life situation to control and overcome his own disturbing "neurotic" reactions, provided that he receives the necessary training and instructions. As far as providing evidence for the effectiveness of the specific procedures described here, however, it must be stressed that such case illustrations are grossly inadequate. Case reports are necessarily incomplete. However, the present reports have value in that they illustrate one possible set of procedures that may account for success with this type of problem. Controlled research must then take over to isolate all of the active ingredients.

The major advantages of a self-controlled approach appear to be the following: (a) reduction in the frequency of counseling sessions, enabling counselors to handle more clients and provide more services, (b) extension of counseling beyond the interview setting, which should significantly reduce the time required for treatment, and (c) reinforcement of active

[12] Editors' Note: Excellent point. Many self-help efforts, such as resolutions to change, fail because of inattention to careful analysis of antecedent and consequent events associated with the problem area. ("What's actually going on?") This failure to critically analyze the environment leads to selecting inappropriate and sometimes problem-enhancing tactics.

self-control of emotions and overt behavior and of independent problem-solving, which should strengthen a sense of personal responsibility and increase feelings of competence and mastery (Cautela, 1966a, 1966b; Homme, 1966). It is important to point out, however, that it is presumptuous to expect that any single therapeutic approach would be equally effective in all cases, even in all cases where the "target problem" is the same, as in the two cases reported here. Studies must be done to investigate not only the effects of self-controlled procedures with a large number of clients, but also the possible differential effects depending upon such factors as type of client (for example, anxiety level, general self-control ability, and other personal-social characteristics) and type of anxiety problem (for example, pervasive, interpersonal, and inanimate).

Three observations about the present case studies might be mentioned in closing which tend to point up the potential value of *in vivo* self-manipulations in desensitization programs. The first is that in the case of Steve a chronic anxiety problem was apparently overcome through the client's own efforts without the help of imaginal desensitization in the counseling room. Secondly, in the case of Frank, anxiety was controlled and overcome in several real-life situations *before* those situations were "desensitized" in counseling. Finally, again in the case of Frank, anxiety was sometimes experienced in life situations *following* "desensitization" of those situations in imagination, which was then controlled and eliminated by self-control.

41

CONTROLLING SEXUAL AND INTERPERSONAL ANXIETIES

David L. Geisinger
BEHAVIOR THERAPY INSTITUTE,
SAUSALITO, CALIFORNIA

The following case is not a typical one. No case is really typical in that each hinges upon a variety of factors which, when considered in their entirety, tend to be unique to a particular client and problem. A case presentation, however, can provide examples or elements which are common to other settings with other clients. One central issue is that of generalizability: what can be learned from this one case that will be applicable to other cases?

LEARNING THE PRINCIPLES

Principles of interaction, intervention and modification, not specific and unvarying techniques, are the elements which are most important to extract from any case study. Each technique is capable of undergoing an almost infinite variety of alterations depending upon the circumstances surrounding its application and the individuals involved.[1] Such alterations, moreover, *should* be made, since counseling must be flexible and individualized if it is to be maximally effective. The flexibility, however, must not be dictated by mere whim, but by a solid familiarity with the principles of human behavior. The case presented here employed techniques based primarily on principles of classical and operant conditioning.

All clients do not progress as smoothly or so positively as this one. Counseling was greatly enhanced in the present instance by the client's high motivation, her diligence in doing the assignments given her, and the splendid co-operation and support of her husband.

In addition, what may be termed "relationship factors" played an influential part in the outcome of this case. The type of relationship involved here was a relaxed one of deep trust, mutual respect, and warmth. In many respects the relationship was more like that of student and teacher than that of client and counselor in the more traditional sense.[2]

THE CASE OF NAOMI

Naomi was a 23-year-old married woman who came from a lower middle-class background. As a child she lived with her grandparents after her parents divorced, returning to live with her mother at the age of 18. Her mother, stepfather, and grandparents were alcoholics, and she was a frequent witness to the vociferous arguments which often occurred when

[1] Editors' Note: The counselor actually needs both. Mastery of a given set of techniques coupled with an understanding of the principles underlying them provides the necessary foundation from which the counselor can build.

[2] Editors' Note: What is termed "relationship factors" indeed may be crucial to what happens. However, this "relationship" actually involves a host of complex present and past behaviors, for example, verbal and nonverbal responses by counselor and client coupled with covert activities such as thoughts, attitudes, and sets. When a counselor acts in a manner producing this "good relationship," he becomes a much more powerful model and reinforcing agent for his client.

they had been drinking. She noted that she was often spanked with a strap or slapped for minor infractions. Her mother and her grandparents had had a puritanical attitude toward sex, and she noted that her parents as well as her grandparents always slept in separate bedrooms. She recalled her mother informing her that her grandfather used to force her grandmother into bed every night. The subject of sex was avoided or, on occasion, talked about in a very pejorative way. As a consequence of her exposure to these and other negative attitudes and experiences she avoided any sexual or romantic involvements during her high school years. After she left high school she found that she was able to interact with members of the opposite sex only when her anxiety was reduced by drinking large amounts of alcoholic beverages. Drinking had not, however, become a problem in later life.

She married at the age of 21. Her husband was a graduate student in the behavioral sciences and was described as a sensitive, thoughtful person who was quite devoted to her. She stated that, in general, she and her husband got along very well.

Sensitivity, Shyness, and Sex

At the time she began counseling there were several areas of concern to her which, because of their pervasiveness, caused her considerable anxiety during much of her waking day. These concerns were (1) an exaggerated sensitivity to criticism from anyone in her environment, particularly from her husband and people in the office where she was a secretary; (2) a marked lack of assertiveness, a shyness, and a tendency to withdraw from social and interpersonal interactions; (3) numerous and persistent feelings of jealousy about her husband which she was aware had no factual basis; (4) painful feelings of discomfort and anxiety about sex, accompanied by a desire to avoid all conversations or situations in which there was even a remote sexual reference.

Her mood was almost always rather gloomy and her facial expression tended to be pained and cheerless. Her physical appearance seemed to mirror this mood: her clothes were drab, unattractive, and ill-fitting; her hair was rarely combed. She was about 40 pounds overweight. In general she conveyed the impression of a person who did not care about her physical appearance, yet in discussion she revealed a definite concern and displeasure with the way she looked. She indicated that she would have liked to take better care of herself, but that most of the time her feelings of self-disgust and her ensuing depressions seemed to rob her of all desire or motivation to work at changing any of these aspects of her appearance.

Concerning her sexual anxiety, she felt that although she loved her husband very much, and although he was a good, attentive, and thoughtful lover, she experienced little pleasure during sex. Most often, intercourse proved to be somewhat painful, although the pain was not especially severe. She was able to experience orgasm sporadically, but most of the time it was accompanied by considerable feelings of guilt. This guilt was related to her inability to put a stop to what she thought might be a "homosexual" fantasy which would drift into her imagination during lovemaking: a nude, faceless woman sexually provoking a faceless man. She felt more stimulated by the image of the woman than by the image of the man. She stated that she had never actually had a homosexual encounter and did not know the origin or reason for this fantasy.

I decided to see her in counseling on a once-a-week basis with the understanding that when the need arose we would see her husband as well. She was told that certain of her problems could most effectively be dealt with by enlisting her husband's support and co-operation. She reported that her husband would be eager to participate in any way he could.

Variety of Techniques

A broad-spectrum approach to counseling was decided upon to deal with the problems of excessive sensitivity to criticism, lack of social assertiveness, and undue sexual anxiety. The following techniques were selected: (1) assertive training, (2) behavior rehearsal, (3) group verbal interaction, (4) thought-stopping, (5) flooding techniques, and (6) systematic desensitization. With regard to desensitization, three separate anxiety hierarchies were constructed in the areas of personal criticism, general sexual stimuli, and jealousy concerning her husband.

The first hour and much of the second were spent in history-taking and in the detailed examination of the circumstances surrounding her various anxieties and depressions. The ongoing behavioral analysis focused on the contingencies of her uncomfortable feelings and maladaptive behavior patterns: when and where did they become manifest, who was present at these times, what was she thinking and doing when they appeared, and what did she do to gain some measure of relief from her discomfort.[3]

[3] Editors' Note: Initial attention to such specifics is very important, and often neglected, in helping the counselor discover what antecedents may be causing the behavior and what consequences may be maintaining the behavior. See Articles 29 and 30.

"THOUGHT-STOPPING" AND COUNTERCONDITIONING

During the second session, in discussing sexual anxiety, I told her in the future to open her eyes during lovemaking and at the final stages of orgasm to look directly at her husband. The point was made that orgasm could, and often did, operate as a powerful positive reinforcement for the stimuli associated with it. Since she had had many orgasms while imagining the homosexual fantasy, this image had become predominant during intercourse. I informed her that in no way did this persistent image mean that she was a homosexual. Opening her eyes during orgasm and looking directly at her husband would interfere with the guilt-producing scene and she would gradually begin to associate her attention and imagination to thoughts of her husband making love to her.[4]

At this point her husband was brought in and both of them were given instructions to engage in as much foreplay as possible prior to intercourse without extending it so far that the situation would begin to become tense and uncomfortable. The relationship between foreplay, vaginal lubrication, relaxation of the muscles in the vaginal walls, and easier, painless intercourse was discussed. Questions that either of them had about sexual technique were solicited and answered in a calm, factual manner.

The following week she reported that she had kept her eyes open during lovemaking and had looked at her husband at the moment of orgasm. She found that she was able to exclude all the former thoughts about her guilt-producing fantasy. She felt a sense of relief about this and also about the fact that the extension of time spent in foreplay had resulted for the first time in the complete absence of pain during intercourse. Orgasm had occurred on both occasions of sexual intercourse during the week.

BEGINNING SYSTEMATIC DESENSITIZATION

The third hour was spent in having her refine and elaborate some of the particular settings in which her anxiety became manifest. A description of the process of desensitization and its rationale was given along with a manual on constructing a hierarchy (Geisinger, 1967).[5] She was asked to begin thinking about specific situations in the areas of criticism, jealousy, and sex. Examples of relevant items within each of these topics were given such as, "Driving home from work with Aaron

---

[4] Editors' Note: Stated differently, the physical act of lovemaking, especially orgasm, would be associated by contiguity with positive visual stimuli, that is, her husband's face rather than with her anxiety producing fantasy.

[5] Editors' Note: See Emery's Article 31 for details of systematic desensitization.

(her husband), you notice him staring at a very attractive woman standing on a corner," and, "You are walking to the store alone and two men drive by slowly and whistle at you."

BEHAVIOR REHEARSAL AND ASSERTIVE TRAINING

During the fourth and fifth sessions behavior rehearsal and assertive training were started. The client reported that her boss had given her an excess amount of work, often resulting in her having to work overtime without compensation in order to finish. She felt angry and resentful about this and was considering leaving her job. I pointed out that she often seemed to take flight from other situations when she felt pressured and abused. It would be helpful for her to learn how to cope more directly with these situations in the future as an alternative to escaping from them.

Using role-playing, I played the part of her employer and she played herself in a typical office interaction. At first her responses were faltering and inadequate and she seemed very ill-at-ease. A tape recording of this behavior rehearsal was played back to her with my suggestions as to how she might improve her communication and be more assertive.[6] She tried again to role-play the same scene. This time she was hostile in a very exaggerated way. Again the tape was played back to her and she laughed when she heard how angrily she had expressed herself. I reversed roles and played her part in the office setting while she played the part of her employer. This modeling technique enabled her to learn in an explicit manner a new way of behaving with her boss. After a few more rehearsals she was able to handle the situation smoothly and comfortably. She was told to practice what she had learned whenever the opportunity arose, both at work and in other settings.

The following week I receive a letter from the client which contained the following passages:

". . . Something that made me feel badly last week was what I interpreted as apathy from you in regard to the notes that I had compiled during the week prior to our last session." (The client often brought in extensive and detailed notes about what had gone on during the week and would read them to me instead of telling me spontaneously what had gone on.) "I had spent quite a bit of time writing down everything I considered important, and when I left your office, I felt that my notes had been a worthless waste of time. In addition, I felt like a guinea pig while reading the notes to you . . . I was very uneasy at the end of the last session concerning your not getting up at the end. I didn't know when the session was over and didn't know when to leave. I felt like I was being put to some kind of test or game."

[6] Editors' Note: Good use of a modeling technique, in this case having the client observe her own behavior.

Lastly, she asked if I would reduce her fee since she was finding it difficult to pay for counseling because her husband was a student and she herself earned only a modest salary. At the bottom of the page, in a postscript, she stated: "I feel guilty for having written this letter."

During the next session I complimented her for having had the courage to write the letter, stating that I knew how difficult it must have been for her to do so. I used the letter as a cogent example of her growing ability to assert herself. I stated that the letter represented an important start in a series of "successive approximations" toward the goal of being able to assert herself in any situation. I then requested that she tell me in person the information she had conveyed in the letter. When she had done this, I complimented her again and told her that I would be happy to reduce the fee as she had requested.[7] I informed her that my not getting up at the end of the last session was not a test or a game but merely an oversight, adding that if she had not had the courage to bring it to my attention, she would have continued to be puzzled by it. Other instances where she failed to ask for clarification of certain matters at her job were called to her attention in order to emphasize the proper time for, and kinds of, assertive behaviors. Further behavior rehearsals concerning this area were practiced near the end of the session.

Continuing Desensitization

Several sessions were then spent in teaching her the technique of progressive relaxation (Jacobson, 1938). She was told to practice this technique at home for two 15-minute periods daily. At about this time she stated that she had always felt particularly anxious at the time of her menstrual periods. She claimed that she would like to be able to have the convenience of using an internal device such as a tampon but found that her anxiety made the insertion of such devices painful. We agreed to include the insertion of such devices as an item on her "general sexual anxiety" hierarchy.

By the twelfth session considerable progress on the desensitization of the hierarchy had been made. Her mood in the office had undergone a perceptible change—she smiled a good deal more and stated that she was feeling more comfortable at work. She reported an instance in which she was able to be more assertive with her boss with no associated anxiety. Work was begun in the desensitization of her sensitivity to innocuous personal criticism and in the area of jealousy about her husband, Aaron.

[7] Editors' Note: This probably was an immediately reinforcing consequence for her being assertive!

During the fourteenth session she said, "Yesterday I was actually joking with Mr. Tomkins (office manager) at the office—I can't believe it!"

Desensitization in the three areas mentioned previously continued during the latter half of each subsequent counseling session. For the most part, several items on each of the three hierarchies were presented to the patient during a given session. The first half of each session was devoted to a review of her progress and a general discussion of other issues that had arisen during the week. When matters of particular significance arose which required longer discussion, the amount of time spent on desensitization proper was reduced.[8]

During the fifteenth session once again Naomi was asked to move to another chair in the office—a large, comfortable recliner chair. The room was darkened a bit by drawing the window blinds. She was then instructed to shut her eyes and recline in the chair while beginning to give herself instructions to relax. Since she had frequently practiced relaxation at home as well as having gone through many relaxation sessions in the office while receiving explicit verbal instructions from me, it was no longer necessary to give her these specific instructions in order to get her to relax. She was now able to reach a deeply relaxed state by herself in only five minutes.

She was told to signal by raising her left index finger when she felt very relaxed. After she had done this I told her that if during the course of any of the imagination sequences she became at all anxious or tense, she was to indicate this to me by raising her right index finger.

Items 23 and 24 from the "general sexual anxiety" hierarchy were presented to her along with item 14 on the "criticism" hierarchy and item 12 on the "jealousy" hierarchy. Each item was repeated until the criterion of three consecutive presentations with no reporting of anxiety was met.[9]

The items were presented for the first time for 5 seconds, the second time for 10 seconds, the third time for 20 seconds. From time to time "perception checks" were made by asking the client to signal if she was able to imagine vividly the item being described to her. These perception checks are a useful adjunct to the desensitization procedure in that they

[8] Editors' Note: This brings up an important question. Would counseling prove just as effective or even more so without these discussions during the first half of each session? The answer may lie in some optimal combination of certain amounts and kinds of discussion with certain types of clients having particular problems.

[9] Editors' Note: An interesting question is raised here, in terms of efficiency and effectiveness, about working on several specific problems. In Naomi's case she was explicitly dealing with her problems of sexual anxiety, criticism, and jealousy. Is it more effective to complete desensitization on one problem before going on to another? Or do concurrent efforts such as working on three hierarchies, as in this case, actually interact to foster more rapid change?

give the counselor feedback as to whether the client has not been signaling because, perhaps, she has not been able to imagine the scenes being described rather than because she didn't experience anxiety. In addition, this technique also permits the counselor to know if, as happens on rare occasions, the client has gradually lapsed into sleep.

The last item presented during the hour was, as always, an item describing an experience in which the client felt particularly calm and peaceful. In Naomi's case this was a description of herself being served breakfast in bed by Aaron during a particular Sunday morning. Having the last scene in the desensitization sequence be a pleasant one tends to ensure that the procedure itself does not become associated with an anxiety-producing experience, since the last item in a chain of events is usually the one which is most clearly remembered.

Evidence of Progress

During the seventeenth session she reported the following progress: (1) she had used a tampon during the second day of her menstrual cycle, after trying unsuccessfully during the first day, and was able to do so quite easily with no pain; (2) while at a new friend's house she played the piano in front of several people though formerly she had been too self-conscious and frightened of making mistakes to do this; (3) she called up a prospective employer who had delayed making a definite commitment to her and told him diplomatically but assertively that she expected to hear from him one way or the other about a particular job.

She entered the next hour stating, "A number of people have told me I've completely changed, that I'm a new person." Though she continued to wear drab, ill-fitting clothing and no make-up, her mood continued to be optimistic and, in contrast to her former appearance, her facial expressions were more animated. In view of the fact that she had no pressing problems that she wanted to discuss, the hour was devoted in its entirety to the desensitization procedure, as were the next two sessions.

Jealousy and Appearance

During the twenty-second session, she indicated that she was still excessively jealous of Aaron's attention. She expressed her discouragement about the fact that the desensitization did not seem to be working in this area. "I still get upset whenever Aaron's concern, time or interest is spent on other people, even other men. I get especially upset whenever Aaron looks at any woman. It seems like a setback." I assured her that it was not a setback but that perhaps it was an indication that we were not working on the most basic dimension relating to her feelings of jealousy. I was unable, however, to arrive at any alternatives at the time and, to some extent, secretly shared her discouragement. I told her, however, that we would continue to explore this subject in future sessions until we could discover the basis for her difficulty.

After thinking about the matter during the intervening week I began to suspect that the patient's jealousy of her husband's attention might be related to her feelings about her own appearance. She had, after all, occasionally hinted about her dissatisfaction with the way she looked, and it was apparent that her self-concept had been a poor one for many years. Aaron, however, prided himself on what he felt was his well-balanced sense of values. He often derogated what he called the "superficial aspects of life," among which was a concern with "mere appearance" such as attractive, stylish clothing and make-up, while laying strong emphasis on matters of intellect. This message was an irritating paradox to the patient because Aaron would often notice other women who were obviously not of shining intellect while commenting enthusiastically about their attractive appearances. Naomi had grown quite reluctant to spend any money on improving her own appearance though it seemed that she would welcome the opportunity to do so if she were not criticized for it.

With this in mind, I began the next session by commenting on how much better she looked since she had been on her diet. I brought up the fact that she would soon have to buy new clothes to accommodate her new figure. She picked up this topic with great enthusiasm and began to elaborate upon it, essentially supporting the hypothesis I had made earlier. She indicated that she was particularly upset by Aaron's criticism and as a result she had gone without any make-up for over a year. She added that she was also in great need of a new coat since the one she now wore was practically falling apart.

We discussed Aaron's inconsistency: that he talked one way but behaved in another in that he was actually very responsive to women who were physically attractive. She decided gradually to improve her physical appearance the following week. In addition, we went through several behavior rehearsals in which I played the part of Aaron and she played herself bringing up the matter of buying new clothes.

Naomi entered the twenty-fourth session wearing a new coat. She noted that Aaron had been "a pushover" and had made no protest whatsoever when she brought up the subject of purchasing new clothing. She had begun to wear eye-liner and some mascara, and even though Aaron did not remark about it one way or the other, she said, "I'm feeling much better about myself." She added that she did not have any feelings of jealousy during the week.

"Flooding" Sex Talk

During the next session, she expressed concern that "sex-talk" in conversation continued to make her quite anxious. "Certain words trigger my anxiety, it seems, especially when Aaron is around." I asked her what these words were and she mentioned among others the following terms: chick, babe, broad, lay, fuck, cunt, whore, prostitute, screw, bubble-dance, tits, knockers, boobs, seduce, make, breasts, figure, shape, nude, shack-up, sexy, voluptuous, orgy, harem, bigamy, knocked-up, piece of ass.

The procedure of "flooding" was described to her and in accord with this she was instructed to read the list of words to herself at least 15 times a day for the next two weeks. She was also told to make up sentences that incorporated these words and to read these sentences aloud to Aaron several times each day, after which Aaron was to read them back to her. It was further suggested that they try to inject some humor into this homework assignment in order to speed up the process of desensitization, since humor is, in most instances, strongly incompatible with anxiety.[10]

Two weeks later she and her husband returned to the office. They had done the exercises diligently and with good results. Her anxiety about the "sex-talk" had diminished markedly, and she was much more comfortable participating in social conversation.

SOME CHANGES

At this time Aaron was graduating from the university and had accepted a job in another city. It was generally agreed that this move fortunately coincided with what seemed to be an appropriate stopping point in counseling. Naomi had changed considerably. She had eliminated several phobias, had become more assertive, was more relaxed in her social interactions, her sex life had improved as did her relationship with her husband in general, and perhaps most importantly, her thoughts and feelings about herself had undergone decided improvement.

[10] Editors' Note: In this example a type of "graduated flooding" is used since Naomi was not asked to say these words in normal social situations. "Flooding" and other techniques based in part on operant extinction such as implosive therapy (see Stampfl & Levis, 1967) may seem quite different from systematic desensitization based on the principle of counterconditioning. Both procedures, however, are quite similar, focusing on the repetitive exposure to stress producing stimuli without aversive consequences. Gradual exposure to stressful stimuli may in the long run prove more effective since excessive anxiety is not aroused and the opportunity for adaptive responses to occur is increased.

An interesting sidelight to this case occurred ten months later. The author and his colleague, who was familiar with the case, were attending a professional meeting and noticed Aaron sitting in the audience on the other side of the room. During the coffee break we approached him to say hello, and I naturally asked how his wife was getting along. He smiled broadly and without saying anything he tapped a young woman on the shoulder who was standing near him chatting with another group of people and said, "You can ask her yourself." When she turned around and greeted us, we found it hard to believe our eyes. It was Naomi. Her hair had been cut and set in an attractive new style, her figure was lithe, she was wearing a bright new dress, tastefully applied make-up, and had even changed her eye-glass frames, from the large, unflattering ones she formerly wore. She seemed poised, outgoing and obviously at ease as she told us how well things had been going for her.[11]

APPENDIX

GENERAL SEXUAL ANXIETY HIERARCHY

1. Patricia (a married woman who works in my office) is flirting with some men in the office; she is calling them "honey," "sweetie," and occasionally holds their hands.
2. I am walking downtown during my lunch hour. There is a man standing up against a building who is staring at a woman as she walks by him. The woman doesn't notice him.
3. I am walking downtown during my lunch hour. There are two men standing on a corner who scrutinize a woman as she walks by them. She doesn't notice them, but after she walks by the men look at each other and grin.
4. I am sitting at my desk at the office. Three men are waiting for the elevator. I look up and notice that they are all looking at me.
5. I am driving to the store alone and see a carload of men trying to pick up two girls. The girls seem slightly self-conscious, but it is obvious that they are enjoying it.
6. I am walking to the store alone and two men drive by and whistle at me.
7. My husband and I go to a new friend's house. In the living room is a profile drawing of a nude (from the waist up).
8. I am with my husband at a friend's house. On a coffee table there is a copy of "Playboy" magazine casually opened to a page containing a color photograph of a voluptuous nude woman.
9. I'm in my office and the door to Mr. Tomkins' (office manager) office is open. I hear him telling a dirty joke on the telephone in a low voice. After telling the joke he laughs heartily and says, "Isn't that awful?"

---

[11] Editors' Note: Some "stories" still do have happy endings!

10. I am in the office with Bob (a junior executive) and Mr. Gordon (my boss). Mr. Gordon says to Bob, "I'd like to do nothing but chase women."
11. I am sitting on the toilet at home. I am beginning to give myself a douche by inserting the nozzle into my vagina.
12. I'm sitting at my desk in the office. As a workman walks by my office, he quickly sticks his head in the door and says, "Hi, beautiful."
13. I'm walking to the store and two men across the street make kissing noises at me.
14. I'm at the office and Bob is explaining procedures to me. While he is talking, he is looking at my breasts.
15. I'm in a small store and it is rather crowded. As a strange man steps past me he casually puts his hands on my waist.
16. Downtown I see a woman wearing heavy makeup who is standing on a corner looking as though she wants to be picked up.
17. At my parents' home, my father says, "A woman's duty is to her husband; he is the master and she'll do as he desires."
18. At my parents' home, my mother and father have just come home from seeing a burlesque show, and they are discussing the shapes of the women performers.
19. I'm at a movie. A woman who is partially clothed is shown on the screen and men in the audience whistle and shout.
20. I'm at a movie. Partially clothed women are shown dancing on the screen. The men in the audience whistle, shout and laugh.
21. Ralph (a friend) is at our house. He's telling of a movie he saw in which a very long line of beautiful girls are waiting to enter the bedroom of the male star.
22. I'm walking down the hall in the office building. Some workmen are doing electrical work and as I walk by they look at my breasts, hips, and thighs.
23. I'm at the office and Mr. Gordon is giving directions to another girl as to how to get to the camera store. He says, "It's right next door to where the topless girls are."
24. I am at home sitting on the toilet putting a tampon in my vagina.
25. I'm walking with another girl downtown. A drunk man staggers out of a bar and says, "Care to spread your legs, honey?"
26. I'm at the doctor's office and he is spreading the opening of my vagina in order to give me a pelvic examination.
27. My husband, our friend Don, and I are driving downtown. Don points to a woman and says, "Boy, that woman has big breasts."
28. While waiting for the bus I see a sign carved into the wooden bus shelter saying, "All waves throw a good fuck."
29. Bob, Mr. Gordon, and I are in the office. Mr. Gordon stands in front of me, looks at my breasts and says, "Never let a challenge go by."

CRITICISM HIERARCHY

1. At the office building Cathy, another secretary, says, "Why don't you wear your hair down?"

2. Mr. Tomkins, the boss, asks, "Have you registered to vote?" I reply, "No," and he says jokingly, "You stinker!"

3. At the office one of my letters is returned to me by Dorothy the district manager's secretary. She has put red marks all over the letter with the statement added, "Please check spelling of names, and counties."

4. At home while playing darts with Aaron I shoot a dart which comes close to the target and Aaron says, "Just a little higher, Hon."

5. At class the teacher says, "Naomi, how can this statement be proven?" I shrug my shoulders and he frowns.

6. Alice, one of the clerks at the office, tells me, "You have a tiny rip in the back of your dress."

7. While doing poorly at darts, Aaron suggests, "Why don't you try holding the dart differently?"

8. At the office, the boss brings back a letter I've composed and says, "Next time it might be better not to be so blunt in telling the customer that he's made an error."

9. Aaron is looking at some math problems I've done at home and says, "These two are right, but in this one you have cancelled the numerators by mistake."

10. At home I receive a letter from my grandmother stating, "You had better start settling down and staying at one job."

11. At home I am telling Aaron of a new route to the bridge. He replies, "That freeway doesn't go to the bridge; it ends up downtown."

12. While shooting darts poorly at home, Ken suggests, "Maybe leaning forward would help."

13. At the office building I go to the mail room to make Xerox copies. As I am leaving the mail room, the clerk sarcastically says, "Don't go out of here without picking up your mail."

14. At the office the mail room clerk brings me the mail and notes that I'm not doing anything. He says, "Here's something for you to do while you're resting."

15. At the office building a man says to me when I'm buying a candy bar, "That's fattening, you know."

16. At the office while taking shorthand, I misunderstand a word and send the letter out with the wrong word in it. The boss's attention is called to the error and he tells me, "You should have caught that."

17. At home I receive a letter from mother after I've told her that I'm drawing unemployment, and she implies I'm a thief by the statement: "People like Dad work hard all their lives putting money into that fund, and then small-time crooks come along and drag it out."

18. At the office I'm talking to an irate man on the phone who says, "What have you people been doing? I've been waiting for my travel orders for a week!"

19. I am crossing the street and am half way to the other side when the light changes to "Don't Walk." A man drives by me and says, "Read the signs!"

20. I am walking out of a post office downtown at the same time a man is entering the building and he says to me, "You're using the wrong door."

21. At home I receive a letter from my grandmother in which she states, "Dad is disgusted with you."
22. At home I am trying to awaken Aaron and am rubbing the bottom of his foot. He irritably says, "That doesn't go over."
23. I start eating a bowl of ice cream at home and Aaron disgustedly looks on and says, "It's not the ice cream so much—it's the amount. I don't know how you can eat so much without getting sick."
24. At home Aaron said, "Your thighs used to be so big that I could see no distinction where your butt ended and your thighs began."

JEALOUSY HIERARCHY

1. Aaron and I are at Ron and Dora's house. Aaron and Ron are talking to each other and laughing.
2. At home I am reading a letter from Aaron's mother and in it she mentions various female relatives of his.
3. At home Aaron tells me that Jack helped him look for apartments all afternoon.
4. Aaron and I are in the supermarket. Aaron bumps into a woman and cordially says, "Pardon me."
5. At home Aaron says he saw the movie "Sound of Music" while I was gone, and he enjoyed it very much.
6. In front of the office building I introduce Aaron to Helen (another secretary), and he is very charming and cordial.
7. At school a girl asks a question in physics class and Aaron looks at her.
8. Aaron and I are at the roller skating rink and he asks a woman of about 50 years of age to skate with him.
9. Ron, Dora, Aaron, and I are at the Xanadu Ballroom and Aaron is waltzing with Dora.
10. I introduce Aaron to Cathy outside the office building and he is very charming.
11. At home Aaron is telling me about his course and says of his female teacher, "She's pretty sharp in some ways."
12. Aaron and I are at Norton's restaurant and Aaron is courteous and pleasant to the attractive waitress.
13. Aaron and I are at a restaurant, and an attractive woman sitting near us keeps staring at him.
14. Aaron and I are at the roller rink. It is the girls' turn to have the floor to themselves for doing tricks, and Aaron watches them intently.
15. Aaron and I are downtown during lunch hour and there are numerous well-dressed, attractive women all around us.
16. Aaron and I are at a dancing studio and the good-looking female dancing instructor is dancing with him.
17. Aaron looks at a billboard in town which shows a sexy-looking woman with a low-cut dress on.
18. Driving home from work, Aaron stares at a woman with a good figure who is standing on the corner.

19. Aaron and I are at Norton's restaurant. A waitress with a good figure swings her hips when she walks by and Aaron looks her up and down.
20. Aaron and I are at Steve's house. We are sitting opposite to Steve and his wife, Lois. Lois is wearing a skirt and has her legs pulled up to her chest so that Aaron can see her crotch area.
21. Aaron and I are at a friend's house. We are about to leave and a woman who boards there comes out to the doorway of her bedroom in her panties and bra. She looks at us and says, "You aren't leaving so early, are you?"

Academic Problems

INABILITY TO CONCENTRATE, difficulties in listening to lectures and taking notes, confusions about organizing and planning the use of time, stress experienced in participating in class discussions, and excessive anxiety in taking examinations are some of the problems labeled as academic. Anything that interferes with the performance of a student in school may be considered an academic problem.

Academic problems are as complex as interpersonal problems, and a single method of helping all students is insufficient. Counselors are in an excellent position to provide very concrete and specific help for students faced with situations that impair academic performance. Counselors need a broad spectrum of techniques to help different kinds of students with different kinds of problems.

In Article 42 Weinstein presents a new group counseling procedure for assisting certain kinds of students suffering from excessive examination anxiety. Using a theory of how different kinds of persons learn, Weinstein categorized some students as extroverts and devised a group procedure called structured group interaction. Other students, identified as introverts, were provided systematic desensitization in groups. The study demonstrates that test-taking anxiety can be reduced in real-life examination situations.

Jones, in Article 43, explored three different group techniques for use with students experiencing problems of studying. Considerable detail of two techniques, group social modeling and group desensitization, is provided along with information on a third treatment called group centered counseling. Jones used a standardized written social model which was individually tailored by each counseling group to fit its own members.

Both these articles suggest that counselors can take concrete and deliberate steps to help clients improve their academic performance. Counselors can individually tailor counseling procedures to fit the particular types of academic problems experienced by different kinds of clients.

42

REDUCING TEST ANXIETY

Francine T. Weinstein
UNIVERSITY OF TENNESSEE

This report describes a project undertaken at Michigan State University to help highly test-anxious college students reduce their excessive fear of examinations (Weinstein, 1968).[1] Two kinds of counseling treatment groups were developed to find out which method worked more effectively with particular types of individuals experiencing the same problem. Students were identified as introverted and extroverted on the basis of the Eysenck Personality Inventory (Eysenck and Eysenck, 1964). The two treatments were termed systematic desensitization and structured group interaction. It was hypothesized that introverts would experience more reduction in test-taking anxiety in the systematic desensitization treatment than would extroverts. In contrast it was hypothesized that extroverts would demonstrate reduced anxiety when counseled in structured group interaction. This report concerns the structured group interaction procedure. Information on the details of the group desensitization has been reported elsewhere (Neuman, 1968; Weinstein, 1968; Leon, 1967; Paul & Shannon, 1966).

STRUCTURED GROUP INTERACTION

The structured group interaction treatment, specifically designed for this study as an alternate to systematic desensitization, was suggested

[1] Carl E. Thoresen participated in conducting this study while at Michigan State University.

from theoretical and experimental studies on the psychological functioning of the extrovert (Eysenck & Rachman, 1965; Peters, 1966; Pavlov, 1957).[2] It was reasoned that a treatment for extroverts should be verbal in nature, demand discussion, require group interaction and activity. For example, examination-taking practice and creating and rehearsing new roles, in general, actively involve the student in the use of all sensory processes. This approach differs from traditional group counseling in terms of its organization, structure, length, breadth of treatment, and underlying philosophy. Structured group interaction attempted to limit the problem to a specific situation and, more importantly, it kept the specified problem as the central focus and task of the treatment by providing session outlines.

A Brief Overview

In constructing the session outlines there was a need to start with the present. The problem of test-taking anxiety was viewed as a "now" problem. The goal was a change in present unsatisfying behaviors, for example, learning to respond to test situations with reduced amounts of stress and anxiety.

Since the emphasis was on the *here and now* and *changing behavior*, the first session concentrated on the counselees' identifying and defining test anxiety as they experienced it, that is, the way in which it incapacitated them in particular current situations.

The first of the five sessions was predominantly concerned with adjustment to the group, identification of the problem elements (particular maladaptive behaviors) and the development of a group hierarchy of maladaptive test-taking behaviors common to the four members.

The second, third, and fourth meetings comprised the core of the sessions. Each session capitalized on the group members' experience that week, self-help attempts, and carrying out of prescribed homework designed for a particular counselee by his group and counselor. These procedures served to maximize the meaning of the one hour allotted per session.

Although meeting in groups served to maximize counselor time and service, the individual counselee within the group was central. There was no one way to reduce test anxiety presented to all group members. The underlying view was "Whatever works to reduce test anxiety, use it!" And of course using it is the most essential element. For example, the third session (see Session Outline) emphasized creating a new, more adaptive role, as a test taker. In one particular group a more general

---

[2] See Weinstein (1968, pp. 6–31) for a summary discussion of the relationship of personality types and conditionability to counseling techniques.

goal was feeling "comfortable" and relaxed immediately preceding the exam. In this group one of the members interpreted this goal as "sitting and reading the student newspaper alone to get his mind off the test." For a second group member the behavior which he felt would be most facilitating in calming him was, "standing outside the exam room talking to some buddies." In both instances the "behaviors" had been suggested to these students during group interaction. The fact that they were suggested as means of warding off test anxiousness is not in itself as important as what was done with the suggestions. It became the responsibility of the two counselees to try out the new behaviors the intervening week before weekly exams.

The following week one boy reported that reading the paper was extremely effective in helping him to remain composed. In fact he happily related to the group that some fellow students had commented that they wished they could feel as unruffled as he apparently looked.

In the second case "talking to buddies outside the exam room" was not as effective and so it was modified with the group's help to: "talking to students who were more tense, anxious or afraid of the exam than he." The modified behavior was again tried the following week and was found to be quite beneficial.

In the above illustrations, as in the experiences of the other 30 students who received help, those who derived the most benefit were those students who tried out the suggestions, modified them in light of subsequent experience, tried out the modifications, and continued this practice until the behaviors felt comfortable and natural. Those students who gained least from the program in terms of the criterion measures (performance on three test-anxiety inventories at the time of the final exam) were those who discussed their blocking, panicking, and fear of examinations in the group but thought in general that practicing responses between sessions would not really help.[3]

The fourth session stressed study skills and effective test preparation, on the assumption that while examination fear may be inappropriate it may also be realistic if preparation for exams was faulty or lacking. This session, then, accented learning as well as relearning. As in the other sessions "homework" was essential and crucial in making the most of a five week period.

The fifth meeting did not introduce anything new but tried to cement the gains and iron out problems. This hour, being a few days before

[3] Editors' Note: Why were some students more enthusiastic about practicing between group sessions, trying out and altering new behaviors, while others tended to focus on verbal expression of their problem? Perhaps previous counseling experiences by some students coupled with expectations about what counseling ought to be characterized the "talkers."

final examinations, served to reinforce the groups' newly gained confidence. At this time many group members were in agreement that the sessions were unique and invaluable in helping to identify the individual's particular maladaptive test-taking actions, demanding that he behave differently by trying out new, less defeating behaviors and at the same time receiving support and advice from other group members.

Session Outlines and Some Simulated Dialogue

The following outlines and scripts provide information on what happened in each session. The three scripts are simulated in that a composite representing the kinds of problems dealt with in most of the groups is presented. The specific examples have been extracted, concentrated, and edited to give you the flavor of what took place.

THE FIRST SESSION

Here is a brief outline and rationale used by the group counselor for the first session:

1. Introduction of self
2. Explanation of rationale and course of treatment—about 10 minutes
3. Introduction of group members and exploration of history and current status of the problem—about 20 minutes
4. Have students help pull together and summarize extent of problem that group is to work with—about 15 minutes
   A. Determine with group what previous attempts at self help, or professional help, have been and their effectiveness
   B. Enlist possible "active" suggestions for working with this group
5. Discuss the nature of anxiety hierarchy and pass out hierarchy sheet (ditto). Get student reaction to list, modifications, suggestions, and so forth—about 15 minutes
6. Remind group of time of next session and necessity of coming without fail. *Stress!*
7. Use the following for explaining rationale:

> The emotional reactions which you experience as a result of your previous experience with testing situations often leads to feelings of anxiety or tenseness that are really inappropriate. As long as you can recall how you've felt in these situations, it is possible to work with your reactions right here in this room by having you imagine yourself in these situations as vividly as possible.
>
> You might say we are going to relive the tense, nervous feelings, in the things we do in here, so that when we actually do face examinations, the stress won't seem as great as it previously did.

We are going to continue to meet in a small group because we have something to offer each other. We all know what that tense, anxious feeling is like. So we're going to share the feeling and benefit from the others' experience with it.

The technique that will be used here is called structured group interaction and each word is a clue to how the sessions will proceed.

Our feeling is that the benefit of this program of help will be greatest for those who really become involved, "active," and contribute to, as well as use, the other group members.

We are going to do a number of things the purpose of which is to create a lot of feelings you have had when taking exams and then to learn to react differently by controlling these feelings so they don't control you. This will mean creating the same situations through practice test-taking, role-playing (explain—for example, reenacting the most anxiety-producing situations for each group member), focusing on what tenseness feels like to us all.

Are there any questions?

This is an example of the interaction in the first session:

Jim: Well, really, I think I'm prepared when I go in to take the test, I mean I studied all my notes, but I get this feeling that maybe I left something out. Then I see the test, look it over and sure enough I spot a question I can't answer and wow, that's the end! I don't know what happens to me from there.

Co: Does this sound familiar to anyone else? I see some heads nodding. You also experience test anxiety like this, Ann?

Ann: I'd call it shaky confidence for myself. But it winds up the same way. I prepare but I'm never really sure what I know. Multiple guess tests can get awfully "picky." So as soon as I see the test I almost look for questions I can't answer. I always find them, too. Then I start to sweat, get dizzy and forget everything.

Co: Bob, what happens to you when you get in there?

Bob: I know what Jim and Ann mean. I've had that feeling but it's not the same kind of problem for me. I'm a clock watcher, and I can't keep my eyes off the clock—I become hypnotized. I watch the minutes tick away and get more and more tense until I can't concentrate at all. I always run out of time and have to just go through and check any answer on the remaining questions. . . . (later in the same session)

Co: Now maybe we have some ammunition to attack the problem. Bob's suggestion might help two of you focus on what you *can* do and *can* answer; and remember Bob, you can only look at the clock three times during the whole exam. Well, making all these promises to yourselves is well intended but they may not work for you when really faced with the exam. Anyone having a quiz between now and next week? O.K., Sue and Jim, try out the suggestions and remember, the rest of us are "anxious" to see if they really help. . . .

SECOND SESSION

This is the outline used by the counselor in conducting the second session.

To reduce anxiety:

1. Change in test-taking behavior
   A. Learning specific, better, more adaptive habits and skills
   B. Reduce physiological and muscular tension through *practice* relaxing posture, breathing exercises, and so forth.
   C. More positive attitudes—"I won't know it all but *much* of it and the rest I can guess on." Therefore, not knowing one answer will not cause panic.

2. Provide verbal reinforcement for positive steps toward changing behavior

3. Encourage use of self-reward and punishment re: satisfactory and unsatisfactory performance on tests

CONTENTS OF THE SECOND SESSION

Sometimes it is difficult to focus on what about tests really gets us tense and nervous, This is especially true when we just *talk* about it from memory, so we are going to create the very same situation and conditions by taking an exam here today.

We must try to make it as close to the real testing situation as possible. O.K. We have a chalk board and I'll write the minutes left on it as the time passes. What other kinds of things would make this situation real for you? (Get suggestions and act upon them if possible, for example, use writing boards on laps, IBM answer sheets and scoring pencils or blue book for essay questions.)

Now that the setting seems right the important thing is the way you view the situation. So let's set some guide lines. The test is in a course that is important to you. It's the last exam and therefore your performance will be very crucial to your final grade. You've studied for this test about as much as you usually do. You have the same kinds of feelings about this test as you usually have about others you have taken like it.

Do you see what we're trying to do? The goal is to experience the same kinds of feelings and reactions here where we can later focus on them while they're still vivid and real. The more you can make this situation like an actual test-taking situation the more you will be able to focus on your usual test-taking behavior and the more you can learn how to deal with it or change it.

You will have 20 minutes for the test. (Give out test and answer sheets, pencils.)

INTRODUCTION (10 MINUTES)

Before test begins, distribute large blank index cards and ask students to write down anything bothering them or interfering with taking exam or distracting them (mentally or physically) from test—anything at all, cue words, free associations, and so forth.

TEST (20 MINUTES)

During test counselor will observe behavior—make notes on characteristic modes for each student; (that is, crossing and uncrossing legs, biting nails, squirming, biting pencil, rigid or awkward posture, perspiring, trembling, pained facial expression, closed eyes or blank stare, or other indications of inefficient behavior).

At the end of 20 minutes stop the test. Begin discussion:

What kinds of reactions do they have to test? What did students feel? How well aware are they of inefficient behavior?

(1) Point out how one or two of them responded (behaviorally) to get the ball rolling, for example, "Dave, how did you feel about the test?" Let him explain. He probably won't be aware of his extraneous but interfering behavior. Tell him how you perceived his test-taking behavior, nervously biting pencil then staring blankly as if frozen.

(2) Go around pointing out maladaptive behavior and encourage interaction by getting members to offer suggestions for how they would *like* to behave—for example, sit relaxed not tense, breathe normally, get non-test thoughts out of mind.

(3) Focus on index cards. What things, feelings, ideas intruded and interfered. Let's name things—not just let it go as vague, diffuse panic or disinterest. If X, Y, and Z things interfered let's *learn* to get rid of them. Be ready to offer concrete, precise suggestions for dealing with them. (Some of these will follow.)

(4) What are the problems encountered?
   a. I look at the first question and can't answer it so I panic.
   b. The test is *long* and this scares me.
   c. Each question has four or five choices—I can't figure out which one is right.
   d. I watch the time tick away and this immobilizes me.

The above items refer to the test situation as the stimulus for anxiety responses. Assuming the students *know* the materials, the goal which seems to be blocked is demonstrating the knowledge.

Some specific suggestions to help counteract the above problems are as follows:

a. Admit to yourself that you will not know *all* the answers. Instead of saying over and over, "I'm afraid I won't know it," say "Some of it I won't know and some of it I will." Thus when you read the first question and don't know the answer you will respond not with the conclusion that you know nothing, not by clutching, but by saying "That's *one* I don't know."

b. Figure out a time schedule. Don't let length scare you, do something constructive about it. Figure amount of time per question and stick to it—leave a few minutes at the end to review or complete test.

c. Go through exam and answer all those items which are easiest and which you are sure of. Then tackle less sure ones. For each question look at choices. Cross out those which are obviously wrong. If left with two choices make an educated guess. Translate items into own words and see if that is what it really says—don't read into item. Accept each at face value.

d. Realize that time will go by anyway—*use* it to your advantage to measure progress—*x* minutes for each item.

e. Suppose all the choices seem true? Perhaps they all are but pick the *one* that *answers the question.*

Factors or problems not related to actual test:

(1) Reducing physiological or muscular tension. Get back to behavioral observations. Encourage students to tell about where or how they felt tension. The counselor may have to get them started by referring to observations made when students were taking test.

    a. To reduce muscle tension—practice relaxation. Counselor demonstrates tensing muscles and relaxing; individualize.

    b. To regulate breathing; to calm down—practice inhaling deeply and exhaling.

    c. For rigid or awkward postures—practice composed, comfortable posture.

    Individualize—allow and encourage each student to practice *his own* anxiety-combating responses.

(2) Getting rid of extraneous, unwanted, or persistent nontest ideas and thoughts.

    a. Interfering thoughts to serve as cue for action—penalty for thinking these is loss of time and points on test. Count each distracting thought as one minute lost.

    b. Decide on punishments for nontest related thoughts, for example, no date Saturday, deny self new shirt or record. Reward self for calm, non-anxious and clear-headed performance—for example, take Saturday afternoon off for fun.

    Homework—practice responding to any tests between the second and third sessions in the above way. Have students keep record of this to focus on in the third session.

Now here is a typical excerpt representing the second session:

Jim: I just can't see how writing down how I felt during this test can help.

Co: What kinds of things did you write down on the card?

Joe: One note I made was, "stuck on number eight, can't move on, frozen." Now that I think of it, I was doing fine until then. I didn't understand number eight but couldn't skip it. I felt compelled to figure it out and spent way too much time on it.

Co: Did anyone else have trouble with that item?

Sue: I didn't with that one, but I started to get the same feeling with a different question and knew I would panic so I said to myself, "No, remember last week, go on to one you can do." So altogether I left a few out, but at least I kept my head.

Co: Maybe taking this test did help by pointing out interfering and self-defeating behaviors. It looks like you may have landed on a good way of preventing panic.

Ann: Yeah, it works here but will it help when I'm faced with the test that counts? Maybe I won't be so brave then.

Bob: I don't know if this will help but I had a quiz Wednesday and said to myself, "Well, it isn't a final and so maybe it's worth a chance. I mean, why am I wasting my time with a group like this if I'm not serious." So I took off my watch, put it on the next seat so I couldn't see it, and forced myself not to look at the room clock more than three times. I still thought about the time too much but at least I finished before time ran out. That's something for me, I didn't leave the room dripping wet.

THE THIRD SESSION

This is the outline used by the counselor.

A. Review of second session (see guide for second session)—10 minutes
   1. Test-taking techniques practiced
      a. doing easy items first
      b. focus on test not clock, and so forth
   2. Relaxation responses—usefulness and attempts at self-induced relaxation
   3. Ridding mind of nontest taking thoughts
   4. Usefulness of index card method for noting "disturbances"
   5. Reaction to last week's test and the use to which techniques were put outside during the week (generalization)
   6. Effectiveness of index cards used while studying or taking "real" exams
   7. Counselor reinforcement of statements pertaining to attempts by student to work on problem outside
B. Content of third session
   1. Get group to discuss ways in which they either did use, or could use, the three kinds of techniques:
      a. test-taking skills and hints

b. relaxation and other physical measures (breathing, assuming and practicing a comfortable posture)

c. getting nagging thoughts out of mind (writing down on cards, self-reward and punishment)

2. Discuss content of students' index cards which were accumulated over week. What specifically prevents John from performing optimally? Focus on each student and try to bring about suggestions from group members to help John change his maladaptive responses. For example, What can John do to change? What behaviors that are different from his present ones (heart beating, looking around aimlessly in test room at others, verbalizing fear to peers) could John engage in (for example, breathe deeply, either don't talk about fear of test to others or play a confident role, be a model of composure)? Importance of creating a new role or self-image as a test-taker.

3. What kind of a role does John want? Just what does he want to do that is different—what behaviors does he want to change?

   a. discuss in general the characteristics of a less defeating role

   b. emphasize importance of individuality since role has to fit or at least feel comfortable—so it will be practiced, which is a crucial element. Point to any common elements which students may identify. "Not all of you want to change the same things or behave the same way on tests but there may be some common denominator."

4. Creation of a new role of test-taker. Just what does it mean (based on foregoing ideas of maladaptive behavior, need to change, characteristics of more adaptive behavior). Based on theory of personal constructs and fixed role therapy.

5. After students understand and have a feel for changing their test-taking role, encourage discussion about construction of a new role. (What elements to emphasize, how to write the "part," how the skills learned in last session fit in.) Make role very specific and detailed and applicable to all possible test situations (the ideal test-taking self). Keep in mind that drastic changes are often easier to bring about than slight changes. Also, the student must really be willing to give the role a try in the real world—modifications may be necessary later on.

6. Allow time for construction of new role. Students will write the new role in counseling room (provide paper)—about 15 minutes.

7. Reading roles, sharing, reacting to one another's role, and discussing ways in which they can be enacted, practiced. Emphasize seriousness of task—try to dispel frivolity relative to role-playing. Focus on any tests which students anticipate in coming week. How will they put new role to work? What to do specifically?—*be* the new role, study it, memorize it and, like a part in a play, live it! Must live it and experience the feelings and reaction to it in real life.

8. Before ending, ask group to talk about the part which studying and present study methods play in creating test-anxiety. (Difficulties might pertain to self-distraction, roommate, or physical environment distractors). Establish need for a session devoted to study habits. Have students

make note throughout the week of such distractors—they might continue to use the index card system of noting distractions. Tell them to bring the cards next week—this should reduce the effect of confounded memory traces.

Interaction representing the third session follows:

Judy: I don't really know what you mean by creating a new role for myself.

Co: O.K. In your case Judy, what would your ideal test-taking behavior be like? How would you most like to feel?

Judy: Calm, collected, cool, and confident!

Co: Yes, that's true for all of us, but I mean what things would you change about what you now do? For example, you probably have a good idea of what you do that makes you anxious.

Judy: Sure, it's those thoughts about how bad I'm going to do, how the two hundred others in the class know as much or more than me and I'll come out at the bottom of the curve. It's all those things that go on in my mind before I even set foot in the exam room.

Co: All right then, those are the thoughts and feelings you want to get rid of. Can anyone help Judy identify some positive, facilitative attitudes and behaviors?

John: It sounds like what you're saying is just to think positively. But I don't see how it can be done. It's kind of false, like acting or making believe. Even if Judy could say to herself, "O.K., I studied and know as much and maybe more than the next guy, and somehow I always manage to get through anyway and maybe if I act confident I'll even perform better," would it really work, would she believe it or would it still be just a bunch of words?

Co: What do you think, Judy? What would it take for you to play the confident role? You seem to have mastered the "I can't succeed" role which apparently has little basis in reality.

Judy: I think I see what you mean. It does sort of start out like play acting but you keep trying it in situations where you used to think the opposite, like in preparing for exams.

Pete: And perhaps it just will make a difference in what she remembers or thinks she knows and maybe that in itself will make her believe the things she's been telling herself.

THE FOURTH SESSION

A. Review of third session

Implementation of the role is seen as a key to change in test-taking behavior. Spend the first 15 minutes exploring what students did to try it out—in test situations, studying, or as extended to total functioning.

1. Explore usefulness or limitations of test-taking role. This assumes that the students have tried the role out and on this basis have comments.

2. Explore with those who had the opportunity to play the role outside but did not; why they didn't.

3. Reinforce positive comments relative to role-playing which was successfully carried out.

   Stress—in order for you to be what you feel is the "ideal test-taker" you must be willing to take a chance, practice and practice still more until this role is as natural as the one of test-anxiousness which you have perfected and are still playing.

B. Emphasis of the fourth session: preparing (studying) for exams

   1. Relevant questions to focus on:

      a. Where does "preparing for the exam" fit into test-anxiety (central, peripheral, not a factor at all)? The responses generated by this question will determine the direction of the session. If preparation plays a part in examination-anxiety, continue by exploring subsequent "thought" questions. If group does not see preparation as a factor in their test-taking fears try to identify, through discussion, the antecedent conditions responsible, for example, inadequate studying, too little time to prepare, simple avoidance or denial of responsibility.

      b. What does "preparation" mean? Seems to imply more than studying, more inclusive, other nonstudy types of activity and behavior.

      c. Is there one *best* way to prepare?

      d. Should one prepare *differentially* depending on the course?

      e. Does preparation for the exam depend on the type of exam, that is, essay versus objective type?

   2. A few points to keep in mind:

      a. While all the students identify themselves as test-anxious, preparation for examinations may be as varied as the number of students. There's no one way to prepare nor would this approach fit everyone.

      b. Talking about, ventilating, the problem is one thing but putting a new plan into action is another. The latter needs emphasis because unless the effort is made outside of the session no benefit is likely to result.

   3. Let the group members do the work—it will be more meaningful that way. Your role here is to: pull in the members, keep discussion close to the topic of preparation for exams (try not to let it wander to studying in general), offer concrete suggestions when members do not, or seem to be incorrect, in their advice.

   4. In line with the notion of the importance of activity and involvement the students will be asked to think about, recall and write down a list of factors, related to preparation, which leads to examination fear and tension. This list should be arranged in a hierarchy of least to most significant problems (noise in room, can't get organized, don't have enough time to review). The goal here is to bring specific problems to light for each individual and identify remedies which can be tried out outside of the session and be adapted or adopted to replace maladaptive methods.

5. After writing these the individuals will take turns presenting their lists and receiving suggestions for improving the conditions. Group should be made aware that it can really help each member by coming up with suggestions that they may have tried and found useful. The leader is only one person—the group can offer three times as much help!
6. Here are some specific problems and possible remedies:
   a. physical distractors (more often excuses!)—remove any articles from desk which cause your mind to wander. Find a time to study when it is most quiet, for example, when your roommate is asleep, or when student is most relaxed but alert, or remove self to a quiet place, for example, stacks in library or other secluded spot like rear of science library (third floor).
   b. the best way to prepare?—this is the most comfortable way. May start with overview of material or review of specifics—whichever serves to get student started.
   c. difficulty in focusing attention or holding attention—review should be active not passive. Not just reading and rereading notes but giving out information, as student will have to on the exam, by reciting it to self, answering own questions.
   d. learning which doesn't follow logical rules—"memory crutch" to learn a series of unrelated items; form a word with the first letter of each item. Another similar device is to repeat two ideas until they become associated—then the first will elicit the second.
   e. The most effective method of learning:

1. Survey	4. Recite
2. Question	5. "Rite"
3. Read	6. Review

   At this point in the term we are only concerned about the last point. It would be almost effortless if the five others were carried out already. In any case, the whole process implies preparation which is active. The method can even be useful in this respect a few days before exams. Motto: Don't be a sponge and expect to learn!
7. Suggestions are to be tried out during week. Students should come to the fifth session ready to discuss what happened in carrying these out.
8. Arrange for change in last session time for those groups meeting on Memorial Day.

THE FIFTH SESSION

This is the guide for the final session:

1. Specific test-taking techniques of second session. Identify any new problems encountered by students since second session. Try to bring group up to date with respect to test-taking skills, that is, get them to bring up and work out any still remaining or recurrent maladaptive, self-defeating behaviors.

2. Review roles of relaxation which can be fostered by:
   a. muscular relaxation (review exercises as needed by individuals in the groups)
   b. confidence as a test-taker and concentration on exam—not on non-test factors.
3. Reinforce the benefits which role-playing the "good test taker" will bring. Encourage sharing of experiences in which role was tried out. As was stressed elsewhere before, to the extent that the role was played by someone in the group and its benefits discussed, the others will be encouraged to do the same.

   Help to rework roles that were found to be ineffective, for example, those that were unrealistic or impossible for students to play. The goal is to create a more comfortable, confident, and less tense test-taker but if the role is too difficult to enact these goals will not be realized.
4. Review and assessment of studying for exams. While this serves as a review of the fourth session it is intended to focus on the week of studying between the fourth session and this one. It is particularly relevant because of its temporal proximity to finals.

   Did students make any observations of their characteristic mode of studying or any new techniques which have implications for test-taking anxiety? What kinds of changes have they made? Have they resisted doing anything other than coming to weekly sessions? Re-emphasize importance of practice—that we cannot offer magical solutions nor do the work for them.

   Deal with persistent poor study methods. What can be done between now and the final exam to correct these? Concentrate on realistic factors such as simply making up a study schedule and sticking to it, going to sleep early before each exam, or not studying immediately before an exam.
5. What are the present concerns about the approach of examination time? The greater portion of this session should enable students to express and deal with current fears and hopes. Being the last week of classes and a week before finals, feelings should probably be running high.

   The goal is not to bring out new, previously unexplored problems but to consolidate the five sessions, encourage students to apply what they learned, to help students face their finals more confidently and better prepared to deal with them—to think clearly and to respond adaptively.

   The counselor's role here is to help every group member to realize the above goal in his own way. You should have the feeling that all of the individuals in your groups are "holding together" all right. Work with those who still seem particularly anxious or unsure of taking exams to overcome this in the time that still remains.
6. About five minutes before the end of the hour formally bring the session to a close and explain that, "we are asking you to fill out some forms to help us look at the 'test-taking anxiety' program from beginning to end. Some of these questionnaires you will recognize because you filled them out before the program began. These you will fill out here in a few seconds. The other three forms which are stapled together will be filled out immediately after your final exam in Psychology 151 on Friday, June 9th. Com-

plete them immediately after you finish the exam (not before). Then bring the materials to the front of the examination room where there will be a container to put them in. If you have any questions at that time or if you forget the forms I will be there with additional ones."

RESULTS

Four instruments were used to evaluate the effectiveness of structured group interaction: S-R Inventory of Anxiousness (Endler, McV. Hunt and Rosenstein, 1962), Text Anxiety Inventory (Neuman, 1968), Test Anxiety Rating Scale (Neuman, 1968) and the Thayer Activation-Deactivation Adjective Checklist (Thayer, 1967). The S-R Test and the Text Anxiety Inventory were completed after the fifth group session while students took the Test Anxiety Rating Scale and the Thayer Adjective Checklist into their final examination and completed it immediately after finishing the examination.[4]

The extroverted students scored lower than introverts on these measures. These differences, however, were not in general statistically significant. Compared to test anxious students who did not receive this counseling the structured group interaction procedures were very effective in reducing test-taking anxiety.[5]

Perhaps more importantly it was found that this type of group counseling is feasible and promising. It is possible to deliberately create a series of specific procedures to assist certain types of individuals with a particular problem. And students are very responsive (the attendance rate at group meetings was excellent!).[6]

[4] Editors' Note: Taking the rating scale and adjective checklist into the exam should permit a more valid self-evaluation. It might have been more revealing, however, to have had students complete them in the examination room just before the exam as well as immediately after.

[5] See Weinstein (1968) for complete presentation of results.

[6] Editors' Note: The concept of "examination anxiety" is quite complex. At this point it seems reasonable to use a variety of criterion measures, such as observer ratings of performance and physiological measures in addition to self-report techniques in efforts to find out what works with which types of clients.

43

IMPROVING STUDY BEHAVIORS

G. Brian Jones[1]
AMERICAN INSTITUTES FOR RESEARCH

Students frequently know how to study but have difficulty once they get into actual study settings. These students experience anxiety over the lack of previous study and sometimes fear of subsequent failure which interferes with effective studying. For others suitable incentives for studying are often not available or accepted. These students indicate that they are "not motivated to study." Something was needed to help college students, something which went beyond the typical study skills class.

In the fall of 1966 three specific group procedures were developed and an experimental-type setting was organized within a college counseling center to give special attention to those students who wanted to improve their study performances. All students received basic study skills information in a regular class conducted by one instructor who used a standardized teaching unit. The 95 students in the lectures were given an opportunity to participate in one-hour, weekly group sessions. The following instructions were read to them by one person:

> Previous experience with this Reading and Study Skills Program has suggested that group sessions for one hour, once a week, can be a useful complement to the large lecture classes. From now until Christmas, groups of seven to eight students will meet with one of three male staff members from the Student Counseling Services. These staff members will be using various group techniques in order to help students perform more effective study behaviors. Attention will be focused on:
>
> A. Independent study behavior
> B. Active intraclass participation
> C. Active extraclass participation

[1] The author gratefully acknowledges the participation of Harold A. Altmann and F. James Hawkes in conducting this project.

D. Efficient use of resource facilities

E. Effective examination behavior

Those of you who wish to participate must be willing to attend all six or seven sessions and to take two or three tests which will be given before and after the series of group sessions. We would like all groups to remain intact throughout the series.

I shall distribute a sheet on which I would like each of you to respond, whether or not you are interested. You are not compelled to participate in the group sessions but we believe you will not receive the full benefit of this total program unless you take time for this project.

Students signed the following written statement:

I agree to participate in all the once-a-week, small-group sessions that will be scheduled from now until Christmas. I understand that these groups will concentrate on aspects of study behavior other than speed reading. Also, I agree to take the two or three tests which will be given before and after this series of sessions.[2]

Sixty-four students signed the statement. That week they received individual notices advising them of their group's number, meeting place, time and date, and counselor.

The students were randomly assigned to one of nine groups, each group numbering seven members. The three counselors, all of whom were experienced group leaders, were then randomly assigned to these groups. Each counselor led groups using all three group approaches.

MODEL REINFORCEMENT GROUP COUNSELING

Modeling was presented in the form of a two-page handout. This symbolic model offered concrete suggestions on such topics as the proper setting for studying, how to handle assignments, how to behave in examination situations and how to study. The model served as the focus for all seven sessions. In the first session the counselor and students overviewed the model which was presented in the form of how a hypothetical student would approach studying. The counselor explained the model in detail encouraging students to suggest any relevant points, errors or omissions. The discussion was individualized by having each student identify which parts of the model were especially significant to him. The handout was set up as follows:

[2] Editors' Note: Use of written (and oral) "contracts" is often a very effective way of creating commitment by clients. Such contracts should be detailed and specific in terms of what is expected and what the anticipated consequences will be. See Articles 8–12 for additional examples of structuring commitments.

EFFECTIVE STUDY BEHAVIOR

I. General Study Behavior
   A. Proper Setting.
      1. Place—has a location which is conducive to concentration; which is free from auditory and visual distraction; and which provides optimal comfort (that is, proper lighting, ventilation and temperature but not so relaxing that drowsiness results).
      2. Time—schedules himself so that class time $+$ study time totals not more than 10 hours a day. Studies not less than 45 hours nor more than 60 hours each week. Works efficiently—tries for 60–90 minutes of concentrated study at a time, then takes a short break. Tries to predict the amount of time he should be taking for certain tasks (this probably will vary for his different subjects) and tries to do his work in the predicted time. Studies early in the day rather than late at night.
   B. Proper Strategy
      1. Uses a study schedule
      2. Assignment procedure
         a. Records assignments in a book. Has a clear conception of what is required and for when it must be completed. If he is not sure he asks questions of his instructor.
         b. Gathers necessary materials. Uses all available resources. Asks librarians and instructors for assistance in locating the most appropriate materials.
         c. Records information on $3'' \times 5''$ note cards which can be arranged advantageously.
         d. For essay writing, makes a rough outline first. Uses large blocks of time when he begins to write. Writes quickly for the rough draft. Puts it aside for 24 hours; then rewrites it. Has someone else read his essay and discusses their comments. Leaves essay for another 48 hours, then prepares final draft for typing.
         e. Does his most difficult assignments during his best concentration periods. Saves his rewriting tasks for periods when his concentration is not as good. Tries simpler assignments first; therefore building up his confidence.
         f. Hands in his assignments on time, every time.
      3. Study procedures
         a. Schedules definite times and outlines specific goals for his study time. Allows at least two hours for every subject each week for a review of notes and text content.
         b. Survey—Surveys a book before he begins reading it. Surveys each chapter before he begins reading it. Briefly looks at all the material that he will be reading during an allotted period of study time.

    c. Question—Asks questions about what should be learned during that study time.

    d. Read—Reads the material. Notes important items of information. Looks for answers to the questions he posed. Realizes that scanning is sufficient in certain areas, while in other places he may need to read more analytically.

    e. Recite—Goes over the content which he wants to remember. Prepares notes on it in order to help his memory.

    f. Review—Asks further questions and then resurveys the material.

II. Specialized Study Behavior

  A. Interactive participation in class

    1. Asks the instructor questions when clarification of lecture points is needed.

    2. Volunteers answers to questions posed by instructor in the class.

    3. Participates in class discussions.

  B. Interactive participation out of class

    1. Asks the instructor (for example, in his office, and so forth) for clarification of lecture information or assignments, or for comments on questions which have arisen from the student's studies.

    2. Engages in formal or informal discussions with classmates on topics relevant to his courses. Clarifies points which had not been clear during lectures or labs. Reviews course content with other students.

    3. Interacts with other resource persons on the campus (for example, librarians, tutorial leaders, course assistants) or in the community.

  C. Note-taking behavior

    1. Previews the lecture topic before he goes to class (that is, uses the text).

    2. Rereads last few days' notes before the class begins.

    3. Listens first; writes second.

    4. Uses the margins of his paper for headings; writes lecture content in the body of the page.

    5. Writes neatly.

    6. Makes special notes of content which the instructor stresses.

  D. Examination behavior

    1. Starts preparation early; follows "Study procedures" mentioned above.

    2. Makes notes of instructor's hints concerning exam content or format.

    3. Discusses with classmates the areas of course which they think are most relevant for the exam.

    4. Reviews library copies of old exams.

    5. Prepares sample test quesions while he studies. Administers these to himself the day before the exam and corrects his responses.

    6. On the day of the exam, he is on time; reads the questions carefully; schedules his time for each question; meets his schedule; begins with the easier test items in order to build up his confidence.

    7. If he finds himself tensing during the exam, closes his eyes and

tries to relax for a moment. Does this by thinking of a relaxing thought. Then goes back to work.

8. Before an exam, does not induce anxiety by talking to fellow students whose questions, or apparent mastery of the course, will upset him.
9. Writes neatly.

Tailoring a Group Model

The major task of the first session was for each group to create a comprehensive model from the written handout which they, as a group, could then seek to emulate. Some details were omitted while others were expanded and elaborated. By the end of the first session each selected one detail from their written group model that he was going to practice during the week. To help each student remember and to generate commitment, before the session ended each student made a written note of what he planned to practice. In addition each student was asked to keep a written record of what he actually did day by day concerning his performance of what he was practicing.

The following excerpt from the counselor's outline entitled "Rationale and Procedures for Model Reinforcement Group Counseling" provides an idea of what occurred during subsequent sessions.[3]

All subsequent sessions would have the following agenda:

1. The counselor should ask all members to outline what they had performed during the previous week in respect to approximating the model. Had they been successful in carrying out their expected responses? The group should be encouraged to decide whether or not each member's weekly performance was an improvement over his previous record.
2. Another section of the written model should be reviewed.
3. Each student should select another relevant studying response which he would like to accomplish during the forthcoming week. Group evaluation should be encouraged—that is, do group members think his expectations are feasible? Too conservative? At the same time, each student should be asked to make a written reminder of the expected response, to keep a record of his weekly performance, and to continue emitting all previously selected behaviors. The counselor should also keep a record of all selected responses.

By the final session, all aspects of the written model must have been covered. This session should be devoted to some type of "accounting" during which each member evaluates the progress that he has—or has not—made

---

[3] Editors' Note: All three group counselors were specifically and carefully trained to provide the three treatments. While the counselors were all experienced in individual and group counseling in general, specialized treatments demand specific training since the counselors were required to behave differently in each treatment.

over the series of meetings. Ways of maintaining improved study behavior should be discussed at this time.

During each session the counselor verbally and nonverbally reinforced students who had successfully practiced an activity from the written model or who stated they intended to practice a particular response. The following excerpt from the counselor's outline provides some detail:

The role of the counselor will be that of discussion-catalyst and dispenser of positive reinforcement for the responses which are to be shaped. Verbal assent and approval, as well as supportive facial expressions and body gestures could be used as social reinforcers. Examples of verbal reinforcers include: "Um hmm," "That's a good idea, Jack," or "I like that point, Fran." An encouraging head nod, an interested leaning forward, or a supportive smile could be construed as nonverbal, positive reinforcers.

Needless to say no generalized verbal or nonverbal reinforcers probably exist. Each counselor will have to learn what reinforcers are valued by group members. For example, some may react with disdain if the counselors continually say "well done" when a desired behavior has been emitted. These same persons may appreciate the counselor simply acknowledging their efforts and then building further group discussion around these efforts.

No attempt should be made to keep the reinforcement at a subtle level —explicit recognition should be given to students who perform model-relevant study behaviors. All subjects will be encouraged to practice overtly the desired form of responding.

Counselors should use the social reinforcers with which they believe they most effectively relay impressions of assent, approval, and support. At the same time—as noted above—an attempt should be made to individualize selection of reinforcers as much as possible. It is anticipated that as group cohesiveness develops and as reinforcement contingencies become recognized, group members will socially reinforce each other's responses as these approximate the model. The counselor should attempt to withdraw his reinforcement efforts at a pace which insures that there is no decrement in the student's response rates.

The concept of successive approximations would be invoked as the counselor—and probably the group—differentially reinforces responses that resemble, and are dissimilar from, the model. Dissimilar responses should be ignored rather than punished (for example, social rebuke). At first, the counselor may have to use frequent social reinforcement (individualizing the selection of reinforcers), but later, intermittent reinforcement principles could be adopted. It is anticipated that as group members find themselves approximating model behaviors closer and closer, their responses will be self-reinforcing or self-controlled (that is, automatic reinforcement) and therefore be less dependent on external (interpersonal) reinforcement.

One important part of each session will be determination of discriminative cues which should be present before group members emit certain response patterns. For example: When are the most appropriate occasions for asking questions in class? When are inappropriate occasions? What environmental conditions are most conducive to the elicitation of individual, book-study behavior? The group should decide which cues are most important, then they should be positively reinforced for emitting model responses when these cues are present. Inappropriate responses could be ignored or the counselor could ask the student to specify what the appropriate response should have been.

DESENSITIZATION GROUP COUNSELING

This procedure involved systematic desensitization.[4] A standardized group hierarchy was developed and modified by suggestions from students. The chosen items for the common hierarchy progressing from the least anxiety-provoking to the most anxiety-provoking were as follows:

Group Anxiety Hierarchy

1. Now imagine yourself leaving for the campus on a bright, warm day. Just take the trip comfortably and leisurely until you get to the building where your first class will be held.
2. Next, imagine yourself in a class. This is one you have enjoyed a lot. It is informative, yet entertaining. See yourself as you sit at your desk watching your professor. Relive that experience as vividly as possible.
3. Go on to imagine yourself leaving the lecture carrying your notes and texts. Then you stop to talk to a close friend and you decide to tell him all about the class you just came out of.
4. Now imagine yourself arriving at your residence carrying your books, feeling good. Just go through the door and take your books to the place where you study and look around the room while your put your books down.
5. You have just enjoyed a good meal and a little relaxation afterwards. Go to your study area and imagine yourself working very hard and productively for three hours.
6. Imagine yourself studying hard in your favorite area and all of a sudden there is a lot of noise. Stop, hear the noise, then return to studying hard.
7. Picture yourself in a lecture where the professor is really boring. It's a waste of time for you to be there.
8. Now imagine yourself in the same boring class, but the person next to you speaks up and asks a question. This livens things up and the lecture takes on added interest.

[4] Editors' Note: See Article 31 by Emery for details of systematic desensitization.

9. Imagine yourself at the beginning of the year in a new class with the professor telling all of you what a tough course this is, and what a hard marker he is.
10. Next, assume that you are in your favorite study place, working hard on this difficult course and feeling very productive. The information is being learned and you enjoy the feeling.
11. The next day you are feeling confident as you walk into the exam in this course. You look at the paper and you get a terrific feeling because you know the answers.
12. Now you are getting back the paper. You have a good mark. You feel so good that you want to know the class average, so you ask for this information.
13. Imagine yourself later that night preparing for your next exam, studying as hard as you can, but you can't seem to grasp the material; however, you continue working at it.
14. The next morning you are talking to a friend just outside the exam room. He asks you a question about one of the basic principles in the course, and you can't give him an answer.
15. Imagine yourself in the exam room reading the paper, and you cannot answer anything. You realize how important this test is for you.
16. You're in the exam room. You have been sitting looking at the paper. Nothing is coming. Time is flying by and you aren't writing anything down.
17. Because you are not doing anything, people are turning around and staring at you. As the instructor comes toward you he is laughing, seemingly making fun of your behavior.
18. Imagine two people you really like sort of sneering at you and intimating that you are stupid as you tell them you have been asked to leave the university because of your failing grades.

All students in the second treatment also received copies of the written model and also reviewed the details of the model. Again as in the first treatment, students specifically indicated what they planned to practice during the forthcoming week. However, less time was spent in discussing these details.

Beginning Desensitization with Relaxation

Following presentation of the model, the following outline was used by the counselors during the first session:

DESENTIZATION RATIONALE AND GENERAL PROCEDURE

1. We believe it is very possible that students become excessively anxious about their study habits and that this anxiety inhibits them from performing effectively. In other words, somehow anxiety becomes connected with various aspects of studying.
2. Therefore, we have concluded that if we can help students to handle, or

even eliminate, this anxiety, then they will be more able to perform better study habits.

3. You will agree that it is impossible for a person to feel relaxed and anxious (tense, fearful) at the same time. Therefore, if we can help you learn to relax yourself—and you learn it well enough so that you are able to do it by yourself in future—then you should be able to gain control over anxiety or tenseness. Relaxation is a skill which can be improved with practice. At first, it will take approximately 30 minutes to go through the entire procedure properly. Eventually you will be able to relax yourself in 10–15 minutes or even less.

4. The basic principle is that when muscles are tensed, and then released, they go into a deeper state of relaxation. It is important to focus your thinking on the particular muscle system which you are relaxing during the exercises.

5. The relaxation exercises also will teach you how to recognize tension and to distinguish it from relaxation and from muscle strain. By learning how to recognize tensions you can readily eliminate them.

6. Once you have learned to relax, we will try the second part of our procedures. When you imagine a scene in a vivid way, your nervous system will react as if you were actually behaving in that way. We shall ask you to imagine a series of scenes which frequently make students anxious about studying. If you imagine these scenes while being in a relaxed state, then relaxation—not tension—should become associated with them.

7. We believe that if you can vividly imagine your reaction to a particular scene, then this will be the same reaction which you would have if that scene occurred in real life.

8. We are not saying that we want you to become overly relaxed in all study settings. An optimal degree of tension is probably necessary for good study behavior. We are saying that if you learn to relax yourselves, then when you become tense and anxious in study settings you will be able to relax yourselves. If the process is really effective, study settings which formerly made you tense up should no longer occasion such a result.

Relaxation training was then conducted for the remaining portion of this initial session. The students were asked to practice the exercises between sessions. While students were comfortably seated in their chairs with their eyes closed, they alternately tensed and relaxed 15 of the major voluntary muscle groups during this 30-minute training period. All during this time the counselors verbalized cues for relaxation ("Relax," "Feeling Calm," "Warm and Relaxed," and so forth) in an attempt to augment the relaxed feelings accompanying the exercises. Once the complete set of exercises had been performed, the counselors counted slowly up to 20 while requesting that the participants take deep breaths on the odd numbers and exhale on the even ones.

Discussion was then encouraged about the nature and effectiveness of this relaxation training for each participant. Questions were asked for while suggestions were offered to those who experienced difficulty relaxing.

Each group chose a total of six exercises which it members felt were most effective for promoting relaxation. These were the only exercises that were used during the relaxation phases of all group sessions.[5]

Instructing Students in Desensitization

Each counselor had a procedural outline to which he adhered during the desensitization process. The outline was as follows:

SPECIFIC DETAILS FOR VISUALIZATION OF SCENES

1. Each scene will be presented for 10, 20, and 30 second intervals, preceded by instructions such as "Now, imagine as vividly as possible that you . . ." and followed by instructions such as "Leave that scene, and continue to concentrate on total relaxation." The item content will be repeated only for the 10 and 30 second interval.
2. Each session will begin by re-presentation of the final scene visualized by the group during the previous session. Each session will end only with the succesful presentation of a scene. If students cannot handle a scene without anxiety, and the time is almost up, go back to a scene lower on the hierarchy and present this one. Do not introduce a new item (which may produce tension) within the last four minutes of a session.
3. Between presentations of the same scene, allow for about 20 seconds of continued relaxation. Instructions about relaxation, letting go, or counting up to six with students breathing in on the odd numbers and out on the even ones, or all of these will be used in order to help the group members attain more relaxed conditions.
4. Group members should raise their left index fingers if they feel themselves becoming less relaxed or becoming afraid. Remind them of this each session, as well as remind them to try to imagine each scene for as long as they have time.
5. About 45 seconds will be taken between the presentation of different hierarchy items.
6. When a group member signals anxiety, the whole group will be asked to "Stop imagining that scene." The counselor will help the members get relaxed again either by relaxation instructions or by having them imagine a scene which they find is very relaxing. Then he will say, "Just signal by raising your right index finger when you have returned to a relaxed state." Once they have all relaxed again, he will have them think only about staying in that state. If they cannot relax, he may have to repeat the counting-to-20 and deep breathing exercise.

---

[5] Editors' Note: Important point. Each person typically has different muscle areas which when tensed and relaxed provide considerable relaxation for him (for example, head and neck area, abdomen and upper legs).

7. After the first anxiety signal on an item, the counselor will always continue with that same item for the same time interval. If anxiety recurs, he will ask the group to leave that scene and relax. Then he will go back and represent the last scene which they all successfully handled. He will work back up to the anxiety-eliciting scene.

8. If anxiety is signaled for a third time on the same item at the same time interval, first the counselor will have the group imagine it for an intermediary time period—that is, 5, 15, 20, or 25 seconds—whichever applies. If the anxiety persists, he will have to employ intermittent scenes (one may suffice) which represent modifications of the hierarchy items. He will present them for the regular time intervals. If this does not work, it will be necessary to talk with the group members in an effort to identify the anxiety cues in the scene.

During the third through the seventh sessions the groups worked through the items on the group hierarchy. The following agenda for each session was followed:

1. (5–10 minutes)—Open discussion of points from previous sessions and students' comments regarding study-related experiences which have occurred during the interim between recent sessions.

2. (10 minutes) —Muscular relaxation procedures using selected exercises plus relaxation deepening instructions through counting-to-20 while deep breathing on odd numbers.
Note: check to make sure all group members have achieved deep relaxation—ask them to signify by raising their right index fingers.

3. (25 minutes) —Visualization of scenes from specified hierarchy of items.

4. (5–10 minutes)—Bring group members back to a normal—that is, no-tension—state by reversing the relaxation deepening instructions and omitting the deep breathing. Conduct any summary discussion which seems necessary including study problems they may wish to discuss. Make continual references to the performance of study behaviors as stated in the written model, "Effective Study Behavior."

GROUP CENTERED COUNSELING

The main factor differentiating this group procedure from the two previously described was its relative lack of structure. Expression of the students' problems and feelings was encouraged. No particular objectives were established other than the fact that the counselors stated that they would like to see the discussion center on study-relevant topics. In the first session, the initial format was the same as for the other two group procedures. This involved the presentation and discussion of the written model for "Effective Study Behavior." As in the other groups, the counselors urged the students to perform as many of these study behaviors as possible over the next seven weeks.

From this point on, discussion was open to the group members with the stipulation that it should be tied in with the content of the written model. The counselors pointed out that they wished only to serve as discussion-catalysts and not as experts in the study skills area. They added that they believed the students could best help each other to improve their study behavior performance.

Each session the counselors asked different students to introduce problems which they felt inhibited their studying effectiveness and then the other members were stimulated to respond. Throughout these sessions, the counselors did not make any consistent, conscious effort to selectively reinforce any student responses. Instead group leaders attempted to respond in ways which would promote group cohesiveness. Group members, it was felt, could provide their own solutions to the problems presented. Frequent counselor statements included direct questions such as: "How do you react to that statement?" "How do you feel about her comment?" "Do you find that is your problem too?" and "Does that bother you?"

Group cohesiveness and student interaction developed but some students seemed dependent on the counselors for problem solutions. They probably would have preferred more of a counselor-centered group procedure. Whether or not their performance of study behaviors would have been significantly different if they had experienced another group procedure is an empirical question which is unanswerable as far as this pilot project is concerned.[6]

SOME OBSERVATIONS

As it stands, I cannot make statements about the relative effectiveness of these three group procedures for improving students' performance of study behaviors.

Two criterion measures were used in an attempt to gather a behavioral indication of observable changes in the students' study performances. Self report measures seemed to be a major improvement over the traditional study habits survey because they required that each student

[6] Editors' Note: This treatment appears to have been more structured than many such groups in that a written model was presented, students were asked to practice ideas from the model between sessions, and to focus on feelings and thoughts about problems directly relevant. Needed are experimentally based studies which explore which types of clients are most effectively and efficiently assisted with which types of group treatment or combination of treatments.

actually keep track of his behavior for one week and record a frequency count of various study behaviors. Students completed the "Study Effectiveness Form" and the "Time Evaluation Form" before the group sessions started. However, on account of timing and some administrative problems many students did not complete these forms afterwards.[7]

This pilot study was successful, however, in providing valuable data on development and feasibility of these group treatments. Students responded positively and enthusiastically. Many reported experiencing meaningful changes in behavior during the course of the weekly sessions. Most students appeared to like the structured and organized format of group social modeling and group desensitization procedures. With training, the counselors were able to offer three types of group treatments. One practical question now to be answered is which students might be best helped with which kind of group counseling?[8]

[7] Editors' Note: This study has been partially replicated by Marilynne Trimble of the Division of Educational Psychology, The University of Calgary under the direction of Dr. Harold A. Altmann.

[8] Editors' Note: It's unfortunate that Jones was unable to obtain information on study behaviors of these students after counseling. However, he has presented valuable data on how counselors confronted with student problems of academic performance can try out new techniques.

References

Addison, R. M. & Homme, L. E. The reinforcing event (RE) menu. *National Society for Programmed Instruction Journal*, 1966, **5** (1), 8–9.

Anderson, D. Application of a behavior modification technique to the control of an hyperactive child. Unpublished M.A. thesis, University of Oregon, 1964.

Arbuckle, D. S. A reader's reactions to Krumboltz's Propositions. *Caps Capsule*, 1968, **1** (No. 3), 3.

Aronfreed, J. The origin of self-criticism. *Psychological Review*, 1964 **71**, 193–218.

Aronfreed, J., & Reber, A. Internalized behavioral suppression and the timing of social punishment. *Journal of Personality and Social Psychology*, 1965, **1**, 3–16.

Ashem, B. The treatment of a disaster phobia by systematic desensitization. *Behaviour Research and Therapy*, 1963, **1**, 81–84.

Ayllon, T., & Michael, J. The psychiatric nurse as a behavioral engineer. *Journal of the Experimental Analysis of Behavior*, 1959, **3**, 323–334.

Bandura, A., Blanchard, E. B., & Ritter, Brunhilde. The relative efficacy of desensitization and modeling treatment approaches for inducing behavioral, effective, and attitudinal changes. Unpublished manuscript, Stanford University, 1968.

Bandura, A., Grusec, J. E., & Menlove, F. Vicarious extinction of avoidance behavior. *Journal of Personality and Social Psychology*, 1967, **5**, 16–23.

Bandura, A., & Huston, A. C. Identification as process of incidental learning. *Journal of Abnormal and Social Psychology*, 1961, **63**, 311–318.

Bandura, A., & Menlove, F. Factors determining vicarious extinction of avoidance behavior through symbolic modeling. *Journal of Personality and Social Psychology*, 1968, **8**, 99–108.

Bandura, A., & Walters, R. H. *Social learning and personality development.* New York: Holt, Rinehart and Winston, 1963.

Becker, W. C., Madson, C. H., Arnold, C. R., & Thomas, D. R. The contingent use of teacher attention and praise in reducing classroom behavior problems. *Journal of Special Education*, 1967, **1**, 287–307.

Bijou, S. W., & Baer, D. M. *Child development.* Volume I. New York: Appleton-Century-Crofts, 1961.

Birnbrauer, J. S., Bijou, S. W., Wolf, M. M., & Kidder, J. D. Programmed instruction in the classroom. In L. Ullmann and L. Krasner (Eds.) *Case studies in behavior modification.* New York: Holt, Rinehart and Winston, 1965. Pp. 358–364.

Blanchard, E. B. The relative contributions of modeling, informational influences, and physical contact in the extinction of phobic behavior. Unpublished doctoral dissertation, Stanford University, 1968.

Bond, I. K., & Hutchinson, H. C. Application of reciprocal inhibition therapy to exhibitionism. *Canada Medical Association,* 1960, **83,** 23–25.

Boocock, S. S. The Life Career Game. *Personnel and Guidance Journal,* 1967, **46,** 328–334.

Cautela, J. R. A behavior therapy approach to pervasive anxiety. *Behaviour Research and Therapy,* 1966, **4,** 99–109. (a)

Cautela, J. R. Treatment of compulsive behavior by covert sensitization. *The Psychological Record,* 1966, **16,** 33–41. (b)

Clark, D. F. The treatment of monosymptomatic phobia by systematic desensitization. *Behaviour Research and Therapy,* 1963, **1,** 63–68.

Cowden, R. C., & Ford, L. I. Systematic desensitization with phobic schizophrenics. *American Journal of Psychiatry,* 1962, **119,** 241–245.

Davison, G. C. A social learning therapy programme with an autistic child. *Behaviour Research and Therapy,* 1964, **2,** 149–159.

Davison, G. C. Elimination of a sadistic fantasy by a client-controlled counterconditioning technique: A case study. *Journal of Abnormal Psychology,* 1968,**73,** 84–90.

Davison, G. C. Appraisal of behavior modification techniques with adults in institutional settings. In C. M. Franks (Ed.), *Behavior Therapies: Assessment and Appraisal.* New York: McGraw-Hill, in press.

Dollard, J., & Miller, N. E. *Personality and psychotherapy.* New York: McGraw-Hill, 1950.

Dreikurs, R. *Children:The Challenge.* New York: Duell, Sloan, and Pearce, 1964.

Dulaney, D. E. Hypotheses and habits in verbal "operant conditioning." *Journal of Abnormal and Social Psychology,* 1961, **63,** 251–263.

Dulaney, D. E. The place of hypotheses and intentions: An analysis of verbal control in verbal conditioning. *Journal of Personality,* 1962, **30,** 102–129.

Dunn, L., & Smith, J. *Peabody language development kit manual for level #1.* Minneapolis: American Guidance Service, 1965.

Ebner, M. An investigation of the role of the social environment in the generalization and persistence of the effect of a behavior modification program. Unpublished doctoral dissertation, University of Oregon, 1967.

Endler, N., McV. Hunt, J., and Rosenstein, A. An S-R Inventory of Anxiousness. *Psychological Monographs,* 1962, 536, #17.

Emery, J. R. An evaluation of standard versus individualized hierarchies in desensitization to reduce test anxiety. Unpublished doctoral dissertation, Stanford University, 1966.

Emery, J. R., & Krumboltz, J. D. Standard versus individualized hierarchies in desensitization to reduce test anxiety. *Journal of Counseling Psychology,* 1967, **14**, 204–209.

Eysenck, H. J. Learning theory and behaviour therapy. *Journal of Mental Science,* 1959, **105**, 61–75.

Eysenck, H. J., & Rackman, S. *The causes and cures of neuroses.* San Diego, California: Knapp, 1965.

Farson, R. Praise reappraised. *Explorations,* 1966, **5**, 13–21.

Ferster, C. B. Positive reinforcement and behavioral deficits in autistic children. *Child Development,* 1961, **32**, 437–456.

Ferster, C. B., Nurnberger, J. I., & Levitt, E. B. The control of eating. *Journal of Mathetics,* 1962, **1**, 87–109.

Freund, K. Some problems in the treatment of homosexuality. In H. J. Eysenck (Ed.), *Behaviour therapy and the neuroses.* New York: Macmillan, 1960. Pp. 312–326.

Geer, J. Phobia treated by reciprocal inhibition. *Journal of Abnormal and Social Psychology,* 1964, **69**, 642–645.

Geisinger, D. L. Constructing an anxiety hierarchy. Mimeographed pamphlet, 1967.

Ginott, H. *Between parent and child.* New York: Macmillan, 1965.

Glasser, W. *Reality Therapy.* New York: Harper & Row, 1965.

Goldiamond, I. Justified and unjustified alarm over behavior control. Paper read at the 71st Annual Convention of the American Psychological Association, Philadelphia, 1963. Reprinted in O. Milton [Ed.] *Behavior disorders: perspectives and trends.* New York: Lippincott, 1965. Pp. 237–262.

Goldiamond, I. Self-control procedures in personal behavior problems. *Psychological Reports,* 1965, **17**, 851–868.

Gray, B. B., England, G., & Mahoney, J. L. Treatment of benign vocal nodules by reciprocal inhibition. *Behaviour Research and Therapy,* 1965, **3**, 187–193.

Haring, N. G. & Hayden, A. H. The program and facilities of the experimental education unit at the University of Washington Mental Retardation and Child Development Center. In M. U. Jones (Ed.) *Special education programs within the United States.* Springfield, Ill.: Charles C. Thomas, 1966.

Hawkins, R. P., Peterson, R. F., Schweid, E., & Bijou, S. W. Behavior therapy in the home: Amelioration of problem parent-child relations with the parent in a therapeutic role. *Journal of Experimental Child Psychology,* 1966, **4**, 99–107.

Hilgard, E. R. *Hypnotic susceptibility.* New York: Harcourt, Brace & World, 1965.

Homme, L. E. System for teaching English literacy to preschool Indian children. Westinghouse Research Laboratories Contract 14-20-065001506. Bureau of Indian Affairs, Final Report, October 11, 1965, 1–15 (a).

Homme, L. E. Perspectives in psychology—XXIV. Control of coverants, the operants of the mind. *Psychological Record,* 1965, **15**, 501–511 (b).

Homme, L. E. Coverant control therapy: A special case of contingency management. Paper read at the Rocky Mountain Psychological Association Convention, Albuquerque, May, 1966.

Homme, L., DeBaca, P., Devine, J., Steinhorst, R., & Rickert, E. Use of the Premack principle in controlling the behavior of nursery school children. *Journal of Experimental Analysis of Behavior*, 1963, **6**, 544.

Jacobson, E. Progressive relaxation. Chicago: University of Chicago Press, 1938.

Jones, Mary C. The elimination of children's fears. *Journal of Experimental Psychology*, 1924, **7**, 383–390. (a)

Jones, Mary C. A laboratory study of fear: The case of Peter. *Pedagogical Seminary*, 1924, **31**, 308–315. (b)

Jourard, S. On the problem of reinforcement by the psychotherapist of healthy behavior. In Franklin Shaw (Ed.), *Behavioral approaches to counseling and psychotherapy*. Montgomery: University of Alabama Press, 1961.

Kanner, L. Autistic disturbances of affective contact. *Nervous Child*, 1943, **2**, 217.

Kanfer, R. H., & Goldfoot, D. A. Self-control and tolerance of noxious stimulation. *Psychological Reports*, 1966, **18**, 79–85.

Keirsey, D. W. Systematic Exclusion: An Experimental Regimen for Chronic Misbehavior. Paper presented to the California Association of School Psychologists and Psychometrists, Pacific Grove, 1957.

Kelly, G. The psychology of personal constructs. New York: Norton, 1955.

Kerr, N., Meyerson, L., & Michael, J. A procedure for shaping vocalizations in a mute child. In L. P. Ullmann & L. Krasner (Eds.), *Case studies in behavior modification*. New York: Holt, Rinehart and Winston, 1965.

Krasner, L. The therapist as a social reinforcement machine. In H. H. Strupp and L. Luborsky (Eds.), *Research in psychotherapy*, Vol. 2. Washington, D.C.: American Psychological Association, 1962. Pp. 61–94.

Krumboltz, J. D. Parable of the good counselor. *Personnel and Guidance Journal*, 1961, **43**, 118–124.

Krumboltz, J. D. Behavioral counseling: Rationale and research. *Personnel and Guidance Journal*, 1965, **44**, 383–387.

Krumboltz, J. D. Behavioral goals for counseling. *Journal of Counseling Psychology*, 1966, **13**, 153–159. (a)

Krumboltz, J. D. Stating the goals of counseling. Monograph No. 1, California Counseling and Guidance Association, 1966. (b)

Krumboltz, J. D. (Ed.) *Revolution in counseling: Implications of behavioral science*. Boston: Houghton Mifflin, 1966. (c)

Krumboltz, J. D. Future directions for counseling research. In John M. Whiteley (Ed.), *Research in Counseling: Evaluation and Refocus*. Columbus, Ohio: Charles E. Merrill, 1967. Pp. 184–203.

Krumboltz, J. D. A behavioral approach to group counseling and therapy. *Journal of Research and Development in Education*, 1968, **1** (No. 2), 3–18.

Krumboltz, J. D., & Goodwin, D. L. Increasing task-oriented behavior: An experimental evaluation of training teachers in reinforcement techniques. School of Education, Stanford University, 1966, Final Report, Office of Education Grant 5-85-095.

Krumboltz, J. D., & Schroeder, W. W. Promoting career exploration through reinforcement. *Personnel and Guidance Journal*, 1965, **44**, 19–26.

Krumboltz, J. D., & Thoresen, C. E. The effect of behavioral counseling in group and individual settings on information-seeking behavior. *Journal of Counseling Psychology*, 1964, **11**, 324–333.

Krumboltz, J. D., Varenhorst, B., & Thoresen, C. E. Non-verbal factors in effectiveness of models in counseling. *Journal of Counseling Psychology*, 1967, **14**, 412–418.

Kushner, M. Desensitization of a post-traumatic phobia. In L. P. Ullmann & L. Krasner (Eds.), *Case studies in behavior modification*. New York: Holt, Rinehart and Winston, 1965.

Lang, P. J., & Lazovik, A. D. Experimental desensitization of a phobia. *Journal of Abnormal and Social Psychology*, 1963, **66**, 519–525.

Lang, P. J., Lazovik, A. D., & Reynolds, D. J. Desensitization, suggestibility, and pseudotherapy. *Journal of Abnormal Psychology*, 1965, **70**, 395–402.

Lavin, N. I., Thorpe, J. G., Barker, J. C., Blakemore, C. G., & Conway, C. B. Behavior therapy in a case of transvestism. *Journal of Nervous and Mental Disease*, 1961, **133**, 346–353.

Lazarus, A. A. New methods in psychotherapy: A case study. *South African Medical Journal*, 1958, **33**, 660–663.

Lazarus, A. A. Group therapy of phobic disorders by systematic desensitization. *Journal of Abnormal and Social Psychology*, 1961, **63**, 504–510.

Lazarus, A. A. The results of behaviour therapy in 126 cases of severe neurosis. *Behaviour Research and Therapy*, 1963, **1**, 69–79.

Lazarus, A. A. The treatment of a sexually inadequate man. In L. P. Ullmann & L. Krasner (Eds.), *Case studies in behavior modification*. New York: Holt, Rinehart and Winston, 1965. Pp. 243–245.

Lazarus, A. A., & Davison, G. C. The reciprocal inhibition concept and desensitization therapy. In R. M. Jurjevich (Ed.), *Handbook of direct and behavior psychotherapies*, in press.

Leary, T. *Interpersonal diagnosis of personality*. New York: Ronald Press, 1957.

Leon, H. Reciprocal inhibition: an evaluation of group procedures with "normal" snake phobic subjects. Unpublished doctoral dissertation, University of Tennessee, 1967.

Lindsley, O. R., & Skinner, B. F. A method for the experimental analysis of the behavior of psychotic patients. *American Psychologist*, 1954, **9**, 419–420.

Lindsley, O. R. An experiment with parents handling behavior at home. *Johnstone Bulletin*, 1966, **9**, 27–36.

Loughmiller, C. *Wilderness road*. Austin, Texas: Hogg Foundation, 1965.

Lovaas, O. I., Freitag, G., Gold, V., & Kassorla, I. Experimental studies in childhood schizophrenia: Analysis of self-destructive behavior. *Journal of Experimental Child Psychology*, 1965, **2**, 67–84.

Madsen, C. H. Positive reinforcement in the toilet training of a normal child. In L. P. Ullmann & L. Krasner (Eds.), *Case studies in behavior modification*. New York: Holt, Rinehart and Winston, Inc., 1965. Pp. 305–307.

Mandler, G., & Watson, D. L. Anxiety and the interruption of behavior. In C. D. Spielberger (Ed.), *Anxiety and behavior*. New York: Academic Press, 1966. Pp. 263–288.

McCully, C. H. The two secrets of the gods. Paper read at Iota Alpha Banquet, Pennsylvania State University, May, 1964.

Menninger, K. *Theory of psychoanalytic technique.* New York: Basic Books, 1958.

Mischel, W. Theory and research on the antecedents of self-imposed delay of reward. In B. A. Maher (Ed.), *Progress in experimental personality research,* Vol. 3. New York: Academic Press, 1965. Pp. 85–132.

Mowrer, O. H., & Viek, P. An experimental analogue of fear from a sense of of helplessness. *Journal of Abnormal and Social Psychology,* 1948, **43,** 193–200.

Newman, D. Professional and subprofessional counselors using group desensitization and insight procedures to reduce examination anxiety. Unpublished doctoral dissertation, Michigan State University, 1968.

Nixon, S. B. Increasing the frequency of attending responses in hyperactive distractible youngsters by use of operant and modeling procedures. Unpublished dissertation, Stanford, Calif.: Stanford University, 1965.

Patterson, G. R. An application of conditioning techniques to the control of an hyperactive child. In L. P. Ullmann and L. Krasner (Eds.), *Case studies in behavior modification.* New York: Holt, Rinehart and Winston, 1965. Pp. 370–375.

Patterson, G. R. Social Learning: An additional base for developing behavior modification technologies. In C. M. Franks (Ed.), *Behavior Therapies: Assessment and Appraisal.* New York: McGraw-Hill, in press.

Patterson, G. R., & Brodsky, G. D. A behavior modification program for a boy with multiple problems. *Journal of Child Psychology and Psychiatry,* 1966, **7,** 277–295.

Patterson, G. R., Gullion, Elizabeth. *Counselors' manual* accompanying *Living with children: A manual for parents and teachers.* Champaign, Ill.: Research Press, 1968.

Patterson, G. R., Hawkins, N., McNeal, S., & Phelps, R. Reprogramming the social environment. *Journal of Child Psychology and Psychiatry,* 1967, **8,** 181–189.

Paul, G. L. *Insight vs. desensitization in psychotherapy: An experiment in anxiety reduction.* Stanford: Stanford University Press, 1966.

Paul, G. L., & Shannon, D. R. Treatment of anxiety through systematic desensitization in therapy groups. *Journal of Abnormal Psychology,* 1966, **71,** 119–123.

Pavlov, J. *Experimental psychology and other essays.* New York: Philosophical Library, 1957.

Peters, J. Typology of dogs by the conditioned reflex method: a selective review of Russian research. *Conditional Reflex: A Pavlovian Journal of Research and Therapy.* 1966, **1,** 235–250.

Peterson, D. R., & Lundon, P. A role for cognition in the behavioral treatment of a child's eliminative disturbance. In L. P. Ullmann & L. Krasner (Eds.), *Case studies in behavior modification.* New York: Holt, Rinehart and Winston, 1965. Pp. 289–295.

Premack, D. Reinforcement theory. In David Levine (Ed.), Nebraska symposium on motivation. Lincoln, Nebraska: University of Nebraska Press, 1965. Pp. 123–188.

Rachman, S. The treatment of anxiety and phobic reactions by systematic desensitization psychotherapy. *Journal of Abnormal and Social Psychology*, 1959, **102**, 421–427.

Ray, R. The training of mothers of atypical children in the use of behavior modification techniques. M.D. thesis, University of Oregon, 1965.

Rickard, H. C. Group problem solving in a therapeutic summer camp. Symposium on Behavior Modification in a Therapeutic Summer Camp. K. F. Newton, Chairman, SEPA, New Orleans, 1966.

Rickard, H. C., & Dinoff, M. Shaping adaptive behavior in a therapeutic summer camp. In L. P. Ullmann & L. Krasner (Eds.), *Case studies in behavior modification.* New York: Holt, Rinehart, and Winston, 1965. Pp. 325–328.

Rimland, B. *Infantile autism.* New York: Appleton-Century-Crofts, 1964.

Ritter, Brunhilde. The treatment of a dissection phobia. Unpublished manuscript, Queens College, 1965.

Ritter, Brunhilde. The group desensitization of children's snake phobias using vicarious and contact desensitization procedure. *Behaviour Research and Therapy*, 1968, **6**, 1–6. (a)

Ritter, Brunhilde. The effect of contact desensitization on avoidance behavior, fear ratings, and self-evaluative statements. *Proceedings, 76th Annual Convention*, American Psychological Association, 1968. (b)

Ritter, Brunhilde. The use of contact desensitization, demonstration-plus-participation, and demonstration alone in the treatment of acrophobia. Unpublished manuscript, Stanford University, 1968. (c)

Ritter, Brunhilde. Treatment of acrophobia with contact desensitization. *Behavior Research and Therapy*, in press.

Ruesch, J. *Disturbed Communications.* New York: Norton, 1957.

Salter, A. *Conditioned reflex therapy.* New York: Creative Age Press, 1961.

Sarason, I. G. Verbal learning, modeling and juvenile delinquency. *American Psychologist*, 1968, **23**, 254–266.

Sheffield, F. D. Theoretical considerations in the learning of complex sequential tasks from demonstration and practice. In A. A. Lumsdaine (Ed.), *Student response in programmed instruction.* Washington, D.C.: National Academy of Sciences—National Research Council, Publication 943, 1961.

Sherman, J. A. Use of reinforcement and imitation to reinstate verbal behavior in mute psychotics. *Journal of Abnormal Psychology*, 1965, **70**, 155–164.

Skinner, B. F. *Science and human behavior.* New York: Macmillan, 1953.

Smith, J. E. Encouraging students to utilize their unscheduled time more effectively through reinforcement and model counseling. Unpublished doctoral dissertation, Stanford University, 1965.

Smith, S., & Guthrie, E. R. *General psychology in terms of behavior.* New York: Appleton-Century-Crofts, 1921.

Stampfl, T. G., & Levis, D. J. Essentials of implosive therapy: A learning theory-based psychodynamic behavioral therapy. *Journal of Abnormal Psychology*, 1967, **72**, 496–503.

Sulzer, E. W. Reinforcement and the therapeutic contract. *Journal of Counseling Psychology*, 1962, **9**, 271–276.

Sutherland, E. H. *Principles of criminology.* Philadelphia: Lippincott, 1955.

Thayer, R. Measurement of activation through self-report. *Psychological Reports* (Monograph Supplement 1-V20), 1967, **20**, 663–678.

Thoresen, C. E. Behavioral counseling: An introduction. *The School Counselor,* 1966, **14**, 13–20. (a)

Thoresen, C. E. Behavioral counseling—the really client-centered approach. Invited address to the Long Island Personnel and Guidance Association, State University of New York at Farmingdale, New York, November 9, 1966. (b)

Thoresen, C. E. The counselor as an applied behavioral scientist. Paper read at the Annual Research in Guidance Institute, University of Wisconsin, Madison, Wisconsin, June, 1968. (a)

Thoresen, C. E. Being systematic about counselor training: Some beginning steps. Paper read at the meeting of the American Personnel and Guidance Association, Detroit, 1968. (b)

Thoresen, C. E., & Krumboltz, J. D. Similarity of models and clients in behavioral counseling: Two experimental studies. *Journal of Counseling Psychology,* 1968, **15**, 393–401.

Thorpe, J. G., Schmidt, E., & Castell, D. A comparison of positive and negative (aversive) conditioning in the treatment of homosexuality. *Behaviour Research and Therapy,* 1963, **1**, 357–363.

Ullmann, L. P. The major concepts taught to behavior therapy trainees. Papers presented at the meeting of the American Psychological Association, Washington, D. C., September, 1967.

Wahler, H. J. *Manual, the Wahler Self-Description Inventory, a measure of favorable and unfavorable self-evaluation.* Los Angeles: Western Psychological Services, in press.

Wahler, R. G., Winkel, G. H., Peterson, R. F., & Morrison, D. C. Mothers as behavior therapists for their children. *Behaviour Research and Therapy,* 1965, **3**, 113–124.

Walker, H. M., & Mattson, R. Development of educational procedures for modifying deviant behavior in children. Submitted to the *Journal of Special Education,* 1968.

Weinstein, F. T. Paper presented at the Annual Meeting of the American Educational Research Association, Chicago, Illinois, February, 1968.

Weinstein, F. T. The effect of personality type on systematic desensitization and structured group interaction in reducing examination anxiety. Unpublished doctoral dissertation, Michigan State University, 1968.

White, R. W. Motivation reconsidered: The concept of competence. *Psychological Review,* 1959, **66**, 297–333.

Wilson, F. W., & Walters, R. H. Modification of speech output of near-mute schizophrenics through social-learning procedures. *Behavior Research and Therapy,* 1966, **4**, 59–67.

Wolberg, L. R. *Medical hypnosis.* New York: Grune & Stratton, 1948.

Wolf, M. M., Risley, T., & Mees, H. Applications of operant conditioning procedures to the behavior problems of an autistic child. *Behaviour Research and Therapy,* 1964, **1**, 305–312.

Wolpe, J. An approach to the problem of neurosis based on the conditioned response. Unpublished M.D. thesis, University of the Witwatersrand, Johannesburg, South Africa, 1948.

Wolpe, J. Objective psychotherapy of the neuroses. *South African Medical Journal*, 1952, **26**, 825–829.

Wolpe, J. *Psychotherapy by reciprocal inhibition.* Stanford: Stanford University Press, 1958.

Wolpe, J. The systematic desensitization of neurosis. *Journal of Nervous and Mental Disorders*, 1961, **112**, 189–203.

Wolpe, J. Isolation of a conditioning procedure as the crucial psychotherapeutic factor: A case study. *Journal of Nervous and Mental Disorders*, 1962, **134**, 316–329.

Wolpe, J. Behavior therapy in complex neurotic states. *British Journal of Psychiatry*, 1964, **110**, 28–34.

Wolpe, J., & Lazarus, A. A. *Behavior therapy techniques.* New York: Pergamon Press, 1966.

Zeilberger, J., Sampen, S., & Sloane, H. Modification of a child's problem behavior in the home with the mother as therapist. *Journal of Applied Behavior Analysis*, 1968, **1**, 42–53.

512   Index

Inner circle strategy, 19–24
Interpersonal problems, 431–469
    and assertive training, 433–441
Interview skills, learning job-seeking, 414–428
In vivo procedures, 442–454
    and systematic desensitization, 443

Jackson, M., 152n
Jacobson, E., 460
Jealousy, systematic desensitization of, 462–463, 468–469
Job-seeking skills
    learning, 414–428
    and Pounce, 399–414
Johnson, R. G., 305n
Jones, G. B., 305n, 486–498
Jones, M. C., 177, 265, 319
Jourard, S., 7
Juvenile delinquent, see Delinquent, juvenile

Kanfer, R. H., 443
Kanner, L., 194
Kassorla, I., 193
Keirsey, D. W., 89–114
Kerr, N., 194
Kidder, J. D., 158
Kirk, R., 178n
Korn, C. V., 45–48
Krasner, L., 321
Krumboltz, J. D., 11, 13, 159n, 161, 202, 234, 236, 293–306
Kusher, M., 268

Lang, P. J., 268
Lavin, N. I., 320
Lazarus, A. A., 20–24, 268, 273, 275, 279, 319–320, 433, 442n, 452
Lazovik, A. D., 268
Leary, T., 323
Leon, H., 471
Levis, D. J., 464n
Levitt, E. B., 443n
Lewis, R., 155n
Life Career Game, 308–319
Lindsley, O. R., 161, 321

Little, R., 155n
Live social models, see Models, social, live
Long, L., 155n
Loughmiller, C., 125
Lovass, O. J., 193

McCully, C. H., 7
McMahon, T-S, 152n
McNeal, S., 155
McV. Hunt, J., 485
Madson, C. H., 161
Magoon, T. M., 343–396
Mahoney, J. L., 443n
Mandler, G., 326
Mattson, R., 158
Mees, H., 155, 194
Menlove, F., 177, 206n
Menninger, K., 124
Meyerson, L., 194
Michael, J., 321
Michaels, J., 194
Miller, N. E., 320, 327
Misbehavior, chronic
    and penalties, 93–95
    and restriction, 94–95
    systematic exclusion and, 89–114
Mischel, W., 323
Model, Effective Problem Solving, 343–396
Models, social, 163–264
    and assertive training, 435–436, 459
    audio taped, 203–207, 211–248, 459
        and assertive training, 459
        and behavior, task-oriented, 234–241
        and reinforcement, 234–241
        and underachievement, 241–248
        and verbal skills, 203–207
        and vocational planning, 213–234
    behavioral method, 249–264
    filmed, 200–210, 419–420
        and behavior, task-oriented, 207–210
        and hyperactivity, 207–210

INDEX

Academic achievement
    and reinforcement, 64–69
    structuring for, 73–78
Academic problems
    multiple techniques and, 470–498
    study behavior, improving, 486–498
    test anxiety, reducing, 471–485
Accounting, problem solving in, 294–295
Ackerman, C., 152n
Addison, R. M., 43
Adler, A., 93
Aggression, modification of, 30–33
Altman, H. A., 486n, 498n
Andresen, J., 152n
Anxiety, reduction of
    academic test, 471–485
    heterosexual, 442–454
    interpersonal, 455–471
    and multiple techniques, 442–471
    sexual, 455–471
    systematic desensitization and, 266–288
Anxiety hierarchy
    construction of, 272–273
    sexual, 465–466
Arbuckle, D. S., 7
Arnold, C. R., 161
Aronfreed, J., 443
Ashem, B., 268

Assertive training
    and anxiety, control of, 459–600
    interpersonal problems and, 433–441
Audio aids and verbal skills, 203–207, see also Models, social, filmed
Audio taped models, see Models, social, audio taped
Autistic children and live models, 193–199
Ayllon, T., 321

Baer, D. M., 442
Baity, L., 152n
Baker, R. D., 305
Bandura, A., 168, 177, 179, 193, 202, 206n, 443
Barker, J. C., 320
Barrett, D., 178n
Beach, A. L., 241–248
Becker, W. C., 161
Behavior
    bizarre, systematic exclusion and, 114–123
    contracts, 87–129, 112–114 ill.
    disruptive, see Classroom, disruptions
    identification of, 54–55
    inappropriate, client awareness and, 16–17

Behavior (*cont.*)
  incompatible, *see* Counterconditioning
  objectives, choice conflict in, 17–18
  rehearsal
    and anxiety, control of, 459–461
    and assertive training, 436–437
  task-oriented
    and models, social, audio taped, 234–241
    and models, social, filmed, 207–210
    see also separate entries
Behavioral consultation, 250–264
Behavioral methods, modeling with teachers, 249–264
Berne, E., 323, 434n
Bijou, S. W., 155, 158, 442
Birnbrauer, J. S., 158
Bizarre behavior, *see* Behavior, bizarre
Blakemore, C. G., 320
Blanchard, E. B., 168, 177
Bond, I. K., 268
Boocock, S., 308
Bourgerie, L., 152n
Brashear, B., 152n
Brodsky, G. D., 155

Callahan, W., 178n
Candy as reinforcer, 131–135, 158–159
Cards as reinforcer, 142–150
Carey, R., 329n
Carlson, P., 178n
Career planning, *see* Vocational planning
Cascadia, 180–193
Castell, D. A., 320
Castle, W. K., 33–36
Castleman, L., 178n
Cautela, J. R., 320, 443n
CD, *see* Contact desensitization
Clark, D. F., 268
Clarke, R., 329n
Classroom(s)
  behavior, reinforcement and, 33–36

disruptions, systematic exclusion and, 84–114
and reinforcement, instruction in use of for, 131–161
Client, identification of, 9–10
Cognitive techniques, 289–428
  confrontation, 397–428
  planning, 328–396
  simulation, 291–327
Conditioning, counter, *see* Counterconditioning
Confrontation, 397–428
Consultation, behavioral, modeling and, 250–264
Contact desensitization (CD), 168–178
Contracts, behavior, *see* Behavior contracts
Conway, C. B., 320
Counseling, career, *see* Vocational planning
Counterconditioning
  and anxiety, sexual, control of, 458
  and desensitization, systematic, 266–288
Cowden, R. C., 268
Criticism hierarchy, 466–468

Dahlum, D., 178n
Daley, M. F., 42–45, 196n
Davison, G. C., 319–327, 442n, 443n
Decision-making
  training in, 328–343
  vocational planning and, 307–319
Delinquents, juvenile, rehabilitation of, 178–193
Denny, D., 178n
Desensitization
  contact, 168–178
  systematic
    and anxiety, reduction of, 266–288
    and *in vivo* procedures, 443
    technique of, 268–278
Dinoff, M., 124–129
Dollard, J., 320, 327

Dreikurs, R., 93, 95, 111
Dunn, L., 45
D'Zurilla, T. J., 442–454

Ebner, M., 159n
Effective Problem Solving (EPS) model, 343–396
Emery, J. R., 168n, 267–288
Employment, *see* Job-seeking skills; Vocational planning
Endler, N., 485
England, G., 443n
Environment, contact desensitization and, 168–178
EPS, *see* Effective Problem Solving model
Erickson, R., 178n
Exclusion, systematic, *see* Systematic exclusion
Experience Tables, 333–338
Explaining Problems, 423–424
Explaining Skills, 421–422
Extinction
  and job-seeking, 46
  see also Reinforcement
Eysenck, H. J., 319, 470, 472

Farson, R., 46
Feelings
  problems expressed as, 11–13
  standards for, realistic comparative, 12–13
  undesired, incompatible action and, 11–12
Ferster, C. B., 321, 443n
Filmed social models, *see* Models, social, filmed
Flooding techniques and anxiety, control of, 464
Ford, L. I., 268
Frazier, M., 152n
Freitag, G., 193
Freund, K., 320
Fuhriman, A., 73–78
Fujikawa, J., 152n
Fullerton, J., 152n

Ganzer, V. J., 178–193
Geer, J., 268
Geisinger, D. L., 454–471
Gelatt, H. B., 329n
Gibbons, J., 178n
Ginott, H., 434n
Glasser, W., 99
Goals
  absence of, 14
  behavior change structure of,
  commitment to, 56–57
  formulation of, 70–73
  difficulties in, 9–19
Gold, V., 193
Goldfoot, D. A., 443
Goldfried, M. R., 442n
Goldiamond, I., 326–327, 442
Goodwin, D. L., 159n, 161, 26
Gorden, W., 152n
Gray, B. B., 443n
Griffin, J. L., 36–40
Group interaction treatmen
  tured, and anxiety,
  test, 471–485
Grusec, J. E., 177, 206n
Gullion, E., 155n, 157
Guthrie, E. R., 319

Hamlow, M., 152n
Haring, N. G., 158
Hawkes, F. J., 486n
Hawkins, N., 155
Hawkins, R. P., 155
Hayden, A. H., 158
Heterosexual anxiety, red
  442–454
Hilgard, E. R., 275
Homme, L. E., 42–43, 327,
Hoopes, M. H., 54–64
Hosford, R. E., 80–83, 152
  207
Howenstine, R., 178n
Huston, A. C., 202
Hutchinson, H. C., 268
Hyperactivity
  and models, social, filme
  and reinforcement, 30–

Models, social (*cont.*)
  of job interviews, 419–420
  and reinforcement, 209–210
  and verbal skills, 202–207
  group, 214–234, 487–492, 496–497
  live, 166–199
    and autistic children, 193–199
    and contact desensitization, 168–178
    and delinquents, juvenile, rehabilitation of, 178–193
    peer groups as, 197–199
Moore, R., 250–259
Mowrer, O. H., 326
Muir, J., 429
Multiple techniques, 429–497
  and academic problems, 470–498
  interpersonal problems, 431–469
Muscular relaxation, training in, 269–272

Nelson, J., 152n
Neufeld, H., 152n
Neuman, D., 433–441, 471
Nixon, S. B., 131, 207–210
Note-taking and assertive training, 437–440
Nurnberger, J. I., 443n

Parents and reinforcement, instruction in use of, 155–161
Patterson, G. R., 155–161, 207, 210n
Paul, G. L., 268, 471
Pavlov, J., 472
Peers, as models, social, 197–199
Penalties, chronic misbehavior and, 93–95
Peters, J., 472
Peterson, R. F., 155
Phelps, R., 155
Phillips, D., 152n
Planning, 328–396
  vocational, *see* Vocational planning
  see also Decision-making
"Pounce," 399–414
Prazak, J. A., 399n, 414–428
Premack, D., 42

Problem identification, 7–19
  and inner circle strategy, 19–24
Problem solving, vocational, 293–306
Problem Solving model, Effective, 343–396
Procrastination, reinforcement and, 58–64
Psychopath, systematic exclusion and, 110
Psychotherapy, systematic exclusion and, 124–129

Rachman, S., 268, 472
Ray, R., 155
Reading, remedial, reinforcement and, 132–136
Reber, J., 443
Reinforcement, 25–28
  and academic performance, 64–69
    structuring for, 73–78
  and aggression, modification of, 30–33
  and behavior contracts, 87–129, 112–114 *ill.*
  and classroom behavior, 33–36
  and goals educational, formulation of, 70–73
  and hyperactivity, modification of, 30–33
  instruction in use of
    for classroom, 131–161
    for parents, 155–161
    for teachers, 152–154
  and job-seeking, 416, 420
  and models, social
    audio taped, 234–241
    filmed, 209–210
  and procrastination, 58–64
  and reading, remedial, 132–136
  refusal of, 45–51
  role-playing and, 79–86
  and soiling behavior, 36–40
  sources of, 57–58, *see also* Reinforcers
  and speaking, public, 80–86
  structuring and, 52–78

Reinforcement (*cont.*)
　and study behavior, improving, 491–492
　and systematic exclusion
　　of behavior, bizarre, 114–123
　　of misbehavior, chronic, 89–114
　and verbal skills, 80–86
Reinforcers
　candy, 131–135
　cards, 142–150
　conditioned, 25–26
　identification of, 41–45
　primary, 25–26
　tokens, 135–136
Responsibility, systematic exclusion and, 124–129
Restriction and misbehavior, chronic, 94–95
Reticence and models, social, filmed, 202–207
Reynolds, D. J., 268
Rice, H., 155
Rickard, H. C., 36–40, 124–129
Rimland, B., 194
Risley, T., 155, 194
Ritter, B., 168–178, 206n
Rogat, N., 399n
Rogers, C., 52, 400n
Role-playing and reinforcement, 79–86
Rosenstein, A., 485
Ryan, T. A., 70–73

Salter, A., 434, 442n
Sampen, S., 155
Sanborn, B., 131–152
Sanguinetti, J., 178n
Sanner, K., 250–259
Sarason, I. G., 178–193
Schmidt, E., 320
Schroeder, W. W., 202
Schuster, W., 131–152
Schweid, E., 155
Scoresby, A. L., 54–58, 64–69
Self-control, systematic exclusion and, 101–132
Sexual anxiety, *see* Anxiety, sexual

Shannon, D. R., 268, 471
Sheppard, L. E., 293–306
Sherman, J. A., 177
Shier, D. A., 114–123
Shyness and models, social, filmed, 202–207
Simmons, J., 152n
Simulation, 291–327
　and decision-making, training in, 328–343
　Effective Problem Solving model and, 343–396
　and vocational planning, 306–319
　by vocational problem solving, 293–306
Skinner, B. F., 155, 321, 442
Sloan, H., 155
Sloat, S., 178n
Smith, J., 45
Smith, J. E., 234–241
Smith, S., 319
Snow, D., 178n
Social models, *see* Models, social
Sociopath, systematic exclusion and, 110
Soiling behavior, reinforcement and, 36–40
Sorenson, D. L., 202–207
Speaking, public, reinforcement and, 80–86
Staging Conference in systematic exclusion, 102–109
Stampfl, T. G., 464n
Sterling, T., 178n
Stewart, N. R., 213–234
Stilwell, W. E., 193–199
Strantz, B., 152n
Structuring and reinforcement, 52–78
Study behavior, improving, 486–498
Subjective unit of disturbance, 273–274
Suiter, S., 152n
Sullivan, H. S., 93
Sulzer, E. W., 124
Sutherland, E. H., 179
Synanon Game, 414n
Systematic desensitization

Systematic desensitization (*cont.*)
and anxiety, sexual, control of, 458–463, 465–466
group, 492–496
and jealousy, 462–463, 468–469
and study behavior, improving, 492–496
Systematic exclusion
arranging for, 109
and behavior, bizarre, 114–123
and misbehavior, chronic, 89–114
and psychotherapy, 124–129
and responsibility, 124–129
and self-control, 101–132
special problems in, 109–110
Staging Conference for, 102–109

Teachers
behavioral methods with, modeling, 249–264
consultation with, behavioral, 250–264
and reinforcement, instruction in, 152–154
Thayer, R., 485
Thomas, D. R., 161
Thoresen, C. E., 8, 202, 214n, 232, 236, 471n
Thorpe, J. G., 320
Tokens as reinforcers, 135–136, 150–159
Tondow, M., 329n
Trimble, M., 498n
Tropp, R., 178n
Tye, V. M., 178n

Ullmann, L. P., 434
Underachievement and models, social, audio taped, 241–248

Vajanasoontorn, C., 42n
Vance, B. J., 30–33
Van Winkle, L., 152n
Varenhorst, B. B., 49–51, 83–86, 202, 306–319
Verbal skills
and models, social
audio taped, 203–207
filmed, 202–207
and reinforcement, 80–86
Viek, P., 326
Visual aids, *see* Models, social, filmed
Vocational planning
and decision-making, 307–319
Effective Problem Solving model and, 343–396
and models, social, audio taped, 213–234
and simulation, 306–319
see also Job-seeking skills
Vocational problem solving and simulation, 293–306

Wahler, R. G., 155
Walker, H. M., 158, 425n
Walters, R. H., 177, 179, 193, 443
Watson, D. L., 326
Weinstein, F. T., 471–485
White, R. W., 326
Wilson, F. W., 177
Winkel, G. H., 155
Wolberg, L. R., 275
Wolf, M. M., 155, 158, 159n, 194
Wolpe, J., 268, 273, 275, 279, 319–320, 433, 442n, 452

Yabroff, W., 329–343

Zeilberger, J., 155